Archaeology of Pacific Oceania

Now in its second edition, this book integrates a region-wide chronological narrative of the archaeology of Pacific Oceania. How and why did this vast sea of islands, covering nearly one-third of the world's surface, come to be inhabited over the last several millennia, transcending significant change in ecology, demography, and society? What can any or all of the thousands of islands offer as ideal model systems toward comprehending globally significant issues of human-environment relations and coping with changing circumstances of natural and cultural history? The new second edition delivers the most updated and comprehensive information for addressing the core fundamental questions about Pacific Oceanic archaeology, based largely on the author's investigations throughout the diverse region.

Mike T. Carson (PhD in anthropology, University of Hawaiʻi, 2002) has investigated the broad geographic range and chronological scope of archaeological landscapes throughout the Asia-Pacific region. He was author of several books about Pacific Oceanic archaeology and ancient landscapes, editor of *Palaeolandscapes in Archaeology: Lessons for the Past and Future* (2022), and coeditor of *Asian Perspectives: The Journal of Archaeology for Asia and the Pacific* (2014–2020). He currently is Associate Professor of Archaeology at the Richard F. Taitano Micronesian Area Research Center at the University of Guam.

Routledge World Archaeology

The Ancient Central Andes
Jeffrey Quilter

Prehistoric Britain
2nd Edition
Timothy Darvill

Ancient Turkey
Antonio Sagona and Paul Zimansky

Ancient Southeast Asia
John Norman Miksic and Goh Geok Yian

Archaeology of the Southwest
3rd Edition
Maxine E. McBrinn and Linda S. Cordell

Archaeology of Pacific Oceania
Inhabiting a Sea of Islands
Mike T. Carson

The Archaeology of Iran
From the Palaeolithic to the Achaemenid Empire
Roger Matthews and Hssann Fazeli Nashli

For more information about this series, please visit: www.routledge.com/Routledge-World-Archaeology/book-series/RWA

Archaeology of Pacific Oceania
Inhabiting a Sea of Islands

Second edition

Mike T. Carson

LONDON AND NEW YORK

Cover image: Beach at the Ritidian Site of Guam.
Photograph by Mike T. Carson, 2019

Second edition published 2024
by Routledge
4 Park Square, Milton Park, Abingdon, Oxon, OX14 4RN

and by Routledge
605 Third Avenue, New York, NY 10158

Routledge is an imprint of the Taylor & Francis Group, an informa business

© 2024 Mike T. Carson

The right of Mike T. Carson to be identified as author of this work has been asserted in accordance with sections 77 and 78 of the Copyright, Designs and Patents Act 1988.

All rights reserved. No part of this book may be reprinted or reproduced or utilised in any form or by any electronic, mechanical, or other means, now known or hereafter invented, including photocopying and recording, or in any information storage or retrieval system, without permission in writing from the publishers.

Trademark notice: Product or corporate names may be trademarks or registered trademarks, and are used only for identification and explanation without intent to infringe.

First edition published by Routledge 2018

British Library Cataloguing-in-Publication Data
A catalogue record for this book is available from the British Library

Library of Congress Cataloging-in-Publication Data
Names: Carson, Mike T., author.
Title: Archaeology of Pacific Oceania : inhabiting a sea of islands / Mike T. Carson.
  Other titles: Inhabiting a sea of islands
Description: Second edition. | Abingdon, Oxon ; New York, NY : Routledge, 2024. | Series: Routledge world archaeology | "First edition published by Routledge 2018." | Includes bibliographical references and index.
Identifiers: LCCN 2023029500 (print) | LCCN 2023029501 (ebook) |
  ISBN 9781032486406 (hbk) | ISBN 9781032486376 (pbk) | ISBN 9781003399025 (ebk)
Subjects: LCSH: Oceania—Antiquities. | Excavations (Archaeology)—Oceania. |
  Human settlements—Oceania.
Classification: LCC DU28 .C37 2024 (print) | LCC DU28 (ebook) | DDC 995—dc23/
  eng/20230701
LC record available at https://lccn.loc.gov/2023029500
LC ebook record available at https://lccn.loc.gov/2023029501

ISBN: 978-1-032-48640-6 (hbk)
ISBN: 978-1-032-48637-6 (pbk)
ISBN: 978-1-003-39902-5 (ebk)

DOI: 10.4324/9781003399025

Typeset in Sabon
by Apex CoVantage, LLC

This book is dedicated to Mustard and Zorro for their vigorous friendship.

Contents

List of figures		ix
Preface		xix
1	Research themes in Pacific Oceanic archaeology	1
2	Regional context and perspectives	25
3	Substance and scope of Pacific Oceanic archaeology	53
4	Hunter-gatherer traditions in the western Asia-Pacific region	67
5	Following the Asia-Pacific pottery trail, 4000 through 800 B.C.	84
6	First contact with the Remote Oceanic environment: the Mariana Islands at 1500 B.C.	149
7	A siege of ecological imperialism: Lapita invasions, 1100 through 800 B.C.	185
8	The end of an era: adjusting to changing coastlines, 1100 through 500 B.C.	209
9	A broad-spectrum revolution? 500 B.C. through A.D. 100	221
10	The atoll highway of Micronesia, A.D. 100 through 500	230
11	Ethnogenesis and polygenesis, A.D. 500 through 1000	245
12	An A.D. 1000 Event? Formalization of cultural expressions	255
13	Expansion and intensification, A.D. 1000 through 1800	304
14	Living with the past: life, lore, and landscape in Pacific Oceania	362
Index		377

Figures

1.1	Pacific Oceania in the world.	2
1.2	Major biogeographic zones of the Asia-Pacific region.	6
2.1	Tectonic plates of the Asia-Pacific region.	26
2.2	Schematic diagram of volcanic "hot spot" formation in the Hawaiian Islands.	27
2.3	Pagan Volcano, Mariana Islands.	27
2.4	Stream-cut valley of Waimea Canyon, the "Grand Canyon of the Pacific" in Kaua'i, Hawaiian Islands.	28
2.5	Schematic diagram of atoll formation.	29
2.6	Limestone plateau, northern Guam.	29
2.7	Coastal freshwater seep at Ritidian, Guam. Photograph provided courtesy of Dr. Hiro Kurashina.	30
2.8	Gondwana model.	31
2.9	Sea-level history. Top: large-scale view in thousands of years. Bottom: detail of the last 4000 years most relevant in Pacific Oceanic archaeology.	32
2.10	General climate zones of the Asia-Pacific region.	34
2.11	Schematic diagram of orographic rain production and rain shadow effect.	35
2.12	Austronesian linguistic phylogeny tree, based on information from Blust (2013).	39
2.13	Asia-Pacific linguistic map, coordinated with approximate settlement dates according to archaeological evidence.	39
3.1	Schematic models of Pacific Oceanic island settlement chronologies.	56
3.2	Idealized models of age systems.	58
3.3	Samoa pottery sequence.	61
3.4	New Caledonia pottery sequence.	61
4.1	Pleistocene landforms and major biogeographic zones of the western Asia-Pacific region.	68
4.2	Callao Cave in northern Luzon, Philippines.	69
4.3	Schematic examples of Paleolithic stone tool types of Southeast Asia.	71
4.4	Baxiandong excavation in eastern Taiwan, September 2014. Lead excavator Dr. Tsang Cheng-hwa is wearing hat and dark glasses, standing beside Dr. Peter Bellwood.	72
5.1	Region-wide incremental growth model.	86
5.2	Asia-Pacific pottery trail.	91
5.3	Borneo in western Island Southeast Asia, noting sites as mentioned in the text.	93

x *Figures*

5.4	Gua Sireh stratigraphy and dating, based on information from Ipoi (1993), Ipoi and Bellwood (1991), and Bellwood et al. (1992).	94
5.5	Schematic diagram of burial formats and associated artifacts at the Niah Caves, based on information from Cole (2012, 2016), Lloyd-Smith (2005, 2009), and Lloyd-Smith et al. (2013).	96
5.6	Approximate distribution of cord-marked pottery sites in coastal China and Taiwan.	98
5.7	Examples of Dabenkeng pottery, Taiwan. Vessels are reconstructed at the on-site museum of the Tainan Science-based Industrial Park (TSIP) in Taiwan.	100
5.8	Early and late Dabenkeng landscapes of Taiwan, based on information from Hung and Carson (2014) and updated.	102
5.9	Changguang site excavation, eastern Taiwan. Lead excavator Dr. Hsiao-chun Hung is recording notes near the back profile, November 2015. Photograph provided courtesy of Dr. Hsiao-chun Hung.	103
5.10	Landscape chronology at Changguang.	103
5.11	Landscape chronology of Taiwan, noting landforms of potential for rain-fed crops in hilly terrain and for wet-field farming in lowland plain formations.	104
5.12	Taiwan archaeological assemblages at 2200–1500 B.C., based on information from Hung (2008).	105
5.13	Fushan pottery tradition, eastern Taiwan, 2500–1500 B.C.	106
5.14	Landscape chronology of Fushan tradition sites.	107
5.15	Beinan stonework features.	109
5.16	Beinan standing megalith.	109
5.17	Beinan tradition pottery and body ornaments, at the Beinan Site Museum in Taiwan.	110
5.18	Map of pottery horizon sites in the Philippines.	111
5.19	Early pottery of the Philippines, similar to Fushan tradition of eastern Taiwan. Photograph provided courtesy of Dr. Hsiao-chun Hung, showing pottery from excavations at the Nagsabaran Site in the Philippines.	112
5.20	Line-impressed pottery from Magapit in Cagayan Valley of Luzon, Philippines. Scale bar is in 1 cm increments.	113
5.21	Finely decorated pottery from Nagsabaran in Cagayan Valley of Luzon, Philippines. Photographs provided courtesy of Dr. Hsiao-chun Hung.	114
5.22	Paddle-impressed pottery from Nagsabaran in Cagayan Valley of Luzon, Philippines. Photograph provided courtesy of Dr. Hsiao-chun Hung.	115
5.23	Cagayan Valley landscape at 2200–1500 B.C. as compared to modern conditions.	119
5.24	Map of pottery horizon sites in Indonesia.	121
5.25	Correlation of pottery associations and radiocarbon dating at Minanga Sipakko and Kamassi in the Karama Valley of Sulawesi, Indonesia, based on information from Anggraeni et al. (2014), Deng et al. (2020), and Bulbeck and Nasruddin (2002).	122
5.26	Locations of the known earliest sites of the Mariana Islands.	125
5.27	Examples of early-period Marianas pottery, 1500–1100 B.C., excavated 2011 and 2013 near House of Taga, Tinian.	126

5.28	Photograph record of the first reported finely decorated pottery in the Mariana Islands, excavated by Marcian Pellett in 1958 near House of Taga, Tinian. The photographic print is in the curatorial archive of the Micronesian Area Research Center, University of Guam.	127
5.29	Earliest Marianas pottery forms and variants, 1500–1100 B.C. Upper right: Ritidian, Guam. Middle row: House of Taga, Tinian. Bottom row: Ritidian, Guam.	129
5.30	Earliest Marianas pottery decorations and design elements. Graphic is adapted from Carson et al. (2013).	131
5.31	Two variants of early-period Marianas paddle-impressed pottery, 1500–1100 B.C., from the Ritidian Site in Guam. Upper piece (A): carved paddle impression. Lower pieces (B, C, D): wrapped paddle impression.	132
5.32	Rare instances of early-period Marianas handles, foot ring, and possible appendage fragment. Upper left and upper middle: handle pieces from House of Taga, Tinian. Upper right: handle piece from Ritidian, Guam. Lower left: foot-ring piece from Ritidian, Guam. Lower right: appendage piece from Unai Bapot, Saipan.	133
5.33	Changing coastal morphology at Unai Bapot, Saipan.	134
5.34	Map of Lapita-associated sites in the Bismarck Archipelago and Near Oceania.	135
5.35	Lapita pottery with decorations excavated from Anir in the Bismarck Archipelago. Photographs provided courtesy of Glenn Summerhayes.	136
5.36	Map of Lapita distribution in Near and Remote Oceania.	137
5.37	Examples of Lapita pottery design motifs.	137
5.38	Locations of reported early sites in Palau.	139
5.39	View of Chelechol ra Orrak, offshore from Babeldaob in Palau.	140
6.1	Radiocarbon dating of earliest sites in the Mariana Islands. Based on information from Carson (2014a) and updated with new information.	151
6.2	Sea-level history in the Marianas region.	154
6.3	Landscape chronology at Ritidian, Guam.	155
6.4	Map of earliest cultural layers, excavated at Unai Bapot, Saipan.	156
6.5	Map of earliest cultural layer, excavated near House of Taga, Tinian.	157
6.6	Excavation survey at Ritidian, Guam, targeting area of potential earliest coastal settlement.	158
6.7	Map of early versus modern landscape conditions at Ritidian, Guam.	159
6.8	Examples of earliest decorated Marianas pottery, 1500–1100 B.C., excavated from Unai Bapot, Saipan.	160
6.9	Examples of non-pottery artifacts from early-period Marianas sites, 1500–1100 B.C.	161
6.10	Examples of "Marianas super-thin" pottery tradition, 1500–1100 B.C., at Ritidian, Guam.	162
6.11	Example of red and black painted pottery, 1500–1100 B.C., at Ritidian, Guam.	162
6.12	Early-period Marianas body ornaments, 1500–1100 B.C., excavated from Ritidian in Guam. A and B: shell bands. C: shell circlet. D and E: thick shell discs. F, G, H: small shell rings. I, J, K: thin shell discs. L: shell pendant. M: pendant of modified tooth of dolphin. N: small round shell beads. O: *Cypraea* sp. shell beads.	163

xii   *Figures*

6.13	Ethnographic examples from Taiwan, showing garments with elements of small cut and polished shell beads. A: robe on display in the Sheng Yue Museum, Taiwan. B: skirt in collection of the Taiwan National Museum of Prehistory. C: leg wrapping in collection of the Taiwan National Museum of Prehistory.	164
6.14	Ethnographic examples from Taiwan, showing elements of shell discs and beads in head dressing. Photograph from approximately 1920–1935, in collection of the Taiwan National Museum of Prehistory.	165
6.15	Ethnographic examples from Taiwan, showing elements of shell discs and beads in shoulder straps, necklaces, and other accessories. A, C, and D are from approximately 1920–1935, in collection of the Taiwan National Museum of Prehistory. B is a head dress on display at the Sheng-yue Museum in Taiwan. E is a shoulder strap in collection of the Taiwan National Museum of Prehistory.	166
6.16	View of excavation at overhang exterior of Ritidian Beach Cave, Guam, during 2016 excavation. Scale bars are in 20 cm increments.	167
6.17	Stratigraphy and dating at Ritidian Beach Cave, Guam. Graphic is based on documentation by Carson (2017a, 2017b, 2017c).	168
6.18	Shell pit-sealing items at Ritidian Beach Cave, Guam. Scale bars are in 1 cm increments.	168
6.19	Decorated pottery from earliest cultural layer at Ritidian Beach Cave, Guam.	169
6.20	Betelnut quid offering at Ritidian Beach Cave, Guam. Offering was part of ceremony for the site's ancestors, led by Jeremy Cepeda, May 2016.	171
6.21	Paleoenvironmental coring profiles from the Mariana Islands.	172
6.22	Island-wide landscape of Guam, showing ancient versus modern conditions. Graphic is based on information from Carson (2011) and updated.	174
6.23	Rock art in the Ritidian Pictograph Cave, showing white-pigment elements overlaying older red-pigment handprints.	175
6.24	Rare black-pigment rock art panels at Ritidian, Guam. Scale bars are in 20 cm increments.	176
7.1	Map of eastern New Guinea, Island Melanesia, and West Polynesia, showing the geographic distribution of Lapita pottery sites at different time intervals of 1500–1100 B.C., 1100–800 B.C., and 800–500 B.C.	186
7.2	Lapita pottery fragments from Vavouto, New Caledonia, excavated by Carson (2003, 2008).	187
7.3	Lapita face motif on pottery fragments from Santa Cruz, Solomon Islands. Illustration by the author, based on documentation by Green (1979a).	189
7.4	Impressions made by different forms of Lapita decoration tools.	191
7.5	Lapita region coordinated with linguistic grouping map.	192
7.6	Lapita landscape versus modern conditions at Vavouto, New Caledonia. Graphic is based on information from Carson (2008).	200
7.7	Examples of Lapita landscapes versus modern conditions in Viti Levu, Fiji. Upper: Natunuka area. Lower: Rove Peninsula area. Graphics are modified from models by Nunn and Heorake (2009).	201
8.1	Formation of beach-ridge following sea-level drawdown at Ritidian, Guam. Graphic is based on information from Carson (2016).	212

Figures xiii

8.2	Lapita pottery from the Ferry Berth Site near Mulifanua in 'Upolu, Samoa. Illustration by the author, based on documentation by Jennings (1974).	213
8.3	Distribution of known Lapita-age sites in Samoa.	213
8.4	Lapita versus post-Lapita shellfish record from Vavouto, New Caledonia. Graphic is adapted from Carson (2008).	214
8.5	Shellfish record chronology of the Mariana Islands, examining the contributing effects of sea-level drawdown and cultural harvesting. Graphic is based on information from Carson (2016).	215
8.6	Pottery chronology of the Mariana Islands. Graphic is adapted from Carson (2016) and updated.	217
9.1	Shift in site distribution about 700–500 B.C. at Ritidian, Guam. Graphic is based on information from Carson (2014).	224
10.1	Map of the inhabited Pacific at A.D. 100–500, noting the role of Central through Eastern Micronesia.	231
10.2	Schematic diagram of sea-level drawdown coordinated with atoll emergence and availability of freshwater lens in Central through Eastern Micronesia. Graphic is based on information from Yamaguchi et al. (2005).	231
10.3	*Rebbelib* chart of the Marshall Islands. This image shows an educational product at the Micronesian Area Research Center, University of Guam.	233
10.4	Bikini Atoll in 1946, during underwater test of an atomic bomb. Photograph is in the collections of the Micronesian Area Research Center, University of Guam.	234
10.5	Beach profile stratigraphy and dating in Tumon, Guam, noting incipient organic horizon of buried ancient beach surface. Scale bar at left is in 20 cm increments.	237
10.6	Map of excavation of ancient beach surface with multiple hearth features in Tumon, Guam. Graphic is adapted from Carson (2011, 2016).	238
10.7	Lamotrek sailing canoe, after arrival in Guam during May 2016.	240
10.8	Sail from Lamotrek canoe, presented as a gift for the University of Guam.	241
11.1	Map of the inhabited Pacific at A.D. 500–1000, noting areas of retaining versus losing pottery, post-raised versus ground-level housing formats, and betelnut-chewing versus kava-drinking traditions.	246
11.2	Samoan archaeology sequence, noting major transitions at A.D. 500–1000. Graphic is adapted from Carson (2014).	248
11.3	Remnants of pre–A.D. 1000 cultural layers beneath surface-visible stonework ruins in Tutuila, American Samoa. Graphic is adapted from Carson (2006).	251
11.4	Map of surface-visible site ruins in Ngatpang, Palau, noting spatially separated distributions of earthen terraces (before A.D. 1000) and stonework villages (after A.D. 1000). Graphic is based on mapping datasets from Republic of Belau, Bureau of Arts and Culture.	252
11.5	Palau earthwork complex in Babeldaob.	253
12.1	Map of the inhabited Pacific after A.D. 1000, noting movements into East Polynesia and the Polynesian Outliers, as well as later movement into New Zealand at A.D. 1300.	256
12.2	Variable scales of stonework elements, features, and complexes in Tutuila, American Samoa. Graphic is adapted from Carson (2005).	260

xiv *Figures*

12.3	Stacked-stone mounds in Honokōhau, Hawai'i Island. Graphics are adapted from Carson (2006).	261
12.4	Stone-filled platform at the edge of Haleakalā Crater, Maui. Scale bar is in 20 cm increments.	262
12.5	Portion of map of surface-visible stonework ruins in Tutuila, American Samoa. Graphic is adapted from Carson (2005).	263
12.6	Monumentality profile, applied to surface-visible stonework ruins in Tutuila, American Samoa. The specific features are shown in Figure 12.5.	264
12.7	Schematic diagrams of terrace and platform constructions.	266
12.8	Pebble and shell floor paving in Mouly, Ouvéa in the Loyalty Islands of New Caledonia, 1999. Left: documenting time-limit collections of beach pebbles and shells. Right: pebble and shell paving at a cooking shed.	266
12.9	Vaitahu valley stonework ruins during 1997 survey in Tahuata, Marquesas Islands.	267
12.10	View of massive front patio stonework in Vaitahu valley of Tahuata, during 1997 documentation, Marquesas Islands.	268
12.11	Grinding basins in patio stonework in Vaitahu valley of Tahuata, during 1997 documentation, Marquesas Islands.	269
12.12	Tuffaceous stone *ke'etu* incorporated into front-facing stonework in Vaitahu valley of Tahuata, during 1997 documentation, Marquesas Islands. This particular stone was carved with a *tiki* image.	269
12.13	Example of traditional *bai* in Babeldaob, Palau.	271
12.14	Detail of stone-filled platform beneath *bai* in Babeldaob, Palau.	271
12.15	Detail of stonework pathway in Babeldaob, Palau.	272
12.16	Photographs of pathway lined with *rai* discs on display in Yap. Photographs are from the Japanese collections, approximately 1925–1935, curated at the Micronesian Area Research Center, University of Guam.	273
12.17	Arrangements of circular hut foundations in Vavouto and Pouémbout, northern province of New Caledonia. Graphic is based on documentation by Carson (2003).	274
12.18	Examples of *latte* construction in plan view, section view, and reconstruction model.	275
12.19	*Latte* of House of Taga in Tinian in 2013.	276
12.20	Setting of the House of Taga in Tinian. Illustration was by Hans Hornbostel (1925).	276
12.21	*Latte* quarry at As Nieves in Rota.	277
12.22	Range of material types of *latte* in the Mariana Islands. Those in Guam, Rota, and Tinian were made of quarried limestone. Those in Pagan were made of beach cobbles (Apansamne'na) or of carved tuffaceous stone (Apansantatte). All scale bars are in 20 cm increments.	278
12.23	Different element configurations of *latte* sets with cleared areas, pavings, borders, grinding mortars, midden areas, and burial pits. All examples (A, B, and C) are from Ritidian, Guam.	279
12.24	Examples of semiportable household-related *lusong* grinding basins in the Mariana Islands. All scale bars are in 20 cm increments.	280
12.25	Examples of immovable permanent bedrock *lusong* grinding mortars in the Mariana Islands. All scale bars are in 20 cm increments.	281

12.26	Examples of pottery from the latte period, A.D. 1000–1700 in the Mariana Islands.	282
12.27	Rat guards on a reconstruction of a traditional Austronesian house in Taiwan. Display is at the Formosan Aboriginal Cultural Village in Nantou, Taiwan.	282
12.28	Example of notch at the base of *haligi* pillar, with surrounding bracing stones in a *latte* set at Ritidian, Guam.	283
12.29	Example of slight socket in *tasa* capital to fit over *haligi* pillar in a *latte* set at Ritidian, Guam. Scale bar is in 20 cm increments.	284
12.30	Badrulchau in Babeldaob, Palau.	285
12.31	Map of Fale o le Fe'e in 'Upolu, Samoa. Graphic is based on documentation by J. Derek Freeman (1944).	286
12.32	Examples of *marae* with an upright slab, at Koutu Ariki Taputapuatea, Cook Islands. Images provided by Dr. Hiro Kurashina.	291
12.33	Four *tiki* heads, carved in stone in real-life size with personal attributes, discovered during 1997 in Vaitahu valley of Tahuata, Marquesas Islands. These *tiki* are now in a curation display at the Tahuata Museum.	292
12.34	Moai at Ahu Tongariki, Rapa Nui, in 1984. Image was provided by Dr. Hiro Kurashina.	293
12.35	Fishing shrine at Ki'ilae, Hawai'i Island. Graphic is adapted from Carson et al. (2004).	294
12.36	Stone object of a fish god idol at Ki'ilae, Hawai'i Island.	295
12.37	Stones associated with fishing lore at Vavouto, New Caledonia. Graphic is based on documentation by Carson (2003).	296
12.38	Pigeon-snaring mound in Tutuila, American Samoa. Graphic is based on documented by Carson (2005).	296
12.39	Portion of the stone city of Nan Madol in Pohnpei.	297
12.40	Map of stonework ruins of Nan Madol.	297
13.1	Map of Polynesian Outliers, noting linguistic subgroupings.	309
13.2	Dating and redating of a hearth feature at Puapua'a, Hawai'i Island. Graphic is based on documentation by Carson (2012b).	311
13.3	Proxies of earliest Hawaiian settlement dating. Graphic is based on information from Athens et al. (2002).	312
13.4	Distribution of radiocarbon dates from archaeological sites of Kaua'i, Hawaiian Islands. The weight of statistical probability increases steadily through time, notably after A.D. 1000–1200. Graphic is based on data from Carson (2005a, 2006a).	313
13.5	Locations of known early Hawaiian sites. Graphic is based on information from Carson (2004).	314
13.6	Wainiha Beach profile chronology. Graphic is based on information from Carson (2004).	314
13.7	Kualoa plan map chronology. Graphic is adapted from Carson and Athens (2007).	315
13.8	Kawaihae plan map chronology. Graphic is adapted from Carson (2012c).	316
13.9	Distribution of archaeological radiocarbon dates from Kaua'i, shown as pie-slice percentage in 100-year increments. The overall probability becomes larger through time, with most probable habitation established by A.D. 1200–1300. Graphic is based on data from Carson (2005a).	318

xvi *Figures*

13.10	View of Haleakalā crater, Maui.	319
13.11	Map of site distribution at Haleakalā summit, Maui. Graphic is adapted from Carson and Mintmier (2006a).	320
13.12	Example of a cave campsite at Haleakalā, Maui, during excavation. Scale bar is in 20 cm increments.	321
13.13	Example of bird bone with butchering or other artificial mark from Haleakalā, Maui.	321
13.14	Example of basalt flake chipping debris at Haleakalā, Maui. Scale bar is in 20 cm increments.	322
13.15	Stacked-stone cairns at Haleakalā, Maui. Scale bar is in 20 cm increments.	322
13.16	Map of stone-ringed campsite complex at Haleakalā, Maui. Graphic is adapted from Carson and Mintmier (2006a).	323
13.17	Example of stone-ringed campsite feature at Haleakalā, Maui, during excavation. Scale bar is in 20 cm increments.	324
13.18	Silhouette model of large flightless *moa* bird of New Zealand, with hunter for relative scale.	325
13.19	Guam island-wide settlement sites. Map is by Erik Reed (1955), modified from notes by Hans Hornbostel (1925), on file at the Micronesian Area Research Center, University of Guam.	328
13.20	Stacked-stone fence boundary in Tutuila, American Samoa. Scale bar is in 10 cm increments.	329
13.21	Schematic diagram of an irrigation field complex, New Caledonia.	330
13.22	Schematic diagram of a yam field complex, New Caledonia.	330
13.23	Yam field in Ouvéa, Loyalty Islands of New Caledonia.	331
13.24	Fencing border of yam field in Ouvéa, Loyalty Islands of New Caledonia.	331
13.25	Map of agricultural sites in a portion of Wainiha Valley, Halele'a District of Kaua'i, Hawaiian Islands. Graphic is adapted from Carson (2003).	332
13.26	Summary of radiocarbon dating of agricultural sites in Halele'a District of Kaua'i, Hawaiian Islands. Graphic is based on data from Carson (2006a).	333
13.27	Varieties of food pounders in Kaua'i, Hawaiian Islands.	334
13.28	Pounding breadfruit paste in Tahuata, Marquesas Islands, 1997.	335
13.29	Kona Field System in section view schematic diagram.	335
13.30	Portion of map of surface-visible stonework ruins at Ki'ilae Village, Hawai'i Island, incorporating dryland cultivation features among a habitation complex. Graphic is adapted from Carson et al. (2004).	336
13.31	Map of He'eia Fishpond in O'ahu, Hawaiian Islands.	338
13.32	Example of fish weir in Yap.	339
13.33	View of 'Alekoko Fishpond in Kaua'i, Hawaiian Islands.	339
13.34	View of *fo'aga* adze-grinding basins near coast in Tutuila, American Samoa. Machete provides scale reference.	340
13.35	Map of house foundation with *fo'aga* adze-grinding basin and adze-working debris in Tutuila, American Samoa. Graphic is adapted from Carson (2005d).	341
13.36	Collection of basalt adzes, presented by Barsinas family in Tahuata, Marquesas Islands, 1997, prior to entering into exhibit in the Tahuata Museum.	342
13.37	Generalized model of the *sawei* exchange network.	342

13.38	Yap chief standing with *rai*. Image is from the Georg Fritz collection, approximately 1899–1911, curated at the Micronesian Area Research Center, University of Guam.	343
13.39	View of Kamehameha Dynasty royal residence at Kawaihae, Hawaiʻi Island.	346
13.40	Mailekini Heiau at Kawaihae, Hawaiʻi Island. Puʻukoholā Heiau is in the background.	347
13.41	Puʻukoholā Heiau at Kawaihae, Hawaiʻi Island.	347
13.42	Excavation profile and dating of stone-ringed campsite feature at Haleakalā, Maui. Graphic is adapted from Carson and Mintmier (2006a).	349
13.43	Slingstone cache from excavation at stone-ringed campsite feature at Haleakalā, Maui.	350
13.44	Approximation of *pā* at Dacre Point, New Zealand.	351
13.45	Map of a refuge cave site in Keauhou, Hawaiʻi Island.	352
13.46	Map of Puʻuhonua o Hōnaunau, noting possible chronological sequence of construction episodes.	353
13.47	Slingstones of the Mariana Islands. Left: limestone. Right: volcanic stone. Both items are from Tumon, Guam.	354
13.48	Diagram of carved bone spear tip from the Mariana Islands. Illustration was by Hans Hornbostel (1925).	354
14.1	Traditional Chamorro blessing ceremony during excavation at Ritidian, Guam, led by Jeremy Cepeda (left) with cultural group I Fanalaiʻan, May 2016.	373
14.2	Community site visit at Ritidan, Guam, March 2016.	374
14.3	Example of "legacy collection" before and after updated curation treatment at the Micronesian Area Research Center, University of Guam.	375

Preface

Now in its second edition, this book aims for readers to engage with Pacific Oceanic archaeology in new ways and to develop more ideas about addressing different questions of their own interest. In my view, the archaeology of Pacific Oceania can contribute substantially toward profound global issues such as how to cope with changing climate and sea level, human migrations, interactive natural and cultural histories, and the processes of creating inhabited landscape systems that may or may not be sustainable. This ambitious work must begin with outlining the regional archaeological record, accounting for its full range of variation both chronologically and geographically, as a substantive basis to address the larger research issues with convincing evidence.

The second edition presents the same order of chapters and topics as in the first edition, and the only major difference has been to add new details that were not available at the time of the first edition. The factual parts of the book have not been changed except to add more detail and nuance. The second edition has allowed for refinement of information and expansion of datasets, including confirmatory findings from newly published studies, extra radiocarbon dates for some sites, and new availability of DNA obtained directly from ancient sites.

I am grateful to several people who made this book possible in its first edition and who graciously supported the second edition. James Bayman encouraged me to undertake this writing project in the first place, and he suggested to open each chapter with a traditional proverb or meaningful quote. Hsiao-chun Hung, Hiro Kurashina, and Glenn Summerhayes graciously offered images from their research. They also shared constructive advice to improve the first edition, as did Peter Bellwood, Rebecca Stephenson, Richard Walter, and anonymous reviewers of both editions. Matt Gibbons and Molly Marler guided me through the process of preparing the first edition for Routledge, and Matt Gibbons suggested to prepare an updated second edition.

I want to thank several people who have supported my research, leading toward the development of this book. At different stages of my career, Barry V. Rolett, Joseph Kennedy, Robert L. Spear, Nancy Farrell, Paul Cleghorn, J. Stephen Athens, John A. Peterson, and Monique Storie provided professional opportunities. I furthermore acknowledge Peter Bellwood, Hsiao-chun Hung, Hiro Kurashina, Patrick Nunn, and Glenn Summerhayes for their continual collaborations and advice.

During the years while preparing the first and second editions of this book, I was fortunate to work with friendly colleagues Vic April, Lufo Babauta, Rosanna Barcinas, Laura Beauregard, Michael Bevacqua, Omaira Brunal-Perry, Lon Bulgrin, Jeried Calaor, Royce Palomo Camacho, John Castro, Jeremy Cepeda, Michael Clement, Doug Comer, Jake Comer, Joey Condit, Gabe Cruz, Jonathan Kawika Davis, Zhenhua Deng, Moñeka De

Oro, Michael Dega, Boyd Dixon, Nicole DeLisle Dueñas, Dietrix Jon Ulukoa Duhaylonsod, Calvin Emesiochel, Don Farrell, Charlene Flores, Joey Flores, Larisa Ford, LaVonne Guerrero-Meno, Anne Hattori, Dorathina Herrero, Fran Hezel, Leonard Iriarte, Mertie Kani, Craig Keenom, Christopher King, Andy Laguana, Brian Leon Guerrero, Ed Leon Guerrero, Victoria Lola Montecalvo Leon Guerrero, Sean Lizama, Patrick Lujan, Carlos Madrid, Al Masga, Sandra Montón-Subías, Kel Muña, Rita Nauta, Kyle Ngiratregd, Sunny Ngirmang, John Diego Palacios, Daniel Pangelinan, Jim Pruitt, Joe Quinata, Marybelle Quinata, Dick Randall, Liz Rechebei, Clynt Ridgell, Ronnie Rogers, Scott Russell, Emily Sablan, Hila'an Pali'i San Nicolas, Carmen Sanchez, Elyssa Santos, Joe Schwagerl, Rlene Steffy, Brett Storie, Kelly Marsh-Taitano, Dominica Tolentino, Herman Tudela, Robert Underwood, and Eric West.

These people, as well as innumerable others over the years and in different places, have enriched my work, and I hope that they can see the results of their influence in this book.

Mike T. Carson

1 Research themes in Pacific Oceanic archaeology

"*Oceania* denotes a sea of islands with their inhabitants."

(Hauʻofa 1994: 153)

This book's second edition strengthens the original content about the archaeology of this large part of the world known as Pacific Oceania. Readers of the first edition will find much of the same core information here, with minor but impactful additions in each chapter to reflect newly available refinements and expanded lines of evidence. For instance, new publications have confirmed the conclusions of the first edition, and new radiocarbon dates have allowed more precision of dating of specific events and periods. Additional new publications have disclosed the studies of DNA directly from ancient sites, thereby expanding the knowledge of the past. These new findings bring greater confidence, depth, and breadth to the presentation of the archaeology of Pacific Oceania.

The Pacific Ocean covers 165 million sq km, nearly one-third of the world's total surface (Figure 1.1), yet its thousands of islands and their diverse cultural histories are scarcely known to the other two-thirds of the world. This sea of islands came to be inhabited as one of the last major population expansions in human history, now detectable through the region's archaeological records. Research has generated impacts far beyond the shores of the individual islands, significantly expanding our knowledge of human migrations, long-distance contacts and trading networks, the roles of coasts and islands in the evolution of human societies, and the development of an inhabited seascape or sea of islands.

For such a sizable portion of the globe, the Pacific region curiously has been underrepresented in world archaeology, thereby prompting the writing of this book and furthermore its second edition. After all, what could be learned from these small and remote points of land, among the last places ever to be inhabited by human beings? The total combined land mass of 300,000 sq km equals less than 0.2% of the surrounding ocean, but in fact the inhabited landscape includes the expansive seascape that indeed constitutes an impressive portion of the world. The ability of people to explore and inhabit this enormous seascape can be recognized as one of the most admirable feats in the human career. The narrative of island settlement and evolving social ecosystems extends more than 3000 years, transcending periods of changing climate, demography, and other factors as discussed in this book.

Paradoxically, the often overlooked Pacific region holds some of the world's most renowned archaeological sites, due in part to public curiosity about how these impressive sites ever existed in their seemingly unlikely places. The sites tend to be sensationalized as isolated anomalies disconnected from the rest of the world, leading to false or incomplete

DOI: 10.4324/9781003399025-1

2 Research themes in Pacific Oceanic archaeology

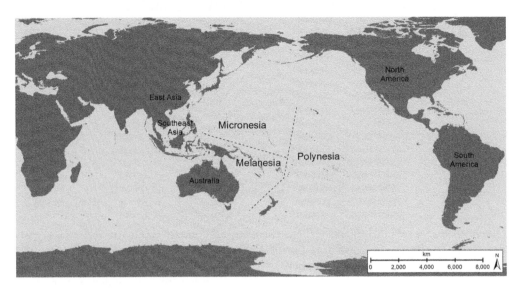

Figure 1.1 Pacific Oceania in the world.

notions of the region's archaeological legacy. For instance, the stone city of Nan Madol in Pohnpei has been regarded as the "Venice of the Pacific," with its canals leading through a labyrinthine network of long-abandoned stonework architecture, but rarely is this site discussed in relation to the many other monumental stonework traditions that developed throughout Micronesia and much of the Pacific all about the same time. Likewise, the towering *moai* stone statues of human figures in Rapa Nui (Easter Island) have inspired countless hypothetical notions and fantasies, but seldom are they portrayed as expressions of the *marae* ceremonial complexes known throughout East Polynesia, in turn related to the *malae* community gathering places of West Polynesia.

The surface-visible megalithic monuments and stonework ruins of the Pacific all date primarily within the last 1000 years, although archaeologists fondly point to a record of more than 3000 years of cultural occupation of the region. Surprisingly little attention has been devoted to the chronological change from initial human settlement through later periods, by default creating an impression of little or no change in the long time scale or *longue durée* of history. Perhaps inadvertently, long-term enduring cultural continuity has been stressed at the cost of undervaluing the substantive change through time in forms of housing, practical techniques and artistic expressions in pottery, and other traditions of diverse material culture.

The region's archaeology extends long before written history entered the Pacific from outside sources. Much can be gained from reading the accounts of Ferdinand Magellan's visit in 1521 and the body of historical literature that has accumulated ever since then, but different kinds of non-written records relate to the more distant past. The unwritten records include not only archaeology but also oral traditions, folklore, linguistic history, and other ways of studying the past. All of these lines of evidence will be considered here, keeping in mind that archaeology uniquely obtains its information directly from the past. Unlike any other discipline, archaeology potentially can provide secure dating and high resolution of chronological control over a long time scale.

Among the sources of knowledge about the past, this book grants priority to the material archaeological evidence in terms of referring to specifically measured objects, locations, and time periods. By establishing these facts in their natural chronological order, this book avoids the problems of misinterpreting or overinterpreting the diverse archaeological record of Pacific Oceania. Ancient site layers have been dated primarily through radiocarbon, thereby allowing a narrative about where people lived at different times and what they did in these places, as reflected in the patterns of their ancient tools, decorative ornaments, food middens, forms of houses, workshops, rock art, ritual caves, religious sites, and more. When the contributions from written history, comparative linguistics, or other fields are relevant for specific places or time periods, then they can be incorporated into the factual chronology.

This book's second edition builds on the central chronological narrative of the first edition. Importantly, nothing from the previous edition has been overturned or proven incorrect, because of the strict adherence to the factual datasets of archaeological sites, layers, and dating. Instead, the second edition retains those strengths of the first edition, while adding the knowledge from newer discoveries. For example, more details of radiocarbon dating are shared here than had been listed in the first edition, and new findings allow for more refined conclusions about the beginning and ending of different time periods. New discoveries are shared for the places that previously had not been surveyed or excavated, in total filling a few gaps and confirming the overall regional chronological sequence. Considerable worldwide attention to ancient DNA studies has in fact included new work in Pacific Oceania, presented here as part of the archaeological record and in the chronological order of relevance.

The chronological narrative provides the basis to address fundamental archaeological questions. While the core questions remain the same as in the first edition, many of the answers now can be clarified with extra details and nuance.

- How and why did people explore this grand ocean and eventually populate its many islands?
- What were the processes of transforming this large part of the world into an inhabited landscape, seascape, or sea of islands?
- What are the roles of islands as case studies for global-scale research issues?
- How can island case studies contribute toward general knowledge of human-environment relations, for instance in terms of coping with changing sea level and coastal ecologies, climate variability, and population growth within inherently limited resource habitats?
- Given the fact that migrations were necessary for people to settle in the remote Pacific Islands, what can Pacific Oceanic archaeology offer toward learning about human migrations and mobility?
- What were the roles of overseas contacts in the development of social networks, economic trade, and population dynamics?
- What do the island archaeological records reveal about coastal settings as part of the larger human experience?
- How does Pacific Oceanic archaeology relate with a broader Asia-Pacific context or with the scope of world archaeology?

These themes will be introduced here briefly, then explored in more detail with relevant material data throughout the next chapters.

Defining Pacific Oceania

Pacific Oceania is an artificial modern name for one large part of the world, where its namesake ocean contains more than 20,000 islands, each with unique yet at some scale interrelated archaeological records. Much like Africa, Asia, and Europe refer to generalized geographic regions encompassing variable internal diversity, Pacific Oceania incorporates considerable variation within its borders, and moreover its borders are not always obvious. All of these regional definitions are based on perceptions of geographic space and cultural history, but they apply only at a rough scale with imperfections.

Three regional names in the Pacific were popularized by the French explorer and naval officer Jules Sébastien César Dumont d'Urville (1832), still in common usage today as Polynesia, Melanesia, and Micronesia. Polynesia ("many islands") refers to the numerous islands of the central and eastern Pacific, where people spoke clearly related languages and maintained many of the same social customs. The term Polynesia in this case has refined the prior usage by Charles de Brosses (1756) to refer to all or most of the Pacific Islands. Melanesia ("black islands") refers to the European impressions of the dark-skinned native islanders in most of the western-central Pacific. Micronesia ("small islands") refers to the province of mostly very small coral atolls in the northwest tropical Pacific.

The three major "culture areas" of Polynesia, Melanesia, and Micronesia today are recognized as convenient names of large geographic portions of the Pacific, and they generally are understood as reflecting only minimal and incomplete aspects of cultural history (Thomas 1989). Pacific Islanders have adopted these words of convenience for modern speech, while most traditional languages refer to "the land" inhabited by "the people." Whatever names are used, the geographic areas of Pacific Oceania incorporate noticeable internal diversity, and their boundaries are blurred with each other. Moreover, significant relationships are evident linguistically, culturally, and biologically between these groups and others living farther westward, for example in New Guinea and throughout Island Southeast Asia.

The Pacific Ocean itself provides the primary basis for defining the island region within it, bounded by the coastlines of surrounding continents or other imposing land barriers. The eastern boundary of the Pacific clearly is delineated by the coastline of the American continents, while the western boundary does not have such a strong marker. In one perspective, the western boundary of the Pacific touches on the shores of East Asia, but in another perspective, it could terminate somewhere around the large land masses of New Guinea, Australia, or Island Southeast Asia.

As will be discussed in Chapters 2 and 4, the complexities of a western boundary in the Pacific apply to geology, native plant and animal communities, and cultural history. The first inhabitants of the remote central and eastern Pacific Islands came from the western side of the Pacific, where their ancestral homeland islands were situated more closely together and where larger land masses were available. When people moved eastward, they moved into a different kind of island world, where the ratio of ocean to land was greater than in any other human experience.

The relative amount of sea versus land provides one way to distinguish Pacific Oceania from other regions of the world. The ratio is extreme in the islands of the Pacific, most obvious when compared to settings of continents like North and South America. The ratio varies somewhat in each island group, and it is more noticeable when comparing the small islands of the eastern Pacific with the larger land masses of Island Southeast Asia.

Looking at the central and eastern zones of the Pacific, nearly all of the islands originated geologically in isolation from continental land masses. Volcanic hills and coral formations emerged entirely in the ocean, and eventually they supported communities of plants and animals that naturally differed from the biomass and biodiversity found in distant continents. The major exceptions to this pattern are the relicts of continental masses in the islands of New Zealand and New Caledonia, separated for millions of years from their geological continental origins.

The remoteness of islands in the central and eastern Pacific has substantiated a naming of Remote Oceania, juxtaposed against the more accessible islands of Near Oceania (Green 1991). In the western Pacific, the Near Oceanic islands are reachable by short water crossings, generally less than 120 km but rarely up to 200 km, always with at least one point of land remaining visible during the water-crossing journey. Many of these islands were at one time interconnected by land bridges during the last major Ice Age, whereas no such land bridges or shelves ever reached as far as the islands of Remote Oceania. The first human settlements in Remote Oceania required ocean-crossing voyages of at least 350 km and beyond the sight of land. Many of these voyaging migrations were much longer, managed only after several days or even weeks at sea.

The peopling of Remote Oceania began about 3500 years ago, around 1500 B.C., made possible by older cultural foundations in the larger and closely packed land masses farther to the west, but again the western boundary of the Pacific defies easy definition. A number of broad regional homelands may be suggested, stretching over thousands of years and over an immense geographic space from New Guinea to East Asia. In contrast to the sudden appearance of archaeological horizons in Remote Oceania within the last 3500 years, innumerable generations of people had lived in New Guinea, Australia, and throughout Island Southeast Asia for about 50,000 years. The search for cultural origins becomes even more complicated when considering the presence of human ancestors such as *Homo erectus* in Indonesia more than 700,000 years ago.

The archaeology of Pacific Oceania is for the most part concerned with the last 3500 years in Remote Oceania, but it interfaces significantly with much older time periods in Near Oceania, Island Southeast Asia, and even as far as East Asia. Pacific Oceania therefore has no clear western geographic limit, and its archaeological record likewise has no exact beginning point in time. These parameters, although necessarily vague at the edges, outline the position of Pacific Oceania in world archaeology.

Islands as laboratories, microcosms, and model systems

Over the last several decades, archaeologists have described islands as laboratories, as microcosms of the world, and as model systems for understanding global processes. These notions arguably make the Pacific Oceanic region exemplary for case studies in world archaeology, notwithstanding several points of criticism. The underlying concepts have been borrowed heavily from biology and biogeography. Significant challenges must be faced when modifying these concepts for archaeological investigation of past human behaviors.

Islands possess two relative values of smallness and isolation that in theory make them ideal settings or virtual laboratories for scientific observations, as highlighted more than 50 years ago in a theory of island biogeography (MacArthur and Wilson 1967). Small islands can incorporate several natural ecological zones within close proximity to each other, such that any plants or animals potentially can adapt to these varied niches all within one island. Meanwhile, greater isolation will decrease the number and variety of plants and animals that reach an island's shores, and henceforth these limited founding populations undergo an exaggerated form of natural selection while adapting to the unique conditions of the remote island setting.

Biogeography was recognized as potentially powerful for cultural anthropology and archaeology in Pacific Oceania (Terrell 1976, 1977, 1997), although, most certainly, human beings could behave in complex ways and overcome the limits of island size and isolation. The remote islands typically did not support all of the culturally desired plant foods and other resources, so people artificially imported multiple crops and domesticated animals across long distances of ocean voyages (Wickler 2004; Yen 1990, 1991). Even the most isolated islands are connected in some way to the outside world, as proved by the fact that people settled the remote Pacific Islands in antiquity. Moreover, the widely separated island societies evidently maintained networks of long-distance ocean-crossing contact and exchange, attested in oral histories and in artifacts such as stone adzes traceable to surprisingly distant geological sources (Weisler 1998).

Despite the good reasons for being cautious about applying the theory of island biogeography to human beings, the basic principles are validated in terms of the large-scale biogeographic zones of plants and animals in the Pacific (Figure 1.2). Approximately during the same time when Charles Darwin found the Galapagos Islands useful as places to observe the speciation of finches (Darwin 1839, 1845, 1859), Alfred Russell Wallace made similar observations about the geographic distributions of animals in the islands of the Indo-Malay Archipelago (Wallace 1869, 1870). Today, the "Wallace Line" or "Wallace's Line" marks the divide between two general biogeographic regions, noting animals of Asian origin to the northwest versus others of Australian origin to the southeast. The line of division coincides with a deep water channel aligned roughly north-south through

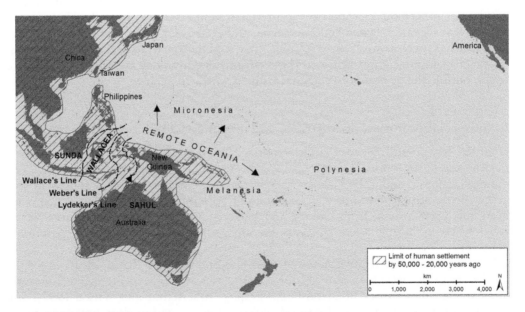

Figure 1.2 Major biogeographic zones of the Asia-Pacific region.

Indonesia, where most animals were unable to cross from one side to the other. The water channel is so deep that it has persisted even through the Last Glacial Maximum when the sea level was much lower than today. During those times when many parts of Island Southeast Asia were joined by land bridges, the deep water zones along Wallace's Line had posed substantial water barriers. In addition to Wallace's Line, other biogeographic divisions have been drawn in Island Southeast Asia, known as Huxley's Line, Weber's Line, and Lydekker's Line.

Today, at least three general regions in Island Southeast Asia are known as Sunda in the northwest, with Asian biota; Sahul in the southeast, with Australian biota; and Wallacea in the middle, with its own distinctive intermediary flora and fauna. The lines of division follow the few notably deep or wide water gaps. Meanwhile, the large regions of overall unity refer to the clustered groupings of numerous islands with much smaller interisland water gaps.

Moving west to east across the Pacific, another biogeographic line may be drawn between Near and Remote Oceania, yet continual gradients in declining biomass and biodiversity are noted incrementally moving west to east into increasingly isolated groups of islands. Of the plants and animals that did reach these remote islands, they tended to evolve with a high degree of endemism, meaning that they evolved into unique species or subspecies not found anywhere else. Just as one example in the Hawaiian Islands, about 4000 km from the nearest continental shores, flowering plants of the Campanulaceae family ("bellflowers") now include six distinct genera with a total of 30 species, all descended from a single introduction (Givnish et al. 1995). The degree of speciation has been remarkably high in those particular islands with the most tightly packed ecological zones or niches, where the founding populations of plants and animals had included very few individual taxa which subsequently diversified locally.

Certainly in biological organisms, a "founder effect" or "bottleneck effect" may be expected in any isolated populations. In principle, when a small population is isolated with little or no outside contact, then those small numbers of founding individuals will produce descendants with a limited range of variability. After some generations, localized speciation or endemism may be expected, as seen in the numbers of endemic plants and animals now living in remote islands. The effects are more pronounced in islands that happen to consist of variable habitat ecology, where the narrow range of a founding population needs to adapt to these special circumstances.

The founder effect in theory operates in human culture, best illustrated in the phylogenetic language groupings of the Pacific. As outlined by linguist Robert Blust (2013), the Austronesian language family diversified into continually different branches as people migrated into farther remote islands across the Pacific. Languages spoken in the more isolated islands of the eastern Pacific, within the area now known as Polynesia, are the easiest to identify as closely related, whereas the languages of farther west islands are more difficult to classify in the language-tree phylogeny. The people in each island group of Polynesia speak their own language, but each separate spoken language very clearly is recognized as part of a unified Polynesian grouping (Marck 1999; Pawley 1966). At a higher phylogenetic level, the languages of Polynesia, Micronesia, most of Melanesia, and much of Island Southeast Asia may be grouped as related elements of Malayo-Polynesian. The largest overarching linguistic unit would be Austronesian, extending the geographic range to Taiwan, presumably with older ancestry in coastal China (Blust 1995). The older ancestry of Austronesian language in coastal China is no longer detectable today, due to replacement by Han Chinese since approximately 2000 years ago, and instead the

Austronesian language history at a large scale has been traced through the unique conditions of the island world.

Based largely on the apparent founder effects in remote islands, the notion of "islands as laboratories" entered the Pacific anthropological literature at least as early as the 1950s. Ward Goodenough (1957) proposed that Pacific Oceania was an ideal place to learn about cultural diversification or phylogeny, noting the potential for examining the development over time from founding ancestral populations into later expressions of diverse cultural descendants. Although this work did not directly advocate "islands as laboratories," it was prefaced by a text composed by Margaret Mead (1957) titled "An introduction to Polynesia as a laboratory for the development of models in the study of cultural evolution." Additional contributions to this theme came from Marshall Sahlins (1957) and Irving Goldman (1957), both providing summary reviews of how present-day variations in Polynesian societies from one island group to another most likely have resulted from the inevitable diversification in their secluded island settings. Following much the same logic a few years later, Andrew Vayda and Roy Rappaport (1963) postulated that island societies have diversified into differential subgroupings according to the degree of limited resources and isolation of the places that they inhabit.

While island societies and ecosystems clearly do not behave like bacteria in petri dishes, islands by definition consist of discrete environments similar to laboratories. Islands can serve as convenient venues with minimal effects of incomplete sampling, external contacts, cross-cultural influence, and other potential complications. In these settings, the necessarily incomplete and often inconclusive archaeological records of past human behaviors arguably are more representative and convincing than typically is the case in larger continents.

The potential for an island to act as a laboratory-like case study depends on the nature of the material being studied, often related to the relative factors of island size and isolation. No island offers a perfect set of circumstances, just like no island consists of an entirely closed system, but each island does offer the potential to minimize complicating factors while maximizing a focus on specific points. As Ben Fitzhugh and Terry Hunt (1997: 381) declared: "At issue is not whether islands make good laboratories, but in what ways are islands good laboratories!" Each island's archaeological record can be assessed for its ability to support a usefully illustrative or representative example of a global or general research topic, but of course not every island offers a convincing or relevant set of data for addressing whatever research question may be desired. The pressure, therefore, is on the archaeologist to justify any particular island as a useful model or example of the specific research issue being addressed.

Although islands are imperfect approximations of laboratories, they potentially are microcosms of the larger and admittedly imperfect world. In theory, the same processes of natural and cultural histories occur everywhere, and they can be encapsulated in neatly observable packages in certain definable microcosms such as in islands. In this case, archaeologists are challenged to find particular islands where the material records most instructively illustrate the key points of interest. For instance, many islands have yielded detailed examples of how human societies have manipulated their fragile environments through introduced domesticated plants and animals, as well as the cultural systems of managing the natural resources, potentially representative of the general processes of human-caused environmental impacts at a global scale (Kirch 2004).

Further considering the capacity of islands as ideal locations for research, Vitousek et al. (2010) described islands as "model systems" that are representative of the world. The scientific model of a *system* should not be mistaken as a direct miniature representation of the world, such as may be the case with a 1:24,000 scale map or a 1:45 ratio of a battlefield terrain model. Rather, in a "model systems" view, the social-natural ecosystems of islands serve as examples of how these kinds of complex systems operate worldwide, much like certain short-lived small insects serve as convenient ways to examine the general principles of biological evolution in action. The insects do not represent the totality of all biological processes, but they allow focus on just the core essence of how an organism can adapt to varied conditions. Likewise, island case studies can allow focus on the particular variables of social-natural ecosystems of general interest for archaeologists and many others.

In principle, the archaeological record of a single site or island can be viewed as representing the record of a larger geographic region or perhaps of a cross-regional theme. If a site truly represents the complete time depth of an island or region, then its material contents could act as a model for the broader island-wide or region-wide chronology. If a site shows evidence of how people adapted to a change in sea level during a particular time period, then those results could be useful when studying the same or similar event in other areas. Not every site can meet these criteria to succeed as a representative model, and therefore the choice of a site-specific model needs to be justified.

Analogies with laboratories, microcosms, and model systems depend on the extent to which the island in question provides compelling evidence about a specific chosen topic. Conceivably, the small size and skewed nature of an island setting have created awkward anomalies, thereby lessening the confidence about representing a larger reality. Furthermore, many islands have supported rather shallow time spans of human occupation, so their short-lived archaeological chronicles may not be so useful toward understanding long-term cultural processes. In other words, if island archaeological records contain so much information compressed into small spaces and often into short time frames, then archaeologists need to demonstrate how these unique situations relate to the larger world.

Human-environment relations

Islands offer productive settings to learn about how people interact with their environments in laboratory-like microcosms or model systems, and especially intriguing studies are possible when tracing the human-environment relations in site records that extend over hundreds or thousands of years. Although no island consists of a purely sealed or closed system, all islands necessarily have boundaries within which an archaeological landscape can be defined as a cohesive unit during each represented time period. Furthermore, if the archaeological site inventory within such a limited space allows clear identification of the timing of first human arrival, then much more can be addressed about the initial human-environment encounters and subsequent chronology of dynamic processes.

Human-environment relations must be understood as mutually affective processes. They are not one-sided reflections of environmental determinism or equally inadequate cultural determinism. People clearly have created impacts, intentionally or not, on their environments, but they also have responded to the given circumstances of their social and natural environments. Both aspects need to be considered simultaneously.

At least two nuanced perspectives have considered how a human-environment relationship operates in the first place. On the one hand, people perceive and experience their environmental circumstances necessarily through human agency, thus enabling a social response as the key unit of study (Lilley 2008). On the other hand, human beings live within preexisting natural environments that now accommodate cultural behaviors in evolving natural-cultural ecosystems (Nunn 2003a, 2003b). These two viewpoints do not necessarily oppose each other, but they serve as reminders that natural and cultural processes tend to be more deeply interconnected than may be apparent superficially.

The time scale of an archaeological record may or may not be sufficient to reveal human-environment interaction, and longer time spans logically can include greater opportunities for learning about significant change through time. Some limited occurrences are detectable as singular events or short windows of a few centuries or less, such as when people after A.D. 1300 or 1400 imported durable crops of sweet potatoes to cope with dry and resource-poor zones, leading to the imposition of new landscape systems in the rain shadows of leeward Hawai'i and Maui islands or in the cool temperate climate of New Zealand (Ballard et al. 2008; Yen 1974). Other aspects are comprehensible only through truly long-term views in the longer-occupied islands of the western Pacific, such as shown in the Mariana Islands sites, transcending fluctuations of sea level, climate, demography, and other factors over extended periods of numerous centuries ever since 1500 B.C. (Carson 2012).

Islands happen to be famously excellent places for documenting human-generated impacts because the unique flora and fauna in these isolated settings evolved in ways that were quite vulnerable to the actions of the human beings who eventually arrived (Fosberg 1963). In the islands of East Polynesia, for instance, people imported suites of plants and animals over long distances across the ocean, leading directly to ecosystem-wide change (Kirch 1983). Island settlers surely would have acted differently, however, if they were moving to occupy islands with the same familiar plant and animal communities as they knew in their homeland, as was the case throughout most of Island Southeast Asia and Near Oceania. Even when crossing major biogeographic zones such as Wallace's Line, people still could recognize several useful plants and animals, and plentiful food resources were available. When crossing into Remote Oceania, and especially in the farther remote islands of East Polynesia, however, people needed to adapt to the extreme paucity of familiar edible terrestrial-based foods, often by importing plants and animals from overseas. Most of the islands actually supported marvelously healthy and productive ecosystems, wherein the only "paucity" was in terms of the specific plants and animals that immigrating people desired in their inhabited landscapes.

Across most of Pacific Oceania, people transported not only the biotic inventories of overseas taxa but also their cultural notions of how to interface with the landscape. The process of a "transported landscape," as first described by Edgar Anderson (1952), has occurred throughout the world, whenever and wherever human groups settled into new regions, and the outcomes have been most visible in remote islands such as in Pacific Oceania. These islands have yielded abundant records of sudden horizons of forest-clearing, imports of new crops and animals, native bird extinctions, and other impacts (Athens et al. 2002; Kirch 2000: 59–62). In the cases of isolated islands with single founding populations of human settlement, the horizons of anthropogenic impacts or transported landscapes can be attributed to specific groups of human immigrants without the ambiguities of cross-cultural influence, borrowing, diffusion, and other factors in the more open-bordered systems of continents.

Much like the historical expansions of European landscape systems which have dominated the face of the world through "ecological imperialism" (Crosby 1986), impressive episodes of transported landscapes have occurred in Pacific Oceania. One of the most profound of these episodes occurred in a concise span of a few centuries, about 1100 through 800 B.C., when Lapita pottery-making groups created irreversible impacts on the fragile Remote Oceanic island ecosystems of Southern Melanesia and West Polynesia. This veritable siege of ecological imperialism will be discussed in Chapter 7, along with an awareness that the process involved a two-way interaction between the Lapita cultural groups and the natural island habitats. The Lapita case in Chapter 7 can be juxtaposed against an earlier event presented in Chapter 6, involving the first contact between human beings and the Remote Oceanic environment about 1500 B.C. in the Mariana Islands of the northwest tropical Pacific.

Human impacts and imprints are exaggerated in island ecosystems, but interpretations of those human exaggerations are at risk of missing the evidence of what had prompted these cultural actions in the first place. This point is most clear in Pacific Oceania, where island ecosystems had evolved for long periods of time without any human presence, so that the first inhabitants necessarily adapted to the given conditions. Human beings could not possibly have caused the natural processes of generating weather patterns, geological landforms, or natural biogeographic zones that had originated long prior to human actions, but instead people certainly have responded to these conditions.

The physical shapes of islands and the compositions of their coastal ecologies have been affected directly by changing sea level, in this case completely unrelated to human agency (except indirectly during the modern era) but definitely triggering cultural response in several cases throughout Pacific Oceania. The cultural groups who targeted narrow ecological niches in certain types of shoreline settings must have been well aware of ever-changing coastal dynamics, but they may not have been prepared for sudden loss of their preferred niches or major shifts in habitat configuration due to rapid sea-level change. These distressing circumstances were magnified when they happened to coincide with increasing resident populations, impacts of overharvesting of nearshore resources, and other factors contributing to an overall resource depression. One such event occurred across the western and central Pacific around 500 B.C., during a drawdown of sea level that had begun around 1100–1000 B.C., very shortly after the first Remote Oceanic settlements, as detailed in Chapter 8. A different event occurred after A.D. 100, when the advancement of sea-level drawdown had allowed hundreds of coral atoll formations to be exposed above sea level and thus supported widespread human habitation for the first time throughout much of Micronesia, as covered in Chapter 10. In a modern context, human actions have accelerated a changing climate and a rising global sea level, and therefore the lessons from the older archaeological examples have become increasingly relevant for modern concerns.

One curiously mixed natural-cultural factor in island geomorphology has been the pattern of slope erosion and redeposition occurring in all islands with appreciable sloping terrain. Slope erosion clearly is a natural process, as is its counterpart of redeposition of the eroded material settling into lower and generally flatter landforms, but the process can be accelerated by cultural activities such as forest clearing and preparing upland zones for cultivation (Spriggs 1997). Forest clearing is recorded in burning episodes preserved occasionally in layers of charcoal flecking on hillslopes, but most definitively in lake-bottom and swamp-bottom sediments, along with pollen and other indicators of reduced native species while introduced taxa and weed growth tend to increase. These records can be correlated with periods of suddenly more rapid buildup of slope-eroded sediments in lowlands such as valley floors and coastal plains, wherein the timing coincides with purported upland forest-clearing activities.

Looking at Pacific Oceania as a whole, the research opportunities for studying human-environment relations are abundant and relevant for comprehending how societies can cope with current and future environmental challenges. An impressive range of habitat diversity is concentrated into the rather small spaces of island ecosystems, thus setting the stage to address several questions about how people adapted to their available niches, created new landscape systems, and coped with ongoing ecological change. Given the variable time depth of human occupation across the region, additional questions may be addressed about how people have adapted successfully or not with changing circumstances of climate and sea level in some islands of older habitation records, whereas different challenges were presented to the inhabitants of other islands with shallower time span of settlement. Further avenues of cross-comparative analysis may consider the differential outcomes of the degrees of island size, ecological diversity, and isolation in numerous islands with similar or different spans of human occupation.

Human migrations

Pacific Oceania has been one of the world's most productive regions for studies of human migrations. Although migration alone lacks ultimate explanatory power in terms of why societies have changed or evolved, real events of migration nevertheless have occurred as part of the cultural histories of all regions of the world (Anthony 1990; Bellwood 2013, 2015). Research of ancient migrations has been ideal in the islands of Remote Oceania and most especially in the eastern provinces of Polynesia, where the instances of first human habitation are well documented in several cases of sudden appearance of material impacts and archaeological signatures. The situation is much more complicated in the longer-occupied areas farther westward in the Pacific, where anatomically modern humans first entered into Island Southeast Asia and into Australia several millennia ago, followed by a number of later movements and meetings of populations in different contexts.

Migration necessarily occurred at a large scale with the peopling of the Pacific, bringing the human species into some of the last habitable places on earth. The region-crossing migration occurred as a series of steps, and each step related to at least one major change in cultural history, such as developments in sailing technology and navigational knowledge, spread of transported landscapes, and adaptations to remote island living. Ancient migration has played a stronger role in Pacific archaeology than has been possible in other regions of the world, where migration typically has been difficult or impossible to assert among the possibilities of internal developments, borrowing, cross-cultural contacts, and other alternative processes that could have resulted in patterns of new material culture horizons emerging in a region. These ambiguities are not applicable in the remote islands of the Pacific, where the first human arrivals very clearly can be associated with distinctive material culture inventories and potentially traced to their approximate homelands.

Migrations into the Pacific began as an extension of *Homo sapiens* dispersals ultimately from a source in Africa, reaching through Southeast Asia and into Australia before 50,000 years ago (Chapter 4). These initial movements occurred at a time of much lower sea level and exposed larger masses of land, with scattered water gaps that people evidently could conquer. A number of later movements of people likely occurred yet cannot be detected clearly in the overall sparse hunter-gatherer sites of this region.

Most abundantly detectable in the material record was the sudden arrival of people producing pottery and living in structured villages, starting at least as early as 2000 B.C. in a few sites of Island Southeast Asia (Chapter 5). The pottery and other artifacts were markedly different from the findings of preceding centuries or millennia in the region, and therefore these assemblages very likely signified an intrusive influence, presumably from a source in Asia where pottery-making and permanent village settlement systems already had been established as cultural traditions for several centuries. Within Island Southeast

Asia, the oldest pottery-bearing horizon at 2200–2000 B.C. began several millennia after the massive post-glacial sea-level rise following 10,000–9000 B.C., so the movement of pottery-making groups (or of their ideas and influences) into the region necessarily involved a significant amount of sea-crossing activity. The continued expansion of the "pottery trail" into Remote Oceania required substantially longer ocean crossings of many hundreds of km for the first time in human history into the Mariana Islands at 1500 B.C. (Chapter 6) and then into Southern Melanesia and West Polynesia about 1100–800 B.C. (Chapter 7).

After 800 B.C., a "pause" occurred in the spread of migrations into the farther remote parts of Pacific Oceania, eventually broken by two major population movements. First was after A.D. 100, when a lowered sea level and emergence of atolls supported new settlements throughout Central and Eastern Micronesia (Chapter 10). Second was after A.D. 1000 with widespread expansion into East Polynesia and leading to more or less complete inhabitation of the Pacific "sea of islands" as it is known today (Chapter 12). Previously, scholars have debated the reasons for a perceived elongated pause between the colonization of West Polynesia at 1100–800 B.C. and much later migrations into East Polynesia at A.D. 1000 (Irwin 1992, 1998). Now with acknowledging the large-scale movements of inhabiting Central and Eastern Micronesia after A.D. 100, the length of the apparent voyaging pause has been shortened, plus the directionality and context are revealed as more complicated than just a singular Polynesian trajectory moving west to east.

Following the premise that migrations alone do not explain cultural change, archaeologists more productively can build stronger understanding of the mechanics of how migrations work and how they interrelate with other events and processes. In addition to considerations of the motivations of migrants seeking new land and opportunities (Bellwood 2013), migrations can be understood as cultural transformations of inhabited homes into exited homelands, of ocean boundaries into navigable sealanes, and of vague notions of faraway islands into inhabitable new homes (Carson and Hung 2014). These kinds of cognitive, transformative shifts occurred repeatedly and in varying forms, and no single formula can be applied to every instance of migration. These processes further can be related to other contemporaneous factors, as facilitated by the chronological narrative in this book, for example seeking possible correlations between migratory events and changing climate, population size and density, modes of resource-use patterns compared to available habitat zones, access to new sailing technologies or navigational knowledge, and developments in social and political operations.

This book depicts the Pacific-wide settlement chronology in terms of a series of sea-crossing migrations, followed by networks of cross-contacts and exchange. In this view of an "incremental growth model," each population movement involved not only the settled islands but also the cultural knowledge of the associated inhabited seascape or sea of islands. This model neatly accommodates the movement of people to and from broad zones rather than pinpointed nodes, as well as the potential for subsequent interaction and cross-contacts across the inhabited regions. Furthermore, the timing of each expansionary growth can be acknowledged as having occurred over a duration, albeit defined as a brief window of time within the limits of archaeologically detectable and datable materials, as illustrated in the Asia-Pacific region-crossing pottery trail (Chapter 5) and then developed further in the chronological narrative of later chapters.

Trade and exchange

After initially settling in islands, people maintained cross-contacts with homelands and potentially throughout ever-expanding networks as a sea of islands took larger and larger shape with new communities established in continually more places across the Pacific. These contacts sometimes have created no durable archaeological trace, but at least some instances have been demonstrated through the material artifacts that must have moved from one place to another. Transported objects have been identified in the stone tools made from known geological sources, the clay recipes and especially certain temper inclusions in pottery fragments, and the distinctive styles of pottery and other artifacts. In addition to the transported materials in themselves, trade partnerships imply other social relations, alliances, and friendships linking the members of the communities involved in these acts of exchange.

Asian and Pacific trading networks consistently were based on using the sea as a means of connectivity, suggesting that the ocean offers more potential to connect than to divide. Coastal groups living on distant shores from one another, such as on opposite sides of a sea, often shared more of their material culture with each other than with their adjacent neighbors living farther inland in the adjoining land mass of an island. Peter Lape (2004) outlined these overseas coastal connections for communities in Island Southeast Asia, and Hung et al. (2013) formally proposed a model of "coastal connectivity" for networking across the South China Sea. The patterns are most striking in larger islands and land masses as in Island Southeast Asia with appreciably large and complex interior zones, where the coastal and inland communities lived in at least some degree of separation. Some of the people living in the highlands of New Guinea or the deep interior of Borneo may never have seen the coast during their lifetime. Meanwhile, smaller islands do not show the same degree of separation of coastal versus inland communities, where, instead, the material culture inventories as a whole tend to reflect only slight differentiation of access to overseas trading.

Differential access to traded items occasionally can be detected in societies wherein certain individuals or groups controlled the raw materials, related labor, or distribution. These patterns could reflect strategies of gaining or at least manipulating the balance of wealth and power in a society (Earle 1997). Such patterns often are easier to accomplish in an island setting with inherently limited internal resources and clear means of controlling external contacts at ports and harbors. At least two archaeological examples of these pathways to power are known within the last 1000 years in Pacific Oceania, including the development of a Tongan "maritime empire" (Campbell 2001) and the antecedents of the historically known Hawaiian Kingdom (Hommon 2013; Kirch 2010). These issues relate with the post–A.D. 1000 formalization of material culture (Chapter 12) and large-scale trends of expansion and intensification that tend to be exaggerated or exacerbated in small islands (Chapter 13).

Interisland trade networks existed during each of the time periods represented in the chapters of this book, and they very clearly have changed chronologically in the arrangement of contact nodes, types of traded commodities, scales, and intensities of activity.

- Earrings, pendants, and other objects made of nephrite (jade) from the distinctive Fengtian source in eastern Taiwan were traded into Mainland and Island Southeast Asia at least since 1000 B.C. (Hung et al. 2007), although the character of the trade changed considerably over time with different producers, end users, and competition with materials from other sources.
- Obsidian and volcanic glass were transported over long distances across Island Southeast Asia for several thousands of years by hunter-gatherer communities, and these

traditions continued later with the groups moving into the islands of Remote Oceania (Spriggs et al. 2011).
- Perhaps as early as 500 B.C. but certainly by A.D. 100, the beginnings of globalized trade entered into parts of Island Southeast Asia, connecting with East Asia, Mainland Southeast Asia, and India (Ardika and Bellwood 1991; Hung et al. 2013). Iron, bronze, gold, glass, and precious stones were traded widely yet did not cross into the networks of interaction among the islands of Remote Oceania.
- Different trading operations were active in the remote Pacific, possibly as precursors to the renowned ethnographic examples such as the *kula* ring in Melanesia (Malinowski 1922) and the *sawei* tribute system connecting Yap with other islands of western Micronesia (Sudo 1996).
- Among the known transported archaeological materials in Pacific Oceania, basalt adzes can be traced to specific volcanic sources, such as the Tatagamatau quarry in Tutuila of American Samoa, whose adzes have been discovered in archaeological sites thousands of km distant and dated mostly within the last 1000 years (Clark et al. 1997; Weisler 1997).

Interisland exchange must be separated analytically from the initial population movements of founding migrations, as they represent two qualitatively different cultural actions of mobility. Most crucially, the later trade and exchange did not involve large-scale movements of populations and their accompanying cultural systems into new territories. The sealanes of first migrations continued to be used for new purposes, while additional routes and connections were discovered as well. Whenever new sailing technology or navigational knowledge became available, then both migrations and trading expeditions suddenly could cover longer distances and occur in greater frequency. The overall picture, thus, was a continually expanding seascape of navigable sealanes and islands.

Interisland exchange further can be conceptualized as occurring at different scales and within variable contexts, including close-neighbor activities and long-range inter-archipelago voyaging. Longer and presumably rarer journeys may have involved restricted numbers of people and certain formalities of special events, in contrast to the more routine practice and public participation of close-neighbor interactions. Closeness of contact very likely affected the degree of shared cultural traditions, for instance as the linguist Jeffrey Marck (1986) noticed in language dialects of Micronesia. The people living in islands within range of overnight voyaging of each other tended to share language dialects, while those separated by longer distances tended to have significantly different language histories. Long voyages indeed were risky and overall rare, requiring extended time at sea, ability to amass wealth and resources to build and maintain sailing craft, skills of remote-distance voyaging and navigation, and, of course, the motivations for people to undertake these extreme journeys.

Coasts and islands

Pacific Oceania may be perceived as an island world within which coasts play a key role. Indeed, coasts have been vital in human evolution and society as a whole, as Jon Erlandson (2001, 2002) has argued through archaeological evidence and as John Gilles (2012) has illustrated in a synthesis of the world history of coasts. Working with related issues, John Mack (2011) proposed an anthropological view of the sea as a culturally perceived entity, intimately involved with the lives of all coastal people yet most profoundly expressed in the lives of coastal people in islands. Given that islands contain a high density of coasts and associated coastal zones, many of the analytic constructs about islands more properly can be reworded as applying to coasts. At the same time, many of the globally significant research topics about coasts can be illustrated most robustly in islands as extreme examples of coastal habitats.

Issues of human migrations into remote islands may be reworded as migrations into dense concentrations of coastal zones that happened to be situated across a large expanse of ocean. Instead of asking the so-far-unanswerable question of why people migrated across the ocean to live in remote islands, scholars may more accurately address the issues of why people migrated long distances to find new coastal habitats. Indeed, the first settlers in Remote Oceania had targeted a narrow range of shoreline niches (Chapters 6 and 7), suggestive of seeking a preferred type of coast rather than seeking any kind of island per se. Moreover, these specific niches had been untouched by any other human beings, so the resource productivity was remarkably high, at least for the first few generations of new inhabitants. The major challenge, though, involved how to provide enough food nutrients for sustaining a large population, particularly in terms of the desired dietary plant foods that might not have existed naturally in the remote islands prior to human-mediated transport.

Coastal routes of human migrations have become recognized as very likely contributing to the spread of anatomically modern humans around the world, as Bailey et al. (2007) noted for the initial movements of *Homo sapiens* from Africa venturing eastward around the Arabian Peninsula. Actual use of any specific type of boat, raft, or other watercraft is uncertain, but ancient humans probably found easier water crossings in places of shorter and shallower channels. Most important was the ability in coastal zones to access vital freshwater sources in low-elevation lenses just above sea level, in seeps near shorelines, in pools inside caves, and in river drainages and deltas. Coastal migration routes likely passed through a series of alluvial fans and other productive natural ecosystems along the edges of the Indian Ocean, continued into Southeast Asia, and eventually reached as far as Australia and New Guinea by 50,000 years ago (Pope and Terrell 2008). The first populations entering the Americas may have followed the Pacific coast as the attractive resource-rich habitats of an ancient "kelp highway" at least as early as 12,500 B.C. (Erlandson et al. 2007), whereas some of the early migrants in Asia and the Pacific may have followed similarly attractive mangroves and other shoreline habitats (Bulbeck 2007) scattered discontinuously over large spaces (Chapter 4).

Instead of thinking about islands, researchers may focus on the "human shore" as the venue for many important events and processes in cultural history (Gilles 2012). Coastal zones comprise the meeting edges of natural resource habitats, where people can benefit from both land and water. Seashores probably are the most contrasting of all coastal environments, as compared to the coasts along rivers or lakes. Although coastal zones notoriously are dynamic through time, coasts, in one way or another, continue to exist and to support human beings as quintessential "edge species" adapted to live at the borders of contrasting environments. These edges constitute their own unique settings or niches, known as ecotones in ecological science (Risser 1995), where people can take advantage of a broader range of resources than in any single ecological habitat.

Islands naturally include more than just coastal zones, and in fact each island contains a series of biomes and transitional ecotones all the way from the exterior shoreline through the upland interior core. These issues will be presented with a range of examples in Chapter 2. In places with pronounced steep slopes of tall mountains, the gradient of ecological zonation can be exceptionally high, passing through numerous ecologies when climbing hundreds of meters of elevation yet contained within just a few km of linear distance. Furthermore, tall mountains can cause rain shadow effects, with dichotomies between wet windward versus dry leeward sides of islands. Island groups or archipelagos, viewed as connected wholes, can incorporate even more ecological diversity if the islands are distributed over some degrees of longitude (east-west) or especially of latitude (north-south) through different areas of climate and weather patterns.

Large numbers of biogeographic zones potentially can be packed closely together within the inherently limited spaces of islands, thus creating unique opportunities for cultural groups who can target specific biomes, ecotones, or assorted combinations of the available ecologies. The range of diversity varies from one island to another, wherein low-lying coral atolls may appear to support a small degree of ecological differentiation as compared to high-rising volcanic cones. The most extreme examples are in the large volcanic masses of islands such as Maui and Hawai'i, reaching into periodically subfreezing temperatures in alpine zones above tree lines at more than 3 km elevation at Haleakalā (Maui) and more than 4 km at Mauna Kea (Hawai'i), in contrast to the subtropical lowlands near the coasts just a few km distant in linear space from those landmark summits.

Landscapes and seascapes

The thousands of islands and islets of Pacific Oceania each hold substantive material records of how people have created landscape systems and adapted to the continually changing aspects of their social-natural landscapes. This scope of study is tied closely to research of initial colonizing episodes and migration patterns, long-term human-environment relations, and other issues that are well represented in islands as exemplary case studies or model systems. The research potential, at its fullest, must recognize landscapes in a broad sense of all of the social and natural conditions of islands and the surrounding ocean.

The complexities of natural-cultural landscape systems arguably can be illustrated most clearly in the idealized model settings of islands. This strategy is particularly instructive in islands where the landscape records transcend multiple periods of changing environmental and social conditions, for instance in the 3500-year record at the Ritidian Site in Guam (Carson 2014). This specific case in Guam has illustrated how a landscape can act as a heritage resource, combining long-term interrelated natural and cultural history. This model is expanded and applied in other island case studies of this book, embracing landscapes as holistically embodying the results of dynamic natural-cultural histories.

Regarding the cultural landscape of Pacific Oceania as a whole, an inhabited sea of islands necessarily developed over time as people explored more and more of the Pacific and gradually populated the region. As proposed by Epeli Hau'ofa (1994), "our sea of islands" refers to Pacific Oceania in terms of island societies connected by a shared ocean, in contrast to the foreign-imposed perception of tiny isolated specks scattered and lost in the grand ocean. This view of Pacific Oceania certainly is valid today, and it can be extended into the past at least as early as the timing of remote-distance ocean-crossing migrations. Nonetheless, as cultural knowledge and experience of the Pacific changed through time, so did the reality of Pacific Oceania as an inhabited landscape.

In a materialist archaeological point of view, the culturally known realm of Pacific Oceania "grew" over time, as outlined in this book by a chronology of island settlement generally from west to east across the Pacific. The chronology of a growing cultural region may be coordinated with definite chronological change in climate, sea level, coastal ecologies, and the modes of human interface with the ever-changing island environments. Depending on the natural and social environmental conditions at the time of first settlement in any given island, the landscapes were inhabited, modified, or created in remarkably diverse ways. The first island colonists before 800 B.C. in the western through central Pacific created substantially different archaeological landscapes than occurred after A.D. 1000 in the eastern Pacific.

In the Pacific region, as can be claimed worldwide, people have perceived of their inhabited landscapes in different ways, ranging from direct use of resources in their natural state to overt rendering of artificial landscape systems. As will be considered in Chapters 4 and 5, groups of hunter-gatherers began low levels of impacts throughout Island Southeast Asia at least 50,000 years ago, and only much later did horticulturalists or agriculturalists create substantially larger impacts there and continuing into the islands of Remote Oceania. The difference in the materially traceable footprints was due in large part to the mode of subsistence economy, wherein food-producing groups of horticulturalists and agriculturalists modified the natural world to a much greater degree than had been the case for food-gathering groups of hunters, fishers, and foragers. The detailed processes in each case were vastly complex and varied (Barker 2006), although the large-scale patterns in the archaeological record may suggest overall rapid spread of new ideas, technologies, and at least some migrating populations, primarily since 2200–2000 B.C., across the Asia-Pacific (Bellwood 2005, 2013). In many parts of Pacific Oceania, the role of terrestrial-based plant food production actually was rather low at first, followed by an apparent increase some centuries later, as happened after 500 B.C. in the western and central Pacific (Chapter 9) and then after A.D. 1000 in East Polynesia (Chapter 13).

Some landscape systems have been more formalized than others and thus have created more substantial and obvious material markers in the archaeological record, as apparently happened throughout Pacific Oceania about A.D. 1000 and continuing thereafter in increasingly intense expressions. A postulated "A.D. 1000 Event" (Chapter 12) involved the affixing of social practice, religious beliefs, and claims of territorial ownership through large-scale and long-lasting stonework productions, monuments, burial traditions, and overall formalized ways of interacting with the landscape. The resulting archaeological signatures have been perhaps overrepresented as durable remnants in accessible surface-visible contexts, even more pronounced when they have been related closely with known ethnohistories of vibrant cultural landscapes (Chapter 14).

The chronological narrative of this book treats landscapes as having evolved over extended periods of time that happen to be represented effectively in the archaeological records of islands. Pacific Oceania offers the possibility of examining how landscape systems have developed or evolved in different ways in numerous ideal cases or model systems of islands. The most powerful lessons come from examining a long time scale of thousands of years, thus accounting for a multitude of concurrently changing factors that otherwise could not be detected in shallow or short-lived records of just a few centuries or decades.

Structure of this book

This book offers a chronological narrative at a region-wide scale. After introducing the key concepts and relevant parameters of Pacific Oceanic archaeology in general, the ordered narrative follows how the region developed into today's fully inhabited landscape and seascape. Within each discernible time period, archaeology and other lines of evidence substantiate a picture of the natural and social environment, how it changed, and what this information can contribute toward larger research questions.

This approach differs from a standard review of Melanesia, Micronesia, and Polynesia as culture areas. The artificially defined culture areas reflect the regional cultural history only partially in the case of Polynesia and hardly at all in the diverse areas of Melanesia and Micronesia. Furthermore, the archaeological records of Island Southeast Asia, Near Oceania, and Remote Oceania need to be drawn closer into a regional synthesis, instead of the separate treatments that have been more popular in past decades.

As in any synthesis of the archaeology of a large portion of the world, the present study seeks to make sense of the major overall trends and patterns among a perplexing morass of datasets, in this case represented in the archaeological records of thousands of islands of the Pacific spread across approximately one-third of the world's surface. Previously published references are cited in the text wherever useful for illustrating the details of specific archaeological discoveries in any geographic area or subregion, major island groups, single islands, or even single sites. These works and others, including the inevitable new contributions postdating this book's publication, serve as the most informative primary sources to learn about the detailed findings of any particular location or area of interest. The current second edition of this book includes several updated references, as well as attention to more of the details in the supporting evidence.

In building the central chronological narrative of this book, key illustrative examples are provided for each time period, beginning with initial human presence at least 50,000 years ago and continuing through historical European contacts as late as the 1700s. Examples are drawn from my own research when relevant and contextualized within the body of existing literature. Although my work has covered most of the major geographic areas and time periods of Pacific Oceanic archaeology, my personal experience cannot possibly account for every nuance. At the same time, a coherently manageable narrative cannot include an exhaustive literature review for its own sake, but the most pertinent findings are brought into the narrative synthesis and updated for this second edition.

Given the general west-to-east pattern in human settlement of the Pacific, the chapters adhere partially to a geographic ordering. The narrative begins with the first peopling of Island Southeast Asia and Near Oceania, follows next with human settlements in the western and central areas of Remote Oceania, and continues into the final stages of human expansion into the eastern Pacific. The narrative does not treat each geographic area as a separate unit, but rather the inhabited portions of the Pacific are discussed as a whole, gradually growing larger and more complicated over time and through the progression of the book's chapters.

Following the present introductory Chapter 1, two more chapters are introductory in character. Chapter 2 considers different perspectives on the past, in a comprehensive view of natural and cultural history that is necessary toward meaningful discussion and interpretation in later chapters. Chapter 3 reviews the kinds of research questions that can be developed with the available materials of the Pacific Oceanic archaeological record.

Chapters 4 through 13 present the major components of the chronological narrative, wherein the content of each chapter provides a material basis to explore the larger research themes that already have been introduced. Chapter 4 opens the presentation with the first groups who entered Island Southeast Asia and evidently migrated as far as Australia and New Guinea by 50,000 years ago, leading to a series of cultural traditions reflected in the archaeological assemblages of hunter-gatherer societies. Chapter 5 follows the evidence of a "pottery trail" connecting Asia and the Pacific over an extended period beginning at least as early as 4000 B.C. and continuing through 800 B.C. Chapter 6 concentrates on humankind's first successful settlement in the Remote Oceanic world, in the Mariana Islands about 1500 B.C. Chapter 7 continues with an account of how Lapita pottery-makers ventured from the Near Oceanic islands such as in the Bismarck Archipelago to the Remote Oceanic islands of Southern Melanesia and West Polynesia about 1100–800 B.C. Chapter 8 then addresses the cultural adaptations to a substantially transforming coastal environment in the western and central Pacific during the centuries of 1100 through 500 B.C. Chapter 9 covers the development of mixed coastal and inland land-use and landscape systems over the period of 500 B.C. through A.D. 100. Chapter 10 considers the roles of Micronesia's hundreds of small coral atolls, evidently all emerging as habitable lands with freshwater lenses above sea level after A.D. 100. Chapter 11 examines the concurrent roles of cultural continuity and change in contributing to the long-term development of cultural traditions in the western and central Pacific, during a critical time of cultural change about A.D. 500 through 1000. Chapter 12 discusses the apparent formalization of cultural practice into stonework complexes and monuments throughout the Pacific beginning about A.D. 1000. Chapter 13 is concerned with the processes of developing social and political complexities, increasingly evident after A.D. 1000 throughout the fully inhabited region of Pacific Oceania.

The concluding Chapter 14 brings the body of archaeological evidence from the other chapters into a modern focus. Questions are addressed about how the past is perceived and experienced as a complex resource of cultural heritage. The book thus concludes in reflecting on what the archaeology of Pacific Oceania actually contributes of practical value for people living in the region today and for people generally interested in world archaeology.

References

Anderson, Edgar, 1952. *Plants, Man and Life*. Little, Brown and Company, Boston.

Anthony, David W., 1990. Migration in archaeology: The baby and the bathwater. *American Anthropologist 92*: 23–42.

Ardika, I. Wayan, and Peter Bellwood, 1991. Sembiran: The beginning of Indian contact with Bali. *Antiquity 65*: 221–232.

Athens, J. Stephen, H. David Tuggle, Jerome V. Ward, and David J. Welch, 2002. Avifaunal extinctions, vegetation change, and Polynesian impacts in prehistoric Hawai'i. *Archaeology in Oceania* 37: 57–78.

Bailey, Geoff N., Nic C. Flemming, Geoffrey C. P. King, Kurt Lambeck, Garry Momber, Lawrence J. Moran, Abdullah Al-Sharekh, and Claudio Vita-Finzi, 2007. Coastlines, submerged landscapes, and human evolution: The Red Sea Basin and the Farasan Islands. *Journal of Island and Coastal Archaeology 2*: 127–160.

Ballard, Chris, Paula Brown, R. Michael Bourke, and Tracy Harwdood (editors), 2008. *The Sweet Potato in Oceania: A Reappraisal*. Ethnology Monographs 19. University of Pittsburgh, Pittsburgh.

Barker, Graeme, 2006. *The Agricultural Revolution in Prehistory: Why Did Foragers Become Farmers?* Oxford University Press, Oxford.

Bellwood, Peter, 2005. *First Farmers: The Origins of Agricultural Societies*. Wiley-Blackwell, Malden, MA.

Bellwood, Peter, 2013. *First Migrants: Ancient Migration in Global Perspective*. Wiley-Blackwell, Malden, MA.

Bellwood, Peter (editor), 2015. *The Global Prehistory of Human Migration*. Wiley-Blackwell, Malden, MA.

Blust, Robert, 1995. The prehistory of the Austronesian-speaking peoples: A view from language. *Journal of World Prehistory* 9: 453–510.

Blust, Robert, 2013. *The Austronesian Languages.* Revised edition. Asia-Pacific Linguistics Open Access Monographs 008. Research School of Pacific and Asian Studies, Australian National University, Canberra.

Bulbeck, David, 2007. Where river meets sea: A parsimonious model for *Homo sapiens* colonization of the Indian Ocean Rim and Sahul. *Current Anthropology* 48: 315–321.

Campbell, Ian C., 2001. *Island Kingdom: Tonga Ancient and Modern.* Revised edition. Canterbury University Press, Christchurch.

Carson, Mike T., 2012. Evolution of an Austronesian landscape: The Ritidian Site in Guam. *Journal of Austronesian Studies* 3: 55–86.

Carson, Mike T., 2014. Contexts of natural-cultural history: A 3500-year record at Ritidian in Guam. In *Guam's Hidden Gem: Archaeological and Historical Studies at Ritidian*, edited by Mike T. Carson, pp. 1–43. British Archaeological Reports International Series 2663. Archaeopress, Oxford.

Carson, Mike T., and Hsiao-chun Hung, 2014. Semiconductor theory in migration: Population receivers, homelands and gateways in Taiwan and Island Southeast Asia. *World Archaeology* 46: 502–515.

Clark, Jeffrey T., Elizabeth Wright, and David J. Herdrich, 1997. Interactions within and beyond the Samoan Archipelago: Evidence from basaltic rock geochemistry. In *Prehistoric Long-Distance Interaction in Oceania: An Interdisciplinary Approach*, edited by Marshall I. Weisler, pp. 68–84. Monograph 21. New Zealand Archaeological Association, Auckland.

Crosby, Alfred W., 1986. *Ecological Imperialism: The Biological Expansion of Europe, 900–1900.* Cambridge University Press, Cambridge.

Darwin, Charles, 1839. *Narrative of the Surveying Voyages of His Majesty's Ships Adventure and Beagle Between the Years 1826 and 1836, Describing Their Examination of the Southern Shores of South America, and the Beagle's Circumnavigation of the Globe, Journal and Remarks 1832–1836, III.* Henry Colburn, London.

Darwin, Charles, 1845. *Journal of Researches into the Natural History and Geology of the Countries Visited During the Voyage of the H. M. S. Beagle Round the World, Under the Command of Captain Fitz Roy, R. N.* Second edition. John Murray, London.

Darwin, Charles, 1859. *On the Origin of Species by Means of Natural Selection, or the Preservation of Favored Races in the Struggle for Life.* John Murray, London.

de Brosses, Charles, 1756. *Histoire des Navigations aux Terres Australes.* Durand, Paris.

Dumont d'Urville, Jules Sébastien César, 1832. Notice sur les îles du Grand Océan et sur l'origine des peoples qui les habitant. *Société de Géographie Bulletin* 17: 1–21.

Earle, Timothy K., 1997. *How Chiefs Come to Power: The Political Economy in Prehistory.* Stanford University Press, Stanford.

Erlandson, Jon M., 2001. The archaeology of aquatic adaptations: Paridigms for a new millennium. *Journal of Archaeological Research* 9: 287–350.

Erlandson, Jon M., 2002. Anatomically modern humans, maritime adaptations, and the peopling of the New World. In *The First Americans*, edited by Nina G. Jablonski, pp. 59–92. California Academy of Sciences, San Francisco.

Erlandson, Jon M., Michael H. Graham, Bruce J. Bourque, Debra Corbett, James A. Estes, and Robert S. Steneck, 2007. The kelp highway hypothesis: Marine ecology, the coastal migration theory, and the peopling of the Americas. *Journal of Island and Coastal Archaeology* 2: 161–174.

Fitzhugh, Ben, and Terry L. Hunt, 1997. Introduction: Islands as laboratories: Archaeological research in comparative perspective. *Human Ecology* 25: 379–383.

Fosberg, F. Raymond (editor), 1963. *Man's Place in the Island Ecosystem.* Bishop Museum Press, Honolulu.

Gilles, John R., 2012. *The Human Shore: Seacoasts in History.* University of Chicago Press, Chicago.

Givnish, T. J., K. J. Sytsma, J. F. Smith, and W. J. Hahn, 1995. Molecular evolution, adaptive radiation, and geographic speciation in *Cyanea* (Campanulaceae, Lobelioideae). In *Hawaiian Biogeography: Evolution on a Hot-spot Archipelago*, edited by W. L. Wagner and V. A. Funk, pp. 288–337. Smithsonian Institution Press, Washington, DC.

Goldman, Irving, 1957. Variations in Polynesian social organization. *Journal of the Polynesian Society* 66: 374–390.

Goodenough, Ward, 1957. Oceania and the problem of controls in the study of cultural and human evolution. *Journal of the Polynesian Society* 66: 146–155.

Green, Roger C., 1991. Near and remote Oceania: Disestablishing "Melanesia" in culture history. In *Man and a Half: Essays in Pacific Anthropology and Ethnobiology in Honour of Raplh Bulmer*, edited by Andrew Pawley, pp. 491–502. The Polynesian Society, Auckland.

Hau'ofa, Epeli, 1994. Our sea of islands. *Contemporary Pacific* 6: 147–161.

Hommon, Robet J., 2013. *The Ancient Hawaiian State: Origins of a Political Society.* Oxford University Press, Oxford.

Hung, Hsiao-chun, Y. Iizuka, P. Bellwood, K. D. Nguyen, B. Bellina, P. Silapanth, E. Dizon, R. Santiago, I. Datan, and J. H. Manton, 2007. Ancient jades map 3000 years of prehistoric exchange in Southeast Asia. *Proceedings of the National Academy of Sciences* 104: 19, 745–819.

Hung, Hsiao-chun, Kim Dung Nguyen, Peter Bellwood, and Mike T. Carson, 2013. Coastal connectivity: Long-term trading networks across the South China Sea. *Journal of Island and Coastal Archaeology* 8: 384–404.

Irwin, Geoffrey J., 1992. *The Prehistoric Exploration and Colonisation of the Pacific.* Cambridge University Press, Cambridge.

Irwin, Geoffrey J., 1998. The colonisation of the pacific plate: Chronological, navigational and social issues. *Journal of the Polynesian Society* 107: 111–143.

Kirch, Patrick V., 1983. Man's role in modifying tropical and subtropical Polynesian ecosystems. *Archaeology in Oceania* 18: 26–31.

Kirch, Patrick V., 2000. *On the Road of the Winds: An Archaeological History of the Pacific Islands Before European Contact.* University of California Press, Berkeley.

Kirch, Patrick V., 2004. Oceanic islands: Microcosms of global change. In *The Archaeology of Global Change: The Impact of Humans on Their Environment*, edited by Charles L. Redman, Steven R. James, Paul R. Fish, and J. Daniel Rogers, pp. 13–27. Smithsonian Books, Washington, DC.

Kirch, Patrick V., 2010. *How Chiefs Became Kings: Divine Kingship and the Rise of Archaic States in Ancient Hawai'i.* University of California Press, Berkeley.

Lape, Peter V., 2004. The isolation metaphor in island archaeology. In *Voyages of Discovery: The Archaeology of Islands*, pp. 223–232. Praeger, Westport, CT.

Lilley, Ian, 2008. Apocalypse now (and avoid the rush): Human dimensions of climate change in the Indo-Pacific. *Archaeology in Oceania* 43: 35–40.

MacArthur, Robert, and Edward O. Wilson, 1967. *The Theory of Island Biogeography.* Princeton University Press, Princeton.

Mack, John, 2011. *The Sea: A Cultural History.* Reaktion Books, London.

Malinowski, Bronislaw, 1922. *Argonauts of the Western Pacific: An Account of Native Enterprise and Adventure in the Archipelagoes of Melanesian New Guinea.* Routledge and Kegan Paul, London.

Marck, Jeffrey C., 1986. Micronesian dialects and the overnight voyage. *Journal of the Polynesian Society* 95: 253–258.

Marck, Jeffrey C., 1999. Revising Polynesian linguistic subgrouping and its culture history implications. In *Archaeology and Language IV: Language Change and Cultural Transformation*, edited by Roger Blench and Matthew Spriggs, pp. 95–122. One World Archaeology and Routledge, London.

Mead, Margaret, 1957. Introduction to Polynesia as a laboratory for the development of models in the study of cultural evolution. *Journal of the Polynesian Society* 66: 145.

Nunn, Patrick D., 2003a. Nature-society interactions in the Pacific Islands. *Geografiska Annaler* 85: 219–229.

Nunn, Patrick D., 2003b. Revising ideas about environmental determinism: Human-environment relations in the Pacific Islands. *Asia Pacific Viewpoint* 44: 63–72.

Pawley, Andrew K., 1966. Polynesian languages: A subgrouping based on shared innovations in morphology. *Journal of the Polynesian Society* 75: 39–64.

Pope, Kevin O., and John E. Terrell, 2008. Environmental setting of human migrations in the circum-Pacific region. *Journal of Biogeography* 35: 1–21.

Risser, Paul G., 1995. The status of the science examining ecotones. *BioScience* 45: 318–325.

Sahlins, Marshall, 1957. Differentiation by adaptation in Polynesian societies. *Journal of the Polynesian Society* 66: 291–300.

Spriggs, Matthew, 1997. Landscape catastrophe and landscape enhancement: Are either or both true in the Pacific? In *Historical Ecology in the Pacific Islands: Prehistoric Environmental and Landscape Change*, edited by Patrick V. Kirch and Terry L. Hunt, pp. 80–104. Yale University Press, New Haven.

Spriggs, Matthew, Christian Reepmeyer, Angraenni, Peter Lape, Leee Neri, Wilfredo P. Ronquillo, Truman Simanjuntak, Glenn Summerhayes, Daud Tanudirjo, and Archie Tiauzon, 2011. Obsidian sources and distribution systems in Island Southeast Asia: A review of previous research. *Journal of Archaeological Science* 38: 2871–2881.

Sudo, Kenichi, 1996. Rank, hierarchy and routes of migration: Chieftainship in the Central Caroline Islands of Micronesia. In *Origins, Ancestry and Alliance: Explorations in Austronesian Ethnography*, edited by James J. Fox and Clifford Sather, pp. 57–72. Department of Anthropology, Research School of Pacific Studies, Australian National University, Canberra.

Terrell, John Edward, 1976. Island biogeography and man in Melanesia. *Archaeology and Physical Anthropology in Oceania* 11: 1–17.

Terrell, John Edward, 1977. Geographic systems and human diversity in the north Solomons. *World Archaeology* 9: 63–81.

Terrell, John Edward, 1997. The postponed agenda: Archaeology and human biogeography in the twenty-first century. *Human Ecology* 25: 419–436.

Thomas, Nicholas, 1989. The force of ethnology: Origins and significance of the Melanesia/Polynesia division. *Current Anthropology* 30: 27–41.

Vayda, Andrew Peter, and Roy A. Rappaport, 1963. Island cultures. In *Man's Place in the Island Ecosystem*, edited by F. Raymond Fosberg, pp. 133–142. Bishop Museum Press, Honolulu.

Vitousek, Peter M., Oliver A. Chadwick, Anthony S. Hartshorn, and Sara C. Hotchkiss, 2010. Intensive agriculture in Hawai'i: The model system approach. In *Roots of Conflict: Soils, Agriculture, and Socio-Political Complexity in Ancient Hawai'i*, edited by Patrick V. Kirch, pp. 31–44. School for Advanced Research Press, Santa Fe.

Wallace, Alfred Russel, 1869. *The Malay Archipelago: The land of the Orang-utan, and the Bird of Paradise. A Narrative of Travel, with Studies of Man and Nature*. MacMillan and Company, London.

Wallace, Alfred Russel, 1870. *Contributions to the Theory of Natural Selection: A Series of Essays*. MacMillan and Company, London.

Weisler, Marshall I. (editor), 1997. *Prehistoric Long-distance Interaction in Oceania: An Interdisciplinary Approach*. Monograph 21. New Zealand Archaeological Association, Auckland.

Weisler, Marshall I., 1998. Hard evidence for prehistoric interaction in Polynesia. *Current Anthropology* 39: 521–532.

Wickler, Stephen K., 2004. Modelling colonisation and migration in Micronesia from a zooarchaeological perspective. In *Colonisation, Migration and Marginal Areas: A Zooarchaeological Approach*, edited by Mariana Mondini, Sebantien Munoz, and Stepehen K. Wickler, pp. 28–40. Oxbow Books, Oxford.

Yen, Douglas E., 1974. *The Sweet Potato in Oceania: An Essay in Ethnobotany*. Bernice Pauahi Bishop Museum Bulletin 236. Bishop Museum Press, Honolulu.

Yen, Douglas E., 1990. Environment, agriculture and the colonization of the pacific. In *Pacific Production Systems: Approaches to Economic Prehistory*, edited by Douglas E. Yen and J. M. J. Mummery, pp. 258–277. Occasional Papers in Prehistory 18. Department of Prehistory, Research School of Pacific Studies, the Australian National University, Canberra.

Yen, Douglas E., 1991. Polynesian cultigens and cultivars: The questions of origin. In *Islands, Plants, and Polynesians: An Introduction Polynesian Ethnobiology*, edited by Paul Alan Cox and Sandra A. Banack, pp. 67–98. Dioscorea Press, Portland.

2 Regional context and perspectives

"One of the worrying consequences of exponential growth in the volume of research and publication . . . is that we know more and more about less and less."

(Ingold 1994: xx)

Tim Ingold wrote these words as part of a preface to an encyclopedia of anthropology, noting that the liberal scope of anthropology had grown fragmented and compartmentalized into narrower and narrower specialisms. Much the same could be said of archaeology, wherein researchers have learned to specialize in a topic, geographic area, or method that achieves greatly detailed results (learning "more and more") yet relevant only to a narrow focus of concern (about "less and less"). When too narrowly focused, investigations produce trivial results, but broad-reaching implications may develop if the varied datasets of different specialisms are brought into a synthesis.

Pacific Oceanic archaeology has been among the most narrowly defined and compartmentalized fields ever to exist, although it certainly has much more to offer in a global perspective. The Pacific region occupies a significant part of the world, so in fact it is just as relevant as any other region in terms of contributing to world archaeology. As mentioned in Chapter 1 and explored more in the next chapters, the substantive findings of Pacific Oceanic archaeology are directly relevant toward several enduring research themes of global significance.

The scope of the Pacific Oceanic past can be studied through several different perspectives, datasets, and specialisms as reviewed in this chapter. Geological processes, climate conditions, natural biogeography, historical contexts, language histories, and genetic lineages all potentially can contribute significantly to our knowledge of the past. A working knowledge of each of these aspects here serves as a prelude to the later chapters, where their individual contributions will be incorporated into a larger narrative.

Geological processes: earth and ocean

In the limited spaces of islands, geology has affected archaeological sites more extremely than has tended to be the case in other settings. The practicalities of bounded space of any island would imply inherently finite opportunities for cultural land use, choice of places most suitable for habitation, and the resulting material patterns of an archaeological landscape. Additionally, the coastal zones of islands are vulnerable even to minor fluctuations in sea level, nearshore ecology composition, and accumulations of slope-eroded sediments that greatly alter the ability of people to live there as well as of archaeologists to find the ancient site layers.

DOI: 10.4324/9781003399025-2

26 *Regional context and perspectives*

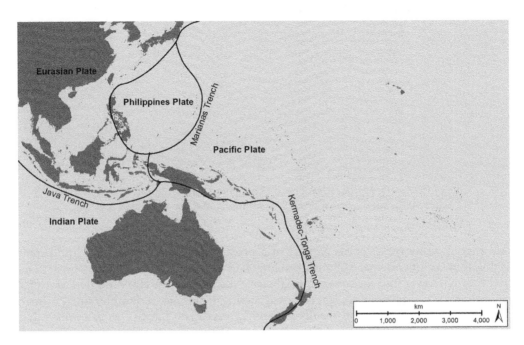

Figure 2.1 Tectonic plates of the Asia-Pacific region.

Pacific regional geology cannot be understood without first acknowledging the roles of the major tectonic plates (Figure 2.1). The extensive Pacific Plate comprises most of the region, and its western margins interface with others such as the Indian Plate and the Philippine Plate. The Pacific Plate overall has been moving northwestward, where it has collided with the other plates in the west and has been driven beneath them. These subduction zones have created deep trenches such as the Marianas Trench, which includes the deepest point of the world's seabed hydrosphere at more than 10 km in Challenger Deep. The plate collisions in some places have caused magma to escape from the earth's core and produce volcanic cone-shaped islands, as well as complicated tectonic movements that have resulted in variable uplift or sometimes subsidence of island masses.

Many islands in the Pacific began geologically as volcanic formations on the seafloor, typically in "hot spots" in the earth's crust where magma was released upward in a cone shape characteristic of most volcanic islands (Figure 2.2). These volcanic masses gradually accumulated upwards, as well as in outer layers called "shields," eventually reaching near the ocean surface. While each hot spot has been stationary in the earth's crust, the tectonic plates have been moving, so that any single hot spot can form a series of volcanoes aligned in reverse with the direction of the plate movement. For example, in the Hawaiian Islands, several volcanoes were formed in a single hot spot of the northwestward-moving Pacific Plate, resulting in the oldest and most severely eroded islands to the northwest and the youngest and still active volcanic islands in the southeast of the archipelago.

In places where volcanic cones have been raised above sea level, they often reach elevations of hundreds of m and occasionally thousands of m (Figures 2.3 and 2.4). The external sloped surfaces of the cones eventually are eroded by flowing water, making stream-dissected valleys running from the central upland interior to the peripheral

Regional context and perspectives 27

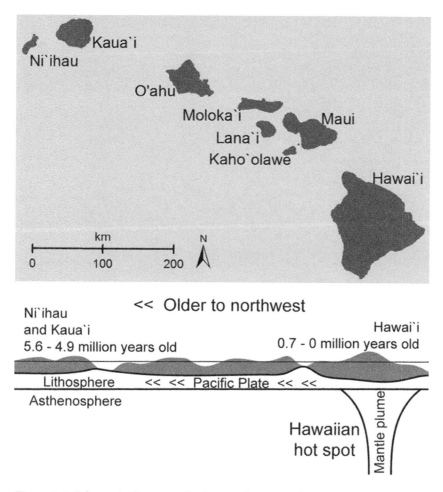

Figure 2.2 Schematic diagram of volcanic "hot spot" formation in the Hawaiian Islands.

Figure 2.3 Pagan Volcano, Mariana Islands.

28 *Regional context and perspectives*

Figure 2.4 Stream-cut valley of Waimea Canyon, the "Grand Canyon of the Pacific" in Kaua'i, Hawaiian Islands.

coastline. Many volcanic islands thus are comprised of "pie slices" of stream-cut valleys and their adjoining high-ground ridges. Each such pie slice contains a series of ecological zones from the shoreline all the way through the upland interior. The seaward-to-landward zones are potentially quite diverse in islands of large size and elevation range.

As volcanic formations neared the ocean's surface in tropical and subtropical climates, corals began to grow over the outward masses just below sea level. These corals continued to grow in horizontally expansive colonies, regardless of whatever was happening with the associated volcano becoming further exposed above sea level or perhaps eroded downward into a submerged seamount. Coral colonies can attach themselves to the sides or to the tops of rock formations, wherever they can grow in horizontal planes within a few meters of sea level and absorb sunlight while submerged in saltwater conditions. Many species of corals can tolerate short times of exposure above water during low-tide episodes, but all corals will die after sustained exposure above water. Corals also cannot grow in areas of fresh water, such as at the mouth of a river drainage or at the discharge of a coastal seepage flow.

One type of coral island is an atoll, technically composed of a set of islands or islets in a crescent shape around one side of a volcanic cone or crater (Figure 2.5). Due to region-wide sea-level drawdown after approximately 1100 B.C., many of the atolls of the Pacific became stable above sea level nearly simultaneously around A.D. 100 (Dickinson 2003), thus changing the practicalities of a cultural landscape of Pacific Oceania. The low-lying

Regional context and perspectives 29

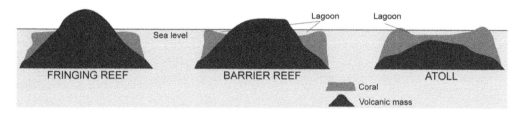

Figure 2.5 Schematic diagram of atoll formation.

Figure 2.6 Limestone plateau, northern Guam.

atolls were just a few m above sea level, but importantly they contained lenses of fresh water floating above the heavier salt water, accessible through shallow pit digging and evidently playing a vital role in atoll habitability (Weisler 1999). Currently rising sea level, however, has been salinizing those freshwater lenses and thus making atolls uninhabitable, in addition to the physical drowning of most of the low-elevation land area.

Another type of coral island formation consists of a coral colony exposed as a massive slab or plateau. These formations can occur attached to a volcanic base as in Guam, with a large limestone plateau in the north and volcanic hills in the south (Figure 2.6). They also can comprise whole islands of limestone plateau formations unto themselves, in some cases resembling large and high-raised atolls.

In the elevated limestone plateau formations, sources of fresh water typically are difficult but not impossible for people to access, and the available practicalities largely have influenced the patterns of cultural land use. The limestone material itself is porous, and rainwater drains quickly through it without opportunities for creating stream drainages. Rainwater settles downward into a level of an aquifer deep inside the limestone's core mass, usually several m below the surface but floating above sea level, inaccessible except through cavernous sinkholes or sometimes through caves that have formed on the exterior flank margins near sea level. The natural aquifers drain out horizontally in seeps just above sea level, and these seeps potentially are accessible in certain locations but not everywhere (Figure 2.7). In rare cases of larger limestone formations, lakes and streams can form in natural depressions and irregularities.

30 *Regional context and perspectives*

Figure 2.7 Coastal freshwater seep at Ritidian, Guam. Photograph provided courtesy of Dr. Hiro Kurashina.

A number of islands in the Pacific do not fit the previously noted geological categories, and instead they originated as parts of continental landforms more than 500 million years ago. An ancient "supercontinent" of Gondwana at one time included the pieces of Antarctica, Australia, India, and South America (Figure 2.8). As Gondwana broke into smaller pieces and continental drift brought those pieces farther apart from each other, the continents as we know them today gradually took shape in their present positions. Islands of New Zealand and New Caledonia were derived from portions of Gondwana, plus Australia and New Guinea represent other large remnants of the ancient supercontinent. Several other pieces now are surviving in the scattered above-water elements of Island Southeast Asia, interspersed with volcanic and coral formations.

In addition to the geological processes that shaped the islands long before human beings ever existed there, other processes have continued during and even after the cultural use of most sites. One such process was change in sea level alternately drowning or exposing areas of land. Another was ongoing slope erosion and redeposition, in most cases magnified at one time or another by human actions of clearing forests in the island interiors.

Sea level in the Pacific for the most part has followed global trends but with localized slight variations (Figure 2.9). These trends were driven primarily by the amounts of water trapped in glaciers and ice sheets during the last major Ice Age of the Pleistocene prior to 10,000 B.C., later released into the world's oceans during the subsequent warmer period of the Holocene, with a number of fluctuations along the way. When the first anatomically

Regional context and perspectives 31

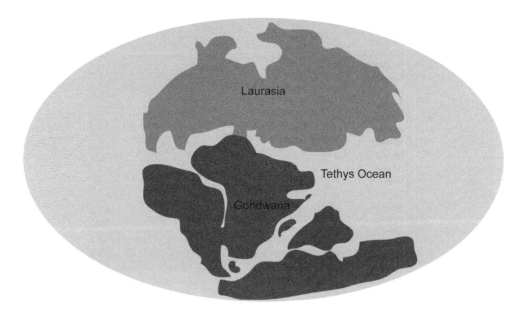

Figure 2.8 Gondwana model.

modern humans (AMH or *Homo sapiens*) ventured as far as Australia and New Guinea by 50,000 years ago, the sea level was more than 80 m lower than today. During the Last Glacial Maximum (LGM) about 22,000 B.C., when the maximum amount of water was frozen, sea level was more than 100 m lower than today. Chapter 4 will consider how extremely large areas of land were joined by natural land bridges and shelves, while some areas were separated by short water gaps. During the Pleistocene conditions, the region from Asia to Australia consisted of three large land mass clusters of Sunda in the northwest, Sahul in the southeast, and Wallacea in the middle with their own compositions and distributions of native plants and animals.

The earth currently is a "drowned world," with higher sea level than generally has been the case over the last several thousands of years (Nunn 2008). Sea level overall has been rising since the LGM, but it rose most rapidly after approximately 10,000–8000 B.C. with the beginning of the generally warmer conditions of the Holocene. By approximately 4000 B.C., the world's oceans reached within a few m of the modern level, and much of the islands and coastlines of the Pacific were approaching their present-day shapes.

Pacific regional sea-level history since 4000 B.C. is quite well documented thanks to visible tidal notches in combination with directly datable coral formations (Dickinson 2001). A highstand of sea level persisted from about 3000 B.C. through approximately 1100–1000 B.C., generally 1.5–2.5 m higher than the modern level, followed by drawdown to current conditions. This point is especially important for understanding the contexts of early settlement sites in the western through central Pacific occurring during or slightly after the highstand (Carson 2011, 2014), followed by significantly changing coastal ecologies just shortly thereafter. By A.D. 100, the rate of drawdown had slowed with sea level nearing its current elevation, coincident with the emergence of most Pacific atolls above sea level and supporting accessible freshwater lenses (Dickinson 2003).

32 *Regional context and perspectives*

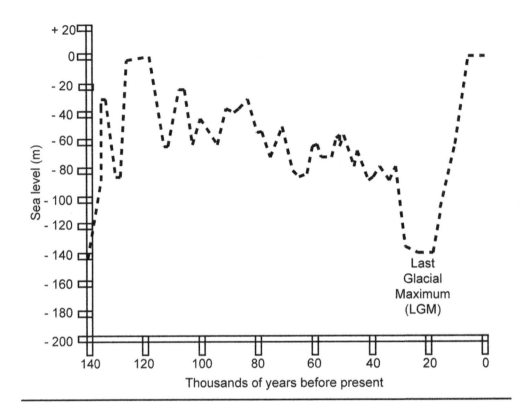

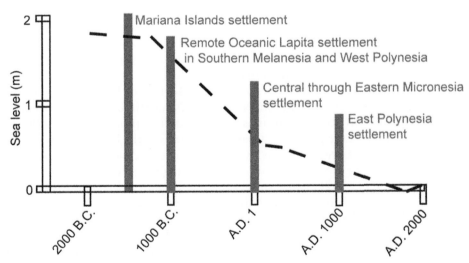

Figure 2.9 Sea-level history. Top: large-scale view in thousands of years. Bottom: detail of the last 4000 years most relevant in Pacific Oceanic archaeology.

In the islands bearing the shortest time spans of human occupation of less than 1000 years (since about A.D. 1000), the typically slow-moving processes of geology and sea-level change realistically had just little time to transform the oldest site settings, but at least some degree of alteration has occurred in almost every case. For instance, in the Hawaiian Islands, with rather brief archaeological records postdating A.D. 1000, the oldest shorefront habitation sites now have been stranded farther inland, buried beneath successive layers of more recent sediments and cultural occupations, and, to some extent, disjointed from their original contexts (Carson 2004, 2012). Searching today's beachfronts with shallow test pits would fail to notice these oldest habitation layers.

In islands with considerably longer spans of habitation, the paleo-terrain or paleo-habitat settings of the oldest sites have been dramatically transformed, so that they have become almost entirely divorced from modern observations. In the Mariana Islands, the first inhabitants at 1500 B.C. lived in specialized shoreline niches when the ocean was about 1.8 m higher than today's level, and subsequently those ancient sites have become stranded more than 100 m inland from today's greatly expanded shorelines and buried 2 m or even deeper beneath newer sedimentary units (Carson 2011, 2014; Carson and Hung 2015, 2022). A drawdown in sea level after 1100–1000 B.C. resulted in progressive enlargement of the coastal plains, accumulations of storm-surge debris and slope-eroded sedimentary layers, major disruption of nearshore ecologies, and significantly different modes of cultural use of the changing landscape. By 500 B.C., coastal habitations had become massively transformed not only in the Mariana Islands but also in other inhabited areas such as New Caledonia (Carson 2008) and Fiji (Nunn 2005). Today, these ancient sites are masked by entirely different coastal landforms and nearshore ecosystems that instead relate to the last 1000 years or less.

Changing coastlines and coastal ecologies certainly have been the most visible of geomorphological transformations in Pacific Oceanic site contexts, but other processes need to be considered in relation to the upland or interior landforms of these islands. Ongoing slope erosion and redeposition have transformed inland zones, and simultaneously they have affected low-lying coastal areas and stream-cut valley floors where the slope-eroded materials tend to accumulate in thick layers. The rate and magnitude of slope erosion typically have increased whenever people started to occupy an island due to artificial clearing of forests and exposure of the ground to rainwater, foot traffic, and other erosional agents (Spriggs 1997). Overall, the redeposited sediments have filled portions of lowlands in valley floors and coastal plains, gradually building more ground surface that happens to be productive for crop growth, so that continually more usable land has been available throughout the periods of human occupations of most islands (Athens and Ward 1993). When these factors are combined with the exposure of coastal sedimentary units due to drawdown in sea level after 1100–1000 B.C., then the total effects can cover several sq km of lowland zones.

While many sites of later periods are visible in surface contexts today, the older and deeper site layers have been obscured through changing depositional and erosional contexts. Where sites remain visible on the surface today, archaeologists need to be aware of the probable recent age and potential superposition over older archaeological deposits. In most islands, the coastal zones originally used as cultural sites have changed substantially due to fluctuating sea level and related transformations of coastal landforms. In some places, such as near rivers or stream drainages, sites have been eroded or exposed to variable extent, perhaps aiding in site identification yet also suggesting at least partial loss of site integrity.

Climate and weather patterns: more than the humid tropics

Most of the inhabitable islands of the Pacific are distributed within tropical or subtropical climate belts with warm temperatures, but a few areas such as in New Zealand extend farther south from the equator into cooler zones (Figure 2.10). Rainfall patterns are quite variable, including some areas with extremely wet conditions year-round and others with unpredictable rain or even periodic drought. In addition to the major climate belts, different portions of the Pacific are characterized by their own dominant patterns of ocean waves and directions of winds, often with seasonal shifts.

Inside each generalized climate zone of the Pacific, weather patterns can vary within an island group or even within a single island. North-south–oriented island arcs potentially can stretch through weather patterns, such as in the Mariana Islands where generally cooler and drier conditions are experienced in farther north latitude as compared to warmer and wetter conditions farther south toward the equator. Regardless of latitude, the taller land masses can generate rainfall through orographic effect on their windward sides, while also creating rain shadows on their leeward sides (Figure 2.11). In many high volcanic islands, as in the Hawaiian archipelago, rain typically falls in windward and upland areas, seldom reaching the rain shadows in the farther leeward coasts. Cultural adaptations in the drought-prone areas have included growing sturdy drought-resistant crops, exchanging resources with other communities in wetter elevations or windward areas, and preserving foods by fermentation or other means.

Monsoon weather patterns and frequent typhoons affect the northwest tropical Pacific. A definite wet-versus-dry season occurs annually. In some areas, the "dry" season still can bring about 40% of annual rainfall, but it is considered dry overall as a season due to the repeated incidents of "mini-droughts" of some days between raining episodes. The wet season is characterized by nearly constant rain sustained for several months.

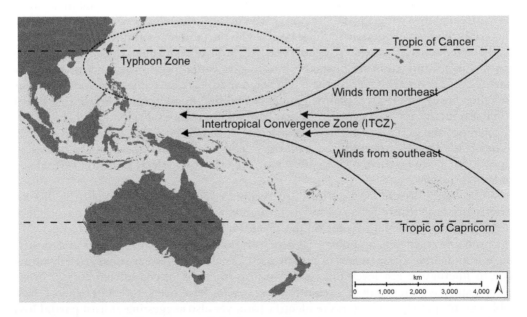

Figure 2.10 General climate zones of the Asia-Pacific region.

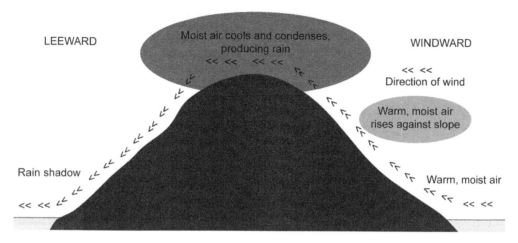

Figure 2.11 Schematic diagram of orographic rain production and rain shadow effect.

Outside the monsoon weather pattern zone of the northwest tropical Pacific, other areas of the Pacific potentially can experience prolonged droughts. The most drought-prone areas are in patches of low-pressure systems and calm winds at the Intertropical Convergence Zone (ITCZ), also known as the "doldrums," extending just a few degrees of latitude both north and south of the equator. Some of the islands in these areas retain ruins of habitation sites postdating A.D. 1000, although they were abandoned by the time of systematic charting and recording in the modern era (DiPiazza and Pearthree 2001a, 2001b). These "mystery islands" were risky places to live due to the unpredictable and restricted water supplies.

Although modern climate and weather patterns serve as important clues of past conditions and the potential for human activities, they certainly have changed in long-term cycles. Inhabitants of the areas of Sunda, Sahul, and Wallacea lived in a few degrees C cooler temperatures for tens of thousands of years until the great warming of the Holocene after approximately 10,000 B.C. By the time people moved into the Remote Oceanic islands, about 1500 B.C. in the Mariana Islands, the general characteristics of modern climate and weather patterns already had been established across the Pacific region for at least some millennia.

Within the long-term overall climate trends, occasionally short-lived climate fluctuations have affected large parts of the world, including the Pacific. One instance involved a sharp but brief drying episode throughout much of the northern hemisphere about 2200 B.C., linked with abandonment of villages in northern China (Yang et al. 2015), curiously at the same time of population movements from Taiwan into Island Southeast Asia (Hung 2008). Another instance involved a shift to cooler, drier, and somewhat unstable conditions of the Little Ice Age (LIA) about A.D. 1300 through 1850, in some cases quite distressing for the societies who had adapted to the warmer, wetter, and generally stable conditions of the Little Climatic Optimum (LCO) about A.D. 1000 through 1300 (Nunn 2000; Nunn et al. 2007).

Pacific regional scholars have debated the role of climate change in contributing to any cultural response (e.g., Fitzpatrick 2011; Nunn and Hunter-Anderson 2011). Debates revolve first around whether or not climate change actually occurred, and then second around whether or not these events were sufficient to trigger different cultural behaviors. Interpretations can be difficult, because although periods of climate change are real facts in the global paleoenvironmental records, nonetheless they necessarily incorporate inconsistencies and irregularities within the large-scale trends and patterns (Ruddiman 2008). In one view, favorable climate or "times of plenty" likely subsidized large and dense populations dependent on certain modes of crop growth and with increasing social and political structuring, later unable to be sustained after a shift to unfavorable climate or "times of less" (Nunn et al. 2007). In other words, changing climate can be considered as one factor in the complex and dynamic relations between people and their environment.

Plant and animal communities: natural and human-mediated

Natural biogeographic zones and gradients have affected the basic parameters of how people have lived in the Pacific region. In some cases, people simply took advantage of the natural resources, but in other cases they engaged in extensive manipulations of the flora and fauna. A large-scale view of the Pacific reveals an overall gradient pattern of decreasing total biomass and increasingly unique speciation when moving farther east into the more remote islands. The overall gradient is punctuated in a few places of larger ocean-crossing gaps that mark the differences between major biogeographic zones, for example, along the boundaries of Sunda, Wallacea, and Sahul as well as between Near and Remote Oceania (see Figure 1.2).

The natural biomass and biodiversity of Island Southeast Asia and Near Oceania evidently supported communities of hunter-gatherers with little or no cultural modification of the available biological taxa and resource zones. A few rare cases have shown evidence of artificial garden plots with ditches to control water and deliberate choice of crop growth, for example, in parts of the New Guinea highlands around 5000–4500 B.C. (Denham et al. 2003). Another key point was the arrival of the dingo (*Canis lupus dingo*) in Australia about 2000–1500 B.C., almost certainly transported by people across the ocean and coinciding with the emergence of new hunting tool technologies (Hiscock 2008). Even when accounting for these cultural modifications of the natural setting, the overall strategies of low-impact and direct-resource usage persisted for several thousands of years, regardless of climate change and other factors.

A mode of low-impact hunting, fishing, and foraging was insufficient to support populations in the islands of Remote Oceania, where instead people needed to depend to some degree on tree and root-tuber crops, most of which needed to be imported from overseas. Animals such as pigs, dogs, and chickens likewise did not exist naturally in Remote Oceania, arriving only by human agency. Perhaps not surprisingly, those islands remained uninhabited for several millennia, while people lived in the islands of Near Oceania with only minimal manipulations of the evidently productive resources of native forests and animal populations.

Wherever rats arrived with people in new territories, they accelerated the impacts of habitat loss and transformation. They may not have been transported deliberately, but they nonetheless traveled almost everywhere in the Asia-Pacific. Most noticeable in the previously uninhabited islands of Remote Oceania, rats joined humans as an invasive species.

The regional landscapes changed dramatically with the arrival of food-producing horticulturalists and agriculturalists in the centuries following 2200 B.C. in parts of Island Southeast Asia. Rice definitely was imported from overseas, dated at least as early as

1400 B.C. along the Cagayan River in Luzon of the northern Philippines (Snow et al. 1986), although rice may not have become a major staple crop until slightly later. Also along the Cagayan River, the most abundant preserved ancient rice grains have been dated around 1100–1000 B.C., found within the earliest pottery-bearing layers that extended as early as 2200–2000 B.C. (Hung et al. 2022: 854–862). Within a similar layer of initial pottery association in Sulawesi of Indonesia, domesticated rice was dated close to 1500 B.C. (Deng et al. 2020).

Whether for rice or for other crops, native forests were being cleared, as implied by increasing numbers of polished adzes and axes used in felling trees (Bellwood 1997: 219), further evidenced by pollen records showing decline of native trees replaced by an influx of disturbance growth grasses (Hope et al. 1999). Many of the foods likely were the same as the locally known bananas, taro, yams, and sago palms already used by indigenous hunter-gatherer groups for several millennia, but the difference now was in establishing permanent village settlements with structured housing and regular access to croplands (discussed in Chapter 4). Additionally, these emerging archaeological layers or horizons in Island Southeast Asia contained the first pottery of the region, signaling a change in the larger cultural context.

This new village-based lifestyle soon would spread throughout Island Southeast Asia, parts of the Near Oceanic islands, and into Remote Oceania (Chapters 4 through 7). When moving into Remote Oceania, people brought suites of plants and often some animals. They imported not just edible foods but other culturally useful products as well. For instance, the initial human impact horizons of forest-clearing in the Mariana Islands, dated at least as early as 1500 B.C., contained the first evidence of pollen of ironwood (*Casuarina equisetifolia*), used for its hard wood, and betelnut (*Areca catechu*), a key ingredient in a chewable narcotic stimulant (Athens and Ward 2006).

People modified the island biota not only through adding new imported taxa but also through reducing or even eradicating many native taxa. Whole landscapes became transformed into managed forests and croplands. Meanwhile, native animals found that their natural habitats were being disturbed, and some of these animals faced further threats of actively being hunted by the human populations. Especially vulnerable were ground-nesting birds and a number of flightless bird taxa, as commemorated in avifaunal extinction horizons in many islands immediately after human arrivals (Steadman 1995).

Historical contexts

Written histories and oral traditions in the Pacific certainly overlap with the scope of archaeological study, but the overlap is only partial. Unlike the archaeological records spanning thousands of years, the oldest known written records relate to Ferdinand Magellan's visit in 1521 at the Mariana Islands. Many parts of the Pacific did not enter the written literature until much later, particularly after Captain Cook's three expeditions from 1768 through 1779. The people of the Marianas already have marked the 500-year remembrance of contact with Ferdinand Magellan's crew, yet the quincentenary of Captain Cook's encounters in the Hawaiian Islands will need to wait for another 250 years or longer. Oral traditions extend deeper into the past in most cases, although they operate within contexts and concepts that are not immediately congruent with material-based archaeological chronologies.

Historical records have been uneven across Pacific Oceania. Depending on the localized character of foreign contacts and interests, some areas have received more visitors than others. Additionally, some visitors kept more careful records than others, and many were sensationalized. The oldest records are especially difficult to decipher in the cases of European visitors in the western Pacific during the 1500s and 1600s, dating to a time when maps, charts, and related information were considered to be proprietary government secrets. Only much later, in the 1700s and especially the 1800s, did some but not all visitors consciously and regularly keep detailed records about the places where they happened to visit.

Most island societies have retained their own oral traditions and views of history, in some cases now preserved in written form. A general field of ethnohistory can be understood as including accounts of both real historical events and mythic traditions, each requiring a different interpretive process (Layton 1999). These records convey certain aspects of direct literal truths of historical facts, but deeper meanings can be extracted from figurative interpretations and contexts. In the Hawaiian Islands, for example, where ethnohistories are closely related with shallow time depths of archaeological records postdating A.D. 1000, many traditions clearly were influenced by political propaganda of Hawaiian historical figures since the A.D. 1400s and most strongly since the late 1700s (Carson 2012), while other traditions convey a more liberal "people's version" of the cultural and mythological landscape (Carson and Athens 2007).

Although the quality of information is uneven, vast amounts of historical and ethnohistorical records, source materials, and reinterpretations are available for most parts of Pacific Oceania. The full body of literature will not be considered here because it mostly refers to contexts postdating the scope of the present book. Works of ethnohistory and social history can address these later contexts and perspectives more effectively than the current book about archaeology. Nonetheless, several sources do relate to deeper traditions of cultural practice, as will be mentioned in the following chapters, most notably when discussing later periods covered in Chapters 12 and 13.

History, historical archaeology, and archaeological history necessarily refer to time periods within the range of their own source materials. An arbitrary time bracket for the historically attested past may be imposed as early as the 1500s in some places but as late as the 1700s in other places of the Pacific. This book concentrates on learning about the archaeological record and asking questions through archaeological datasets that, for the most part (but not entirely), refer to ancient contexts prior to the reach of historical documents and ethnohistories.

Linguistic histories

The Pacific region has provided one of the world's classic examples of historical linguistic studies (Figures 2.12 and 2.13), in particular tracing the phylogenetic relationships of Austronesian-speaking communities as they spread and diversified across the island region (Blust 1995, 2013). As was mentioned in Chapter 1, founder effects or bottleneck effects, in principle, work with language groupings. Language communities will diverge over time depending on how long they have been isolated from one another, for example, when speakers of a single language become separated in different islands. The island setting of Pacific Oceania makes this region an ideal model case for studying the processes of language splitting and divergence.

Over time, separate island populations have developed their own distinctive linguistic features that are not shared with each other, although they continue to share some other features retained from their common origin. For example, the languages spoken in

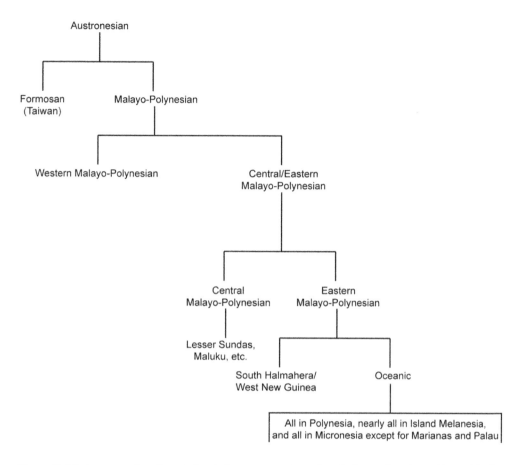

Figure 2.12 Austronesian linguistic phylogeny tree, based on information from Blust (2013).

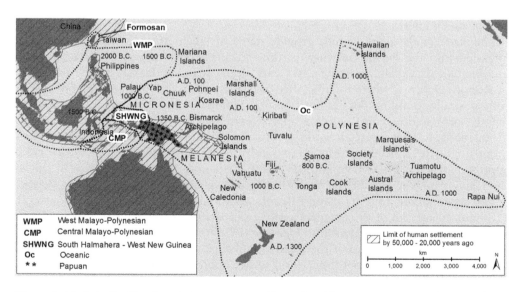

Figure 2.13 Asia-Pacific linguistic map, coordinated with approximate settlement dates according to archaeological evidence.

Tahiti, the Tuamotu Archipelago, and the Marquesas Islands all can be grouped together as members of Central East Polynesian (CEP). An ancestral form of CEP, hypothetically reconstructed as Proto CEP (or PCEP), once was spoken before its members split into different island populations. The ancestors who once spoke PCEP were the original settlers in these islands around A.D. 1000, but they brought their language with them from a homeland elsewhere, probably in West Polynesia, where another even older protolanguage can be reconstructed as Proto Nuclear Polynesian (PNP). The same logic can be applied incrementally farther back through levels of the Austronesian language family, with internal levels and splits corresponding with the major episodes of migrations and breakup of language communities.

Linguists, archaeologists, and others have recognized the vast geographic distribution of Austronesian languages over 210 degrees longitude and 75 degrees latitude, evidently the most widespread of any group at the time when Magellan's crew explored around the globe in 1519–1522. The oldest Austronesian linguistic features have been retained in Taiwan, while the most diverged descendant variations are known in the margins of East Polynesia in the Hawaiian Islands, Rapa Nui (Easter Island), and Aotearoa (New Zealand). Another Austronesian-speaking group, Malagasy, settled in Madagascar, marking the farthest westward boundary of the known Austronesian world near the east coast of Africa.

Austronesian languages are not spoken in Australia or New Guinea, where instead the native languages collectively are classified as non-Austronesian (NAN) and with several groupings and subgroupings. In this case, the Austronesian-speaking groups who entered Remote Oceania could not have been descended from NAN-speaking groups in Australia or New Guinea. Rather, Austronesian linguistic origins must have come from elsewhere, eventually spreading over most of the Asia-Pacific region but somehow not affecting the NAN-speaking areas of Australia and New Guinea. Following this logic, the NAN-speaking groups most likely have descended from the original human inhabitants of Sahul during the Pleistocene, and related NAN-speaking groups once had lived in Sunda and Wallacea until the arrival of Austronesian-speaking groups much later.

Linguistic study alone cannot provide dates of when Austronesian-speaking groups migrated into the Pacific or when certain ancestral protolanguages were spoken, but archaeological evidence in some cases can supply relevant dating. In any island group of Remote Oceania, where today's Austronesian-speaking groups presumably descended from a single founding population, the archaeological dates of first human settlement may be proposed as corresponding approximately to the divergence from an ancestral protolanguage. This approach works very well in Remote Oceania, where the major subgroup linguistic branches correspond to the chronological order of human settlement from approximately 1500 B.C. through A.D. 1300 (Bellwood 1991; Blust 2013). In this view, the Chamorro language of the Mariana Islands split from a Proto Malayo-Polynesian (PMP) source about 1500 B.C., and Palauan separated from a different PMP source about 1100 B.C. Nearly all of the languages spoken in Remote Oceania, except for Chamorro and Palauan, diverged from a Proto Oceanic (POc) source, beginning perhaps as early as 1400–1300 B.C. At the end of the linguistic history narrative, the New Zealand Maori language split from a Proto Tahitic (PTa) source about A.D. 1300. The approach becomes more difficult when extending farther westward and farther back in time in Island Southeast Asia, where people had been living for tens of thousands of years prior to the overlays of Austronesian languages.

Given that the first people entering Remote Oceania brought a distinctive style of dentate-stamped pottery with them, the homeland origin of that pottery style potentially can reveal the migration route of those people and thus of the Austronesian-speaking communities. This pottery trail will be discussed in Chapter 5, but the key point for linguistic history is that pottery-making traditions first entered into Island Southeast Asia suddenly after 2200–2000 B.C. and came from an older established homeland source in Taiwan (Bellwood et al. 2011; Carson et al. 2013; Hung et al. 2011). This scenario matches the proposal of Austronesian linguistic origins in Taiwan, wherein traditions had spread from there into Island Southeast Asia before proceeding onward into Remote Oceania (Bellwood 1991; Blust 1995).

Austronesian origins in Taiwan are abundantly clear in linguistics, noting that the oldest features of the Austronesian language family are retained in the aboriginal Formosan languages of Taiwan and not shared with any other group outside Taiwan (Blust 1995, 2013). Similar Austronesian-speaking groups very likely had lived across the Taiwan Strait in coastal China, but these groups have been replaced by more recent layering since the Han Dynasty overprinted the native populations around 206 B.C.–A.D. 220. In this case, a large portion of the most ancient linguistic history of Austronesian (An) or Proto Austronesian (PAn) is now missing, and the oldest surviving remnants are restricted to Taiwan.

The major expansion of Austronesian-speaking groups actually occurred outside Taiwan, and, in fact, all of the daughter languages outside Taiwan belong to a unified grouping of Malayo-Polynesian. Notions of an Austronesian diaspora may be described more accurately in relation to the Malayo-Polynesian subgroup of populations that had exited Taiwan and then later gained their greatest momentum in the context of the Malayo-Polynesian (MP) language communities in Island Southeast Asia and beyond. The first generations of speakers of MP or Proto Malayo-Polynesian (PMP) spread rapidly through much of Island Southeast Asia and as far as the Mariana Islands by 1500 B.C., and their descendants later spread into parts of Near Oceania, throughout Remote Oceania, and even as far as Madagascar.

Whenever the Austronesian or Proto Malayo-Polynesian languages entered into Island Southeast Asia, they must have blended with or replaced other languages that had been spoken by the hunter-gatherer groups living in the region for the previous several thousands of years. Very little, if any, trace of non-Austronesian (NAN) language exists today in Island Southeast Asia, but rather, the NAN languages are found most clearly among the native people of Australia and New Guinea. These NAN languages may be considered as having descended from the groups who lived in the region long before any Austronesian-speaking groups arrived and likely involved a number of different speech communities across the diverse areas of Sunda, Wallacea, and Sahul.

Genetics lineages

Within the last few decades, genetics research has made enormous advances in reading DNA and interpreting large datasets, and the Asia-Pacific region has been in the spotlight of some of the leading studies. As summarized by Murray Cox (2015), the central concern has been how to explain the apparently shared phenotype of Asians in the west and Polynesians in the east, somehow bypassing the Australo-Melanesian or Papuan region in the middle of this wide geographic distribution. Genetics research potentially can address some of the enduring questions as posed by linguists and archaeologists about the past populations of the Asia-Pacific region, although DNA is inherited through different mechanisms and with different time scales than can be seen in language or material culture. The results of DNA research therefore do not always parallel the findings of linguistic or archaeological investigations, especially when attempting to use the DNA of modern-day living people as a way to reconstruct the past.

In terms of integrating DNA research with archaeology, a productive approach has become possible only within the last decade, involving the examination of the truly ancient DNA (aDNA), obtained directly from the ancient skeletons and burial sites that have been preserved in the archaeological record. This approach has added an important new tool in the tool kit of archaeologists in collaboration with DNA analysts. While very few aDNA studies so far have been attempted in Pacific Oceania, the results have corroborated the views based on the archaeological evidence and historical linguistics, for instance noting an East Asian origin of the Austronesian populations who moved into the region with the initial pottery-bearing horizon, so far proven in the Mariana Islands (Pugach et al. 2021; see also Liu et al. 2022), Vanuatu, and Tonga (Skoglund et al. 2016).

Currently, with modern computational advancements, analysts can examine the extensive datasets of whole genomes, instead of relying on isolation of one or a few key markers. The whole genome logically provides the greatest confidence in representing a DNA profile, knowing for sure that nothing has been missed or overlooked. Moreover, the results of multiple whole genomes can be compared for the fullest view of the DNA of a population. The extremely large datasets can be analyzed objectively through computational procedures, such as principal component analysis (PCA), for identifying the specific points within the whole genomes that covary with each other or that carry the most statistical weight for distinguishing one population from another.

A key breakthrough by Hertzberg et al. (1989) identified a variant in DNA that appeared to characterize most Polynesian individuals as well as many Asian groups that occurred only very rarely among people living in Australia, New Guinea, or Melanesia. According to the geographic distribution of the "Polynesian motif" or Lineage B4a1a1a, people of an Asian homeland brought little or no genetics effect into the Australo-Melanesian region while migrating eventually into the remote islands of the Pacific as in Polynesia. When including the Lineage B4a1a1a with the "E" haplogroups and others of Asia-derived DNA ancestry, the results are seen in nearly 100% of Austronesian groups in Taiwan, merely 20% in Island Melanesia, and about 80% in Polynesia (Friedlaender et al. 2008; Kayser et al. 2008). Increasingly detailed DNA analysis has refined the overall picture through examining maternally inherited mitochondrial DNA (mtDNA), paternally inherited Y chromosome, and complete human genome or autosomal chromosomes (Delfin et al. 2012; Melton et al. 1998; Sykes et al. 1995).

The Asian-Polynesian connection in genetics has been difficult for the DNA analysts alone to interpret while accommodating the significantly different Melanesian or Australo-Melanesian genetic ancestry, and here some clues from linguistics and archaeology help to make sense of the geographic patterns in the DNA lineages. Linguistically, the people of Island Melanesia are members of the Oceanic (Oc) language community, shared at an equal level in the Austronesian phylogeny with all others in Polynesia as well as in Micronesia, except as has been noted in the Mariana Islands and Palau. Archaeologically, the first people migrating into West Polynesia about 1100–800 B.C. produced a diagnostic style of pottery that also was made by the first people moving into Southern Melanesia at the same time. Moreover, they all shared an immediate older ancestry farther northwest in Melanesia, specifically in the Bismarck Archipelago east of New Guinea about 1350 B.C., all within the geographic range of the Oceanic-speaking language communities (Chapter 6).

The combined lines of evidence reflect a complicated culture history connecting Near and Remote Oceania. Austronesian-speaking groups definitely passed through some but not all parts of Melanesia, and some stayed there, as Oceanic-speaking descendants are present today. The older-established biological populations in Melanesia, however, evidently were influenced only very minimally by the overlay of Asia-derived populations passing through the region. While people in Melanesia evidently adopted Austronesian languages and many aspects of material culture, they retained their own biological characteristics and Australo-Melanesian (Papuan) DNA lineages. Some of these Australo-Melanesian groups now populate the islands of Remote Oceania in parts of Island Melanesia in the southeast Solomon Islands, New Caledonia, Vanuatu, and Fiji. Others, carrying mostly the Asia-derived DNA lineages, today live farther in the Remote Oceanic islands in parts of Polynesia in Tonga and Samoa. These patterns presumably reflect the initial founding populations of groups with Melanesian and Polynesian DNA lineage markers, although the effects of later population movements would need to be considered.

People with Asia-derived (or sometimes termed "Mongoloid") DNA were not the only people who ventured into the islands of Remote Oceania. According to the DNA evidence, at least some members of those founding populations came from Melanesia or from the greater Australo-Melanesian region. The Australo-Melanesian groups very likely had inhabited all of Island Southeast Asia, the continental masses of Australia and New Guinea, and the islands of Near Oceania since the Pleistocene. After post-glacial sea-level rise and forced separation of land masses by large-scale flooding of coastal lowlands, the widespread Australo-Melanesian groups began to diverge more and more significantly from one another biologically, linguistically, and culturally so that many of their individually distinguished characteristics most likely can be dated roughly in the range of 8000–6000 B.C. When Asian-related "Mongoloid" groups moved through the region much later during the Holocene after 2200 B.C., different outcomes prevailed from one place to another in terms of interacting with the preexisting indigenous Australo-Melanesian populations.

The Asia-derived DNA lineages evidently contributed just minimally to the genetic populations in the islands of Near Oceania and Melanesia, but their dispersals through Island Southeast Asia were much more dramatic. Even so, their arrivals did not constitute a 100% population replacement. The Asia-related DNA lineages are overall dominant now in the region of Island Southeast Asia and coincide geographically with Austronesian-speaking groups, but small traceable amounts of quite different lineages include groups directly traceable to human dispersals from Africa, presumably during the Pleistocene. These Africa-derived groups are attested in maternally inherited mitochondrial DNA (mtDNA) Haplogroups P and Q (Van Oven and Kayser 2009) and in paternally inherited Y chromosome Haplogroup C (Karafet et al. 2008). These DNA lineages have survived in greatest abundance farther east in Indonesia, also found regularly in New Guinea and Australia, while they are less prominent farther west and north toward the Asian continent (Karafet et al. 2010).

The conclusions of DNA studies often have been difficult for archaeologists to accept when the formal publications have lacked clarity about how the results were interpreted, especially when they were interpreted from modern-day DNA samples of living people. Critics correctly can point to the traditions of interisland exchange and the possibility of small amounts of crossover mixtures of lineages from otherwise separate communities. Perhaps more important, though, is the fact that native populations in almost all islands declined radically after European contact, thereby creating a drastically reduced representation of the genetics lineages in the surviving populations today. All of these issues feed the doubts of cynical archaeologists concerned with knowing secure chronological contexts and associations of specific materials and, in this case, of DNA. Even in the rare cases of obtaining ancient DNA from archaeological bones, those results need to be evaluated against the more extensive datasets of modern-day DNA samples.

Despite the limitations, modern and ancient DNA studies confidently can identify the unique genetic mutations or markers that represent real biological "events" in a population's history. Those genetic markers have been inherited by the successive descendant generations of people, regardless of any concerns of cross-migration flow or historically reduced biological diversity. Cross-migration flow often can be detected due to the level of a genetic marker relative to others in the total population. Following the collapsed biological populations in many of the postimperial contexts of the Pacific Islands, less opportunities have remained to examine the diversity that once existed within the pre-imperial societies, but the surviving genetic markers still are just as valid as any others.

Until recently, with ancient DNA studies, the dating of past genetic lineage events has relied to some extent on archaeological dating of when human populations first entered different regions of the world. Geneticists have proposed different ways of estimating a "molecular clock" of the numbers of human reproductive generations needed to create a mutation in the DNA of a population (e.g., Dover 1987; Li and Tanimura 1987; Li et al. 1987; Vawter and Brown 1986). Occasionally, the molecular clock can be calibrated with samples of ancient DNA obtained from dated archaeological contexts close to the timing of purported migration episodes, but these are extremely rare even in the Pacific where migrations must have occurred.

So far in Pacific Oceania, ancient DNA studies have been rare, because nearly all of the known burials postdated the timing of first human inhabitation of the islands, thereby belonging to contexts separate from the major point of interest for learning about the original founding populations. Prior to about A.D. 1000, across the region, the few known burial sites consistently have been in ritual caves or other specially designated areas set apart from the regular residential habitation sites. As will be presented in Chapter 12, the tradition of burial at a house or village site became popular after A.D. 1000, as part of a broader cultural practice of formalization of villages and territories, portrayed in this book as an "A.D. 1000 Event." Furthermore, this later context after A.D. 1000 involved the region's most extensively inhabited sea of islands, necessarily including the most opportunities for cross-contact interactions among populations that likely would complicate the ability to identify the original founding populations among DNA profiles.

At the time of preparing this book's second edition, the only published studies of ancient DNA in Pacific Oceania have involved the skeletons from the sites of Vanuatu, Tonga, the Mariana Islands, and a sampling of areas in Micronesia. Of these studies, the skeletons from Vanuatu and from Tonga related to the founding populations in those areas, dated around 1100–700 B.C. and 700–200 B.C. respectively (Skoglund et al. 2016). A study in Guam of the Mariana Islands provided the complete genome sequencing of two individuals at a ritual cave burial dated around 300–200 B.C. (Pugach et al. 2021), although the archaeological record at this site and many others of the Marianas have demonstrated permanent residential habitation sites at least as old as 1500 B.C. Another study extended the time depth of Guam's burial population back to 700–500 B.C., while also examining numerous later-aged and historical burial sites from varied parts of Micronesia (Liu et al. 2022).

The ancient DNA studies so far have confirmed the same chronological narrative of Pacific Oceanic archaeology that had been presented in the first edition of this book, and the relevant details have been added in Chapters 6, 7, 12, and 13. The founding population of people making pottery for the first time in the region has been verified as originating from a homeland of East Asian affinity and linked with the modern-day Austronesian-speaking groups of Taiwan. The ancient DNA findings indicate a population movement from Taiwan through Island Southeast Asia, then next into different parts of Pacific Oceania. The peopling of the Mariana Islands can be traced to a direct source in the Philippines of Island Southeast Asia, and this event occurred earlier and separately from the other events of Pacific Oceania, congruent with the earlier archaeological dating and separate non-Oceanic language group in the Marianas (Pugach et al. 2021; see also Liu et al. 2022). The major population movement associated with Lapita pottery and Oceanic-speaking language groups, as in Vanuatu and in Tonga, occurred primarily after 1100 B.C., and this context involved people of Austronesian ancestry along with others of Australo-Melanesian or Papuan ancestry from the long-inhabited Melanesian areas of eastern New Guinea and nearby islands (Skoglund et al. 2016).

Additional future studies of ancient DNA likely will not change the current knowledge other than to add extra details and refinement. Stoneking et al. (2023) noted that ancient DNA research may yet reveal more of the diversity of individual people who lived within the broader overall populations during specific time periods, so far known only from limited numbers of individuals for representing those larger populations. Other contributions still could be possible with examining the burial populations from later time periods and cross-contact population movements. With attention to the chronological narrative of the Pacific-wide context, as presented in this book, ancient DNA studies potentially can clarify the population histories of islands in the order of the initial founding events, followed by various later population movements, contacts, and changing circumstances.

Role of archaeology

Archaeology is uniquely suited for drawing a wealth of datable material evidence directly from the past in a manner that is not possible through written history, linguistics, or other approaches. Instead of reaching from the present into the past, archaeology can bring the past forward into the present. Accordingly, the following chapters provide a chronological narrative exposing how the natural and cultural contexts of Pacific Oceania have changed through time.

Long before archaeology developed as a discipline, people were asking questions about the cultural history of Pacific Oceania that are still being addressed today by archaeologists and others. In this regard, one of the most famous historical quotes comes from Captain James Cook during his second voyage into the Pacific, when he was near Rapa Nui (Easter Island) in 1774: "It is extraordinary that the same Nation should have spread themselves over all of the isles in this vast Ocean from New Zealand to this island which is almost a fourth part of the circumference of the globe" (in Beaglehole 1969: 354). Following Cook, Horatio Hale (1846), Edward S. C. Handy (1930), Sir Peter Buck, also known as Te Rangi Hiroa (1938), and others proposed different ideas about the "Polynesian problem" of how the many people speaking clearly related Polynesian languages came to colonize (in the biological sense) such a widespread portion of the Pacific, with further relationships connecting to the communities living in Island Southeast Asia. Moreover, how was this large-scale migration possible while an apparently independent culture history unfolded in most of the Australo-Melanesian region? Finally, when did people make the remote-distance colonizing voyages into different parts of the Pacific, not only in Polynesia but also elsewhere?

Although archaeological excavations had begun in Pacific Oceania as early as 1872 in New Zealand (Von Haast 1872) and 1887 in the Mariana Islands (Marche 1889), the early scholars addressing the "Polynesian problem" relied mostly on observations of language and ethnographic knowledge of traditional material culture. Hale (1846) was among the first explicitly to outline a west-to-east progression of migrations across the Pacific, in stages from Island Southeast Asia through Melanesia and eventually into Polynesia, although at the time the prevailing wisdom suggested that Melanesians and Polynesians were separate and unrelated racial groups. Handy (1930) postulated layers of cultural influence from India, Mainland Southeast Asia, and China flowing directly into Polynesia, including an earlier "Brahmanical" and a later "Buddhistic" association, although certainly neither Brahmanic Hinduism nor Buddhism were practiced as formal religions traditionally in Polynesia. Hiroa (1938) rejected both of these models, and instead he proposed a movement of people from Island Southeast Asia, moving through Micronesia on the way to Polynesia, completely circumventing any connection with the seemingly different racial grouping of Melanesia. Of these three proposals, the model by Horatio Hale has been upheld by modern archaeological, linguistic, and genetics research while the others have been proven inaccurate.

Archaeology did not contribute much toward solving any chronology-related questions in the Pacific until after World War II with the popularization of systematic stratigraphic excavations, soon to be coupled with the ability to obtain radiocarbon dates starting in the 1950s. Before these advancements in the field, archaeology was subsumed within ethnography by most practitioners in the region. Archaeology was embraced as a tool in the ethnographer's kit to learn more about the native cultures that had been "disappearing" due to infectious disease, warfare, and other impacts following European contacts and colonial impositions. Time has shown that the indigenous people of the Pacific did not tragically vanish, and in fact they continue to survive and to maintain their own lively cultural traditions. Meanwhile, archaeologists were busy with documenting site ruins and monuments, occasionally excavating at some of these sites or inside caves, and the material findings generally were viewed as filling the picture of ethnographic material culture inventories in museum exhibits or curated collections.

By focusing attention on surface-visible ruins and engaging in little or no excavations, archaeologists before World War II in the Pacific essentially were reaching from the present into the accessible past. Working from surface observations, the pioneering efforts in archaeology primarily validated and expanded just slightly upon what already had been known from museum-curated ethnographic collections, language subgrouping relations, oral histories, and place-name traditions. Even today, many archaeological investigations focus on the recent past within the reach of ethnography and history, and often the research questions and primary datasets involve little or no archaeology at all.

Beginning in the 1950s in several parts of Pacific Oceania, stratigraphic excavations aimed to recover sequences of cultural occupations beyond the surface-visible site ruins, and radiocarbon dates supplied absolute ages that were astonishing for anyone who previously thought of just a very shallow time depth of cultural presence in the Pacific. One of the first known radiocarbon dates from the Pacific, however, was not part of a systematic search for ancient sites, but rather it was due to Kenneth Emory's curiosity in Willard Libby's new technique of radiocarbon dating. Emory supplied a sample of charcoal from a hearth that he had excavated inside the Kuliʻouʻou Rockshelter in Oʻahu of the Hawaiian Islands, and it produced an unexpectedly old dating of approximately A.D. 1000 (Emory et al. 1959). Following this surprise, archaeologists began to rethink the possibilities of their investigations in the region. Awkwardly, the museum-curated materials from the Kuliʻouʻou excavation have been redated and found to belong to contexts postdating A.D. 1400 (Kahn et al. 2014), but the notions of potentially old dating already had revolutionized the field of Pacific archaeology.

Although an age of A.D. 1000 in the Hawaiian Islands was celebrated as remarkable when it was published in 1959, considerably older dates already had been reported from other parts of Pacific Oceania. In the Mariana Islands, Alexander Spoehr (1957) documented deeply buried subsurface layers containing red-slipped and decorated pottery at least as early as 1000 B.C. In New Caledonia, Gifford and Shutler (1956) documented an age of approximately 800 B.C. for dentate-stamped pottery at a site that they called "Lapita," now giving its name to an entire cultural assemblage found across an impressively broad region of the Pacific. These findings have been known since the 1950s, but their implications about early Marianas settlement, Lapita origins, and Island Southeast Asia relations have been variably ignored or disputed for some decades as discussed in Chapter 5.

Armed with radiocarbon dating and control of stratigraphic layers, archaeologists began producing dated sequences of material culture inventories in numerous island groups. Excavations produced a proliferation of descriptive chronologies about archaic versus later forms of pottery, stone adzes, and fishing gear. Today, these classifications and typologies may be regarded as quaint reminders of an old-fashioned cultural historical approach in archaeology, but they have created the fundamental basis of all modern archaeological practice. Although the naming of periods as archaic or classic may be shunned today, the chronological ordering has proven necessary in making sense of the past. The proposed names of time periods can be disregarded while still learning about the material facts of sites and artifacts of those time periods toward comprehending the key issues of change through time.

Material culture chronologies do not in themselves solve any urgent problems about understanding laws of human behavior or about the place of humanity in the world. Rather, they constitute the necessary raw data toward addressing questions about the past. In other words, the true research significance can be realized only through linking with some other question, problem, theme, or idea. In this regard, the possibilities are limitless, but they must begin with real tangible material substance from the archaeological record. Otherwise, the questions and the datasets are not in fact related to archaeology at all.

The approach of material culture chronology is fundamental to any archaeological inquiry, or else no basis exists for addressing anything else. These issues will become self-evident through the next chapters. Without referring to material assemblages from dated contexts of the past, archaeology in the Pacific or anywhere in the world becomes trapped in a mode of reaching from the present into the past, doomed to add very little, if anything, to the fields of ethnography and social history.

With the surge of chronologically oriented research since the 1950s, archaeologists have leveraged their descriptive catalogs of artifacts toward restructuring thoughts of how cultures have changed or evolved through time. Within the Pacific Oceanic region, one such influential approach was formulated by Robert Suggs (1961) in the Marquesas Islands, which looked not only at the sequence of different forms of artifacts over time but rather more holistically at how those artifact-based chronologies could be coordinated with changing forms of housing, settlement structure, and ecology. This broadened view resonated well with emerging notions at the time about culture process, and it demonstrated that archaeology was capable of addressing a vibrant range of chronology-related topics.

Since the 1960s, archaeologists in the Pacific, like their colleagues worldwide, continually have expanded their research in partnership with other disciplines, and indeed the nature of archaeology requires an interdisciplinary approach. The material categories of artifacts, middens, and settlement ruins can be viewed as uniquely within the scope of archaeology, yet the techniques, methods, and theories for studying these materials rely on other disciplines. Archaeological field and laboratory techniques are borrowed from geology and other sciences, reapplied toward examining archaeological datasets, and redirected methodologically and theoretically toward addressing social, anthropological, and other questions. Many of the research questions and theoretical paradigms have grown from notions extraneous to the field of archaeology itself, such as related to structural Marxism, Darwinian evolutionary theory, biogeography, and ecological principles. The analytical and interpretive methodologies of linking technique and theory, however, tend to be developed mostly within the bounds of archaeological thought and practice, although many notions of archaeology are based in interdisciplinary paradigms, whether explicitly or implicitly.

Interdisciplinary programs have been most productive in addressing questions about how people adapted to the unique environmental and social conditions of living in small and remote islands of Pacific Oceania. The region's archaeology today would be unimaginable without the information learned from hybrid specialisms of archaeobotany, zooarchaeology, ethnoarchaeology, geoarchaeology, archaeometry, and more. Although at risk of learning "more and more about less and less," Pacific archaeology no longer is part of the tool kit of ethnography, but rather it works with an ever-growing tool kit of its own.

Another interdisciplinary trend in the Pacific has been a "triangulation approach," combining archaeology with ethnography and linguistics, as advanced by Kirch and Green (2001). The three lines of evidence are coordinated so as to point to a single target of interest in the past, thus revealing a more accurate picture than any of these perspectives could achieve independently. These studies primarily have been aimed at illustrating the cultural context in West Polynesia prior to the major population expansions into East Polynesia about A.D. 1000, but secondarily they have been applied toward depicting an older Ancestral Polynesian Society (APS) that may have existed some centuries earlier, possibly even as early as the first inhabitants making dentate-stamped Lapita-style pottery in West Polynesia about 1100–800 B.C. In any case, attention to chronology is critical, or else the different lines of evidence may in fact point to separate contexts and thereby produce misleading conclusions and anachronisms.

Regardless of changing paradigms and techniques over the last several decades, Pacific archaeology has contributed significantly to the world's knowledge about long-term human-environment relations, Asia-Pacific migrations, development of trade and exchange systems, emergence of social-political complexities, and other research themes as mentioned in Chapter 1. In principle, rich cultural contexts can be recovered through interdisciplinary programs, triangulation, and other studies in a chronological sequence of time periods. The following chapters work toward these goals, leaving the doors open for others to pursue the research avenues more fully.

References

Athens, J. Stephen, and Jerome V. Ward, 1993. Environmental change and prehistoric settlement in Hawai'i. *Asian Perspectives* 32: 205–223.

Athens, J. Stephen, and Jerome V. Ward, 2006. *Holocene Paleoenvironment of Saipan: Analysis of a Core from Lake Susupe*. Micronesian Archaeological Survey Report Number 35. Commonwealth of the Northern Mariana Islands Division of Historic Preservation, Saipan.

Beaglehole, John Cawte (editor), 1969. *The Journals of Captain James Cook on His Voyages of Discovery: The Voyage of the Resolution and Discovery, 1776–1780*. 2 volumes. Hakluyt Society, Cambridge.

Bellwood, Peter, 1991. The Austronesian dispersal and the origin of languages. *Scientific American* 265: 88–93.

Bellwood, Peter, 1997. *Prehistory of the Indo-Malaysian Archipelago*. Revised edition. University of Hawai'i Press, Honolulu.

Bellwood, Peter, Geoffrey Chambers, Malcolm Ross, and Hsiao-chun Hung, 2011. Are 'cultures' inherited? Multidisciplinary perspectives on the origins and migrations of Austronesian-speaking peoples prior to 1000 BC. In *Investigating Archaeological Cultures: Material Culture, Variability, and Transmission*, edited by Benjamin Roberts and Marc Vander Linden, pp. 321–354. Springer, New York.

Blust, Robert, 1995. The prehistory of the Austronesian-speaking peoples: A view from language. *Journal of World Prehistory* 9: 453–510.

Blust, Robert, 2013. *The Austronesian Languages*. Revised edition. Asia-Pacific Linguistics Open Access Monographs 008. Research School of Pacific and Asian Studies, Australian National University, Canberra.

Carson, Mike T., 2004. Resolving the enigma of early coastal settlement in the Hawaiian Islands: The stratigraphic sequence of the Wainiha Beach Site in Kaua'i. *Geoarchaeology* 19: 99–118.

Carson, Mike T., 2008. Correlation of environmental and cultural chronology in New Caledonia. *Geoarchaeology* 23: 695–714.

Carson, Mike T., 2011. Palaeohabitat of first settlement sites 1500–1000 B.C. in Guam, Mariana Islands, western Pacific. *Journal of Archaeological Science* 38: 2207–2221.

Carson, Mike T., 2012. Ethnohistoric and geoarchaeological landscape chronology at Kawaihae, leeward Hawai'i Island. *Geoarchaeology* 27: 385–409.

Carson, Mike T., 2014. Paleoterrain research: Finding the first settlement sites of Remote Oceania. *Geoarchaeology* 29: 268–275.

Carson, Mike T., and J. Stephen Athens, 2007. Integration of coastal geomorphology, mythology, and archaeological evidence at Kualoa Beach, windward O'ahu, Hawaiian Islands. *Journal of Island and Coastal Archaeology* 2: 24–43.

Carson, Mike T., and Hsiao-chun Hung, 2015. On the beach in Remote Oceania. In *Field Archaeology from around the World: Ideas and Approaches*, edited by Martin Carver, Bisserka Gaydarska, and Sandra Monton-Subias, pp. 133–136. Springer, New York.

Carson, Mike T., and Hsiao-chun Hung, 2022. 3500 years in a changing landscape: The house of Taga in the Mariana Islands, western Micronesia. In *Palaeolandscapes in Archaeology: Lessons for the Past, Present, and Future*, edited by Mike T. Carson, pp. 340–376. Routledge, London.

Carson, Mike T., Hsiao-chun Hung, Glenn Summerhayes, and Peter Bellwood, 2013. The pottery trail from Southeast Asia to Remote Oceania. *Journal of Island and Coastal Archaeology* 8: 17–36.

Cox, Murray P., 2015. Southeast Asian islands and Oceania: Human genetics. In *The Global Prehistory of Human Migration*, edited by Peter Bellwood, pp. 293–301. Wiley Blackwell, Malden, MA.

Delfin, Frederick, Sean Myles, Ying Choi, David Hughes, Robert Illek, Mannis van Oven, Brigitte Pakendorf, Manfred Kayser, and Mark Stoneking, 2012. Bridging near and Remote Oceania: MtDNA and NRY variation in the Solomon Islands. *Molecular Biological Evolution* 29: 545–564.

Deng, Zhenhua, Hsiao-chun Hung, Mike T. Carson, Adhi Agus Oktaviana, Budianto Hakim, and Truman Simanjuntak, 2020. Validating earliest rice farming in the Indonesian archipelago. *Scientific Reports 10*: 10984. DOI https://doi.org/10.1038/s41598-020-67747-3

Denham, Tim P., Simon Haberle, Carol Lentfer, Richard Fullagar, Judith Field, M. Therin, N. Porch, and Barbara Windsborough, 2003. Origins of agriculture at Kuk Swamp in the highlands of New Guinea. *Science* 301: 189–193.

Dickinson, William R., 2001. Paleoshoreline record of relative Holocene sea levels on Pacific islands. *Earth-Science Reviews* 55: 191–234.

Dickinson, William R., 2003. Impact of Mid-Holocene hydro-isostatic high stand in regional sea level on habitability of islands in Pacific Oceania. *Journal of Coastal Research* 19: 489–502.

DiPiazza, Anne, and Erik Pearthree, 2001a. An island for gardens, and island for birds and voyaging: A settlement pattern for Kiritimati and Tabuaeran, two "mystery islands" in the northern Lines, Republic of Kiribati. *Journal of the Polynesian Society* 110: 149–170.

DiPiazza, Anne, and Erik Pearthree, 2001b. Voyaging and basalt exchange in the Phoenix and Line Archipelagoes: The viewpoint from three mystery islands. *Archaeology in Oceania* 36: 146–152.

Dover, Gabriel A., 1987. DNA turnover and the molecular clock. *Journal of Molecular Evolution* 26: 47–58.

Emory, Kenneth P., William J. Bonk, and Yosihiko H. Sinoto, 1959. *Hawaiian Archaeology: Fishhooks.* Special Publication 46. Bernice Pauahi Bishop Museum, Honolulu.

Fitzpatrick, Scott M., 2011. Defending the defensible or offending the sensible? *Journal of Pacific Archaeology* 2: 100–105.

Friedlaender, Jonathan S., Françoise R. Friedlaender, Floyd A. Reed, Kenneth K. Kidd, Geoffrey K. Chambers, Rodney A. Lea, Jun-Hun Loo, George Koki, Jason A. Hodgson, D. Andrew Merriwether, and James L. Weber, 2008. The genetic structure of the Pacific Islanders. *PLoS Genetics* 4, e19. DOI: 10.1371/journal.pgen.0040019.

Gifford, Edward Winslow, and Richard Shutler, Jr., 1956. *Archaeological Excavations in New Caledonia.* Anthropological Records 18, Part 1. University of California Press, Berkeley.

Hale, Horatio, 1846. *Ethnography and Philology.* United States Exploring Expedition Volume 6. Sherman, Philadelphia.

Handy, E. S. Craighill, 1930. The problem of Polynesian origins. *Bernice Pauahi Bishop Museum Occasional Papers* 9: 1–27.

Hertzberg, M., K. N. P. Mickelson, S. W. Serjeantson, J. F. Prior, and R. J. Trent, 1989. An Asian-specific 9-bp deletion of mitochondrial DNA is frequently found in Polynesians. *American Journal of Human Genetics* 44: 504–510.

Hiroa, Te Rangi, 1938. *Vikings of the Sunrise.* Frederick Stokes, New York.

Hiscock, Peter, 2008. *Archaeology of Ancient Australia.* Routledge, London.

Hope, Geoffrey, Dominique O'Dea, and Wendy Southern, 1999. Holocene vegetation histories in the western Pacific: Alternative records of human impact. In *Le Pacifique de 5000 à 2000 avant le Présent: Suppléments à l'Histoire d'une Colonisation,* edited by Jean-Christophe Galipaud and Ian Lilley, pp. 387–404. Institut de Récherche pour le Développement, Paris.

Hung, Hsiao-chun, 2008. *Migration and Cultural Interaction in Southern Coastal China, Taiwan and the Northern Philippines, 3000 BC to AD 100: The Early History of Austronesian-Speaking Populations.* Doctoral dissertation, School of Archaeology and Anthropology, Australian National University, Canberra.

Hung, Hsiao-chun, Mike T. Carson, Peter Bellwood, Frediliza Campos, Philip J. Piper, Eubesio Dizon, Mary Jane Louise A. Bolunia, Marc Oxenham, and Zhang Chi, 2011. The first settlement of Remote Oceania: The Philippines to the Marianas. *Antiquity* 85: 909–926.

Hung, Hsiao-chun, Cheng-hwa Tsang, Zhenhua Deng, Mary Jane Louise A. Bolunia, Rey A. Santiago, Mike T. Carson, and Peter Bellwood, 2022. Preceramic riverside hunter-gatherers and the arrival of Neolithic farmers in northern Luzon. *Antiquity* 96: 848–867.

Ingold, Tim, 1994. Preface. In *Companion Encyclopedia of Anthropology: Humanity, Culture and Social Life,* edited by Tim Ingold, pp. xiii–xxii. Routledge, London.

Kahn, Jennifer G., Timothy M. Rieth, Patrick V. Kirch, J. Stephen Athens, and Gail Murakami, 2014. Re-dating of the Kuli'ou'ou Rockshelter, O'ahu, Hawai'i: Location of the first radiocarbon date from the Pacific Islands. *Journal of the Polynesian Society* 123: 67–90.

Karafet, Tatiana M., Brian Hallmark, Murray P. Cox, Herawati Sudoyo, Sean Downey, J. Stephen Lansing, and Michael F. Hammer, 2010. Major east-west division underlies Y chromosome stratification across Indonesia. *Molecular Biology and Evolution* 27: 1833–1844.

Karafet, Tatiana M., Fernando L. Mendez, Monica B. Meilerman, Peter A. Underhill, S. L. Stephen L. Zegura, and Michael F. Hammer, 2008. New binary polymorphisms reshape and increase resolution of the human Y chromosomal haplogroup tree. *Genome Research* 18: 830–838.

Kayser, Manfred, Oscar Lao, Kathrin Saar, Silke Brauer, Xingyue Wang, Peter Nürnberg, Ronald J. Trent, and Mark Stoneking, 2008. Genome-wide analysis indicates more Asian than Melanesian ancestry of Polynesians. *American Journal of Human Genetics* 82: 194–198.

Kirch, Patrick V., and Roger C. Green, 2001. *Hawaiki: Ancestral Polynesia: An Essay in Historical Anthropology.* Cambridge University Press, Cambridge.

Layton, Richard, 1999. Folklore and world view. In *Archaeology and Folklore*, edited by Amy Gazin-Schwartz and Cornelius Hastorf, pp. 26–34. Theoretical Archaeology Group. Routledge, London.

Li, W. H., and M. Tanimura, 1987. The molecular clock runs more slowly in man than in apes and monkeys. *Nature 326*: 93–96.

Li, W. H., M. Tanimura, and P. M. Sharp, 1987. An evaluation of the molecular clock hypothesis using mammalian DNA sequences. *Journal of Molecular Evolution* 25: 330–342.

Liu, Yue-chen, Rosalind Hunter-Anderson, Olivia Cheronet, Joanne Eakin, Frank Camacho, Michael Pietrusewsky, Nadin Rohland, Alexander Ionnidis, J. Stephen Athens, Michele Toomay Douglas, Rona Michi Ikehara-Quebral, Rebecca Bernardos, Brendan J. Culleton, Matthew Mah, Nicole Adamski, Nasreen Broomandkhoshbacht, Kimberly Callan, Ann Marie Lawson, Kisten Mand, Megan Michel, Jonas Oppenheimer, Kritsin Stewardson, Fatma Zalzala, Kenneth Kidd, Theodore G. Schurr, Kathryn Auckland, Adrian V. S. Hill, Alexander J. Mentzer, Consuelo D. Quinto-Cortés, Kathryn Robson, Douglas J. Kennett, Nick Patterson, Carlos D. Bustamante, Andrés Moreno-Estrada, Matthew Spriggs, Miguel Vilar, Mark Lipson, Ron Pinhasi, and David Reich, 2022. Ancient DNA reveals five streams of migration into Micronesia and matrilocality in early Pacific seafarers. *Science* 377: 72–79.

Marche, Antoine-Alfred, 1889. Rapport general sur une mission aux Îles Mariannes. *Nouvelles Archives des Missions Scientifiques et Littéraires, Nouvelle Série 1*: 241–280.

Melton, T., R. Peterson, A. J. Redd, N. Saha, A. S. Sofro, J. Martinson, and M. Stoneking, 1998. Polynesian genetic affinities with Southeast Asian populations as identified by mtDNA analysis. *American Journal of Human Genetics* 57: 403–414.

Nunn, Patrick D., 2000. Environmental catastrophe in the Pacific Islands around A.D. 1300. *Geoarchaeology 15*: 715–740.

Nunn, Patrick D., 2005. Reconstructing tropical shorelines using archaeological data: Examples from the Fiji Archipelago, southwest Pacific. *Journal of Coastal Research Special Issue 42*: 15–25.

Nunn, Patrick D., 2008. *Vanished Islands and Hidden Continents of the Pacific.* University of Hawai'i Press, Honolulu.

Nunn, Patrick D., and Rosalind L. Hunter-Anderson, 2011. Defending the defensible. *Journal of Pacific Archaeology 2*: 92–99.

Nunn, Patrick D., Rosalind L. Hunter-Anderson, Mike T. Carson, Frank Thomas, Sean Ulm, and Michael J. Rowland, 2007. Times of plenty, times of less: Last-millennium societal disruption in the Pacific Basin. *Human Ecology 35*: 385–401.

Pugach, Irina, Alexander Hübner, Hsiao-chun Hung, Matthias Meyer, Mike T. Carson, and Mark Stoneking, 2021. Ancient DNA from GBuam and the peopling of the Pacific. *Proceedings of the National Academy of Sciences 18*: e2022112118. https://doi.org/10.1073/pnas.2022112118

Ruddiman, William F., 2008. *Earth's Climate: Past and Future.* Second edition. W. H. Freeman, New York.

Skoglund, Pontus, Cosimo Posth, Kendra Sirak, Matthew Spriggs, Frédérique Valentin, Stuart Bedford, Geoffrey R. Clark, Christian Reepmeyer, Fiona Petchey, Daniel Fernandes, Qiaomei Fu, Eadaoin Harney, Mark Lipson, Swapan Mallick, Mario Novak, Nadin Rohland, Kristin

Stewardson, Syafiq Abdullah, Murray P. Cox, Françoise R. Friedlaender, Jonathan S. Friedlaender, Toomas Kivisild, George Koki, Pradiptakati Kusuma, D. Andrew Merriwether, François X. Ricaut, Joseph T. S. Wee, Nick Patterson, Johannes Krause, Ron Pinhasi, and David Reich, 2016. Genomic insights into the peopling of the southwest Pacific. *Nature* 538: 510–513.

Snow, Bryan E., Richard Shutler, Jr., D. E. Nelson, J. S. Vogel, and J. R. Southon, 1986. Evidence of early rice cultivation in the Philippines. *Philippine Quarterly of Culture and Society* 14: 3–11.

Spoehr, Alexander, 1957. *Marianas Prehistory: Archaeological Survey and Excavations on Saipan, Tinian and Rota*. Fieldiana: Anthropology, Volume 48. Chicago Natural History Museum, Chicago.

Spriggs, Matthew, 1997. Landscape catastrophe and landscape enhancement: Are either or both true in the Pacific? In *Historical Ecology in the Pacific Islands: Prehistoric Environmental and Landscape Change*, edited by Patrick V. Kirch and Terry L. Hunt, pp. 80–104. Yale University Press, New Haven.

Steadman, David W., 1995. Prehistoric extinctions of Pacific Island birds: Biodiversity meets zooarchaeology. *Science* 267: 1123–1131.

Stoneking, Mark, Leonardo Arias, Dang Liu, Sandra Oliveira, Irina Pugach, and Jae Joseph Russell B. Rodriguez, 2023. Genomic perspectives on human dispersals during the Holocene. *Proceedings of the National Academy of Sciences* 120: e2209475119. https://doi.org/10.1073/pnas.2209475119

Suggs, Robert C., 1961. *Archaeology of Nukuhiva, Marquesas Islands, French Polynesia*. Anthropological Papers, Number 1. American Museum of Natural History, New York.

Sykes, Bryan, Andrew Leiboff, Jacob Low-Beer, Susannah Tetzner, and Martin Richards, 1995. The origins of the Polynesians: An interpretation from mitochondrial lineage analysis. *American Journal of Human Genetics* 57: 1463–1475.

Van Oven, M., and M. Kayser, 2009. Updated comprehensive phylogenetic tree of global human mitochondrial DNA variation. *Human Mutation* 30: E-386–394.

Vawter, L., and W. M. Brown, 1986. Nuclear and mitochondrial DNA comparisons reveal extreme rate variation in the molecular clock. *Science* 234: 194–196.

Von Haast, Julius, 1872. Moas and moa hunters. *Transactions of the New Zealand Institute* 4: 66–107.

Weisler, Marshall I., 1999. The antiquity of aroid pit agriculture and significance of buried A horizons on Pacific atolls. *Geoarchaeology* 14: 621–654.

Yang, Xiaoping, Louis A. Scuderi, Xulong Wang, Louis J. Scuderi, Deguo Zhang, Hongwei Li, Steven Forman, Qinghai Xu, Ruichang Wang, Weiwen Huang, and Shixia Yang, 2015. Groundwater sapping as the cause of irreversible desertification of Hunshandake Sandy Lands, Inner Mongolia, northern China. *Proceedings of the National Academy of Sciences* 112: 702–706.

3 Substance and scope of Pacific Oceanic archaeology

Whāia te iti kahurangi ki te tūohu koe me he maunga teitei (New Zealand Maori proverb), translates into English as "Seek the treasure that you value most dearly. If you bow your head, then let it be to a lofty mountain."

This *whakataukī* (proverb) is one of many recalled by the people of Aotearoa ("long white cloud," also known as New Zealand) with layered meaning. It encourages to "aim high" for valuable goals, while it also warns that some goals are not realistically attainable. For instance, a "lofty mountain" may stand in the way of what a person is seeking. Anything less than such a majestic power, however, should not prevent a person from achieving a worthy goal and to accomplish something spectacular.

Pacific Oceanic archaeologists certainly have lofty goals of contributing to world knowledge, but their jargon and particularistic datasets need to be decoded for the world's scholars to comprehend. Otherwise, the tendency to accumulate specialized and narrowly focused knowledge of "more and more about less and less" (sensu Ingold 1994: xx) becomes an obstacle rather than the broad-reaching achievement that had been intended. Food-producing field systems of tree and root-tuber crops may be discussed as evidence of intensive agriculture. Rosters of imported plants and animals are understood implicitly as proxies of cultural manipulations of the environment. Sets of stacked-rock walls and platforms may be viewed as territorial markers, as symbols of chiefly power, or even as evidence of state-level societies. A single stone adze may be regarded as demonstrating the far overseas reach of a maritime chiefdom or perhaps an empire. The present chapter will begin to demystify how these investigations have been possible.

Scholars working in other regions of the world may be surprised that the sites of Tahiti, Hawai'i and other islands of East Polynesia typically contain very few stone flakes or perhaps no portable artifacts at all, whereas the sites of the Mariana Islands, New Caledonia, and other western Pacific Islands contain abundant broken pottery among other diverse assemblages. In nearly every island, middens of discarded shells, animal bones, and wood charcoal constitute mountains of material for incredibly detailed analysis. In many island groups, stonework ruins comprise the primary units of archaeological attention, although they overrepresent later periods in surface-visible contexts completely unrelated to the older periods of initial seafaring migrations and island settlement.

Most archaeologists can appreciate that different questions can be addressed when studying a shell midden, a complex of stone monuments and statues, a surface concentration of a handful of stone flakes, or an excavation of thousands of pieces of pottery. Accordingly, most inventories of material culture are reported in categories of portable artifacts, food remains, and structural features so that each such category can be discussed with its own set of research issues. Depending on what happens to be discovered during an investigation, other categories may need to be added, for instance, accommodating the findings of burials, caves, or rock art. For studies at larger scales, analysis could consider settlement systems or even whole landscapes.

Range of materials and questions

The archaeological material records of Pacific Oceania have supported a wide range of research questions regarding what can be inferred about past social life, about human-environment relations, and about other issues that can be addressed through the available assemblages of artifacts, midden compositions, structural features, and other surviving evidence. Strictly speaking, archaeological research *must* involve material culture records from datable contexts of the past as the essential substance of the discipline, or else the questions and their answers would exist outside the scope of archaeology. While maintaining this central focus, archaeological research worldwide has become increasingly interdisciplinary, drawing on other lines of evidence to generate new ideas and to test hypotheses, and Pacific Oceania has very much been part of this global trend.

In principle, Pacific Oceanic archaeology follows the same approach as in other regions, beginning with an awareness of the available material records, how they appear to be composed, and how they express variation geographically and chronologically. Geographical and chronological variations obviate questions about how and why those variations occurred, for instance, as seen in the use or nonuse of red slip on pottery, lenticular versus quadrangular or other section-view shapes of adzes, or preference for different types of shellfish in site middens. Other potential investigations may concentrate on the practical and social performance characteristics of stone versus shell adzes, cooking in pots versus earth ovens, or building houses on elevated posts versus ground-level foundations. Further research programs involve greater reliance on intellectual inference and interpretation, such as when addressing issues of social functioning, political organization, ideological systems, and other aspects of past societies that are not immediately observable in the material site records today.

In practice, Pacific Oceanic archaeology differs from what occurs in other regions and involves its own unique sets of material inventories that support some research questions more reasonably than others. The relative values of smallness and isolation make Pacific Islands convenient venues for studying environmental change and especially human-caused impacts in the fragile island ecosystems by relying on pollen records, animal bones, and other proxy evidence that may or may not be coordinated convincingly (if at all) with archaeological material. Remoteness of islands further can support research about human migrations, pending the ability to detect artifacts or other material evidence traceable to a homeland source. Likewise, long-distance trade and exchange can be studied in geographically separate islands, granted that distinctive materials can be traced to a specific external source.

In terms of the archaeological assemblages themselves, the findings in Pacific Oceania consist of variable series of pottery in some but not all islands, polished adzes and chisels, assorted flaked stone and shell tools, ground stone implements, fishing gear, numerous locally specific personal body ornaments, and remnants of dry masonry stonework features. In islands where sites contain maybe just a few stone flakes as the only artifacts, most information is gained from the discarded shells, animal bones, and wood charcoal found in site middens. Additionally, surface-visible stonework ruins offer plentiful information about the last time when people occupied a place, but typically these insights refer to the contexts just prior to (or even during) the years of written histories with European visitors and colonialists, while the records of older periods are the least accessible and tend to be underrepresented.

While some regions of the world boast nicely preserved sites of all ages on or near the surface, such is extremely rare in Pacific Oceania, where, instead, archaeologists find excellent records of later-aged sites and only limited subsurface views of older periods. Given the inherently restricted land masses of islands, increasing sizes of human populations eventually have occupied every usable patch of land, so the surface-accessible site components invariably reflect these later periods of widespread settlement and land-use patterns. Additionally, the oldest site layers tended to be in positions of ancient seashores that have transformed due to change in sea level, overlaying sediments, and other factors in total burying these layers deep beneath the ground and stranded some distance from present-day shorelines. The oldest site layers cannot be observed on the surface, and often they have been obscured or disturbed by successive episodes of intensive crop cultivation, reworking of stonework foundations, and other intensive use of limited land with typically shallow rocky deposits, in total resulting in less knowledge of older periods while overrepresenting later periods.

Pacific Oceanic settings typically offer informative views of past cultural systems as known ethnohistorically and reflected in surface-associated site ruins, but the scope and detail of knowledge become increasingly sparse in older time frames. The older periods are represented only through the inherently limited sizes of excavations revealing layers with collections of broken artifacts and midden associated with scattered remnants of hearths, post molds, and occasional vestiges of stonework features. By comparison, the later periods typically postdating A.D. 1400 are represented through extensive and open views of surface-accessible stonework ruins of settlement and land-use patterns, assemblages of artifacts and midden directly linked with rich ethnographic documentation, and plentiful ethnohistoric traditions about place-names and about the historical and mythical events that occurred in each of those places.

In the eastern Pacific Islands where cultural chronologies extend only to A.D. 1000, most research programs focus on synchronic issues of how societies functioned during short time frames, and any concerns with chronology are addressed much differently than in other parts of Pacific Oceania. In the Hawaiian Islands, for example, as will be discussed in Chapter 13, so far no research program at all has been designed expressly to seek the oldest sites that date probably around A.D. 1000, but instead the period of A.D. 1000 through 1400 is known mostly through pollen and charcoal particles found in lake-bottom and swamp-bottom sediments, along with bones of rats and birds found in natural sinkholes and other locales (Athens et al. 2002). Very few of the known Hawaiian archaeological sites contain subsurface layers predating A.D. 1400, and they clearly preceded the better known ethnohistoric contexts of the superimposed layers with stonework ruins, as at Wainiha in Kaua'i (Carson 2003, 2004), Kualoa in O'ahu (Carson and Athens 2007), and Kawaihae in Hawai'i (Carson 2012). Hawaiian settlement as early as A.D. 1000 has been based largely on the paleoenvironmental proxies and on statistical modeling of the available radiocarbon dates from the few known earlier archaeological sites (Dye 2015). Meanwhile, most Hawaiian research programs focus on the surface-accessible sites that can be documented most easily and can be related clearly with ethnohistoric traditions, always with fascinating results yet, by definition, separate from the potential contributions of chronology-oriented research.

Chronologically sensitive research has been applied most strongly in the longer-occupied islands in the western through central Pacific by working directly with buried site layers dating to specific periods in long sequences. Given adequate radiocarbon dating of hearths and other features within discrete layers, cultural sequences of pottery types and other materials have been formulated as old as 1500 B.C. in the Mariana Islands (Chapter 6), approximately 1000 B.C. in many islands of Southern Melanesia and West Polynesia (Chapter 7), and A.D. 100 in most of Central through Eastern Micronesia (Chapter 10). Within each identifiable site layer, appreciable amounts of broken pottery serve as the most abundant time-sensitive markers, along with whatever other observations are possible in the overall small windows of excavation samples.

Framework of cultural chronologies

While inconsistently following or ignoring the conventions of Paleolithic, Neolithic, and other age terminologies, the Pacific archaeological literature is replete with examples of localized chronologies, usually involving an initial founding settlement period, followed by a time of population growth and expansion, a subsequent time of intensification of land use and social tension, and a later period of classic material culture that continued through the period of foreign contacts and colonial encounters (Figure 3.1). The exact dated years for each period can be debated ferociously, and, of course, they vary from one island group to another. The individual time periods sometimes are assigned names that may be meaningful locally but incompatible cross-regionally. Colleagues outside the Pacific wonder why the "founding settlement" period in East Polynesia occurred more than 2000 years later than initial "settlement" in the western and central Pacific, at the same time of "monument building" in Eastern Micronesia.

The standard culture history sequence conveys a general idea of population growth and related processes, but different frameworks are needed for discussing other issues. Notions of "founding settlement" and "expansion" rarely can define the relevant contexts when

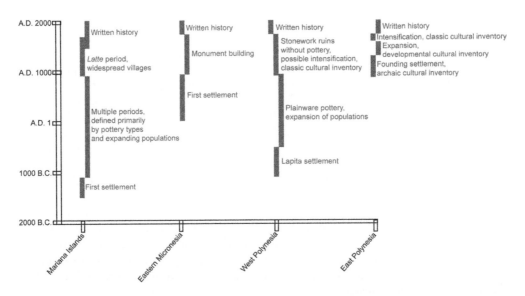

Figure 3.1 Schematic models of Pacific Oceanic island settlement chronologies.

studying change in pottery decoration, shellfish-collection strategy, or size distribution of charcoal particles. During an "intensification" period, surely people engaged in plenty of activities other than intensifying their behaviors. Periods of "developmental" and "intermediary" probably should be discarded in most cases, as they tend to ignore the events of their actual time range and instead fill a gap between an earlier "archaic" period and a later "classic" period that ring hollow in a cultural relativist perspective.

Regardless of how the individual cultural periods may be named, most international colleagues will want to know at least the basics of how to conceptualize the archaeological assemblages in relation to notions of Paleolithic, Neolithic, and Metal Ages that are applicable only unevenly in the Asia-Pacific region (Figure 3.2). The scope of Remote Oceanic archaeology could be termed Neolithic if this word refers to sedentary populations relying mostly on artificial food production rather than hunting-gathering subsistence, but most Pacific archaeologists would point to the indispensable roles of fishing, shellfish gathering, and bird hunting plus, of course, the long traditions of seafaring and mobility as not necessarily fitting expectations of the residential lifestyle of the Neolithic. Some of these characteristics may appear not much different from the scenes at Paleolithic hunter-gatherer sites in Island Southeast Asia and Near Oceania dating thousands of years earlier, but those contexts did not witness any human expansion into the islands of Remote Oceania. In the remote Pacific Islands, the cultural sequence began after a kind of sedentary mode of Neolithic lifestyle already had started in Island Southeast Asia. Many of the Pacific Islands first were settled long after a Metal Age had operated throughout Asia, even though no such Metal Age ever occurred in the Pacific Islands.

Anthropologically sensitive modern archaeologists may be suspicious of portraying human cultures as if they passed through evolutionary stages of Paleolithic, Neolithic, and other ages. These categories should not be misconstrued as evolutionary stages, but rather they refer to different modes of economies. Nothing at all needs to be implied about evolutionary trajectories in order to appreciate that cultural groups engage in different strategies of obtaining their foods, making their settlements, structuring their communities, and interfacing with their inhabited world. These considerations allow archaeologists to focus on the material contents of sites as reflecting economic practice and other aspects of a fully functioning society.

Even without resorting to the conventions of Neolithic and other age categories, the notion of an "archaeological culture" facilitates discussion of the materials of an identified geographic area and time range. Archaeological cultures have become unfashionable and ridiculed in some theoretical perspectives, but they continue to be applied worldwide "in order to make sense of potentially coherent assemblages" (Roberts and Vander Linden 2011: 1). The silently understood caveat is that an archaeologically defined ancient culture is incomplete and artificially constructed on the basis of the limited surviving evidence. The actual people of the past probably defined themselves much differently than how archaeologists refer to them as makers of certain types of pottery and stone tools, consumers of different shellfish catchments, and builders of distinctive stonework monuments. They certainly did not think of themselves as representing archaic, developmental, intermediary, preclassic, or classic time periods.

The concept of an "archaeological culture" often has been misapplied and misunderstood, so the original reference as formulated by V. Gordon Childe (1929: v–vi) may be worth examining:

> We find certain types of remains – pots, implements, burial rites and house forms – constantly recurring together. Such as a complex of associated traits we shall call a

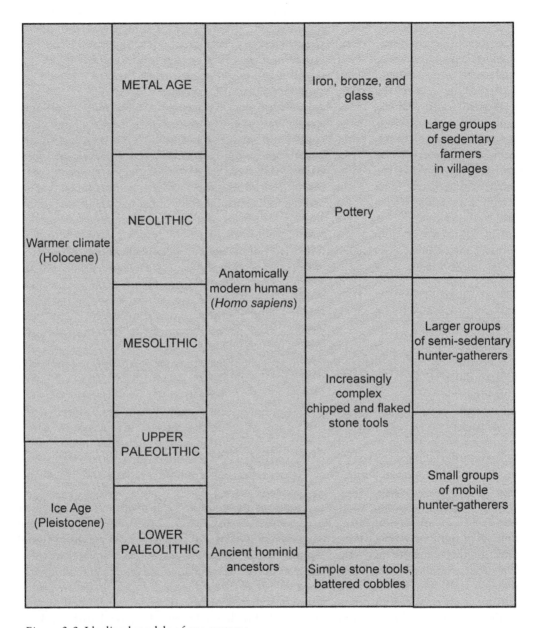

Figure 3.2 Idealized models of age systems.

"cultural group" or just a "culture". We assume that such a complex is the natural expression of what today we would call a "people".

As described here, an archaeological culture includes at least two important characteristics. First, it refers to a recurring set of materials from a definable place and time, and therefore it must be identifiable at multiple sites within a confirmable geographic area and time range. Second, it reflects only the durable material remains of a past human society, and therefore many of the aspects of a living cultural system are inferred rather than observed directly.

Perhaps a blessing and a curse, notions of archaeological cultures overall have been defined only rarely and vaguely in Pacific Oceania. The single successful application of such a concept has followed Roger Green's (1979a) proposal of a "Lapita Cultural Complex" for the sites with dentate-stamped pottery in Melanesia and West Polynesia around 1000 B.C. The "cultural complex" in this case expressly acknowledged the numerous other artifacts and associated cultural behaviors beyond what could be directly observed in the dentate-stamped pottery itself. This understanding of a Lapita Cultural Complex effectively built on Jack Golson's (1961: 176) prior suggestion that the dentate-stamped pottery across much of Melanesia and West Polynesia in total reflected "some early community of culture linking New Caledonia, Samoa and Tonga." Today's literature is flooded with references to the Lapita Cultural Complex and the "Lapita People" (Kirch 1997), although the actual material evidence does not necessarily meet the criteria of an archaeological culture. Criticisms and cautionary tales periodically emerge about the logical problems of defining such a "cultural complex" and especially an entire "people" on the basis of incomplete archaeological materials divorced from their original behavioral contexts (Terrell 2003, 2009).

In the western and central Pacific Islands, pottery typologies give some of the appearance of sequences of archaeological cultures, but only very rarely are they presented as such. As noted, the only formally defined culture in this sense has been the Lapita Cultural Complex, yet the classic diagnostic signature of dentate-stamped pottery in fact represents only one small part of a diverse cultural system. In the islands where Lapita pottery occurs, it is viewed as transitioning directly into later forms or styles generally known as "post-Lapita." The terminology becomes difficult for referring to different post-Lapita archaeological sequences and assemblages in dozens of separate islands.

Further vexing, many scholars refer to a long-term sustained continuity between Lapita sites and present-day living cultural groups, such that an ancestral "Lapita culture" never truly ended but rather changed just superficially and slowly, preserving its essential core identity throughout the long time scale or *longue durée* of history. Proponents of this view refer to Roger Green's (1979b) astute observations of the ethnographically known designs of tattooing and bark cloth (*tapa*) decorations in Polynesia that very convincingly mirrored the designs as documented in dentate-stamped Lapita pottery. In this view, the descendants of Lapita pottery-makers continued the same cultural, linguistic, and other traditions as inherited from their ancestors, with variable modifications through time. Even with accepting this premise, the end of dentate-stamped Lapita pottery about 500 B.C. certainly marked a profound cultural change and can be linked with other changing conditions in ancient society and ecology, and this definite cultural change deserves serious archaeological study.

Notions of a *longue durée* sometimes have been misunderstood in the literature, thus leading to false orthodoxies about little or no change in certain deep social structures that endured throughout a long time scale. In François Simiand's (1903) original formulation, varied aspects of social history could change concurrently and at multiple different paces and scales. Using these ideas, Fernand Braudel (1949) later published his more famously cited works that illustrated the slow-moving or "long-enduring" elements of a *longue durée* in contrast to the fast-moving elements of "event-based history" (*histoire événementielle*). The slow-moving aspects of the *longue durée* were viewed as the most stable profound depths of the ocean with little internal movement, whereas the fast-moving aspects of *histoire événementielle* were viewed as the ever-active ripples over the ocean's surface.

If the evident chronological change in pottery types and other aspects of material culture are dismissed as superficial *histoire événementielle* and extraneous to the *longue durée* as the preferred topic of interest, then the resulting picture of long-term cultural continuity, in effect, does little more than to extend ethnography and social history into an archaeological context. This approach reaffirms the paradigm of reaching from the present into the past. At its best, this approach justifies drawing on the rich body of ethnographic, linguistic, and other knowledge of an "ethnographic present" as applicable to an unchanging cultural context regardless of chronological issues and potential anachronisms. At its worst, this approach makes use of artifacts as theatrical props when discussing prechosen anthropological theories, and opportunities are disallowed for the archaeological record in its own right to contribute toward new ideas.

If chronology is embraced as a central strength of archaeology, then the notion of a slow-moving *longue durée* can be accepted as just one of the many aspects of ever-changing conditions co-occurring at different paces and scales. This view is compatible with the role of archaeology to learn about how human cultures have changed through time. Accordingly, each identifiable archaeological time period can be characterized in terms of its material culture and associated behaviors and contexts, in total representing an "archaeological culture" with all of its limitations and caveats. This approach, based on real material evidence in datable contexts, allows a means for the past to represent itself in its descriptive content. After the material of an archaeological culture can be defined, then various analytical and interpretive procedures can be applied toward building larger knowledge and answering research questions that truly are relevant to the actual archaeological material.

When considering the validity of the "archaeological culture" concept in Pacific Oceania, the region's most celebrated example of the Lapita Cultural Complex has proven to be not the best example after all. The singular indisputable diagnostic characteristic of dentate-stamped pottery constitutes a rather rare and specialized element in Lapita sites overall, and therefore it probably does not represent the larger cultural system accurately. The cultural role of dentate-stamped Lapita pottery was restricted to a narrow range of activities, whereas other forms of pottery were used more broadly and therefore were more typical of the archaeological culture being defined. Dentate stamping occurred in small numbers of pots, usually less than 5% of any site's total pottery collection, and it was completely absent in many sites of the same age range where instead only plain pottery has been found. Plainware pottery continued to be produced for several centuries after the Lapita style had terminated about 500 B.C. in most islands, sometimes known as the "Polynesian plainware" tradition (Burley and Clark 2003).

Two examples help to illustrate the limitations of defining the Lapita Cultural Complex by its dentate-stamped pottery, and they are instructive of how multiple cultural contexts may coexist within any defined archaeological culture or assemblage (Figures 3.3 and 3.4).

- The first and most extreme example is seen in Samoa (Carson 2014), where only a single site so far has yielded dentate-stamped Lapita pottery, at the Ferry Berth Site near Mulifanua and dated near the end of the Lapita expansionary movement about 800 B.C. (Dickinson and Green 1998; Jennings 1974; Leach and Green 1989; Petchey 2001). Other sites of 800 B.C. in Samoa reveal plainware pottery, entirely lacking the

Substance and scope of Pacific Oceanic archaeology 61

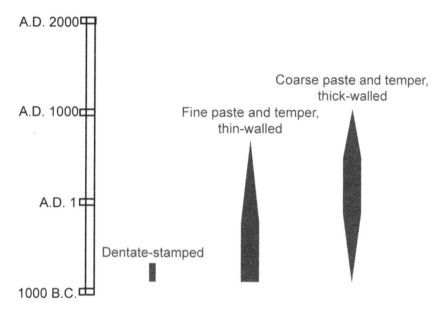

Figure 3.3 Samoa pottery sequence.

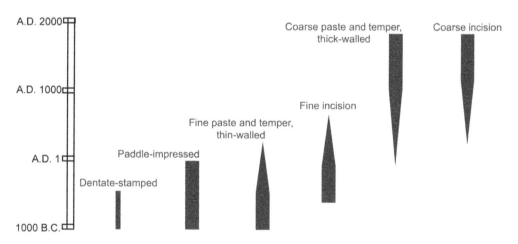

Figure 3.4 New Caledonia pottery sequence.

dentate-stamped signature of Lapita and therefore defining a cultural context different from Lapita pottery.
- Another informative example is seen in New Caledonia, where plainware pottery and paddle-impressed pottery both occurred in the same sites alongside dentate-stamped pottery but also in many other sites without dentate-stamped Lapita pottery (Galipaud 1996; Sand 1996, 1999). Furthermore, the pottery was made with different manufacturing techniques and raw materials (Galipaud 1992), thus suggesting that people engaged in different kinds of contexts simultaneously in the region and challenging the notion of a singular "Lapita people."

In the eastern Pacific Islands with shallow time depths of less than 1000 years and curiously lacking pottery, not too many "archaeological cultures" or "phases" realistically can be distinguished at all. Given that much of Pacific Oceanic archaeology has been written from the perspective of practitioners in Hawai'i (with oldest sites about A.D. 1000) and New Zealand (with oldest sites about A.D. 1300), the concepts of archaeological cultures and phases have not been exercised to their fullest potential. Instead, the short time spans of archaeological records can be interpreted vibrantly from the perspective of ethnohistory and abundant written chronicles since the late 1700s, and nearly all of the material records are accessible in surface-visible contexts or in single undifferentiated cultural layers. Much of Hawaiian and Polynesian archaeology has involved questions generated from historical perspectives not actually related to archaeological material in a strict sense. Moreover, in these particular island groups without pottery, the only definable artifacts are stone, shell, and bone objects that overall exhibit very little chronological variation. This skewed perspective has promulgated an unfortunate misrepresentation of the *longue durée*.

Compounded with the short-lived and ethnographically defined cultural histories of East Polynesia, U.S.-based archaeologists over the last several decades have spearheaded a growing international skepticism of defining "archaeological cultures" and an implicit distrust of "cultural phases," mostly for good reasons. The good reasons involve an awareness that collections of artifacts do not in themselves exhibit human behaviors, but rather they allow modern-day inferences about what kinds of behaviors most likely occurred in the past. Tides of literature have stressed how today's observed archaeological materials potentially can be interpreted as reflecting limited portions of the original contexts of cultural behavioral systems, for example, as reviewed by LaMotta (2012) and by Schiffer (2010). Whether adopting one school of thought or another, students learn that "pots are not people" (Kramer 1977) and that "pots don't breed" (Brew 1946).

In a global perspective, most of the Pacific Islands archaeological assemblages may be characterized as belonging to Neolithic cultural groups, although almost no practitioners in the Pacific today use the terms Paleolithic or Neolithic. As early as 1500 B.C., the oldest sites of the Mariana Islands contain finely decorated pottery and remains of formal housing structures. By 1100–800 B.C., convincing evidence is available about domesticated plants and animals translocated by people into Island Melanesia and West Polynesia. These hallmarks of sedentary lifestyle are accepted as defining a Neolithic culture in other parts of the world, but the term "Neolithic" is notably absent in most of the literature of the remote Pacific Islands.

Concepts of Neolithic culture have been influential not so much within the Pacific region but rather at a larger scale encompassing the Asia-Pacific and concerning the initial population movements from Southeast Asia into Remote Oceania, as will be discussed in Chapters 4 through 7. In particular, the decorative pottery styles of the first Remote Oceanic sites can be traced back to older traditions in Island Southeast Asia (Carson et al. 2013) and further linked with other lines of evidence about the language history, genetics, and other aspects of an ancestral Neolithic culture (Bellwood et al. 2011). Even so, the definition of "Neolithic" is debatable because the degree of reliance on domesticated versus wild foods was highly variable in these oldest known sites. Furthermore, traditions of long-distance ocean-crossing could suggest nomadism and mobility of lifestyle, contrary to the expectations of sedentary Neolithic communities, but they equally could demonstrate permanent settlement of a seascape. In any case, the initial settlers in Remote Oceania constructed formal housing and settlement systems, and their descendants continued to live in the islands permanently, so at least these aspects of a Neolithic culture can be acknowledged.

Concepts of the Neolithic, however they are defined, become less relevant in later-aged sites when all of the inhabitants of every Remote Oceanic island definitely were living in their places permanently with sedentary landscape systems. From an internal view within the remote Pacific Islands, the traditional populations "always" lived there and must have engaged in permanent sedentary lifestyle, or else nobody ever could have lived in these isolated places at all. Additionally, pottery-making traditions ended by A.D. 1000 in Eastern Micronesia and all of Polynesia, so this classic indicator of a Neolithic culture is actually missing in much of Pacific Oceanic archaeology, notably in the areas of Hawai'i, Tahiti, Rapa Nui (Easter island), and Aotearoa (New Zealand), whose archaeological literatures dominate in the region.

When expanding the view of Pacific archaeology to relate with the islands of Near Oceania and Island Southeast Asia, a much older time depth extends at least 50,000 years and includes evidence of Paleolithic hunter-gatherer groups. Over this very long time scale and diverse geography, numerous variations are observable in the archaeological record and cannot be categorized summarily as a singular Paleolithic Age. Several cultural assemblage types have been proposed, mostly based on the forms of stone tools as the predominant material findings. Just to give one example, the Hoabinhian culture is characterized by flaked pebbles and cobbles, mentioned since the 1920s for sites of Vietnam (Ha Van Tan 1978) but with similar findings throughout much of Mainland and Island Southeast Asia, at least as old as 25,000 B.C. in caves of eastern Taiwan (Tsang et al. 2009, 2011) and continuing as recently as 1000 B.C. in some places (Bellwood 1997: 158).

Within the many millennia of the Paleolithic Age in Southeast Asia and Near Oceania, a major distinction can be identified approximately around 10,000 B.C., at the transition from the last Ice Age conditions of the Pleistocene into the new warmer conditions of the Holocene. Dating of this transition realistically should be extended over a period of roughly 12,000 through 9000 B.C., accommodating a set of climatic fluctuations eventually leading to the continued warming of the Holocene. The "new" conditions of the Holocene generally allowed greater reliability of plants and animals and of fresh water, thus supporting new opportunities for the groups who relied on those resources.

Concepts of a Mesolithic Age have been slow to develop in the Asia-Pacific region and have been proposed as part of a "Para-Neolithic" context (Bellwood 2017). In other regions, for example, as originally defined in Europe, the term Mesolithic refers to hunter-gatherers during the Holocene who were beginning to live in settled housing with less frequent mobility, experimentally manipulating edible plants instead of simply gathering whatever happened to be available, and developing social systems more suitable for living in semi-sedentary communities of larger numbers of people than had been the case during the Paleolithic Age. Mesolithic or Para-Neolithic groups generally are viewed as the inheritors of Paleolithic hunter-gatherer ancestry and living alongside Paleolithic counterparts for some time. These groups actively adopted new forms of semi-formalized and semi-sedentary residence, along with limited management or experimental manipulation of the plants and animals in their natural resource catchments.

In Southeast Asia, pottery-bearing sites signaled an obvious change in the archaeological sequence, usually interpreted as the beginning of a Neolithic Age overlaying several millennia of a deeply established Paleolithic Age and possibly a Mesolithic or Para-Neolithic Age. These details will be discussed in Chapters 4 and 5, wherein pottery-making technologies were very clearly imported from outside sources, presumably coming with associated cultural traditions and with at least some numbers of migrant people. Southeast Asian Neolithic sites show evidence of sedentary housing and increasing reliance on different forms of agriculture, horticulture, or arboriculture generally labelled as a food-producing economy. Meanwhile, the older preexisting material signatures of mobile hunter-gatherers markedly decreased, even though the indigenous descendants of those groups must have continued living there while adopting the pottery-making, housing forms, and other characteristics of a Neolithic society.

The Paleolithic-Neolithic transition varied in its pace and timing, material components, and geographic distribution to such an extent that scholars need to contend with multiple concurrent processes of the emergence of Neolithic societies in Southeast Asia and eventual dispersal into the Pacific. As in all parts of the world, the overall spread of Neolithic materials and behaviors can be debated as having involved one degree or another of intrusive population movements, local adoption of the new materials and ideas, independent inventions of Neolithic lifestyles, and variable blending of external and internal factors. The processes of intrusion, integration, and innovation likely functioned together, as Roger Green (1991, 2000) proposed in a "triple-I" model for the development of the Lapita Cultural Complex as one expression of Neolithic society.

Issues of the "Neolithic" continue to be examined in the Asia-Pacific region, but the relevant research issues differ from one area to another. An overlay or spread of Neolithic lifestyle has been investigated most intensively in Island Southeast Asia and Near Oceania for the period 2000 through 1000 B.C. Further of interest are the initial settlement episodes in Remote Oceania, occurring first in the western margins at 1500 through 800 B.C., and then diminishing in relevance farther eastward into the Pacific at later periods. Each of these areas reveals its own material signatures of artifact types, settlement system, land-use pattern, and subsistence practice that have changed through time.

A "Metal Age" was unknown in the Pacific Islands, but it constituted a highly visible cultural change and set of new developments in Island Southeast Asia. Bronze, iron, and glass entered the material records of Island Southeast Asia simultaneously, as early as 500 B.C., followed by evidence of inscriptions and writing systems in a few places. No such indicators are known in the remote islands of the Pacific prior to the foreign intrusions following Magellan's passage in 1521. Complicated trading networks, centrally controlled polities, and organized religions emerged in Island Southeast Asia that had no equivalents in Remote Oceania.

The later periods of many islands after A.D. 1000 have been given various names implying a Classic Age overlapping with an ethnographic or historically documented period. These later periods are characterized as times of increasingly complex social structuring, politically driven economies, materialization of power in imposing monuments, and growing populations approaching the limits of island carrying capacity, as will be discussed in Chapters 12 and 13. The archaeological and historical records in some parts of Pacific Oceania have been highlighted as exemplary cases of how chiefs and other leaders gain power (Earle 1997), at least in a functional sense of how these processes occur, not to be conflated with other separate issues such as the emergence of urbanism, intensive agrarian systems, and state-level societies as seen in other regions.

References

Athens, J. Stephen, H. David Tuggle, Jerome V. Ward, and David J. Welch, 2002. Avifaunal extinctions, vegetation change, and Polynesian impacts in prehistoric Hawai'i. *Archaeology in Oceania* 37: 57–78.

Bellwood, Peter, 1997. *Prehistory of the Indo-Malaysian Archipelago.* Revised edition. University of Hawai'i Press, Honolulu.

Bellwood, Peter, 2017. *First Islanders.* Wiley-Blackwell, Malden, MA.

Bellwood, Peter, Geoffrey Chambers, Malcolm Ross, and Hsiao-chun Hung, 2011. Are 'cultures' inherited? Multidisciplinary perspectives on the origins and migrations of Austronesian-speaking peoples prior to 1000 BC. In *Investigating Archaeological Cultures: Material Culture, Variability, and Transmission*, edited by Benjamin Roberts and Marc Vander Linden, pp. 321–354. Springer, New York.

Braudel, Fernand, 1949. *La Méditerranée et la Monde Méditerranéan à l'Époche de Philippe II.* 3 volumes. Armand Collin, Paris.

Brew, John Otis, 1946. *The Archaeology of Alkali Ridge, Southeastern Utah, with a Review of the Prehistory of the Mesa Verde Division of the San Juan and Some Observations of Archaeological Systematics.* Papers of the Peabody Museum of American Archaeology and Ethnology, Volume 21. Harvard University Press, Cambridge.

Burley, David V., and Jeffrey T. Clark, 2003. The archaeology of Fiji/Western Polynesia in the post-Lapita era. In *Pacific Archaeology: Assessments and Prospects*, edited by Christophe Sand, pp. 235–254. Cahiers de l'Archéologie en Nouvelle-Calédonie 15. Département d'Archéologie, Services des Musées et du Patrimoine de Nouvelle-Calédonie, Nouméa.

Carson, Mike T., 2003. Integrating fragments of a settlement pattern and cultural sequence in Wainiha Valley, Kaua'i, Hawaiian Islands. *People and Culture in Oceania* 19: 83–105.

Carson, Mike T., 2004. Resolving the enigma of early coastal settlement in the Hawaiian Islands: The stratigraphic sequence of the Wainiha Beach Site in Kaua'i. *Geoarchaeology* 19: 99–118.

Carson, Mike T., 2012. Ethnohistoric and geoarchaeological landscape chronology at Kawaihae, leeward Hawai'i Island. *Geoarchaeology* 27: 385–409.

Carson, Mike T., 2014. De-coding the archaeological landscape of Samoa: Austronesian origins and Polynesian culture. *Journal of Austronesian Studies* 5: 1–41.

Carson, Mike T., and J. Stephen Athens, 2007. Integration of coastal geomorphology, mythology, and archaeological evidence at Kualoa Beach, windward O'ahu, Hawaiian Islands. *Journal of Island and Coastal Archaeology* 2: 24–43.

Carson, Mike T., Hsiao-chun Hung, Glenn Summerhayes, and Peter Bellwood, 2013. The pottery trail from Southeast Asia to Remote Oceania. *Journal of Island and Coastal Archaeology* 8: 17–36.

Childe, V. Gordon, 1929. *The Danube in Prehistory.* Oxford University Press, Oxford.

Dickinson, William R., and Roger C. Green, 1998. Geoarcheological context of Holocene subsidence at the Ferry Berth Lapita Site, Mulifanua, Upolu, Samoa. *Geoarchaeology* 13: 239–263.

Dye, Tom S., 2015. Dating human dispersal in Remote Oceania: A Bayesian view from Hawai'i. *World Archaeology* 47: 661–676.

Earle, Timothy K., 1997. *How Chiefs Come to Power: The Political Economy in Prehistory.* Stanford University Press, Stanford.

Galipaud, Jean-Christophe, 1992. Un ou plusieurs peoples potiers en Nouvelle-Calédonie? Analyse physico-chimique des poteries préhistoriques de Nouvelle-Calédonie. *Journal de la Société des Océanistes* 95: 185–200.

Galipaud, Jean-Christophe, 1996. New Caledonia: Some recent archaeological perspectives. In *Oceanic Culture History: Essays in Honour of Roger Green*, edited by Janet Davidson, Geoffrey Irwin, Foss Leach, Andrew Pawley, and Dorothy Brown, pp. 297–305. New Zealand Archaeological Society, Auckland.

Golson, Jack, 1961. Report on New Zealand, Western Polynesia, New Caledonia, and Fiji. *Asian Perspectives* 5: 166–180.

Green, Roger C., 1979a. Lapita. In *The Prehistory of Polynesia*, edited by Jesse D. Jennings, pp. 27–60. Harvard University Press, Cambridge.

Green, Roger C., 1979b. Early Lapita art from Polynesia and Island Melanesia: Continuities in ceramic, barkcloth, and tattoo decorations. In *Exploring the Visual Art of Oceania: Australia, Melanesia, Micronesia, and Polynesia*, edited by Sidney M. Mead, pp. 13–31. University of Hawai'i Press, Honolulu.

Green, Roger C., 1991. Near and Remote Oceania: Disestablishing "Melanesia" in culture history. In *Man and a Half: Essays in Pacific Anthropology and Ethnobiology in Honour of Raplh Bulmer*, edited by Andrew Pawley, pp. 491–502. The Polynesian Society, Auckland.

Green, Roger C., 2000. Lapita and the cultural model for intrusion, integration and innovation. In *Australian Archaeologist: Collected Papers in Honour of Jim Allen*, edited by Atholl Anderson and Tim Murray, pp. 372–392. Coombs Academic Publishing, Australian National University, Canberra.

Ha Van, Tan, 1978. The Hoabinhian in the context of Vietnam. *Vietnamese Studies* 46: 127–197.

Ingold, Tim, 1994. Preface. In *Companion Encyclopaedia of Anthropology: Humanity, Culture and Social Life*, edited by Tim Ingold, pp. xiii–xxii. Routledge, London.

Jennings, Jesse D., 1974. The Ferry Berth site, Mulifanua, Upolu. In *Archaeology in Western Samoa*, edited by Roger C. Green and Janet M. Davidson, Volume 2, pp. 176–178. Bulletin 7. Auckland Institute and Museum, Auckland.

Kirch, Patrick V., 1997. *The Lapita Peoples: Ancestors of the Oceanic World*. Blackwell Publishers, Cambridge.

Kramer, Carol, 1977. Pots and peoples. In *Mountains and Lowlands: Essays the Archaeology of Greater Mesopotamia* edited by L. D. Levine and T. C. Young, Jr., pp. 91–112. Bibliotecha Mesopotamia 7. Undena, Malibu.

LaMotta, Vincent M., 2012. Behavioral archaeology. In *Archaeological Theory Today, Second Edition*, edited by Ian Hodder, pp. 62–92. Polity Press, Cambridge.

Leach, Helen M., and Roger C. Green, 1989. New information for the Ferry Berth Site, Mulifanua, Western Samoa. *Journal of the Polynesian Society* 98: 319–329.

Petchey, Fiona J., 2001. Radiocarbon determinations from the Mulifanua Lapita Site, Upolu, Western Samoa. *Radiocarbon* 43: 63–68.

Roberts, Benjamin W., and Marc Vander Linden, 2011. Investigating archaeological cultures: Material culture, variability, and transmission. In *Investigating Archaeological Cultures: Material Culture, Variability, and Transmission*, edited by Benjamin W. Roberts and Marc Vander Linden, pp. 1–21. Springer, New York.

Sand, Christophe, 1996. Recent developments in the study of New Caledonia's prehistory. *Archaeology in Oceania* 31: 45–71.

Sand, Christophe, 1999. Lapita and non-Lapita ware during New Caledonia's first millennium of Austronesian settlement. In *La Pacifique de 5000 à 2000 Ans avant le Présent: Suppléments à l'Histoire d'une Colonisation*, edited by Jean-Christophe Galipaud and Ian Lilley, pp. 139–159. Institut de Recherche pour le Développement, Paris.

Schiffer, Michael B., 2010. *Behavioral Archaeology: Principles and Practice*. Equinox, London.

Simiand, François, 1903. Méthode historique et science social. *Revue de Synthèse Historique* 16: 113–137.

Terrell, John Edward, 2003. Archaeological inference and ethnographic analogies: Rethinking the Lapita cultural complex. In *Archaeology Is Anthropology*, edited by Susan D. Gillespie and Deborah L. Nichols, pp. 69–76. Archeological Papers of the American Anthropological Association, Volume 13. American Anthropological Association, Arlington.

Terrell, John Edward, 2009. Return to the entangled bank: Deciphering the Lapita cultural series. In *Lapita: Ancestors and Descendants*, edited by Peter J. Sheppard, Tim Thomas, and Glenn R. Summerhayes, pp. 255–269. Monograph 28. New Zealand Archaeological Association, Auckland.

Tsang, Cheng-hwa, W. S. Chen, K. T. Li, and Y. X. Zeng, 2009. *Report of the Baxiandong Cave Sites, Changbin, Taidong County, the First Year*. Academia Sinica, Taipei. (in Chinese).

Tsang, Cheng-hwa, W. S. Chen, K. T. Li, and Y. X. Zeng, 2011. *Report of the Baxiandong Cave Sites, Changbin, Taidong County, the Second Year*. Academia Sinica, Taipei. (in Chinese).

4 Hunter-gatherer traditions in the western Asia-Pacific region

"Those who lose dreaming are lost."
(Australian Aboriginal proverb)

The tradition of "dreaming" or of the "dream time" is uniquely Australian today, but it raises questions about similar traditions that may have existed among related cultural groups who once lived in the broader geography of the western Asia-Pacific region. For the Aboriginal Australian people, the act of dreaming links a person to the memories of the landscape, with dreamlike archives of ancient times and events that have made the world into what it is today. With access to the dream time, people can situate themselves in both space and time, or else they can become "lost." Some aspects of the dreaming refer to geological formations and processes of a Pleistocene landscape of Sahul, when northern Australia was connected to the land mass of New Guinea during a period of much lower sea level. In certain cases, rock art panels may be interpreted as reflecting past events of the dreaming, and successive layers of rock art demonstrate the changing contexts of people living and dreaming in the Australian landscape over several millennia.

The regional landscape history has been crucial for comprehending where people could have lived at different points in time, where to look for sites of those particular ages, and how people may have related with each other and their surrounding environment through time. For these reasons, ancient landscape studies have proven to be productive with archaeological investigations (Shaw 2022). Meanwhile, indigenous traditions have referred to the ancient settings of coastal landforms that no longer exist today, although they have been remembered through stories and ascertained through observations of the modern-day landscapes (Nunn 2021).

People have been living in Australia and New Guinea for approximately 50,000 years, obviating that other groups lived at least for this length of time if not longer throughout the nearby and adjacent lands of an ancient Pleistocene world (Figure 4.1). Due to a lower global sea level during the Ice Age conditions of the Pleistocene (described in Chapter 2), people could travel across exposed coastal lowlands and shelves, land bridges, and short water crossings. The areas of modern-day Australia through New Guinea were connected as "Sahul." The islands of modern-day Island Southeast Asia were either attached together or else separated by short distances in zones of "Sunda" and "Wallacea."

The precise dating may never be known of when *Homo sapiens* first arrived in this region of the world, but the evidence so far supports a date around 50,000 years ago. The foot bone of member of the *Homo* genus was dated close to 60,000 years old in Callao Cave of the northern Philippines (Mijares et al. 2010) (Figure 4.2), but later studies questioned if perhaps the foot bone belonged to *Homo sapiens* or perhaps a different species

DOI: 10.4324/9781003399025-4

68　*Hunter-gatherer traditions in the western Asia-Pacific region*

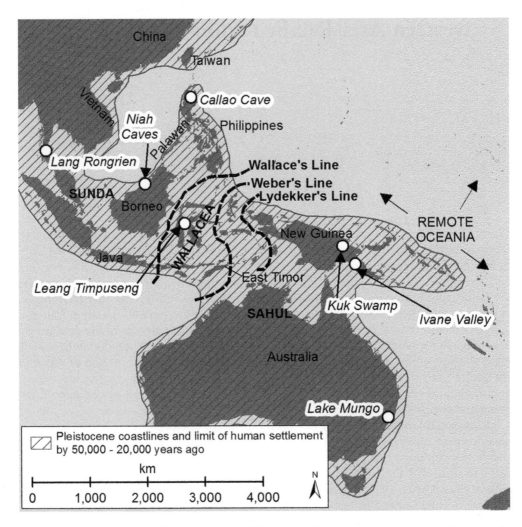

Figure 4.1 Pleistocene landforms and major biogeographic zones of the western Asia-Pacific region.

proposed as *Homo luzonensis* (Détroit et al. 2019). Australia's oldest known human skeletal remains have been dated between 50,000 and 46,000 years old at Lake Mungo (Bowler et al. 2003). By 40,000 years ago in Indonesia, people were making hand stencils and other rock art, including some of the world's oldest examples at Leang Timpuseng in Sulawesi (Taçon et al. 2014). These findings hint at a deep cultural tradition among the people who once lived over a much larger extent of the western Asia-Pacific. Rock art in western Australia has been dated at least 33,000 years old and potentially could be much older (O'Connor and Fankhauser 2001).

This proposed time depth accords with a global-scale view of the origin of anatomically modern *Homo sapiens*, wherein the species first had migrated outside Africa at some point after 80,000 years ago and prior to 50,000 years ago (Stoneking 2021). In populations of Island Southeast Asia, the numbers of mutations in DNA lineages suggest human arrivals

Figure 4.2 Callao Cave in northern Luzon, Philippines.

primarily after 70,000 years ago (Soares et al. 2012). For purposes of this book, a dating can be accepted at least as early as approximately 50,000 years ago.

Over the course of tens of thousands of years, the western Asia-Pacific region has accumulated layers of population distributions, varied cultural traditions, and different material archaeological signatures transcending human evolutionary history, global climate change, and a long series of adaptations through millennia of dynamic natural and cultural history. The oldest known evidence pertains to *Homo erectus*, a now-extinct ancient hominin ancestor who ventured at least as far as Java in Indonesia as much as 1.5 million years ago and lived near estuarine habitats at that time (Bettis et al. 2009; Huffman 2009; Huffman et al. 2006; Joordens et al. 2009). Anatomically modern humans (AMH or *Homo sapiens*) evolved later and entered into the regions of Sunda, Wallacea, and Sahul around 50,000 years ago or possibly earlier, partly overlapping with other species of the same Genus, whose fossils and ancient DNA continue to be studied.

At the time when external visitors and scholars began to write in the late 1700s about the people of the Asia-Pacific region, thousands of years of human occupation and dynamic developments already had taken place, resulting in puzzling geographic distributional patterns of linguistic and cultural groups. The broadly shared language family and cultural traditions of the Austronesian world stretched across most of the Asia-Pacific region, yet different languages and traditions persisted in the middle of this geographic distribution in Australia and New Guinea, loosely labelled as Papuan or non-Austronesian. Moreover, those indigenous inhabitants of Australia and New Guinea lived as hunter-gatherers, at least in the areas where the Europeans had visited, in contrast to the islanders elsewhere in the Pacific who lived in dense populations in organized villages and maximized the productivity of their formalized farmlands and cropping systems.

Today, the Aboriginal Australian and New Guinean populations are recognized as the descendants of the original human inhabitants of the region. Like their distant ancestors, they belong to an Australo-Melanesian or Australo-Papuan biological phenotype that once extended over a large portion of the world, now found primarily in Australia, New Guinea, and most of Island Melanesia. Ancient skeletal remains indicate that Australo-Melanesian people previously lived throughout Mainland and Island Southeast Asia as a "first layer" or "foundational layer" of the regional population, prior to a much later "second layer" of an influx of Asia-derived or Mongoloid populations (Matsumura and Hudson 2005). In most interpretations of this "two-layer hypothesis," the arrival of Mongoloid (Asian) phenotypes coincided with the spread of farming and sedentary lifestyles generally regarded as signaling the Neolithic horizon of Southeast Asia and eventually extending into Pacific Oceania (Bellwood 2013; Matsumura et al. 2008). These findings resonate with research of DNA lineages, as discussed in Chapter 2.

The deep chronologies and changing cultural contexts of East Asia through Australia and New Guinea are difficult to unravel and are beyond the scope of this book, but at least a basic understanding is necessary in order to begin a study of Pacific Oceanic archaeology. Before people made the first successful movements to live in the islands of Remote Oceania about 1500 B.C. and continuing in multiple ocean-crossing migrations during later centuries, their ancestors had lived in numerous parts of the islands of Near Oceania and Island Southeast Asia. Multiple groups have inhabited this diverse part of the world over many thousands of years, and the picture is even more complex when considering ancient hominin ancestors.

Overlaying the numerous millennia of human presence in the region, pottery-making traditions of a Neolithic horizon entered into parts of Island Southeast Asia about 2200–2000 B.C., with direct links to the Austronesian-speaking groups who now inhabit all of the Remote Oceanic islands and indeed much of the Asia-Pacific region overall. The pottery trail and its implications will be discussed in Chapter 5, but first the general context must be understood as entailing more than an intrusive overlay movement of people, materials, and ideas of a Neolithic society overprinting long-established Paleolithic hunter-gatherer traditions that had persisted for thousands of years in the western Asia-Pacific region. In fact, the preexisting hunter-gatherer groups likely contributed significantly to the origins and development of what archaeologists now recognize as the Neolithic horizon in Island Southeast Asia, with later developments observable in the islands of Near Oceania and Remote Oceania.

Dated prior to the emergence of pottery-bearing sedentary village sites, the archaeologically attested cultures of the western Asia-Pacific region are represented primarily through different assemblages of stone tools (Figure 4.3), augmented by limited information from other rarely preserved materials. The stone tools happen to be most durable over thousands of years, while evidence is notably sparser in terms of the infrequently discovered traces of shell and bone tools, food middens, and ancient botanical remains. The necessarily limited evidence imposes constraints on what can be inferred about the cultural groups who existed in the distant past, with the cautions as introduced in Chapter 3 concerning the archaeological material reflections of Paleolithic, Neolithic, and other societies.

Following the premise of "those who lose dreaming are lost," an archaeological overview tour of the western Asia-Pacific region needs to clarify the landmarks of what kinds

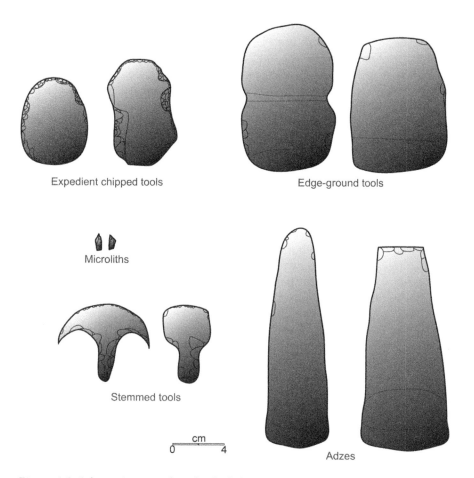

Figure 4.3 Schematic examples of Paleolithic stone tool types of Southeast Asia.

of evidence have been found, where, and referring to what time periods. The discernible categories of evidence may seem arbitrary to outside observers, yet they are based on the actual findings that have been reported so far. Instead of reliving the memories of an ancient landscape through the dreaming, archaeologists have characterized past cultural groups in terms of their basic tool technologies, relationships with naturally available plants and animals, burial practice, and economic patterns of subsistence and resource usage. While a thoroughly detailed review is outside this book's concern with Pacific Oceania, the key points of evidence are considered toward contextualizing the next chapters.

Expedient chipped tools

Small stone flakes, related flaking cores, and a few chipped pebbles and cobbles comprise the oldest-known stone tools in the western Asia-Pacific region. The flakes could have been used for general utility of cutting and slicing, while the chipped pebbles and cobbles were probably more effective for chopping through thick meat and bone of animal carcasses, tree trunks, or other hard materials. Although not the oldest currently known, one of the best documented assemblages was reported from excavations by Douglas Anderson (1990, 1997) in Lang Rongrien Rockshelter in the Malay Peninsula, technically in modern-day Peninsular Thailand, within Pleistocene layers spanning a period of roughly 41,000 through 25,000 B.C. Some of the flakes exhibit bifacially worked surfaces, shaped on two sides, indicative of formal tools that may have been intended for piercing and slicing actions. Other flakes very likely represent the debitage from manufacturing the bifacial tools. The few examples of chipped pebbles and cobbles were made by chipping on limited portions of the stones, suggestive of expedient manufacture. Similar forms of limited chipping were reported on the ends and sides of pebbles in sites of Vietnam, locally considered to represent a Son Vi (or Sonvian) Culture, dated roughly 20,000 through 9000 B.C. and predating the subsequent Hoa Binh (or Hoabinhian) culture (Ha Van Tan 1991).

The Southeast Asian stone tools known as Hoabinhian are characterized by chipping all around large pebbles and small cobbles. At the Lang Rongrien Rockshelter, these kinds of tools all postdated 10,000 B.C. and related to a broadened range of activities during the warmer conditions of the Holocene (Anderson 1990). Smaller numbers of Hoabinhian chipped tools may be as old as 16,000 B.C. in sites of Vietnam (Ha Van Tan 1991) or as old as 25,000 B.C. in caves of eastern Taiwan (Tsang et al. 2009, 2011) (Figure 4.4).

Among the oldest of all stone artifacts now known in the region, chipped stone tools have been documented in the highlands of New Guinea and dated in the range of 47,000 through 42,000 B.C. in the Ivane Valley (Summerhayes et al. 2010). People used these tools in an upland zone at 2000 m elevation and several km inland from the coast, further implying active use of the diverse Pleistocene landscapes of Sunda, Wallacea, and Sahul at a similarly early date. These ancient tools consisted of simple chipped pebbles and cobbles, but at least two items exhibited midsection trimming or waisted shapes diagnostic of a "waisted axe" most likely used for tree-felling or other heavy working.

Figure 4.4 Baxiandong excavation in eastern Taiwan, September 2014. Lead excavator Dr. Tsang Cheng-hwa is wearing hat and dark glasses, standing beside Dr. Peter Bellwood.

These general-utility chopping tools have been found in Paleolithic hunter-gatherer sites throughout much of Mainland and Island Southeast Asia, continuing in use until the emergence of pottery-bearing sedentary village sites as late as 1000 B.C. in some areas. The primary characteristic involved expedient use of locally available cobbles and pebbles, chipped just enough to create a usable edge or set of cutting surfaces, often with some of the stone's unmodified original cortex still visible. These tools were not edge-ground or polished, but rather they were produced entirely through chipping.

Edge-grinding and other formal developments

Formal edge-ground stone tools have been dated at least 35,000 years old in Australia (Geneste et al. 2010; Hiscock et al. 2016), and presumably a related technology was known more broadly among hunter-gatherers living in the inhabited Asia-Pacific land masses of Sunda, Sahul, and Wallacea during the Pleistocene. These objects generally resemble the blades of axes, and many were made with slight notching that would be suitable for hafting or lashing of a handle. Most of these objects are flat tabular pieces with rounded perimeters, ground on one or two of the rounded ends to produce a cutting edge. The edge-grinding in most cases was confined to the working edge, at least superficially viewed as different from fully polished blades that generally appeared much later in Island Southeast Asia.

Edge-ground tools began to comprise substantial portions of Southeast Asian site assemblages after 9000 B.C. and generally postdated the Pleistocene-Holocene transition (Bellwood 1997: 161), known in Mainland Southeast Asia as the index markers of a Bacsonian culture named after sites in the Bac Son Province north of the Red River in Vietnam. The much older discoveries in Australia, however, reveal that edge-ground tools were part of the Asia-Pacific technological repertoire for many thousands of years prior to the Holocene. Even within Vietnam, where the classic Bacsonian edge-ground tools have been described, the oldest dates of these tools could be near 16,000 B.C. within site layers locally considered to represent early components of Hoabinhian culture (Pham Ly Huong 1994). Given the overlap of tool assemblages, Bellwood (1997: 161) proposed that the Bacsonian tools comprised "in reality just an aspect of the Hoabinhian characterized by a high proportion of edge-ground tools."

The edge-grinding technology was replaced much later by full polishing in most parts of Island Southeast Asia, subsequently becoming part of the toolmaking traditions carried into all of the islands of Pacific Oceania after 1500 B.C. Before that happened, however, edge-grinding gradually increased in popularity during the Holocene in all inhabited areas. Edge-grinding was applied primarily for making stone axes, but it was employed occasionally for making heavy shell adzes in parts of Island Southeast Asia in contexts prior to the pottery-bearing horizons and therefore older than 1500–1000 B.C. (Bellwood 1997: 187–188). Ages of edge-ground shell adzes could extend as old as 10,000 B.C. by direct radiocarbon dating of the shells (O'Connor 2006), although in-built old age of fossil shell cannot be corrected in the absence of other dating of the associated archaeological layers. The large shells of giant clams and similar thick-bodied shells often do not show obvious visual clues about being from fossil reefs or from habitats with in-built old ages, and therefore the direct radiocarbon dating inconsistently reflects fossil-related old ages in some but not all cases. In the cave sites where both the shell adzes and other materials have been dated in the same layers, the radiocarbon ages of shell adzes are some thousands of years older than the dating results of charcoal samples, but the offset difference is inconsistent and unpredictable (Bellwood et al. 1998).

Concurrent with the overall increasing role of edge-grinding through the Holocene, other developments occurred in stone, shell, and bone tool-production technologies. Several localized tool complexes have been described, mostly on the basis of flaked stone tools that comprise the numerically dominant artifacts in these assemblages. The chipped pebbles and cobbles of a generic Hoabinhian Paleolithic continued to be used broadly, often with hints of waisted profiles or even definitely pronounced waisting for a handle lashing of an axe. Traditions of waisted axes apparently varied from one area to another, with uneven dating and associations, but overall they became more popular through time. New shapes of bifacial points, most likely used as knives or spear tips, developed in many parts of Mainland and Island Southeast Asia by 5000 B.C. (Bellwood 1997: 171–200; Higham 2014: 52–67). Meanwhile, bone pick-like tips and spatula-shaped tools were common in most of the sites where bone materials have been preserved, and chipped pieces of hard shells have been described in most coastal sites.

Microliths and small flaked stone tool traditions

A change in stone tool technology occurred around 5000–3000 B.C. in Island Southeast Asia with the creation of particular forms of small blades known as microliths (Glover 1976, 1978; Mulvaney and Soejono 1971). Microliths technically existed prior to this time in several places, but site layers beginning 5000–3000 B.C. in Sulawesi of Indonesia have yielded assortments of crescent-shaped, serrated, and back-blunted blades known locally as the diagnostic markers of the Toalean culture assemblages (van Heekeren 1972). Other forms of back-blunted blades are known as "backed blades" in Australia (beginning as early as 3000–2000 B.C.), and they generally are regarded as independently invented within Australia (Mulvaney and Kamminga 1999). Additional stone tools of the same age included more simply prepared blades of chert and their associated flaking cores. They are known broadly through Island Southeast Asia, for instance, as described by Robert Fox (1970) in Palawan of the Philippines and by Peter Bellwood (1985) in the Talaud Islands of Indonesia.

Although not always termed "microliths," numerous small flaked tools, flaking cores, and debitage of obsidian and other types of volcanic glass are known throughout Island Southeast Asia and in many of the Pacific Islands. In places where volcanic glass was unavailable, local sources of chert or other cryptocrystalline stone could provide nearly the same sharpness for similar kinds of small cutting tools. Many geological sources evidently were prized for their high quality of products that were traded thousands of km over sea-crossing networks (Reepmeyer et al. 2011; Spriggs et al. 2011). Interisland transport of chert has been difficult to identify except impressionistically by the color and texture of material types, as compared to the elemental composition of volcanic glass that happens to be ideal for X-ray fluorescence (XRF) and other analysis matching with the geochemistry of known sources. Among the oldest dated obsidian tools so far are those reported from rockshelters in East Timor, found in layers extending as early as 40,000 B.C. (Ambrose et al. 2009). Interisland transport of obsidian occurred at least as early as 10,000–8000 B.C. within the Admiralty Islands northeast of New Guinea, where people obtained obsidian from the Lepong source and distributed it to a number of other sites (Summerhayes et al. 2014). The obsidian source in Talasea, in the Bismarck Archipelago east of New Guinea, may have been used for toolmaking and mobilized into interisland trade as early as 10,000 B.C. (Specht et al. 1988).

By the time of the influx of pottery-making and other traditions of a Neolithic context after 2000 B.C., the high-quality sources of toolmaking stone already were well known and traded broadly. The difference after 2000 B.C. was that the materials were used in new contexts with the availability of more trading opportunities, especially with new populations established in previously uninhabited islands after 1500 B.C. In particular, Talasea obsidian has been identified as the origin of flaked tools found more than 3000 km farther westward at Bukit Tengkorak in Borneo at 800 B.C., if not earlier (Bellwood and Koon 1989), and it was transported more than 1000 km eastward into Lapita pottery-bearing sites of Island Melanesia about 1100–800 B.C. (Kirch 1997).

Stemmed tools

Stemmed tools of obsidian have been found in sites of eastern New Guinea and nearby islands. In some cases, the tools are more than 10 cm long and regarded as ceremonial objects (Araho et al. 2002). They are dated by positions relative to tephra deposits at least as early as 4000 B.C., and they either ceased or radically declined by 1300–900 B.C. (Torrence and Swadling 2008). The decline of this tradition occurred around the beginning of dentate-stamped Lapita pottery and an associated Lapita Cultural Complex in the same region, so a fascinating research topic may yet be addressed about the roles of different kinds of objects in acts of presentation and exchange before, during, and after the Lapita horizon. The large stemmed artifacts of obsidian apparently were exchanged between communities in different islands, as verified by geochemical provenance studies (Torrence and Swadling 2008).

Adzes

Among the formal edged tools, adzes occupy a special place in Asia-Pacific archaeology. Found in every island group, adzes exhibit morphological types that largely correspond to geographic areas and sometimes to chronological periods. Fully polished adzes were part of the inherited technology of people moving into the islands of Remote Oceania beginning at 1500 B.C., but the older roles of adzes in Island Southeast Asia and Near Oceania have been difficult to ascertain. Following several thousands of years of edge-ground axes and chipped pebble-cobble tools, the earliest confirmable dates of polished adzes in the region have been reported about 3000 B.C. in Duyong Cave of Palawan in the Philippines (Fox 1970). The oldest adzes of the region thus predated the horizon of pottery-making and sedentary settlements at 2200–2000 B.C., so they could not have been introduced solely as part of a "Neolithic package" associated with massive forest-clearing in support of sedentary village farmers. At least some polished adzes already had been used prior to the Southeast Asian Neolithic horizon, but certainly these objects appeared in considerably greater frequency with pottery-bearing sites generally postdating 2000 B.C. and then later throughout the cultural sequences of all islands in Remote Oceania.

Plant foods

So far the oldest known direct evidence of plant use in the Pacific region comes from starch grains clinging to the surfaces of chipped stone tools in the highlands of New Guinea, dated in the range of 47,000 through 42,000 B.C. (Summerhayes et al. 2010). These particular starch grains most closely resemble the remains of different kinds of yams (*Disocorea* spp.). Additionally, charred pieces of edible *Pandanus* sp. nuts were found in the same archaeological layer, thus indicating a mixed diet generally using the naturally available root-tuber plants and fruit-bearing or nut-bearing trees.

In terms of knowing more generally about the kinds of plant communities that once supported hunter-gatherers in Island Southeast Asia and Near Oceania, useful baseline information has been compiled from pollen and other preserved materials in coring profiles taken from lake-bottom and swamp-bottom sediments reflecting the overall patterns of vegetation growth. The native vegetation throughout most of the region consisted of mixed palms, ferns, and plentiful trees bearing edible fruits and nuts. People must have taken advantage of these resources, although evidently they did not create large-scale transformations of the forest, as instead they cleared small areas or else simply used and managed the available forest resources with little or no clearing at all.

The regional pollen and sedimentary core records typically show prolonged periods of low-level or no impact in the native vegetation composition for several millennia prior to pottery-bearing contexts of 2000–1000 B.C. (Hope et al. 1999). In some cases, though, increased levels of secondary weedy growth, influx of burned charcoal particles, and other forest disturbance are seen as evidence of hunter-gatherers affecting the natural forests, for example, as documented in the Ivane Valley of the New Guinea highlands as early as 39,000–36,000 B.C. (Hope 2009). Similar instances of burning and clearing are noted in other parts of the New Guinea highlands at much later dates, such as near Kuk Swamp at 5000 B.C. (Haberle et al. 2012). In the rainforests of Sarawak in Malaysian Borneo, possible forest clearing may have occurred as early as 4500 B.C. when hunter-gatherers lived in this area and buried their deceased at the Niah Caves complex, followed by slightly more convincing evidence of forest clearing after 800 B.C. and within the date range of pottery-making traditions (Jones et al. 2013). The strongest indicators of human-caused forest manipulations, however, occurred much later in the context of increasingly intensive rice-farming systems that apparently postdated A.D. 700 in Sarawak (Jones et al. 2013). Similar evidence has been reported in Java of Indonesia, where a trans-Holocene environmental record shows thousands of years of little or no human-caused disturbance of the rainforest until the impacts of intensive rice-farming endeavors postdating A.D. 500 (Sémah and Sémah 2012).

The tropical forests of Island Southeast Asia and parts of New Guinea offer naturally abundant edible plant foods and economically useful plants. Perhaps most importantly, dietary starch was available in sago palms (*Metroxylon* spp., *Eugeissona* spp., and others), certain cycads (*Cycas* spp.), varieties of breadfruit (*Artocarpus* spp.) in some but maybe not all places, several types of bananas (*Musa* spp., *Eumusa* spp., and *Australomusa* spp.), nuts of *Canarium* spp., and many more. Additionally, important resources included coconuts (*Cocos nucifera*) and the fruits of durian (*Durio* sp.) and numerous others. Root-tuber crops such as yams and taro could grow interspersed with forest trees or in small clearings, and they provided reliable starches throughout the Pleistocene and Holocene sequences of hunter-gatherer presence in the region.

Given that the low-intensity managed forests could provide a wealth of plant foods for hunter-gatherer groups, the material signature of sustained and obvious forest-clearing activity has been sporadic and often ambiguous prior to the emergence of sedentary villages relying on fixed units of land for food production. Quite simply, the Neolithic horizon of sedentary farmers has been more visible and dominant in the archaeological record, and it coincided with more frequent and more widespread clearing of forests. Certainly, people manipulated their forests and encouraged some plants to grow more than others, and evidently, people cleared at least some areas for habitations and for growing root-tuber crops such as varieties of yams and taro. Nonetheless, the hunter-gatherer groups of Island Southeast Asia did not engage in large-scale removal of native rainforests, as the trees themselves provided the most abundant and reliable food resources. Furthermore, the forests comprised the supporting natural habitat for birds, bats, and other animals that evidently were hunted regularly.

Of course, some groups engaged in more intensive management and manipulation of the tropical rainforests than is evident in the overall pattern for the region's hunter-gatherer populations, and in fact a few instances could suggest formalized artificial rendering of the landscape as expected of agriculturalists. One of the more noteworthy examples is at Kuk Swamp along the Wahgi River in the highlands of New Guinea, where people made shallow water-carrying ditches through a patchwork of artificial raised beds or mounds of earth, dated as early as 5000 B.C. and continuing in phases of overlaying mounds and ditches (Denham et al. 2003). The swampy lands around the Wahgi River had been cleared of native forest, and then preserved indicators of bananas followed in high concentrations throughout the sequence of artificial ditches and mounds (Haberle et al. 2012).

While forest management and manipulation had been intense in some cases, it apparently did not extend over large geographic areas of the landscape prior to the appearance of the pottery-bearing sites of the Southeast Asian Neolithic. Only after this time and postdating 2000–1000 B.C. have the paleoenvironmental records revealed large-scale land clearing and conversion of native forests into artificially controlled, economically manipulated compositions. As shown in this brief review, much of the strongest evidence of a transformed landscape actually occurred much later, thus suggesting a continuation of the preexisting hunter-gatherer traditions of managed forests for some length of time after the initiation of a Neolithic horizon. Meanwhile, at least some forms of intensive management and purposeful manipulation of the forests already had occurred in some places, hinting at more complex origins of food-producing modes of arboriculture, horticulture, and agriculture.

Animal life

Along with the abundant plant foods, diverse animals have inhabited the rainforests of Island Southeast Asia through Near Oceania. Although their skeletal remains have been preserved unevenly in archaeological contexts, numerous animals certainly were targeted by hunter-gatherers, while some may have entered into site middens as scavengers. In the deep deposit of Ille Cave with layers as old as 12,000 B.C. in Palawan of the Philippines, preserved animal bones belong to several kinds of rats, bats and flying foxes, deer, wild pigs, a kind of tiger, leopard cats, macaques and other primates, porcupine, badger, otter, and other animals (Piper et al. 2011). In the Niah Caves complex of Borneo, layers as old as 30,000 B.C. have yielded the remains of assorted fish, reptiles, rats, macaques, gibbons, orangutans, pangolins, porcupines, leopards and other wild cats, wild pigs, deer, rhinoceros, and others (Piper and Rabett 2009). Numerous faunal studies could add to this picture, but these two long-term records demonstrate that people in the tropical rainforests successfully hunted a broad range of small, medium, and large animals in different forest habitat zones.

Domesticated animals are unknown in the regional faunal records prior to pottery-bearing layers beginning about 2200–2000 B.C., but at least some taxa moved across water gaps between islands. While rats may have been uninvited stowaways on canoes, other larger animals must have been transported deliberately. When looking at the faunal records of islands of eastern Indonesia through New Guinea and Near Oceania, certain taxa of phalangers, bandicoots, and other marsupials appear suddenly at different points in time, and their arrivals may be attributed to the actions of people (White 2004). The timing of these events ranged from nearly 18,000 B.C. through 5000 B.C., definitely prior to the pottery-bearing horizons in the region and prompting questions of why people would translocate these animals. None of these animals were domesticated, and apparently, they were released to live freely in the managed forests, thus suggesting that people practiced varying degrees of managing the plants and the animals of the tropical rainforests long before formalized agricultural economies.

Forest-dwelling animals were plentiful for the region's hunter-gatherers, yet site middens confirm that fish and shellfish provided the most reliable sources of protein in easily accessible areas near the shores of the ocean, lakes, and rivers. In most cases, the near-shore resources dominate in the midden deposits, while deep-sea or pelagic fish bones tend to be absent until much later and overlapping with the contexts of people making long-distance ocean-crossing migrations after 2000 B.C. At least some deep-sea explorations are reflected in the fish remains prior to 2000 B.C., although, definitely, these activities were in the minority overall. The region's oldest evidence of pelagic fishing appears to have been found in the form of thousands of bones of sharks and tuna, along with shell fishhooks in East Timor, possibly more than 42,000 years old (O'Connor 2015; O'Connor et al. 2011). These traditions were known even if they were rare for many millennia prior to the first peopling of the Remote Oceanic islands at 1500 B.C.

Burial practice

Early hunter-gatherer burial practice is known from scattered instances of disturbed skeletal remains and sometimes from the remnants of flexed-position interments. Little information is ascertainable about the mortuary rituals, but the known burial sites so far are confined to caves that clearly were separated from the ordinary habitation zones. Many of these caves continued to be used during later Neolithic and Metal Age contexts with overlaying patterns of grave pits, jar burials, and ritual offerings.

Extended-position burials with grave goods apparently became popular during a later period of pottery-bearing Neolithic sites, mirroring the same transition that had occurred in coastal China by 3000 B.C. (Zhang and Hung 2012). In coastal China and in Taiwan, an older tradition of flexed-position burial among hunter-gatherers was replaced eventually by a new tradition of extended-position burial among sedentary villagers making pottery and relying to some degree on farming modes of subsistence (Hung and Carson 2014). In Island Southeast Asia, the timing of this transition is unclear because very few burials are known at all from the earliest pottery-bearing Neolithic layers prior to 500 B.C., and furthermore, the indigenous hunter-gatherers apparently continued their preexisting tradition of flexed-position burial at least for some time overlapping with the emergence of Neolithic societies in the region (Lloyd-Smith 2009; Lloyd-Smith et al. 2013).

Patterns of resource use

The region's ancient hunter-gatherer sites could have supported small groups, likely composed of a few families in each inhabited place, drawing their food and other resources from broad catchment areas ranging through diverse ecological zones. No formal village sites have been discovered yet prior to the pottery-bearing horizons, by default suggesting a very long tradition over thousands of years when people did not invest substantially in longevity of year-round habitations but rather engaged in continual mobility in their landscapes. The faunal remains in particular indicate that people fished, trapped, hunted, or scavenged animals from numerous different patches of riverine, coastal, and forest habitats and brought those mixed resources back to the campsites.

The known sites have been discovered mostly in the shelters of large cave overhangs and rarely in open areas of riverbanks or valley floors now covered by deep sedimentary layers. All of these cases so far have shown dispersed middens of general living areas. One particularly informative example has been along the alluvial banks of the Cagayan River in Luzon, the Philippines, where the deepest and oldest layers with stone tools and mixed animal bones extended back to 5000 B.C., and later they were covered by pottery-bearing layers and even later again by massive shell mounds generally postdating 2200 B.C. (Hung et al. 2022). The deepest layers here reflected general hunter-gatherer activities at dispersed points along the river valley floor, so far lacking evidence of formalized housing structures or a village settlement pattern.

If small groups of people obtained their food and other resources from rather large areas with access reaching into multiple ecological settings, then overall the population density must have been at a low ratio of people to land. Precise estimates are impossible on the basis of limited archaeological evidence, but at least a few hectares of mixed ecological zones would have been needed for each group of people to acquire enough starchy plant foods, fruits, protein-rich animals, fresh water, wood and fibers, stone toolmaking material, medicinal and therapeutic supplies, and other resources. Depending on seasonal change in rainfall and other variables, people may have shifted their habitations from time to time in order to live closer to their essential resources, not necessarily coming back to the same location later.

The concept of a managed forest may be expanded to accommodate cultural management of whole ecosystems. People certainly manipulated the composition of native vegetation at least informally, with episodes of forest-clearing and encouraging growth of preferred food-giving or otherwise useful plants. They additionally were responsible, intentionally or not, for moving certain animals between islands, altering the natural food webs, and creating new relationships among the diverse plant and animal communities of the tropical rainforests.

Issues of managed ecosystems, human-environment relations, and developing a culturally inhabited landscape will be revisited in the next chapters in the context of discussing the origins and spread of Neolithic communities in Island Southeast Asia and eventually into Remote Oceania. The preexisting patterns among the region's hunter-gatherers, however, can be understood as having developed through some millennia of low-level population density and access to broad and diverse natural resource zones. Questions will endure about how to conceptualize the hunter-gatherer groups as Paleolithic, Mesolithic, Para-Neolithic, or other kinds of societies, and realistically, various different groups inhabited the region and developed their own unique traditions that later contributed to the emergence of Neolithic societies discussed in the following chapters.

References

Ambrose, Wal, Charlotte Allen, Sue O'Connor, Matthew Spriggs, Nuno Vasco Oliveira, and Christian Reepmeyer, 2009. Possible obsidian sources for artifacts from Timor: Narrowing the options using chemical data. *Journal of Archaeological Science* 36: 607–615.

Anderson, Douglas D., 1990. *Lang Rongrien Rockshelter: A Pleistocene, Early Holocene Site from Krabi, Southwestern Thailand*. University Museum Monograph 71. The University Museum, Philadelphia.

Anderson, Douglas D., 1997. Cave archaeology in Southeast Asia. *Geoarchaeology* 12: 607–638.

Araho, Nick, Robin Torrence, and J. Peter White, 2002. Valuable and useful: Mid-Holocene stemmed obsidian artefacts from West New Britain, Papua New Guinea. *Proceedings of the Prehistoric Society* 68: 61–81.

Bellwood, Peter, 1985. Holocene flake and blade industries of Wallacea and their predecessors. In *Recent Advances in Indo-Pacific Prehistory*, edited by Virendra Nath Misra and Peter Bellwood, pp. 197–206. IBH Publishing Company, New Delhi.

Bellwood, Peter, 1997. *Prehistory of the Indo-Malaysian Archipelago*. Revised edition. University of Hawai'i Press, Honolulu.

Bellwood, Peter, 2013. *First Migrants: Ancient Migration in Global Perspective*. Wiley Blackwell, Malden, MA.

Bellwood, Peter, and Peter Koon, 1989. Lapita colonists leave boats unburned: The question of Lapita links with Island Southeast Asia. *Antiquity* 63: 613–622.

Bellwood, Peter, G. Nitihaminoto, Geoffrey Irwin, Gunadi, A. Waluyo, and Daud Tanudirjo, 1998. 35,000 years of prehistory in the northern Moluccas. In *Bird's Head Approaches*, edited by Gert-jan Bartstra, pp. 233–275. Modern Quaternary Research in Southeast Asia 15. Balkema, Rotterdam.

Bettis, E. A., III, A. K. Milius, S. J. Carpenter, R. Larick, Y. Zaim, Y. Rizal, R. L. Ciochon, S. A. Tassier-Surine, D. Murray, Suminto, and S. Bronto, 2009. Way out of Africa: Early Pleistocene paleoenvironments inhabited by *Homo erectus* in Sangiran, Java. *Journal of Human Evolution* 56: 11–24.

Bowler, James M., Harvey Johnston, Jon M. Olley, John R. Prescott, Richard G. Roberts, Wilfred Shawcross, and Nigel A. Spooner, 2003. New ages for human occupation and climatic change at Lake Mungo, Australia. *Nature* 421: 837–840.

Denham, Tim P., Simon Haberle, Carol Lentfer, Richard Fullagar, Judith Field, M. Therin, N. Porch, and Barbara Windsborough, 2003. Origins of agriculture at Kuk Swamp in the highlands of New Guinea. *Science* 301: 189–193.

Détroit, Florent, Armand Salvador Mijares, Julien Corny, Guillaume Daver, Clément Zanolli, Eusebio Dizon, Emil Robles, Rainer Grün, and Philip J. Piper, 2019. A new species of *Homo* from the late Pleistocene of the Philippines. *Nature* 568: 181–186.

Fox, Robert B., 1970. *The Tabon Caves: Archaeological Explorations and Excavations on Palawan Island, Philippines*. Monograph Number 1. Philippines National Museum, Manila.

Geneste, Jean-Michel, Bruno David, Hugues Plisson, Chris Clarkson, Jean-Jacques Delannoy, Fiona Petchey, and Ray Whear, 2010. Earliest evidence for ground-edge axes: 35,400±410 cal BP from Jawoyn Country, Arnhem Land. *Australian Archaeology* 71: 66–69.

Glover, Ian, 1976. Ulu Leang cave, Maros: A preliminary sequence of post-Pleistocene cultural development in south Sulawesi. *Archipel* 11: 113–154.

Glover, Ian, 1978. Survey and excavation in the Maros District, south Sulawesi, Indonesia. *Bulletin of the Indo-Pacific Prehistory Association* 1: 60–102.

Ha Van Tan, 1991. New researches on the Stone Age sites pregviously excavated by French archaeologists in Viet Nam. In *Recherches en Archéologie en Thaïlande, Deuxième Symposium Franco-Thai*, pp. 166–171. Silpakorn University, Bangkok.

Haberle, Simon, Carol Lentfer, Shawn O'Donnell, and Tim Denham, 2012. The palaeoenvironments of Kuk Swamp from the beginnings of agriculture in the highlands of Papua New Guinea. *Quaternary International* 249: 129–139.

Higham, Charles, 2014. *Early Mainland Southeast Asia, from First Humans to Angkor*. River Books, Bangkok.

Hiscock, Peter, Sue O'Connor, James Balme, and Tim Maloney, 2016. World's earliest ground-edge axe production coincides with human colonisation of Australia. *Australian Archaeology* 82: 2–11.

Hope, Geoffrey, 2009. Environmental change and fire in the Owen Stanley Ranges, Papua New Guinea. *Qauternary Science Reviews* 28: 2261–2276.

Hope, Geoffrey, Dominique O'Dea, and Wendy Southern, 1999. Holocene vegetation histories in the western Pacific: Alternative records of human impact. In *Le Pacifique de 5000 à 2000 avant le Présent: Suppléments à l'Histoire d'une Colonisation*, edited by Jean-Christophe Galipaud and Ian Lilley, pp. 387–404. Institut de Récherche pour le Développement, Paris.

Huffman, O. Frank, 2009. Geologic context and age of the Perning/Mojokerto *Homo erectus*, east Java. *Journal of Human Evolution* 40: 353–362.

Huffman, O. Frank, Yahdi Zaim, John Kappelman, D. R. Ruez, Jr., J. de Vos, Y. Rizal, F. Aziz, and C. Hertler, 2006. Relocation of the 1936 Mojokerto skull discovery site near Perning, east Java. *Journal of Human Evolution* 50: 431–451.

Hung, Hsiao-chun, and Mike T. Carson, 2014. Foragers, fishers and farmers: Origins of the Taiwan Neolithic. *Antiquity* 88: 1115–1131.

Hung, Hsiao-chun, Cheng-hwa Tsang, Zhenhua Deng, Mary Jane Louise A. Bolunia, Rey A. Santiago, Mike T. Carson, and Peter Bellwood, 2022. Preceramic riverside hunter-gatherers and the arrival of Neolithic farmers in northern Luzon. *Antiquity* 96: 848–867.

Jones, Samantha E., Chis O. Hunt, Huw Barton, Carol Lentfer, and Paula J. Reimer, 2013. Forest disturbance, arboriculture and the adoption of rice in the Kelabit Highlands of Sarawak, Malaysian Borneo. *The Holocene* 23: 1528–1546.

Joordens, J. C. A., F. P. Wesselingh, J. de Vos, H. B. Vonhof, and D. Kroon, 2009. Relevance of aquatic environments for hominins: A case study from Trinil (Java, Indonesia). *Journal of Human Evolution* 57: 656–671.

Kirch, Patrick V., 1997. *The Lapita Peoples: Ancestors of the Oceanic World*. Blackwell Publishers, Cambridge.

Lloyd-Smith, Lindsay, 2009. *Chronologies of the Dead: Later Prehistoric Burial Practice at the Niah Caves, Sarawak*. Doctoral dissertation, University of Cambridge, Cambridge.

Lloyd-Smith, Lindsay, Graeme Barker, Huw Barton, Judith Cameron, Franca Cole, Patrick Daly, Chris Doherty, Chris Hunt, John Krigbaum, Helen Lewis, Jessica Manser, Victor Paz, Philip J. Piper, Ryan J. Rabett, Garry Rushworth, and Katherine Szabo, 2013. "Neolithic" societies c. 4000–2000 years ago: Austronesian farmers? In *Rainforest Foraging and Farming in Island Southeast Asia: The Archaeology of the Niah Caves, Sarawak*, edited by Graeme Barker, Volume 1, pp. 255–298. McDonald Institute for Archaeological Research, University of Cambridge, Cambridge.

Matsumura, Hirofumi, and Mark J. Hudson, 2005. Dental perspectives on the population history of Southeast Asia. *American Journal of Physical Anthropology* 127: 182–209.

Matsumura, Hirofumi, Marc F. Oxenham, Yukio Dodo, Kate Domett, Nguyen Kim Thuy, Nguyen Lan Cuong, Nguyen Kim Dung, Daien Huffer, and Mariko Yamagata, 2008. Morphometric affinity of the late Neolithic human remains from Man Bac, Ninh Binh Province, Vietnam: Key skeletons with which to debate the "two layer" hypothesis. *Anthropological Science* 116: 135–148.

Mijares, Armand Salvador, Florent Détroit, Philip Piper, Rainer Grün, Peter Bellwood, Maxime Aubert, Guillaume Champion, Nida Cuevas, Alexandra De Leon, and Eusebio Dizon, 2010. New evidence for a 67,000-year-old human presence at Callao Cave, Luzon, Philippines. *Journal of Human Evolution* 59: 123–132.

Mulvaney, D. John, and Johan Kamminga, 1999. *Prehistory of Australia*. Revised edition. Smithsonian Institution Press, Washington, DC.

Mulvaney, D. John, and R. P. Soejono, 1971. Archaeology in Sulawesi, Indonesia. *Antiquity* 45: 26–33.

Nunn, Patrick D., 2021. *Worlds in Shadow: Submerged Lands in Science, Memory, and Myth*. Bloomsbury, London.

O'Connor, Sue, 2006. Unpacking the Island Southeast Asian Neolithic package, and finding local complexity. In *Uncovering Southeast Asia's Past: Selected Papers from the Tenth International Conference of the European Association of Southeast Asian Archaeologists*, edited by Elizabeth A. Bacus and Ian Glover, pp. 74–87. National University of Singapore Press, Singapore.

O'Connor, Sue, 2015. Crossing the Wallace Line: The maritime skills of the earliest colonists in the Wallacean Archipelago. In *Emergence and Diversity of Modern Human Behavior in Paleolithic Asia*, edited by Yosuke Kaifu, Masami Izuho, Ted Goebel, Hiroyuki Sato, and Akira Ono, pp. 214–224. Texas A&M University, College Station.

O'Connor, Sue, and Barry Fankhauser, 2001. Art at 40,000 BP? One step closer: An ochre covered rock from Carpenter's Gap Shelter 1, Kimberley Region, western Australia. In *Histories of Old Ages: Essays in Honour of Rhys Jones*, edited by Atholl Anderson, Ian Lilley, and Sue O'Connor, pp. 287–301. Pandanus Books, Canberra.

O'Connor, Sue, Rintaro Ono, and Chris Clarkson, 2011. Pelagic fishing at 42,000 years before the present and the maritime skills of modern humans. *Science* 334: 1117–1121.

Pham Ly Huong, 1994. Radiocarbon dates of the Hoabinh Culture in Vietnam. *Vietnam Social Sciences* 5(43): 9–21.

Piper, Philip J., Janine Ochoa, Emil C. Robles, Helen Lewis, and Victor Paz, 2011. Palaeozoology of Palawan Island, Philippines. *Quaternary International* 233: 142–158.

Piper, Philip J., and Ryan J. Rabett, 2009. Hunting in a tropical rainforest: Evidence from the terminal Pleistocene at Lobang Hangus, Niah Caves, Sarawak. *International Journal of Osteoarchaeology* 19: 551–565.

Reepmeyer, Christian, Matthew Spriggs, Anggraeni, Peter Lape, Leee Neri, Wilfredo P. Ronquillo, Truman Simanjuntak, Glenn Summerhayes, Daud Tanudirjo, and Archie Tiauzon, 2011. Obsidian sources and distribution systems in Island Southeast Asia: New results and implications from geochemical research using LA-ICPMS. *Journal of Archaeological Science* 38: 2995–3005.

Sémah, Anne-Marie, and François Sémah, 2012. The rain forest in Java through the Quaternary and its relationships with humans (adaptation, exploitation and impact on the forest). *Quaternary International* 249: 120–128.

Shaw, Ben, 2022. Palaeolandscapes, radiocarbon chronologies, and the human settlement of southern lowland and island Papua New Guinea. In *Palaeolandscapes in Archaeology: Lessons for the Past and Future*, edited by Mike T. Carson, pp. 215–290. Routledge, London.

Soares, Pedro, Farida Alshamali, Joana B. Pereira, Veronica Ferdandes, Nuno M. Silva, Carla Alfonso, Marta D. Costo, Eliska Musilova, Vincent Macaulay, Martin B. Richards, Viktor Cerny, and Luisa Pereira, 2012. The expansion of mtDNA haplogroup L3 within and out of Africa. *Molecular Biology and Evolution* 29: 915–927.

Specht, Jim, Richard Fullagar, Robin Torrence, and Neville Baker, 1988. Prehistoric obsidian exchange in Melanesia: A perspective from the Talasea sources. *Australian Archaeology* 27: 3–16.

Spriggs, Matthew, Christian Reepmeyer, Angraenni, Peter Lape, Leee Neri, Wilfredo P. Ronquillo, Truman Simanjuntak, Glenn Summerhayes, Daud Tanudirjo, and Archie Tiauzon, 2011. Obsidian sources and distribution systems in Island Southeast Asia: A review of previous research. *Journal of Archaeological Science* 38: 2871–2881.

Stoneking, Mark, 2021. Genomic insights into the Out-of-Africa dispersal(s) of modern Humans. In *Human Migration: Biocultural Perspectives*, edited by Maria de Lourdes Muñoz-Moreno and Michael H. Crawford, pp. 9–19. Oxford University Press, Oxford.

Summerhayes, Glenn R., Jean Kennedy, Elizabeth Matisso-Smith, Herman Mandui, Wal Ambrose, Charlotte Allen, Christian Reepmeyer, Robin Torrence, and François Wadra, 2014. Lepong: A new obsidian source in the Admiralty Islands, Papua New Guinea. *Geoarchaeology* 29: 238–248.

Summerhayes, Glenn R., Matthew Leavesley, Andrew Fairbairn, Herman Mandui, Judith Field, Anne Ford, and Richard Fullagar, 2010. Human adaptation and plant use in Highland New Guinea 49,000 to 44,000 years ago. *Science* 330: 78–81.

Taçon, Paul S. C., Noel Hidalgo Tan, Sue O'Connor, Ji Xueping, Li Gang, Darren Curnoe, David Bulbeck, Budianto Hakim, Iwan Sumantri, Heng Than, Im Sokrithy, Stephen Chia, Khuon Khun-Neay, and Soeung Kong, 2014. The global implications of the early surviving rock art of greater Southeast Asia. *Antiquity* 88: 1050–1064.

Torrence, Robin, and Pamela Swadling, 2008. Social networks and the spread of Lapita. *Antiquity* 82: 600–616.

Tsang, Cheng-hwa, W. S. Chen, K. T. Li, and Y. X. Zeng, 2009. *Report of the Baxiandong Cave Sites, Changbin, Taidong County, the First Year.* Academia Sinica, Taipei. (in Chinese).

Tsang, Cheng-hwa, W. S. Chen, K. T. Li, and Y. X. Zeng, 2011. *Report of the Baxiandong Cave Sites, Changbin, Taidong County, the Second Year.* Academia Sinica, Taipei. (in Chinese).

Van Heekeren, H. R., 1972. *The Stone Age of Indonesia.* Second edition. Nijhoff, The Hague.

White, J. Peter, 2004. Where the wild things are: Prehistoric animal translocation in the Circum New Guinea Archipelago. In *Voyages of Discovery: The Archaeology of Islands*, edited by Scott M. Fitzpatrick, pp. 147–164. Praeger, Westport, CT.

Zhang, Chi and Hsiao-chun Hung, 2012. Later hunter-gatherers in southern China, 18,000–3000 B.C. *Antiquity* 86: 11–29.

5 Following the Asia-Pacific pottery trail, 4000 through 800 B.C.

"*Kapag may usok, may apoy*" (Filipino Tagalog saying), translates into English as "Where there is smoke, there is fire."

The first inhabitants of the remote Pacific Islands must have traversed the ocean from a distant homeland, and they potentially brought certain forms of pottery and other artifacts, languages, and cultural practices that can be traced to homeland sources in neighboring regions such as Near Oceania and Island Southeast Asia. For example, the oldest known sites in Southern Melanesia and West Polynesia (about 1000 B.C.) contained dentate-stamped Lapita-style pottery linked to a slightly older pottery tradition in the Bismarck Archipelago of Near Oceania just a few centuries earlier. Similar pottery has been found in even older sites dating from about 1500 B.C. in the Mariana Islands, and then still older (about 1800–1600 B.C.) in the Philippines of Island Southeast Asia. The existence of any pottery at all in Island Southeast Asia began about 2200–2000 B.C., traceable to origins in Taiwan and eventually farther back to coastal southeast China prior to 4000 B.C.

Following the principle of "where there is smoke, there is fire," a material effect like an area's first pottery-bearing horizon can be attributed to a real cause, such as an event of establishing a new cultural tradition in that area. In the Remote Oceanic islands, the initial pottery-bearing sites happen to constitute the oldest evidence of any human presence at all, so the distinctive material assemblage of dentate-stamped Lapita pottery can be assigned to a homeland of the people who made it, for instance, in Near Oceania or in Island Southeast Asia. In both Near Oceania and Island Southeast Asia, however, people with varied hunter-gatherer Paleolithic or perhaps Mesolithic lifestyles already had occupied these landscapes for thousands of years prior to the appearance of the oldest pottery in a Neolithic horizon, thus raising questions about the spread of people, materials, and ideas independently or in concert.

The "smoke" of a pottery-bearing horizon does not need to be assigned to a single "fire" of its reasons for existence in each case. In fact, the spread of a pottery through Island Southeast Asia and eventually into Pacific Oceania involved great diversity of geography, cultural setting, and dated contexts. Pottery appeared as early as 2200–2000 B.C. in the northern Philippines, but it entered as late as 800 B.C. in Samoa. For each localized occurrence of the first entry of pottery into the archaeological record, research has been able to identify the similarities or differences in the forms and styles of pottery, natural environments, and social contexts.

While a definite pottery-bearing horizon is evident in Island Southeast Asia and Pacific Oceania, it can be recognized as unified only at a quite large scale while involving several internal components at smaller scales with their own different ages, geographic areas, and associated contexts. Archaeological research has advanced sufficiently to acknowledge

DOI: 10.4324/9781003399025-5

that the spread of pottery-making traditions, along with other aspects of a Neolithic horizon, involved different circumstances across the diverse space of the Asia-Pacific and through the several centuries assigned to the known archaeological sites. The temptation to apply one area's particular circumstances toward explaining the totality of the Asia-Pacific pottery-bearing horizon must be rejected as nothing more than a "smoke screen" that masks the real picture. Similarly, Paul Gorecki (1992) cautioned that a "Lapita smoke screen" prevented researchers from learning about other information beyond the allure of this one variety of dentate-stamped pottery.

By focusing on the oldest pottery made in each island group, a "pottery trail" emerges as the set of footprints of where and when ocean-crossing migrations occurred in the distant past (Carson et al. 2013). Tracking the pottery trail requires attention to secure chronological contexts that can be compared cross-regionally, now possible with advancements in precision and reliability of radiocarbon dating, although the dating results have been questioned or misunderstood in many cases. Additional debates have emerged in terms of how to define the pottery artifacts as convincingly diagnostic or representative of an ancient cultural group. The findings in each area need to be scrutinized in order to clarify what kind of pottery was made, how it related to a larger material culture inventory, and exactly when the responsible cultural group produced those materials.

The Asia-Pacific pottery trail has been among the most crucial foundational components for understanding the earliest archaeological sites, layers, and contexts in the remote islands of Pacific Oceania. Given the crucial role of this evidence, the present chapter includes updated references and additional details for the second edition. Additional supporting evidence has become available from most areas to confirm the prior conclusions. In a few cases, new studies have clarified about the pottery assemblages and radiocarbon dating at site layers in Sarawak of Borneo, in the Cagayan Valley of Luzon in the Philippines, and in the Karama Valley of Sulawesi in Indonesia.

When depicting the pottery trail on a map, problems are evident about how to know for sure where to draw the connections and what dates to assign. The exact lines of movement never can be known precisely, and the proposed dates of cross-regional connections never can be too narrowly defined. In this book, cross-regional connections and movement are depicted according to an "incremental growth model," viewed as a series of ever-growing zones of cultural knowledge and potential contacts (Figure 5.1). These zones became larger and more diverse through time, covering increasingly more geography of islands and surrounding oceans. In this view, the pottery trail does not necessarily link one specific point to another, but rather it links one geographic zone with another, involving multiple potential points of contacts within each of those inhabited zones.

Perspectives and scales of origins

The Asia-Pacific pottery trail here is proposed in a unified cross-regional view, incorporating all of its internal segments or steps, yet alternative interpretations of the pottery trail have depended on using narrow points of view and scale of analysis, combined with incomplete or misrepresented datasets. These alternative proposals have been proven to be incorrect on the basis of material evidence and chronometric dating, as will be demonstrated in this chapter. For instance, many researchers have sought a Lapita homeland proximately in the Bismarck Archipelago of Near Oceania, while wrestling with notions of Lapita as attributable to migrants from Southeast Asia versus a locally generated tradition in situ within Near Oceania (Allen 1996; Allen and Gosden 1996; White et al. 1988).

86 *Following the Asia-Pacific pottery trail*

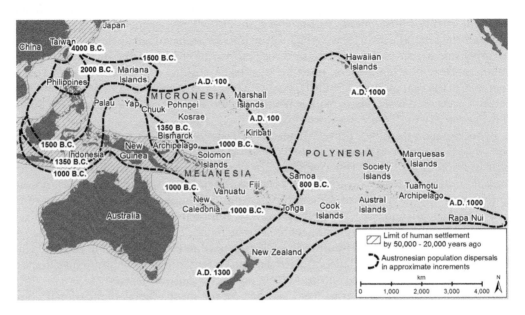

Figure 5.1 Region-wide incremental growth model.

Meanwhile, investigations throughout different parts of Island Southeast Asia occasionally identified apparent Lapita-like ancestral pottery with similar dentate-stamping and other designs, notably in the northern through central Philippines and parts of Indonesia, yet the associated dating often was questionable (Bellwood 1997: 234–235). Similarly, claims of early dating of dentate-stamped pottery in the Mariana Islands were questioned as validly predating Lapita in Near or Remote Oceania, or else they were viewed as marginal to the discussion of Lapita origins within Oceania (Kirch 2000: 170–173). Research of the last few decades has accumulated abundant evidence of the earlier dating of dentate-stamped and other pottery traditions at multiple sites of the Mariana Islands around 1500 B.C. (Carson 2020; Carson and Kurashina 2012) and in the northern Philippines even earlier (Hung 2008; Hung et al. 2022), thereby invalidating the claims that the dentate-stamped pottery tradition had originated within Near Oceania or perhaps in Indonesia.

The ability to retrace the pottery trail cross-regionally has been possible with four concurrent research developments, each involving secure and precise radiocarbon dating associated with large collections of materials in pottery-bearing horizons. Each of these four points has reset the clock of when a pottery-making tradition first appeared within a particular island group in relation to others, and then these updated baseline parameters have allowed cross-regional tracing of the pottery trail.

- First, the oldest known Lapita pottery has been confirmed at 1350 B.C. in the Bismarck Archipelago of Near Oceania, while a possibility exists of accepting a date range of 1500–1350 B.C. (Summerhayes 2007).
- Second, movement of Lapita pottery-makers into the Remote Oceanic islands of Southern Melanesia and West Polynesia has been dated firmly after 1200 B.C. and mostly in the range of 1100–800 B.C. (Denham et al. 2012).

- Third, the earliest sites of the Mariana Islands conclusively have been dated at 1500 B.C. and defined as containing red-slipped pottery with dentate-stamped designs highlighted by white lime infill (Carson 2014, 2020; Carson and Kurashina 2012). Details are offered in Chapter 6.
- Fourth, the oldest-known pottery in Island Southeast Asia has been dated about 2200–2000 B.C. in the northern Philippines, matching with the contemporaneous red-slipped and fine cord-marked pottery of Taiwan, followed by a later development of dentate-stamped designs locally within the Philippines by 1800–1600 B.C. (Hung 2008; Hung et al. 2011, 2022).

Unfortunately, these dating refinements have tended to be reported in their own particularistic or localized significance, and the larger regional picture has been slow to develop as a cohesive synthesis.

Prior to the formalized clarity of the cross-regional pottery trail chronology (Carson et al. 2013; Hung et al. 2011), uneven geographic survey coverage and uncertain dating allowed a perpetuation of different unproven hypotheses about a Lapita Homeland and other issues. For instance, much of the international research program of the "Lapita Homeland Project" was predicated on the notion of seeking Lapita origins in the pre-pottery layers of hunter-gatherer societies prior to 1500 B.C. locally within the Near Oceanic region of eastern New Guinea and nearby islands. Sites within the targeted search region were investigated most intensively in the 1980s and continuing through the 1990s (Allen 1996; Allen and Gosden 1996; White et al. 1988). Much of the research was framed in a view that the pottery-making traditions of Lapita developed indigenously within a Near Oceanic regional context, possibly adopted through trade or other contacts with foreign pottery-using groups. Furthermore in this view, Lapita pottery's apparent similarities with Southeast Asian pottery could be dismissed as superficially insignificant, or else the undated or vaguely dated direction of influence could be interpreted as having originated in the Bismarck Archipelago or eastern New Guinea and then dispersing westward into Island Southeast Asia.

Now knowing that the dentate-stamped Lapita pottery designs in Near Oceania emerged no earlier than 1500–1350 B.C. and definitely postdated a related dentate-stamped tradition extending as early as 1800–1600 B.C. in the northern Philippines, the prior decades of debating about a Lapita Homeland need to be reconsidered. In particular, Roger Green's (1991, 2000) "Triple I" model continues to bear relevance today, wherein Lapita may be viewed as having emerged through processes of intrusion, integration, and innovation. According to all of the evidence now available, Lapita could not possibly have developed exclusively in situ within Near Oceania, but equally it cannot be attributed entirely to a foreign intrusive group of immigrants (Spriggs 1997). In this case, the indigenous populations were very likely active agents in the emergence and developments of a Neolithic cultural context that archaeologists now recognize as the pottery-bearing Neolithic horizon of a Lapita Cultural Complex.

As more site discoveries are reported throughout Island Southeast Asia and Pacific Oceania, the picture of regional archaeology continually grows more precise. Importantly, increased precision allows clarity such as situating Lapita settlement in the Bismarck Archipelago very close to 1350 B.C. or perhaps within a potential range of 1500–1350 B.C., instead of the prior reference to a vague geographic scope of Near Oceania within a potential range of 1500–1000 B.C. (Summerhayes 2007). This increased precision is qualitatively different from a case of overturning prior claims, such as needing to counteract false statements about Lapita settlement originating all at once across Near and Remote Oceania at 1500 B.C.

Unfortunately, the repeated new discoveries may trigger suspicions that perhaps the region's archaeological record remains largely unknown and therefore cannot yet support any definitive statements, such as regarding the origins and dating of pottery-bearing horizons. Skeptics may wonder if ancient buried archaeological layers are hidden from view or not yet discovered in the large land masses of Island Southeast Asia, but the last several decades of research have provided reasonable coverage to identify the major patterns and regional chronology. While the site-specific findings tend to be reported singly and not always noticed in larger regional synthesis narratives, the baseline information is nonetheless available in one form or another, albeit with all of the frustrations of accessing and deciphering the details. As in any region of the world, more sites eventually will be discovered, especially now with practical methodologies to excavate several m deep into ancient landscape layers that previously were either unknown or else very poorly documented. Likewise, the previous literature made vague age estimates such as "postglacial" or "Holocene" that could span thousands of years and incorporate numerous different cultural contexts and material assemblages, but now much finer precision allows statements about specific kinds of pottery and other artifacts associated with calibrated date ranges of a few centuries each.

Notions of population dispersals into Island Southeast Asia during the Holocene are now understood as having occurred since 2200–2000 B.C. in terms of movements associated with the oldest pottery-bearing horizons, some thousands of years after the major postglacial sea-level rise that had marked the beginning of the Holocene about 10,000–8000 B.C. Surely, other population movements occurred prior to the appearance of the pottery-bearing site layers, but those episodes can be appreciated as having occurred in very different contexts. Prior to the oldest pottery-bearing horizon in Island Southeast Asia at 2200–2000 B.C., the archaeological record reflected the activities of varied hunter-gatherer groups as outlined in Chapter 4. Several important social, technological, and other developments had occurred prior to the emergence of a pottery-bearing Neolithic association, and these dynamic contexts continued.

By 8000 B.C., the early Holocene flooding of coastal lowlands contributed to isolation of populations and subsequent divergence of their DNA lineages, language groupings, and material culture inventories, thus creating a complex mosaic of cultural communities long established before the emergence of Island Southeast Asia's oldest Neolithic horizon at 2200–2000 B.C. Wherever any Neolithic immigrants might have made contact in Island Southeast Asia or Near Oceania after 2200–2000 B.C., they must have encountered indigenous groups who spoke their own languages, expressed their identities, and engaged with their environments in their own ways. In the archaeological record, the most visible difference was that pottery had been entirely absent for several millennia, followed by a sudden appearance and then a subsequent geographic spread across the region.

For several decades, archaeologists have perceived the Asia-Pacific pottery trail in reverse, looking at the later-aged expressions of dentate-stamped Lapita pottery in Melanesia and Polynesia and then seeking deeper origins. This reserve-chronology strategy has been productive for identifying the oldest Lapita sites in the Bismarck Archipelago just east of New Guinea about 1350 B.C., where the lavishly decorated pottery vessels display the same motifs and design principles of a clearly unified Lapita tradition, yet the trail ends there in terms of the classically defined Lapita pottery. Older dated sites with dentate-stamped pottery are well known now in Island Southeast Asia, definitely older than Lapita by some centuries, but the specific designs and motifs are most certainly not the same as in the Lapita world. Whatever happened in the Bismarck Archipelago at

1350 B.C. had resulted in a unique new expression of dentate-stamped pottery in the forms recognized today as Lapita, developed locally from the older ancestral links in Island Southeast Asia.

When reordering the pottery trail chronologically from beginning to end, Lapita becomes exposed as the end of the narrative. The beginning of the story did not involve dentate-stamped pottery, but rather it emphasized cord-marked pottery prior to 4000 B.C. and then an escalating popularity of red-slipped pottery by 2200 B.C. Only later did dentate-stamped designs, applied to the red-slipped vessels and often highlighted by white slaked lime infilling, gain prominence locally within Island Southeast Asia, perhaps as early as 1800–1600 B.C., but most strongly evidenced and spreading cross-regionally after 1500 B.C. This large-scale view of the chronological evidence reveals that the Lapita pottery of Melanesia and Polynesia developed at the end of the pottery trail.

Even now, with a confidently defined archaeological pottery trail, the mapped and dated geographic spread does not in itself equate with the ancient movement of the actual people who made the pottery. In a critical viewpoint, the spread of a pottery horizon could have involved down-the-line transference of ideas and knowledge such that the indigenous groups in the Philippines, Indonesia, or New Guinea each adopted pottery-making and other traits through their ability to access knowledge about overseas communities. Most realistically, the archaeological record reflects the past movement of people, materials, and ideas in varying degrees across the areas of Island Southeast Asia and Near Oceania where people had been living for many thousands of years prior to the pottery-bearing horizons. All three of these factors (people, materials, and ideas) must have coincided when people first moved to inhabit the islands of Remote Oceania, but the situation was considerably more fluid in the longer-inhabited areas of Island Southeast Asia and Near Oceania.

Now with the ability to interconnect the pieces of the pottery trail in concisely dated parameters, some erroneous conclusions can be avoided. The dating of oldest pottery in Island Southeast Asia obviates an origin of pottery-making from Asia moving through the region generally from northwest to southeast. The Bismarck Archipelago no longer makes sense as a completely self-contained in situ homeland of a Lapita Cultural Complex. Furthermore, the pottery-making traditions in Taiwan can be recognized in a long chronological sequence since at least 4000 B.C., within which one portion after 2200 B.C. branched into a connection with the northern Philippines in Island Southeast Asia. In all of these cases, lingering notions of an older or younger dispersal from any other source now can be rejected. The chronological outline carries further implications for studies of language histories and of genetics lineages that do not in themselves involve direct dating.

Given the chronologically distinguishable steps of the pottery trail in separate geographic areas of the Asia-Pacific region, each such step can be associated with localized expressions and developments of the pottery-making traditions and other traits of a larger material culture inventory. Each step in the trail may be equated with a movement from one geographic zone to another, such that the total set of zones has grown larger through time in the "incremental growth model." As research continues, the internal steps of the pottery trail are being traced more precisely, and some new steps are being discovered in places that previously lacked information. The present summary will not be the final statement of its kind, but it incorporates the most updated details previously not available for an integrated synthesis. Furthermore, the pottery evidence can be accepted as reflecting one highly visible and durable portion of the diverse material culture of each area being studied, and a more comprehensive analysis may yet account for other cultural traits.

Pottery as a diagnostic element of an archaeological horizon

The archaeological evidence of the Asia-Pacific pottery trail relies on the ability to define the diagnostic characteristics and dated parameters of the first instance of a pottery-bearing horizon in each island group. In certain frustrating instances, undecorated or plainware pottery may not bear any distinguishing characteristics, other than obviating the existence of pottery itself as a material trait, whereas decorative elements potentially represent unique signatures. In some cases, the mere existence of pottery can be enough to demonstrate its first appearance in any area, most strikingly in the islands of Remote Oceania where the first human presence of any kind was marked by pottery-bearing archaeological layers. In order to relate any single area's first pottery assemblage with a potential homeland region, however, something more specific needs to be observed in the form or style of the pottery in question. Additionally, the dates of pottery-bearing horizons need to be clarified in chronological order, or else the cross-regional patterns become lost in muddled anachronisms.

Regardless of the valid criticisms about the meaning of "Neolithic" in the Asia-Pacific or any other region, pottery in fact entered the archaeological record abruptly as a new material trait in Island Southeast Asia and Pacific Oceania. Logically speaking, pottery alone does not equate with sedentism, farming, domestication, or other traits typically assigned to a Neolithic society, but rather it belongs to a horizon containing pottery among other elements of an assemblage that may or may not be labelled as Neolithic. The oldest pottery in some cases has not been found with specifically definable housing formats, but often it coincided with generalized evidence of formal residential habitations and villages, overall suggesting sedentary groups with investment in their lands or habitat niches. Meanwhile, the character of subsistence food economy in the earliest pottery-bearing periods typically lacked formalized field systems as might be expected of land-dependent Neolithic farmers, and in fact it involved heavy reliance on coastal and marine foods, balanced with managed forests, continued hunting of wild animals with uneven use of domesticated livestock, and varied roles of slash-and-burn or shifting-field swidden horticulture.

While recognizing that pottery comprises just one of many material items in a cultural horizon, pottery nonetheless occurs in bounteous quantity and with ample opportunity for observing unique diagnostic traits, such that a pottery assemblage can support a practical tracing of the Asia-Pacific pottery trail. The pottery trail first can be outlined as a factual material record in chronological order, and then interpretive theories and methods can be applied toward further interrogation of those facts. As part of developing those interpretative frameworks, the conclusions about the abundant pottery assemblages can be augmented, refined, or tested by comparing with other kinds of artifacts, food middens, and categories of evidence that tend to be less prominent than the pottery records.

In a logical approach, the pottery trail shows the geographic spread of a pottery-making tradition in several incremental steps across the Asia-Pacific region, and then various hypotheses can be proposed and ideally tested about what may have caused those expansions. The evidence of a pottery trail may continue to be questioned as reflecting migrations of intrusive farming societies, local adoption of pottery and other traits by preexisting indigenous groups, or expansion of people escaping population pressure or other threats. These and other questions do not need to be tied to the ability to identify the pottery trail in itself, and more productively, they should be separated as possible hypotheses that could be tested.

Following the Asia-Pacific pottery trail 91

The Asia-Pacific pottery trail now can be understood as originating at least as early as 4000 B.C. in Taiwan and with older roots in coastal China, followed by regional movements into Island Southeast Asia after 2200 B.C., eventually with new traditions expanding at a larger scale and reaching into the islands of Remote Oceania some centuries later (Figure 5.2). With each step in the incremental growth model, expanding from one zone to another, the material signature changed somewhat in the archaeological assemblage of pottery and other artifacts. For instance, the movement from Taiwan into the Philippines at 2200–2000 B.C. involved different forms and styles of pottery than seen later in the incremental growths into other areas. Although Taiwan may be regarded as instrumental in the origins of the groups eventually settling in the farthest remote islands of the Pacific, those links developed indirectly through a series of expansions over several centuries. The motivation or reason for the pottery trail expansion may have differed in each incremental step, given the differences in time period, cultural context, and associated environment.

This book's focus on Pacific Oceania concentrates on the regional movement from Taiwan after 2200 B.C., yet this flow from Taiwan was not alone in the world. Another expansion of pottery-making traditions spread from southern China into Mainland Southeast

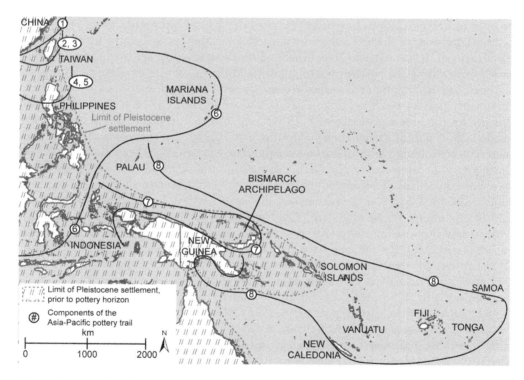

Figure 5.2 Asia-Pacific pottery trail.

1 = varied traditions over time, including coarse cord-marked pottery by 5000 B.C.; 2 = coarse cord-marked pottery by 4000 B.C.; 3 = varied traditions over time, including red-slipped pottery by 2500 B.C.; 4 = red-slipped pottery by 2000 B.C.; 5 = finely decorated red-slipped pottery by 1800 B.C.; 6 = red-slipped pottery by 1500 B.C., including finely decorated farther north and plain or coarsely decorated farther south; 7 = dentate-stamped pottery by 1350 B.C.; 8 = dentate-stamped pottery and other traditions by 800 B.C.

Asia by 1800 B.C., outside the scope of the present book. The Taiwan-associated flow refers to the pottery assemblages that can be tracked in a clear set of steps in the pottery trail from coastal China to Taiwan by 4000 B.C., into Island Southeast Asia by 2200–2000 B.C., and subsequently farther into the Remote Oceanic islands of the Pacific.

Possible early pottery in Sarawak of Borneo

Before proceeding with the central narrative of the pottery trail evidence spreading from Taiwan and into the broader region, the possibility of a separate pottery route into Borneo needs to be addressed directly, given the arguments for this hypothesis in both linguistics (Blench 2010) and in archaeology (Simanjuntak 2017). So far, extremely sparse archaeological evidence of pottery prior to 1000 B.C. from Borneo has shown no significant difference from the overall expansion of a red-slipped pottery horizon that will be described later in this chapter. In fact, the emergence of a pottery-bearing horizon in Borneo may have occurred slightly later than in other parts of Island Southeast Asia, along with the slightly later dates as seen at other sites along the southeast margin of the South China Sea.

The massive island of Borneo contains considerable internal diversity and happens to occupy a key place in the western side of Island Southeast Asia (Figure 5.3), where various cross-regional interactions have occurred over the last several thousands of years. Today's political divisions of Borneo reflect the natural geography as well as the historical cultural differences of the people who have inhabited the diverse landscape, including Sabah in the north, Sarawak in the northwest, the small-sized Brunei within a corner of Sarawak, and the extensive Kalimantan covering the center, south, and east.

An early pottery-bearing horizon in Sarawak of Borneo has been claimed as involving potentially the oldest evidence of both pottery and rice in all of Island Southeast Asia around 2000 B.C. or earlier (Bellwood et al. 1992). The two sites with the most relevant materials are among the most curiously enigmatic in Island Southeast Asian archaeology, namely at Gua Sireh and at the Niah Caves Complex. The pottery assemblages notably have been described as not including the red-slipped and dentate-stamped pottery as documented more broadly in the region, but instead they have been defined as cord-marked and basket-impressed earthenware (Ipoi and Bellwood 1991; Lloyd-Smith et al. 2013). More recent observations, however, have revealed at least some instances of red slip in the earlier pottery, and the age may have been more recent than had been claimed previously.

The proposed early age, possible role of rice, and distinctive pattern-impressed pottery in total could be viewed as the result of an early and separate origin of the pottery-bearing horizon in Sarawak, distinguished apart from the larger pattern elsewhere in Island Southeast Asia. This hypothesis has been presented in terms of a migration of Austroasiatic-speaking people, moving from Mainland into Island Southeast Asia, prior to the time of another migration of Austronesian-speaking populations into other parts of Island Southeast Asia (Blench 2010; Simanjuntak 2017). If this view is correct, then possible origins could be across the South China Sea, in Mainland Southeast Asia, where so far the oldest securely dated pottery has postdated about 2000 B.C. and mostly appeared around 1800–1500 B.C. (Higham 2014: 106–129).

Reexamination projects have changed the prior assertions about the earliest pottery in Borneo, and the new evidence effectively argues against the notion of a Mainland Southeast Asian origin for the pottery-bearing horizon here (Hung and Bellwood 2023). Radiocarbon dating and associated contexts at Guah Sireh probably postdated 1500 B.C. and did not include domesticated rice for farming (Barron et al. 2020). A dating close

Following the Asia-Pacific pottery trail 93

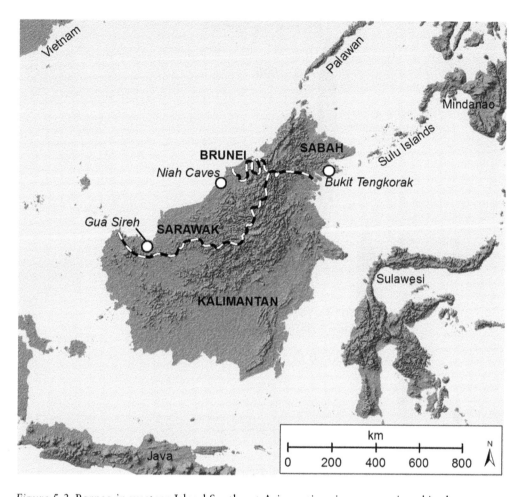

Figure 5.3 Borneo in western Island Southeast Asia, noting sites as mentioned in the text.

to 800 B.C. has been confirmed at Niah Caves (Cole 2012, 2016). Moreover, the earliest pottery fragments at Niah Caves indeed belonged to the broader regional red-slipped tradition (Cole 2012).

The cave deposits of Gua Sireh have been excavated several times since the 1950s, most productively by Ipoi Datan in 1989 (Ipoi 1993; Ipoi and Bellwood 1991), whose work disclosed a sequence of pre-pottery layers with stone tools at least 20,000 years old, covered by pottery-bearing layers with a number of internal components extending into historical contexts of the A.D. 1500s or later (Figure 5.4). The pottery mostly displayed impressed geometric patterns as typical in the surrounding region during the centuries of approximately A.D. 700 through 1500, as confirmed by direct radiocarbon dating of a rice husk in one potsherd from Gua Sireh. Another potsherd with a qualitatively different type of decoration, specifically a kind of basket-impressed exterior surface, contained a rice husk with a direct radiocarbon dating at some point within a broad potential range calibrated at 3013–1632 B.C. – surprisingly old when compared to the overall pottery assemblage

94 *Following the Asia-Pacific pottery trail*

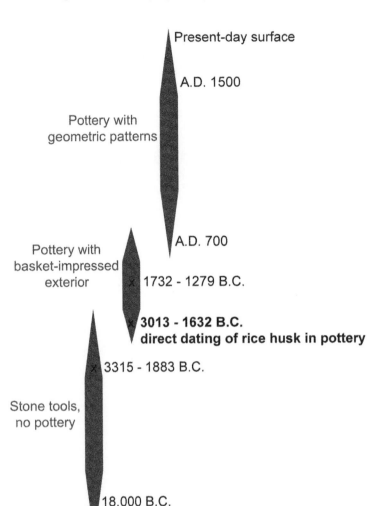

Figure 5.4 Gua Sireh stratigraphy and dating, based on information from Ipoi (1993), Ipoi and Bellwood (1991), and Bellwood et al. (1992).

(Bellwood et al. 1992). The wide dating range can be constrained by a result for an older pre-pottery context calibrated at 3315–1883 B.C. and by a stratigraphically later-aged context calibrated at 1732–1279 B.C.

A formal reexamination of the Gua Sireh evidence has clarified that the oldest rice impressions were probably from wild, non-domesticated rice, and that the pottery horizon probably started later than had been claimed previously (Barron et al. 2020). Apparently, varieties of wild rice were part of the natural environment where people made the pottery that later was deposited at Gua Sireh. The dating of the pottery horizon has not yet been resolved. While the oldest basket-impressed pottery could not be redated, other pottery fragments from the next superimposed layers had been dated much later, postdating 100 B.C. and extending perhaps as late as A.D. 500 (Bellwood et al. 1992).

The evidence from Gua Sireh reveals the influence of a basket-impressed pottery-making tradition different from the overall regional pattern of red-slipped earthenware that dominated elsewhere. Its dating and its origins are unclear, and curiously, it seems to have ended in Sarawak of Borneo. The attested early type of basket-impressed pottery did not spread through a broader geographic region in later periods, nor did it last for very long locally at Gua Sireh. Meanwhile, the evidently wild rice here was not associated with deliberate farming of domesticated rice. Instead, the role of rice farming gained traction in Borneo several centuries later. For whatever reasons, quite different cultural contexts developed after the earliest enigmatic pottery-bearing layers at Gua Sireh.

At least one other site in Sarawak has produced potentially early pottery comparable with the findings at Gua Sireh, but these archaeological discoveries have been notoriously puzzling at the Niah Caves Complex. This chapter will present only the confirmable findings from the Niah Caves. Nonetheless, various other dates and interpretations have been proposed for the pottery-bearing horizon, often without evidence or contradictory to the available evidence.

As summarized by Graeme Barker (2013), during the 1950s and 1960s, Tom and Barbara Harrison commandeered international attention with their excavations at the Niah Caves, where they found dozens of human burials spanning an astonishing range from 40,000 years ago all the way through the last few centuries. The original documentation was scattered in innumerable reports one by one, without attempting overall coherence at that time. Decades later, since the year 2000, Graeme Barker and his colleagues have engaged in reanalysis of the available curated Niah materials, plus controlled re-excavation at the site, with several research goals, not the least of which involved a reassessment of when a pottery-bearing horizon or other indications of a Neolithic context might be attested in the site records (Barker 2013).

The Niah Caves contain several human burial features of multiple time ranges and cultural associations (Figure 5.5), including the time of a regional pottery-bearing horizon, now reexamined in detail by Franca Cole (2012, 2016) and by Lindsay Lloyd-Smith (2005, 2009; see also Lloyd-Smith et al. 2013). Variable frequencies of broken pottery were found with many of the burials, wherein the oldest layers have been associated with dates as early as 800 B.C. and continuing through about 200 B.C. (Cole 2016). These dating results can now be confirmed, instead of relying on any of the previous suggestions or interpretations.

The pottery-bearing horizon coincided with diverse burial practices after 800 B.C. A flexed-position format continued for some of the interments, sustaining a tradition that had started many thousands of years earlier and predating the pottery-bearing horizon. New burial practices after 800 B.C., however, included extended-position formats, secondary reburial, jar burial, and cremation.

The oldest pottery at Niah Caves, in the rage of 800 through 200 B.C., has been described as either plain or "red pigmented" (Cole 2012, 2016). Most revealing, the red pigment resembles the classic red-slipped pottery that had gained popularity throughout other areas of Island Southeast Asia and as far as the Mariana Islands by 1500 B.C. Much of the earliest pottery at Niah Caves was undecorated, but some pieces displayed impressions from textiles or baskets, paddle-marked impressions, and other forms of treatment.

The window into the oldest pottery-bearing context at the Niah Caves has clarified a substantial difference apart from the claims of earliest pottery at Gua Sireh. At the Niah Caves, the pottery-bearing horizon emerged around 800 B.C. and with red-slipped pottery as part of the earliest tradition (Cole 2012). In contrast, the pottery-bearing horizon at

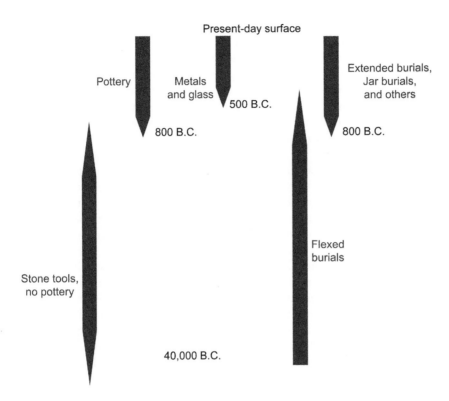

Figure 5.5 Schematic diagram of burial formats and associated artifacts at the Niah Caves, based on information from Cole (2012, 2016), Lloyd-Smith (2005, 2009), and Lloyd-Smith et al. (2013).

Gua Sireh may have started somewhat earlier, associated with basket-impressed pottery and without the use of red slip (Barron et al. 2020; Ipoi and Bellwood 1991).

When interpreting the evidence from Gua Sireh and the Niah Caves, the unique settings of caves should not be mistaken as representative of the usual patterns of ordinary daily life. Light-zone domes and overhangs in some cases, such as at Gua Sireh, may be convenient places for temporary camping, but inner dark-zone chambers are not suitable for regular habitation or living by human beings. The Niah Caves, like many caves worldwide, were the venues of specialized rituals and ceremonies that were intentionally kept spatially and cognitively separate from the realms of daily living, as seen in the evidence of mortuary events, consultation with ancestors, and overall unusual artifact assemblages unlike the findings in regular habitation sites. Whether used for temporary camping or for formalized ceremonies, caves worldwide tend to contain artifacts, food remains, and other evidence notably different from the expectations of regular daily activities.

A question still lingers about how the pottery-bearing horizon in Sarawak may have differed from the overall pattern of red-slipped pottery as witnessed elsewhere in Borneo and more widely throughout Island Southeast Asia, primarily after about 1500 B.C. At the very least, the dating in Sarawak seems to be later than expected, closer to 800 B.C. in the case of Niah Caves, contrary to the prior claims of exceptionally early dating here and at Gua Sireh. Possible cultural origins in Mainland Southeast Asia previously may have been claimed on the basis of early dating of basket-impressed or textile-impressed pottery, but now the later evident dating and the presence of red-slipped pottery would negate those older notions (Hung and Bellwood 2023). These issues within Sarawak still can be clarified further, ideally through documenting the pottery-bearing horizon at different sites with distinguished stratigraphic layers.

Outside Sarawak, caves and non-cave "open" sites in other parts of Borneo have produced red-slipped pottery and assemblages aligned very closely with the overall patterns seen more broadly in the initial pottery-bearing horizon of Island Southeast Asia. As presented later in this chapter, the classically defined dentate-stamped red-slipped pottery layers have been found elsewhere in Borneo, best documented at Bukit Tengkorak in Sabah and dated at least as old as 811–544 B.C. (Bellwood and Koon 1989). Varied traditions of coarsely decorated and non-decorated pottery developed after 500 B.C. in different areas. The older origins of red-slipped pottery, however, can be traced father north in the Philippines as early as 2200–2000 B.C., and then even farther north in Taiwan in older contexts, ultimately attributable to cord-marked pottery traditions of coastal China prior to 4000 B.C.

Coastal China

After clarifying about the findings in Sarawak of Borneo as noted, the Asia-Pacific pottery trail consists of a number of steps that can be traced back at least as early as 4000 B.C. in Taiwan and with even deeper ancestry in coastal China (Figure 5.6). These ancient archaeological assemblages did not relate directly to anything in Pacific Oceania, but they made the foundations of the cultural traditions that would enter into the islands of Remote Oceania a few thousands of years later. Over the course of some millennia, the pottery-making and other behaviors of coastal communities in China underwent a series of developments and transformations as descendant communities inherited these traditions, modified them, and created their own lifeways in different areas across the Asia-Pacific region.

By 4000 B.C., a pottery-bearing horizon appeared at several sites in Taiwan, signifying an influence coming from across the Taiwan Strait in coastal China (Hung and Carson 2014). Cord-marked earthenware was the key diagnostic component in the material assemblage, although other material contributions included small amounts of red-slipped pottery, polished stone adzes, stone bark cloth beaters, shell harvesting knives, and other objects. These assemblages were produced by communities living in coastal zones and engaged in mixed subsistence economies of fishing, foraging, managed forests, and varied forms of horticulture or agriculture.

Rice and millet definitely were grown in southeast coastal China as early as 3000–2800 B.C. (Yang et al. 2018) and in Taiwan after 2800 B.C (Deng et al. 2022), appearing as an abrupt new horizon in archaeological layers. Older site layers have disclosed cord-marked pottery in these areas, but those older layers so far have not disclosed any evidence of either rice or millet contributing to the local diets, land-use patterns, and social complexes in these areas. Much older evidence of rice and millet farming can be traced to the rich landscapes of the Yellow and Yangtze River valleys in China, where people had begun manipulating and experimenting with seeds and plants at least as early as 10,000 B.C. (Zhang and Hung 2008, 2010) and developed systems with strong reliance on formally domesticated crops by 7000 B.C. (Fuller et al. 2009; Zhang and Hung 2013). Meanwhile, people already had been making pottery in parts of China during the preceding several

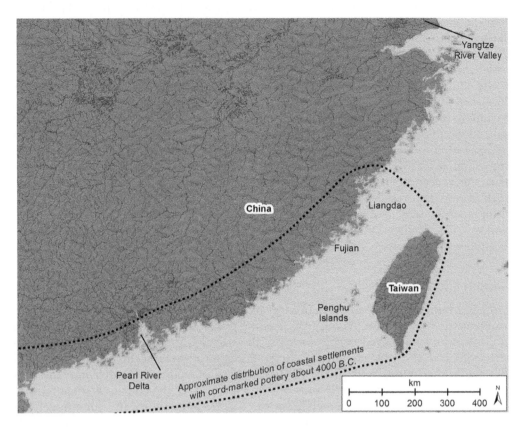

Figure 5.6 Approximate distribution of cord-marked pottery sites in coastal China and Taiwan.

thousands of years (Wu et al. 2012). Varied traditions of cord-marked designs, red-slipped surfaces, and other expressions had characterized the material assemblages of numerous communities by 7000 B.C.

Within the time range of relevance for linking coastal China with the first pottery-bearing horizon in Taiwan about 4000 B.C., the archaeological record of coastal southeast China depicts several communities that lived outside the direct influence of land-dependent farming populations. Until about 3000 B.C., hunter-gatherer groups continued to inhabit most of the southeast coast (Zhang and Hung 2012), specifically in the areas most likely to have been linked with Taiwan's earliest pottery-making groups. Their sites have shown cord-marked pottery and an emphasis on coastal and marine food resources.

The coastal communities of southeast China at 4000 B.C. were living with an awareness of the growing popularity of rice and millet farming among their neighbors who rapidly were consuming more and more land for their farms. Since 7000 B.C., sedentary agriculturalists had been expanding into adjacent territories, beginning in the inland river valleys and established at the coastal zones of those major river valleys about 5000–4000 B.C. While these large-scale expansions and transformations of the landscape were underway, many coastal zones continued to support groups engaged in mixed hunting, gathering, and fishing economies (Liu and Chen 2012: 169–212). The factors of a changing landscape, farming economy, and high-density population did not enter significantly into the orbit of the communities of coastal southeast China until 4000 B.C., about the time when some of those people must have crossed the Taiwan Strait and brought their cord-marked pottery-making and other traditions into Taiwan for the first time. The coastal communities nearest to the crossing of the Taiwan Strait adopted rice and millet farming somewhat later, around 3000–2800 B.C. (Yang et al. 2018).

Prior to the proliferation of horizontally expansive rice-farming systems about 3000 B.C., southeast coastal China offered landforms that were unsuitable for wetland rice paddies. At 5000 through 3000 B.C., the terrain consisted of rough hillslopes meeting the water, narrow beach pockets, estuaries with deep inlets, and marshlands often with scattered small offshore islets. In these kinds of environments, small amounts of rice and millet potentially may have been grown in rain-fed dryland plots or at the edges of natural wetlands, among the preexisting practices of mixed horticulture and managed forests, but large-scale systems of wet-field rice farming were impractical. Prior to 3000 B.C., lowland sediments had not yet begun to accumulate as seen in today's ideal rice-farming lands of broad coastal plains, tablelands, and wide valley floors in coastal China. At that time, the best opportunities for wetland rice and millet farming were situated along the major river valleys, mostly in farther inland settings where sedimentary buildup already had filled large valley floors well prior to 4000 B.C. In coastal zones, sedimentary profiles show that significant alluvial and colluvial buildup began after 3000 B.C., most likely accelerated by inland forest-clearing and agricultural activities, leading to new opportunities of land-use systems that clearly postdated the origins of Taiwan's oldest pottery horizon.

Sites with coarse cord-marked pottery at 5000–4000 B.C. were distributed widely along China's southeast coast and offshore islands, and so far, no single place can be demonstrated as the exclusive origin point of the pottery traditions transferring across to Taiwan at 4000 B.C. Perhaps multiple communities were involved and contributed varied cultural components. The current reality in coastal China no longer retains clues about where people may have spoken Austronesian-related languages prior to the influence of the Han Dynasty.

The search can be narrowed by looking for places where coastal groups used at least one form of artifact besides just the cord-marked pottery that could be associated with an Austronesian cultural tradition. In this regard, perhaps the most distinctive artifact may be the engraved stones of bark cloth beaters, so far confirmed as early as 4800 B.C. in the Pearl River Delta (Tang 2012). Moreover, the genetics origin of the paper mulberry (*Broussonetia papyrifera*), the most popular tree for making bark cloth, has been traced to southern China, with subsets of its genetic diversity found in Taiwan and eventually transported into the remote Pacific Islands as far as the eastern margins of Polynesia (Chang et al. 2015).

After the initial spread of the cord-marked pottery horizon from coastal China to Taiwan around 4000 B.C., the cross-strait contacts fluctuated at least a few times. At first the connections sustained for several centuries, then declined drastically after 2200 B.C., and much later regained strength under very different cultural contexts after perhaps A.D. 1000. At 2200 B.C., sites in the Penghu Islands (in the Taiwan Strait) were abandoned and therefore no longer supported trade and other interactions between coastal China and Taiwan (Tsang 1992). This timing coincided with the greatly increased role of rice farming in coastal China as well as in much of Taiwan. It also coincided with a new direction of sea-crossing communications, specifically with links between eastern Taiwan and the Philippines. The Penghu Islands thereafter supported no permanent residential settlement until after another several centuries.

The decline of cross-strait contacts after 2200 B.C. resulted in overall independence of the communities in Taiwan from the cultural events and processes in China. For instance, the emergence of a Bronze Age by 1700 B.C. and an Iron Age by 600 B.C. in China did not transfer across to Taiwan. Instead, a singular Metal Age (combined bronze and iron technologies) began in Taiwan all at once at a later date after 500 B.C. and linked with Mainland Southeast Asia (Hung and Chao 2016). Taiwan's overseas trading economy developed more strongly with Mainland and Island Southeast Asia in networks crossing the South China Sea (Hung et al. 2013). The economic relations with China resumed long after the rise and fall of the Han Dynasty (206 B.C.–A.D. 220) and the major transformations making the foundations of Chinese society as it is known today.

With the cultural independence of Taiwan from coastal China increasing after 2200 B.C., the later-dated developments within China created no effects in the pottery trail as seen in eastern Taiwan, Island Southeast Asia, and Pacific Oceania. In each of these areas, the archaeological records, linguistic histories, and other lines of evidence should not be expected to reflect the post-2200 B.C. contexts of Mainland China. Regular exchange between China and Taiwan recommenced only much later and in historical contexts disconnected from this book's archaeological narrative of Pacific Oceania.

Taiwan

Taiwan's oldest site layers with pottery were characterized by coarse cord-marked vessels (Figure 5.7) locally known as the diagnostic signature of "TPK culture," as first defined by K. C. Chang (1969). This particular archaeological culture was named after the Tapenkeng Site (abbreviated as TPK), now recognized as Dabenkeng in today's *pinyin* system. After some decades of research, a few dozen sites with coarse cord-marked pottery have been verified, and the dating spanned from as early as 4000 B.C. through as late as 2200 B.C., incorporating components of "early" and "late" TPK or Dabenkeng Culture (Hung and Carson 2014).

The appearance of pottery in Taiwan at 4000 B.C. must be attributed to an external source because Taiwan at that time had been an island separated from the land mass of

Figure 5.7 Examples of Dabenkeng pottery, Taiwan. Vessels are reconstructed at the on-site museum of the Tainan Science-based Industrial Park (TSIP) in Taiwan.

East Asia for a few thousand years. In Taiwan, the pottery horizon marked a clear disjuncture against the prior records of stone tools in campsites of caves and rock shelters in evidence from 25,000 B.C. through 4000 B.C. (Tsang et al. 2009, 2011). The final episodes of non-pottery-bearing sites overlapped in time slightly with the first instances of pottery-bearing sites, hinting at a period of interaction between long-established indigenous groups and any new immigrants who brought pottery and other cultural traits into Taiwan.

Within the extended period of coarse cord-marked pottery from 4000 B.C. through 2200 B.C., the material assemblages underwent degrees of change from early to late components. The transition occurred around 3000–2800 B.C., best seen in different forms of incised decorations on pottery rims, as well as reduction through time in the frequency of pronounced ridges on rims, the thickness of rim profiles, and the exaggerated forms of carinations. In other aspects of material culture, the transition has been unclear due to poor preservation of the older site layers that cannot be compared with the excellent preservation of water-logged deposits that generally postdated 2800 B.C. Among those water-logged site layers, such as at Nanguanli and Nanguanlidong in southwest Taiwan (Tsang et al. 2006), the records of community burials, whole or reconjoinable pots, polished stone adzes, shell harvesting knives, dog burials, storage concentrations of rice and millet, and other materials characterized the later component of 2800 through 2200 B.C. Overall in Taiwan, domesticated rice and millet have been confirmed as early as 2800 B.C. (Deng et al. 2022). By comparison, much less has been known about the earlier contexts of coarse cord-marked pottery that date at least as early as 4000 B.C.

The transition of cultural context at 3000–2800 B.C. may be clarified in terms of the landscape setting (Figure 5.8). Within the time range of the Dabenkeng assemblages in Taiwan, the older sites from 4000 B.C. were situated on low hilltops and on a few scattered beach ridges and berms, and then the later sites after 2800 B.C. were situated in newly available coastal plains just beginning to take shape at that time. These conditions would continue to change, such that the Dabenkeng sites today are found in contexts very different from their original settings of when they had been inhabited.

Most of Taiwan's oldest pottery-bearing habitations prior to 3000 B.C. were situated on roughly level areas of hilltops and ridges, such as at Fengbitou and other sites, originally overlooking coastal waters of their time, although today these locations have been stranded far inland and separated from the ocean by impressively wide coastal plains of alluvial deposits that have developed only after 3000 B.C. Additionally, a few incipient beach ridges or berms were occupied by 4000 B.C. along the eastern coast of Taiwan, for instance at the Changguang Site, yet most of these landforms did not stabilize until some centuries later (Figures 5.9 and 5.10). In all of these cases, the sites originally had been inhabited when they were in coastal settings, but today they are found some km inland due to changing sea level, increased sedimentation rates, and localized tectonic movements.

By 2800 B.C., alluvial sediments began to accumulate most noticeably on Taiwan's western coast, likely due to increased slope erosion prompted by forest-clearing, and residential sites began to develop in these new landforms. These sites of 2800 B.C. and later, such as at Nanguanli and Nanguanlidong in the Tainan Science-based Industrial Park (TSIP), now are buried under 5–7 m of more recent alluvial sediments and stranded some km inland from today's coastline of western Taiwan (Tsang 2005). Later, alluvial deposits continued to accumulate over the abandoned sites, and a drawdown of sea level after 1000 B.C. magnified the extent of the alluvial plain now exposed above sea level (Chen et al. 2004). These combined factors created a substantially different coastal landscape today than had

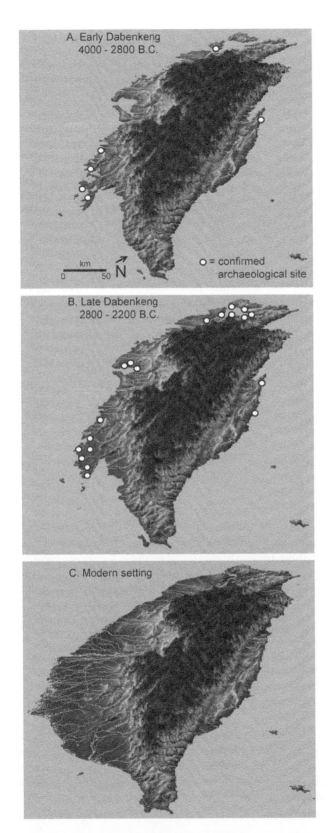

Figure 5.8 Early and late Dabenkeng landscapes of Taiwan, based on information from Hung and Carson (2014) and updated.

Figure 5.9 Changguang site excavation, eastern Taiwan. Lead excavator Dr. Hsiao-chun Hung is recording notes near the back profile, November 2015. Photograph provided courtesy of Dr. Hsiao-chun Hung.

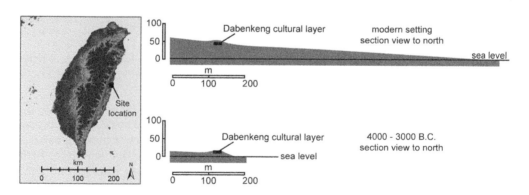

Figure 5.10 Landscape chronology at Changguang.

been inhabited at 2800 B.C. and even more dramatically different from the landscape of 4000 B.C.

The changing landscape of Taiwan reveals the different opportunities for rice farmlands and other modes of land use, concurrent with the chronology of pottery types and other aspects of the archaeological assemblages (Figure 5.11). Overall, the wide coastal terraces most suitable for wetland farming of rice and millet developed after 3000 B.C. and primarily in western Taiwan, whereas similar opportunities developed after 1500 B.C. in eastern

104 *Following the Asia-Pacific pottery trail*

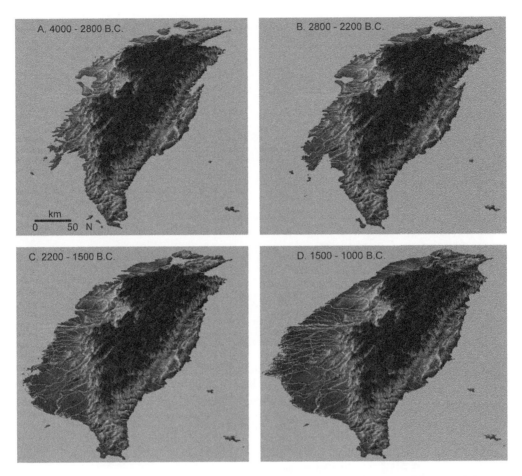

Figure 5.11 Landscape chronology of Taiwan, noting landforms of potential for rain-fed crops in hilly terrain and for wet-field farming in lowland plain formations.

Taiwan. In each of those areas, prior to the availability of the wide coastal terraces, people occupied low hill ridges and a few scattered patches of beach ridges or berms most amenable for subsistence systems of fishing, managed forests, and mixed horticulture. Much the same changing landscape context as occurred in coastal southeast China was mirrored in western Taiwan at the same time about 3000 B.C. and then again much later in eastern Taiwan about 1500 B.C.

Taiwan's oldest pottery-bearing assemblages of the Dabenkeng associations can be defined primarily by coarse cord-marked pottery, but at least two other aspects of the pottery collections must be acknowledged. First, small amounts of earthenware vessels were red-slipped. Second, the cord-marking overall transitioned gradually from coarse to fine. This trend toward finer cord-marking had begun at least as early as 2600 B.C. at some sites. By 2200 B.C., coarse cord-marked pottery was absent in Taiwan, and instead new localized archaeological assemblages can be identified in different parts of the island, signifying separate community identities. Moreover, the trend of fine cord-marked pottery soon began to decline, overtaken steadily by increasingly popular red-slipped pottery without any cord-marked designs.

During the time range of 2200 through 1500 B.C., when the first connections can be noted between Taiwan and Island Southeast Asia, the pottery assemblages in Taiwan already had diversified in the communities in geographically different parts of the island (Figure 5.12). As early as 2600–2500 B.C. and overlapping with the later-aged components of the Dabenkeng sites, at least five geographically distinguished "Middle Neolithic" assemblages may be characterized by their varied forms and relative amounts of fine cord-marked and red-slipped earthenware vessels. Taiwan's Middle Neolithic associations are locally known as Xuntangpu in the northwest, Niumatou in the central west, Niuchouzi in the southwest, Fushan in the southeast, and Hongmaogang in the north through central west. In each of the pottery collections, coarse cord-marking was absent or extremely minimal, replaced instead by fine cord-marking and variable amounts of red-slipped pottery. By 2200 B.C., the cord-marking of any kind had been declining and nearing its termination, in some cases quite radically as in the Fushan assemblages of southeast Taiwan.

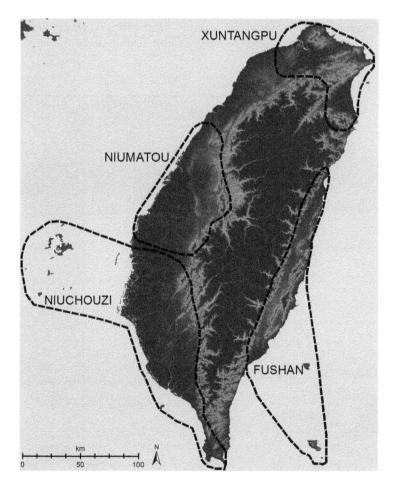

Figure 5.12 Taiwan archaeological assemblages at 2200–1500 B.C., based on information from Hung (2008).

106 *Following the Asia-Pacific pottery trail*

At the Fushan-associated sites of southeast Taiwan that bear the strongest potential for linking with sites in Island Southeast Asia after 2200 B.C., the site records contain mostly red-slipped pottery with only very small amounts of cord-marked pottery (Figure 5.13). Many of the vessels were made with carinated shoulders, such that the upper neck was slightly restricted leading up to the lip of a tall rim. Others were simple open bowls. Both of these forms sometimes were produced with options of a foot-ring base attached to a rounded bottom. These same characteristics are found in the oldest pottery horizons in the northern Philippines after 2200 B.C., as will be presented later in this chapter.

Within the geographic scope of the Fushan sites of southeast Taiwan, the landscape at 2500–1500 B.C. differed significantly from other contemporaneous parts of Taiwan (see Figure 5.11). Elsewhere, such as on the western coast with its broad alluvial plains, residential village complexes relied heavily on rice and millet farming, but the eastern coast at this time consisted of sloped hilly terrain surrounded by aquatic habitats. In eastern Taiwan, today's wide coastal plains and riverbank terraces did not begin to emerge and stabilize above sea level until 1500 B.C. Those most productive lowlands for rice and millet farming, associated with sites such as Beinan at 1500–300 B.C., did not exist during the time of the Fushan-associated cultural sites.

At 2500–1500 B.C., communities lived on the roughly level hilltops along Taiwan's eastern-facing coast (Figure 5.14), at sites such as Fushan and Chaolaiqiao (Carson and

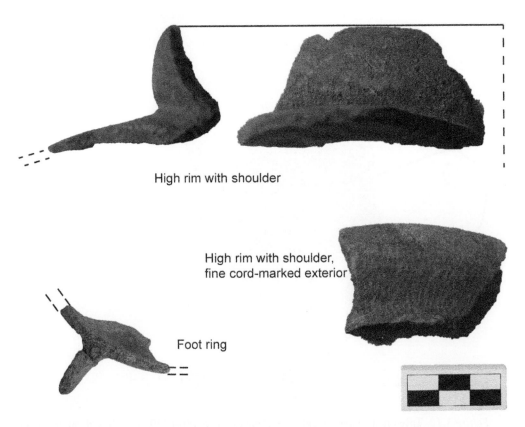

Figure 5.13 Fushan pottery tradition, eastern Taiwan, 2500–1500 B.C.

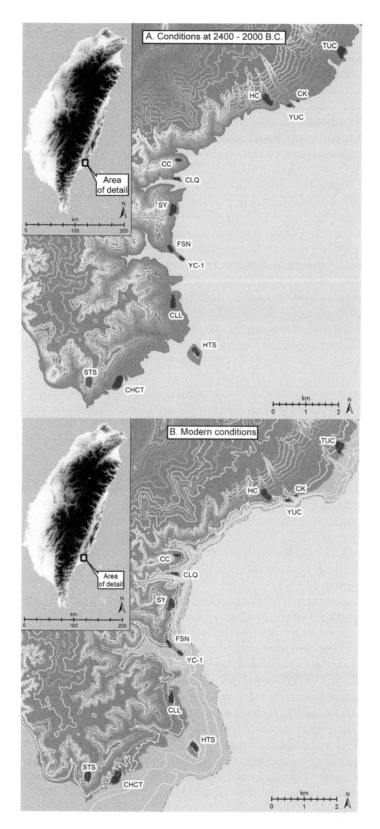

Figure 5.14 Landscape chronology of Fushan tradition sites.

Hung 2018; Hung 2008). Today, these sites are about 40–50 m above sea level and far removed from the shoreline, but at 2200 B.C., they were at 5–15 m elevation, prior to massive tectonic uplift. The local rate of uplift has been among the most rapid in the world, about 7–9 mm per year in the south and 4–6 mm per year in the north of the mountain range (Liew et al. 1993). The inhabited small hills on their eastern sides had met with the adjacent ocean, while their other edges had bordered with streams and marshlands. In those ancient settings, the Fushan communities could access diverse habitats and natural resources.

Around 2200–2000 B.C., when the oldest links can be noticed between the Fushan-associated sites of southeast Taiwan and others in the northern Philippines of Island Southeast Asia, a distinctive inhabited landscape had developed in eastern Taiwan. By that time, most of the other communities of Taiwan had been engaging in increasingly intensive farming of rice and millet, already making use of enlarging lowland terraces and plains for some centuries. Meanwhile, the mountainous terrain of eastern Taiwan persistently was best suited for economies of fishing, forest management, and mixed horticulture. Very few opportunities for rice and millet were available in eastern Taiwan prior to 1500 B.C., either in small rain-fed plots on the lowest hilltops or else in other small patches at the edges of streams and marshlands along the bases of the inhabited hills. Nevertheless, grains of rice have been verified at sites such as Chaolaiqiao in layers dated at 2200–2000 B.C. (Deng et al. 2017), thus signifying the role of rice among a broader spectrum of foods and land-use patterns.

The archaeological records throughout Taiwan depict much more numerous and larger-sized residential habitations, beginning about 1500 B.C., long after the initial connections of a pottery trail had been made between Taiwan and the Philippines, all with increasing reliance on rice and millet farmlands. Specifically, in eastern Taiwan, lowland sediments began to accumulate over riversides and coastal zones, for the first time providing the basis for horizontal expansions of farmlands in this particular area that was associated with sites such as Beinan bearing large-scale stonework village features, slate-lined coffins, and tall megalithic columns (Figures 5.15 and 5.16). Beinan's pottery at 1500 through 500 B.C. was made of orange clay paste, fashioned into varied shapes often with strap handles, and very much different from the older forms of pottery found at the Fushan cultural sites (Figure 5.17). Additionally, nephrite (commonly called "jade") of the Fengtian source in eastern Taiwan became increasingly popular for fashioning ear ornaments, pendants, and other jewelry.

Of the cultural changes that occurred in Taiwan after 1500 B.C., many were mirrored or shared in the archaeological records of the Philippines and other parts of Island Southeast Asia, as well as in limited fashion in parts of Mainland Southeast Asia. These traditions continued to operate and to transform over several centuries, for instance, as seen in the geographic distributions of certain forms and styles of objects made of iron, bronze, and glass after 500 B.C. Communities of Taiwan, especially in the southeastern coastal areas of the island, were involved in sea-crossing trade with other coastal groups distributed all around the edges of the South China Sea (Hung et al. 2013). Several material links can be demonstrated through time as reflections of the cultural histories, economic systems, and social contexts interconnecting the coastal groups of this broad region, but they need to be separated into their distinct chronological units and recognized as certainly postdating the initial connections of the oldest pottery-bearing horizons. These overseas connections so far have not been documented as ever having extended into Pacific Oceania, except for the possibility of shared similarities in shell ornaments seen in the earliest site layers of the

Figure 5.15 Beinan stonework features.

Figure 5.16 Beinan standing megalith.

Figure 5.17 Beinan tradition pottery and body ornaments, at the Beinan Site Museum in Taiwan.

Mariana Islands at 1500–1100 B.C. (Chapter 6) yet lacking other definitive materials such as Taiwan nephrite.

Philippines

A pottery-bearing horizon in the Philippines has been dated as old as 2200–2000 B.C. at a few sites in the far north and closest to Taiwan, followed by more numerous sites in an expanding geographic range by 1500 B.C. (Figure 5.18). The oldest instances of Philippines pottery resembled the Fushan assemblages in southeast Taiwan, which used red slip on vessels with carinated shoulders and foot-ring bases (Figure 5.19). The later instances included these same characteristics, plus new additions locally within the Philippines not shared with Taiwan at that time, such as designs made by dentate-stamped, circle-stamped, and fine-line incised patterns highlighted by white lime infilling. Other forms of pottery have been noted during both the older and later components, including wide bowls or platters among other variants.

The emergence of a pottery horizon in the Philippines can be understood as a process that began at 2200–2000 B.C. and continued through 1500 B.C. or even later in many cases, thus involving variability both chronologically and geographically. Pottery-making and other cultural traditions did not appear suddenly everywhere at once, but rather they spread through the movements of people or of their materials and ideas. In each localized area, regardless of dating older or younger than one another, the initial pottery-bearing layers occurred at habitation sites with dense food middens and indications of house structures, contrasting against the older preexisting patterns of campsites at caves and rock shelters defined primarily by their stone tool industries. The strong contrast resulted in a highly visible archaeological horizon, although the specific attributes of this horizon

Following the Asia-Pacific pottery trail 111

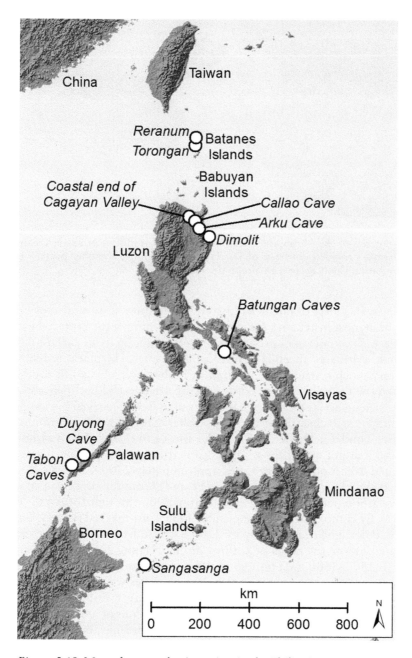

Figure 5.18 Map of pottery horizon sites in the Philippines.

varied from one site to another due to chronological differences that developed while the pottery-making and other traditions spread geographically over the course of some centuries.

The oldest dated pottery in the Philippines so far has been reported at 2200–2000 B.C. in the Batanes Islands, north of the large land mass of Luzon, as well as at sites along

Figure 5.19 Early pottery of the Philippines, similar to Fushan tradition of eastern Taiwan. Photograph provided courtesy of Dr. Hsiao-chun Hung, showing pottery from excavations at the Nagsabaran Site in the Philippines.

the riverside of the Cagayan Valley of northern Luzon. The findings at several sites in the Cagayan Valley have been most instructive for clarifying the timing of the pottery-bearing horizon, overlaying the older contexts of pre-pottery layers, pointing to an earliest dating around 2200–2000 B.C. (Hung et al. 2022). At all of these sites, the oldest red-slipped earthenware vessels very much resemble the findings in Fushan assemblages of southeast Taiwan at a time when the tradition of fine cord-marking already had declined and had become virtually nonexistent. So far only very few pieces of fine cord-marked pottery have been found in the Philippines, exclusively at two cave shelters (Torongan and Reranum) in the Batanes Islands (Bellwood and Dizon 2013). At the Torongan cave shelter, a sample of residue on one potsherd (but not one of those rare cord-marked pieces) produced a radiocarbon dating calibrated over a potential range of approximately 2500–2000 B.C., while the associated archaeological layers at both Torongan and Reranum contained marine shell debris with radiocarbon dating spread generally from 2000 through 1000 B.C. (Bellwood and Dizon 2013). By comparison, the frequency of fine cord-marked pottery at sites in southeast Taiwan had declined dramatically by 2200 B.C. and had become nonexistent at the Fushan-associated sites in the range of 2000–1500 B.C. (Hung 2008).

Beginning as early as 1800–1600 B.C., pottery-making transitioned to include different vessel forms and decorative patterns, and these new characteristics were sustained at least through 1000 B.C. while the pottery horizon spread through an ever-broadening geographic expanse. The vessel shapes followed the preexisting traditions of red-slipped earthenware, mostly with carinated shoulders and sometimes with foot rings, but new variants were made in two ways. First, many, but certainly not all, of the upper rims were everted with lips oriented horizontally outward. Second, the shoulder carinations were made in variable degrees of sharp or rounded edges. The rising popularity of these new variants coincided with a declining frequency of open bowls and platters with line-impressed exteriors that typically lacked red slip (Figure 5.20). Meanwhile, very small proportions of the red-slipped vessels, typically less than 5% in site collections, were decorated with highly distinctive designs made by dentate-stamping, circle-stamping, and fine-line incision usually enhanced by white lime infilling for a white-on-red contrast (Figure 5.21).

Figure 5.20 Line-impressed pottery from Magapit in Cagayan Valley of Luzon, Philippines. Scale bar is in 1 cm increments.

Although the decorated red-slipped pottery was made in low frequency among a larger field of plain red-slipped pottery, it can be appreciated as a diagnostic marker of a unique tradition. The red slip alone was applied on pottery over a very broad region and through many centuries, but the addition of decorative elements in the Philippines created a distinctive expression. Zones of various shapes were filled with dentate-stamping, produced by a pointed comb-like tool similar to a tattooing needle or chisel. Rows and clusters of circles were either hand-drawn or else stamped by a circle-tipped cut piece of bamboo or plant stem. Fine-line incisions could have been drawn by any finely tipped tool. Even further distinguishing this decorative tradition, the patterns in many cases were filled with white slaked lime, made by heating shells or coral into a powder and then mixing the powder with water.

The cultural use of slaked lime preceded the appearance of pottery in the Philippines and is related to betelnut-chewing as a deep indigenous cultural tradition of the region. The white powder material already had been well known and later applied to the new medium of pottery. The white powder of lime is one key ingredient in preparing betelnut quids (Fitzpatrick et al. 2003). Betelnut (from the *Areca catechu* palm tree) acts as a narcotic stimulant when chewed as a quid with slaked lime and the leaf of a *Piper betle* shrub,

114 *Following the Asia-Pacific pottery trail*

Figure 5.21 Finely decorated pottery from Nagsabaran in Cagayan Valley of Luzon, Philippines. Photographs provided courtesy of Dr. Hsiao-chun Hung.

wherein all three ingredients interact for this effect (Zumbroich 2008). The biological origin of *Areca catechu* has been suggested in the Philippines prior to a much broader dispersal aided by human travelers to various destinations throughout Asia and the West Pacific (Zumbroich 2008). The oldest known shell container with residue of slaked lime has been found in the Philippines, specifically in Duyong Cave of Palawan, dated by association with a human burial feature as old as 2700 B.C. and a hearth as old as 3700 B.C. (Fox 1970: 62–65), long prior to the emergence of a pottery-making tradition in the region.

The decorated red-slipped pottery signified a unique material signature that later would spread as part of the archaeologically traceable pottery trail. Radiocarbon dates of 1800–1600 B.C. have been reported for a layer containing these kinds of decorated potsherds at the Nagsabaran Site in the Cagayan Valley of northern Luzon (Hung 2008; Hung et al. 2011). Dates closer to 1500 B.C. are known at other sites, such as in the Batanes Islands north of Luzon (Bellwood and Dizon 2013). These decorative styles continued through 1000 B.C., as evidenced at several sites of the region, and then they declined in frequency until approximately 500 B.C.

The distinguishing decorations were applied to small percentages of the total pottery collections, suggestive of narrowly defined cultural contexts that emphasized presentation of the bowls or of their contents. These characteristics may be expected of ceremonies and

Figure 5.22 Paddle-impressed pottery from Nagsabaran in Cagayan Valley of Luzon, Philippines. Photograph provided courtesy of Dr. Hsiao-chun Hung.

feasts in general, although the specific activities cannot be ascertained on the basis of the surviving material evidence. The decorated elements tended to be added over the most easily visible portions of pots, for instance, around the lip and above a shoulder carination in the portions facing upward. In cases of outcurving rim profiles, the decorations could extend over the lip and into the interior of a pot with an everted or otherwise open top. In cases of foot-ring attachments, the foot ring was often decorated in the exterior ring portion facing outward. Curiously, even the underside of a foot-ring base could be decorated in rare instances, although such a position could not have been visible except under special circumstances.

Aside from the decorated pottery as described, extremely few pieces have been identified as paddle-impressed at the Nagsabaran Site (Hung 2008). These examples hint at the larger diversity of technical and artistic factors involved in pottery-making traditions. Paddle-beating in a technical sense helps in compacting the clay wall of a pot for greater strength during final shaping of the body, but it can create markings that potentially can be incorporated into artistic expressions. In the few known cases at the Nagsabaran Site, the impressions were made by a carved paddle beaten against the exterior of the pot (Figure 5.22). The markings show that the paddle had been carved with long parallel grooves, such that the ridges between those grooves impressed into the pot's exterior surface.

As has been noted, the decorated potsherds are rare in the known site collections, and large excavations are essential for producing enough material with any realistic opportunity to identify these rarities. At present, the two sites with the largest collections of red-slipped and decorated pottery are Nagsabaran and Magapit, both situated in the lower (north) end of Cagayan Valley in Luzon, within the Lal-lo area known for its many shell mounds and middens. Radiocarbon dating has clarified that the pottery-bearing horizon initiated around 2200–2000 B.C., followed by a series of transitions in the pottery forms and other artifacts, including a definitive Metal Age after 500 B.C. and continuing through A.D. 1000 or later (Hung et al. 2022). Focusing on the early pottery and the role of the dentate-stamped expressions, the excavations at the Nagsabaran Site have revealed the oldest pottery around 2200–2000 B.C. and then the earliest distinctive decorated varieties around 1800–1600 B.C. (Hung 2008; Tsang et al. 2002). Another case was the mound of shells on the hilltop of Magapit containing unexpectedly high frequencies of decorated red-slipped pottery and dated by radiocarbon mostly around 1000 B.C. (Aoyagi et al. 1993, 1997; Ogawa 2005) and overlaying a sedimentary unit of clay with even older decorated pottery that so far has been undated. Other sites in the Cagayan Valley have been dated by radiocarbon but with rather small collections of red-slipped pottery, not necessarily including any decorated pieces at all, such as those reported at 1500–1300 B.C. for Irigayen (Ogawa 2005), at 1950–1400 B.C. for Andarayan (Snow et al. 1986), at 1900–1700 B.C. for Pamittan (Tanaka and Orogo 2000), and at 1900–1800 B.C. for Gaerlan (Ogawa 2005).

The Nagsabaran Site in particular and the lower Cagayan Valley in general may be appreciated as having disclosed the best documentation so far available of the oldest decorated pottery assemblage in the Philippines, but similar findings should be acknowledged as potentially existing in other sites. In theory, the early decorated pottery tradition developed in a larger geographic scope including Nagsabaran and other places since 1800–1600 B.C., and most likely it emerged within a time span of a few centuries and in multiple sites distributed through the northern and central Philippines. For instance, archaeological layers with decorated red-slipped and lime-infilled pottery have been dated at least as old as 1500 B.C. in the Batanes Islands north of Luzon (Bellwood and Dizon 2013). Other decorated pottery has been described at the Batungan Caves in Masbate Island of the central Philippines, notably including red-slipped potsherds with dentate-stamped zone-filling and circle-stamped rows, highlighted by white lime infill (Solheim 1955, 1968). From a context overlaying these particular potsherds in one cave, a charcoal sample at 12 inches (~30.5 cm) depth produced a radiocarbon date of 1190–550 B.C. (Broecker et al. 1956: 164), presumably younger than the pottery found at 24 inches (~61 cm) depth.

The Batungan Caves in Masbate contained examples of a few different pottery styles, mostly but not entirely separated in stratigraphic order within the cave sediments, although the findings sometimes have been viewed as representing a single pottery-making tradition. At the time of the excavations, Solheim (1957) considered all of the pottery to relate to a unified Kalanay tradition, named after findings in the Kalanay Cave of Masbate Island. The scroll-like design motifs of the Kalanay pottery matched with discoveries of Sa Huynh pottery in Vietnam, indicating that a broad-reaching Su Huynh-Kalanay Complex once extended across the South China Sea.

Today, the Sa Huynh-Kalanay pottery complex has been substantiated definitively as part of a Metal Age trading network that operated from 500 B.C. through A.D. 100 (Hung et al. 2013). A few of the pottery design elements likely derived from much older traditions, as did at least some of the trading network contacts across the South China Sea. In any case, the pottery from the Batungan Caves included several specimens from this period, as well as others with dentate-stamped motifs that were deposited much earlier. This example underscores the fundamental role of chronological ordering of material assemblages. In this case the stratigraphic position of the radiocarbon sample calibrated at 1190–550 B.C. clarifies that the earliest forms of decorated red-slipped pottery in fact occurred prior to the Metal Age components of the Kalanay assemblages in the Batungan Caves. Equally as important, the Sa Huynh-Kalanay pottery complex must be accepted as a later development of the Metal Age context after 500 B.C.

Given the rarity of any decorated pieces within a red-slipped assemblage, the non-decorated findings potentially can expand knowledge of the geographic distribution of the larger cultural contexts, but the associated dating often has been vague or problematic. Perhaps the most reliable radiocarbon dates are available for the red-slipped pottery layers of sites in the Cagayan Valley as already mentioned, and one instance in particular at the Andarayan Site deserves special attention for the direct radiocarbon dating of a rice husk in a potsherd, calibrated at 2050–1400 B.C. and corroborated by a date on a charcoal sample calibrated at 1950–1050 B.C. (Snow et al. 1986). Other occurrences of red-slipped pottery are difficult to relate with specific radiocarbon dating samples due to the high probability of disturbance inside caves and rock shelters of Palawan (Fox 1970) and of islands around the Sulu Sea (Spoehr 1973). Additional cave findings in limestone hills of Luzon have suggested the localized adoption of red-slipped pottery by preestablished hunter-gatherer groups, such as in the undated assemblage at Arku Cave (Thiel 1986) and in the vaguely dated layers at Callao Cave that could be assigned to any point in the range of 2000–500 B.C. (Mijares et al. 2010). On the eastern coast of Luzon, the Dimolit Site contained a layer rich with red-slipped pottery (Peterson 1974), yet the results of three radiocarbon samples indicate three different chronological associations that may not at all relate to the pottery calibrated at 4500–3300 B.C., 2900–1950 B.C., and 1900–1300 B.C.

The cave sites will require future study to clarify how people had been using these places through time, specifically in terms of the traditions sustained from older practices of indigenous hunter-gatherer groups in comparison to the newer traditions related with the contexts of pottery and other material culture. The rare decorated pieces of red-slipped pottery and specialized ornaments in particular reflect narrow contexts typical of ritual or ceremony, and their occurrences in caves or rock shelters certainly differed from the potential ceremonial events at residential villages. Some older site records, such as those for Callao Cave where deeper layers definitely predated the pottery horizon (Mijares et al. 2010), indicate that people had used these places for thousands of years as recurring campsites. The layers of a pottery-bearing horizon show local adoption of red-slipped pottery, along with new forms of earrings and body ornaments. For example, Arku Cave in Luzon contains human skeletal remains indicating a place of burial (Thiel 1986), with undecorated red-slipped pottery, ear ornaments, possible tattooing chisels, and other items that were deposited most likely during ceremonies of the burial events or of visiting and consulting with the ancestors of this place. Other cases, such as at the Batungan Caves in Masbate, have revealed rarities of finely decorated red-slipped pottery and other specialized items (Solheim 1955, 1968) indicative of a narrow range of the traditions that operated within the larger contexts of contemporaneous residential habitation sites. Although the dating is imprecise for each of these sites, the caves certainly were being used during the emergence of a pottery horizon generally in the range of 2000–1000 B.C., wherein the pottery and other artifacts were being used at non-habitation sites of their own specialized contexts.

The chronological information from the Philippines reveals at least two key components in the regional pottery trail.

- First, the initial instances of the pottery horizon appeared as early as 2200–2000 B.C. in the northern areas of the Philippines, closest to Taiwan, and demonstrating the same vessel shapes and styles as seen in the contemporaneous Fushan sites of southeast Taiwan.
- Second, the highly distinctive decorated varieties developed locally within the Philippines, beginning as early as 1800–1600 B.C. in the north and then spreading through

much of the northern and central Philippines by 1500 B.C. This second component became part of the repertoire of cultural traits broadcast over an ever-widening geographic coverage during the next few centuries.

Later components, for instance after 1000 B.C., lacked the finely made decorations, and instead they showed broad-line incisions and coarse punctate-stamped designs. Even later, after 500 B.C. and during a Metal Age, scroll-like patterns and other elements of the Sa Huynh-Kalanay pottery complex were unrelated to the foundational horizon of the pottery trail crossing into Pacific Oceania. Also after 500 B.C., numerous pieces of pottery fragments had been broken from portable stoves, much like those stoves used in boats and on land even today in many parts of the Philippines, although the portable stove tradition may have existed earlier.

Within the range of the emerging pottery horizon in the Philippines at 2200–1500 B.C., reconstructions of the ancient site settings indicate four different categories in the patterns of settlement and land use, and perhaps more yet will be identified in future research.

- First was a continuation of the use of caves involving modified traditions of indigenous hunter-gatherer groups with new traditions developing in the context of the pottery horizon.
- Second was a targeting of habitats close to the water level of river valley floors, for example, as seen at sites such as Nagsabaran and Andarayan in the Cagayan Valley.
- Third was a limited use of elevated terrain of low hilltops and ridges in positions overlooking water sources, such as at Magapit overlooking the Cagayan River.
- Fourth was habitation at the beachfronts along ancient seashores, currently hidden from view due to changing sea level and sedimentary units that cover these ancient site layers, so far documented solely at Dimolit on the eastern coast of Luzon.

Regarding the reconstructions of paleo-landscapes at 2200–1500 B.C., the available site records from the Cagayan Valley in Luzon offer the most coverage of any place investigated so far in the Philippines (Figure 5.23). The reported depths and dates of site layers can be coordinated with knowledge of a sustained higher sea level about 1.5–2 m higher than present at 3000 through 1000 B.C., such that much of today's low-elevation terrain around the seashore and valley floor could not have existed prior to 1000 B.C. During the time of the initial pottery-bearing horizon, the coastal zone and the riverside areas included marshy habitats close to the ancient slightly higher water level. Among the freshwater and saltwater marshlands, a few small mounded areas supported stilt-raised houses close to the water level, such as reflected in arrangements of post molds at Nagsabaran as early as 2000 B.C. (Hung 2008). The nearby low hills offered stable rocky surfaces well elevated above the river, such as at Magapit, inhabited at least some centuries prior to 1000 B.C. Meanwhile, the seashores did not yet offer stable coastal plains before the sea-level drawdown that began only after 1000 B.C., so the ancient oceanfront included only a few narrow sandy fringes and unstable beach berms still in initial stages of formation close to sea level, where archaeological subsurface survey has yet to be performed. Clues from the Dimolit site, on the eastern-facing coast of Luzon, suggest that similar ancient beachfront habitations have been buried up to 2 m beneath more recent sediments and now stranded at least 200 m farther landward from today's shorelines.

The sites of an emerging pottery horizon in the Philippines reflect a definite ancestral link with traditions in southeast Taiwan, which, over time, developed a set of locally

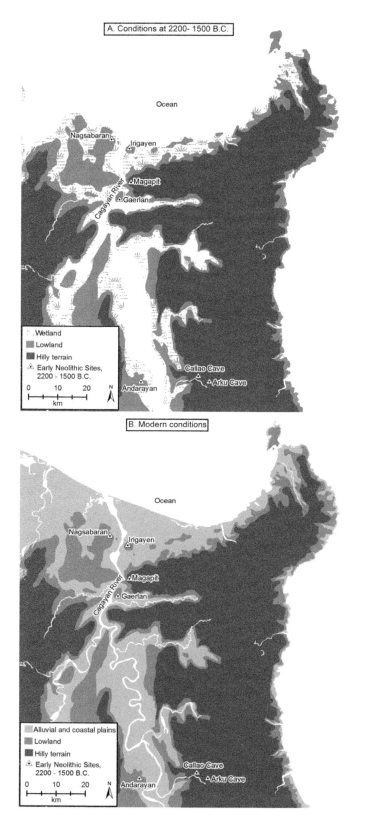

Figure 5.23 Cagayan Valley landscape at 2200–1500 B.C. as compared to modern conditions.

unique characteristics. The pottery assemblage underwent a chronological transition to include additional forms with outcurved rims and with finely decorated designs. The site settings involved more than the low hilltop settlements seen in southeast Taiwan's sites, such as Fushan and Chaolaiqiao dated 2200–2000 B.C., and they accommodated a range of habitat niches, such as seen along the large and diverse shorelines and river valley floors of Luzon.

Prior to 1000 B.C. in the Philippines, the pottery-bearing sites were occupied in ecological settings that could support a broad spectrum of fishing, shellfishing, horticulture, and managed forests similar to the situation as described for southeast Taiwan prior to 1500 B.C. Preserved remains of domesticated rice and millet have been confirmed among the crops imported into the Philippines, at least as early as 1000 B.C. at Nagsabaran and Magapit (Carson and Hung 2018; Hung et al. 2022), and rice husks were dated in pottery around 1950–1400 B.C. at Andarayan (Snow et al. 1986). These crops most likely were grown in small plots near the edges of rivers and marshlands as in the Cagayan River Valley, mirroring the evidence of limited rice farming at the edges of streams and wetland zones in southeast Taiwan prior to 1500 B.C. This situation would begin to change a few centuries later, after drawdown of sea level and buildup of lowland sediments created extensive horizontal plains and terraces just slightly above the water table and ideal for wetland rice farming.

The locally developed variabilities in pottery and settlement locales in the Philippines are evidenced at least as early as 1800–1600 B.C. and therefore existed as parts of the cultural repertoire transported with the pottery trail moving into other areas at 1500–1000 B.C. A few centuries later, after 1000 B.C., significantly different kinds of conditions existed due to lowering of sea level, accumulation of lowland sediments, and substantive change in the pottery and other artifacts. In other words, after 1000 B.C., the material culture and the natural landscape had changed so much as to characterize a different context. The later context after 1000 B.C. postdated the initial spread of the pottery horizon relevant to the Philippines portion of the cross-regional pottery trail.

Indonesia

The dating of a pottery horizon in Indonesia (Figure 5.24) has been among the most misunderstood topics in all of Asia-Pacific archaeology, especially regarding the appearance of decorated red-slipped pottery that could potentially be linked with the dentate-stamped traditions found in the Philippines, in the Mariana Islands, and in Lapita sites of Melanesia and Polynesia. Some decades ago, prior to the availability of cross-regional information reported in this present chapter, the most famous decorated pottery assemblage in Island Southeast Asia had been recognized in the Karama Valley of Sulawesi in Indonesia, first identified in 1931 by van Stein Callenfels (1951) and later pursued more vigorously in 1949 by van Heekeren (1972). Now, after some decades of research, several other sites with red-slipped pottery have been documented throughout Indonesia as in the Philippines, but decorated varieties are so far rare and mostly postdating the initial pottery-bearing horizon.

In the Kalumpang area of Karama Valley, van Heekeren (1972: 119) proposed that decorated potsherds related to "a later horizon of influence, since comparable specimens are known from Early Metal settlements in Cambodia." Specifically, van Heekeren (1972: 119) noted that "the decoration on this pottery with rectangular figures, squares, spirals, circlets and rosettes resembles those from the upper layers from the Samrong Sen

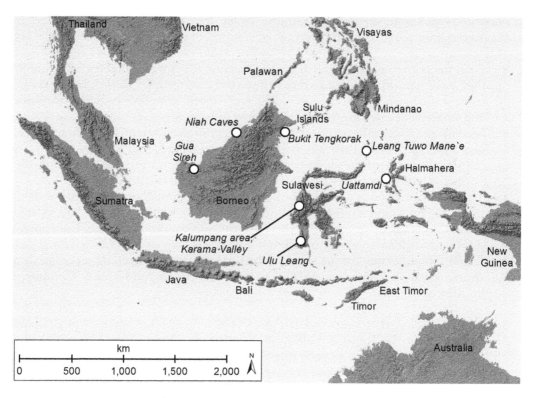

Figure 5.24 Map of pottery horizon sites in Indonesia.

collection in Cambodia." These comparisons are upheld today after some decades of focused research, and they indicate a context postdating 500 B.C., likely related to the Sa Huynh-Kalanay interaction networks of Metal Age communities across the South China Sea (Hung et al. 2013). Indeed, Solheim (1957, 1968) regarded these decorated pieces as typical of the Sa Huynh-Kalanay tradition, but he proposed a rather old age that now has been proven incorrect. Flavel (1997) recorded about 40 decorative motifs on potsherds from the Kalumpang area that resembled motifs in the more definitively known Sa Huynh-Kalanay assemblages now dated at 500 B.C.–A.D. 100. More recently, Prasetyo (2008) identified a total of 20 major decorative motifs with 70 sub-elements, and he concluded a clear relation with the repertoire of motifs otherwise characterizing the Sa Huynh-Kalanay Complex.

Radiocarbon dates are available from very few of the red-slipped pottery layers in Indonesia, often with ambiguous results, but at least two such dated sites in the Kalumpang area of Karama Valley are known as Minanga Sipakko and Kamassi. The material culture assemblages probably overlap with a portion of the findings previously reported by van Heekeren (1972) and likely postdating 500 B.C. The most recent study at Minanga Sipakko has confirmed the emergence of red-slipped pottery horizon, along with domesticated rice, as early as 1500 B.C., (Deng et al. 2020). Previously, however, the dating had been vague, noting a general range of 1500–1000 B.C. for several dating samples that were not always consistent with their stratigraphic positions (Simanjuntak 2008: 236–238).

Before considering the older radiocarbon dates approaching 1500 B.C. for red-slipped pottery in the Kalumpang area of Karama Valley, four points need to be clarified about the stratigraphic sequences and depositional contexts of the relevant archaeological layers.

- First, the pottery-bearing sites along the Karama River were inhabited at a time when they were natural riverside terraces close to the water level of the river and its side tributaries. Later, they were covered by more recent materials of both river flooding and slope-eroded detritus from the adjacent hillslopes.
- Second, the pottery-bearing sedimentary units in the ancient riverside terraces display a gradual change vertically within their accumulated sedimentary columns, with red-slipped potsherds in the lowest and oldest depths, transitioning into non-slipped potsherds in the uppermost and later-aged depths (Hakim 2014).
- Third, when viewed as a whole, the pottery horizon throughout Indonesia undeniably postdated the long-established traditions of stone tool industries that had existed for many thousands of years, and it preceded the appearance of bronze, iron, gold, and glass in evidence surely by A.D. 100 but perhaps as early as 500 B.C.
- Fourth, some portions of the layers in the Karama Valley sites contain potsherds most clearly associated with assemblages such as the Sa Huynh-Kalanay Complex that postdated 500 B.C.

Some of the radiocarbon dates validate pre–1000 B.C. ages for portions of the pottery-bearing layers in the Karama Valley, specifically at Minanga Sipakko and Kamassi, although the precise dating associations have been problematic until now (Figure 5.25). A recent study at Minanga Sipakko clarified that the pottery-bearing horizon started around 1500 B.C. and then continued to accumulate thereafter (Deng et al. 2020). Otherwise, prior studies met difficulties in obtaining dating samples from secure contexts, and instead the dating was suggested as early as 1391–1091 B.C. (Anggraeni et al. 2014) or as late as 916–840 B.C. (Bulbeck and Nasruddin 2002). Nonetheless, multiple other dates were both older and younger, often inconsistent with their stratigraphic positions. Additionally at the Kamassi site, one radiocarbon date for charcoal at 160–170 cm depth was calibrated at 1126–416 B.C., but the pottery-bearing deposit extended much lower

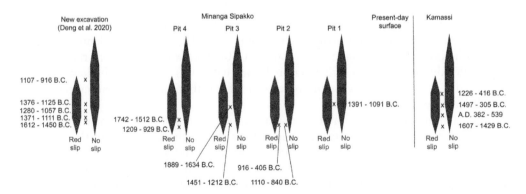

Figure 5.25 Correlation of pottery associations and radiocarbon dating at Minanga Sipakko and Kamassi in the Karama Valley of Sulawesi, Indonesia, based on information from Anggraeni et al. (2014), Deng et al. (2020), and Bulbeck and Nasruddin (2002).

and was dated only by unreliable *Melanoides* sp. freshwater gastropod shells, calibrated as 1497–1305 B.C. at 210–220 cm depth, as A.D. 382–539 at 230–240 cm depth, and as 1607–1429 B.C. at 240–250 cm depth (Anggraeni et al. 2014).

The radiocarbon results from the Karama Valley sites overall indicate that the individual pieces of materials of different ages must have become displaced and commingled within the riverside sedimentary units through a series of episodes spanning more than 1000 years. Within the definable scale of the sedimentary units, the oldest component by radiocarbon calibration is confirmable around 1500 B.C. Thereafter, as documented in detail by Hakim (2014), the internal site stratigraphic sequences indicate a gradual transition from an older component of red-slipped pottery to a later component of non-slipped pottery. While the pottery fragments mostly appeared in a steady stratigraphic order, some of the charcoal and other samples for radiocarbon dating evidently had been intermixed vertically within the sedimentary matrix.

The sites in the Karama Valley exhibit a definite initial pottery-bearing horizon with variable forms of red-slipped earthenware sustained over several centuries with unclear potential of differentiation in the represented vessel shapes and decorative elements. Of the decorated potsherds, the observed designs almost all indicate a post-500 B.C. association as identified in prior studies (Flavel 1997; Prasetyo 2008). So far, only one potsherd from the Kamassi Site, reported by Anggraeni et al. (2014), has shown the coarse or bold versions of dentate-stamped and circle-stamped patterns that were most popular around 1000–500 B.C., lacking the extremely fine decorative designs as seen in the dentate-stamped pottery of the northern through central Philippines and of the Mariana Islands around 1500 B.C. (Hung et al. 2011).

The pottery horizon in the Karama Valley appears to have emerged as mostly generic red-slipped earthenware, including a very low-frequency contribution of the decorated varieties that quickly vanished from the overall repertoire. Given the probable specialized cultural context of the decorated pottery, it may have been produced in very small numbers at these particular sites. According to the extreme rarity in the known sites, the role of decorated pottery evidently was minimal among the local cultural groups in the Karama Valley.

Finely dentate-stamped and circle-stamped red-slipped pottery may not have been popular in the Karama Valley, but it has been documented in some spectacular findings at the site of Bukit Tengkorak in Sabah of Borneo (Bellwood and Koon 1989). Fragments of an ornately decorated vessel and accompanying lid, among other pieces, were recovered from a sealed subsurface layer outside a shelter cave, where three radiocarbon dates produced results overlapping at 811–544 B.C. The individual dating results all have wide potential ranges, calibrated as 1187–544 B.C., 811–2 B.C., and 1004 B.C.–A.D. 211, in total suggesting an extended occupation of several centuries. The cross-confirmed overlap range therefore indicates the most confident minimum age of the pottery-bearing horizon.

If the age of the Bukit Tengkorak pottery is accepted as postdating 1200 B.C., then it can be associated with the changing decorative styles as seen in other areas. By 1000 B.C., the dentate stamping and circle stamping had transitioned into broader and coarser expressions in areas farther to the north, specifically in the Philippines and in the Mariana Islands. Meanwhile, the more finely executed designs, as seen at Bukit Tengkorak, sustained through 500 B.C. in areas farther to the east, specifically in the Lapita-associated realm of Melanesia and West Polynesia. In this larger cross-regional view, the decorated pottery at Bukit Tengkorak may suggest links with the eastward locales of Lapita-associated sites generally in the range of 1200–500 B.C.

An eastward Lapita connection for Bukit Tengkorak becomes more convincing when accounting for the artifacts other than the pottery. In particular, pieces of obsidian have been sourced geologically to the Talasea area in New Britain of the Bismarck Archipelago (Bellwood and Koon 1989). Pieces of obsidian from Talasea were transported as far westward as in this discovery in Borneo and as far eastward as Fiji at Lapita pottery-bearing sites dated about 1100–800 B.C. (Reepmeyer et al. 2011; Spriggs et al. 2011). The 6500-km-long reach, from Borneo in the west to Fiji in the east, substantiated one the most widely distributed raw materials in the world at 1000–500 B.C. During this same time range, decorated Lapita pottery was making its first intrusions along the southern coast of New Guinea at sites dated about 800 B.C. (McNiven et al. 2011), within the middle of the east-west geographic distribution of Talasea obsidian and suggestive of sea-crossing links among distant communities.

While the decorated pottery varieties were rare overall in Indonesia, the generalized red-slipped tradition has been documented throughout the islands of Indonesia and the Philippines as being widespread by 1200–1000 B.C. (Bellwood 1997: 229–234; Spriggs 2007). Given the extensive geographic spread of red-slipped pottery at 1000 B.C., in principle, almost any locale within Island Southeast Asia could have been involved in overseas components of a pottery trail at this time or later. Most likely, multiple coastal communities were connected by sea-crossing trade as evidenced by the widely mobilized Talasea obsidian. Traditions of long-distance seafaring must have existed at least as early as 1000 B.C. in order to account for the sea-crossing migrations into the islands of Remote Oceania, likely connecting back with communities in Island Southeast Asia as well.

The emergence of a pottery horizon in Indonesia can be viewed as an extension of the red-slipped traditions with rare decorated varieties that had originated in the Philippines about 1800–1600 B.C., evidently spreading quite rapidly to reach several places by 1500 B.C. and then expanding throughout most of the islands of the Philippines and Indonesia by 1200–1000 B.C. During this time range, the pottery trail did not follow a singular path from one discrete point to another, but rather it expanded in multiple directions concurrently throughout Island Southeast Asia. The rapid and multidirectional spread must have been enabled by sea-crossing voyages and traditions of seafaring among the closely packed islands, with mostly short water crossings between one coastal community and the next.

Starting around 1500 B.C., an expansive growth of the red-slipped pottery horizon accords with an event of a widespread Malayo-Polynesian branching of the Austronesian language family throughout most of Island Southeast Asia (Blust 2013). The many individual Malayo-Polynesian languages within this region apparently branched out around the same time and subsequently diversified. The "event" in the Malayo-Polynesian language communities involved several population movements, reflected in the emergence of pottery-bearing layers in different places, starting around 1500 B.C. and continuing through about 1000 B.C. Only a few of the instances can be distinguished from each other in chronological order, such as identifying a date of 1500 B.C. at Minanga Sipakko versus dates closer to 1000 B.C. at most other sites. The numerous sites with dating closer to 1000 B.C. produced radiocarbon dating within standard error ranges of each other, thereby portraying a scene of rapid expansion of the pottery-bearing horizon in multiple directions at once, similar to the multi-branching event in the Malayo-Polynesian language communities.

Given the grand size of Indonesia and the even larger geography of Island Southeast Asia, the possibility always will persist that pottery-bearing sites have not yet been discovered. Whether or not those particular unknown sites contain critical information for rewriting the archaeological narrative of Island Southeast Asia and Pacific Oceania, however, cannot be entertained unless scholars rely on pure speculation without tangible evidence. Even so, new methodologies may yet be enacted to search for pottery-bearing site layers now buried and hidden from the view of most surface-scanning surveys, as illustrated in this chapter for other areas and then discussed more fully in Chapter 6 regarding the Mariana Islands. Instead of relying on happenstance to find potsherds eroding from riverbanks or inside unusual contexts of caves, more effort of subsurface exploratory survey can be directed into searching for ancient landform surfaces of the seashores and riversides that now are obscured beneath more recent sedimentary layers. Until more of this scope of work can be accomplished, the present summary of the pottery trail in Indonesia can be regarded as accurate in the most general parameters that may yet be refined.

Mariana Islands

The pottery horizon in the Mariana Islands marked the first cultural presence of any kind in the islands of Remote Oceania, thereby allowing an equation of the pottery trail with both a specific cultural tradition and a long-distance ocean-crossing migration. Beginning by 1500 B.C., the red-slipped pottery assemblage has been documented in at least nine sites of three different islands in the Marianas (Figure 5.26). The rare decorated varieties match exactly with the finely dentate-stamped, circle-stamped, and white lime-infilled occurrences at contemporaneous and slightly older sites in the northern and central Philippines

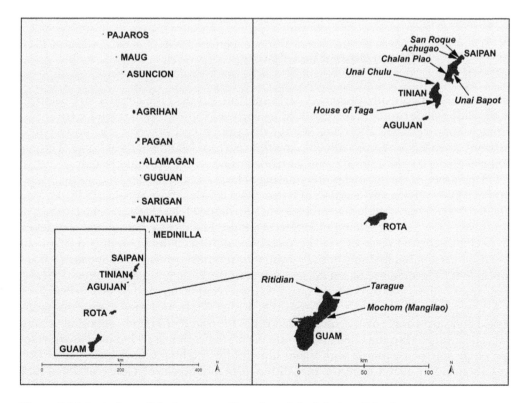

Figure 5.26 Locations of the known earliest sites of the Mariana Islands.

126 *Following the Asia-Pacific pottery trail*

Figure 5.27 Examples of early-period Marianas pottery, 1500–1100 B.C., excavated 2011 and 2013 near House of Taga, Tinian.

(Figure 5.27). As already presented earlier in this chapter, the counterpart occurrences in the Philippines can be traced at least as early as 1800–1600 B.C. and were sustained through approximately 1000 B.C. Within this time range, however, the pottery-bearing horizon expanded geographically into multiple parts of Island Southeast Asia. The expansion was underway by 1500 B.C. and extended as far as the Mariana Islands.

The presence of red-slipped pottery dating at least as early as 1000 B.C. in the Marianas has been known for many decades, first described by Alexander Spoehr (1957) as "Marianas Red." While most of the assemblage was red-slipped but otherwise undecorated, a few rare items showed white lime-infilled decorations. The precise dating and the definition of specific decorated varieties have been clarified only much more recently (Carson 2014). Based on the limited findings initially available about Marianas Red, Spoehr (1957: 174) concluded: "The presence of red pottery wares in the Philippines may link with Marianas Red, and I believe that through these red wares a relationship will be established."

A few years after Spoehr's field research, Father Marcian Pellett discovered a deeply buried and surprisingly dense cultural deposit in the island of Tinian containing a substantial collection of Marianas Red and its rare decorated variants, including dentate-stamped and circle-stamped patterns with white lime-infilled highlighting (Figure 5.28). The site was about 30 m inland from the megalithic *latte* monument of House of Taga, and the oldest cultural deposit was more than 2 m deep, in a context certainly prior to the *latte* period occupation. Radiocarbon dating was not attempted at the time of this work, but Pellett and Spoehr (1961: 323) recognized the importance of the discovery:

Following the Asia-Pacific pottery trail 127

Figure 5.28 Photograph record of the first reported finely decorated pottery in the Mariana Islands, excavated by Marcian Pellett in 1958 near House of Taga, Tinian. The photographic print is in the curatorial archive of the Micronesian Area Research Center, University of Guam.

The significance of these sherds is that their distinctive decoration should prove of substantial aid in relating the Marianas to other pottery-making islands where this type of decoration will one day surely be found and reported. We strongly suspect a tie with the Philippines.

The notion of a homeland source in Island Southeast Asia soon gained solid support by discoveries of red-slipped pottery in a few sites in Palawan (Fox 1970) and in the Sulu Archipelago (Spoehr 1973), in the west-southwest Philippines around the Sulu Sea. With this information, Spoehr (1973: 274) proposed:

Although the archaeological evidence is limited, work has now progressed to the point where a systematic attack can be made on the question of the prehistoric relations of Micronesia with Island Southeast Asia. The time level involved in these relations remains uncertain, but I believe will be found to antedate 1,000 B.C. and may well have commenced at a much earlier date. In addition to the Philippines, the northern

Celebes, Moluccas, and Halmahera must be brought within the sphere of archaeological investigation of the problem.

Despite the crucial role of the Marianas pottery horizon in clarifying the ancestral links between Island Southeast Asia and Remote Oceania, the Marianas case often has been regarded as anomalous and extraneous to the central narrative of Lapita pottery in Pacific Oceania. As Patrick Kirch (2000: 171) summarized correctly: "Although both Marianas Red and the lime-filled decorated variants have been compared to Lapita assemblages, they are probably not directly related, but rather stem from a common, older tradition in island Southeast Asia." While the early pottery assemblages began to be excavated and published in more detail, for instance by Brian Butler (1994) regarding the Achugao Site in Saipan and by John Craib (1993, 1999) regarding Unai Chulu in Tinian, the Marianas case was recognized as divergent from the orthodox narrative of Lapita as the origin of Pacific Oceanic culture.

By casting doubt on the radiocarbon dating associated with the early pottery horizon in the Marianas, these findings are easy to dismiss from the narrative theme of Lapita as essential in Pacific archaeology. These doubts no longer have been tenable after the clarification of the lowest cultural layers at Unai Bapot in Saipan at 1500 B.C. or slightly earlier (Carson 2008, 2020; Carson and Hung 2017), along with critical assessment of other early site dating and stratigraphy throughout the Mariana Islands (Carson and Kurashina 2012). As will be substantiated more in Chapter 6, the results indicate earliest settlement with red-slipped pottery and rare decorated pieces by 1500 B.C. In this case, the early pottery in the Marianas was produced at a time equal in age or older than the earliest Lapita horizon in the Bismarck Archipelago dated at 1500–1350 B.C. (Denham et al. 2012).

As outlined in this chapter, the Marianas case does not need to be discounted from the mainstream narrative of Lapita origins, and, in fact, the Marianas record occupies one key part in the pottery trail that predates the later expressions known as Lapita. For each step in the pottery trail moving into an island group for the first time, whether in the Marianas or in the Lapita-associated islands, the potential homeland can be appreciated as a large geographic zone with a degree of internal diversity. Origins of the pottery horizon in the Marianas can be traced to a zone in Island Southeast Asia prior to 1500 B.C., whereas the potential homeland zone for Near Oceanic Lapita included much the same possibilities in Island Southeast Asia plus the Mariana Islands. In other words, Lapita origins in the Bismarck Archipelago may have involved input from multiple sources, including the Mariana Islands as one of those potential sources to be considered along with others.

A homeland for the first Mariana Islanders must have been in a region where red-slipped pottery included a distinctive set of decorations prior to 1500 B.C. This date range indisputably occurred prior to the emergence of dentate-stamped Lapita pottery in Melanesia and Polynesia (Denham et al. 2012), and it has been described as a "smoking gun" of an Island Southeast Asian origin of dentate-stamping and further of pottery-making in general spreading into the Remote Oceanic islands (Spriggs 1999: 20, see also 2007: 113–114). Several possible candidate sites exist in the Philippines and perhaps arguably in Indonesia, but the pottery trail as portrayed in this present chapter points most strongly to an ancestral origin in the northern through central Philippines.

Regarding the earliest Marianas pottery assemblages, excavations now have produced sufficient collections to define of the range of variants within the parameters of red-slipped earthenware (Figure 5.29). In particular, larger material collections have allowed more conclusive studies of the rare items of highly specialized decorative traits within the larger

Following the Asia-Pacific pottery trail 129

Figure 5.29 Earliest Marianas pottery forms and variants, 1500–1100 B.C. Upper right: Ritidian, Guam. Middle row: House of Taga, Tinian. Bottom row: Ritidian, Guam.

general-utility repertoire. Additional rare objects, such as finely made shell beads and other ornaments, will be considered in Chapter 6 for situating the Mariana Islands more clearly within a context of cross-regional connections.

The early-period pottery vessels all were small, nearly all made with openings of 15–20 cm diameter, but a few are much smaller at 5–10 cm diameter. The small size could accommodate unusually thin vessel walls, consistently less than 4 mm thickness but including one type of bowl made with walls as thin as 1 mm or sometimes even thinner. In later periods, pottery became much thicker. The oldest rim profiles were made in forms of slightly outcurved through horizontally everted, as seen in some of the Philippines pottery after 1800–1600 B.C. None were made incurving, although incurved rims would become dominantly popular in later-aged contexts. The early-period pottery bodies often, but not always, included carinated shoulders, and the bases could be either flat or rounded.

The small and overall simple pottery shapes represented a subset of the full scope of variably simple and complex forms seen in the potential homeland range of Island Southeast Asia at this time. The Marianas collections so far have revealed no lids at all, one possible disc-shaped appendage, and only a single definite instance of a foot-ring appendage. Three extremely rare occurrences have been documented of narrow handles, and handles were entirely unknown in later periods. All of these characteristics and more have been verified in pottery assemblages of equal and earlier time periods in the Philippines.

The early pottery mostly was red-slipped, within which rare decorated pieces indicated the same repertoire as known in the Philippines, using elements of dentate-stamping, circles, and fine-line incision often with white lime infilling (Figure 5.30). Again, as seen in the Philippines collections, the decorations were added onto the most visible upward-facing portions of vessels at the lip, rim, and portions above a carinated shoulder. The individual elements were produced in juxtaposition to one other, effectively creating rows or other clusters of filled or unfilled space in variable combinations. Given the fragmentary nature of the thin-walled and friable earthenware, the total pictures of the motifs have not yet been clarified, but sufficient partial views allow a reasonable assessment of the range of designs involved in the early-period traditions.

Among the rarest of all of the early-period pottery forms, paddle-impressed pottery has been confirmed in two distinctive versions (Figure 5.31). Both of these paddle-impressed wares display paddle marks that deliberately were retained on the vessel surfaces and thus indicate artistic expression beyond simply acting as by-products of technical process. One form was made by a carved paddle impressed directly against the pot, paralleled with other cases as documented in the Philippines. Another form was made by a paddle wrapped by thin vines or rattan, so far identified in just a single location outside a cave at the Ritidian Site in Guam and suggestive of a ceremonial context.

A number of curiously "missing" elements may be mentioned in the Marianas early site records. These characteristics are found commonly in Taiwan and the Philippines, yet they are either extremely rare or absent in the Marianas. Details will be discussed in Chapter 6, but in brief summary, this situation can be explained by the exceptionally remote distance of the Marianas as responsible for a bottleneck subset of the ancestral material culture inventory. Foot rings and handles were known by the earliest pottery-makers and then quickly abandoned from the traditions in the Marianas (Figure 5.32). Bark cloth beaters, spindle whorls, and domestic animals may never have been present at all in the Mariana Islands. Materials of nephrite and slate so far have not been found in any Marianas sites of any age, although they had been traded from Taiwan into overseas communities such as in the Philippines.

As will be presented in Chapter 6, the earliest Marianas settlement at 1500 B.C. was very much shoreline oriented and targeted a narrow range of ecological habitats. People lived directly at the ancient seashores, with access to *Anadara* sp. arc clams in shallow-water zones, yet people drew resources, to a limited extent, from inland forests, deep-sea zones, and other areas. The overall patterns indicate a narrowed focus of the larger diversity seen in the Philippines where the ancient pottery-bearing sites reflected variable possibilities of targeting near-water riverside patches, low-elevation hilltops and ridgetops, sandy beaches at seashores, and ritual use of caves. By comparison to the diverse options in the Philippines, the early-period Marianas sites reflected a narrow range of specialized shoreline niche-targeting, with equally specialized use of a few caves for ceremonial purposes.

The ancient shoreline conditions found at 1500 B.C. existed only for a short time of a few centuries after the initial settlement in the Marianas due to a change in sea level that directly affected those ancient settings (Figure 5.33). Prior to the sea-level drawdown beginning about 1100 B.C., people lived in stilt-raised houses over intertidal or shallow subtidal zones on the seaward borders of rough limestone terrain, where sandy beach fringes had only just begun to form as unstable patches and incipient ridges. Broad coastal plains began to form later, through the combined effects of sea-level drawdown,

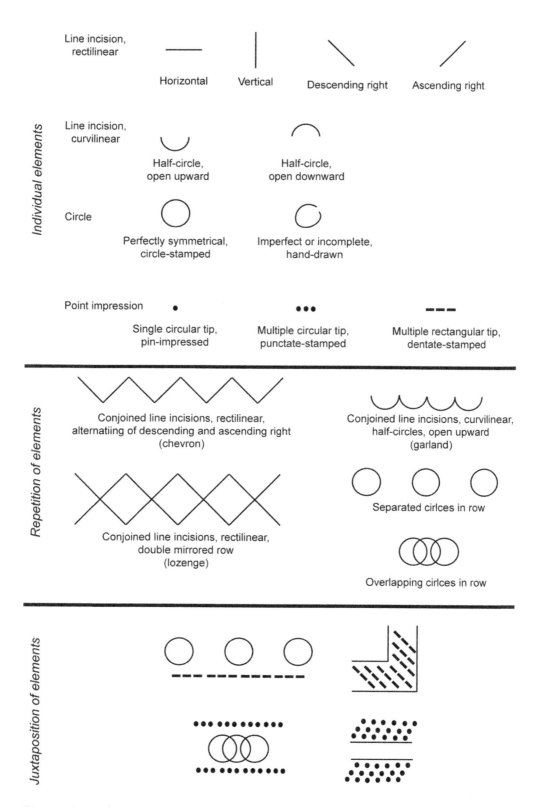

Figure 5.30 Earliest Marianas pottery decorations and design elements. Graphic is adapted from Carson et al. (2013).

132 *Following the Asia-Pacific pottery trail*

Figure 5.31 Two variants of early-period Marianas paddle-impressed pottery, 1500–1100 B.C., from the Ritidian Site in Guam. Upper piece (A): carved paddle impression. Lower pieces (B, C, D): wrapped paddle impression.

accumulations of massive sand units due to frequent storm-surge events, and slope-eroded sediments from the upland areas. Meanwhile, the nearshore habitats began to transform and no longer could support healthy populations of *Anadara* sp. shellfish and other preferred food resources, so people were forced to adapt with substantially different modes of life thereafter.

Following the Asia-Pacific pottery trail 133

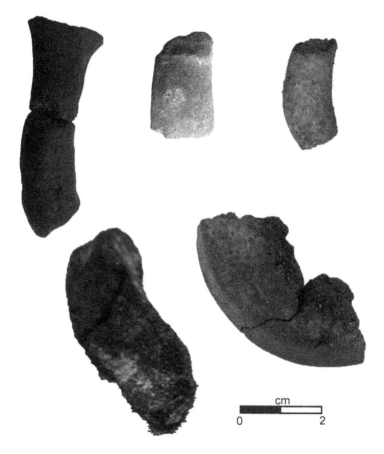

Figure 5.32 Rare instances of early-period Marianas handles, foot ring, and possible appendage fragment. Upper left and upper middle: handle pieces from House of Taga, Tinian. Upper right: handle piece from Ritidian, Guam. Lower left: foot-ring piece from Ritidian, Guam. Lower right: appendage piece from Unai Bapot, Saipan.

The early-period Marianas sites can be framed neatly in a window of 1500 through 1100 B.C., setting the chronological parameters for the earliest pottery assemblage as well as for the natural environmental setting, cultural use of the landscape, and other factors that will be presented fully in Chapter 6. The key point for tracing a pottery trail, however, is that the characteristics in the Mariana Islands at 1500 B.C. were sustained through 1100 B.C. and thereby can be considered among the potential homeland range for other steps in the cross-regional pottery trail within this time range. Equally important, a potential homeland zone for the Marianas settlement must have been situated in Island Southeast Asia prior to 1500 B.C. and involving the highly distinctive decorative expressions as outlined here.

Bismarck Archipelago

The Bismarck Archipelago figures prominently in Pacific Oceanic archaeology, in particular involving the appearance of dentate-stamped Lapita pottery and an associated Lapita

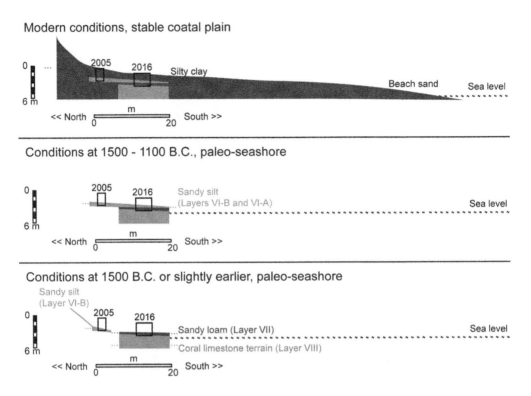

Figure 5.33 Changing coastal morphology at Unai Bapot, Saipan.

Cultural Complex. Several sites have been documented here (Figure 5.34), yielding appreciable collections of exquisitely decorated pottery, assorted stone and shell tools, shell ornaments, shell and bone food refuse, preserved botanical remains, and vestiges of stilt-raised houses over ancient shallow-water seashore niches. This archaeological signature was established most certainly by 1350 B.C. at the Kamgot Site and others, according to critical reviews of radiocarbon dating (Summerhayes 2007; see also Denham et al. 2012). Dates as old as 1500 B.C. have been claimed for Talepakemalai and nearby sites in Mussau (Kirch 2001), thus suggesting a possible date range of 1500–1350 B.C. for the earliest Lapita horizon. According to the most recent summary of the Mussau sites by Kirch et al. (2015), the dentate-stamped pottery layers are dated as early as 1350 B.C. at Talepakemalai, a potential range of 1520–1300 B.C. at Etakosarai, perhaps 1500 B.C. or else 1300 B.C. at Etapakengaroasa, and a potential range of 1200–800 B.C. at Epakapaka.

As seen in the Mariana Islands, the oldest pottery-bearing sites in the Bismarck Archipelago were situated in a narrow range of nearshore habitats that later were transformed due to change in sea level, localized tectonic movements, and accumulations of other later-dated sedimentary layers (Summerhayes 2022). Access to certain kinds of shellfish influenced the choice of specific housing locations, in particular with preference for *Anadara* sp. clams that thrived in shallow-water and marshy areas. The sedimentary units of the site layers had accumulated within lagoons, nearshore coral reefs, and similar ecological settings of their time (Gosden and Webb 1994). Occasionally, the locations of stilt-raised houses can be traced through arrangements of post molds in the site layers and shell

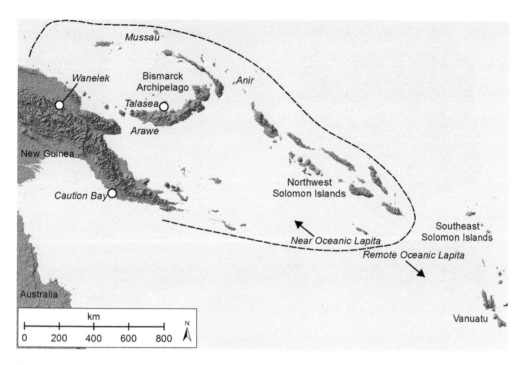

Figure 5.34 Map of Lapita-associated sites in the Bismarck Archipelago and Near Oceania.

middens piles beneath and around those ancient houses. Most often, the ancient shoreline contexts are evident in the sedimentary matrix and through documenting the original elevation of an ancient layer relative to the sea level of its time period (Summerhayes 2022). When the sea level began its stage of drawdown after 1100 B.C., people in some sites adjusted their housing locations to follow the shifting habitat zone of their preference, for example, as illustrated at the Talepakemalai Site (Kirch 2001).

Regardless of the similarities of the natural environments, the cultural context of a pottery horizon in the Bismarck Archipelago differed from the remote-distance Marianas case and instead was more similar to the situation in the Philippines and Indonesia, namely involving the pottery horizon as a new tradition overlaying thousands of years of preestablished cultural presence. In this sense, Lapita developed in a multicultural venue in the Bismarck Archipelago, entailing the interplay of cultural elements that Roger Green (1991, 2000) has described as combining intrusion, integration, and innovation. The multicultural interactions, of course, varied in each case across the diverse cultural areas of the Philippines, Indonesia, and the Near Oceanic islands such as in the Bismarck Archipelago.

Lapita pottery is recognized as unique in terms of its elaborate decorations (Figure 5.35), which added extraordinary characteristics to the older and contemporaneous decorative expressions in the Philippines and the Mariana Islands. A human face motif, among other symbols, signified a definitely specialized character of Lapita that did not occur anywhere else in the pottery trail previously. The technical components of pottery-making and specifically of the decorative elements all were derived from the traditions that occurred earlier in the Philippines and in the Mariana Islands, but the decorations were made into significantly more elaborate forms in the Lapita sites of the Bismarck Archipelago.

Figure 5.35 Lapita pottery with decorations excavated from Anir in the Bismarck Archipelago. Photographs provided courtesy of Glenn Summerhayes.

Southern Melanesia and West Polynesia

After 1200 b.c., the Lapita pottery horizon in Southern Melanesia and West Polynesia indisputably descended from Near Oceanic Lapita such as seen in the Bismarck Archipelago. All dated within a few centuries, many dozens of Lapita sites across these islands reflect a sudden dispersal of people into this previously uninhabited realm of Remote Oceania (Figure 5.36). Dates of initial human presence are predominantly within a concise frame of 1100 through 800 b.c., while a date of 1200 b.c. may be regarded as a maximum oldest parameter by a yet-to-be-confirmed singular case in the Southeast Solomon Islands (Denham et al. 2012).

Across the varied Near Oceanic and Remote Oceanic islands of the Lapita geographic distribution, the pottery decorative motifs display remarkable similarities, including the famed Lapita face as well as a labyrinth and other distinguished designs (Figure 5.37). This portion of the pottery trail very clearly shows a link between Near and Remote Oceanic Lapita. A number of localized distinctions, of course, can be outlined for each island group, but the context of decorated Lapita pottery suggests a consistent and unifying factor, as in Jack Golson's (1961: 176) depiction of a cross-regionally shared "community of culture."

The Lapita-associated archaeological record represented a sudden impact on the natural environment, especially in the previously uninhabited Remote Oceanic Islands. Large numbers of people spread into multiple locations within a very narrow time frame,

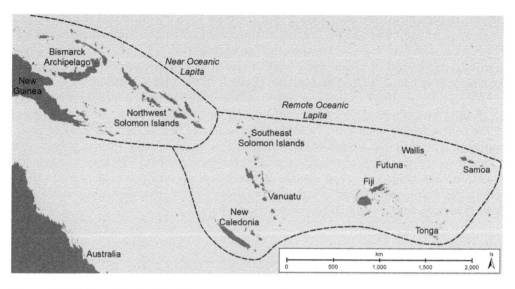

Figure 5.36 Map of Lapita distribution in Near and Remote Oceania.

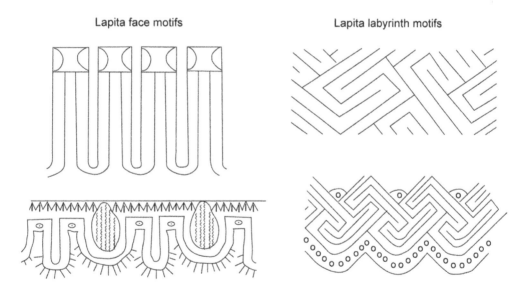

Figure 5.37 Examples of Lapita pottery design motifs.

effectively acting as an invasive species. They brought not only their numbers but also their cultural ways of inhabiting an environment, carrying their concepts and their materials such as translocated animals and plants, forever changing the landscapes. This apparent siege of ecological imperialism will be discussed in Chapter 7.

The seashore-oriented Lapita site contexts represented a bottlenecked subset of the larger diversity of ecologies as known in pottery-bearing horizon sites of Island Southeast Asia, thus hinting at a narrower range of land-use and resource-use systems in the Lapita world. Other narrowing episodes had already been witnessed in the Mariana Islands and in the Near Oceanic Lapita sites of the Bismarck Archipelago. The nearshore niche-targeting evidently gained widespread success with the broad dispersal of Lapita sites after 1200 B.C., in this case not at all involving any traces of rice or millet agricultural economy that had been present in Island Southeast Asia and perhaps in the Mariana Islands.

Although the seashore niche-targeting was linked with the success of the spread of Lapita groups, the associated traditions could not be sustained for more than a few centuries. About 500 B.C., the conditions of a lowering sea level had altered the coastal ecologies that were central to the Lapita site inhabitants, thus forcing people to engage more heavily in land-based activities of horticulture and forest management (Nunn and Carson 2015). This timing coincided with the demise of finely dentate-stamped pottery and other cultural traits that were replaced by other expressions, not only in the Lapita world but also in the Mariana Islands, as will be presented in Chapter 8.

New Guinea

Lapita pottery layers now have been verified about 900–800 B.C. on the south coast of New Guinea (David et al. 2011; McNiven et al. 2011), and other pottery-bearing layers have been dated as old as 1000 B.C. in the New Guinea highlands (Gaffney et al. 2015). These discoveries clarify that people with pottery-making traditions must have passed through the land mass of New Guinea and effectively settled in a few locales within the time range of the Lapita diaspora. Prior to these discoveries, however, extremely little was known about possible ancient pottery layers in New Guinea, and the paucity of information by default suggested that Lapita and other early pottery-making groups mostly avoided this area.

The pottery horizon in New Guinea reflects a later end of the Lapita range, at a time when the Lapita-associated traditions already had been sustained for some centuries in adjacent areas such as in the Bismarck Archipelago. By 1000 B.C., the Lapita expansion was nearing its maximum coverage, such that New Guinea occupied one portion of the larger geography of the Lapita world. The earlier spread of Lapita evidently brought people into coastal niches that were not being heavily used by the preestablished indigenous groups, but a substantially different situation existed in the main land mass of New Guinea where populous groups had been living long prior to the appearance of Lapita in their orbit.

Palau

At the same time of Lapita intrusions into Melanesia and Polynesia, the first human presence in Palau in far western Micronesia (Figure 5.38) appeared about 1100–900 B.C., although the associated artifacts and material assemblages have not yet been clarified (Liston 2005). The most secure early dating has been reported for several graves in a cave of Chelechol ra Orrak, as old as 1100–1000 B.C. (Fitzpatrick 2003; Fitzpatrick and Nelson 2011; Nelson and Fitzpatrick 2006). Two other sites definitively contain cultural layers, dated approximately 1100–900 B.C. at Ulong (Clark et al. 2006) and slightly older at Ngatpang (Liston et al. 1998). In all cases, pottery fragments have been mentioned as plainware yet not described in much detail, therefore lacking information about potentially linking with the traditions of neighboring areas. Although only very little currently

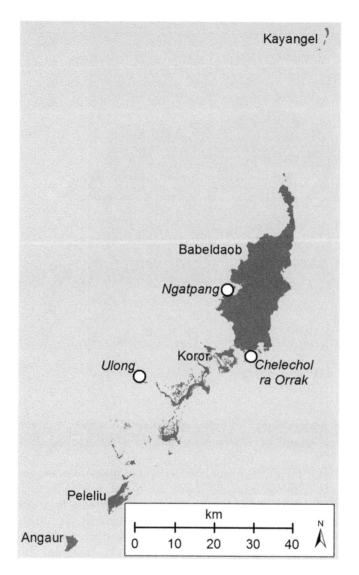

Figure 5.38 Locations of reported early sites in Palau.

is known of the oldest pottery horizon in Palau, it cannot be attributed to any particular homeland other than most likely within a vague scope of the eastern islands of Indonesia closest to Palau.

While the site of Chelechol ra Orrak so far offers the best documentation of the initial pottery horizon in Palau, the site must be contextualized as a burial cave of its own unique association. The cave is situated in a small limestone islet (Figure 5.39), unsuitable for regular habitation, and accordingly it was used as a place of burial and not as a place of residence. This particular rock islet is within close range of the large land mass of Babeldaob, vastly more encouraging for large-scale settlement. At a much later date, probably after A.D. 1000, a stacked-stone causeway connected the offshore islet with the

Figure 5.39 View of Chelechol ra Orrak, offshore from Babeldaob in Palau.

island of Babeldaob, but today, only a portion of this causeway has survived intact. At 1100–1000 B.C., however, access would have been possible by a short crossing through shallow water.

Archaeological research has been intensive throughout Palau for some decades, yet the methodologies have proven ineffective for learning about the oldest sites. The surfaces of ancient coastal landforms of 1200–1000 B.C. now have become buried 1 m or deeper beneath more recent sedimentary layers, most likely about 100 m inland from present-day shorelines. These conditions of ancient site layers can be estimated according to the depths, radiocarbon dating, contexts, and locations of other cultural layers of similar age, as documented in other Pacific Oceanic islands, for instance, as illustrated in the Mariana Islands (Chapter 6). Independently, the same conditions were estimated by regional modeling of sea-level change and available sediment coring records in Palau (Dickinson and Athens 2007).

Disconnected from archaeological site layers, Athens and Ward (2002) proposed that Palau's oldest preserved charcoal particles could approximate the date of first human settlement. In this research strategy, sediment cores from the bottoms of swamps provided records of the pollen and other materials that settled into the bottoms of those swampy zones over long periods of time, including the oldest traces of charcoal particles that had been produced most likely by deliberate clearing and burning of native forests. The associated radiocarbon dates point to ages as old as 2000 B.C. or as young as 1000 B.C. (Welch 2008), and ultimately they are not useful for refining the dating of the initial cultural habitation sites in Palau.

So far only a single site in Palau has produced evidence of an apparent residential habitation at an ancient coastline of a large land mass, specifically in the Ngatpang area of the island of Babeldaob. A subsurface layer in just one location, about 1.5 m deep, produced charcoal with a radiocarbon dating calibrated at 1410–998 B.C. (Liston et al. 1998). The contents of this layer were reported unclearly, but they most likely included pieces of broken pottery among other materials. The excavation was prompted by observing subsurface layers in the profile of a twentieth-century Japanese-era trench, conveniently affording quick and efficient excavation of a fresh trench extension more suitable for updated archaeological documentation down to 1.9 m depth. If a pre–1000 B.C. pottery-bearing cultural layer can be verified at 1.5 m depth in this location, then it would constitute the most important substantive information toward searching for Palau's oldest archaeological sites.

More broadly across Micronesia

Other than in the Mariana Islands and in Palau as noted, the islands of Micronesia appear to have been inhabited after about A.D. 100, associated with a horizon of plain pottery, as will be presented in Chapter 10. The placement within the larger regional pottery trail has remained unclear at the time of this book's second edition, for three primary reasons.

- First, the plain pottery potentially could relate to nearly anywhere in Island Melanesia or West Polynesia, where these traditions were established at least since about 500 B.C.
- Second, the dating around A.D. 100 is substantially later than the prior steps in the pottery trail, and this time gap likely involved numerous localized developments in pottery traditions that have not yet been clarified.
- Third, outside the low-lying atolls of Micronesia, the larger and higher island masses in Yap, Chuuk, Pohnpei, and Kosrae conceivably may have supported earlier cultural habitations, prior to A.D. 100, although no such early-dated archaeological layers have yet been documented.

Tracking the pottery trail

The Asia-Pacific pottery trail overall points to a broadly shared ancestral tradition that spread incrementally across a large geographic expanse, resulting in a series of unique area-specific expressions along the successive steps of the trail. The chronological range began at least as early as 4000 B.C. in coastal China, then proceeded in components through Taiwan, Island Southeast Asia, and Pacific Oceania, all with their own distinctive internal assemblages enduring through about 500 B.C. The pottery assemblages at the beginning and end of the pottery trail were substantially different from each other, as well as distanced from one another by thousands of years, but striking consistencies are noted within each of the steps of the pottery trail and individually constrained time intervals.

A large-scale view and confident radiocarbon dating in concert have enabled clearer understanding of how the pottery trail developed cross-regionally and extended over some centuries. Research has advanced more than sufficiently to overturn prior vague chronologies and unclearly described pottery assemblages, so that the pottery collections in each island group can be defined and dated securely. Equally important, the cross-regional connections can be identified through real material evidence, rather than viewing each localized pottery horizon as its own unique and in situ occurrence.

The pottery trail is essential for comprehending the foundation and context of Pacific Oceanic archaeology that will be developed more fully in the next chapters. The pottery trail constitutes the datable substantive connection between Asian and Pacific archaeological records, generally following steps from west to east across this immense region. The middle to eastern steps of this trail entered into the geography generally understood as Pacific Oceania, but the entire trail from west to east first needs to be outlined as in the foregoing chapter.

References

Allen, Jim, 1996. The pre-Austronesian settlement of Island Melanesia: Implications for Lapita archaeology. In *Prehistoric Settlement of the Pacific*, edited by Ward H. Goodenough, pp. 11–27. Transactions 86, Part 5. American Philosophical Society, Philadelphia.

Allen, Jim, and Chris Gosden, 1996. Spheres of interaction and integration: Modelling the culture history of the Bismarck Archipelago. In *Oceanic Culture History: Essays in Honour of Roger Green*, edited by Janet M. Davidson, Geoffrey Irwin, B. Foss Leach, Andrew Pawley, and Dorothy Brown, pp. 183–197. New Zealand Journal of Archaeology Special Publication. New Zealand Archaeological Association, Dunedin.

Anggraeni, Truman Simanjuntak, Peter Bellwood, and Philip Piper, 2014. Neolithic foundations in the Karama Valley, west Sulawesi, Indonesia. *Antiquity* 88: 740–756.

Aoyagi, Yoji, Melchor L. Aguilera, Jr., Hidefumi Ogawa, and Kazuhiko Tanaka, 1993. Excavation of hill top site, Magapit Shell Midden in Lal-lo Shell Middens, Northern Luzon, Philippines. *Man and Culture in Oceania* 9: 127–155.

Aoyagi, Yoji, Hidefumi Ogawa, and Kazuhiko Tanaka, 1997. Excavation and ornaments discovered at the Magapit shell-midden site in northern Luzon. *The Journal of Sophia Asian Studies* 15: 167–180.

Athens, J. Stephen, and Jerome V. Ward, 2002. Paleo-environmental evidence for early human settlement in Palau: The Ngerchau core. In *Pacific 2000: Proceedings of the Fifth International Congress on Easter Island and the Pacific*, edited by Christopher M. Stevenson, Georgia Lee, and Frank J. Morin, pp. 165–177. Easter Island Foundation, Los Osos, CA.

Barker, Graeme (editor), 2013. *Rainforest Foraging and Farming in Island Southeast Asia: The Archaeology of the Niah Caves, Sarawak, Volume 1.* McDonald Institute for Archaeological Research, University of Cambridge, Cambridge.

Barron, Aleese, Ipoi Datan, Peter Bellwood, Rachel Wood, Dorian Q. Fuller, and Tim Denham, 2020. Sherds as archaeobotanical assemblages: Gua Sireh reconsidered. *Antiquity* 94: 1325–1336.

Bellwood, Peter, 1997. *Prehistory of the Indo-Malaysian Archipelago*. Revised edition. University of Hawai'i Press, Honolulu.

Bellwood, Peter, and Eusebio Dizon (editors), 2013. *4000 Years of Migration and Cultural Exchange: The Archaeology of the Batanes Islands, Northern Philippines*. Terra Australis 40. Australian National University E Press, Canberra.

Bellwood, Peter, R. Gillespie, Gill B. Thompson, J. S. Vogel, I. Wayan Ardika, and Ipoi Datan, 1992. New dates for prehistoric Asian rice. *Asian Perspectives* 31: 161–170.

Bellwood, Peter, and Peter Koon 1989. Lapita colonists leave boats unburned: The question of Lapita links with Island Southeast Asia. *Antiquity* 63: 613–622.

Blench, Roger, 2010. Was there an Austroasiatic presence in Island Southeast Asia prior to the Austronesian expansion? *Bulletin of the Indo-Pacific Prehistory Association* 30: 133–144.

Blust, Robert, 2013. *The Austronesian Languages*. Revised edition. Asia-Pacific Linguistics Open Access Monographs 008. Research School of Pacific and Asian Studies, Australian National University, Canberra.

Broecker, W. S., J. L. Kulp, and C. S. Tucek, 1956. Lamont natural radiocarbon measurements III. *Science* 124: 154–165.

Bulbeck, F. David, and Nasruddin, 2002. Recent insights on the chronology and ceramics of the Kalumpang site complex, south Sulawesi, Indonesia. *Bulletin of the Indo-Pacific Prehistory Association* 22: 83–99.

Butler, Brian M., 1994. Early prehistoric settlement in the Mariana Islands: New evidence from Saipan. *Man and Culture in Oceania* 10: 15–38.

Carson, Mike T., 2008. Refining earliest settlement in Remote Oceania: Renewed archaeological investigations at Unai Bapot, Saipan. *Journal of Island and Coastal Archaeology* 3: 115–139.

Carson, Mike T., 2014. *First Settlement of Remote Oceania: Earliest Sites in the Mariana Islands*. Springer, New York.

Carson, Mike T., 2016. *Achaeological Landscape Evolution: The Mariana Islands in the Asia-Pacific Region*. Springer International, Cham, Switzerland.

Carson, Mike T., 2020. Peopling of Oceania: Clarifying an initial settlement horizon in the Mariana Islands at 1500 BC. *Radiocarbon* 62: 1733–1754.

Carson, Mike T., and Hsiao-chun Hung, 2017. *Substantive Evidence of Initial Habitation in the Remote Pacific: Archaeological Discoveries at Unai Bapot in Saipan, Mariana Islands*. Archaeopress, Oxford.

Carson, Mike T., and Hsiao-chun Hung, 2018. Learning from paleo-landscapes: Defining the land-use systems of the ancient Malayo-Polynesian homeland. *Current Anthropology* 59: 790–813.

Carson, Mike T., Hsiao-Chun Hung, Glenn Summerhayes, and Peter Bellwood, 2013. The pottery trail from Southeast Asia to Remote Oceania. *Journal of Island and Coastal Archaeology* 8: 17–36.

Carson, Mike T., and Hiro Kurashina, 2012. Re-envisioning long-distance Oceanic migration: Early dates in the Mariana Islands. *World Archaeology* 44: 409–435.

Chang, Chun-hsiang, Yousuke Kaifu, Masanaru Takai, Reiko T. Kono, Raier Grun, Suhji Mastuura, Les Kingsley, and Liang-kong Lin, 2015. The first archaic *Homo* from Taiwan. *Nature Communications* 6: 6037.

Chang, Kwang-Chi, 1969. *Fengpitou, Tapenkeng, and the Prehistory of Taiwan*. Yale University Press, New Haven.

Chen, Wen-shan, Shih-hua Sung, Leh-chyun Wu, Hao-de Hsu, and Hsiao-chin Yang, 2004. Shoreline changes in the coastal plain of Taiwan since the Last Glacial Epoch. *Chinese Journal of Archaeological Science* 94: 40–55. (in Chinese).

Clark, Geoffrey, Atholl Anderson, and Duncan Wright, 2006. Human colonization of the Palau Islands, western Micronesia. *Journal of Island and Coastal Archaeology* 1: 215–232.

Cole, Franca, 2012. *Communities of the Dead: Practice as an Indicator of Group Identity in the Neolithic and Metal Age Burial Caves of Niah, North Boreno*. Doctoral dissertation, University of Cambridge, Cambridge.

Cole, Franca, 2016. Earthenware ceramics, chronology and use at Niah c. 2800–500 BP (c. 800 BC – AD 1500). In *Archaeological Investigations in the Niah Caves, Sarawak: The Archaeology of the Niah Caves, Sarawak*, edited by Graeme Barker and Lucy Farr, Volume 2, pp. 329–344. McDonalnd Institute for Archaeological Research, University of Cambridge, Cambridge.

Craib, John L., 1993. Early occupation at Unai Chulu, Tinian, Commonwealth of the Northern Mariana Islands. *Bulletin of the Indo-Pacific Prehistory Association* 13: 116–134.

Craib, John L., 1999. Colonisation of the Mariana Islands: New evidence and implications for human settlement in the western Pacific. In *Le Pacifique de 5000 à 2000 avant le Présent: Suppléments à l'Histoire d'une Colonisation*, edited by Jean-Christophe Galipaud and Ian Lilley, pp. 477–485. Institut de Récherche pour le Développement, Paris.

David, Bruno, Ian J. McNiven, Thomas Richards, Sean P. Connaughton, Matthew Leavesley, Bryce Barker, and Cassandra Rowe, 2011. Lapita sites in the central province of Papua New Guinea. *World Archaeology* 43: 576–593.

Deng, Zhenhua, Su-chiu Guo, Mike T. Carson, and Hsiao-chun Hung, 2022. Early Austronesians cultivated rice and millet together: Tracing Taiwan's first Neolithic crops. *Frontiers in Plant Science* 13: Article 962073. https://doi.org.10.3389/fpls.2022.962073

Deng, Zhenhua, Hsiao-chun Hung, Mike T. Carson, Peter Bellwood, Shu-ling Yan, and Houyuan Lu, 2017. The first discovery of Neolthic rice remains in eastern Taiwan: Phytolith evidence from the Chaolaiqiao site. *Archaeological and Anthropological Sciences*, first online 6 February 2017. https://doi.org/10.1007/s12520-017-0471-z

Deng, Zhenhua, Hsiao-chun Hung, Mike T. Carson, Adhi Agus Oktaviana, Budianto Hakim, and Truman Simanjuntak, 2020. Validating earliest rice farming in the Indonesian Archipelago. *Scientific Reports 10*: 10984. https://doi.org/10.1038/s41598-020-67747-3

Denham, Tim, Christopher Bronk Ramsey, and Jim Specht, 2012. Dating the appearance of Lapita pottery in the Bismarck Archipelago and its dispersal to Remote Oceania. *Archaeology in Oceania 47*: 39–46.

Dickinson, William R., and J. Stephen Athens, 2007. Holocene paleoshoreline and paleo environmental history of Palau: Implications for human settlement. *Journal of Island and Coastal Archaeology 2*: 175–196.

Fitzpatrick, Scott M., 2003. Early human burials in the western Pacific: Evidence for a c. 3000-year-old occupation on Palau. *Antiquity 77*: 719–731.

Fitzpatrick, Scott M., and Greg C. Nelson, 2011. Purposeful commingling of adult and child cranial elements from the Chelechol ra Orrak Cemetery, Palau. *International Journal of Osteoarchaeology 21*: 360–366.

Fitzpatrick, Scott M., Greg C. Nelson, and Ryan Reeves, 2003. The prehistoric chewing of betel nut (*Areca catechu*) in western Micronesia. *People and Culture in Oceania 19*: 55–65.

Flavel, Ambika, 1997. *Sa Huynh-Kalanay: Analysis of the Prehistoric Decorated Earthenware of South Sulawesi in an Island Southeast Asian Context*. B.S. thesis, Centre for Archaeology, University of Western Australia, Perth.

Fox, Robert B., 1970. *The Tabon Caves: Archaeological Explorations and Excavations on Palawan Island, Philippines*. Monograph Number 1. Philippines National Museum, Manila.

Fuller, Dorian Q., Ling Qin, Yunfei Zheng, Zhijun Zhao, Xugao Chen, Leo Aoi Hosoya, and Guoping Sun, 2009. The domestication process and domestication rate in rice: Spikelet bases from the lower Yangtze. *Science 323*: 1607–1610.

Gaffney, Dylan, Glenn R. Summerhayes, Anne Ford, James M. Scott, Tim Denham, Judith Field, and William R. Dickinson, 2015. Earliest pottery on New Guinea mainland reveals Austronesian influences in highland environments 3000 years ago. *PLoS One 10*: e0134497. DOI: 10.1371/journals.pone.0134497.

Golson, Jack, 1961. Report on New Zealand, Western Polynesia, New Caledonia, and Fiji. *Asian Perspectives 5*: 166–180.

Gorecki, Paul, 1992. A Lapita smokescreen? In *Poterie Lapita et Peuplement*, edited by Jean-Christophe Galipaud, pp. 27–47. ORSTOM, Nouméa.

Gosden, Chris, and John Webb, 1994. The creation of a Papua New Guinean landscape: Archaeological and geomorphological evidence. *Journal of Field Archaeology 21*: 29–51.

Green, Roger C., 1991. Near and remote Oceania: Disestablishing "Melanesia" in culture history. In *Man and a Half: Essays in Pacific Anthropology and Ethnobiology in Honour of Raplh Bulmer*, edited by Andrew Pawley, pp. 491–502. The Polynesian Society, Auckland.

Green, Roger C., 2000. Lapita and the cultural model for intrusion, integration and innovation. In *Australian Archaeologist: Collected Papers in Honour of Jim Allen*, edited by Atholl Anderson and Tim Murray, pp. 372–392. Coombs Academic Publishing, Australian National University, Canberra.

Hakim, Budianto, 2014. Archaeological traces of Austronesian ancestors at the Kamansi Site of the Karama River Valley in west Sulawesi, Indonesia. *Journal of Austronesian Studies 5*: 73–95.

Higham, Charles, 2014. *Early Mainland Southeast Asia: From First Humans to Angkor*. River Books, Bangkok.

Hung, Hsiao-chun, 2008. *Migration and Cultural Interaction in Southern Coastal China, Taiwan and the Northern Philippines, 3000 BC to AD 100: The Early History of Austronesian-Speaking Populations*. Doctoral dissertation, School of Archaeology and Anthropology, Australian National University, Canberra.

Hung, Hsiao-chun, and Peter Bellwood, 2023. Archaeological correlations for the dispersal of the Malayo-Polynesian languages of Southeast Asia, western Micronesia and Madagascar. In *The Oxford Guide to the Malayo-Polynesian Languages of Asia and Madagascar*, edited by Alexander Adelaar and Antoinette Schapper, forthcoming in August 2023. Oxford University Press, Oxford. DOI: 10.1093/oso/9780198807353.003.0006.

Hung, Hsiao-chun, and Mike T. Carson, 2014. Foragers, fishers and farmers: Origins of the Taiwan Neolithic. *Antiquity* 88: 1115–1131.

Hung, Hsiao-chun, Mike T. Carson, Peter Bellwood, Frediliza Campos, Philip J. Piper, Eubesio Dizon, Mary Jane Louise A. Bolunia, Marc Oxenham, and Zhang Chi, 2011. The first settlement of Remote Oceania: The Philippines to the Marianas. *Antiquity* 85: 909–926.

Hung, Hsiao-chun, and Chin-yung Chao, 2016. Taiwan's early metal age and engagement with world trading systems. *Antiquity* 90: 1537–1551.

Hung, Hsiao-Chun, Kim Dung Nguyen, Peter Bellwood, and Mike T. Carson, 2013. Coastal connectivity: Long-term trading networks across the South China Sea. *Journal of Island and Coastal Archaeology* 8: 384–404.

Hung, Hsiao-chun, Cheng-hwa Tsang, Zhenhua Deng, Mary Jane Louise A. Bolunia, Rey A. Santiago, Mike T. Carson, and Peter Bellwood, 2022. Preceramic riverside hunter-gatherers and the arrival of Neolithic farmers in northern Luzon. *Antiquity* 96: 848–867.

Ipoi, Datan, 1993. *Archaeological Excavations at Gua Sireh (Serian) and Lubang Angin (Gunung Mulu National Park), Sarawak, Malaysia. Sarawak Museum Journal Volume 45*, Special Monograph 6. Sarawak Museum, Kuching.

Ipoi, Datan, and Peter Bellwood, 1991. Recent research at Gua Sireh Serian) and Lubang Angin (Gunung Mulu National Park), Sarawak, Malaysia. *Bulletin of the Indo-Pacific Prehistory Association* 11: 386–405.

Kirch, Patrick V., 2000. *On the Road of the Winds: An Archaeological History of the Pacific Islands Before European Contact*. University of California Press, Berkeley.

Kirch, Patrick V. (editor), 2001. *Lapita and Its Transformations in Near Oceania: Archaeological Investigations in the Mussau Islands, Papua New Guinea, 1985–88, Volume 1: Introduction, Stratigraphy, Chronology*. Archaeological Research Facility Contributions Number 59. University of California, Berkeley.

Kirch, Patrick V., Scarlett Chiu, and Yu-yin Su, 2015. Lapita ceramic vessel forms of the Talepakemalai Site, Mussau Islands, Papua New Guinea. In *The Lapita Cultural Complex in Time and Space: Expansion Routes, Chronologies, and Typologies*, edited by Christophe Sand, Scarlett Chiu, and Nicholas Hogg, pp. 49–61. Archeologia Pasifika 4. Institut d'Archéologie de la Nouvelle-Calédonie et du Pacifique, Nouméa.

Liew, P. M., P. A. Pirazzoli, M. L. Hsieh, M. Arnold, J. P. Barusseau, M. Fontugne, and P. Giresse, 1993. Holocene tectonic uplift deduced from elevated shorelines, eastern coastal range of Taiwan. *Tectonophysics* 222: 55–68.

Liston, Jolie, 2005. An assessment of radiocarbon dates from Palau, western Micronesia. *Radiocarbon* 47: 295–354.

Liston, Jolie, Tina M. Mangieri, David G. Grant, Michael W. Kaschko, and H. David Tuggle, 1998. *Archaeological Data Recovery for the Compact Road, Babeldaob Island, Republic of Palau: Historic Preservation Investigations Phase II, Volume II, Fieldwork Reports*. Report prepared for U.S. Army Corps of Engineers. International Archaeological Research Institute, Inc., Honolulu.

Liu, Li, and Xingcan Chen, 2012. *The Archaeology of China: From the Late Paleolithic to the Early Bronze Age*. Cambridge University Press, New York.

Lloyd-Smith, Lindsay, 2005. *Prehistoric Jar Burials in the West Mouth of Niah Cave, Sarawak: Assessing the Concept of the "Jar Burial Tradition" in Southeast Asia*. M.Phil. thesis, University of Cambridge, Cambridge.

Lloyd-Smith, Lindsay, 2009. *Chronologies of the Dead: Later Prehistoric Burial Practice at the Niah Caves, Sarawak*. Doctoral dissertation, University of Cambridge, Cambridge.

Lloyd-Smith, Lindsay, Graeme Barker, Huw Barton, Judith Cameron, Franca Cole, Patrick Daly, Chris Doherty, Chris Hunt, John Krigbaum, Helen Lewis, Jessica Manser, Victor Paz, Philip J. Piper, Ryan J. Rabett, Garry Rushworth, and Katherine Szabo, 2013. "Neolithic" societies c. 4000–2000 years ago: Austronesian farmers? In *Rainforest Foraging and Farming in Island Southeast Asia: The Archaeology of the Niah Caves, Sarawak, Volume 1*, edited by Graeme Barker, pp. 255–298. McDonald Institute for Archaeological Research, University of Cambridge, Cambridge.

McNiven, Ian J., Bruno David, Thomas Richards, Ken Aplin, Brit Asmussen, Jerome Mialanes, Matthew Leavesley, Patrick Faulkner, and Sean Ulm, 2011. New direction in human colonisation of the Pacific: Lapita settlement of south coast New Guinea. *Australian Archaeology* 72: 1–6.

Mijares, Armand Salvador, Florent Détroit, Philip Piper, Rainer Grün, Peter Bellwood, Maxime Aubert, Guillaume Champion, Nida Cuevas, Alexandra De Leon, and Eusebio Dizon, 2010. New evidence for a 67,000-year-old human presence at Callao Cave, Luzon, Philippines. *Journal of Human Evolution* 59: 123–132.

Nelson, Greg C., and Scott M. Fitzpatrick, 2006. Preliminary investigations of the Chelechol ra Orrak, Republic of Palau: I, skeletal biology and paleopathology. *Anthropological Science* 114: 1–12.

Nunn, Patrick D., and Mike T. Carson, 2015. Sea-level fall implicated in profound societal change around 2570 cal yr BP (620 BC) in western Pacific Island groups. *Geo: Geography and Environment* 2: 17–32.

Ogawa, Hidefumi, 2005. Typological chronology of pottery assemblages from the Lal-lo shell middens in northern Luzon, Philippines. *Journal of Southeast Asian Archeology* 25: 1–29.

Pellett, Marcian, and Alexander Spoehr, 1961. Marianas Archaeology: Report on an excavation on Tinian. *Journal of the Polynesian Society* 70: 321–325.

Peterson, Warren, 1974. Summary report of two archaeological sites from north-eastern Luzon. *Journal of Archaeology and Physical Anthropology in Oceania* 9: 26–35.

Prasetyo, Bagyo, 2008. Pottery from the Neolithic sites on the bank of the Karama River. In *Austronesian in Sulawesi*, edited by Truman Simanjuntak, pp. 77–92. Center for Prehistoric and Austronesian Studies, Depok, Indonesia.

Reepmeyer, Christian, Matthew Spriggs, Anggraeni, Peter Lape, Leee Neri, Wilfredo P. Ronquillo, Truman Simanjuntak, Glenn Summerhayes, Daud Tanudirjo, and Archie Tiauzon, 2011. Obsidian sources and distribution systems in Island Southeast Asia: New results and implications from geochemical research using LA-ICPMS. *Journal of Archaeological Science* 38: 2995–3005.

Simanjuntak, Truman (editor), 2008. *Austronesian in Sulawesi*. Center for Prehistoric and Austronesian Studies, Yogyakarta, Indonesia.

Simanjuntak, Truman, 2017. The western route migration: A second probable Neolithic diffusion to Indonesia. In *New Perspectives in Southeast Asian and Pacific Prehistory*, edited by Philip Piper, Hirofumi Matsumura, and David Bulbeck, pp. 201–211. The Australian National University E Press, Canberra.

Snow, Bryan E., Richard Shutler, Jr., D. E. Nelson, J. S. Vogel, and J. R. Southon, 1986. Evidence of early rice cultivation in the Philippines. *Philippine Quarterly of Culture and Society* 14: 3–11.

Solheim, Wilhelm G., II, 1955. Notes on the archaeology of Masbate. *University of Manila Journal of East Asiatic Studies* 4: 47–50.

Solheim, Wilhelm G., II, 1957. The Kalanay pottery complex in the Philippines. *Artibus Asiae* 20: 279–288.

Solheim, Wilhelm G., II, 1968. The Batungan Cave Site, Masbate, Philippines. In *Asian and Pacific Archaeology Series*, edited by Wilhelm G. Solheim, II, Volume 2, pp. 20–62. Social Science Research Institute, University of Hawai'i, Honolulu.

Spoehr, Alexander, 1957. *Marianas Prehistory: Archaeological Survey and Excavations on Saipan, Tinian and Rota*. Fieldiana: Anthropology, Volume 48. Chicago Natural History Museum, Chicago.

Spoehr, Alexander, 1973. *Zamboanga and Sulu: An Archaeological Approach to Ethnic Diversity.* Ethnology Monographs, Number 1. Department of Anthropology, University of Pittsburgh, Pittsburgh.

Spriggs, Matthew, 1997. *The Island Melanesians.* Wiley-Blackwell, Cambridge, MA.

Spriggs, Matthew, 1999. Archaeological dates and linguistic sub-groups in the settlement of the Island Southeast Asian-Pacific region. *Indo-Pacific Prehistory Association Bulletin* 18: 17–24.

Spriggs, Matthew, 2007. The Neolithic and Austronesian expansion within Island Southeast Asia and into the Pacific. In *From Southeast Asia to the Pacific: Archaeological Perspectives on the Austronesian Expansion and the Lapita Cultural Complex*, edited by Scarlett Chiu and Christophe Sand, pp. 104–140. Center for Archaeological Studies, Research Center for Humanities and Social Sciences, Academia Sinica, Taipei.

Spriggs, Matthew, Christian Reepmeyer, Angraenni, Peter Lape, Leee Neri, Wilfredo P. Ronquillo, Truman Simanjuntak, Glenn Summerhayes, Daud Tanudirjo, and Archie Tiauzon, 2011. Obsidian sources and distribution systems in Island Southeast Asia: A review of previous research. *Journal of Archaeological Science* 38: 2871–2881.

Summerhayes, Glenn R., 2007. The rise and transformations of Lapita in the Bismarck Archipelago. In *From Southeast Asia to the Pacific: Archaeological Perspectives on the Austronesian Expansion and the Lapita Cultural Complex*, edited by Scarlett Chiu and Christophe Sand, pp. 141–184. Center for Archaeological Studies, Research Center for Humanities and Social Sciences, Academia Sinica, Taipei.

Summerhayes, Glenn R., 2022. Kisim save long graun: Understanding the nature of landscape change in modelling Lapita in Papua New Guinea. In *Palaeolandcapes in Archaeology: Lessons for the Past and Future*, edited by Mike T. Carson, pp. 291–312. Routledge, London.

Tanaka, Kazuhiko, and Alfredo Orogo, 2000. The archaeological excavation at the Pamittan Site. *Journal of Environmental Studies of Keiai University, Chiba* 8: 113–141.

Tang Chung (editor), 2012. *Origins of Clothes: Barkcloth Exhibition Catalogue.* Chinese University of Hong Kong, Hong Kong. (in Chinese).

Thiel, Barbara, 1986. Excavations at Arku Cave, northeast Luzon, Philippines. *Asian Perspectives* 27: 229–264.

Tsang, Cheng-hwa, 1992. *Archaeology of the Penghu Islands.* Special Publication 95. Academia Sinica, Taipei.

Tsang, Cheng-hwa, 2005. Recent discoveries at the Tapenkeng culture sites in Taiwan: Implications for the problem of Austronesian origins. In *The Peopling of East Asia: Putting Together Archaeology, Linguistics and Genetics*, edited by Laurent Sagart, Roger Blench, and Alicia Sanchez-Mazas, pp. 63–73. Routledge Curzon, London.

Tsang, Cheng-hwa, W. S. Chen, K. T. Li, and Y. X. Zeng, 2009. *Report of the Baxiandong Cave Sites, Changbin, Taidong County, the First Year.* Academia Sinica, Taipei. (in Chinese).

Tsang, Cheng-hwa, W. S. Chen, K. T. Li, and Y. X. Zeng, 2011. *Report of the Baxiandong Cave Sites, Changbin, Taidong County, the Second Year.* Academia Sinica, Taipei. (in Chinese).

Tsang, Cheng-hwa, K. T. Li, and Y. C. Chu, 2006. *Footprints of Ancestors: Archaeological Discoveries in Tainan Science-based Industrial Park.* Tainan Countey Government, Tainan, Taiwan.

Tsang, Cheng-hwa, Rey Santiago, and Hsiao-chun Hung, 2002. *Report on Archaeological Exploration in Northern Luzon, Philippines, 1996–2002.* Annual report for the program of Asian and Pacific Study. Academia Sinica, Taipei. (in Chinese).

van Heekeren, H. R., 1972. *The Stone Age of Indonesia.* Second edition. Nijhoff, The Hague.

van Stein Callenfels, Pieter Vincent, 1951. Prehistoric sites on the Karama River. *University of Manila Journal of East Asiatic Studies* 1: 82–97.

Welch, David J., 2008. Archaeological and paleo environmental evidence of early settlement in Palau. *Bulletin of the Indo-Pacific Prehistory Association* 22: 161–173.

White, J. Peter, Jim Allen, and Jim Specht, 1988. Peopling of the Pacific: The Lapita Homeland Project. *Australian Natural History* 22: 410–416.

Wu, Xiaohong, Zhang Chi, Paul Goldberg, David Cohen, Yan Pan, Trina Arpin, and Ofer Bar-Yosef, 2012. Early pottery at 20,000 years ago in Xianrendong Cave, China. *Science* 336: 1696–1700.

Yang, Xioyan, Quihe Chen, Yongchao Ma, Zhao Li, Hsiao-chun Hung, Qianglu Zhang, Zhiwei Jin, Suiqiang Liu, Zhenyu Zhou, and Xianguo Fu, 2018. New radiocarbon and archaeobotanical evidence reveal the timing and route of southward dispersal of rice farming in South China. *Science Bulletin Beijing* 63: 1495–1501.

Zhang, Chi, and Hsiao-chun Hung, 2008. The Neolithic of southern China: Origin, development, and dispersal. *Asian Perspectives* 47: 299–329.

Zhang, Chi, and Hsiao-chun Hung, 2010. The emergence of agriculture in southern China. *Antiquity* 84: 11–25.

Zhang, Chi, and Hsiao-chun Hung, 2012. Later hunter-gatherers in southern China, 18,000–3000 B.C. *Antiquity* 86: 11–29.

Zhang, Chi, and Hsiao-chun Hung, 2013. Jiahu 1: Earliest farmers beyond the Yangtze River. *Antiquity* 87: 46–63.

Zumbroich, Thomas J., 2008. The origin and diffusion of betel chewing: A synthesis of evidence from South Asia, Southeast Asia and beyond. *Electronic Journal of Indian Medicine* 1: 63–116.

6 First contact with the Remote Oceanic environment
The Mariana Islands at 1500 B.C.

Long ago, when Puntan was about to die, he made a plan and instructed his sister Fu'uña to use his body to create components of the world. Fu'uña used her power to bring life to her brother's body parts, thus making the world that was thereafter inhabited by the Chamorro people.

This Chamorro tradition of creation has many variants, but this version is paraphrased from accounts by Chamorro language and cultural practitioner Leonard Iriarte, as he told me on several occasions from our first meeting in June 2009 until the time of writing this book. Additionally, I have learned more nuances and implications about this story from language expert and cultural practitioner Jeremy Cepeda. Every time we discuss the Chamorro origin story or any other tradition, we focus on the most essential core elements that have been consistent throughout the multitude of possible interpretations. Our collaborations over the last several years have grown along with our increasing knowledge about archaeology, language history, and cultural traditions that force us to think in new ways about the past and what all of this information could mean for us today.

According to the Chamorro creation story, the landforms of the Mariana Islands were made from the bodies of the founding ancestral pair of Fu'uña and Puntan, so people everywhere today can appreciate physical reminders of the act of creation that gave them a place and purpose in the world. Every part of the island world owes its existence to the ancestors who sacrificed their own lives to make the world into a livable place for later descendant generations. Richly varied interpretations of the story are remembered today when visiting at Fouha Rock, also known as Creation Rock, near Umatac Bay in southern Guam, and related elements are remembered when viewing other landforms associated with the body parts of Fu'uña and Puntan. Now whenever people work in the land and sea, they repeat the themes of imbuing the physical world with the essence of their labor that will endure for future generations.

Among the numerous ways to interpret the Chamorro creation story, Fu'uña and Puntan may be viewed as representing the first people who came to live in the Mariana Islands. In this view, the name of the female founder, Fu'uña, could be a version of the Chamorro word *fo'na*, meaning "going ahead" or "being first" (Topping et al. 1975: 72), befitting of her role as a primary ancestor in this previously uninhabited place of the Mariana Islands. The founding male figure, Puntan, may have represented a version of the Chamorro word *pontan*, referring to a ripe coconut that has fallen from its tree and has rolled to a new location (Topping et al. 1975: 170) where it will try to establish roots for a new life.

The story of Fu'uña and Puntan reminds us today about the individual people who were responsible for the first inhabitation of the Mariana Islands. We can imagine the hardships that they faced, and we can appreciate the labor that they devoted into shaping the island

DOI: 10.4324/9781003399025-6

world for future generations. Now through examining buried site layers and their contents, we are learning more about what people actually did during this ancient time that made everything else since then into a reality.

By 1500 B.C., if not earlier, in the Marianas, pottery-bearing habitation sites confirm that people lived successfully for the first time in this region of Remote Oceania that required long-distance sea voyaging and new ways of coping with these strange environments where no other people ever had lived previously. These events were occasioned by an ocean-crossing migration of more than 2000 km that set a world record of its time. As outlined in Chapter 5, the next effective settlements of the Remote Oceanic world needed to wait for another few centuries. The earliest Marianas sites have provided windows into an exquisite episode in the human experience of making contact with a truly pristine island environment.

Earliest Marianas sites

Before considering issues about the settlement process and the viability of remote-distance island colonization, the baseline information of earliest Marianas sites needs to be substantiated. Given the importance of the primary datasets, extra details have been included in this second edition of the book. Alternative hypothetical proposals about different dating have been excluded, because they have been contradicted and rejected by the factual evidence.

The material records refer to nine earliest site layers so far known in three islands (see Figure 5.26), each yielding diagnostic early pottery and other materials verified in subsurface cultural layers with radiocarbon dating (Carson 2014a; Carson and Kurashina 2012). The dating clusters around 1500 B.C. for the initial episodes of cultural presence, although naturally the results varied somewhat from one case to another (Figure 6.1). Radiocarbon dating actually is prior to 1500 B.C. at Unai Bapot in Saipan, and a few other sites have produced dating results of potentially earlier age as well. The age of 1500 B.C. may be regarded as the time when people were definitely living in the Mariana Islands, although future research may yet verify slightly older dating.

The radiocarbon results have been scrutinized in terms of

- the raw materials of the dated samples, including direct pairing of short-lived charcoal with specific taxa of *Anadara* sp. shells in multiple contexts for avoiding any inbuilt errors or unpredictability of the results;
- attention to the stratigraphic positions and integrity of referring to specific ancient cultural events within the initial pottery-bearing horizon; and
- ability to refine, corroborate, or constrain a dated range of a layer according to multiple samples within each layer and in directly overlying (postdating) and underlying (predating) stratigraphic positions.

These oldest site layers of the Marianas had been situated in unstable shorelines near the ancient tidal zones of their time prior to 1100 B.C., where the charcoal has been poorly preserved and therefore either unavailable or unreliable for radiocarbon dating. In this case, a marine reservoir correction (ΔR) of -152 ± 58 has been calculated specifically for *Anadara* sp. shells paired with charcoal in multiple secure contexts, thereby establishing a directly measurable and reliable dating and expressly avoiding any potential issues of inbuilt older or younger age in the shells. The direct pairings were from three different contexts at the Ritidian Site in Guam (Carson 2010, 2017a, 2020), another such pairing in

First contact with the Remote Oceanic environment 151

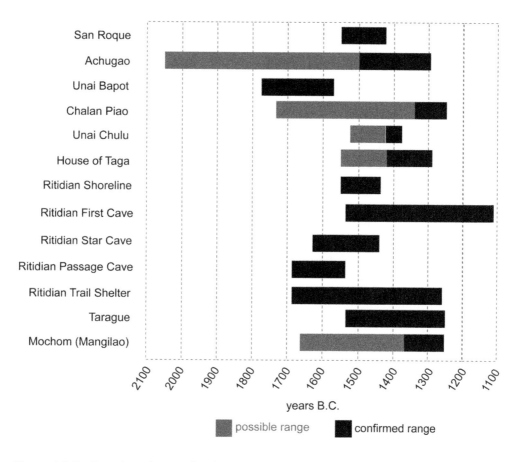

Figure 6.1 Radiocarbon dating of earliest sites in the Mariana Islands. Based on information from Carson (2014a) and updated with new information.

a hearth at Unai Bapot of Saipan (Carson and Hung 2017), and one additional pairing in a hearth at House of Taga in Tinian (Carson and Hung 2022). All of the results overlapped significantly with each other, and they all showed no unexpected isotope ratios or other indicators of anomalies. Currently, this ΔR calculation is among the most robustly proven by independent cross-checking in the Pacific Oceanic region, and the calculation has been updated with the most recent marine curve calibration dataset of Marine20 (Heaton et al. 2020). Also important, the datable *Anadara* sp. shells dominated the ancient food middens as definite cultural materials belonging to the age range of interest.

According to these analytic protocols with the radiocarbon dates, at least nine early sites can be confirmed in the larger southern islands of the Marianas (see Figure 5.26). Each site has revealed at least one distinctive layer, bearing red-slipped pottery and other diagnostic markers of early cultural habitation.

- At Mochom (Mangilao Golf Course) in southern Guam, eight charcoal samples from "Layer IIIg2" were dated as early as 1668–1259 B.C. (Beta-67871) and as late as

1056–809 B.C. (Beta-67874) (Dilli et al. 1998). However, this layer's dating bracket can be constrained by dates from the next superimposed layer at 1200–1000 B.C.

- At Tarague in northern Guam, the lowest pottery-bearing layer was dated by limpet shells (Patellidae) around 1520–1263 B.C. (Beta-4897), referring to an ancient beachfront (Kurashina and Clayshulte 1983; Kurashina et al. 1981).
- At Ritidian (Litekyan) in northern Guam, five distinct localities have produced early dating of a pottery-bearing layer within an ancient shoreline context (Carson 2017a, 2020). First, a deeply buried layer of a habitation area (Paleo-beach habitation) was dated by *Anadara* sp. shell (Beta-253681) at 1605–1165 B.C., referring to the cultural food midden. Within the natural matrix of this earliest cultural layer, short-lived *Halimeda* sp. algal bioclasts (Beta-253682) were dated at 1717–1172 B.C., and Uranium-Thorium dating of the same bioclasts independently confirmed the accuracy of the radiocarbon dating. The date range of this layer was constrained by dates in lower and upper layers, in total pointing to a most likely range of 1535–1439 B.C. for the earliest cultural presence.
- Second at Ritidian, a deep layer outside a ritual cave area (First Cave, also known as "Ritidian Beach Cave") was dated by two *Anadara* sp. shells (Beta-424686 and -433371) and one *Halimeda* sp. bioclast sample (Beta-500161), all overlapping significantly with each other at 1522–1107 B.C.
- Third at Ritidian, another ritual cave (Star Cave, also known as "Ritidian Pictograph Cave") with extensive pictographs revealed a subsurface layer at its overhang exterior, dated by *Ctena* sp. shell (Beta-649290) at 1733–1312 B.C. This date range was refined by dating of *Halimeda* sp. bioclasts in the matrix and other dating from earlier and later layers, pointing to a most likely range at 1621–1440 B.C.
- Fourth at Ritidian, the initial cultural layer at a cave shelter (Passage Cave) did not contain datable material within it, but the next superimposed and later-aged layer was dated by *Gafrarium* sp. shell (Beta-630708) at 1531–1117 B.C. Moreover, the initial cultural layer and the next superimposed layer both corresponded with the layers at the nearby locality of Trail Shelter.
- Fifth at Ritidian, a buried layer at another cave shelter (Trail Shelter) was dated by *Anadara* sp. shell (Beta-630710) at 1691–1271 B.C. and *Tellina* sp. shell (Beta-630711) at 1626–1210 B.C. The stratigraphic layers at this cave shelter correspond with the layers at the nearby Passage Cave, and potentially, the dating of the later-aged layer can provide a constraint on the earliest cultural layer in both cases.
- Inland from the famous House of Taga in Sanhalom of Tinian, the earliest cultural layer was dated by *Anadara* sp. shell (Beta-316283) paired with charcoal (Beta-313866) in a hearth at 1417–1259 B.C. (Carson and Hung 2022). The initial cultural layer can be confirmed as prior to about 1200 B.C., according to dates from the next superimposed layer.
- At Unai Chulu in northern Tinian, one excavation (Craib 1993) recovered four *Anadara* sp. shells from the earliest layer, wherein the oldest three (Beta-6203, -6205, and -6206) overlapped at 1418–1380 B.C., and one other (Beta-6204) was dated as 1297–824 B.C. Another excavation at the same site (Haun et al. 1999) recovered 13 charcoal samples from the lowest pottery-bearing layer, all overlapping with each other, wherein the earliest result was 1517–1045 B.C. (Beta-81947), and the latest result was 1311–970 B.C. (Beta-81949).
- At Chalan Piao in Saipan, Spoehr (1957) obtained a radiocarbon date for oyster shell (Chicago-699) in a position postdating the lower pottery-bearing horizon at

1743–755 B.C., and a later project (Moore et al. 1992) dated charcoal flecks that post-dated the same horizon, including results of 1325–907 B.C. (Beta-33390) and 1696–1255 B.C. (Beta-33391).

- Unai Bapot in Saipan has revealed a set of pottery-bearing layers with remains of post-raised houses and other features, definitively predating 1100 B.C. and extending prior to 1500 B.C. (Carson 2008; Carson and Hung 2017). The most secure stratigraphic contexts of radiocarbon dates have been calibrated at 1787–1385 B.C. (Beta-448701) for the lowest and oldest cultural layer (Layer VII), constrained significantly by the dating from the next superimposed and postdating layer (Layer VI-B) at 1691–1271 B.C. (Beta-461341), at 1786–1334 B.C. (Beta-202722), and at 1941–1466 B.C. (Beta-216616), all overlapping at 1691–1466 B.C. for the range that must have postdated the deeper and older Layer VII.
- At Achugao in northern Saipan, the apparently intermixed sediments of the ancient beachfront produced dates for charcoal at least as old as 1498–1296 B.C. (Beta-36191) and potentially as old as 2053–1503 B.C. (Beta-36190) (Butler 1994, 1995).
- Either nearby or arguably part of the Achugao site in Saipan, within an area known locally as San Roque, charcoal in the ancient pottery-bearing layer was dated at 1539–1425 B.C. (Beta-445267) at 166–179 cm depth, entirely preceding the age of charcoal in a higher stratigraphic position of 136–156 cm, calibrated at 1420–1263 B.C. (Beta-445266) (Dixon et al. in press).

Now with establishing the chronometric dating of the earliest Marianas site layers, this chapter can proceed to consider the ancient shoreline contexts and the range of artifacts, food remains, and other evidence within those contexts.

Ancient inhabited shorelines

The first generations of Mariana Islanders lived at several shoreline-oriented communities, where they found vital freshwater sources, lagoons and reefs with their preferred shellfish and other foods, and nearby island interior terrain and forests. All of the deepest cultural layers occurred during a time of higher sea level prior to 1100 B.C., thereby allowing definition of a large part of the ancient natural setting. Within those contexts, the surviving archaeological evidence has shown that people lived in post-raised houses, created stone bracings around those posts, produced exquisite pottery and other artifacts, harvested diverse foods primarily but not exclusively from the immediate coastal habitats, engaged in rituals or ceremonies at nearby specialized caves, and accessed various inland forest timbers, birds and fruit bats, and clay and rock sources in the island interiors.

The earliest formal residential sites were constrained to the larger southern-arc islands bearing the largest and most diverse natural habitats, biomass, and sources of fresh water. In addition to the streams of southern Guam and southeast Saipan, caves in the limestone terrain enabled collection of ceiling-drip water and collection of water from pools. Cave pools at Ritidian (Litekyan) in Guam were notably slightly higher at 1500 B.C. when the freshwater lens floated above a sea level that was about 1.8 m higher than today's level (Carson 2017b, 2017c). Additionally, the southern islands tend to receive more of the monsoon-pattern rainfall each year than in the farther north latitudes of the Marianas.

Studies of sea-level history have been instrumental in clarifying earliest Marianas settlement (Figure 6.2) because the changing sea level directly affected the shapes and configurations of coastal landforms and ecologies where people potentially could have lived

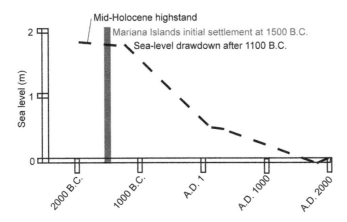

Figure 6.2 Sea-level history in the Marianas region.

(Figure 6.3). The Mariana Islands, like many islands of the tropical Pacific, offer a unique situation for observing ancient tidal notches along coastlines in conjunction with emerged coral reefs that together can provide direct radiocarbon dating associated with measured elevations of former sea level. By coordinating these observations, Kayanne et al. (1993) and then later Dickinson (2000, 2001, 2003) illustrated that sea level was about 1.8 m higher in the Mariana Islands at 3000 through 1100 B.C., followed by a period of drawdown over the next several centuries. The Marianas sea-level history has been verified by deep excavations uncovering ancient corals and lagoon beds in different locations, again with direct dating and measured elevations (Carson 2011, 2014b).

With the sea-level drawdown beginning about 1100 B.C., people no longer could live in the same shoreline niches that had characterized the early Marianas settlement period. Initial signs of change were evident at 1100 B.C., and significantly more pronounced change occurred by 500 B.C., not only in the Marianas but also throughout the inhabited islands of Pacific Oceania, as will be presented in Chapter 8. In immediate practical terms, people adjusted to the changing coastal ecologies, accordingly harvested different kinds of shellfish, began to rely more on inland forest management instead of too narrowly focused on their coastal zones, and shifted their housing into slightly different situations. Meanwhile, people produced less of the finely decorated pottery and shell ornaments and eventually abandoned the crafts entirely.

Scope of artifacts and material findings

While each of the initial settlement sites has provided significant information about the period of 1500–1100 B.C., three sites in particular have been most productive, namely at Unai Bapot in Saipan, at House of Taga in Tinian, and at Ritidan in northern Guam. Unai Bapot has revealed deep cultural layers prior to 1100 B.C. (Carson and Hung 2017), all containing discrete hearths and others features for secure radiocarbon dating extending just prior to 1500 B.C. in the oldest cultural layer (Figure 6.4). So far the largest contiguous hand-excavated investigation uncovered about 90 sq m of an ancient living surface near House of Taga in Tinian (Figure 6.5), thus providing the most information about the ancient material culture assemblage (Carson and Hung 2022). Extensive test pits and a

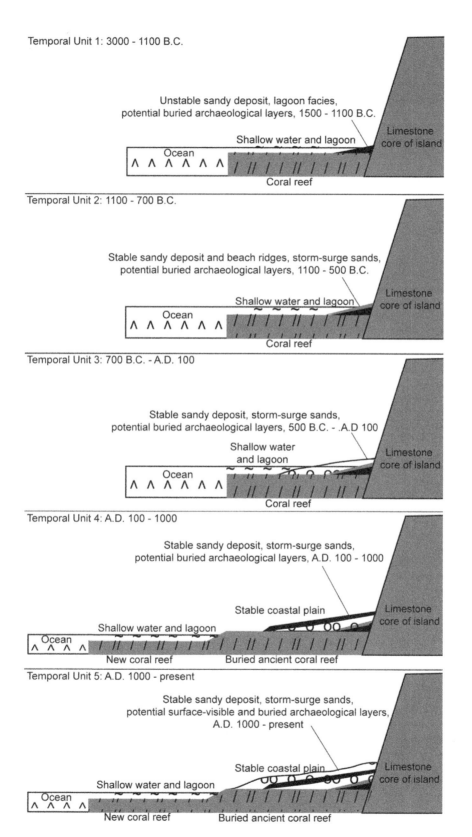

Figure 6.3 Landscape chronology at Ritidian, Guam.

156 *First contact with the Remote Oceanic environment*

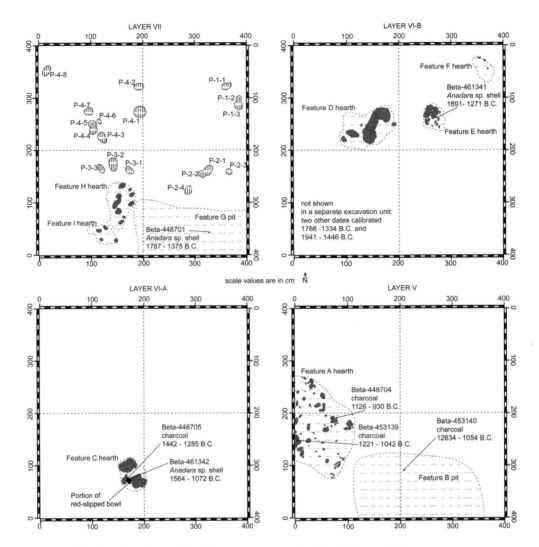

Figure 6.4 Map of earliest cultural layers, excavated at Unai Bapot, Saipan.

few larger blocks of excavations throughout the Ritidian Site in northern Guam have built a cohesive picture of the ancient use of the coastal habitat (Figure 6.6) (Carson 2017a), including a small residential occupation in a shallow subtidal or intertidal zone, recruitment of natural resources from a broad catchment area, ritual contexts at two nearby caves, and access to another two cave shelters (Figure 6.7).

The earliest material culture of the Marianas included the decorated pottery, as noted in Chapter 5, among plentiful undecorated pottery, assorted stone and shell tools, rare bone tools, various shell ornaments, fishing hooks and net weights, large amounts of food refuse dominated by shellfish remains, and instances of housing structural ruins (Figures 6.8 and 6.9). Most of this material appears consistent with a subset of somewhat more diverse findings in the Philippines prior to 1500 B.C., specifically involving a narrowed range of

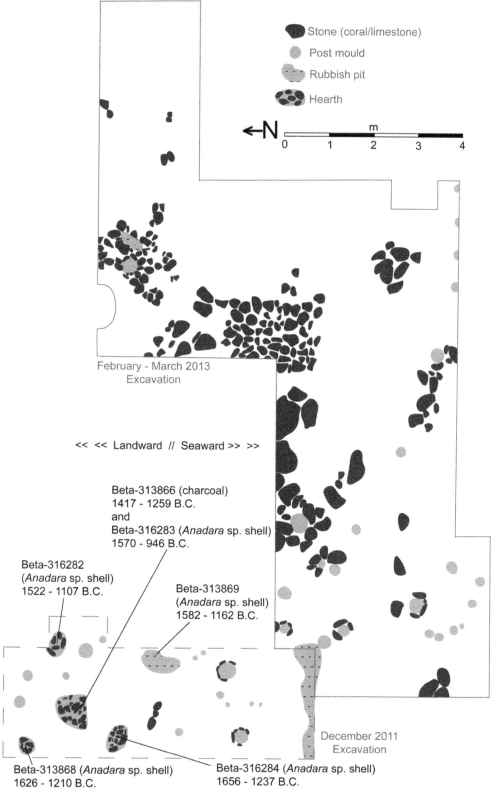

Figure 6.5 Map of earliest cultural layer, excavated near House of Taga, Tinian.

158 *First contact with the Remote Oceanic environment*

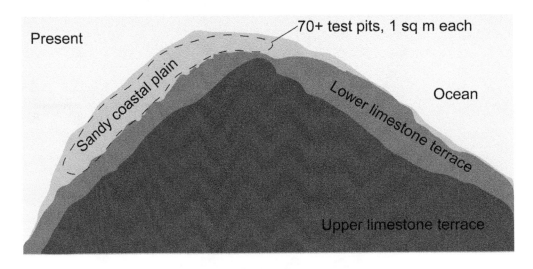
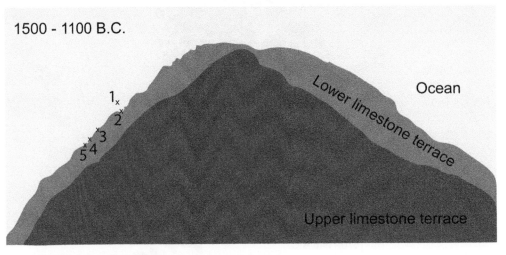
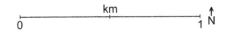

1 = Paleo-shore habitation, excavated 2 sq m
2 = First Cave, excavated 9 sq m
3 = Star Cave, excavated 11 sq m
4 = Passage Cave, excavated 1 sq m
5 = Trail Shelter, excavated 1 sq m

Figure 6.6 Excavation survey at Ritidian, Guam, targeting area of potential earliest coastal settlement.

contexts in seashore habitats of the Marianas. Some of the shell ornaments may suggest farther links with coastal communities in eastern Taiwan, hinting at a larger interconnected homeland geography and the mobility of ocean-crossing people. A few characteristics appear to be local inventions uniquely within the Marianas environment, such as the

First contact with the Remote Oceanic environment 159

Figure 6.7 Map of early versus modern landscape conditions at Ritidian, Guam.

cut and drilled shell portions of compound-piece octopus lure riggings that so far have been the oldest such artifacts known in the world at 1500 B.C. (Carson and Hung 2021).

While the distinctive decorations on the earliest Marianas pottery point very certainly to ancestral traditions in the northern through central Philippines, other characteristics reveal how Marianas pottery-making developed as an isolated bottlenecked offshoot. The Marianas pottery was rather small as compared to contemporaries and predecessors in the Philippines and in Taiwan, generally 15–20 cm in diameter and in some cases even smaller. The small size allowed for an option of extremely thin-walled pottery (Figure 6.10), about 1 mm thickness, as one of the localized variants in the Marianas, and so far not known elsewhere. In addition to the super-thin red-slipped pottery, another unique localized expression was a form of paddle-impressed pottery made with a vine-wrapped or rattan-wrapped paddle, while another option of using a carved paddle could be linked with rare examples in the Philippines (see Figure 5.31). Rare instances of black and red painted pottery can be recognized as different from the usual red slip (Figure 6.11), not yet verified in the Philippines and possibly suggesting a specialized crafting group or context.

In terms of the vessel forms, the Marianas collections displayed very little or no usage of lids, foot rings, and handles that had been fairly popular in the Philippines and in Taiwan. The Marianas pottery was made with alternatives of flat or rounded bottoms, without a foot ring or pedestal except in just two rare fragments (see Figure 5.32). Although occurring in fair quantity in the Mariana Islands, flat-bottomed bowls and platters were rare in other areas where instead foot rings and pedestals were more popular. Similarly, only three handle pieces have been recovered from these earliest cultural layers in the Marianas (see Figure 5.32).

Baked clay at this early time was used exclusively for pottery, unlike the more popular use of baked clay in East and Southeast Asia for making spindle whorls, varied forms of net weights, ear ornaments, and other items. A few rare baked-clay objects have been found in much later-aged site layers, postdating about A.D. 1000, including large sizes of net weights and sling stones. Otherwise, the Marianas early site layers so far have not shown any evidence of the traditions of using baked clay for other products that were known in East and Southeast Asia.

160 *First contact with the Remote Oceanic environment*

Figure 6.8 Examples of earliest decorated Marianas pottery, 1500–1100 B.C., excavated from Unai Bapot, Saipan.

Pottery fragments of portable stoves have not been found at any site of any time period in the Marianas, perhaps curious given the role of such stoves among sea nomads and in the kinds of cultural associations that may have been involved in remote-distance Marianas settlement. The age of Marianas settlement at 1500 B.C., however, preceded the popularity of the baked-clay stoves in Island Southeast Asia after 500 B.C. These kinds of stoves still are used today, and they have been documented in use by the Bajau Laut and other sea nomads (Sather 1985). No such stoves are known in the islands of Pacific Oceania, so the tradition seems to have been limited to portions of Island Southeast Asia and most likely postdating the departure of people moving into the Remote Oceanic islands.

The early-period Marianas artifacts, of course, included much more than pieces of broken pottery vessels (see Figure 6.9). Bone was used only very rarely for producing

First contact with the Remote Oceanic environment 161

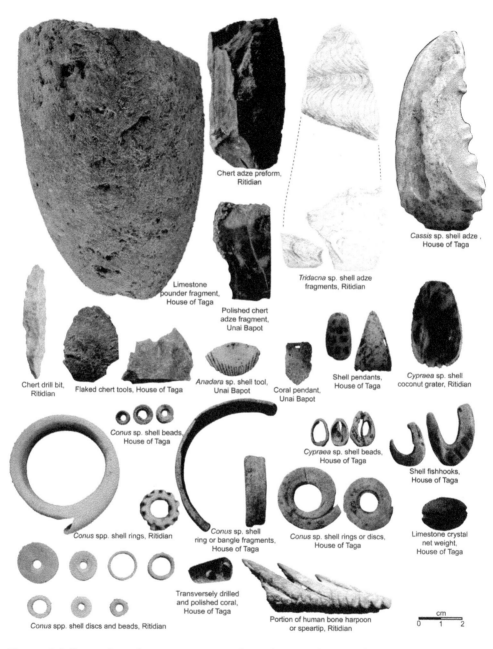

Figure 6.9 Examples of non-pottery artifacts from early-period Marianas sites, 1500–1100 B.C.

points, and so far just one extraordinary example has been found of a carved harpoon piece, although human bone was used more frequently in later periods. Stone artifacts included limestone cobbles fashioned into heavy pounders, chert used for varied flaked tools and sometimes polished into adzes, and volcanic rock made into scrapers and other tools. Volcanic stone later became more popular for producing adzes and other

162 *First contact with the Remote Oceanic environment*

Figure 6.10 Examples of "Marianas super-thin" pottery tradition, 1500–1100 B.C., at Ritidian, Guam.

Figure 6.11 Example of red and black painted pottery, 1500–1100 B.C., at Ritidian, Guam.

tools, but chert and other materials were preferred for making adzes during the earliest centuries in the Marianas. Shells of the giant clam, *Tridacna* sp., were convenient as adze-making material during all periods. Other shells with shiny nacreous surfaces were favored for making fishing hooks. A single adze in the Marianas has been identified as made of *Cassis cornuta* shell, whereas this particular kind of shell was quite popular in

First contact with the Remote Oceanic environment 163

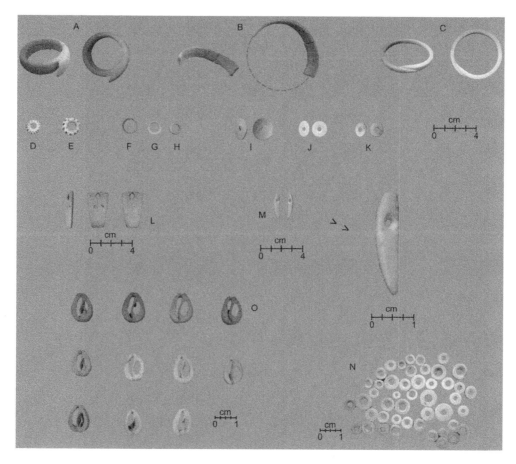

Figure 6.12 Early-period Marianas body ornaments, 1500–1100 B.C., excavated from Ritidian in Guam. A and B: shell bands. C: shell circlet. D and E: thick shell discs. F, G, H: small shell rings. I, J, K: thin shell discs. L: shell pendant. M: pendant of modified tooth of dolphin. N: small round shell beads. O: *Cypraea* sp. shell beads.

parts of Indonesia and Micronesia many centuries later and generally postdating A.D. 100. Assorted shells were chosen for making beads, discs, and pendants through cutting and polishing, often with labor-intensive work for the numbers of individual shells that would be required.

The oldest shell ornaments displayed forms and styles that did not last for more than a few centuries in the Marianas, much like seen in the finely made pottery decorations that were not sustained after 1100 B.C. (Figure 6.12). Tiny pieces of *Conus* sp. shells (and possibly other shell taxa such as *Tridacna* sp., not yet authenticated) were cut and polished and made in large quantities as suitable for producing necklaces, skirts, and leg coverings, as have been documented historically among Taiwan's aboriginal Austronesian tribes (Figure 6.13). These tiny beads became much less popular after 1100 B.C. but were produced in smaller numbers through as late as 500 B.C. Small *Cypraea* sp. shells, more tightly constrained in time and definitely before 1100 B.C., were cut and polished into beads that so far have not been identified outside the Mariana Islands.

164 *First contact with the Remote Oceanic environment*

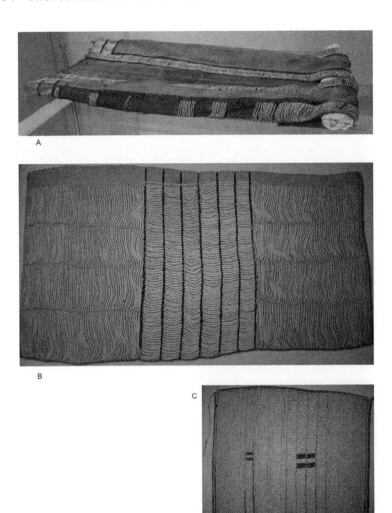

Figure 6.13 Ethnographic examples from Taiwan, showing garments with elements of small cut and polished shell beads. A: robe on display in the Sheng Yue Museum, Taiwan. B: skirt in collection of the Taiwan National Museum of Prehistory. C: leg wrapping in collection of the Taiwan National Museum of Prehistory.

Other overseas similarities are seen in the many discs and rings that were exhibited in head gear, ear lobe plugs, belts, or shoulder straps (Figures 6.14 and 6.15). Unique pendants have been recovered, most likely belonging to specific people and expressing individuality as compared to the other shell ornaments that resemble more broadly shared group-membership values.

The shell ornament inventories were present in variable quantities at most of the early-period habitation sites, but they appeared in impressively high concentration at the entrance of the Ritidian Beach Cave (Figure 6.16), interpreted as a place of specialized ceremony or ritual at 1500–1100 B.C. (Carson 2017b, 2017c). In this context, the shell ornaments may have been ritual offerings or somehow involved in the specialized activities at this location. The unique context is evident in a set of small ash-filled pits (Figure 6.17), each sealed by

First contact with the Remote Oceanic environment 165

Figure 6.14 Ethnographic examples from Taiwan, showing elements of shell discs and beads in head dressing. Photograph from approximately 1920–1935, in collection of the Taiwan National Museum of Prehistory.

large shells (Figure 6.18) and containing rare items such as the noted shell ornaments, a piece of carved human bone, other human bone points, unusually dense occurrence of decorated pottery, extremely rare pottery forms, yellow and red pigment nodules, and a fragment of cremated human bone with residue of red ochre dust (Figure 6.19; see also Figures 6.9 and 6.12). Additional such items were found in the general cultural layer, not just within the defined ash pits, along with unusual compositions of shellfish remains unlike the expectations of a regular habitation site.

The early-period shell ornaments may be understood as most likely related to ceremonial regalia reserved for special occasions. These traditions were short-lived, as none of these specialized items continued in the Marianas some centuries later. The older shell finery objects evidently declined in popularity by 1100 B.C. and disappeared altogether by 500 B.C., perhaps due to a change in the associated cultural traditions that were not sustained through larger transformations in the natural environment and social setting (discussed in detail in Chapter 8).

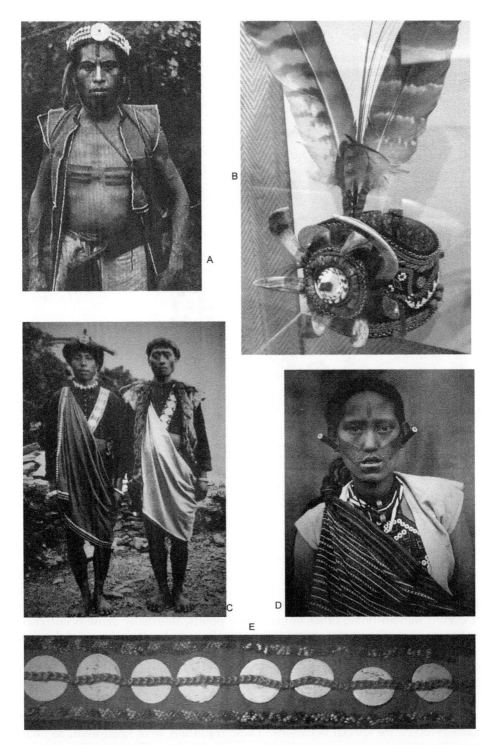

Figure 6.15 Ethnographic examples from Taiwan, showing elements of shell discs and beads in shoulder straps, necklaces, and other accessories. A, C, and D are from approximately 1920–1935, in collection of the Taiwan National Museum of Prehistory. B is a head dress on display at the Sheng-yue Museum in Taiwan. E is a shoulder strap in collection of the Taiwan National Museum of Prehistory.

First contact with the Remote Oceanic environment 167

Figure 6.16 View of excavation at overhang exterior of Ritidian Beach Cave, Guam, during 2016 excavation. Scale bars are in 20 cm increments.

168 First contact with the Remote Oceanic environment

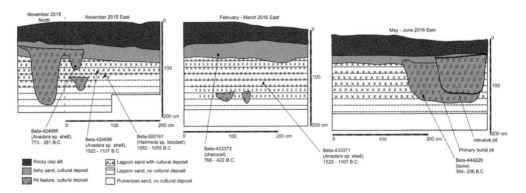

Figure 6.17 Stratigraphy and dating at Ritidian Beach Cave, Guam. Graphic is based on documentation by Carson (2017a, 2017b, 2017c).

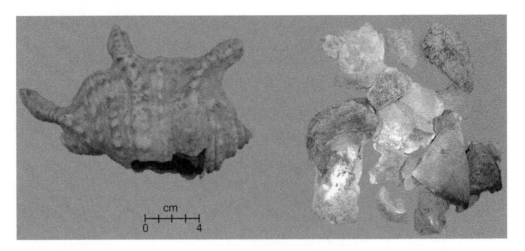

Figure 6.18 Shell pit-sealing items at Ritidian Beach Cave, Guam. Scale bars are in 1 cm increments.

Historically, no woven-fabric clothing at all was reported in the Marianas, other than scant coverings and hats. Moreover, no spindle whorls or bark cloth beaters ever have been reported in the Marianas, so these two most frequent indicators of clothing production in Southeast Asia were curiously not parts of the Marianas cultural repertoire. In this case, the early-period shell finery most likely had been strung or woven into sennit, plaited mats, vines, rattan, or other plant fiber products.

The Mariana Islands evidently were outside the reach of the ocean-crossing trade networks that operated in Island Southeast Asia. Although remote-distance contacts probably occurred as rare events periodically, they did not involve the routine or repeated regularities of trade and communications networks seen farther to the west. In particular, specialized ornaments made of Taiwan nephrite (jade) were entirely unknown in the Marianas, although they were quite popular in many coastal sites of the Philippines at least as early as 1500 B.C. (Hung et al. 2007). Other precious greenstone sources, such as muscovite, were quarried in the Philippines and elsewhere to produce similar decorative objects as made of the Taiwan nephrite, but again none of these items were transferred to

First contact with the Remote Oceanic environment 169

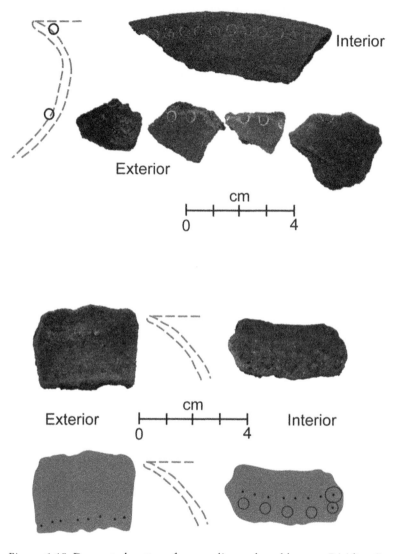

Figure 6.19 Decorated pottery from earliest cultural layer at Ritidian Beach Cave, Guam.

the Marianas. Indeed, the various ear pendants and rings known in Taiwan and Island Southeast Asia were never produced in the Marianas in any kind of material. Other shell beads and discs, as already noted, resembled the objects of special-use traditions that endured all the way through historical times in Taiwan and possibly shared with coastal communities in the Philippines not yet well known archaeologically, but these traditions were abandoned shortly after the first few centuries of settlement in the Mariana Islands.

Characteristics of the inhabited setting

During the first centuries of Marianas settlement, several communities lived independently from their overseas homeland and thus developed their own unique cultural expressions in the context of seashore-oriented lifestyle in the world's most remote inhabited islands of their time. Somewhat different seashore niches were inhabited about 1500 B.C. in a few sites known in the islands of Ludao and Lanyu, off the east coast of Taiwan, with preference for sandy-fringed embayments at the base of hillslopes, but these settings did not incorporate the specifically defined shallow-water habitats as preferred in the Marianas at that time. A larger scale of a sandy beach embayment seems to have been inhabited at the Dimolit Site of Palanan Bay in eastern Luzon (Peterson 1974), but overall not enough yet is known from the paleo-seashore settings in the Philippines prior to 1500 B.C. that might offer relevant parallels with the oldest Marianas habitations.

In the known Marianas early sites, people lived at the limited available scattered patches of beaches with immediate access to shallow-water nearshore resource zones, managed forest lands, and sources of fresh water. Post molds at both Unai Bapot and House of Taga have revealed post-raised houses close to the ancient tidal zone. The findings at House of Taga have revealed that the wooden posts were braced by stones and associated with artificial stonework surfaces that supported areas for cooking, toolmaking and maintenance, and other activities (Carson and Hung 2022). At all of the oldest sites, clamshells of *Anadara* sp. provided the major source of protein, augmented by chitons, limpets, sea urchin, and other shellfish taxa. In terms of essential nutrition of starchy foods, people needed to rely on various trees and root-tubers available naturally and through cultural management of the island forest ecosystems.

Given the remote coastal habitation contexts of the earliest Marianas sites at 1500–1100 B.C., the overall land-use and resource-use patterns accordingly reflected strong emphasis on nearshore habitats, with infrequent but greatly important access to other zones that should not be underestimated. Among the defining characteristics of this early period, the residential sites were surrounded by extensive uninhabited spaces that were available as social buffers and as resource supplements, both at land and at sea. People definitely were clearing and burning some areas of inland forests, resulting in layers of charcoal flecking and disturbance preserved in sedimentary records at the bottoms of lakes and swamps (Athens and Ward 2004; Athens et al. 2004). At the same time, people must have explored the islands extensively in order to find the best clay deposits for making pottery, as well as sources of chert and other stones for making adzes and flaked tools.

Limited numbers of small communities maintained nearshore residential patterns close to their primary resources, augmented by traditions of managed forests and supplemental resource zones at variable distance from the residential locales. Entire islands of the northern-arc group of the Marianas were uninhabited until perhaps A.D. 1000, although they were available for periodic access to forest trees, birds, fruit bats, turtles, and other resources. In theory, these same islands could offer refuge for birds and other animals that otherwise might have been depopulated by the sudden impact of hunting, trapping, and disturbance of native forest habitats. Accordingly, the first ever instance of Remote Oceanic settlement in the Marianas may not have involved the profound and irreversible impacts of deforestation and faunal extinctions brought by the Lapita infiltrations into Southern Melanesia and West Polynesia (Chapter 7). Additionally, the first Marianas settlers did not transport any of the domesticated animals such as pigs, dogs, and chickens that were important for Lapita settlers, so these factors did not affect the Mariana Islands ecologies. Even the seemingly inevitable stowaway rats were excluded from the Marianas until much later, close to A.D. 1000 (Wickler 2004).

At least a few plants were transported into the Marianas, and people certainly were clearing inland forests to prepare for their cultural management of the island habitats. An obvious human impact horizon has been preserved in lake-bottom and swamp-bottom coring records in Guam, Tinian, and Saipan (Athens and Ward 2004, 2006; Athens et al. 2004), where charcoal flecking indicates forest burning at 1500 B.C. but possibly slightly older. Within the sedimentary layer of initial human impact, pollens of both betelnut palms (*Areca catechu*) and ironwood trees (*Casuarina equisetifolia*) appeared for the first time, so at least these two plants were introduced as part of the first human settlement of the islands. Notably, the betelnut was essential for the nut's value as a key ingredient in chewing a narcotic quid (Figure 6.20), and ironwood was valued for its hard and dense wood. If people imported these taxa that were extraneous to basic food requirements, then they likely imported other items.

While the coring records consistently reveal a human impact horizon, unfortunately, the preserved pollen grains and charcoal flecks were not dated directly, so the only available radiocarbon dates have been reported for shells and other materials within the associated sedimentary units. In some cases, the dating results contradicted their stratigraphic positions in the coring columns, but overall they verified long spans of time for each sedimentary unit (Figure 6.21). When accounting for intermixture of material within each sedimentary unit as a whole, the dating results must be regarded cautiously as referring to the extended periods of a sedimentary unit's accumulation. In the coring records from Laguas in Guam (Athens and Ward 1999) and from Susupe in Saipan (Athens and Ward

Figure 6.20 Betelnut quid offering at Ritidian Beach Cave, Guam. Offering was part of ceremony for the site's ancestors, led by Jeremy Cepeda, May 2016.

172 *First contact with the Remote Oceanic environment*

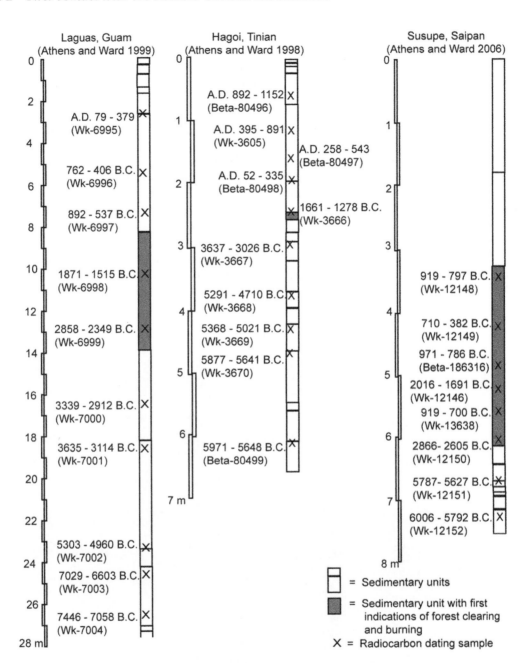

Figure 6.21 Paleoenvironmental coring profiles from the Mariana Islands.

2006), the impact horizons are the most ambiguously defined within unusually thick sedimentary units (more than 6 m thick at Laguas and about 2.5 m thick at Susupe), and accordingly, the radiocarbon dates are the most widely diffuse and with stratigraphic incongruities, potentially as old as 2800 B.C. or as young as 900 B.C. By comparison, the coring record from Hagoi in Tinian (Athens and Ward 1998) reveals an impact horizon within a thin sedimentary unit (less than 50 cm in thickness) dated at 1661–1278 B.C. and reasonably matched with archaeological dating of first human settlement at 1500 B.C.

Edible plant foods in the Marianas included some naturally available taxa, as well as others that must have been introduced from overseas, although the hard evidence is not yet verified through preserved ancient botanical remains in securely dated contexts. The endemic seeded breadfruit (*Artocarpus mariannensis*) biologically did not exist outside the Mariana Islands, except perhaps in Palau, until later when it was transported by people and hybridized with the seedless species (*Artocarpus altilis*) eventually distributed widely across Micronesia (Zerega et al. 2004, 2006). The natural presence of such nutritious and high-yield trees like the seeded breadfruit in the Marianas may have enabled the first settlers to survive, while the seedless breadfruit trees may have needed some time to be nurtured into healthy producers after being transported from overseas. Additional naturally existing trees with edible products included cycads, such as the *fadang* (Frederico palm or *Cycas micronesica*), among others. Certain seaweeds likely were eaten, although they have been so far unidentifiable in the archaeological layers. While the botanical origins still are murky, perhaps a few varieties of thorny-vined yams and wild elephant-ear taro may have existed naturally in the islands, but most of the preferred root-tuber crops must have been imported deliberately. Bananas certainly were carried by people.

Most of the edible plant foods were suitable for low-labor management of forests and gardens, but curiously, rice may have been grown in a limited fashion that would have required a different mode of land management. Chamorro traditions consistently refer to rice as a rare item used only in special circumstances, and it contributed only minimally to the local diet. Although its primary role was non-dietary, rice had been attested historically during the 1600s, and linguistically it is attributed to an archaic Malayo-Polynesian source implying a deep cultural value in the Marianas.

Ancient landforms of the Marianas did not include extensive coastal lowlands or riverside terraces that would have been suitable for wetland rice cultivation (Figure 6.22), and no rice field structures are known of any time period prior to the A.D. 1900s. Indeed, no agricultural field systems of any kind are known in the Marianas at all in premodern contexts, and instead the traditional systems of food production must have involved low-labor strategies of managed forests and ecosystems. Arboriculture and horticulture may have been spatially extensive, but they did not constitute labor-intensive or formalized structured systems. Rice may have been grown in small plots of a few sq m size, but these activities never resulted in transformations of the landscape and island ecologies as has been the case in rice-farming lands of East and Southeast Asia. Perhaps only a few people grew rice, whereas almost every household needed to attend to horticultural gardens, orchards, and forests with varying degrees of management, again without creating permanent structural alterations.

Earliest Marianas settlement involved more than just the practicalities of where to live and how to obtain food, and, in fact, aspects of ritual ceremony can be traced in the oldest sites. While living in their shoreline habitations at 1500 B.C., people accessed nearby limestone caves that were just slightly above sea level at that time, likely for obtaining fresh water but also probably for ritual purposes (Carson 2017b, 2017c). Where the oldest cave records have been documented at Ritidian in Guam, the deepest dark-zone interiors were kept clean at the elevations and positions that would have held freshwater pools prior to 1100 B.C., while the outer twilight chambers and exterior light-zone overhang sheltered areas were used for specialized activities. Food refuse at the caves was notably different than in the nearby habitation area at Ritidian, including little or no *Anadara* sp.

174 *First contact with the Remote Oceanic environment*

A. Modern conditions

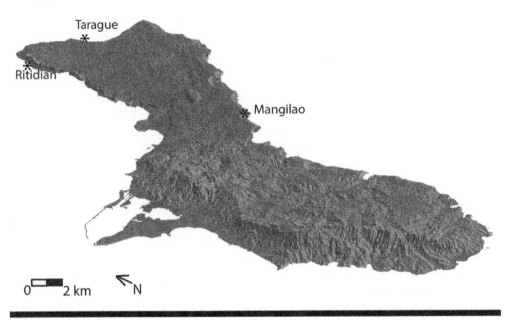

B. 1500–1000 B.C. conditions

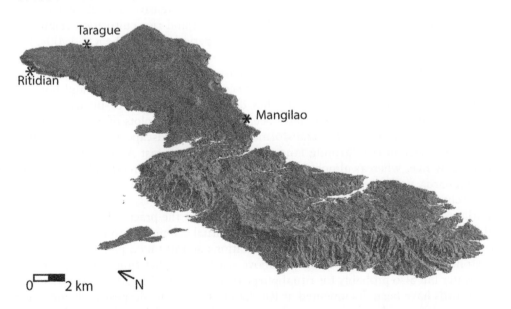

Figure 6.22 Island-wide landscape of Guam, showing ancient versus modern conditions. Graphic is based on information from Carson (2011) and updated.

clamshells that ordinarily dominated at the residential habitation middens of the oldest time periods. The pottery and other artifacts were different as well, including extremely rare and unusual items, overall suggesting that people recognized the caves as significantly different venues than their shoreline-oriented habitations.

The Ritidian caves contain pictographs made in bright red, dull reddish brown, black, and white pigments that were produced in multiple time periods, potentially including a few rock art panels from the earliest settlement period of 1500–1100 B.C. Direct dating has not yet been attempted due to concerns of physical preservation and cultural sensitivity at the site, but the archaeological layers at the exterior overhangs of Ritidian Beach Cave (also called "First Cave") and Pictograph Cave (also called "Star Cave") both have confirmed specialized activities with rare objects ever since 1500 B.C. Relative chronological ordering is evident in superimposed layering of white-pigment figures overlaying the bright red (Figure 6.23), so the white figures may be interpreted as most likely postdating the earliest settlement period.

Potentially, the oldest rock art at Ritidian appears to be constrained to the black-pigment figures (Figure 6.24). At the Ritidian Beach Cave, black-pigment figures were the only rock art at all. At both the Beach Cave and Pictograph Cave, black-pigment motifs were drawn only above head level and requiring stepping on portions of cave walls or stalagmite formations to extend an arm's reach, and they depicted human shapes, distorted human shapes, or other unknown images. Furthermore, the black-pigment figures are the only examples of rock art at Ritidian found exclusively within the dark zones, linked with the otherworldly settings of these caves, whereas all other rock art panels were drawn in twilight zones of more ordinary access or transitional context.

Figure 6.23 Rock art in the Ritidian Pictograph Cave, showing white-pigment elements overlaying older red-pigment handprints.

Figure 6.24 Rare black-pigment rock art panels at Ritidian, Guam. Scale bars are in 20 cm increments.

This greatly abbreviated introduction to earliest Marianas sites opens a door toward answering at least three research questions of broad-reaching impact.

- First, what cultural actions were involved in the process of the world's first rendering of Remote Oceania into an inhabited landscape and seascape?
- Second, what made the Marianas case successful as a viable remote island settlement for the first time in human history?
- Third, how can the early-period Marianas settlement be situated in a larger Asia-Pacific context?

Migration and settlement process

In the case of Remote Oceanic settlement in the Mariana Islands, an overseas migration must have occurred, and the archaeological evidence points to a timing of 1500 B.C. with connections to a homeland in Island Southeast Asia. While the precise motivations for this remote-distance migration cannot be known today, certainly it did occur, and the archaeological records of the Marianas and cross-regionally reveal the factual context of whatever had happened in order to make the migration possible. Circumstances likely differed for each person or group involved in a migration, much like what can be observed today among people who migrate for greatly mixed reasons of push and pull factors, ways of making the journey, and degree of success in establishing a new life or lifestyle.

Rather than speculate wildly about the motivations of ancient sea-crossing migrants more than 3000 years ago, a theoretical framework can be brought to bear on the issues of island settlement process. The process involved an awareness of islands across the ocean, availability of sailing technology and navigational knowledge, motivation and capability to make a journey, and ability to live successfully in an isolated setting for the first time. Each of these factors can be studied in detail independently, but the settlement process as a whole can be understood most productively as a unison of its interrelated components. Most archaeological evidence refers to the material results after an island already was populated effectively by a founding group, necessarily postdating the actual settlement process, so archaeology in itself may not be effective in learning about the settlement process.

Before considering how people managed to live successfully in the Remote Oceanic setting of the Marianas, the mechanisms of the migration process need to be outlined. In this view, the migration process preceded and partly overlapped with the settlement process. In other words, making the sea-crossing voyage was one major achievement, and then the successful establishment of a viable community in the Marianas was another such achievement involving a different set of skills, circumstances, and material signature.

In general terms, any migration may be understood as a multicomponent process made possible by coordinating three factors.

- First, a homeland must be recognized not only as a home but rather as a place that can be exited, possibly with no future return.
- Second, a conduit of travel, such as the ocean in the case of the Marianas settlement, must be perceived not only as a resource zone or type of barrier, but rather it must be perceived as an effective means of transportation whose implied barriers can be crossed.
- Third, notions of a faraway land need to be transformed to accommodate thoughts of living successfully in this place.

The three essential components of a migration can be regarded as cognitive transformations, effectively activating a homeland, gateway, and receiver in unison. These elements always existed, but they became transformed from inert to active modes analogous to the mode-switching of semiconductors. An aptly named semiconductor theory in migration (Carson and Hung 2014) clarifies the mechanisms of how a migration has occurred as the basis to explore the varied explanations of why it may have happened.

Exiting a homeland may seem contradictory to most notions of sedentary lifestyle of Neolithic societies that lived in structured village communities, produced their food with a degree of formality more than hunting-gathering, modified their surrounding environments, and created pottery and other artifacts typical of investing in long-term residence. Nevertheless, seafaring traditions throughout Island Southeast Asia and Pacific Oceania obviate that mobility was a fact of life for many people exiting their homes periodically but usually returning or at least maintaining some kind of contact. For those who exited permanently, the archaeological evidence shows that they enacted much the same mode of residential habitation and land-use systems as in their homeland range, but the Marianas case indicates a highly specialized mode of seashore-oriented lifestyle that necessarily involved more mobility than would be practiced by inland-dwelling groups.

Remote ocean-crossing to the Marianas may be viewed as a form of inhabiting the seascape or as embracing a growing sense of a sea of islands. In this view, people cognitively transformed their perception of the ocean not only as a highway to be crossed but also to be incorporated into active living. The ocean still retained its qualities of acting as a set of resource zones, and barriers or borders still could be recognized between resource zones and cultural territories. Under certain circumstances, those implied barriers could be crossed, as indeed such crossing would have been necessary in order to reach the Mariana Islands or any other Remote Oceanic island group. As people learned more about their surrounding oceans, longer ocean-crossing voyages became increasingly possible.

Realistically, a migration cannot occur unless people first can clarify a concept of where they will go to live, possibly based at first on vague notions of a faraway land, but eventually this overseas place must be recognized as a suitable new home. This kind of knowledge must have existed before people could organize a long-distance migration at sea for a few weeks from Island Southeast Asia to the Mariana Islands, furthermore bringing sufficient men, women, and supplies for a viable settlement. In this case, advance scouting knowledge most likely was reported by seafaring individuals who first sighted the islands as a compelling "proof of concept" prior to the actual first migration of a fully viable population into the Marianas.

In order to support a successful migration, all three transformative aspects needed to be activated in unison, yet they were not necessarily driven by the same motivations. They may have developed at different times and for unrelated reasons. Moreover, they may have been configured differently for separate individuals or groups of people who eventually settled in the same island region.

Instead of seeking a one-size-fits-all explanation, every instance of a migration can be viewed more realistically as bringing several different individuals into a shared experience. In the case of first Marianas settlement, the individual migrants must have included diverse men and women, possibly coming from different villages. The migrating group as a whole included people from varied backgrounds, possessing enough skills and knowledge to manage the ocean-crossing voyage and then to enact a sustainable settlement in a remote island setting.

Despite the differences of individual people within the initial founding population, the archaeological evidence reveals a coherence of the material culture inventory in each of the earliest Marianas habitation sites at 1500 B.C., such that the migrants must have shared a significant amount of cultural practice and tradition. The sharing of highly distinctive traits, such as the dentate-stamped red-slipped pottery with white lime infilling, is most remarkable for having been distributed among communities living over a broad geography of Island Southeast Asia and then in the Mariana Islands by 1500 B.C., thus reflecting a cultural context that transcended diverse settings. The commonality of cultural traits in these diverse settings may have been stressed through community assembly events likely involving the rare objects of finely decorated pottery and shell finery in special-occasion contexts. These issues may have been most important for group identity and cohesion during the earliest settlement period in the Marianas or any other area, but the meaning clearly changed after some centuries.

Successful settlement and viability

The early-period Marianas sites prove that people successfully established a viable community in the Remote Oceanic environment at 1500 B.C. involving adaptations that no other human beings had made until this time. The viability of the community can be understood as biological in terms of producing new generations of people, but it also was cultural in terms of enabling social functioning. At least a few hundred people can be estimated in total for the earliest-known sites, evidently with enough women to give birth to new descendant generations. Among those people, the specific individuals possessed the sets of skills and knowledge as attested in the material record of house-building, pottery-making, tool production, securing food resources, cooking, and managing the native forest composition. Some individuals may have been responsible for the social factors that are not directly visible in the archaeological record, such as for maintaining social order, resolving conflicts, keeping track of history, and more.

Settlement in the Marianas at 1500 B.C. succeeded under unique circumstances, some centuries prior to settlement in any other part of Remote Oceania, and in a significantly more isolated place at more than 2000 km from the nearest potential homeland. The Marianas case brought people into one set of islands, unlike the geographically widespread dispersal into multiple island groups and archipelagos as seen later in the Lapita-associated movement into Southern Melanesia and West Polynesia. Also different from the Lapita case, the earliest Marianas settlement involved a low degree of anthropogenic impact and transformation of the island environment, thus lacking the severity of impacts that otherwise might be expected of Remote Oceanic settlement.

The uniqueness of the Marianas case resulted from at least three factors.

- First, the record-setting voyage beyond 2000 km must have involved unprecedented navigational knowledge, sailing skill, and endurance of voyaging at sea for a few weeks before reaching the Mariana Islands, and then additional innovative skills were needed for living in greater isolation than had been known before this time.
- Second, the unbroken chronological record of a sustained population in the Marianas obviates that most people actually stayed in the islands multi-generationally, although most probably a few people continued to make overseas journeys and contacts occasionally, and indeed the Marianas archaeological record shows little or no

influence from external sources other than the essential contribution of the founding population.
- Third, the earliest settlement sites appeared in several locations of separate islands, but they were constrained to a narrowly defined seashore niches in the larger southern islands, with little or no direct ecological impacts enacted by small groups of people who only occasionally accessed the large expanses of uninhabited territories and the smaller northern islands.

Marianas settlement at 1500 B.C. reflects a movement of people seeking specific types of coastal habitats, and they found such places at the shores of remote overseas islands of the Marianas. Similar seashore habitats certainly existed in the Philippines and in Island Southeast Asia generally, but evidently, one group of people chose to make an extraordinary long-distance voyage to live in the particular seashore niches of the Mariana Islands. In this sense, earliest Marianas settlement sites may be viewed as constituting a faraway and isolated extension of the larger groups of people living in more diverse contexts of Island Southeast Asia prior to 1500 B.C. and specifically referring to a subset of ancient seashore-oriented contexts.

Situating earliest Marianas settlement in the Asia-Pacific region

At 1500 B.C., few options existed that could have been a potential homeland of the first Marianas settlers who made the distinctive forms of decorated pottery and shell ornaments while living in specifically targeted seashore niches. The only known sites bearing this diagnostic pottery tradition prior to 1500 B.C. so far have been identified in the northern through central Philippines. Some of the shell ornaments may be linked with a broader range including coastal Taiwan, but the relevant areas of ancient seashore habitats in the Philippines have not yet been explored sufficiently to evaluate how well the Marianas findings might be matched with such sites. At present, the artifact inventories from riverside areas such as in the Cagayan Valley of Luzon of the Philippines have provided the best dating and definition of the ancestral pottery-making and other traditions prior to Marianas settlement, traceable here as early as 1800–1600 B.C., soon thereafter found in a number of other areas by 1500 B.C. (Chapter 5).

In terms of seeking potential beachfront homeland parallels in the Philippines, limited pottery-bearing sites have been reported in coastal or near-coastal areas potentially predating 1500 B.C. at the Tabon Caves in Palawan (Fox 1970), the Batungan Caves in Masbate (Solheim 1955, 1968), Sanga Sanga Rockshelter in the Sulu Archipelago (Spoehr 1973), and the Dimolit Site in eastern Luzon (Peterson 1974). All of these cases have produced ambiguous dating, and the contexts of the archaeological materials are questionable. As best as can be ascertained, the coastal-adapted materials at these sites with potential Marianas parallels include the use of giant clam *Tridacna* sp. shells for making polished adzes, using tops of *Conus* spp. shells as pieces in personal adornments, and using *Anadara* sp. clamshells as containers for holding slaked lime. Additionally, house structural remains at Dimolit indicate a stilt-raised house with a bordering fenceline.

The timing of Marianas settlement at 1500 B.C. coincided with an apparent spread of the pottery horizon into multiple parts of the Philippines and a few parts of Indonesia, as reviewed in Chapter 5. So far the definitive decorated pottery tradition as seen in the Marianas has been clarified prior to 1500 B.C. only in the northern through central Philippines, specifically involving red-slipped pottery with finely dentate-stamped, circle-stamped, and line-incised decorations highlighted by white lime infilling. Red-slipped pottery without the fine decorations has been confirmed in parts of Indonesia as early as 1500 B.C. in a few cases but closer to 1000 B.C. in most other cases. Roughly similar pottery-bearing sites in a broader geographic range of Island Southeast Asia appear to postdate the potential Marianas homeland age, and so far they have lacked the particular early variants of the finely decorated expressions. Instead, these later contexts, especially in parts of Indonesia, refer to the continuing spread of the pottery horizon and related cultural traditions through 1000 B.C. or even more recently.

A specifically pinpointed homeland of the first Marianas settlers may never be known, and the homeland may have involved multiple places instead of a solitary point. As has been noted, the successful settlement in the Mariana Islands most likely was occasioned by the cooperation of people possessing a diverse set of skills and knowledge and who potentially came from varied backgrounds, perhaps from a few distinctly different biological families, and perhaps from separate village areas. Furthermore, in the context of an increasing popularity of pottery-making and associated cultural contexts spreading into more and more areas at 1500 B.C., the remote-distance Marianas settlement could be attributed potentially to any of those increasingly numerous homeland locales within a rapidly broadening geographic range, most likely in the northern through central Philippines.

The "incremental growth model" accounts for the potential of composite origins from a large zone of inhabited space, traceable in the archaeological record of a pottery trail as illustrated in Chapter 5, as well as suggested by linguistic and genetic studies. Linguistic studies of the Chamorro language refer to origins at the time of the initial breakup of Malayo-Polynesian languages within the Austronesian family outside Taiwan, which spread over a large geographic range in the northern through central Philippines and intruded into parts of Indonesia at the time when the Chamorro language diverged from this ancestry (Blust 2013). Likewise, the genetic markers retained in modern populations indicate that the Chamorro genetic lineages in the Marianas must have diverged from a source of population in Island Southeast Asia, today found in scattered parts of the Philippines and Indonesia (Vilar et al. 2013), and analysis of full genomes in ancient DNA from Guam have indicated a source in the northern through central Philippines (Pugach et al. 2021). Notably, these ancestral aspects of the founding populations in the Marianas still continue among the indigenous Chamorro people living today, thereby stressing a direct and unbroken connection through time.

While people were living in the Marianas and perpetuating their distinctive pottery traditions since 1500 B.C. if not earlier, other groups began making related dentate-stamped pottery in the Near Oceanic islands of the Bismarck Archipelago, certainly by 1350 B.C. but perhaps as early as 1500 B.C. According to the logic of the incremental growth model, the pottery horizon in the Bismarck Archipelago may be attributed to a large potential zone of Island Southeast Asia and the Mariana Islands, with the possibility of different contributing cultural elements coming from multiple sources. The pigs, dogs, and chickens brought into Lapita sites could not have come from the Mariana Islands where no such animals had existed, so a prospective influence from the Mariana Islands could not have been the only source contributing to Lapita origins in the Bismarck Archipelago.

Beyond the possible role in the emergence of a pottery horizon in Near Oceanic Lapita sites, the groups living in the Mariana Islands since 1500 B.C. have shown no long-term sustained contact with the Lapita world. A few people may have been involved in overseas contacts such as in initiating the Lapita horizon along with people from other areas, but of course large numbers of people stayed permanently in the Mariana Islands for multiple generations and experienced little or no contact with communities outside the Marianas until much later, notably after A.D. 1000. The Lapita Cultural Complex developed as its own unique expression in many ways, including a high degree of embellishments of pottery decorations, a rapid and widespread program of severe ecological impacts, and a divergence of language into the Oceanic subgrouping not shared with any of the potential Malayo-Polynesian ancestral areas in Island Southeast Asia or in the Mariana Islands.

References

Athens, J. Stephen, Michael F. Dega, and Jerome V. Ward, 2004. Austronesian colonisation of the Mariana Islands: The palaeoenvironmental evidence. *Bulletin of the Indo-Pacific Prehistory Association* 24: 21–30.

Athens, J. Stephen, and Jerome V. Ward, 1998. *Paleoenvironment and Prehistoric Landscape Change: A Sediment Core Record from Lake Hagoi, Tinian, CNMI*. Report prepared for United States Naval Facilities Engineering Command. International Archaeological Research Institute, Inc., Honolulu.

Athens, J. Stephen, and Jerome V. Ward, 1999. *Paleoclimate, Vegetation, and Landscape Change on Guam: The Laguas Core*. Report prepared for United States Naval Facilities Engineering Command. International Archaeological Research Institute, Inc., Honolulu.

Athens, J. Stephen, and Jerome V. Ward, 2004. Holocene vegetation, savannah origins and human settlement of Guam. In *A Pacific Odyssey: Archaeology and Anthropology in the Western Pacific: Papers in Honour of Jim Specht*, edited by Val Attenbrow and Richard Fullagar, pp. 15–30. Records of the Australian Museum, Supplement 29. Australian Museum, Sydney.

Athens, J. Stephen, and Jerome V. Ward, 2006. *Holocene Paleoenvironment of Saipan: Analysis of a Core from Lake Susupe*. Micronesian Archaeological Survey Report Number 35. Commonwealth of the Northern Mariana Islands Division of Historic Preservation, Saipan.

Blust, Robert, 2013. *The Austronesian Languages*. Revised edition. Asia-Pacific Linguistics Open Access Monographs 008. Research School of Pacific and Asian Studies, Australian National University, Canberra.

Butler, Brian M., 1994. Early prehistoric settlement in the Mariana Islands: New evidence from Saipan. *Man and Culture in Oceania* 10: 15–38.

Butler, Brian M. (editor), 1995. *Archaeological Investigations in the Achugao and Matansa Areas of Saipan, Mariana Islands*. Micronesian Archaeological Survey Report 30. Commonwealth of the Northern Mariana Islands, Division of Historic Preservation, Department of Community and Cultural Affairs, Saipan.

Carson, Mike T., 2008. Refining earliest settlement in Remote Oceania: Renewed archaeological investigations at Unai Bapot, Saipan. *Journal of Island and Coastal Archaeology* 3: 115–139.

Carson, Mike T., 2010. Radiocarbon chronology with marine reservoir correction for the Ritidian Archaeological Site, northern Guam. *Radiocarbon* 52: 1627–1638.

Carson, Mike T., 2011. Palaeohabitat of first settlement sites 1500–1000 B.C. in Guam, Mariana Islands, western Pacific. *Journal of Archaeological Science* 38: 2207–2221.

Carson, Mike T., 2014a. *First Settlement of Remote Oceania: Earliest Sites in the Mariana Islands*. Springer, New York.

Carson, Mike T., 2014b. Paleoterrain research: Finding the first settlement sites of Remote Oceania. *Geoarchaeology* 29: 268–275.

Carson, Mike T., 2017a. *Rediscovering Heritage through Artefacts, Sites, and Landscapes: Translatign a 3500-year Record at Ritidian, Guam*. Archaeopress, Oxford.

Carson, Mike T., 2017b. Cultural spaces inside and outside caves: A study in Guam, Western Micronesia. *Antiquity* 91: 421–441.

Carson, Mike T., 2017c. Inhabiting remote tropical seashores at 1500–1100 B.C.: Water, practicalities, and rituals in the Mariana Islands. *Journal of Field Archaeology 42*.

Carson, Mike T., 2020. Peopling of Oceania: Clarifying an initial settlement horizon in the Mariana Islands. *Radiocarbon* 62: 1733–1754.

Carson, Mike T., and Hsiao-Chun Hung, 2014. Semiconductor theory in migration: Population receivers, homelands and gateways in Taiwan and Island Southeast Asia. *World Archaeology* 46: 502–515.

Carson, Mike T., and Hsiao-chun Hung, 2017. *Substantive Evidence of Initial Habitation in the Remote Pacific: Archaeological Discoveries at Unai Bapot in Saipan, Mariana Islands*. Archaeopress, Oxford.

Carson, Mike T., and Hsiao-chun Hung, 2021. Let's catch octopus for dinner: Ancient inventions of octopus lures in the Mariana Islands of the remote tropical Pacific. *World Archaeology* 53: 599–614.

Carson, Mike T., and Hsiao-chun Hung, 2022. 3500 years in a changing landscape: The House of Taga in the Mariana Islands, western Micronesia. In *Palaeolandscapes in Archaeology: Lessons for the Past and Future*, edited by Mike T. Carson, pp. 340–376. Routledge, London.

Carson, Mike T., and Hiro Kurashina, 2012. Re-envisioning long-distance Oceanic migration: Early dates in the Mariana Islands. *World Archaeology* 44: 409–435.

Craib, John L., 1993. Early occupation at Unai Chulu, Tinian, Commonwealth of the Northern Mariana Islands. *Bulletin of the Indo-Pacific Prehistory Association* 13: 116–134.

Dickinson, William R., 2000. Hydro-isostatic and tectonic influences on emergent Holocene paleoshorelines in the Mariana Islands, western Pacific Ocean. *Journal of Coastal Research* 16: 735–746.

Dickinson, William R., 2001. Paleoshoreline record of relative Holocene sea levels on Pacific islands. *Earth-Science Reviews* 55: 191–234.

Dickinson, William R., 2003. Impact of Mid-Holocene hydro-isostatic highstand in regional sea level on habitability of islands in Pacific Oceania. *Journal of Coastal Research* 19: 489–502.

Dilli, Bradley J., Alan E. Haun, Susan T. Goodfellow, and Brian Deroo, 1998. *Archaeological mitigation program, Mangilao Golf Course Project Area, Mangilao Municipality, Territory of Guam*. Report prepared for Jetan Sahni. Paul H, Rosendahl, Ph.D., Inc., Hilo, Hawai'i.

Dixon, Boyd, Michael Dega, Darlene Moore, and Judith R. Amesbury, in press. Archaeological research at the early pre-latte period site of San Roque of Saipan, ca. 1500–1100 BC. *Journal of Island and Coastal Archaeology* in press, advance copy online in June 2022, DOI: 10.1080/15564894.2022.2048284.

Fox, Robert B., 1970. *The Tabon Caves: Archaeological Explorations and Excavations on Palawan Island, Philippines*. Monograph Number 1. Philippines National Museum, Manila.

Haun, Alan E., Joseph A. Jimenez, Melissa A. Kirkendall, and Susan T. Goodfellow, 1999. *Archaeological investigations at Unai Chulu, Island of Tinian, Commonwealth of the Northern Mariana Islands*. Report prepared for Commander, Pacific Division, US Naval Facilities Engineering Command. Paul H, Rosendahl, Ph.D., Inc., Hilo, Hawai'i.

Heaton, Timothy J., Peter Köhler, Martin Butzin, Edouard Bard, Ron W. Reimer, William E. N. Austin, Christopher Bronk Ramsey, Pieter M. Grootes, Konrad A. Hughen, Bernd Kromer, Paula J. Reimer, Jess Adkins, Andrea Burke, Mea S. Cook, Jesper Olsen, and Luke C. Skinner, 2020. Marine20: The marine radiocarbon age calibration curve (0–55,000 cal BP). *Radiocarbon* 62: 779–820.

Hung, Hsiao-chun, Y. Iizuka, P. Bellwood, K. D. Nguyen, B. Bellina, P. Silapanth, E. Dizon, R. Santiago, I. Datan, and J. H. Manton, 2007. Ancient jades map 3000 years of prehistoric exchange in Southeast Asia. *Proceedings of the National Academy of Sciences* 104: 19, 745–819.

Kayanne, Hajime, Teruaki Ishii, Eiji Matsumoto, and Nobuyuki Yonekura, 1993. Late Holocene sea-level change on Rota and Guam, Mariana Islands, and its constraint on geophysical predictions. *Quaternary Research* 40: 189–200.

Kurashina, Hiro, and Russell N. Clayshulte, 1983. Site formation processes and cultural sequence at Tarague, Guam. *Bulletin of the Indo-Pacific Prehistory Association* 4: 114–122.

Kurashina, Hiro, Darlene Moore, Osamu Kataoka, Russell Clayshulte, and Erwin Ray, 1981. Prehistoric and protohistoric cultural occurrences at Tarague, Guam. *Asian Perspectives* 24: 57–68.

Moore, Darlene R., Rosalind L. Hunter-Anderson, Judith R. Amesbury, and Eleanor F. Wells, 1992. *Archaeology at Chalan Piao, Saipan, Report prepared for José Cabrera*. Micronesian Archaeological Research Services, Mangilao. Guam.

Peterson, Warren, 1974. Summary report of two archaeological sites from North-Eastern Luzon. *Journal of Archaeology and Physical Anthropology in Oceania* 9: 26–35.

Pugach, Irina, Alexander Hübner, Hsiao-chun Hung, Matthias Meyer, Mike T. Carson, and Mark Stoneking, 2021. Ancient DNA from GBuam and the peopling of the Pacific. *Proceedings of the National Academy of Sciences* 18: e2022112118. https://doi.org/10.1073/pnas.2022112118

Sather, Clifford, 1985. Boat crews and fishing fleets: The social organization of maritime labor among the Bajau Laut of southeastern Sabah. In *Contributions to Southeast Asian Ethnography*, edited by Anthony R. Walker, pp. 165–214. Double Six Press, Singapore.

Solheim, Wilhelm G., II, 1955. Notes on the archaeology of Masbate. *University of Manila Journal of East Asiatic Studies* 4: 47–50.

Solheim, Wilhelm G., II, 1968. The Batungan Cave Site, Masbate, Philippines. In *Asian and Pacific Archaeology Series*, edited by Wilhelm G. Solheim, II, Volume 2, pp. 20–62. Social Science Research Institute, University of Hawai'i, Honolulu.

Spoehr, Alexander, 1957. *Marianas Prehistory: Archaeological Survey and Excavations on Saipan, Tinian and Rota*. Fieldiana Anthropology Volume 48. Chicago Natural History Museum, Chicago.

Spoehr, Alexander, 1973. *Zamboanga and Sulu: An Archaeological Approach to Ethnic Diversity*. Ethnology Monographs, Number 1. Department of Anthropology, University of Pittsburgh, Pittsburgh.

Topping, Donald M., Pedro M. Ogo, and Bernadita C. Dungca, 1975. *Chamorro-English Dictionary*. University of Hawai'i Press, Honolulu.

Vilar, Miguel G., Chim W. Chan, Dana R. Santos, Daniel Lynch, Rita Spathis, Ralph M. Garruto, and J. Koji Lum, 2013. The origins and genetic distinctiveness of the Chamorros of the Mariana Islands: An mtDNA perspective. *American Journal of Human Biology* 25: 116–122.

Wickler, Stephen K., 2004. Modelling colonisation and migration in Micronesia from a zooarchaeological perspective. In *Colonisation, Migration and Marginal Areas: A Zooarchaeological Approach*, edited by Mariana Mondini, Sebantien Munoz, and Stepehen K. Wickler, pp. 28–40. Oxbow Books, Oxford.

Zerega, Nyree J. C., Diane Ragone, and Timothy J. Motely, 2004. Complex origins of breadfruit (*Artocarpus altilis*, Moraceae): Implications for human migration in Oceania. *American Journal of Botany* 91: 760–766.

Zerega, Nyree J. C., Diane Ragone, and Timothy J. Motely, 2006. Breadfruit origins, diversity, and human-facilitated distribution. In *Darwin's Harvest: Origins, Evolution, and Conservation of Crop Plants*, edited by Timothy J. Motely and Nyree J. C. Zerega, pp. 213–238. Columbia University Press, New York.

7 A siege of ecological imperialism
Lapita invasions, 1100 through 800 B.C.

Ni dau vakamacalataki edua na ka se i tukutuku vakamatai lalai, ka kilai vinaka ka matata na kenai balebale (Fijian proverb), paraphrased in English as "When ripe or well cooked with its skin still attached, the cooking banana's skin is easy to peel and the fruit is good to eat."

A Fijian proverb expresses that when someone explains well about how to do something properly, then everyone can enjoy the results, as may have happened when Lapita pottery-making people infiltrated through a wide geographic range of Remote Oceania. In the case of this proverb, the cooking banana (sometimes called a "plantain") is a wonderfully nutritious and tasty food, but it cannot be eaten like the common banana. The edibility is easily managed but needs clear instruction. Likewise, the Lapita settlement of Remote Oceania brought significant rewards enjoyed by many people, but this outcome was possible only after foreplanning and the development of requisite skills and knowledge.

Serious preparation and clear instructive explanation must have transpired prior to the rapid human settlement of the Remote Oceanic islands all across Southern Melanesia and West Polynesia within an archaeological "blink of an eye" of a few centuries about 1100–800 B.C. (Figure 7.1). The Lapita groups acted as invasive species who transported not only themselves but also a full system for artificially rendering the islands of Remote Oceania into culturally inhabited landscapes. Native forests were replaced by introduced taxa, birds and other animals were depopulated, and long-distance translocated plants and animals came to dominate the local environments. Overall, the impact of human settlement may be characterized as a form of ecological imperialism in support of a rapid and widespread human invasion of this part of Remote Oceania.

The Lapita movement into Remote Oceania at 1100–800 B.C. has been substantiated in multiple cases too numerous to present individually. Compilations of site findings have been examined elsewhere (Kirch 1997), with periodic updates as research has continued (Bedford 2015; Bedford et al. 2019). The most securely dated Remote Oceanic Lapita site layers have been reported with well defined assemblages of Lapita pottery and other artifacts in New Caledonia (Sand 1997, 2010), Vanuatu (Bedford 2006), Tonga (Burley 2023; Burley and Connaughton 2007, 2010; Burley and Dickinson 2010; Burley et al. 2010), and Fiji (Irwin et al. 2011; Nunn and Petchey 2013). Additionally, Lapita sites in the Solomon Islands have been found in both Near and Remote Oceanic settings, all postdating 1200 B.C. and mostly in the range of 1100–800 B.C. (Walter and Sheppard 2017).

Remote Oceanic Lapita must be understood as an expansive outgrowth from older Lapita origins within Near Oceania, such as at the older Lapita sites of the Bismarck Archipelago and other sites at the east side of New Guinea, dating back to 1500–1350 B.C. (Chapter 5). Lapita traditions already had developed for several generations within Near Oceania,

186 *A siege of ecological imperialism*

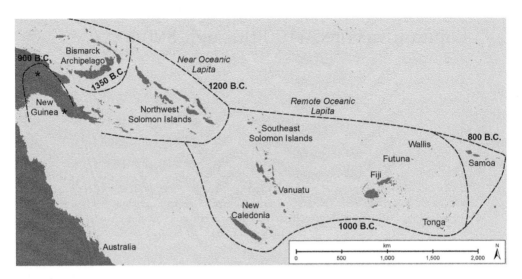

Figure 7.1 Map of eastern New Guinea, Island Melanesia, and West Polynesia, showing the geographic distribution of Lapita pottery sites at different time intervals of 1500–1100 B.C., 1100–800 B.C., and 800–500 B.C.

prior to the migrations of later descendants across the ocean into the remote-distance islands shores of Southern Melanesia and West Polynesia. The roles of intercommunity interaction and adaptation to a natural and social environment were substantially different for the people in a pre-inhabited Near Oceanic setting versus their later descendants living as the first people in a remote-distance island setting.

The effective expansion of Lapita groups involved large-scale transformations of the Remote Oceanic world according to preconceived notions of how the world should be inhabited and made into familiar configurations of habitats with culturally useful plants, animals, named places, and roles of new founding lineages. Many of those transformations followed ideas that were shared with the Lapita ancestors who lived in Near Oceania prior to the expansion into the Remote Oceanic islands, so the records of both Near and Remote Oceania need to be considered when studying the overall picture of a siege of ecological imperialism and everything related with this context. Each island group reveals its own slightly different circumstances in how the Lapita people brought their transformative ideas into action, including not only the impacts on the natural environment but also the full set of cognitive, social, and other ways of creating an inhabited landscape.

A broad view of the social-ecological contexts of Lapita sites has been most productive when considering that the diagnostic Lapita style of dentate-stamped pottery comprises only a very small percentage of the total content of any Lapita site. The dentate-stamped designs remain the foremost material marker of Lapita groups and continue to be investigated in several ways, yet they must be understood as only some of the elements of a larger repertoire of cultural traits, as in Roger Green's (1979a) definition of a Lapita Cultural Complex, already mentioned in Chapter 3 and elsewhere. In total, the surviving archaeological records and other lines of evidence enable a strong sense of how Lapita groups created their particular mode of inhabited landscape in terms of ecological, social, and other impacts in unison.

Meaning of Lapita?

Before discussing anything about Lapita sites, the defining dentate-stamped pottery needs to be considered (Figure 7.2). These decorated pieces constitute the essence of verifying an archaeological layer or collection as representing the Lapita Cultural Complex or the Lapita people, so their details need to be recognized as part of the parameters of any further study. Given that the highly specialized decorated pottery tradition was transported with the people who spread rapidly through several islands, it may be appreciated as a fundamental part of the larger cultural contexts, including the ecological impacts among other aspects.

Scholars never will agree about their answers to questions such as "What does Lapita mean?" In one point of view, the cultural meaning existed only in the past and in the action of making or using the diagnostic dentate-stamped pottery more than 2500 years ago, whereas archaeologists today are able to examine only the surviving material remnants of broken potsherds without access to the original behavioral contexts. Within the limits of what the material evidence does reveal, however, the observable patterns can suggest the kinds of cultural contexts of how the pottery was used, yet, of course, multiple interpretations are possible.

Over several decades, different systems have been devised for categorizing the dentate-stamped Lapita motifs and designs, at first examining the tiny available potsherds

Figure 7.2 Lapita pottery fragments from Vavouto, New Caledonia, excavated by Carson (2003, 2008).

as pieces of a curious puzzle, then later recognizing the fuller sense of motifs in large pieces and in rare occurrences of whole or reconjoinable pots. Advancements in computer database technology have allowed management of vast amounts of information, including the coding of specific design motifs and cross-referencing with other attributes. Pattern-recognition software may yet prove useful when applied to digital photographic image archives of pottery designs.

Pattern-recognition principles have been central in studies of Lapita design motifs for many decades, even if archaeologists did not explicitly use these terms. In one of the most clearly outlined studies, Sidney Mead (1975a, 1975b) proposed a framework of how to conceptualize an artistic design system in general, then applied the concepts specifically to Lapita pottery designs. In this framework, the *technical execution* refers to the tools and practical ways of making decorations, such as using a dentate stamp, circle stamp, or single-tipped incising tool that can create specific kinds of *design elements*, such as a row of dots, a circle, or an incised line. Next, the *design principles* refer to the notions of symmetry or asymmetry, rules of juxtaposition, and other logic guiding the ways of applying each individual element of technical execution. Finally, the *design motifs* refer to the full sets of images that are created by the ordering of the design principles in concert.

When examining the scattered small bits of broken Lapita pottery, Mead's (1975a, 1975b) framework tended to be applied primarily toward generating inventories of design elements, motifs, or partial motifs to the extent that they could be observed. Although often difficult to distinguish between the analytic scales of individual elements or composite motifs, impressive inventories were demonstrated for Lapita pottery collections from Fiji (Shaw 1975) and from Santa Cruz in the Solomon Islands (Donovan 1973). Using different criteria of composite elements as more realistic units of analysis, Dmitri Anson (1983) produced an extensive inventory of motif components found in Lapita pottery of the Bismarck Archipelago.

In theory, the logical ordering or rules of Lapita designs could be deciphered from close examination of the individual elements and ways of combining the motifs, much like the rules of language grammar can be ascertained through paying attention to patterns of speech. Certain words tend to be used together, and then groups of words furthermore tend to be used together in different scales composing the patterns of a language. According to this analogy, the individual decorative elements and motifs in Lapita pottery may be recognized in variable scales mirroring the levels of phonemes, words, and phrases. Going even farther with this line of thought, perhaps groups of pots may be interpreted as conversations.

Catalogs of the Lapita design system can vary considerably, depending on the unit and scale of analysis. Practical issues need to be addressed about how to differentiate the specific design elements, combinations of those elements, larger motifs, and combinations of motifs. One solution is to identify units at the smallest scale possible, taking advantage of the power of digital storage space and computer processing power, and then eventually working toward systematic analysis at multiple scales. Nancy Sharp (1993) developed one such attribute-based system for a database of Lapita decorations, but ultimately, the actual use of any database depends on having access to raw data. The encoding system may work quite well, but the ability to examine spatial patterns or chronological trends always will be limited by the available datasets inputted into the database. Partly addressing these issues, Scarlett Chiu (2011) started to compile a database of Lapita decorative attributes as observable in the collections from a few selected sites, beginning with the smallest visible elements. In terms of accounting for design elements as part of a logical data structure of a

A siege of ecological imperialism 189

design system, Arnaud Noury (2005) developed a comprehensive management framework of general utility for examining any possible individual Lapita decorations within a meaningful context (see also Noury and Galipaud 2011).

While archaeologists were struggling to make sense of the artistic organization or meaning of Lapita designs, one of the most significant discoveries to emerge has been the recognition of the "Lapita face" motif (Figure 7.3), now joined by several other motifs as preserved in the larger pottery fragments, rejoined pieces, and whole vessels. As expected, each artistic motif was composed of several individual contributing elements, potentially matching with the catalogs or inventories in a database. Roger Green (1979a) noticed that among the first of the more popularized discoveries was the depiction of a human face in a Lapita potsherd from the Solomon Islands, composed of several individual elements in combination. Another important advancement was the recognition of different forms or styles of the face motif (see Figure 5.37), evidently made in repeated and sometimes interlocked sets of faces and drawn around the perimeter of a pot (Spriggs 1990). The design paradigm involved a central frieze of the Lapita face or other motif, with supplementary or

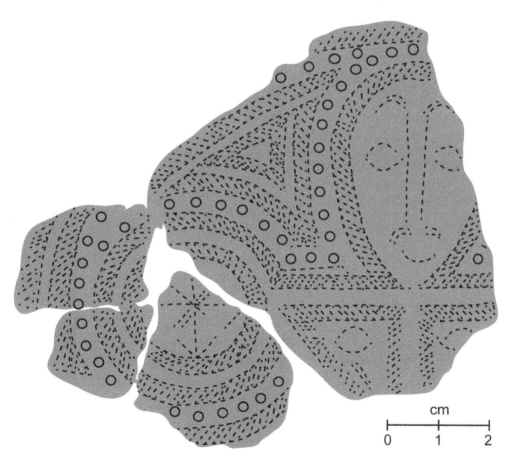

Figure 7.3 Lapita face motif on pottery fragments from Santa Cruz, Solomon Islands. Illustration by the author, based on documentation by Green (1979a).

annex zones mirroring around the sides for symmetry and balance (Noury and Galipaud 2011).

Among the most informative Lapita pottery collections is the rare case of a Lapita cemetery at the Teouma Site in Vanuatu which has been excavated extensively, revealing a set of whole pots or large portions of pots with decorated surfaces (Bedford et al. 2007). These findings of full motifs at Teouma and at a few other Lapita sites have shown precisely how the individual elements were combined toward the larger artistic expressions, thereby enabling the best representation of the decorative design systems. The Lapita face, labyrinth, and other motifs now have been well established. Even if only small portions happen to be preserved in a few potsherds at any particular site, the association with a definite larger artistic motif can be appreciated, and often the specific motif can be ascertained according to the corpus of regional Lapita pottery knowledge.

Naturally, some degree of variation must have occurred in Lapita designs, although overall they are quite striking in their consistent similarities over a large geographic extent and through some centuries of a sustained tradition. Localized provinces of Lapita style may be outlined as northwest, central, south, east, and other areas within the Lapita world. Within each such province, however, a certain amount of chronological variation followed the geographic spread of the pottery horizon generally from west to east, as outlined by Glenn Summerhayes (2000a, 2000b).

At least six observations can clarify the chronology of Lapita:

- The oldest Lapita sites in the Bismarck Archipelago show a chronological change in pottery through time, beginning with finely decorated pieces at 1500–1350 B.C. and then generally becoming coarser in later periods through 500 B.C.
- Beginning by 1100 B.C. and partway through the sequence as seen in the Bismarck Archipelago, the Lapita horizon spread eastward and southeastward with the movement of people into various islands, resulting in the middle and later variants of Lapita designs as seen in parts of the Solomon Islands, New Caledonia, Vanuatu, and Fiji generally post-dating 1100 B.C. and continuing through 500 B.C.
- Approaching the eastern end of the Lapita distribution in Tonga, only a single site of Nukuleka contained pottery with the earlier decorative motifs and was dated close to 900 B.C., and the other Lapita sites in Tonga have disclosed pottery with the later Lapita designs (Burley 2023).
- Sites in Samoa exhibit the final stages of Lapita expression after 800 B.C.
- Discoveries of late Lapita pottery on the southern coast of New Guinea can additionally be included in the post–1000 B.C. contexts and in the post–800 B.C. inventory characterized by minimal and coarse decorations.
- The Lapita-like dentate-stamped pottery pieces in some parts of Indonesia appear most similar to the middle through late range of Lapita, about 1100 through 500 B.C., with an increased frequency in some areas about 800 B.C.

Given the variation of Lapita through time, the cultural meaning likely changed through variable contexts, further differentiated in each island group according to localized circumstances and developments. Whatever Lapita meant to people in the Bismarck Archipelago at 1200 B.C., their later descendants at 900 B.C. held different perceptions, as did other people living in New Caledonia at 800 B.C. or in Fiji at 600 B.C. Ultimately, Lapita ended about 500 B.C. in its strictest definition, so its range of cultural contexts and meanings no longer survived in the same ways thereafter. Nevertheless, given the consistency of the dentate-stamped tradition across the Lapita world for some centuries, a unified core meaning can be postulated to have existed, even if it produced diverse expressions.

One aspect of Lapita design variation may be seen in the high degree of multicultural interaction in Near Oceanic islands, such as in the Bismarck Archipelago, versus necessarily very different settings of entering otherwise uninhabited lands in Remote Oceanic sites. The multicultural setting in Near Oceania may have prompted the need to negotiate cultural identity in the displays of lavishly decorated Lapita pottery (Summerhayes 2000a). If the decorated pots were used as parts of identity-signaling encounters, then the postulated events likely were rare occurrences mirroring the small percentage of decorated pieces in the larger pottery assemblages. The face motif certainly evokes notions of ancestors and lineages linked with the overall theme of identity signaling. Specialized ritual events furthermore are indicated by the higher concentrations of decorated pots in the undoubtedly ceremonial context of a cemetery at the Teouma Site in Vanuatu.

As has been noted, part of the "meaning" of Lapita may relate to the actions of decorating the pots, thus bringing attention to the tool kits involved in making those decorations (Figure 7.4). Impressions and incisions were created in the wet or leather-hard skin of a pot before it was dried and ready for firing, similar in technical execution to the tattooing of a body or to the production of bark cloth patterns (Green 1979b). By examining the markings in Lapita pottery decorations, Jean-Pierre Siorat (1990, 1999) and Wal Ambrose (1999, 2007, 2012) have reconstructed the working tips of the tools that originally had produced the rows of dentate-stamped points, individual circles, and incised lines. Pieces of bone and turtle carapace were fashioned into comb-tipped tools with different numbers of points making dentate-stamped lines of short, medium, and long markings. Narrow pieces of bamboo or plant stems most likely were used as stamps for impressing circles, but some circles were hand-drawn by a pointed tool. The same kind of pointed tool could create the various incised lines.

The meanings of Lapita decorations may not be known clearly at this time, but their contexts can be defined or refined by knowing more about the attendant material culture assemblages. The available records so far offer a picture of specialized ritual contexts within a larger scene of profound ecological impacts, enacted over a large geographic range and within a rather short time span. Additional knowledge can be gained from other lines of evidence, including the many contributions from linguistics and from human biology and genetics, yet the fundamental material of the archaeological record should not be overlooked.

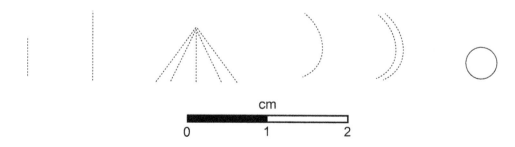

Figure 7.4 Impressions made by different forms of Lapita decoration tools.

Linguistic perspective

The mapped distribution of the Lapita archaeological signature corresponds very closely with the Oceanic-speaking communities of the Austronesian language family (Figure 7.5; see also Figure 2.13), thus stressing the central role of linguistics in the regional culture history (Pawley and Ross 1993). In scattered places nearest to New Guinea, a few Papuan-speaking (non-Austronesian) groups live in areas where Lapita sites have been reported, but the overwhelming pattern shows non-Austronesian languages in the areas of New Guinea and Australia outside the scope of Lapita. Meanwhile, a strong correspondence is maintained between ancient Lapita sites and present-day Oceanic-speaking language communities. This correspondence is especially noteworthy in the Remote Oceanic component of Lapita, where no people had lived prior to 1100 B.C., such that the closely related Oceanic languages in each of these separate island groups can be traced to a commonly shared source.

Today's Oceanic languages can be traced to an origin within the Near Oceanic Lapita world prior to 1100 B.C., at a time when the definitive characteristics of the Oceanic subgrouping began to diverge from an older Malayo-Polynesian ancestry. This divergence of the Oceanic grouping must have occurred separately from the developments of the non-Oceanic Malayo-Polynesian languages spoken in Island Southeast Asia, the Mariana Islands, and Palau (Blust 2013). Given the fact that the Oceanic languages can be grouped so tightly together, they must have branched from a single shared ancestral language group, necessarily spoken prior to the dispersal of its speakers into the Remote Oceanic islands of Southern Melanesia and West Polynesia.

Prior to the dispersal of Oceanic-speaking people who carried Lapita pottery traditions into several islands after 1100 B.C., an archaic version of Oceanic (Oc) can be viewed as a protolanguage called Proto Oceanic (POc) spoken within the Near Oceanic islands that served as the immediate or proximate homeland of the Lapita diaspora (Ross 1988). POc no longer is spoken today, yet many of its features can be reconstructed through

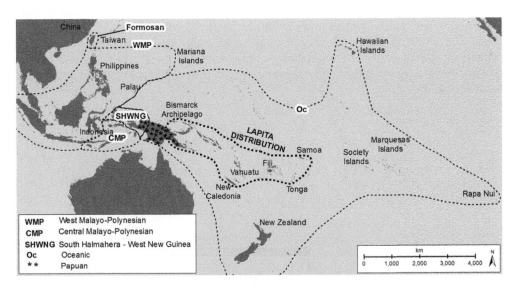

Figure 7.5 Lapita region coordinated with linguistic grouping map.

cross-comparison of phonemes, cognates in word lists, and grammatical structure in modern-day living languages. Although each language of Oc is distinctive today, the cross-comparative consistencies are compelling toward recognizing that they all derived from a shared ancestry of a POc community.

At some point prior to 1100 B.C. in the Bismarck Archipelago, people speaking a form of Malayo-Polynesian language developed distinctive linguistic features resulting in a POc language. As the linguist Andrew Pawley (2003: 25) summarized: "We can infer that the early Lapita peoples of the Bismarck Archipelago spoke Proto Oceanic, that stage of Oceanic which was spoken by a more or less unified Oceanic speech community immediately prior to its decisive breakup." The "breakup" in this case refers to the fact that the Oceanic-speaking groups today maintain their separate languages that had "broken up" from a shared ancestral source of a Proto-Oceanic language. The most likely scenario involved a meeting of Malayo-Polynesian immigrant groups with indigenous Papuan (non-Austronesian) groups, traceable archaeologically in the emergence of the Lapita pottery horizon as early as 1500–1350 B.C. Within a few generations and necessarily prior to 1100 B.C., the POc language had developed its distinguishing features that would be carried with the Lapita expansion into Southern Melanesia and West Polynesia.

If POc developed in a multicultural context of early Lapita sites in Near Oceania, then the possible contributions of non-Austronesian Papuan language may be considered. Moreover, at least some of the people involved in cultural actions at Lapita sites were from indigenous Papuan-speaking groups, and the total inventory of cultural traits of the Lapita Cultural Complex most realistically resulted from a blending of Malayo-Polynesian and Papuan traditions. Linguistically, however, the vast majority of features of POc must have derived from Malayo-Polynesian as the source of the syntax structure, vocabulary, and phonemic inventory that developed into POc. This language history could not have occurred unless speakers of Malayo-Polynesian language lived in appreciable numbers and used their language in the majority of cultural contexts. Most important would have been the opportunity to speak with infants and children during early language-learning stages. By comparison, any contributions from non-Austronesian Papuan languages have been minimal and nearly impossible to detect. Following the dynamic interactions during the initial development of POc within Near Oceania, a unified cultural context was established prior to the spread of the Lapita horizon into Remote Oceania.

Linguistic history parallels archaeological evidence quite well in Pacific Oceania, especially in the Remote Oceanic islands where the only language groups have descended from neatly definable founding populations. While island communities probably never were entirely isolated, at least some degree of isolation evidently resulted in the differentiation of languages through time. Interisland contacts must have occurred, but they did not persist to such an extent that would sustain exactly the same language features among all members of the communities living in different islands over hundreds of years. A degree of breakup of linguistic similarity developed through time, as attested in the diversification of Oceanic languages.

A breakup of a shared ancestral language community may be viewed as part of a "network-breaking model" as proposed by Pawley and Green (1984). This model acknowledges that people in different communities, villages, or islands shared a common language during the periods when they lived in networks of close contact with one another, followed by eventual diversification of their language histories after their degree of contact lessened. The key point here is to situate a linguistic change in terms of larger cultural events of the communities that spoke a shared language. A shared language in this sense may be viewed as reflecting the networking of the community speaking this language and implying other shared cultural traits within the network, such as pottery decorative traditions, forms of shell ornaments, and preferences for living in certain types of ecological habitat niches. In this context, the cultural events of remote island colonization occasioned the breakdown of the ability to maintain shared languages, and other aspects of the previously networked cultural groups presumably developed independently as well.

Reconstructed POc dictionaries provide lists of the words that people once spoke when referring to their pottery, house constructions, and other aspects of a material world of interest to archaeologists (Ross et al. 1998, 2003). In addition to the attraction of attaching POc words to specific items in the archaeological record, the POc word lists potentially can offer clues about how people referred to their nonmaterial aspects of social structure, political organization, and ideological beliefs. As an important caution, the existence of a proto word in itself does not convey the precise cultural significance or meaning of whatever is being expressed, and therefore the pursuits of cultural meaning must consider context, which is just as applicable in linguistic study as in archaeology. For instance, cognate words of *qa-riki* may be glossed as referring to a kind of hereditary chief, but the actual authority and cultural role of a group's leader may vary from one case to another. The definition of a "chief," just like for any other kind of group leader, depends on the particular context open to variation. The same logic applies to other words in the protolanguage dictionaries and at all levels within the Austronesian family.

Human biology and genetics

Substantial evidence now can refer to the Lapita people as a biological group, based on studies of ancient skeletal remains, interpretive analysis of modern patterns in DNA of living people today, and rare glimpses into the preserved ancient DNA from ancient skeletons at Lapita-aged sites. These studies consistently show the diversity of Lapita communities, in particular as a mixture of intrusive Asian or "Mongoloid" lineages, now identified as "Austronesian," with indigenous Australo-Melanesian or Papuan lineages (Chambers and Edinur 2015; Cox 2015). Today, the Austronesian phenotypes and DNA lineages are represented strongly in the Polynesian end of the Lapita distribution, as well as in the later-settled areas of Polynesia and Micronesia. Meanwhile, the Australo-Melanesian features of darker skin, thalassemia condition with resistance against malaria, and different inherited DNA markers are most prevalent in the Near Oceanic and Southern Melanesian islands of the Lapita distribution, as well as dominant throughout New Guinea and Australia. Viewed at a large scale, the Australo-Melanesian or Papuan traits appear to be retained from the oldest human ancestors of the region extending at least 50,000 years ago, overlain by later-aged arrivals of Austronesian lineage traits postdating 2200 B.C.

The situation within the Lapita realm can be clarified by referring to the larger picture of physical anthropology and genetics in the Asia-Pacific region, as outlined in Chapter 2. This larger picture shows how East Asia-derived Austronesian groups moved through Island Southeast Asia and into Pacific Oceania, intermixing to varying degrees with long preestablished indigenous Australo-Melanesian groups. The Austronesian features are found in the highest percentages among the indigenous Formosan populations in Taiwan, progressively declining while moving outward from Taiwan into Island Southeast Asia, appearing in lowest frequencies in Near Oceania and Southern Melanesia, and then regaining higher frequency in West Polynesia.

The meeting of Austronesian and Australo-Melanesian individuals in the Near Oceanic Lapita world was not the first time when such a meeting occurred between different cultural, linguistic, and biological communities. The steps of an incrementally spreading pottery horizon, as illustrated in Chapter 5, brought immigrant Austronesian groups into varying degrees of contact with indigenous Australo-Melanesians on several occasions in Taiwan, in the Philippines, and in Indonesia. Such events had occurred prior to the emergence of the Lapita horizon in the Bismarck Archipelago at 1500–1350 B.C., meaning that the incoming pottery-making groups already had developed with a mixture of lineages and heritage that would contribute to the formulation of a Lapita Cultural Complex. The new arrivals in Near Oceania after 1500 B.C. met with indigenous Australo-Melanesian groups that were different in some ways from others who had lived in Island Southeast Asia, and perhaps a few groups could have been distinguished just within the Bismarck Archipelago.

After some generations of interaction within the Near Oceanic portion of the Lapita world, descendants of those multicultural groups became the first people ever to live in the Remote Oceanic islands of Southern Melanesia and West Polynesia. After 1100 B.C., the Remote Oceanic components of the Lapita communities must have inherited a mixture of Austronesian and Australo-Melanesian traits and DNA markers, congruent with the modern DNA signatures (Chambers and Edinur 2015). Today, the Australo-Melanesian features are by far the most dominant in Island Melanesia, while they occur in rather low frequency in West Polynesia. In West Polynesia and all subsequently later-settled areas of Pacific Oceania, Austronesian traits and DNA markers are dominant, in effect showing a stronger link with the Austronesian and Malayo-Polynesian groups in Taiwan and Island Southeast Asia than with the Melanesian populations living in the immediate proximate Lapita homeland of Near Oceania.

During the Lapita era, the exact relationships cannot be known for sure between the Austronesian and Australo-Melanesian groups that composed the Lapita populations. At the beginning of the Lapita horizon in Near Oceania after 1500 B.C., the incoming influence of Austronesian DNA-carrying people in a biological sense likely was outnumbered by that of the indigenous Australo-Melanesian population. This balance must have been different some centuries later when descendants of those groups moved into the Remote Oceanic Islands, and very likely the balance was different in each island's founding population and furthermore varied through subsequent generations. The patterns today show that the Austronesian phenotype traits have become numerically stronger with greater distance from the Near Oceanic Lapita homeland.

If the balance of Austronesian and Australo-Melanesian (Papuan) individuals changed through time, then ancient DNA (aDNA) from Lapita-age skeletons may clarify about the ancient context. So far, the only aDNA studies of Lapita-age skeletons have indicated little or no trace of Papuan (Australo-Melanesian) traits in three individuals buried in Vanuatu and another one buried in Tonga (Skoglund et al. 2016). Although the sample size is small, the findings are greatly informative for comparing the ancient populations in a modern-day Australo-Melanesian area (Vanuatu) versus a modern-day Austronesian-derived Polynesian area (Tonga).

The aDNA results are sufficient for making two inferences (Skoglund et al. 2016).

- First, Australo-Melanesian or Papuan individuals initially were outnumbered in Vanuatu during the Lapita settlement period, and they later outnumbered the Austronesian

individuals as seen today in Vanuatu's indigenous population of Australo-Melanesians who retain only very small amounts of Austronesian DNA.
- Second, Australo-Melanesian or Papuan individuals probably never lived in large numbers in Tonga, where instead people apparently have been mostly of Austronesian lineages ever since the first Lapita settlement.

In terms of refining the search for a genetic homeland of the Austronesian-related DNA in the Lapita-associated skeletons in Vanuatu and Tonga, the DNA datasets from other areas so far have shown the closest match among ancient skeletons and modern-day populations of the Mariana Islands and Island Southeast Asia (Pugach et al. 2021). These similarities accord with a rapid and multidirectional dispersal of the Malayo-Polynesian branching of Austronesian people around 1500 B.C. throughout parts of Island Southeast Asia and into the Mariana Islands, followed shortly thereafter by a migration from this preestablished multipart zone into the Near Oceanic Lapita region such as in the Bismarck Archipelago (Stoneking et al. 2023). Next, Austronesian-related Lapita groups had lived for some generations among or nearby the indigenous Papuan groups in the Bismarck Archipelago, where they developed a proto-Oceanic language community, and their later Lapita descendants migrated across to the Remote Oceanic Lapita areas such as in Vanuatu and Tonga.

Given the Near Oceanic context of a few generations of Austronesians and Papuans living together, both of those DNA lineages may be expected in combination among the later generations of Lapita people moving to live in Remote Oceanic areas of Southern Melanesia and West Polynesia. However, the aDNA findings have shown primarily an Austronesian DNA signature among the people who migrated into Remote Oceanic Lapita sites. Austronesian DNA was prevalent among the Lapita-age populations in both Vanuatu and Tonga, with only a small percentage of Papuan DNA in Vanuatu and nearly none at all in Tonga (Skoglund et al. 2016). In separate and later post-Lapita contexts, the Papuan DNA ancestry became much more prevalent in Vanuatu, today recognized as an Australo-Melanesian area, while the Austronesian DNA ancestry continued as the nearly singular component in Tonga, today recognized as a Polynesian area.

If the cultural contexts of pottery, and especially of the finely decorated varieties, were regarded as essential for the people who migrated into new islands with the spread of the Lapita horizon, then those cultural contexts need to be recognized as originating from the Malayo-Polynesian-speaking groups that mostly possessed Austronesian physical traits and DNA lineages. In the places where indigenous Papuan populations were involved in Lapita contexts, Malayo-Polynesian languages were adopted and contributed to the formation of the Oceanic subgroup. The decorated pottery and Oceanic subgroup of Malayo-Polynesian language became completely dominant in the Lapita world, while the biological situation naturally was somewhat different. The necessarily intrusive Austronesian lineages did not make too much impact overall in Near Oceania or even in the closest Remote Oceanic islands of Southern Melanesia, but they became dominant in West Polynesia at the far eastern and later-aged end of the Lapita distribution, as seen in cranial morphology (Pietrusewsky 2006) and in DNA markers (Cox 2015).

Endemic malaria in New Guinea and Near Oceania probably affected the ability of Austronesian-derived groups to live there, whereas the indigenous Australo-Melanesian or Papuan groups already had developed genetic traits that afforded partial resistance against malaria. These issues were not relevant in the Remote Oceanic islands where malaria was absent. Malaria is considered endemic because it continues in perpetuity, in contrast to an outbreak of an epidemic such as smallpox that occurs as a single definable event. Malaria can be deadly to adults and especially to infants and children, so a genetically inherited resistance would be beneficial overall for a population's survival, even if it entailed a blood disorder such as thalassemia (Clark and Kelly 1993). Thalassemia indeed is present in a significant proportion of the Australo-Melanesian populations in the malaria-affected areas, yet it is virtually absent among the Austronesians of Taiwan, Malayo-Polynesians of Island Southeast Asia, Micronesians, and Polynesians.

While the large-scale picture of genetics always will need to be framed by the cautions of representative sampling and logical inference, physical anthropological analysis of ancient skeletal remains in dated contexts slowly has been providing more information directly about the people who lived in the past. Lapita-age burial features are quite rare overall, but observations have clarified that Lapita populations included people of both Austronesian and Australo-Melanesian physical types (Pietrusewsky 2006). Most informatively in recent decades, the discovery of a dense cemetery at the Teouma Site in Vanuatu has afforded a unique opportunity to examine more than 40 Lapita-age burials in comparison to more than 30 immediately post-Lapita burials (Valentin et al. 2009, 2011). The mortuary practice involved special treatment of heads or skulls. For example, skulls or skull fragments had been repositioned around the remains of other individuals, and secondary burials were inside large pottery vessels (Valentin et al. 2015).

Among the dozens of burial features at the Teouma Site, five skulls were identified as sufficiently intact for a detailed craniofacial study, and they exhibited a close match with Polynesian morphology rather than with the Australo-Melanesian morphology of today's indigenous people of Vanuatu (Valentin et al. 2016). Adding to the aDNA of three individuals of mostly Austronesian type as already mentioned (Skoglund et al. 2016), the craniofacial findings suggest that people of Austronesian-derived Polynesian physical type definitely were among the founding Lapita population in Vanuatu, yet eventually they became outnumbered by people of Australo-Melanesian physical type as seen today in Vanuatu. Additionally, these particular individuals at the Teouma Site were buried with attention to grave goods suggesting high social status, but these contexts did not continue into the post-Lapita era after the loss of finely decorated pottery and other transformations by 500 B.C. (Chapter 8).

Transported landscapes

The combined archaeological, linguistic, biological, and ecological information enables a rich illustration of how people transformed diverse islands into familiar habitats, in some ways transported or transplanted from overseas homeland traditions but in other ways developed locally as new expressions of the Lapita horizon. From a Remote Oceanic perspective, a rapid and widespread Lapita settlement occurred as a unified phenomenon that brought a fully operational cultural system and effectively inhabited landscape and seascape. These behaviors must have been imported or transported from proximate Lapita origins in Near Oceania, wherein people translocated their material artifacts, economically useful plants, domesticated animals, and ways of thinking about the island world. Many of those ideas and behaviors could be traced to even older ancestry in Island Southeast Asia, as seen in the pottery trail and related evidence discussed in Chapter 5, but other elements of a Lapita Cultural Complex developed locally within Near Oceania or even later in Remote Oceanic contexts.

With refined radiocarbon dating of multiple Lapita sites across Near and Remote Oceania, at least three stages can be defined, furthermore clarifying the context of a transported landscape.

- The first stage of Lapita emergence in Near Oceania occurred as early as 1500–1350 B.C. and continued through 1200–1100 B.C. in islands where pottery-making groups met with preestablished populations. The elaborate dentate-stamped designs and vessel shapes likely related to acts of presentation and display, suggestive of signaling cultural identity during cross-cultural encounters.
- The second stage involved localized developments of Lapita decorations, along with learning and sharing of knowledge about the indigenous pre-Lapita cultural practice as combined with new Lapita-associated traditions, beginning about 1200–1100 B.C. and continuing through perhaps 800 B.C. While those processes were underway in Near Oceania, new population movements brought Lapita groups into the Remote Oceanic islands of Southern Melanesia and West Polynesia, primarily in the range of 1100–800 B.C.
- The third stage entailed further area-specific diversification of Lapita groups, beginning about 800 B.C. throughout the inhabited islands of the Lapita world and sustained until the end of Lapita about 500 B.C. in the context of sea-level drawdown and compound effects of a transforming natural and cultural environment.

Within the three-part chronological resolution within the Lapita period, the notion of a siege of ecological imperialism in Remote Oceania can be ascertained as having occurred during a few centuries between 1100 B.C. and 800 B.C. These events necessarily postdated some centuries of earlier developments locally within Near Oceania during the emergence and establishment of the Lapita tradition and associated Lapita Cultural Complex. Significant blending of cultural knowledge and practice already had occurred within Near Oceania, and the resulting new traditions of Lapita postdating 1200 B.C. can be identified as the repertoire of traits potentially transported into the Remote Oceanic islands as part of the rapid and widespread social and ecological impact of the later Lapita diaspora.

In both Near and Remote Oceania, the Lapita communities lived in shoreline-oriented settlements, very much as had been seen in the seashore habitat niche-targeting of the earliest Mariana Islands sites (Chapter 6). The timing of Remote Oceanic Lapita settlements after 1100 B.C., however, coincided with the beginning of sea-level drawdown and initial transformations of precisely those seashore habitats that were preferred for the habitation sites. The Remote Oceanic Lapita settlers needed to adapt to changing coastal ecologies concurrently with their creation of transported landscapes. Meanwhile, their counterparts in Near Oceania and in the Mariana Islands already had been established for some time prior to these potentially distressing conditions of a changing environment.

The deliberate targeting of specific coastal niches was part of an older ancestral tradition, applied and reapplied in different settings of the Asia-Pacific region, whenever people moved for the first time to inhabit new areas and especially in the island world of Pacific Oceania. These island settings happen to contain densely packed coastal areas of diverse ecologies, with high concentrations of the kinds of habitat niches preferred by the early settlers. The nearshore zones provided immediate access to vital resources of freshwater seeps, small fish, and abundant shellfish such as *Anadara* sp. clams.

The ancient geographic settings of Lapita sites naturally varied somewhat from one place to another, depending on the localized availability of usable landforms and resource zones such as coral reefs and mangroves. In general terms, the Lapita-age habitation sites consistently were situated very close to the ancient shorelines and often in shallow subtidal or intertidal zones, but local conditions would have dictated the ability to select places with access to protected lagoons, fringing reefs, swamps, and other types of habitats that were beneficial in different ways. Other consistent factors included access to the ocean for canoe transport, proximity to interior land masses for forest resources and cultivable lands, and availability of fresh water in seeps, streams, or caves. Daniel Frimigacci (1980) suggested that archaeologists should seek to understand those consistencies in the choices of ancient site locations, with attention to the original conditions that may look much different from today's settings, but this scope of research would need to wait for more than a decade while the regional sea-level history was not yet understood clearly.

With solid information now available about changing sea level regionally and globally, considerable efforts over the last few decades have concentrated on reconstructing the Lapita site settings during the time of their inhabitation. Reconstructions have been possible by coordinating knowledge about the depths of subsurface layers, origins of their associated sedimentary units, and the state of sea level during the measured time interval (Figure 7.6). This strategy successfully depicted the original contexts of Lapita sites in the Bismarck Archipelago (Summerhayes 2022), Tonga (Dickinson et al. 1994), New Caledonia (Carson 2008), and Fiji (Nunn 2005). Nunn and Heorake (2009) expanded this work to depict the range of seashore niches that once had been inhabited at varied places in Fiji and elsewhere (Figure 7.7).

In places where localized tectonics have counteracted the effects of regional sea-level change, Lapita pottery and other materials potentially can be found in settings similar to their original deposition. For instance, concentrations of Lapita-associated artifacts have been reported on the surfaces of coral reefs in the Solomon Islands, with little or no sedimentary deposit and with apparently little or no net change in sea level since the time of their cultural use (Sheppard and Walter 2009). In other cases, exceptional magnitude of localized subsidence or uplift may have created unusual conditions in some localities, such as the submerged setting of a Lapita site offshore of 'Upolu in Samoa (Dickinson and Green 1998).

While nearshore resources were accessible directly within the proximities of the early Lapita village settlements, other resource zones were important for survival. Perhaps most essentially, people needed to gain a portion of their nutrition from plants, and especially starchy plants, yet the Remote Oceanic islands did not naturally offer the same range of edible plant foods as could be found more abundantly in the forests of Near Oceanic islands. Clearly seen in botanical records as part of a sudden human impact horizon, the roster of overseas imported plants was quite impressive, not only for food products but also for construction wood, therapeutic medicines, and other cultural usage. At the far eastern end of the Lapita distribution in the islands of Samoa, at least 49 plants are recognized as early cultural imports (Whistler 2000), despite the great distance from an original source in Near Oceania.

In addition to the dozens of plants, people translocated a set of animals as significant components in creating an entirely new ecological balance in the islands where they appeared abruptly. Most important in the artificially imposed food production systems were the pigs, dogs, and chickens that people had imported into most of the islands. The notable exceptions, such as in New Caledonia lacking imported pigs and dogs, are regarded as curious anomalies departing from the overall pattern. People may not have imported rats intentionally, but rats nonetheless became active agents of ecological

200 *A siege of ecological imperialism*

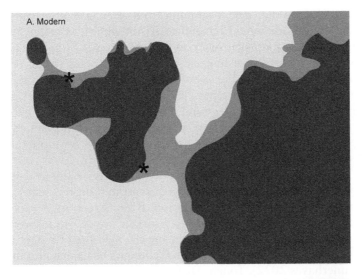

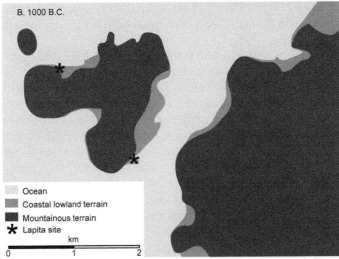

Figure 7.6 Lapita landscape versus modern conditions at Vavouto, New Caledonia. Graphic is based on information from Carson (2008).

impacts in the islands, with magnified results in the fragile settings of Remote Oceanic islands.

The suite of imported plants and animals became established partly at the expense of native species. People cleared native forests to make new growing space for their preferred plant communities, and gradually the artificially manipulated and managed compositions dominated throughout the inhabited zones of each island. Furthermore, the disturbance or removal of the original habitats affected native birds, bats, and other animals that mostly had evolved without natural defense against predators such as humans and rats. Pigs, dogs, and chickens brought their own impacts on the environment as well.

A siege of ecological imperialism 201

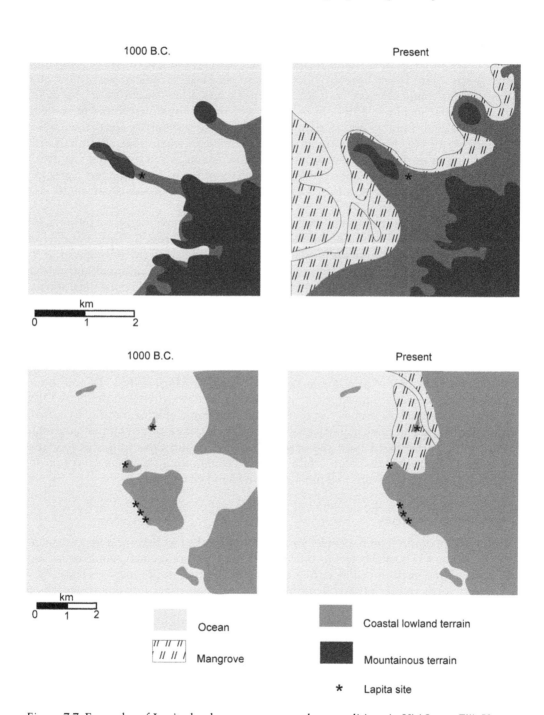

Figure 7.7 Examples of Lapita landscapes versus modern conditions in Viti Levu, Fiji. Upper: Natunuka area. Lower: Rove Peninsula area. Graphics are modified from models by Nunn and Heorake (2009).

Faunal and botanical records depict rapid decline and often outright extinction of native taxa rather quickly as part of the horizon of first human appearance of Lapita groups in Remote Oceania. Centuries later, this pattern would be repeated again in almost every other remote island of the Pacific. Among the records of depopulation of native species, bird bones have provided some of the clearest indications of how quickly the island environments were transformed within just a few centuries or less of initial human arrivals (Steadman 1995). Bones of now-extinct animals are found in contexts of ancient food, indisputably implicating people as largely responsible for their demise. To some extent, the effects on the animal world depended on what range of animals already had been living in the particular Remote Oceanic island in question, but the available records so far indicate extinctions of several species of birds, including large megapodes in some islands, as well as kinds of tortoise, crocodiles, and others (Bedford 2006; Dye and Steadman 1990; Sand 1995).

The narrative of anthropogenic impacts is strong and compelling, yet caution is advisable to avoid overinterpretation. Faunal and botanical records, by their nature, reflect human impacts on the animal and plant populations, wherein the only question is the degree of impact being represented in each instance. Records of minimal anthropogenic impact are difficult to prove, yet they have been evident in the Mariana Islands, starting at an earlier dating around 1500 B.C. and sustaining the minimal level of effects until much later, around A.D. 1000 (Chapter 6). Further restraint is necessary about overstating the Lapita case to the point of cultural determinism that can be just as problematic (if not more so) than environmental determinism.

In a chronological view, the Remote Oceanic Lapita impacts represented a departure from the older example of minimal impacts in the remote Mariana Islands, and so far the degree of human-caused impact seems to have been not so extreme in the Near Oceanic Lapita sites as well. This perspective reveals that the people moving into the Remote Oceanic Lapita world had implemented a substantially different mode of human-environment interaction than ever had been the case previously among their immediate or distant ancestors. Conceivably, the later Lapita context brought an anomalous exception to the preestablished pattern of minimal impacts in an island environment.

Lapita contemporaries

Any discussion of the "Lapita people" must account for the fact that the diagnostic dentate-stamped pottery of Lapita refers to only one narrow kind of context, while other aspects of the social and environmental setting may represent ancient life more realistically. This awareness, furthermore, raises a concern about defining other possible groups (or subgroups) living contemporaneously with the Lapita phenomenon. Many sites show no dentate-stamped pottery at all, as in Samoa where so far only a single site has yielded classic Lapita pottery and, in fact, all of the other known Lapita-age sites in Samoa involved solely plainware pottery. Meanwhile in New Caledonia, paddle-impressed pottery of the Podtanéan tradition was made simultaneously with Lapita and was found at the same sites plus others where no Lapita pottery has yet been found, thus suggesting different contexts that operated at the same time. In all of these sites, most of the reflected cultural activities did not involve dentate-stamped pottery, but rather people used large amounts of other pottery types, built houses, collected fish and shellfish, and used assorted shell and stone tools.

The apparent minority of dentate-stamped Lapita pottery signifies a constrained cultural context, and potentially it could be interpreted as reflecting its own "archaeological culture" as implied by referring to a Lapita Cultural Complex. Depending on how scholars conceptualize an archaeological culture (see Chapter 3), the material inventories may be leveraged to infer different cultural contexts or different sets of people during the Lapita era using dentate-stamped pottery versus other forms and styles of pottery. Given the mix of different groups of people involved in the initial colonizing events in the Remote Oceanic islands, perhaps the role of dentate-stamped pottery was more important for some people than for others.

In a larger view of Pacific Oceanic archaeology, Lapita groups were not the only inhabitants of Remote Oceania as a whole, even though they dominated in Island Melanesia and West Polynesia. As shown in Chapter 6, ancestrally related people had been living in the Mariana Islands at least as early as 1500 B.C., where definite change in material culture occurred by 1100 B.C. in terms of pottery forms and decorations, shell ornaments, stone tools, housing locations, and use of a transforming coastal ecology. Additionally, while the Lapita expansion was underway, another sea-crossing migration occurred in an entirely different area of far western Micronesia, specifically with the settlement of Palau about 1100–1000 B.C. (mentioned in Chapter 5). The Lapita groups probably experienced very little and indirect contact with these other groups in the Mariana Islands and in Palau, but this larger picture reveals more about the regional context of the Lapita phenomenon.

While the early settlements of the Mariana Islands and Palau involved groups of Malayo-Polynesian speakers separate from the Proto Oceanic communities of the Lapita realm, another possible early settlement in Yap (in west-central Micronesia) may have been related more closely with Lapita around 1000 B.C. No such site ever has been discovered in Yap, but the linguistic origins of Yapese point to an origin at a time of a breakup of the oldest Oceanic-speaking groups inferred as having occurred when Lapita pottery-making groups spread into Remote Oceania (Ross 1996). Archaeological surveys in Yap so far have concentrated on the surface-visible village ruins of known ethnohistoric contexts, whereas any older buried site layers of 1000 B.C. would require a different strategy of subsurface exploration with attention to ancient landscape settings. In the absence of archaeological data, paleoenvironmental proxies suggest an anthropogenic impact horizon older than any attested archaeological sites, in this case estimated around 1000 B.C. (Dodson and Intoh 1999) and admittedly intriguing yet sorely needing further research.

The findings at the western fringe of Micronesia clarify that Lapita was not alone in Remote Oceania. People very certainly were living in the Mariana Islands and in Palau, although their separate language histories and material culture sequences indicate overall independence from the Lapita world and from each other. A few low-level contacts may have occurred with Lapita communities but without affecting the overall culture histories in the Marianas and Palau, while a possible early settlement in Yap hypothetically would have related to the same Oceanic-speaking communities as were associated with Lapita. At least some east-west contacts must have occurred in order to account for the presence of Talasea obsidian coming from a source in the Bismarck Archipelago and distributed as far west as Borneo and as far east as Fiji (Bellwood and Koon 1989; Reepmeyer et al. 2011; Spriggs et al. 2011), but the western contact points seem to have been concentrated in Indonesia rather than in western Micronesia at this time.

Along with these developments of Lapita communities expanding the inhabited landscape and seascape in Remote Oceania, people naturally continued living in Near Oceania and Island Southeast Asia, and some of the geographic spread of pottery-making traditions still was continuing in Indonesia, as outlined in Chapter 5. In particular, sites with dentate-stamped pottery began to emerge in scattered areas of Indonesia as late as 1100–800 B.C.

Several other sites at this time and continuing through 500 B.C. began to be inhabited yet showed undecorated red-slipped pottery lacking the diagnostic dentate-stamped motifs. As has been mentioned, the long-distance transport of Talasea obsidian clearly linked at least some of the Indonesian sites of this period with the Lapita world.

A final caution must be mentioned about drawing conclusions from the available site records, specifically in terms of accepting the fact that new discoveries may yet alter the knowledge base. For instance, the potential for an early site record in Samoa has not been explored thoroughly, and the narrative of Lapita in this area may need to be rewritten. If the few presently known Lapita-age sites in Samoa truly are representative, then they offer a picture of a single dentate-stamped founding settlement at 800 B.C., immediately followed by a more widespread plainware horizon at 800–500 B.C. The possibility persists, however, that today's landscape is obscuring an unknown number of sites of 800 B.C. or older, now hidden beneath sedimentary layers perhaps 1.5 m or deeper.

The search will need to continue for the oldest site layers in Samoa, for instance, by following the strategy in the Mariana Islands for identifying and contextualizing sites of 1500–1100 B.C. in relation to the sea level, coastal ecology, and other conditions of their time (Chapter 6). This approach works for any time period by coordinating the local sea-level history, sedimentary unit formation, coastal morphology, and other factors as shown in a full chronological sequence of landscape evolution at the Ritidian Site in Guam (Carson 2012, 2017) and elsewhere in the Marianas (Carson 2011, 2014; Carson and Hung 2022). Accordingly, the same practical approach, as well as the same paradigm of natural-cultural landscape evolution, proved successful in documenting the plainware Samoan site layer of 800–500 B.C. in Ofu Village (Quintus et al. 2015). Independently, geoarchaeological research clarified the sequence of sedimentary units and other factors involved in the formation of the plainware occupation at Aganoa, dated about 800–500 B.C. (Pearl and Sauck 2014). Based on these findings so far, a similar scope of research surely can be broadened in Samoa, as well as in Yap and elsewhere, toward resolving the questions of possible settlement in the available landforms and habitats at 800 B.C. or earlier.

References

Ambrose, Wal, 1999. Curves, tines, and scutes in Lapita ware. In *The Western Pacific, 5000 to 2000 BP: Colonisations and Transformations*, edited by Jean-Christophe Galipaud and Ian Lilley, pp. 119–126. Institut de Récherche pour le Dévéloppement, Paris.

Ambrose, Wal, 2007. The implements of Lapita ceramic stamped ornamentation. In *Oceanic Explorations: Lapita and Western Pacific Settlement*, edited by Stuart Bedford, Christophe Sand, and Sean P. Connaughton, pp. 213–221. Australian National University E Press, Canberra.

Ambrose, Wal, 2012. Oceanic tattooing and the implied Lapita ceramic connection. *Journal of Pacific Archaeology 3*: 1–21.

Anson, Dmitri, 1983. *Lapita Pottery of the Bismarck Archipelago and Its Affinities*. Doctoral dissertation, Department of Anthropology, University of Sydney, Sydney.

Bedford, Stuart, 2006. *Pieces of the Vanuatu Puzzle: Archaeology of the North, South and Centre*. Terra Australis 23. The Australian National University E Press, Canberra.

Bedford, Stuart, 2015. Going beyond the known world 3000 years ago: Lapit exploration and colonization of Remote Oceania. In *The Lapita Cultural Complex in Time and Space: Expansion Routes, Chronologies, and Typologies*, edited by Christophe Sand, Scarlett Chiu, and Nicholas Hogg, pp. 25–47. Archeologia Pasifika 4. Institut d'Archéologie de la Nouvelle-Calédonie et du Pacifique, Nouméa.

Bedford, Stuart, Matthew Spriggs, Dave Burley, Christohe Sand, Peter Sheppard, and Glenn R. Summerhayes, 2019. Debating Lapita: Distribution, chronology, society and subsistence. In *Debating Lapita: Chronology, Society and Subsistence*, edited by Stuart Bedford and Matthew Spriggs, pp. 5–53. Terra Australis 52. The Australian National University E Press, Canberra.

Bedford, Stuart, Matthew Spriggs, Ralph Regenvanu, Colin Macgregor, Takaronga Kuautonga, and Michael Sietz, 2007. The excavation, conservation and reconstruction of Lapita burial pots from the Teouma Site, Efate, central Vanuatu. In *Oceanic Explorations: Lapita and Western Pacific Settlement*, edited by Stuart Bedford, Christophe Sand, and Sean P. Connaughton, pp. 223–240. Terra Australis 26. The Australian National University E Press, Canberra.

Bellwood, Peter, and Peter Koon, 1989. Lapita colonists leave boats unburned: The question of Lapita links with Island Southeast Asia. *Antiquity* 63: 613–622.

Blust, Robert, 2013. *The Austronesian Languages*. Revised edition. Asia-Pacific Linguistics Open Access Monographs 008. Research School of Pacific and Asian Studies, Australian National University, Canberra.

Burley, David V., 2023. *The Birth of Polynesia: An Archaeological Journey through the Kingdom of Tonga*. Archaeology Press, Simon Fraser University, Burnaby, Canada.

Burley, David V., Andrew Barton, Willian R. Dickinson, Sean P. Connaghton, and Karine Taché, 2010. Nukuleka as a founder colony for West Polynesian settlement: New insights from recent excavations. *Journal of Pacific Archaeology* 1: 128–144.

Burley, David V., and Sean P. Connaughton, 2007. First Lapita settlement and its chronology in Vava'u, Kingdom of Tonga. *Radiocarbon* 49: 131–137.

Burley, David V., and Sean P. Connaughton, 2010. Completing the story: A late Lapita denate-stamped pot from Sigatoka, Fiji. *Archaeology in Oceania* 45: 144–146.

Burley, David V., and William R. Dickinson, 2010. Among Polynesia's first pots. *Journal of Archaeological Science* 37: 1020–1026.

Carson, Mike T., 2003. *Phase Two Archaeological Study, Koniambo Project, Regions of Voh, Koné, and Pouémbout, Northern Province, New Caledonia*. Report prepared for Projet Koniambo. International Archaeological Research Institute, Inc., Honolulu.

Carson, Mike T., 2008. Correlation of environmental and cultural chronology in New Caledonia. *Geoarchaeology* 23: 695–714.

Carson, Mike T., 2011. Palaeohabitat of first settlement sites 1500–1000 B.C. in Guam, Mariana Islands, western Pacific. *Journal of Archaeological Science* 38: 2207–2221.

Carson, Mike T., 2012. Evolution of an Austronesian landscape: The Ritidian Site in Guam. *Journal of Austronesian Studies* 3: 55–86.

Carson, Mike T., 2014. Paleoterrain research: Finding the first settlement sites of Remote Oceania. *Geoarchaeology* 29: 268–275.

Carson, Mike T., 2017. *Rediscovering Heritage through Artefacts, Sites, and Landscapes: Translatign a 3500-year Record at Ritidian, Guam*. Archaeopress, Oxford.

Carson, Mike T., and Hsiao-chun Hung, 2022. 3500 years in a changing landscape: The House of Taga in the Mariana Islands, western Micronesia. In *Palaeolandscapes in Archaeology: Lessons for the Past and Future*, edited by Mike T. Carson, pp. 340–376. Routledge, London.

Chambers, Geoffrey K., and Hisham A. Edinur, 2015. The Austronesian diaspora: A total synthetic evidence model. *Global Journal of Anthropology Research* 2: 53–65.

Chiu, Scarlett, 2011. Lapita-scape: Research possibilities using the digital database of Lapita pottery. *People and Culture in Oceania* 27: 39–63.

Clark, Jeffrey T., and Kevin M. Kelly, 1993. Human genetics, paleoenvironments, and malaria: Relationships and implications for the settlement of Oceania. *American Anthropologist* 95: 612–630.

Cox, Murray P., 2015. Southeast Asian islands and Oceania: Human genetics. In *The Global Prehistory of Human Migration*, edited by Peter Bellwood, pp. 293–301. Wiley-Blackwell, Malden, MA.

Dickinson, William R., David V. Burley, and Richard Shutler, Jr., 1994. Impact of hydro-isostatic Holocene sea-level change on the geologic context of island archaeological sites, northern Ha'apai Group, Kingdom of Tonga. *Geoarchaeology* 9: 85–111.

Dickinson, William R., and Roger C. Green, 1998. Geoarcheological context of Holocene subsidence at the Ferry Berth Lapita Site, Mulifanua, Upolu, Samoa. *Geoarchaeology* 13: 239–263.

Dodson, John, and Michiko Intoh, 1999. Prehistory and palaeoecology of Yap, Federated States of Micronesia. *Quaternary International* 59: 17–26.

Donovan, Lorna J., 1973. *A Study of the Decorative System of the Lapita Potters in Reefs and Santa Cruz Islands*. M.A. thesis, Department of Anthropology, University of Auckland, Auckland.

Dye, Tom S., and David W. Steadman, 1990. Polynesian ancestors and their animal world. *American Scientist* 78: 207–215.

Frimigacci, Daniel, 1980. Localisation éco-géographique et utilization de l'éspace de quelques sites Lapita de Nouvelle-Calédonie: Essai d'interprétation. *Journal de la Société des Océanistes* 36: 5–11.

Green, Roger C., 1979a. Lapita. In *The Prehistory of Polynesia*, edited by Jesse D. Jennings, pp. 27–60. Harvard University Press, Cambridge.

Green, Roger C., 1979b. Early Lapita art from Polynesia and Island Melanesia: Continuities in ceramic, barkcloth, and tattoo decorations. In *Exploring the Visual Art of Oceania: Australia, Melanesia, Micronesia, and Polynesia*, edited by Sidney M. Mead, pp. 13–31. University of Hawai'i Press, Honolulu.

Irwin, Geoffrey J., Trevor H. Worthy, Simon Best, Stuart Hawkins, Jonathan Carpenter, and Sepeti Matararaba, 2011. Further investigations at the Naigani Lapita Site (VL 21/5), Fiji: Excavation, radiocarbon dating and palaeofaunal extinction. *Journal of Pacific Archaeology* 2: 66–78.

Kirch, Patrick V., 1997. *The Lapita Peoples: Ancestors of the Oceanic World*. Blackwell Publishers, Cambridge.

Mead, Sidney M., 1975a. The decorative system of the Lapita potters of Sigatoka, Fiji. In *The Lapita Style of Fiji and Its Associations*, edited by Sidney M. Mead, Lawrence Birks, Helen Birks, and Elizabeth Shaw, pp. 19–43. Memoir 38. The Polynesian Society, Wellington.

Mead, Sidney M., 1975b. The relationships of the decorative systems of Fiji. In *The Lapita Style of Fiji and Its Associations*, edited by Sidney M. Mead, Lawrence Birks, Helen Birks, and Elizabeth Shaw, pp. 56–68. Memoir 38. The Polynesian Society, Wellington.

Noury, Arnaud, 2005. *Le Reflet de l'Âme Lapita, Tome 1: Essai d'interprétation des décors des potteries Lapita en Mélanésie et Polynésie Occidentale entre 3000 et 2700 BP*. Aurnaud Noury, Versailles.

Noury, Arnaud, and Jean-Christophe Galipaud, 2011. *Les Lapita, Nomades du Pacifique*. IRD Éditions, Institut de Recherche pour le Développement, Marseille.

Nunn, Patrick D., 2005. Reconstructing tropical shorelines using archaeological data: Examples from the Fiji Archipelago, southwest Pacific. *Journal of Coastal Research Special Issue* 42: 15–25.

Nunn, Patrick D., and Tony Ahikau Heorake, 2009. Understanding the place properly: Palaeogeography of selected Lapita sites in the western tropical Pacific Islands and its implications. In *Lapita: Ancestors and Descendants*, edited by Peter J. Sheppard, Tim Thomas, and Glenn R. Summerhayes, pp. 235–254. Monograph 28. New Zealand Archaeological Association, Auckland.

Nunn, Patrick D., and Fiona J. Petchey, 2013. Bayesian re-evaluation of Lapita settlement in Fiji: Radiocarbon analysis of the Lapita occupation at Bourewa and nearby sites on the Rove Peninsula, Viti Levu Island. *Journal of Pacific Archaeology* 4: 21–34.

Pawley, Andrew K., 2003. Locating proto Oceanic. In *The Lexicon of Proto Oceanic: The Culture and Environment of Ancestral Oceanic Society 7. Volume 2: The Physical Environment*, edited by Malcolm Ross, Andrew Pawley, and Meredith Osmond, pp. 17–34. Pacific Linguistics 545. The Australian National University E Press, Canberra.

Pawley, Andrew K., and Roger C. Green, 1984. The Proto Oceanic language community. *Journal of Pacific History* 19: 123–146.

Pawley, Andrew K., and Malcolm Ross, 1993. Austronesian historical linguistics and culture history. *Annual Review of Anthropology* 22: 425–459.

Pearl, Frederic B., and William A. Sauck, 2014. Geophysical and geoarchaeological investigations at Aganoa Beach, American Samoa: An early archaeological site in Western Polynesia. *Geoarchaeology* 29: 462–476.

Pietrusewsky, Michael, 2006. The initial settlement of Remote Oceania: The evidence from physical anthropology. In *Austronesian Diaspora and the Ethnogenesis of People in the Indonesian Archipelago*, edited by T. Simanjuntak, I. H. E. Pojoh, and M. Hisyam, pp. 320–347. Indonesian Institute of Sciences, Jakarta.

Pugach, Irina, Alexander Hübner, Hsiao-chun Hung, Matthias Meyer, Mike T. Carson, and Mark Stoneking, 2021. Ancient DNA from GBuam and the peopling of the Pacific. *Proceedings of the National Academy of Sciences* 18: e2022112118. https://doi.org/10.1073/pnas.2022112118.

Quintus, Seth, Jeffrey T. Clark, Stephanie S. Day, and Donald P. Schwert, 2015. Landscape evolution and human settlement patterns on Ofu Island, Manu'a Group, American Samoa. *Asian Perspectives* 54: 208–237.

Reepmeyer, Christian, Matthew Spriggs, Anggraeni, Peter Lape, Leee Neri, Wilfredo P. Ronquillo, Truman Simanjuntak, Glenn Summerhayes, Daud Tanudirjo, and Archie Tiauzon, 2011. Obsidian sources and distribution systems in Island Southeast Asia: New results and implications from geochemical research using LA-ICPMS. *Journal of Archaeological Science* 38: 2995–3005.

Ross, Malcolm D., 1988. *Proto Oceanic and the Austronesian Languages of Western Melanesia*. Pacific Linguistics, Series C, Number 98. Department of Linguistics, the Australian National University, Canberra.

Ross, Malcolm D., 1996. Is Yapese Oceanic? In *Reconstruction, Classification, Description: Festschrift in Honor of Isidore Dyen*, edited by Bernd Nothofer, pp. 121–166. Abera, Hamburg.

Ross, Malcolm D., Andrew Pawley, and Meredith Osmond (editors), 1998. *The Lexicon of Proto Oceanic. Volume 1, Material Culture: The Culture and Environment of Ancestral Oceanic Society*. Pacific Linguistics. Research School of Pacific and Asian Studies, the Australian National University, Canberra.

Ross, Malcolm D., Andrew Pawley, and Meredith Osmond (editors), 2003. *The Lexicon of Proto Oceanic: The Culture and Environment of Ancestral Oceanic Society 2: The Physical Environment*. Pacific Linguistics. The Australian National University E Press, Canberra.

Sand, Christophe, 1995. *Le Temps d'Avant: La préhistoire de la Nouvelle-Calédonie*. L'Harmattan, Paris.

Sand, Christophe, 1997. The chronology of Lapita ware in New Caledonia. *Antiquity* 71: 539–547.

Sand, Christophe, 2010. *Lapita Calédonien: Archéologie d'un Premir Peuplement Insulaire Océanien*. Collection Travaux et Documents Océanistes 2. Société des Océanistes, Paris.

Sharp, Nancy D., 1993. The computer graphic database as an aid to recording and analyzing pottery decoration. In *Archaeometry: Current Australiasian Research*, edited by Barry L. Fankhauser and J. Roger Bird, pp. 69–76. Occasional Papers in Prehistory 22. Department of Prehistory, Research School of Pacific Studies, the Australian National University, Canberra.

Shaw, Elizabeth, 1975. The decorative system of Natunuku, Fiji. In *The Lapita Style of Fiji and Its Associations*, edited by Sidney M. Mead, Lawrence Birks, Helen Birks, and Elizabeth Shaw, pp. 44–55. Memoir 38. The Polynesian Society, Wellington.

Sheppard, Peter J., and Richard Walter, 2009. Inter-tidal late Lapita sites and geotectonics in the western Solomon Islands. In *Lapita: Ancestors and Descendants*, edited by Peter J. Sheppard, Tim Thomas, and Glenn R. Summerhayes, pp. 73–100. Monograph 28. New Zealand Archaeological Association, Auckland.

Siorat, Jean-Pierre, 1990. A technological analysis of pottery decoration. In *Lapita Design, Form, and Composition*, edited by Matthew Spriggs, pp. 59–82. Occasional Papers in Prehistory 19. Department of Prehistory, Research School of Pacific Studies, the Australian National University, Canberra.

Siorat, Jean-Pierre, 1999. Les formes et les décors du matériel céramique du site WBR001 de Nessadiou. In *La Pacifique de 5000 à 2000 Ans avant le Présent: Suppléments à l'Histoire d'une Colonisation*, edited by Jean-Christophe Galipaud and Ian Lilley, pp. 105–115. Institut de Recherche pour le Développement, Paris.

Skoglund, Pontus, Cosimo Posth, Kendra Sirak, Matthew Spriggs, Frédérique Valentin, Stuart Bedford, Geoffrey R. Clark, Christian Reepmeyer, Fiona Petchey, Daniel Ferdandes, Qiaomei Fu, Eadaoin Harney, Mark Lipson, Swapan Mallick, Mario Novak, Nadin Rohland, Kristin Stewardson, Syafiq Abdullah, Murray P. Cox, Françoise R. Friedlaender, Jonathan S. Friedlaender, Toomas Kivisild, George Koki, Pradiptajati Kusuma, D. Andrew Merriwether, François-X. Ricaut, Joseph T. S. Wee, Nick Patterson, Johannes Krause, Ron Pinhasi, and David Reich, 2016. Gemonic insights into the peopling of the Southwest Pacific. *Nature* 538: 510–526.

Spriggs, Matthew, 1990. The changing face of Lapita: Transformation of a design. In *Lapita Design, Form, and Composition*, edited by Matthew Spriggs, pp. 83–122. Occasional Papers in Prehistory 19. Department of Prehistory, Research School of Pacific Studies, the Australian National University, Canberra.

Spriggs, Matthew, Christian Reepmeyer, Angraenni, Peter Lape, Leee Neri, Wilfredo P. Ronquillo, Truman Simanjuntak, Glenn Summerhayes, Daud Tanudirjo, and Archie Tiauzon, 2011. Obsidian sources and distribution systems in Island Southeast Asia: A review of previous research. *Journal of Archaeological Science* 38: 2871–2881.

Steadman, David W., 1995. Prehistoric extinctions of Pacific Island birds: Biodiversity meets zooarchaeology. *Science* 267: 1123–1131.

Stoneking, Mark, Leonardo Arias, Dang Liu, Sandra Oliveira, Irina Pugach, and Jae Joseph Russell B. Rodriguez, 2023. Genomic perspectives on human dispersals during the Holocene. *Proceedings of the National Academy of Sciences* 120: e2209475119. https://doi.org/10.1073/pnas.2209475119

Summerhayes, Glenn R., 2000a. *Lapita Interaction*. Terra Australis 15. Department of Archaeology and Natural History and Centre of Archaeological Research, the Australian National University, Canberra.

Summerhayes, Glenn R., 2000b. Far western, western, and eastern Lapita: A re-evaluation. *Asian Perspectives* 39: 109–138.

Summerhayes, Glenn R, 2022. Kisim save long graun: Understanding the nature of landscape change in modelling Lapita in Papua New Guinea. In *Palaeolandcapes in Archaeology: Lessons for the Past and Future*, edited by Mike T. Carson, pp. 291–312. Routledge, London.

Valentin, Frédérique, Stuart Bedford, Matthew Spriggs, and Hallie R. Buckley, 2009. Une analyse diachronique des pratiques funéraires préhistoriques du centre du Vanuatu. *Journal de la Société des Océanistes* 128: 39–52.

Valentin, Frédérique, Jeong-in Choi, Hsiuman Lin, Stuart Bedford, and Matthew Spriggs, 2015. Three-thousand-year-old jar burials at the Teouma Cemetery (Vanuatu): A Southeast Asian-Lapita connection? In *The Lapita Cultural Complex in Time and Space: Expansion Routes, Chronologies, and Typologies*, edited by Christophe Sand, Scarlett Chiu, and Nicholas Hogg, pp. 81–101. Archeologia Pasifika 4. Institut d'Archéologie de la Nouvelle-Calédonie et du Pacifique, Nouméa.

Valentin, Frédérique, Florent Détroit, Matthew Spriggs, and Stuart Bedford, 2016. Early Lapita skeletons from show Polynesian craniofacial shape: Implications for Remote Oceanic settlement and Lapita origins. *Proceedings of the National Academy of Sciences* 113: 292–297.

Valentin, Frédérique, Matthew Spriggs, Stuart Bedford, and Hallie R. Buckley, 2011. Vanuatu mortuary practices over three millennia: Lapita to the early European contact period. *Journal of Pacific Archaeology* 2: 49–65.

Walter, Richard, and Peter Sheppard, 2017. *Archaeology of the Solomon Islands*. University of Hawai'i Press, Honolulu.

Whistler, W. Arthur, 2000. *Plants in Samoan Culture: The Ethnobotany of Samoa*. Isle Botanica, Honolulu.

8 The end of an era
Adjusting to changing coastlines, 1100 through 500 B.C.

'Oua lau e kafo kae lau e lava (Tongan proverb), translates into English as
"Stay positive and count your blessings."

This quote serves as a reminder to be thankful of what we have, as well as to keep moving productively in our lives, rather than to concede to despair and defeat in the face of a challenge. For instance, when Pacific Islanders, on numerous occasions, have found that their coastal environments and lifestyles were being threatened by changing sea level and other forces beyond their control, they could rely on other strengths and strategies in order to persevere. One such example occurred in the centuries following 1100 B.C., when a period of sea-level drawdown created region-wide effects on coastal ecologies and people responded by refocusing their energies into alternatives of interior forests, terrestrial habitats, and land-based food resources.

Within a few centuries after Remote Oceanic settlement, the descendants of the first island immigrants found that the worlds of their immediate ancestors were beginning to transform or even to disappear, and they needed to adapt to new circumstances of lowering sea level and altered coastal ecologies. For some generations, people had targeted highly specialized and productive nearshore ecological niches that did not survive the changing environmental conditions. The preferred cultural lifeways eventually became unsustainable due to the compound effects of changing sea level and human-caused impacts on sensitive resources. Initial signs of change began as early as 1100 B.C. in some island groups such as the Marianas, and cross-regional responses were in full effect by 500 B.C. throughout the inhabited island groups of Pacific Oceania, simultaneously involving shifts in residential placements, decreasing reliance on coastal resources, increasing use of inland and land-based resource zones, and termination of finely decorated pottery traditions.

Regardless of how much the coastlines and habitats have changed through time, coastal zones consistently have played essential roles in island life. The shapes of coastlines and configurations of resource areas have changed, but people repeatedly have adjusted according to the new conditions. Some of those adjustment periods have been more difficult than others, for example, when preestablished coastal lifestyles became unsustainable within brief time frames and forced people quickly to engage in radically different lifestyles.

In an archaeological perspective, a "rapid" period of radical readjustment could refer to a window of some centuries, and the "radical" factor of the readjustment must be acknowledged as somewhat subjective. One such challenge now confronts the modern world with predictions of global warming and sea-level rise, already noticed in the low-lying atolls of Micronesia with salinization of the water table and flooding of many coastal lands.

DOI: 10.4324/9781003399025-8

A different kind of challenge confronted Pacific Islanders after 1100 B.C. during a period of sea-level drawdown.

In Pacific Oceania, the effects of a sea-level-driven change in coastal ecology at 1100–500 B.C. were compounded with the cultural impacts occurring during the centuries following initial island settlement. At that time, the first generations of remote-distance islanders had targeted a narrow range of nearshore habitats that happened to be situated precisely in the same locales most severely affected by a lowering sea level after 1100 B.C. While people were learning to live in the Remote Oceanic islands for the first time, they were forced to adjust their preferred modes of life that had been instrumental in the island settlement process.

Along with the practical shift in resource-use patterns during the period of 1100–500 B.C., the finely decorated pottery styles such as Lapita were abandoned by 500 B.C. These outcomes point to a significant change of cultural contexts among societies when people were adapting to the effects of their transforming coastal zones. By 500 B.C., the preexisting lifeways were not sustainable, and instead people shifted their habitation locales, relied on different mixed food resources, and engaged with their natural and social worlds in new ways. Coastal zones remained essential for island life, but the next generations of people needed to learn new modes of living with their transformed coasts.

A profound social and ecological system-wide change by 500 B.C. contradicts notions of long-term continuity and overall stability of slow-changing cultural traditions of a *longue durée*. If such a significant transformation occurred in the natural environment and cultural way of inhabiting the environment, then certainly, the later historically known ethnographies of the Pacific cannot be imposed as an interpretive lens when examining the archaeological records prior to this substantive transformation that had been in effect by 500 B.C. Linguistic histories furthermore illustrate how the languages in different island groups have diverged from their shared ancestries, thereby reflecting at least some degree of independent culture histories that each have undergone important change through time. The archaeological material records have shown the definite end of dentate-stamped Lapita pottery, coinciding with substantial transformation of coastal morphology and other aspects of the ancient environment, so a significant change absolutely must be acknowledged.

Site records after 500 B.C. refer to diverse patterns of settlement and use of coastal and inland resource areas of islands, as compared to the older patterns of activities that had relied heavily on narrowly defined seashore niches. The older patterns as associated with first island settlement were presented in Chapters 6 and 7, and the later patterns after 500 B.C. will be treated in Chapter 9. The present chapter concentrates on the processes of transition in social and ecological systems, extended over a period of approximately 1100 through 500 B.C., when Pacific Oceanic communities were forced to adapt to critical change in their island worlds.

Coastal morphologies and ecologies

Changing sea level has been the primary factor in affecting the shapes of coastlines and configurations of resource zones, and therefore the records of global, regional, and local sea-level histories have been indispensable in Pacific Oceanic archaeology (see Figure 2.9). Most relevant for the present chapter, the timing of a period of sea-level drawdown is essential for tracing the chronology of changing coastal ecologies in Pacific Oceania. Specifically, this drawdown followed the extended period of a mid-Holocene highstand of sea level that was 1.5–2.5 m higher than the present level. The precise elevations of sea level varied slightly across the Pacific Basin, and the timing of rise or fall varied as well. The highstand had begun approximately 3000 B.C. and continued through 1100 B.C. in the northwest tropical Pacific, yet the timing may have been slightly delayed by 100 years farther to the central and eastern portions of the Pacific.

When sea level began its period of drawdown after 1100 B.C., the results entailed some potential benefits of increased spatial extent of usable coastal landforms, but the drawdown meanwhile brought a certain amount of unpredictability and instability. For several centuries prior to the drawdown, the long period of the mid-Holocene highstand had afforded stability and reliability of coastal conditions and resources, implying good opportunities for people to develop highly specific cultural adaptations to the available coastal niches. These kinds of cultural adaptations were reflected in the targeting of narrowly defined seashore niches that evidently subsidized the first successful habitations of the Remote Oceanic islands in the Marianas (Chapter 6). Much the same scope of seashore niche-targeting continued in Lapita-associated settlements at least through 1100 B.C. (Chapter 7), but then circumstances began to change increasingly over the next centuries.

After the drawdown conditions began, coastal habitats naturally adjusted but with different layouts of landforms, shallow versus deeper water zones, areas of coral reef growth, potential areas of swamps or mangroves, and freshwater outflows at the shorelines. Some of those eventual outcomes may have been beneficial centuries later, but meanwhile, the period of transition necessarily was a time of instability. The components of the ecosystem underwent structural shifts, but the rate of change and the magnitude depended on localized variables in each area. By 500 B.C., the degree of change had become substantial enough to result in qualitatively different coastal ecologies throughout the region.

Sea-level drawdown contributed most obviously to the exposure of coastal landforms, gradually enlarging. As the sea level lowered, patches of sand were stranded above sea level, often in the shapes of berms or ridges in parallel with the shoreline (Figure 8.1). These ridges and berms at first formed as unstable masses just above the lowering water level, but gradually they became more stable as the sea level continued to lower, wherein each ridge stood atop a broader base of plain-like landform. Often, a series of ridges could form in progression with the lowering sea level, one by one forming by virtue of being stranded at the ever-moving edge of the lowering water.

While the sea level lowered and coastal landforms effectively expanded, the various habitat niches within coastal zones were altered, directly affecting the compositions of plants, animals, and resource catchments. The upper elevation portions of coral reefs could not survive above sea level, while new coral growth occurred in the outer portions of reefs. Similarly, the upper elevations of swamps and mangroves began to transition into dry non-wetland habitats, and new wetland zones developed in some, but not all, areas of lower elevations. Access to fresh water meanwhile was affected, in particular with a lowering of an aquifer or freshwater lens floating over the falling sea level, such that water pools may have become less abundant inside caves yet more abundant in coastal seeps in the newly forming coastal plain landforms.

Depending on the timing of human settlement in an island relative to the state of sea level, people established different kinds of shoreline habitations and subsequently adapted to the changing conditions. Prior to 1100 B.C., the preferred habitations were directly at the paleo-shorelines. After 1100 B.C., people took advantage of the emergent beach berms and ridges that formed only after the sea-level drawdown. After 800 B.C., habitation areas could be installed over broadening coastal landforms, often with a series of stabilized

212 *The end of an era*

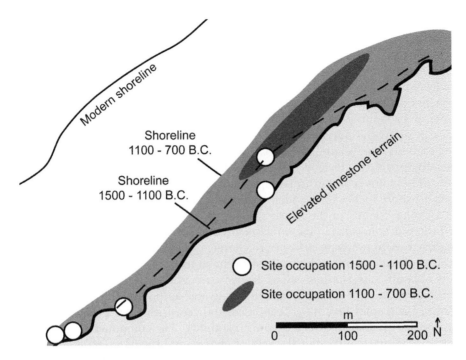

Figure 8.1 Formation of beach-ridge following sea-level drawdown at Ritidian, Guam. Graphic is based on information from Carson (2016).

ridges stranded in parallel lines. By 500 B.C., the lines of old ridges stood over contiguous plain-like accumulations of progressively stranded sands, with additional layering and buildup of storm-surge deposits, and they began to resemble true beach dune formations.

Records of older settlements prior to 1100 B.C. in the Mariana Islands and in the Bismarck Archipelago are especially instructive toward appreciating what happened in the numerous islands of Remote Oceania inhabited after 1100 B.C. Overall, as opportunities diminished and eventually disappeared for people to occupy shallow subtidal or intertidal zones, they shifted their attention to the next closest types of available habitats. Clusters of stilt-raised houses needed to be rebuilt while chasing after the lowering water level, wherein the emergent yet still unstable beach berms and ridges offered ideal places to install new stilt-raised houses.

Virtually all of the Lapita settlements in Southern Melanesia and West Polynesia were initiated in the range of 1100–800 B.C., when the sea level just had begun its period of drawdown. This time range is verified by radiocarbon dating at Lapita sites throughout the islands, as evidenced most abundantly in New Caledonia (Sand 1997, 2010), Vanuatu (Bedford 2006), Tonga (Burley 2023; Burley and Connaughton 2007; Burley and Dickinson 2010; Burley et al. 2010), and Fiji (Irwin et al. 2011; Nunn and Petchey 2013). Among the more informative sites, Bourewa in the Rove Peninsula of Viti Levu, Fiji, has shown an arrangement of post molds, where the traces of stilt-raised house posts were identifiable within thick shell middens (Nunn 2007). The piles of shellfish debris had accumulated around the lower portions of the house posts, evidently within a mucky saltwater matrix. Overall, the Lapita sites in Fiji were occupied when they were very close to ancient sea level (see Figure 7.7) on the edges of small offshore islets, tombolo, and other settings of unique nearshore habitat configurations that no longer existed just a few centuries later (Nunn and Heorake 2009). Similar intertidal contexts have been identified for other Remote Oceanic Lapita sites, such as Vavouto in New Caledonia (Carson 2008) and Nukuleka in Tonga (Burley 2016, 2023: 55–104; Dickinson and Burley 2007). All of these findings indicate a continuation of the seashore niche-targeting as seen at older Near Oceanic Lapita sites (Kirch 2001; Summerhayes 2022) and in the Mariana Islands (Carson 2011, 2014).

In Samoa, so far only one site near Mulifanua is known with dentate-stamped Lapita pottery (Figure 8.2), and others of slightly later age have shown no dentate-stamped pottery (Figure 8.3). Today the Ferry Berth Site near Mulifanua is submerged beneath the ocean, and it most likely had been inhabited when this particular locale was very close to sea level and possibly a shallow subtidal zone. In the oldest cultural layer dated about 800 B.C. (Petchey 2001), the diagnostic Lapita pottery fragments were discovered within a thick deposit of shell midden and tidal debris (Dickinson and Green 1998). Other Samoan sites with plainware pottery but lacking the characteristic dentate-stamped pottery were occupied slightly later during the range of 800–500 B.C., apparently along the newly stabilized beach ridges or berms that had formed with the beginning of sea-level drawdown, as found at the sites of 'Aoa (Clark and Michlovic 1996), Aganoa (Pearl and Sauck 2014), To'aga (Kirch and Hunt 1993), and Ofu Village (Quintus et al. 2015).

As seen at several sites in Fiji and at the Ferry Berth Site in Samoa, the Lapita settlements of New Caledonia, Vanuatu, and Tonga were situated originally at the edges of small offshore islets and similar settings with access to shallow-water zones or swamps with plentiful *Anadara* sp. shellfish and other resources. Although actual stilt-raised house

Figure 8.2 Lapita pottery from the Ferry Berth Site near Mulifanua in 'Upolu, Samoa. Illustration by the author, based on documentation by Jennings (1974).

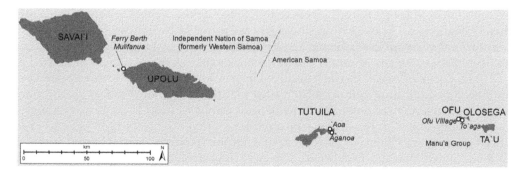

Figure 8.3 Distribution of known Lapita-age sites in Samoa.

214 *The end of an era*

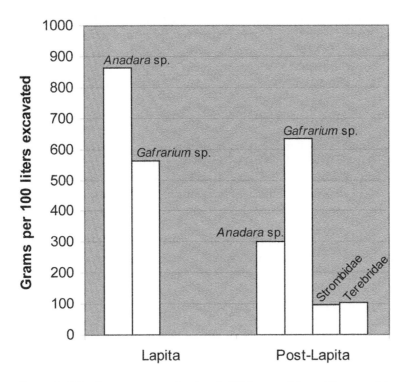

Figure 8.4 Lapita versus post-Lapita shellfish record from Vavouto, New Caledonia. Graphic is adapted from Carson (2008).

structures have not yet been documented specifically at most sites, the contexts definitely were shallow subtidal or intertidal settings at first, soon thereafter undergoing significant transformation with lowering sea level and buildup of more recent sedimentary layers. By 500 B.C., notable decline of *Anadara* sp. shells may be viewed as a result of lowering sea level changing faster than the associated mangroves or other nearshore habitats could adjust (Figure 8.4). Mangroves continued to exist at the edges of expanding coastlines in many places, but the conditions as seen today cannot be mistaken as reflecting the environments of 500 B.C. or earlier.

The change in coastal ecology may be viewed as a form of nearshore resource depression resulting from both natural environmental change and human-caused impacts. An example in the Mariana Islands serves well to illustrate the combined natural and cultural drivers (Figure 8.5). Sea-level drawdown was the major factor in reshaping coastlines and transforming the available habitats, and it was the primary cause of declining *Anadara* sp. shellfish throughout the islands. Even in the coasts that were not directly inhabited prior to 1100 B.C., *Anadara* sp. shellfish occurred in very low frequencies in later-aged deposits and then not at all some centuries later, such that the decline of *Anadara* sp. directly followed the sea-level drawdown. Meanwhile, cultural harvesting of certain other preferred shellfish contributed to the declines in several taxa that might not have been so severely affected just by the change in sea level itself. Cultural harvesting is implicated as the cause of declining chitons, sea urchins, and limpets in every locale within a few centuries of initial occupation, regardless of the condition of sea level at the time of any particular site

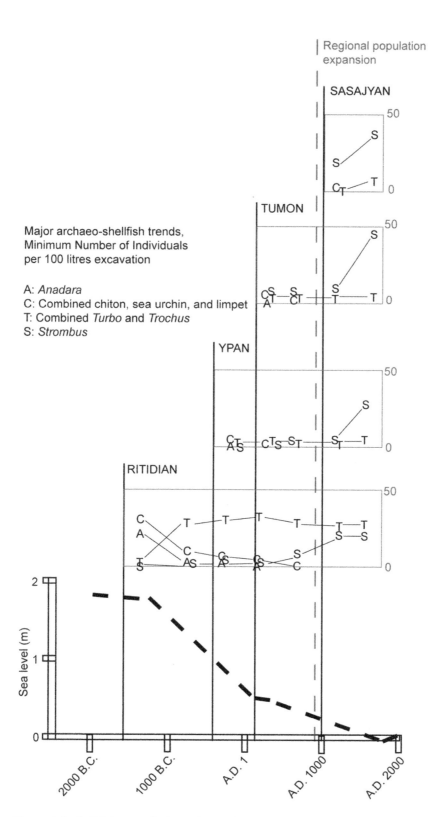

Figure 8.5 Shellfish record chronology of the Mariana Islands, examining the contributing effects of sea-level drawdown and cultural harvesting. Graphic is based on information from Carson (2016).

habitation. When these factors of sea-level drawdown and cultural harvesting coincided, however, they contributed to nearshore resource depression by 1100 B.C., compensated by relying more on shellfish taxa such as *Turbo* spp. and *Trochus* spp. in the middle through outer lagoon and reef zones.

Shifting contexts in nature and society

Coinciding with the change in coastal ecology following 1100 B.C., the role of finely decorated pottery diminished and eventually vanished by 500 B.C. (Nunn and Carson 2015). Dentate-stamped pottery and thin red-slipped wares became replaced by thicker and coarser pottery, often undecorated but occasionally with bolder or broader design elements. These trends can be matched with the end of direct shoreline housing, notable shifts in shellfish resource collection, and increased reliance on terrestrial foods. The same timing correlated with the termination of some of the locally specific decorative shell rings and other ornaments in different island groups, thus indicating a broader change in material culture beyond just the pottery.

In terms of material culture traits, the end of Lapita's most definitive characteristics occurred around 500 B.C. due to factors that already had been at work for some centuries previously. The precise timing of a demise of Lapita varied from one island community to another, but 500 B.C. can be accepted as the approximate timing overall. Moreover, the same shift in material culture is witnessed cross-regionally in correlation with the environmental change, so a region-wide driving factor must have been involved.

The Marianas chronological sequence reveals the same sea-level drawdown and change in coastal ecology as seen in the Lapita realm, but the cultural response began there immediately at 1100 B.C. As people had been living in the Mariana Islands since 1500 B.C., the cultural setting differed from the circumstances of Lapita communities moving into Island Melanesia and West Polynesia for the first time about 1100 B.C. In the Marianas case, the very finely made and decorated pottery varieties had terminated about 1100 B.C., as did many of the specialty ornaments, such as the small beads made of *Cypraea* sp. shells. Thicker and coarser pottery then displayed new variants of lime-infilled decoration in simple incisions and bold circle-stamped designs, which drastically reduced in production by 500 B.C. and entirely disappeared by 200 B.C. (Figure 8.6). Additionally, one type of small polished shell bead continued to be produced through 500 B.C. and then suddenly ceased.

The cross-regional evidence indicates a significant change in island societies over the period of a few centuries and reaching a critical threshold at 500 B.C., correlating with the noted sea-level drawdown and impacts on coastal ecologies. In different locations, people responded in very similar ways to their changing coastal environments. As the preferred habitats of earliest settlement disappeared, people were forced to adapt according to the new conditions and contexts, no longer able to sustain the same kinds of activities as their ancestors had done during the immediately preceding centuries. Meanwhile, resident population sizes must have been increasing at a multigenerational scale following initial island settlement episodes, so people were under more stress to produce enough food and resources during a time of environmental instability.

The change in island life around 500 B.C. may be viewed as a profound systemic transformation in natural and social context, wherein the natural-cultural environment underwent fundamental transformation as a functioning system. Sea-level drawdown did not directly cause the end of finely decorated pottery traditions, but rather the change in coastal habitat caused people to shift their activities and develop different traditions. The

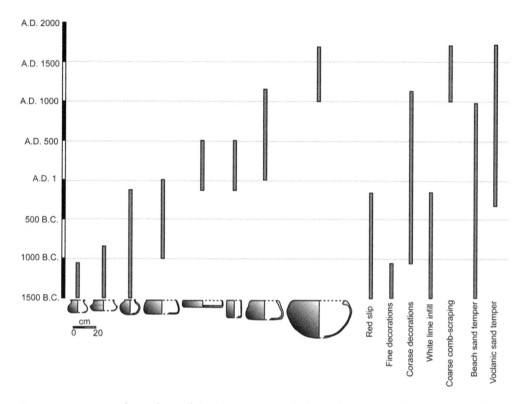

Figure 8.6 Pottery chronology of the Mariana Islands. Graphic is adapted from Carson (2016) and updated.

cultural roles of dentate-stamped pottery and other material traits of earliest island settlement became less and less relevant in a changing world, as the contexts of island life underwent major transformation.

By 500 B.C., people no longer could live in the same shoreline houses, rely on the same kinds of shellfish resources, or relate with their coastal environments in the same way as had been possible for their ancestors in prior centuries. Instead, the new generations of people needed to shift significant portions of their activities into slightly landward locales, harvest different kinds of coastal and marine foods, and rely increasingly on land-based foods and resources. While the coasts persisted as important parts of island life, the coasts in themselves were changing, and people developed new kinds of relationships with their coasts as well as with their island interiors. People, of course, continued to use both coastal and inland resources in all time periods, but the difference was in the overall balance of food types and use of habitat zones.

An increased use of island interiors, forests, and cultivable lands by 500 B.C. is evident when comparing the earlier and later site records. Most instructive are the sites with distinguishable components over continuous spans of some centuries, such as at the Teouma Site in Vanuatu with its internal components of a Lapita-age layer at 1100–500 B.C. and a directly post-Lapita layer at 500–100 B.C. The records from Teouma show an early reliance on nearshore foods and wild forest plants and animals, shifting to a later emphasis on mixed coastal foods and increasingly more cultivated plant and animal foods, as consistently documented in the site's faunal remains (Bedford 2006), stable isotope signatures of diet in human and animal bones (Kinaston et al. 2014; Valentin et al. 2010), and residues of foods preserved in dental calculus (Horrocks et al. 2014). These chronological trends at the Teouma Site potentially could be refined into internal divisions outlining a prolonged process, for example, when noticing that the use of dentate-stamped Lapita pottery may have started to decline as early as 800 B.C., with increasing popularity of other decorative styles thereafter (Bedford 2009).

The ability of communities to rely on land-based foods, especially domesticated plants and animals, was underwritten by the earlier overseas imports coming with the first island settlers. Those imported food options may not have been intended at the outset to substantiate the majority of a population's diet, and indeed all archaeological indicators of ancient diets have shown that they contributed very little during the first few centuries of island settlements. Although used in small overall quantities, the transported food resources had been essential for nutrition and for creating familiar landscapes ever since the very beginning of island settlement in each case, and then they became increasingly significant for survival when the coastal resources began to decline.

The region-wide timing of a change in coastal ecology correlated with a change in social behaviors of subsistence, housing, resource-use patterns, pottery decorative designs, and other aspects of material culture. Beginning as early as 1100 B.C. and reaching a critical threshold by 500 B.C., several factors of natural and cultural history had changed substantially and in concert, to the extent that the total natural-cultural system became recognizably different from its previous state of functioning during earliest island settlement. Factors of sea level, coastal ecology, role of land-based food production, and material culture expressions had been changing at different paces and magnitudes, yet they coincided for a deep impact in the social-ecological system as a whole, with continuing effects over the next several centuries.

References

Bedford, Stuart, 2006. *Pieces of the Vanuatu Puzzle: Archaeology of the North, South and Centre.* Terra Australis 23. The Australian National University E Press, Canberra.

Bedford, Stuart, 2009. Les traditions potières Erueti et Mangaasi du Vanuatu central: Réévaluation et comparaison qurante ans après leur identification initiale. *Journal de la Société des Océanistes 128*: 25–38.

Burley, David V., 2016. Reconsideraton of sea level and landscape for first Lapita settlement at Nukuleka, Kingdom of Tonga. *Archaeology in Oceania 51*: 84–90.

Burley, David V., 2023. *The Birth of Polynesia: An Archaeological Journey through the Kingdom of Tonga.* Archaeology Press, Simon Fraser University, Burnaby, Canada.

Burley, David V., Andrew Barton, Willian R. Dickinson, Sean P. Connaghton, and Karine Taché, 2010. Nukuleka as a founder colony for West Polynesian settlement: New insights from recent excavations. *Journal of Pacific Archaeology 1*: 128–144.

Burley, David V., and Sean P. Connaughton, 2007. First Lapita settlement and its chronology in Vavaʻu, Kingdom of Tonga. *Radiocarbon 49*: 131–137.

Burley, David V., and William R. Dickinson, 2010. Among Polynesia's first pots. *Journal of Archaeological Science 37*: 1020–1026.

Carson, Mike T., 2008. Correlation of environmental and cultural chronology in New Caledonia. *Geoarchaeology 23*: 695–714.

Carson, Mike T., 2011. Palaeohabitat of first settlement sites 1500–1000 B.C. in Guam, Mariana Islands, western Pacific. *Journal of Archaeological Science 38*: 2207–2221.

Carson, Mike T., 2014. Paleo-terrain research: Finding the first settlement sites of Remote Oceania. *Geoarchaeology 29*: 268–275.

Carson, Mike T., 2016. *Archaeological Landscape Evolution: The Mariana Islands in the Asia-Pacific Region*. Springer International, Cham, Switzerland.

Clark, Jeffrey T., and Michael G. Michlovic, 1996. An early settlement in the Polynesian homeland: Excavation at 'Aoa Valley, Tutuila Island. *Journal of Field Archaeology 23*: 151–167.

Dickinson, William R., and David V. Burley, 2007. Geoarchaeology of Tonga: Geotechtonic and geomorphic controls. *Geoarchaeology 22*: 231–261.

Dickinson, William R., and Roger C. Green, 1998. Geoarcheological context of Holocene subsidence at the Ferry Berth Lapita Site, Mulifanua, Upolu, Samoa. *Geoarchaeology 13*: 239–263.

Horrocks, Mark, Michel K., Nieuwoudt, Rebecca Kinaston, Hallie Buckley, and Stuart Bedford, 2014. Microfossil and Fourier Transform Infrared analyses of Lapita and post-Lapita human dental calculus from Vanuatu, southwest Pacific. *Journal of the Royal Society of New Zealand 44*: 17–33.

Irwin, Geoffrey J., Trevor H. Worthy, Simon Best, Stuart Hawkins, Jonathan Carpenter, and Sepeti Matararaba, 2011. Further investigations at the Naigani Lapita Site (VL 21/5), Fiji: Excavation, radiocarbon dating and palaeofaunal extinction. *Journal of Pacific Archaeology 2*: 66–78.

Jennings, Jesse D., 1974. The Ferry Berth Site, Mulifanua, Upolu. In *Archaeology in Western Samoa, Volume 2*, edited by Roger C. Green and Janet M. Davidson, pp. 176–178. Bulletin 7. Auckland Institute and Museum, Auckland.

Kinaston, Rebecca, Hallie Buckley, Frédérique Valentin, Stuart Bedford, Matthew Spriggs, Stuart Hawkins, and Estelle Herrscher, 2014. Lapita diet in Remote Oceania: New stable isotope evidence from the 3000-year-old Teouma Site, Efate Island, Vanuatu. *PLoS One 9*: e90376. DOI: 10.1371/journal.pone.0090376

Kirch, Patrick V. (editor), 2001. *Lapita and Its Transformations in Near Oceania: Archaeological Investigations in the Mussau Islands, Papua New Guinea, 1985–88, Volume 1: Introduction, Stratigraphy, Chronology*. Archaeological Research Facility Contributions Number 59. University of California, Berkeley.

Kirch, Patrick V., and Terry L. Hunt (editors), 1993. *The To'aga Site: Three Millennia of Polynesian Occupation in the Manu'a Islands, American Samoa*. Contribution 51. Archaeological Research Facility, University of California, Berkeley.

Nunn, Patrick D., 2007. Echoes from a distance: Progress report on research into the Lapita occupation of the Rove Peninsula, southwest Viti Levu island, Fiji. In *Oceanic Explorations: Lapita and Western Pacific Settlement*, edited by Stuart Bedford, Christophe Sand, and Sean P. Connaughton, pp. 163–176. Terra Australis 26. The Australian National University E Press, Canberra.

Nunn, Patrick D., and Mike T. Carson, 2015. Sea-level fall implicated in profound societal change around 2570 cal yr BP (620 BC) in western Pacific Island groups. *Geo: Geography and Environment 2*: 17–32.

Nunn, Patrick D., and Tony Ahikau Heorake, 2009. Understanding the place properly: Palaeogeography of selected Lapita sites in the western tropical Pacific Islands and its implications. In *Lapita: Ancestors and Descendants*, edited by Peter J. Sheppard, Tim Thomas, and Glenn R. Summerhayes, pp. 235–254. Monograph 28. New Zealand Archaeological Association, Auckland.

Nunn, Patrick D., and Fiona J. Petchey, 2013. Bayesian re-evaluation of Lapita settlement in Fiji: Radiocarbon analysis of the Lapita occupation at Bourewa and nearby sites on the Rove Peninsula, Viti Levu Island. *Journal of Pacific Archaeology 4*: 21–34.

Pearl, Frederic B., and William A. Sauck, 2014. Geophysical and geoarchaeological investigations at Aganoa Beach, American Samoa: An early archaeological site in western Polynesia. *Geoarchaeology 29*: 462–476.

Petchey, Fiona J., 2001. Radiocarbon determinations from the Mulifanua Lapita Site, Upolu, Western Samoa. *Radiocarbon* 43: 63–68.

Quintus, Seth, Jeffrey T. Clark, Stephanie S. Day, and Donald P. Schwert, 2015. Landscape evolution and human settlement patterns on Ofu Island, Manu'a Group, American Samoa. *Asian Perspectives* 54: 208–237.

Sand, Christophe, 1997. The chronology of Lapita ware in New Caledonia. *Antiquity* 71: 539–547.

Sand, Christophe, 2010. *Lapita Calédonien: Archéologie d'un Premir Peuplement Insulaire Océanien*. Collection Travaux et Documents Océanistes 2. Société des Océanistes, Paris.

Summerhayes, Glenn R, 2022. Kisim save long Graun: Understanding the nature of landscape change in modelling Lapita in Papua New Guinea. In *Palaeolandcapes in Archaeology: Lessons for the Past and Future*, edited by Mike T. Carson, pp. 291–312. Routledge, London.

Valentin, Frédérique, Hallie R. Buckley, Estelle Herrscher, Rebecca Kinaston, Stuart Bedford, Matthew Spriggs, Stuart Hawkins, and Ken Neal, 2010. Lapita subsistence strategies and food consumption patterns in the community of Teouma (Efate, Vanuatu). *Journal of Archaeological Science* 37: 1820–1829.

9 A broad-spectrum revolution? 500 B.C. through A.D. 100

'O le ua na fua mai Manu'a (Samoan saying), translates into English literally as
"The rain comes from Manu'a."

This quote refers to something that is known to happen regularly, but somehow the event leads to an important change. In Samoa, people can observe rain clouds from a distance or predict that rains will come generally from the direction of the prevailing winds from the Manu'a Islands, but they may or may not be compelled to prepare for the raining event. On rare occasions, a seemingly ordinary rainfall potentially could prompt major change. Most of the time, people are comfortable to make adjustments whenever an event actually happens. In the infrequent cases of more severe effects, lack of preparation can force people to suffer, while they may not receive much sympathy from others who have invested in advance preparation.

The long-term perspective of archaeology reveals real examples of how people have been variably prepared or not to survive through periods of hardship. Changing sea level and coastal ecology continued as an ongoing process after 1100 B.C. (outlined in Chapter 8), and people were forced to adapt, leading to substantially different patterns of settlement and land use by 500 B.C. The events from these centuries continued to exert effects thereafter in strategies of diversified resource use – in some cases more diversified than others – but in all cases no longer risking overspecialization in too narrowly focused modes of subsistence and economy.

By 500 B.C., evidence began to emerge for addressing issues of generalist versus specialist adaptations, long-term versus short-term resilience, and strategies of sustainability that were perhaps magnified in the innately bounded and vulnerable settings of islands. During and after the necessary adjustments of coastal ecologies over some centuries, settlement and resource-use patterns were diversified in various configurations of coastal and inland zones. Separate groups developed broad-spectrum usage of natural resources, with long-lasting effects on the evolution of social-ecological systems.

Any subsistence and land-use patterns can be characterized along a spectrum from narrow to broad use of resources, which is most useful in a relativist perspective of comparing what makes any one system narrower or broader than another. A broader spectrum may be indicated by cultural use of a greater diversity of landforms and habitats, of greater numbers of plant foods, or of more numerous types of shellfish from different ecological settings. These relative values require at least two entities to compare in different geographic settings or in different time periods.

This chapter focuses on a chronological characterization of resource-use patterns in Pacific Oceania, in particular, involving an evident broadening of those patterns by 500 B.C.

DOI: 10.4324/9781003399025-9

and increasingly broadened over the next centuries. An earlier emphasis on nearshore resources expanded to incorporate increasing input from both coastal and land-based resources by 500 B.C. Archaeological investigations have generated relevant information in the size and distribution of sites across a landscape, in types of plant and animal remains, in stable isotopes in bones as indications of diet, in soil chemistry suggestive of past land use, and in reconstructions of ancient landforms suggestive of potential habitats during specific time periods.

Whether intentional or not, a broad-spectrum approach may be effective as a strategy of planning in advance to cope with periodic and unpredictable disasters. Given an expectation of frequent typhoons in most of Micronesia, land-use patterns developed without overspecializing in formalized field systems that very easily could be destroyed. Quite different weather and storm patterns affected Southern Melanesia and West Polynesia, where field systems developed in variable ways. Evolutionary biology teaches us that generalists survive through numerous challenges, while specialists may thrive under their ideal circumstances yet suffer or perish when those conditions eventually change. As a case in point, the earlier pre–500 B.C. focus on narrowly defined shoreline niches proved to be unsustainable, transitioning into more diversified use of island ecosystems that evidently became more sustainable in a long-term perspective.

Ecological zones in large and small Islands

Islands are notable for the different ecological habitats within defined areas, so that people can find diverse resources within a single island. As a general rule, larger islands provide environments with more biomass and diversity of resources and habitats, where people could find more opportunities than in smaller islands. Total land area and elevation range directly influence the configuration of ecological zones, and they may serve as efficient proxies for estimating the potential for resource-use strategies. Greater variation of land-use practice therefore may be expected in larger or taller islands, whereas less variation could be supported in smaller and especially low-lying islands.

In many island settings, ecological zonation tends to be reduced to a simple dichotomy of coastal versus inland, but these categories need to be tempered with an awareness of scale. A coastal zone may be conceptualized as the area inside the access range of a coastally residing person within a few minutes, one hour, a day's journey, or other unit of time, accounting for degree of slope and elevation change between the coastline and anywhere farther inland. Depending on the standards being used, a house situated 1 km from the coastline and at 200 m elevation could be regarded as "inland" in an analytic sense, while the occupants of that house potentially could think of themselves as having easy access to coastal resources and not necessarily locked in an inland setting. The combined effects of linear distance and elevation need to be acknowledged as creating differential resource zones, as well as the cultural perceptions of those zones as categories of coastal or inland. Furthermore, broad categories of coastal or inland may contain internal subdivisions definable by landforms, soil types, forest growth, bird habitats, water sources, or other factors.

Depending on local conditions in any island, the relationship between coastal and inland zones can vary from virtually nonexistent to effectively separate entities. Small and low-lying atolls, for instance, allow people to move easily across all available ecological habitats without any daunting physical barriers, and moreover, those available habitats are not so greatly different from one another. On the other hand, tall mountainous masses such as in New Caledonia or New Guinea incorporate multiple quite different ecological habitats ranging from coastal lowlands through remote uplands, and people can live in any part of this diverse range while experiencing minimal or zero contact with people living in other parts.

In most islands of Pacific Oceania, people realistically could access different resource zones with little or no detectable restrictions. Nonetheless, during the last few centuries, many island traditions have emphasized the procedures of respectfully asking for permission before entering into a territory. Access may have become more difficult with larger populations and fixed territories belonging to certain groups while excluding outsiders, as apparently began to happen after A.D. 100 in many places and became more formalized after A.D. 1000 (Chapters 12 and 13). No obvious territory-marking features of walls or formalized field systems have been described in contexts before A.D. 100, so these older contexts probably did not involve serious competition over land and resources in most cases.

Following the change in sea level and coastal ecologies over the period 1100–500 B.C., people needed to rely more on the available non-coastal habitats and resource areas. The potential options were more limited in the smaller islands of Remote Oceania than in the larger land masses of Island Southeast Asia and Near Oceania. Especially after people had invested heavily in specialized coastal niches during the initial centuries of remote island settlement, the markedly reduced productivity of those same niches forced a broadening into other habitats by 500 B.C., necessarily involving greater investment in island interior zones.

Roles of fishing, foraging, and farming

In some cases, simply knowing the settings and distributions of sites can depict the land-use patterns during a specific time period, granted the ability to achieve sufficient survey coverage. Otherwise, site layers with poor or uneven preservation of faunal and botanical materials can produce inaccurate pictures about the kinds of foods that people obtained from different sources. One example is seen at the Ritidian site in northern Guam (Figure 9.1), where extensive subsurface exploration identified the distributions of habitation areas in a full chronological sequence of continuous time intervals, noting a clear shift in the pattern around 700–500 B.C. (Carson 2012, 2014). Habitations prior to this point had been situated on the changing shoreline-oriented landforms, but then habitations after this point had shifted to cliff-base locales farther from the shoreline. Meanwhile, after 500 B.C., the Marianas archaeological records overall show an increased total number of habitations, including the first signs of limited occupations in island interior zones of elevated limestone plateau terrain and in the volcanic hills of southern Guam.

In sites bearing well preserved food remains, analysis can reveal the contributions of varied types of foods coming from definable habitat zones or from different modes of subsistence practice. The best opportunities for preservation of shell and animal bone are in coastal habitations with beach sand layers, but these sites naturally would contain more foods from coastal zones than from island interiors. Even with these cautions in mind, disruption in coastal resource collection is clear, as at Ritidian with a strong shift in favor of *Turbo* spp. and *Trochus* spp. shellfish that had been more resilient than other taxa through the changing coastal ecology (Carson 2012). In places with imported domesticated animals, such as at the Teouma Site in Vanuatu, the post–500 B.C. records contain significantly

224 *A broad-spectrum revolution? 500 B.C. through A.D. 100*

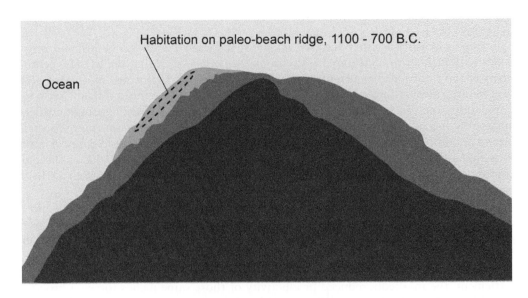

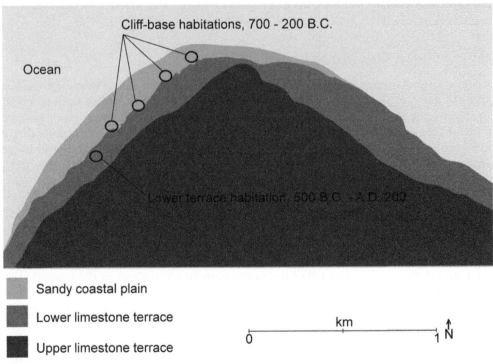

Figure 9.1 Shift in site distribution about 700–500 B.C. at Ritidian, Guam. Graphic is based on information from Carson (2014).

denser remains of those animals (especially pigs) than had been present earlier, along with decreased amounts of wild animal remains (Bedford 2006; Hawkins 2015).

The growing role of land-based foods did not eradicate the importance of coastal and marine resources, but instead this trend may be understood in terms of the relative values in a total diet of mixed resources. Fish and shellfish continued to supply essential components of the diet yet in a different way than had been practiced during earlier centuries. People collected different shellfish taxa, while plant foods and often domesticated animals contributed more and more to the local diets through time and especially after 500 B.C.

The beach sites with good preservation of animal bones tend to be poor in their preservation of ancient plant remains. Pieces of starch and other microscopic plant parts may adhere to the surfaces of stone tools or pottery, but they tend to be washed or drained through beach sand layers. Terrigenous silts and clays generally provide the best preservation of ancient botanical materials, but these soil formations are different from the beach sand deposits where animal bones and shellfish remains are preserved more abundantly. The two types of sedimentary units (beach sands versus terrigenous silts or clays) are found in separate sites or else in separate dated layers.

Plant food production in Pacific Oceania often is portrayed as "agriculture," but this term may seem awkward when referring to the growth of taros, yams, bananas, coconuts, and breadfruits. In other regions, these forms of food production may be termed horticulture, arboriculture, or part of forest management. In any case, the deliberate cultural action of producing food can be appreciated as categorically different from collecting wild foods, underscored by the fact that people intentionally translocated a roster of plants. Many of the overseas imports were domesticated varieties, including not only plants but also animals in most islands.

In comparison to the later periods with increased emphasis on land-based food production, earlier periods of horticulture and arboriculture aligned more closely with the notion of a managed forest without formalized field systems or investment in fixed territories. The oldest formalized field systems in Pacific Oceania appeared after A.D. 100 in some but not all islands, for instance, in New Caledonia, and then they became most abundantly evidenced much later in sites postdating A.D. 1000 (Sand 2002). Limited hints of land-clearing and slope-retention features have been dated in Samoa as early as A.D. 100–200, followed by more extensive garden fields and orchards, often with walled borders, postdating A.D. 1000 (Carson 2006).

The patterns of land and resource use prior to A.D. 100 resembled overall an informal use of land and an ability to accommodate a broad-spectrum approach. No evidence so far points to specialization in particular crops to the extent of excluding others, but rather multiple foods contributed to a diverse diet. Similarly, site locations were distributed broadly in diverse types of coastal and inland zones.

In a context of increasing emphasis on land-based food production, the continued absence of rice in Pacific Oceania may appear curious. In much of East and Southeast Asia in the Austronesian world ancestral to the inhabitants of Pacific Oceania, rice and millet farming had dominated land-use patterns, yet rice farming systems did not contribute to the transported landscapes of Pacific Oceania. The single possible exception was the presence of rice in the Mariana Islands, although it was regarded historically as a special ritual food and without any formalized fields, while the major plant foods were comprised of mixed root-tuber and tree crops in informally managed forests and gardens.

Rice and millet farmlands indicate a narrow-range specialization in a group's subsistence and land-use system. This kind of narrow-range specialization could be beneficial for increasing annual yields per unit of land area, but generally it is considered risky in places with unpredictable rainfall. Accordingly, Dewar (2003) proposed that the more variable and unreliable rainfall patterns in the Pacific made rice farming impractical and too precarious. The Pacific regional variability in rainfall perhaps can be described more realistically in terms of unpredictable storminess and other conditions.

As a further consideration, rice and millet may not have been dominant in the diets and land-use systems of the groups directly responsible for the eventual migrations into the remote Pacific Islands following 1500 B.C. Evidently, the first island settlers focused on specific seashore niches that were unsuitable for intensive wetland rice farming (Chapters 5 and 6). While rice in particular was farmed in Island Southeast Asia at least as early as 1400 B.C. along the banks of the Cagayan River in the Philippines (Snow et al. 1986) and as early as 1500 B.C. in the Karama Valley of Sulawesi in Indonesia (Deng et al. 2020), it may not have been the dominant crop until sometime later, postdating the sea-crossing migration episodes into the Mariana Islands at 1500 B.C. and into the Near Oceanic Lapita world around 1500–1350 B.C. For instance, the evidence of domesticated rice and millet became most abundant in the Cagayan River Valley starting around 1000 B.C. (Hung et al. 2022). Furthermore, those few sites with early rice evidence were situated somewhat inland, and rice may not have been the main focus of seashore-oriented communities whose people ventured into the islands of Remote Oceania.

The contributions of fishing, foraging, and farming were part of life ever since the beginning of Pacific Oceanic settlement, but the balance by 500 B.C. shifted to accommodate a stronger role of "farming" in its variable definitions. In the Pacific Islands, farming may be understood as a deliberate cultural investment in producing foods through horticulture, arboriculture, and forest management. Importantly, the category of forest management could involve more than gathering plant products and may include strategies of hunting or trapping birds, bats, and other animals. Additionally, many island groups raised domesticated pigs, dogs, and chickens as part of their food-producing systems.

Along with the broadened use of landscapes and resources, people used more general-utility plain pottery without the specialized decorative varieties of earlier periods. Plainware pottery had been made from the beginning of each island's settlement, but it was joined at first by finely decorated varieties that ceased in production by 500 B.C., such that plainware by default became the standard general-utility pottery thereafter. Similarly, the first island settlers relied mostly on specialized shoreline niches during their first centuries of settlement, with lesser use of the plants and animals that they had transported from overseas, later transitioning to broad-spectrum use of all available resources.

The region-wide trends after 500 B.C. would set the parameters for some island societies to invest in specialized or formalized field systems during later centuries, while other groups continued to emphasize more generalist and informal land-use strategies of managed forests and low-labor input horticulture. In all cases, however, the relative roles of different food resources had fluctuated through time, typically shifting at key points when conditions changed in the natural environment, social system, or both. One of those key shifts can be identified by 500 B.C. cross-regionally.

Sustainability, resilience, and collapse

The evident transformation in Pacific Oceanic societies after 500 B.C. raises questions about long-term continuity versus change that are relevant for the region's scholarship overall, as well as for global issues of sustainability, resilience, and collapse. Much of

Pacific Oceanic archaeology scholarship has stressed the importance of the slow-moving or even purported long-term unchanging aspects of a *longue durée*, as opposed to the quicker pace of change in superficial aspects of society referring to *histoire événementielle*. An extremist stance would allow for direct application of historical or modern ethnographic knowledge into the contexts of ancient archaeological sites. Even when accepting such an argument, the long-term sustained cultural traits tend to be practical and applicable throughout diverse contexts, such as using waterworn pebbles or seashells to cover a house floor, growing taro in wet zones while growing yams in dry zones, or creating villages in locations with access to diverse natural resources. Meanwhile, the shorter-lived traits such as seen in decorative pottery styles cannot be dismissed as superficial, and indeed the chronological transitions in pottery forms and styles reflect larger contexts of cultural change.

In a long-scale view, successive generations of people continued living in the islands despite the periods of minor and major change, yet they did so with significantly transformed or altered modes of life through time. Minor fluctuations are noticed continually, as seen in climate records and in subtle changing frequencies of different types of artifacts, food remains, and other materials. At certain points, however, major change at a dramatic scale pervaded through multiple aspects of landscape and society, such as with the shift toward land-based resources about 500 B.C., coincident with a change in settlement locations, loss of finely decorated pottery, and other aspects of deep cultural change. These kinds of events occur over extended periods of time, perhaps more properly understood as processes rather than as events, and they necessarily involve periods of change that do not fit neatly in most definitions of *longue durée* or *histoire événementielle*.

Another view of cultural change may consider the sustainability of behaviors through time, such as when considering the sustainability of a pottery style, subsistence strategy, or entire cultural system. Very simply, some traits can be sustained longer than others, through changing conditions of climate, sea level, population density, and other factors. Traits such as general-utility pottery and broad-spectrum food production are capable of enduring through periods of changing conditions, and thus they may be considered resilient. Traits with more narrowly focused or specialized values tend to be unsustainable when their supporting contexts undergo significant change, such as was seen in Pacific Oceania by 500 B.C.

When considering the sustainability of an artifact style, land-use pattern, or social group, problems arise in defining the responsible operating system and what it can accommodate before undergoing systemic transformation, internal splitting into different parts, or apparent collapse. For instance, dentate-stamped Lapita pottery ceased around 500 B.C. and may have signified a collapse of this particular pottery-making industry or of its evidently narrowly defined cultural context of an operating system, even if the inner workings of that system are unclear today. Meanwhile, other types of plain and general-utility pottery persisted through periods of change, apparently successful across multiple different systems. This perspective is congruent with the notion of long-term survivability of a generalist or broad-spectrum approach, as compared to the tendency for shorter life span of a tightly focused specialization.

When multiple aspects of a society undergo a major transformational change simultaneously, as what happened about 500 B.C. in Pacific Oceania, then a system-wide change can be acknowledged, but at least some elements of the island societies must have been sustained while the biological populations continued to live in these islands. The new emphasis on land-based foods and general-utility pottery was possible largely because those traits already had existed, yet in low frequency, during earlier periods, and they proved to be effective through the changing conditions that made previous lifeways unsustainable. Traits such as shoreline-oriented housing, targeting of specialized nearshore resources, and use of finely decorated pottery could not be sustained, but the descendants of the actual people survived. When their descendants continued to use much of the same plainware pottery as had been produced for many centuries previously, then they did so in qualitatively different contexts and operating within arguably different cultural systems.

The endurance of a biological population does not logically require persistence or continuity of cultural practice. In fact, successive generations of people generally tend to do things differently than their predecessors, as seen in the archaeological records of Pacific Oceania and indeed worldwide in repeated instances. Major cultural change does not need to be equated with a societal collapse or a population replacement, but rather it signifies that a society crossed a threshold of needing to undergo deep structural change in order to survive through radically different conditions before and after this threshold point. One such event unfolded around 500 B.C. in the inhabited islands of Pacific Oceania.

In Pacific Oceania, the continued presence of human populations could imply a sustained continuity of at least some aspects of society enduring through periods of significant change. As shown in this chapter, those long-term sustained cultural traits most often belong to categories of generalist behaviors such as growing mixed crops of overall low-labor input and making plain pottery of basic utility that can characterize almost any cultural group cross-regionally and throughout time in Pacific Oceania. In contrast, the forms of material culture expression and lifestyles that characterize clearly distinguishable cultural groups, such as seen through habitat niche-targeting and distinctive pottery decorative motifs, are, by definition, narrowly structured and unable to be sustained through significantly changing conditions.

Contexts after 500 B.C. in Pacific Oceania refer to people investing in broad usage of their island worlds, with decreased overseas contacts, and importantly, no new expansionary migrations occurred into previously uninhabited portions of the Pacific until A.D. 100. Meanwhile, significant events in Island Southeast Asia created no noticeable effects in the Pacific Islands in terms of strengthened trade networks and mobilization of new commodities made of iron, bronze, and glass. Additionally, in parts of Island Southeast Asia, the archaeological records of this period reveal an emergence of new cultural traditions of jar burials, much denser populations in more highly structured villages, and signs of political hierarchies. These trends would continue in later centuries with increasing evidence of globalized economic systems linking Island Southeast Asia with other parts of the world, but these spheres of influence did not extend into Pacific Oceania. Instead, Pacific societies developed with their own cultural histories that came to define life in this sea of islands.

References

Bedford, Stuart, 2006. *Pieces of the Vanuatu Puzzle: Archaeology of the North, South and Centre.* Terra Australis 23. The Australian National University E Press, Canberra.

Carson, Mike T., 2006. Samoan cultivation practices in archaeological perspective. *People and Culture in Oceania* 22: 1–29.

Carson, Mike T., 2012. Evolution of an Austronesian landscape: The Ritidian Site in Guam. *Journal of Austronesian Studies* 3: 55–86.

Carson, Mike T., 2014. Contexts of natural-cultural history: A 3500-year record at Ritidian in Guam. In *Guam's Hidden Gem: Archaeological and Historical Studies at Ritidian*, edited by Mike T. Carson, pp. 1–43. British Archaeological Reports International Series 2663. Archaeopress, Oxford.

Deng, Zhenhua, Hsiao-chun Hung, Mike T. Carson, Adhi Agus Oktaviana, Budianto Hakim, and Truman Simanjuntak, 2020. Validating earliest rice farming in the Indonesian Archipelago. *Scientific Reports 10*: 10984. DOI https://doi.org/10.1038/s41598-020-67747-3

Dewar, Robert E., 2003. Rainfall variability and subsistence systems in Southeast Asia and the western Pacific. *Current Anthropology* 44: 369–388.

Hawkins, Stuart, 2015. *Human Behavioural Ecology, Anthropogenic Impact and Subsistence Change at the Teouma Lapita Site, Central Vanuatu, 3000–2500 BP.* Doctoral dissertation, Department of Archaeology and Natural History, the Australian National University, Canberra.

Hung, Hsiao-chun, Cheng-hwa Tsang, Zhenhua Deng, Mary Jane Louise A. Bolunia, Rey A. Santiago, Mike T. Carson, and Peter Bellwood, 2022. Preceramic riverside hunter-gatherers and the arrival of Neolithic farmers in northern Luzon. *Antiquity* 96: 848–867.

Sand, Christophe, 2002. Creations and transformation of prehistoric landscapes in New Caledonia, the southernmost Melanesian Islands. In *Pacific Landscapes: Archaeological Approaches*, edited by Thegn N. Ladefoged and Michael W. Graves, pp. 11–34. Bearsville Press, Los Osos, CA.

Snow, Bryan E., Richard Shutler, Jr., D. E. Nelson, J. S. Vogel, and J. R. Southon, 1986. Evidence of early rice cultivation in the Philippines. *Philippine Quarterly of Culture and Society* 14: 3–11.

10 The atoll highway of Micronesia, A.D. 100 through 500

Ia kwe (Marshallese phrase), translates into English as "You are a rainbow."

According to Marshallese legend, the words *ia kwe* were pronounced by the creator Loa when he looked with pleasure at the islands, especially the most beautiful island of Bikini Atoll (Flood et al. 2002: 174). Today this expression refers to anything that is beautiful, and it has become the beloved Marshallese greeting *yokwe*. The atolls of Micronesia represent idyllic microcosms, and together they give shape and character to a large portion of Pacific Oceania.

Within a few centuries starting about A.D. 100, the vast area of Central through Eastern Micronesia transformed into an inhabited seascape (Figure 10.1). The physicality of the Pacific had changed due to the new habitability of hundreds of tiny and low-lying atolls that later would inspire the naming of Micronesia as a region of "small islands." Sea level had lowered enough to expose the land surfaces at stable elevations above the ocean (Figure 10.2). Essential sources of fresh water were accessible in lenses within those land masses floating over the lowered sea level.

Not only the atolls but also the "high islands" received their first human inhabitants at this time, as expressed in a shared Nuclear Micronesian language history (Bender et al. 2003a, 2003b) and near-simultaneity of the overall archaeological evidence of initial settlement (Intoh 1997; Rainbird 1994, 2004). A major population expansion undoubtedly was linked to the opening of the "atoll highway." Availability of atolls created new opportunities for short-range voyages, thus enabling settlements in the atolls and supporting staging grounds for farther voyaging to the high islands. The overall pattern indicates widespread settlement within a few centuries, much like what had been the case during the Lapita-associated expansion into Remote Oceania earlier (Chapter 7).

The inhabitation of Central through Eastern Micronesia needs to be clarified as a separate and later occurrence than what has happened in the far western margins of Micronesia in the Mariana Islands and in Palau. The shared ancestral language grouping of Nuclear Micronesian was a branching of the Oceanic language family, deriving or descending from the older Lapita-associated communities in Near Oceania, Island Melanesia, and West Polynesia. This language grouping was separate from the much older-derived Malayo-Polynesian groups in the Mariana Islands and in Palau that had originated prior to the development of the Oceanic grouping. Furthermore, the archaeological layers in the Marianas and in Palau have shown considerably older inhabitation than has been documented so far in the islands of Central through Eastern Micronesia.

A possibility needs to be recognized that older settlement sites have not yet been discovered in the higher islands of Pohnpei, Kosrae, Chuuk, and Yap. Survey methodology so far

DOI: 10.4324/9781003399025-10

The atoll highway of Micronesia, A.D. 100 through 500   231

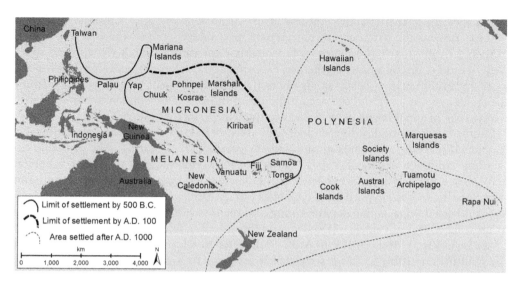

Figure 10.1 Map of the inhabited Pacific at A.D. 100–500, noting the role of Central through Eastern Micronesia.

A. Conditions after A.D. 100

B. Conditions approximately 1000 B.C.

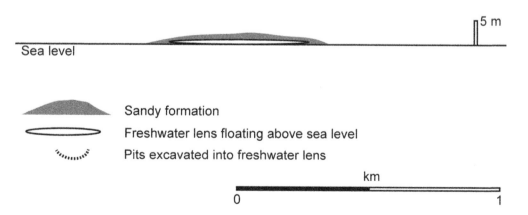

Figure 10.2 Schematic diagram of sea-level drawdown coordinated with atoll emergence and availability of freshwater lens in Central through Eastern Micronesia. Graphic is based on information from Yamaguchi et al. (2005).

has focused on surface-visible site ruins instead of searching for buried layers of ancient landscapes. In particular, any cultural layers of ancient seashore habitations older than 500 B.C. now would have become buried perhaps 1 m deep and stranded several dozens of m inland from today's shorelines. A reasonable exploratory search would need to assess each island locality in terms of where to excavate and how deep to continue until reaching a pre-cultural matrix of beach sands or corals. This assessment would need to account for the change in sea level and the accumulation of more recent sedimentary units that have covered the original layers of the initial settlement period.

Hints of possibly undiscovered older sites are seen in language history, noncultural environmental records, and unusual outlying early radiocarbon dating. The probable earlier Oceanic language origin of Yapese (Ross 1996) would suggest an earlier inhabitation here when compared with other areas of the Nuclear Micronesian language communities. Additionally, in Yap, hypothetical dating as old as 1000 B.C. has been implied by possible human-caused impacts in paleoenvironmental records without artifacts, food middens, or other archaeological evidence (Dodson and Intoh 1999). Outside Yap, surprising old dates of sparse cultural layers in Bikini Atoll could refer to a limited use of an unstable emerging landform at 1000 B.C. and some centuries prior to formalized residential settlement (Streck 1990), furthermore suggestive of the role of Bikini as the most perfectly formed and ideal atoll since the time of Loa's creation.

A rapid dispersal of founding settlement throughout Central and Eastern Micronesia is reflected in the tightly unified language grouping, even when accepting Yapese as a separate but related branch of the Oceanic (Oc) languages. Micronesian language histories indicate a closely shared ancestry and likely a degree of continued cross-contact through time (Bender et al. 2003a, 2003b). The short-range distances of overnight sailing canoe voyages coincide with the mapping of the Micronesian language subgroupings (Marck 1986). Languages tend to be shared within areas of most frequent contact of short-range voyaging, as compared to language divergence between areas separated by rare and specialized contexts of long-range voyaging.

Micronesian seafaring is among the most complex and sophisticated in the world. Knowledge of a sea of islands has been encoded in intricate cognitive maps of the paths of stars, types of clouds, patterns of winds, characteristics of waves, and other factors. The learning process may extend over many years, and in a sense it continues indefinitely with the constant accrual of new information and experience. Certain elements of the navigational knowledge base can be fixed into standardized learning aides, such as the charts known as *rebbelib* in the Marshall Islands, made of wooden sticks and *Cypraea* spp. (cowrie) shells. In a *rebbelib*, the cowrie shells indicate the positions of several islands, while the diagonal and curved sticks indicate the major regional ocean swells and wave patterns (Figure 10.3). The vertical and horizontal sticks serve as a practical support framework. A more advanced chart, known as the *mattang*, contains more detailed information about the swell movements around one particular island or set of islands.

Micronesian seafaring has been part of the regional cultural identity of strong interconnectivity among the numerous island societies spread over an impressively large part of the Pacific Ocean. Today, air travel and other modern technologies have changed the way that people can be mobile between islands, and many aspects of modern economies have altered the ability of people to undertake interisland voyages. Despite these historical and modern transformations, many people maintain various kinds of interisland connections at different geographic scales and levels of intensity, mirrored in the complex webs of exchange systems, including formalized tribute and circulation rituals, as well as informal

The atoll highway of Micronesia, A.D. *100 through 500* 233

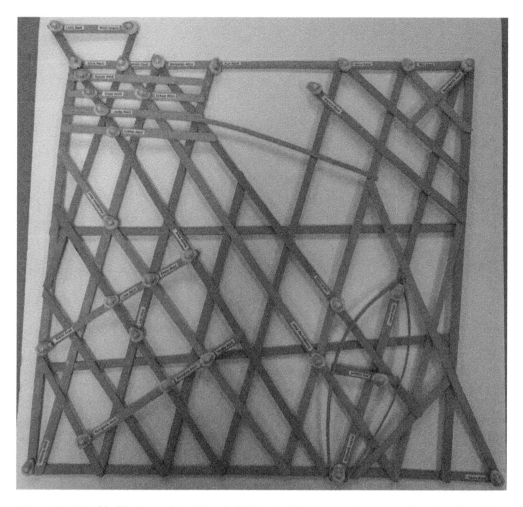

Figure 10.3 Rebbelib chart of the Marshall Islands. This image shows an educational product at the Micronesian Area Research Center, University of Guam.

encounters. The historically known multiple overlapping scales and contexts of interisland exchange suggest the likelihood of other complex systems in the more distant past associated with the archaeological records.

Unlike in many other parts of Pacific Oceania, Micronesian people sustained their traditional seafaring and other lifeways through periods of foreign imperialism, although this situation has been changing more recently. The central and eastern island groups of Micronesia were marginalized for the most part during the era of Spanish galleon trade (A.D. 1565–1815) that relied instead on bases of operation in the Philippines and eventually in the Mariana Islands. Large-scale imprints of foreign imperialism began primarily in the twentieth century with Japanese occupation, World War II devastation, and further alterations by U.S. actions during postwar control, atomic bomb testing, and continued military and economic interests today (Figure 10.4). The impacts have been greatly distressing and raise questions of human rights violations, yet the islanders have adapted

Figure 10.4 Bikini Atoll in 1946, during underwater test of an atomic bomb. Photograph is in the collections of the Micronesian Area Research Center, University of Guam.

while maintaining their ways of life, including their seafaring traditions. Within the last several decades, Micronesian navigators have been recruited in programs of reviving other Pacific seafaring experiments and traditions that now have lives of their own.

Currently, Micronesia is at the forefront of international research of the effects of global warming and sea-level rise. In the delicate balance of life in the low-lying atolls, the slightest fluctuation of sea level can bring disastrous consequence, and in theory, similar effects eventually will be seen in other regions of higher-elevated land masses after a larger magnitude of sea-level rise. The effects are illustrated spectacularly in the physical erosional loss of large portions of coastlines, but, in fact, most distressing so far has been the salinization of the freshwater lenses. The elevated ocean level has altered the freshwater lenses and already has started to cause failure of food crops and concerns about the health of drinking water.

Throughout the time range of human presence, the Micronesian atolls have been exceptionally vulnerable to environmental impacts. Human settlement in itself had posed threats to the fragile island ecologies. Additional impacts have persisted with the frequent typhoons that run through this region. Complicated webs of interisland connectivity have allowed groups to overcome periodic catastrophe, while at the same time building the seafaring traditions that have defined much of the cultural identity of the region. Archaeological remnants of artificial landfill constructions, water-crossing causeways, and offshore fish traps are gaining more attention today as examples of how people in the past had coped with the fragility of life in the atolls.

Early site contexts

Widespread Micronesian settlement at A.D. 100–500 involved a rapid movement of people across a large expanse of Pacific Oceania, wherein in at least three aspects can be defined in the social and environmental context.

- First, a large population dispersal of closely related Oceanic-speaking people may have been motivated by diminishing opportunities in homeland communities of Melanesia and West Polynesia, where people had been coping with significantly transforming coastal ecosystems and developing new modes of life at least since 500 B.C.
- Second, those Oceanic-speaking groups by A.D. 100 used mostly general-utility pottery and other artifacts lacking the highly distinctive forms of earlier periods, and overall, the material culture inventories at A.D. 100–500 depicted generalized and broad-spectrum living in Pacific Islands.
- Third, temporary stability of sea level and coastal conditions during the first few centuries A.D. likely supported more reliable use of coastal resources and evidently made more coastal areas suitable for habitation in Central and Eastern Micronesia.

Now with securely dated archaeological layers in several different islands, the major population movement into the region can be situated confidently in a range of A.D. 100–500. These oldest layers in some cases contain no more than sparse charcoal and debris of shells and fish bones, but in other cases they contain dense concentrations of broken pottery, shell and stone tools, hearth features, and other materials. The more secure dating results of A.D. 100–500 have been reported for buried archaeological layers in Pohnpei (Athens 1990a; Ayres 1990; Galipaud 2001), Kosrae (Athens 1990b), Kwajalein (Shun and Athens 1990), Majuro (Yamaguchi et al. 2005, 2009), Kiribati (Thomas 2009), and Mokil (Poteate et al. 2016). General survey data from other islands, referring primarily to Yap and Chuuk and their several neighboring islands, have focused mostly on later-aged surface-visible site ruins, yet scattered subsurface deposits have confirmed the existence of an earlier settlement period consistent with the regional pattern (Craib 1983, 1984; Intoh 2008; Intoh and Leach 1985; Sinoto 1984).

While the archaeological dating so far indicates a large-scale regional settlement after A.D. 100, the possibility still exists of finding older evidence in places that have not yet been searched thoroughly for deeply buried archaeological layers. Certainly coming from a homeland source in Melanesia or West Polynesia, the unified Oceanic linguistic history and rather generic plainware pottery could be traced potentially as early as 500 B.C. Even older dating at 1000 B.C. may be possible if groups had departed from Lapita-associated communities, and perhaps such hypothetical voyages could have been more realistic in the context of sea-crossing contacts with the early settlement areas of the Mariana Islands and Palau at that time. None of these conjectured scenarios so far can be substantiated with hard evidence from archaeological sites in Central and Eastern Micronesia.

If earlier settlement episodes occurred prior to A.D. 100 at small scales, then they have been overwritten by more abundant records of widespread populations settling in these islands after A.D. 100. Any such older settlement sites would have preceded the lowered sea-level conditions, and relevant archaeological layers now would be buried deeply and stranded far inland from the modern coastlines, obscured by more recent sedimentary units covering today's coastal landforms. Additional complications have involved subsidence of volcanic masses of the larger and higher islands, such as in Pohnpei (Sefton et al. 2022), where large portions of volcanic coastline have subsided and sunk beneath sea level.

Lowering sea level made the low-lying coral atolls inhabitable not only because of the emerged land mass but more importantly because of the accessibility of a freshwater lens floating just above the newly lowered sea level (Dickinson 2003). For some centuries of falling sea level, the surfaces of atolls were available as patches of variably stable or unstable land, but the water table was not yet positioned at a suitable level for supporting large groups of people. Given the window of time involved in these processes, minor discrepancies have occurred in the precise dating in each island case, yet the overall patterns conform to a tight time frame in the first centuries A.D.

In the atolls of Central and Eastern Micronesia, a mostly stable sea level at A.D. 100–500 is attested in excavation profiles of sedimentary units. Layers of beach sands, containing directly datable foraminifera, do not include interruptions or nonconformity transitions that otherwise characterize more dynamic beach settings. Instead, the massive units of undifferentiated sands reflect singular periods of sustained conditions, and the dated materials all point to a period of approximately A.D. 100–500 (Yamaguchi et al. 2009). These dates correspond with the ages of artificial pits dug into the floating water lens for the purpose of growing swamp taro, an activity especially well documented in the Marshall Islands (Weisler 1999, 2001). Given the limited habitat zones of atolls, the ability to grow swamp taro was vital for survival, especially if it could be grown in high-density production.

The stability of atolls by A.D. 100 coincided with a region-wide stability of sea level affecting the high islands as much as the atolls. While the atolls were probably not habitable at all prior to this time, the coasts of higher islands had been habitable yet unstable until close to A.D. 100. This period of temporary sea-level stability occurred within a portion of the continuing drawdown, specifically wherein the rate of drawdown had slowed considerably during the first few centuries A.D. It may be described as a period of very slow drawdown, not fully at a stand-still.

Evidence of this temporary coastal stability has been most clear in Guam at the far northwest edge of Micronesia, in particular at sites within the sandy beach fringe along Tumon Bay. Long landward-seaward section exposures of beach profiles have shown an incipient organic horizon, occurring as a thin layer of less than 5 cm thickness, draped over a former beach surface that had sloped downward to the former shoreline (Figure 10.5). Within this incipient organic horizon that must have formed during a period of temporary stability, two samples of charcoal have produced cross-corroborating radiocarbon dates calibrated at A.D. 23–222 and at A.D. 127–344. Another portion of the same ancient beach surface had preserved an area of several hearth features (Figure 10.6) containing dense charcoal chunks ideal for radiocarbon dating, including two dates from one hearth overlapping at A.D. 141–338, another two from a separate hearth overlapping at A.D. 53–136, and finally one other hearth charcoal sample at A.D. 131–377. The hearths had been emplaced over an older layer of lagoon sands composed of *Halimeda* sp. algal bioclasts directly dated at 341 B.C.–A.D. 9. Shortly after the cultural use of the hearths, a layer of tidal-surge debris was dated directly by its constituent bioclasts at A.D. 5–305, most probably near the middle to end of this range in order to accommodate the multiple dates of the hearths that must have preceded the tidal-surge event.

At present, no large-format excavations have exposed the details of the initial habitation floors in Central and Eastern Micronesia, but the sample windows of test pits and trenches have been sufficient to confirm initial settlements about A.D. 100–500. Buried cultural layers contain broken pieces of pottery, stone and shell tools, and food midden. Possible house forms and other details are not yet clarified prior to A.D. 1000 in these islands.

Pottery-making evidently ceased about A.D. 1000 in most of Central Micronesia and all of Eastern Micronesia, as had happened in West Polynesia at the same time, but so far the oldest pottery fragments do not reveal any particularly distinctive forms or styles. Rather, they were broken from general-utility "plainware" bowls of practical values. Rare instances display simple incisions or impressions, but mostly the pottery shows no

Figure 10.5 Beach profile stratigraphy and dating in Tumon, Guam, noting incipient organic horizon of buried ancient beach surface. Scale bar at left is in 20 cm increments.

decoration at all, much like the utilitarian plainware that survived through the changing contexts of the post-Lapita transformations in Melanesia and Polynesia (Chapter 9).

Especially in small coral and limestone islands, people have used shells more frequently than stones for making tools, simply because these environments offer plentiful shells but do not naturally include the geological formations with the most useful types of stone raw materials. Adzes usually were fashioned from the hard shells of the giant clam of the Tridacnidae family (mostly *Tridacna* spp. but also *Hippopus* sp. in some areas) as seen more broadly in the western Pacific region. Another form of shell adze, made from *Cassis cornuta* shell, was widespread throughout Micronesia after A.D. 100, and counterparts have been found at the same date range in parts of Indonesia and rarely in a few isolated cases in Polynesia. A narrow gouge or chisel sometimes was made of a *Terebra* sp. shell.

Interisland connectivity

Historically, Micronesia has been known for its sea-crossing trade and tribute systems that likely developed from much earlier roots. The most ancient archaeologically known period of A.D. 100–500 so far has not produced hard evidence of interisland transport of pottery or other commodities. The movement of people in general is attested in the effective settlement of the islands, but the overseas trade and exchange systems likely developed through extended periods of time.

Material evidence of interisland exchange in Micronesia appears to postdate A.D. 1000 and will be discussed in more detail in Chapter 13. Older evidence in the range of A.D. 100–500 may yet be discovered, but more research will be needed in order to obtain sufficient relevant archaeological materials, especially pottery with clay pastes or temper

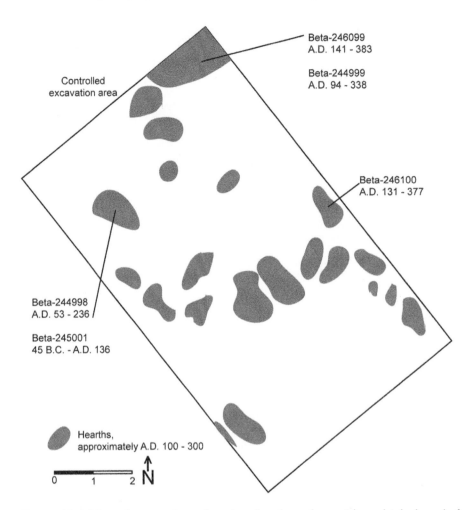

Figure 10.6 Map of excavation of ancient beach surface with multiple hearth features in Tumon, Guam. Graphic is adapted from Carson (2011, 2016).

inclusions that can be traced geologically to specific island sources. The later-aged evidence, however, shows that people from Yap quarried large stone money discs (*rai*) from geological sources in Palau, so far dated well after A.D. 1000 (Fitzpatrick 2002). A complex interisland tribute system of the *sawei* involved circulation of goods through a hierarchy of communities (Sudo 1996), but none of those material elements yet have been found in contexts older than the last few centuries (Descantes 2005). This same time range after A.D. 1000 and most abundantly after A.D. 1400 corresponds with the mobilization of stone adzes into far-reaching sea-crossing events, mostly involving Polynesian communities but extending into other parts of the Pacific as well (Weisler 1997).

Hybridization of seeded and seedless breadfruits required an east-west crossing of Micronesia, but a relevant dating is unclear (Zerega et al. 2004, 2006). The east-west movement is inferred from the hybridization of the seeded *Artocarpus mariannensis* that was native only to the Mariana Islands (and possibly Palau) in the far west of Micronesia with the seedless *Artocarpus altilis* and then distributed across Micronesia. These events likely occurred during the earliest settlement period in Central and Eastern Micronesia as a means to provide more food resources for the resident populations. Notably, these outcomes must have involved at least some form of contact between the non-Oceanic-speaking groups in the Marianas (or in Palau) and the Oceanic-speaking groups of the Nuclear Micronesian communities.

Breadfruit has been useful for long-term survival through difficulties of unpredictable storminess, drought, and other conditions. Fermented breadfruit paste could be preserved through extended periods, and accordingly breadfruit storage pits and paste foods have been significant cultural traditions in eastern Micronesia (Petersen 2006, 2009). Moreover, breadfruit is well suited to survive through the limited water-table supplies that are common in parts of Micronesia.

Breadfruit in Micronesia traditionally has been more than just an edible item, and Glenn Petersen (2006, 2009) identified breadfruit as an essential defining characteristic of Micronesian societies. In this view, breadfruit has been instrumental in shaping dietary nutrition, gift exchange, social networks, and more. Breadfruit is an expected part of most feasting events, and it makes an effective gift, especially when a particular variety offers a different size, shape, taste, texture, seasonality, or other quality appreciated by the people receiving the feast or gift. In certain areas of Eastern Micronesia, traditions of breadfruit pounders and pounding boards reveal more of the material culture associated with a complex set of behaviors, while their uneven geographic distribution could reflect the diversity of localized traditions across Micronesia.

Interisland connections may be viewed as ways to reduce the risks of living in an uncertain place such as Micronesia, for example, by providing access to food, land, transplantable crops, more people, and other resources. In Micronesia, more than any other part of Pacific Oceania, typhoons pose a serious threat on a regular basis, and people have learned to expect a devastating episode at least once every few years. Along with the destruction to homes, typhoon winds and tidal surges can destroy farmlands and forests, and they can result in blights lasting long after the storm events. In addition to the punctuated storminess, the region is prone to unpredictable droughts that can threaten the sustainability of subsistence crops and water supplies. All of these factors have persisted through the entire time of people living in Micronesia, so they formed part of the multi-generationally inherited context of maintaining interisland networking.

The inhabitation of most of Micronesia after A.D. 100 constituted the necessary environment for the Micronesia-wide traditions of overseas networking and interisland connectivity. The geographic extent of the inhabited world of Pacific Oceania remained stable for several centuries while people in each island group developed more of their own localized cultural practices, artistic expressions, and language history. These issues will be discussed more in Chapter 11, but part of what came to define Micronesia, as distinguished from neighboring areas, was the strength of interisland voyaging and connectivity traceable to a much older origin.

Contributions of Micronesia in Pacific-wide voyaging

Notions of a "pause" in Pacific exploration and settlement can be redefined by acknowledging that Micronesia occupies a large part of Pacific Oceania, where an extensive population dispersal occurred at A.D. 100–500. Otherwise, an apparent chronological break is difficult to comprehend between Lapita settlement in West Polynesia at 1100–800 B.C. and the next Polynesian population expansion into East Polynesia about A.D. 1000. The currently accepted dating of A.D. 1000 would indicate a "long pause" of nearly 2000 years.

An older settlement date would indicate a "short pause" that is easier to reconcile with the expectation of more or less continuous human exploration of the Pacific Ocean. In particular, Geoff Irwin (1992, 1998) has proposed that people persistently explored the Pacific by sailing canoes, accruing more and more knowledge of the sea and a potentially inhabitable sea of islands.

Rather than a "long pause" or a "short pause," the real evidence points to a *faux pas* (false step) in academic views of Pacific Oceania preoccupied with the "Polynesian problem" of how to explain an apparent continuity of culture from Island Southeast Asia through East Polynesia. Despite the great advances in Polynesian archaeology and ethnography, Pacific-wide voyaging clearly cannot be confined to Polynesians, especially when knowing the strong seafaring traditions in Micronesia (Figures 10.7 and 10.8). Polynesian ancestry has been traced through Lapita sites, linked proximately with Melanesia and more remotely with Island Southeast Asia, yet the role of Micronesia has been missing from most regional synthesis narratives.

Micronesian population dispersal at A.D. 100 was just as rapid and covered more geographic space than the Lapita-associated expansion a few centuries earlier. Shortly after the descendants of Lapita settlers adjusted to the unstoppable transformations of their island worlds with lowering sea level, the same lowering sea level opened the "atoll highway" of Micronesia. Another few centuries later, groups expanded farther eastward into

Figure 10.7 Lamotrek sailing canoe, after arrival in Guam during May 2016.

The atoll highway of Micronesia, A.D. 100 through 500 241

Figure 10.8 Sail from Lamotrek canoe, presented as a gift for the University of Guam.

East Polynesia as the next major episode of Pacific Oceanic population movement. According to this evidence, any pause in Pacific-wide voyaging was rather brief and lasted only long enough for people to adjust to new environmental conditions and to become comfortable with their newly settled sea of islands before investing in another major event of ocean-crossing migrations.

The role of Micronesia within the middle of Pacific-wide exploration needs to be stressed as categorically different from an older notion once proposed by Sir Peter Buck, also known as Te Rangi Hiroa. Without access to the archaeological information and dating now available, Hiroa (1938) postulated that Polynesians migrated from Southeast Asia and through Micronesia on their way to Polynesia, bypassing Melanesia entirely and thereby explaining the racial and ethnic differentiation between Melanesians and Polynesians. This proposal has been proven incorrect for several decades now, with the revelation of Lapita-associated settlement through Melanesia and Polynesia confirming a shared ancestry cross-regionally. A few centuries after the Lapita expansion, some of the

Oceanic-speaking people from this broad region moved to inhabit the islands of Central and Eastern Micronesia.

Pacific-wide voyaging certainly was not unidirectional from one singular point to another but rather caused the inhabited world to grow incrementally in broad zones of geographic coverage and with internally linked communities. Whenever a new area was occupied, it did not need to become the only possible launching point for the next ocean-crossing migration. For instance, people settled in the Mariana Islands by 1500 B.C., but the Marianas were probably not the sole source of people later moving into the Lapita realm. Rather, the origins of Lapita groups may have included some contribution from the Marianas as well as from Island Southeast Asia. Likewise, the expansion of people into Central and Eastern Micronesia at A.D. 100 resulted in an increased area of inhabited seascape and more navigational knowledge of the Pacific, but then the next major population movement into East Polynesia at A.D. 1000 did not need to come solely from Micronesia. In fact, the major source of East Polynesian settlement can be attributed to groups originating from West Polynesia, according to language history, material culture, oral traditions, and genetics studies.

References

Athens, J. Stephen, 1990a. Non Madol pottery, Pohnpei. In *Recent Advances in Micronesian Archaeology*, edited by Rosalind L. Hunter-Anderson, pp. 17–32. Micronesica Supplement 2. University of Guam Press, Mangilao.

Athens, J. Stephen, 1990b. Kosrae pottery, clay and early settlement. In *Recent Advances in Micronesian Archaeology*, edited by Rosalind L. Hunter-Anderson, pp. 171–186. Micronesica Supplement 2. University of Guam Press, Mangilao.

Ayres, William S., 1990. Pohnpei's position in Eastern Micronesian prehistory. In *Recent Advances in Micronesian Archaeology*, edited by Rosalind L. Hunter-Anderson, pp. 187–212. Micronesica Supplement 2. University of Guam Press, Mangilao.

Bender, Byron W., Ward H. Goodenough, Frederick H. Jackson, Jeffrey Marck, Kenneth L. Rehg, Ho-min Sohn, Stephen Trussel, and Judith W. Wang, 2003a. Proto-Micronesian reconstructions – 1. *Oceanic Linguistics* 42: 1–110.

Bender, Byron W., Ward H. Goodenough, Frederick H. Jackson, Jeffrey Marck, Kenneth L. Rehg, Ho-min Sohn, Stephen Trussel, and Judith W. Wang, 2003b. Proto-Micronesian reconstructions – 2. *Oceanic Linguistics* 42: 271–358.

Carson, Mike T., 2011. Palaeohabitat of first settlement sites 1500–1000 B.C. in Guam, Mariana Islands, western Pacific. *Journal of Archaeological Science* 38: 2207–2221.

Carson, Mike T., 2016. *Archaeological Landscape Evolution: The Mariana Islands in the Asia-Pacific Region*. Springer International, Cham, Switzerland.

Craib, John L., 1983. Micronesian prehistory: An archaeological overview. *Science* 219: 922–927.

Craib, John L., 1984. Settlement on Ulithi Atoll, western Caroline Islands. *Asian Perspectives* 24: 47–56.

Descantes, Christophe, 2005. *Integrating Archaeology and Ethnohistory: The Development of Exchange Between Yap and Ulithi, Western Caroline Islands*. British Archaeological Report International Series Number 1344. Archaeopress, Oxford.

Dickinson, William R., 2003. Impact of Mid-Holocene hydro-isostatic highstand in regional sea level on habitability of islands in Pacific Oceania. *Journal of Coastal Research* 19: 489–502.

Dodson, John, and Michiko Intoh, 1999. Prehistory and palaeoecology of Yap, Federated States of Micronesia. *Quaternary International* 59: 17–26.

Fitzpatrick, Scott M., 2002. A radiocarbon chronology of Yapese stone money quarries in Palau. *Micronesica* 34: 227–242.

Flood, Bo, Beret E. Strong, and William A. Flood, 2002. *Micronesian Legends*. Bess Press, Honolulu.
Galipaud, Jean-Christophe, 2001. Le peuplement initial de Pohnpei. *Journal de la Société des Océanistes 112*: 49–60.
Hiroa, Te Rangi, 1938. *Vikings of the Sunrise*. Frederick Stokes, New York.
Intoh, Michiko, 1997. Human dispersals into Micronesia. *Anthropological Science 105*: 15–28.
Intoh, Michiko, 2008. Ongoing archaeological research on Fais, Micronesia. *Asian Perspectives 47*: 121–138.
Intoh, Michiko, and Foss Leach, 1985. *Archaeological Investigations in the Yap Islands, Micronesia: First Millennium B.C. to the Present Day*. British Archaeological Reports International Series 277. Archaeopress, Oxford.
Irwin, Geoffrey J., 1992. *The Prehistoric Exploration and Colonisation of the Pacific*. Cambridge University Press, Cambridge.
Irwin, Geoffrey J., 1998. The colonisation of the Pacific Plate: Chronological, navigational and social issues. *Journal of the Polynesian Society 107*: 111–143.
Marck, Jeffrey C., 1986. Micronesian dialects and the overnight voyage. *Journal of the Polynesian Society 95*: 253–258.
Petersen, Glenn, 2006. Micronesia's breadfruit revolution and the evolution of a culture area. *Archaeology in Oceania 41*: 82–92.
Petersen, Glenn, 2009. *Traditional Micronesian Societies: Adaptation, Integration, and Political Organization in the Central Pacific*. University of Hawai'i Press, Honolulu.
Poteate, Aaron S., Scott M. Fitzpatrick, William S. Ayres, and Adam Thompson, 2016. First radiocarbon chronology for Mwoakilloa (Mokil) Atoll, Eastern Caroline Islands, Microensia. *Radiocarbon 58*: 169–178.
Rainbird, Paul, 1994. Prehistory of the north-west tropical Pacific: The Caroline, Mariana, and Marshall Islands. *Journal of World Prehistory 8*: 293–349.
Rainbird, Paul, 2004. *The Archaeology of Micronesia*. Cambridge University Press, Cambridge.
Ross, Malcolm D., 1996. Is Yapese Oceanic? In *Reconstruction, Classification, Description: Festschrift in Honor of Isidore Dyen*, edited by Bernd Nothofer, pp. 121–166. Abera, Hamburg.
Sefton, Juliet P., Andrew C. Kemp, Simon E. Englehart, and Mark D. McCoy, 2022. Implications of anomalous relative sea-level rise for the peopling of Remote Oceania. *Proceedings of the National Academy of Sciences 119*: e2210863119. https://doi.org/10.1073/pnas.2210863119
Shun, Kanalei, and J. Stephen Athens, 1990. Archaeological investigations at Kwajalein Atoll, Marshall Islands, Micronesia. In *Recent Advances in Micronesian Archaeology*, edited by Rosalind L. Hunter-Anderson, pp. 231–240. Micronesica Supplement 2. University of Guam Press, Mangilao.
Sinoto, Yosihiko H. (editor), 1984. *Caroline Islands Archaeology: Investigations on Fefan, Faraulep, Woleai, and Lamotrek*. Pacific Anthropological Records 35. Department of Anthropology, Bernice Pauahi Bishop Museum, Honolulu.
Streck, Charles S., 1990. Prehistoric settlement in eastern Micronesia: Archaeology on Bikini Atoll. In *Recent Advances in Micronesian Archaeology*, edited by Rosalind L. Hunter-Anderson, pp. 247–260. Micronesica Supplement 2. University of Guam Press, Mangilao.
Sudo, Ken-ichi, 1996. Rank, hierarchy and routes of migration: Chieftainship in the Central Caroline Islands of Micronesia. In *Origins, Ancestry and Alliance: Explorations in Austronesian Ethnography*, edited by James J. Fox and Clifford Sather, pp. 57–72. Department of Anthropology, Research School of Pacific Studies, Australian National University, Canberra.
Thomas, Frank R., 2009. Historical ecology in Kiribati: Linking past with present. *Pacific Science 63*: 567–600.
Weisler, Marshall I. (editor), 1997. *Prehistoric Long-Distance Interaction in Oceania: An Interdisciplinary Approach*. Monograph 21. New Zealand Archaeological Association, Auckland.
Weisler, Marshall I., 1999. The antiquity of aroid pit agriculture and significance of buried A horizons on Pacific atolls. *Geoarchaeology 14*: 621–654.

Weisler, Marshall I., 2001. Precarious landscapes: Prehistoric settlement of the Marshall Islands. *Antiquity* 75: 31–32.

Yamaguchi, Toru, Hajime Kayanne, and Hiroya Yamano, 2009. Archaeological investigation of the landscape history of an Oceanic atoll: Majuro, Marshall Islands. *Pacific Science* 63: 537–565.

Yamaguchi, Toru, Hajime Kayanne, Hiroya Yamano, Yayoi Najima, Masahi Chikamori, and Hiromune Yokoki, 2005. Excavation of pit-agriculture landscape on Majuro Atoll, Marshall Islands, and its implications. *Global Environmental Research* 9: 27–36.

Zerega, Nyree J. C., Diane Ragone, and Timothy J. Motely, 2004. Complex origins of breadfruit (*Artocarpus altilis*, Moraceae): Implications for human migration in Oceania. *American Journal of Botany* 91: 760–766.

Zerega, Nyree J. C., Diane Ragone, and Timothy J. Motely, 2006. Breadfruit origins, diversity, and human-facilitated distribution. In *Darwin's Harvest: Origins, Evolution, and Conservation of Crop Plants*, edited by Timothy J. Motely and Nyree J. C. Zerega, pp. 213–238. Columbia University Press, New York.

11 Ethnogenesis and polygenesis, A.D. 500 through 1000

Fag heta 'es ia pau (Rotuman saying), translates into English as "The fish trap is full of fish."

This Rotuman saying refers to an event that attracts many people, implying that something has baited the people to attend the event, like fish attracted to a fish trap (Inia 1998: 11). Pacific Oceania is known for its feasting events involving copious amounts of foods and attracting large crowds, often entire village populations, or even attendance from other villages or distant islands. Some of these events are orchestrated to justify claims of social rank or political leadership, as well as to maintain positions and sometimes to overthrow others. In many ways, feasts can control the outcomes of social histories, and furthermore they encapsulate the definitive aspects of a cultural group's identity.

During the period of A.D. 500–1000, the inhabited islands of Pacific Oceania were becoming full of people, like fish filling nets or traps (Figure 11.1). The previous period of sea-level drawdown was nearly complete, and new coastal ecologies were growing stable and reliable with abundant resources capable of supporting large populations. Meanwhile, people had inherited several generations of knowledge and traditions adapted to the local conditions of each island group. Communities exercised proficiency in maximizing the broad spectrum of coastal and land-based resource zones, managing through periodic devastating storms and other cataclysms, and maintaining complex networks of overseas trading and other partnerships.

No major sea-crossing migrations spread into previously uninhabited islands during this period, but rather hundreds of communities maintained their residence in the islands of the western through central Pacific. In each of these island communities, population growth was increasing internally, encouraged by the capacity of the stabilizing coastal ecologies plus the cultural use of a broad range of island resource habitats. Meanwhile, the archaeological record shows that people continued living in the same islands without release of population through migrations into other parts of the Pacific.

Feasting events likely served to sustain social cohesion, especially during a time when people were living in greater demographic density of inherently limited island space. The physical evidence of Pacific feasting events became much more prominent after A.D. 1000, for instance, as seen in the large community-serving earth ovens throughout Polynesia after this time, but these developments can be traced back to the preceding centuries. Although lacking specific dating, the traditions of drinking kava (a depressant drug, made from the roots of *Piper methysticum*) often involved community gatherings with varying degrees of formal ceremony in parts of Island Melanesia, West Polynesia, and Eastern Micronesia. The period of A.D. 500–1000 overall was characterized by increasing intensity of island habitation, supporting localized developments of unique traditions in each island group, as reflected both in the differentiation of language groups and in the diversified expressions of material culture.

DOI: 10.4324/9781003399025-11

246 *Ethnogenesis and polygenesis, A.D. 500 through 1000*

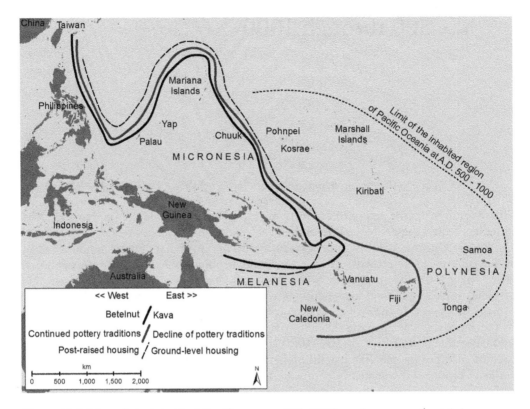

Figure 11.1 Map of the inhabited Pacific at A.D. 500–1000, noting areas of retaining versus losing pottery, post-raised versus ground-level housing formats, and betelnut-chewing versus kava-drinking traditions.

By A.D. 1000, archaeological assemblages revealed different material culture characteristics in the separate island groups of Pacific Oceania, especially distinctive within West Polynesia. Leading up to that point and beginning around A.D. 500, pottery-making traditions diminished and eventually disappeared entirely in Eastern Micronesia and West Polynesia, while they continued in other regions farther to the west in Micronesia and Melanesia. The decline of pottery-making coincided with a rising popularity of large-sized community-serving earth ovens in Polynesia. Other simultaneous shifts are noticed in transitions from earthen-filled to stone-filled house foundations, as well as in forms of residential settlement structure. The linguistic subgroup splitting of Polynesian communities must have occurred during this period as well, accounting for the linguistic phylogeny associated with Polynesian expansion into other parts of the Pacific at A.D. 1000, furthermore indicating similar differentiation of other language subgroups that could be defined separately by this time in Melanesia and Micronesia.

The period of A.D. 500–1000 was a crucial time in the shaping of cultural identity, often perceived as a process of ethnogenesis or alternatively of polygenesis. David Burley (2013) has stressed that cultural identities in Fiji and West Polynesia have developed not through single pathways of ethnogenesis but rather through a more complex process that he described as polygenesis. In this view, polygenesis incorporates multiple factors and extends over a period of time. This clarification serves well to accommodate the cultural change in the region, especially during the centuries of A.D. 500 through 1000 when shifts evidently occurred in material culture expressions that eventually created a set of clearly distinctive Polynesian traits distinguished from Melanesian and Micronesian neighbors by A.D. 1000.

The cultural transformations during A.D. 500–1000 resulted in the contextual setting of Polynesian culture just prior to the explosive radiation of population dispersal into all of East Polynesia as well as into the Polynesian Outliers. These later Polynesian sites are characterized by extensive stonework foundations, ground-level housing, formally structured village settlement systems, large monuments, community assembly centers, large group-serving earth ovens, and absence of pottery that in total act as a collective assemblage contrasting strongly against the material culture inventories seen in older periods. In other words, the distinguishing traits of Polynesian culture, as known ethnohistorically and continuing today, had developed through a transformative period at A.D. 500–1000 within West Polynesia, later extended into the Polynesian Outliers and East Polynesia nearly simultaneously after A.D. 1000.

The dying art of pottery and other cultural transformations

The loss of pottery before A.D. 1000 constituted one of the most curious puzzles in Pacific Oceanic archaeology, occurring throughout Polynesia and also in Eastern Micronesia. While people continued pottery-making traditions in islands farther westward in both Melanesia and Micronesia, the cessation in the east has been difficult to comprehend. Without access to the archaeological records, ethnographic and historical knowledge alone would suggest that pottery-making never had been part of a Polynesian identity, even to the point of questioning the cultural associations of older pottery-bearing archaeological layers.

Pottery-making was not sustained as part of the cultural repertoire by people living in East Polynesia, where settlement sites now are accepted dating no earlier than A.D. 1000. In this case, pottery must have been a dead or dying art in the homeland of those Polynesian settlers prior to A.D. 1000, for instance, in the islands of West Polynesia, such as in Samoa and Tonga where, in fact, pottery was mostly absent in sites postdating A.D. 1000. Most tellingly in East Polynesia, extremely rare potsherds were documented in the Marquesas Islands in unclear contexts, and those few pieces contained mineral inclusions typical of islands farther to the west and likely carried aboard an early long-distance voyage (Dickinson et al. 1998). Other than those few potsherds hinting at the very first traces of cultural presence in East Polynesia, no pottery at all has been found in the definite settlement contexts ever since A.D. 1000.

Although not yet dated clearly, the scant instances of pottery fragments in the Marquesas Islands probably represented the final chapter of pottery-making traditions that were disappearing just at the cusp of initial East Polynesian settlement. Substantial settlement prior to A.D. 1000 would appear unlikely, given the existing evidence of faunal extinctions and other anthropogenic impacts in definitely non-pottery-bearing layers of A.D. 1000–1200 that resemble the contexts of first cultural settlement in the Marquesas Islands (Rolett 1998). Alternatively, if those few potsherds in the Marquesas Islands are proven to date significantly older than A.D. 1000, then other layers of such an early settlement would need to be explored in paleo-landscapes that have not yet been defined.

Dating of the end of pottery-making in West Polynesia has been quite clear and sudden in Tonga yet irregular over an extended period in Samoa. Tongan sites indicate loss of pottery well prior to A.D. 1000 and likely close to A.D. 500, apparently all at once in a singular horizon-like event (Burley and Clark 2003). Most Samoan sites indicate the same date range of a pre–A.D. 1000 loss of pottery, with limited outlying later-dated instances of a few centuries later, thus suggesting an uneven decline of pottery-making across different communities (Carson 2014; Clark 1996).

The disappearance of pottery can be understood best in relation to other material culture traits that declined at the same time, while other traits still gained popularity and replaced them (Figure 11.2). In Samoa, the older pottery-bearing sites consisted of earthen-filled terraces that likely supported post-raised houses, later replaced by stone-filled house foundations for ground-level housing entirely lacking pottery. Additionally, large earth ovens gained great popularity after A.D. 1000 and would indicate a new form of cooking without pots along with new social contexts of community feasting again without pots (Leach 1982, 2007).

Knowing about this larger context of a shift in material culture during the centuries prior to A.D. 1000, the loss of pottery-making can be understood as one part of the larger cultural transition. Several ideas have been proposed about the declining inaccessibility of suitable clays to make pottery, changing roles of skilled potters within Polynesian society, and emerging popularity of earth ovens for cooking without pots. Accessibility of clays may have been a concern for some atoll communities if they could not gain access to clays

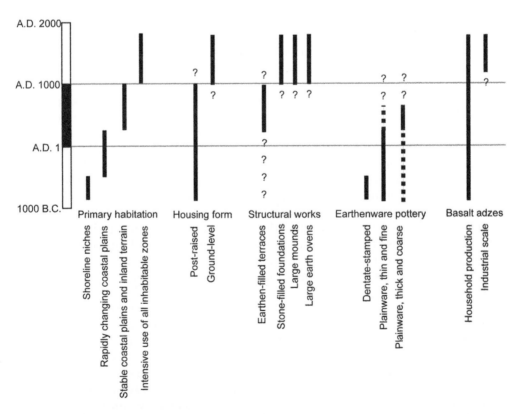

Figure 11.2 Samoan archaeology sequence, noting major transitions at A.D. 500–1000. Graphic is adapted from Carson (2014).

or to pottery makers on other islands (Claridge 1984), but it would not have affected most communities. A possible changing role of pottery specialists may have been related to other new conditions that demanded those people to invest their time in other activities (le Moine 1987; Marshall 1985), such as the apparent rising popularity of earth ovens. The eventual dominance of large earth ovens certainly fits with the timing of the decline of pottery-making (Leach 1982, 2007) and with implications about the technical utility as well as the social performance characteristics of pottery versus earth ovens.

The rising popularity of large earth ovens corresponded with other new constructions generally postdating A.D. 1000 that will be discussed in Chapter 12. In brief, the new constructions entailed stone-filled house foundations, as well as large-scale stonework monuments. The emergence of formalized village structures and monuments clearly signified a new set of cultural traditions that characterized West Polynesia and later would be carried into East Polynesia. Parallel events occurred in Melanesia and Micronesia as well, and each island group developed a unique expression of this broadly shared general pattern.

The role of feasting should not be underestimated, for example, as the large community-serving earth ovens were designed to attract people "like fish filling a fish trap." The dying art of pottery-making coincided with the rising art of feasting, in this case formalized in prominent earth oven features. The emergence of large stonework monuments, furthermore, may have served as attractions for tribute and other ritual events linked broadly with feasts.

Related with feasting activities but missing from the archaeological material record, kava-drinking became popular within the geographic area where pottery was lost in Eastern Micronesia and West Polynesia. Kava-drinking traditions have been absent in the western Pacific where betelnut-chewing instead has been practiced. Cultural use of kava (made from the processed root of *Piper methysticum*) did not correspond completely with a loss of pottery, given that kava has been an important cultural tradition in Fiji and Vanuatu where pottery-making continued. Only partially has the distribution of kava-drinking corresponded with the areas where pottery-making declined and where other traditions emerged. Several rules and regulations apply to kava ceremonies, clearly within the scope of specialized events and conceivably linked with feasting behaviors, often performed in meeting halls or at religious monuments where the ritual aspects are enhanced.

Traditions such as kava-drinking have functioned centrally in developing distinctive cultural identities, although precise archaeological dating has not yet been possible of kava remains or residues. The geographic distribution of kava-drinking in the central and eastern Pacific suggests a later development as compared to betelnut-chewing in the west. Betelnut-chewing may have originated with hunter-gatherers in Island Southeast Asia, thereafter imported both westward and eastward, and linked with the first human settlements into Remote Oceania. Kava evidently developed later and with more rigidly defined contexts of ceremonial performance, possibly originating in Vanuatu. Communities in western Micronesia continued traditions of betelnut-chewing, pottery-making, and post-raised housing as compared to the groups in eastern Micronesia and West Polynesia who, by A.D. 1000, practiced different traditions of kava-drinking, absence of pottery-making, and new formats of ground-level housing.

Changing house forms and settlement systems

The distinctively Polynesian house forms can be understood as components of a social settlement structure, famously documented by Roger Green (1967, 1970, 1986, 1993) as the elements of a shared Ancestral Polynesian Society (APS). Traditional Polynesian settlements have consisted of separate dwelling and cooking houses, often with designated men's versus women's houses, a dedicated "god house" for religious ritual, a central community event area, and usually a canoe shed. These components have been documented mostly through ethnographic observation, correlated with archaeological sites that consistently postdated A.D. 1000, as will be presented in a later chapter (Chapter 12). According to this chronological view, the unified sense of a distinctively Polynesian type of settlement structure by A.D. 1000 most likely had been under development during a transformative period of A.D. 500–1000.

The Polynesian type of settlement structure can be seen convincingly in the stonework ruins found everywhere in surface-visible contexts of Polynesia, but so far this connection cannot be extended into contexts older than A.D. 1000. Instead, the deeper and older pottery-bearing layers were associated with earthen-filled terraces that were most suitable for post-raised houses rather than for ground-level housing. This overall shift in housing form and other aspects of material culture brought the emergence of the formalized Polynesian settlement structure as it came to be known ethnohistorically.

The notion of an Ancestral Polynesian Society clearly applies in the post–A.D. 1000 contexts of expansion into East Polynesia and the Polynesian Outliers, and the origins may be attributable to the developments that occurred just prior to A.D. 1000 within West Polynesia. As illustrated in this chapter, however, the time depth of those specific traits cannot be extended much earlier, and, in fact, these traits developed into their known ethnographic forms primarily during the centuries of A.D. 500–1000. During this same period when Polynesian cultural traditions were becoming distinguished, parallel developments of distinctive cultural identity were underway in all of the inhabited island groups of Pacific Oceania, expressed in language histories as well as in archaeological material assemblages.

By A.D. 1000, housing features in West Polynesia were constructed with stone-filled foundations directly supporting the houses at ground level. This format replaced an older tradition of post-raised housing for elevated superstructures, as had been practiced in Island Southeast Asia and in western Micronesia. The new developments of ground-level housing required stone-filled foundations of terraces and platforms as a matter of practical necessity. Meanwhile, even in the areas farther westward where post-raised housing continued, people began to construct extensive stonework features associated with those houses as well as with pathways and other features, notably defining the traditional villages as in Palau, Yap, and Chuuk.

Given the preponderance of post–A.D. 1000 stonework ruins covering most surfaces today, the remnants of older housing and settlement structures prior to A.D. 1000 are, by comparison, sparsely documented throughout Pacific Oceania (Figure 11.3). With repeated reuse of inherently constrained island masses, older cultural layers tend to be disturbed at least partially and often rather extensively in shallow rocky sediments with little opportunity for stratigraphic separation. Nevertheless, numerous site layers predating A.D. 1000 have yielded plenty of information to dispel notions of a "dark age" that previously had been poorly known (Rieth and Addison 2008).

Palau offers an exception to the overall rule of needing to search in subsurface layers for site remnants prior to A.D. 1000. In the large island of Babeldaob, the stonework ruins of post–A.D. 1000 villages were constructed in roughly level terrain, spatially separated from older sites that had occupied rugged hilltops and ridges (Figure 11.4). On these hilltops and ridges, people had built large earthwork complexes as early as 100 B.C. but mostly in the range of A.D. 500–1000 (Liston 2009; Wickler 2002). These complexes involved massive earth-moving efforts, implying organized labor (Figure 11.5). Their positions could be

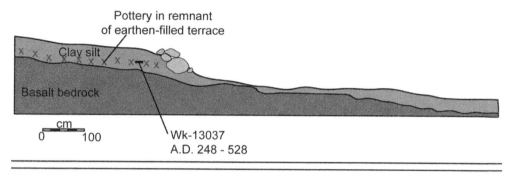
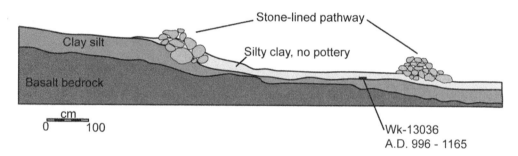

Figure 11.3 Remnants of pre–A.D. 1000 cultural layers beneath surface-visible stonework ruins in Tutuila, American Samoa. Graphic is adapted from Carson (2006).

defended, if necessary, further implying a degree of centralized control of each settlement unit. They did not include the same clear elements of men's and women's houses and other structures matching with ethnographic traditions and later stonework sites, but they functioned as largely self-sufficient settlements with apparently general-purpose housing and other activity areas.

In a large-scale view, the period of A.D. 500–1000 can be recognized as vital in the ethnogenesis or polygenesis of each island group and in the resulting differentiation of language communities, archaeological material inventories, and cultural traditions that eventually characterized each island society individually by A.D. 1000. These developments were made possible by the combined effects of

- overall stable ecological conditions;
- established cultural strategies of broad-spectrum use of coastal and land-based habitats and resources; and
- consecutive centuries of people living within constrained island spaces.

In each island community, population densities increased with people caught like fish filling a trap, soon to start filling other traps with a new population expansion into other parts of the Pacific after A.D. 1000.

252 *Ethnogenesis and polygenesis*, A.D. 500 through 1000

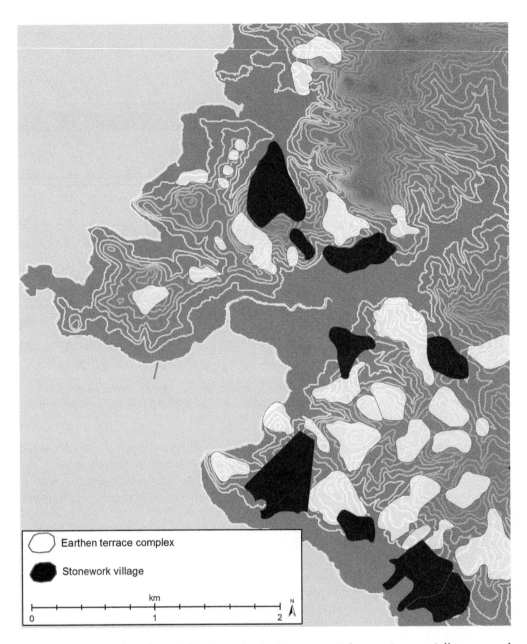

Figure 11.4 Map of surface-visible site ruins in Ngatpang, Palau, noting spatially separated distributions of earthen terraces (before A.D. 1000) and stonework villages (after A.D. 1000). Graphic is based on mapping datasets from Republic of Belau, Bureau of Arts and Culture.

Figure 11.5 Palau earthwork complex in Babeldaob.

References

Burley, David V., 2013. Fijian polygenesis and the Melanesian/Polynesian divide. *Current Anthropology* 54: 436–462.

Burley, David V., and Jeffrey T. Clark, 2003. The archaeology of Fiji/Western Polynesia in the post-Lapita era. In *Pacific Archaeology: Assessments and Prospects*, edited by Christophe Sand, pp. 235–254. Cahiers de l'Archéologie en Nouvelle-Calédonie 15. Département d'Archéologie, Services des Musées et du Patrimoine de Nouvelle-Calédonie, Nouméa.

Carson, Mike T., 2006. Samoan cultivation practices in archaeological perspective. *People and Culture in Oceania* 22: 1–29.

Carson, Mike T., 2014. De-coding the archaeological landscape of Samoa: Austronesian origins and Polynesian culture. *Journal of Austronesian Studies* 5: 1–41.

Claridge, Graeme G. C., 1984. Pottery in the Pacific: The clay factor. *New Zealand Journal of Archaeology* 6: 37–46.

Clark, Jeffrey T., 1996. Samoan prehistory in review. In *Oceanic Culture History: Essays in Honour of Roger Green*, edited by Janet Davidson, Geoffrey Irwin, Foss Leach, Andrew Pawley, and Dorothy Brown, pp. 445–460. New Zealand Archaeological Association, Auckland.

Dickinson, William R., Barry V. Rolett, Yosihiko H. Sinoto, Mara Elena Rosenthal, and Richard Shutler, Jr., 1998. Temper sands in exotic Marquesan pottery and the significance of their Fijian origin. *Journal de la Société des Océanistes* 107: 119–133.

Green, Roger C., 1967. Settlement patterns: Four case studies from Polynesia. In *Archaeology at the Eleventh Pacific Science Congress*, edited by Wilhelm G. Solheim, II, pp. 101–132. Asian and Pacific Archaeology Series 1. Social Science Research Institute, University of Hawai'i, Honolulu.

Green, Roger C., 1970. Settlement pattern archaeology in Polynesia. In *Studies in Oceanic Culture History*, edited by Roger C. Green and Marion Kelly, Volume 1, pp. 13–32. Pacific Anthropological Records Number 11. Department of Anthropology, Bishop Museum, Honolulu.

Green, Roger C., 1986. Some basic components of the Ancestral Polynesian settlement system: Building blocks for more complex Polynesian societies. In *Island Societies: Archaeological Approaches to Evolution and Transformation*, edited by Patrick V. Kirch, pp. 50–54. New Directions in Archaeology. Cambridge University Press, Cambridge.

Green, Roger C., 1993. Community-level organisation, power and elites in Polynesian settlement pattern studies. In *The Evolution and Organisation of Prehistoric Society in Polynesia*, edited by Michael W. Graves and Roger C. Green, pp. 9–12. Monograph Number 19. New Zealand Archaeological Association, Auckland.

Inia, Elizabeth F. K. (compiler and translator), 1998. *Fäeg 'Es Fuaga: Rotuman Proverbs*. Institute of Pacific Studies, University of the South Pacific, Suva, Fiji.

le Moine, Genevieve, 1987. The loss of pottery in Polynesia. *New Zealand Journal of Archaeology* 9: 25–32.

Leach, Helen M., 1982. Cooking without pots: Aspects of prehistoric and traditional Polynesian cooking. *New Zealand Journal of Archaeology* 4: 149–156.

Leach, Helen M., 2007. Cooking without pots – again. In *Vastly Ingenious: The Archaeology of Pacific Material Culture in Honour of Janet M. Davidson*, edited by Atholl Anderson, Kaye Green, and Foss Leach, pp. 53–68. Otago University Press, Dunedin, New Zealand.

Liston, Jolie, 2009. Cultural chronology of earthworks in Palau, Western Micronesia. *Archaeology in Oceania* 44: 56–73.

Marshall, Yvonne, 1985. Who made the Lapita pots? A case study in gender archaeology. *Journal of the Polynesian Society* 94: 205–233.

Rieth, Timothy, and David J. Addison, 2008. How dark are they? The Samoan Dark Ages, ~1500–1000 BP. In *Recent Advances in the Archaeology of the Fiji/West Polynesia Region*, edited by David J. Addison and Christophe Sand, pp. 87–96. University of Otago Studies in Prehistoric Anthropology 21. University of Otago, Dunedin, New Zealand.

Rolett, Barry V., 1998. *Hanamiai: Prehistoric Colonization and Cultural Change in the Marquesas Islands, French Polynesia*. Department of Anthropology and the Peabody Museum, Yale University, New Haven.

Wickler, Stephen K., 2002. Terraces and villages: Transformation of the cultural landscape in Palau. In *Pacific Landscapes: Archaeological Approaches*, edited by Thegn N. Ladefoged and Michael W. Graves, pp. 63–96. Bearsville Press, Los Osos, CA.

12 An A.D. 1000 Event? Formalization of cultural expressions

E haere iho a te pape i roto i te tahora (Tahitian proverb), translates into English as "Water flows only into rivers."

This chapter's opening quote implies that wealth always seems to go to the people who already have it, but it means more than the adage of "the rich get richer." The sentiment stresses an awareness of social and economic imbalance between the few wealthy elites who control resources versus the more numerous members of the population who can access only a small portion of those resources. In many parts of Polynesia, the most vital and precious natural resource of fresh water is equated with wealth. For example, when the Hawaiian word for "water" (*wai*) is doubled as *waiwai*, then it means "wealth." When wealth flows into the hands of the wealthy, then it accords with the principles of how water flows into a river, in a sense justifying the elite concentration of wealth as a natural condition of the world.

Evidence of wealth and status differential began to crystallize in formalized ways throughout Pacific Oceania about A.D. 1000, as part of a broader formalization of culture in a general sense. In numerous islands, the archaeological records have shown the emergence of monument-making traditions, clearly structured village complexes, burial of individuals at their houses, and a strong sense of permanence in fixed territories linking specific groups of people with their own units of land. Each island group developed a unique localized expression, in some cases accompanied by terrain-altering agricultural systems, industrial scale of stone material quarries, religious institutions justifying political power, and other creations.

The post–A.D. 1000 records have revealed a formalization of culture literally fixed in stone. House structures mostly were made at ground level with stone-filled foundations in varied terrain settings, instead of the older patterns of stilt-raised houses primarily at seashores. Post-raised housing still was practiced in some places, such as in western Micronesia, but these later constructions involved prominent use of stone in the foundation elements. Stone was used not only for housing foundation terraces and platforms but also for many other elements, such as pathway paving or lining, boundary-marking of fences or walls, mounds or platforms of burial or other ceremonial monuments, and varied rings, terraces, and mounds in gardens or cultivation fields. Additionally, items previously made of wood now became increasingly popular in stone, such as grinding mortars, pestles or pounders, and statues.

When Pacific Oceanic societies began to demonstrate these patterns of cultural formalization all at once about A.D. 1000, the timing followed the immediately preceding centuries of in situ development of cultural identity within each inhabited island group of the

256　An A.D. 1000 Event? Formalization of cultural expressions

western and central Pacific (Chapter 11). In this context, each island group already had developed distinguishing characteristics in language and in material culture, so the records after A.D. 1000 reflected formalization of those preexisting characteristics. Those material culture traits in West Polynesia were especially well defined and carried into East Polynesia, but parallel cases occurred in Melanesia and Micronesia, as will be discussed in this chapter.

The cross-regional timing at A.D. 1000 indicates that the numerous island societies developed a similar set of solutions to their mutually shared conditions at the same time, perhaps related to the preceding centuries of population growth, a period of overall climatic stability, or other factors generally affecting the whole region. Increasing densities of island populations created a need for managing access and distribution of land, food, and resources. Limits of population growth, at least socially if not in terms of physical carrying capacity of island ecosystems, could be indicated by the flood of population dispersal into the remote-distance islands of East Polynesia as well as into the Polynesian Outliers, all proceeding after A.D. 1000 (Figure 12.1). Meanwhile, a period of overall climatic stability of warm temperature and steady rainfall sustained from A.D. 1000 through 1300, likely supporting even more population growth and investment in labor-intensive behaviors of building monuments, constructing large-scale and long-lasting village complexes, and ultimately creating systems of linking people with defined territories.

After A.D. 1000, stonework villages dominated the landscapes of all island groups. These records imply large resident populations, in many cases expanding into marginal resource zones such as in the far northern Mariana Islands, generally lacking groundwater supplies and forcing people to rely on rainwater collection. Population growth further is implied by the constructions of large-scale monuments that must have involved the labor of impressive numbers of people to move the masses of stones.

Toward explaining this apparent "A.D. 1000 Event," opinions vary about the effective roles of family lineages, distribution of wealth and resources, region-wide

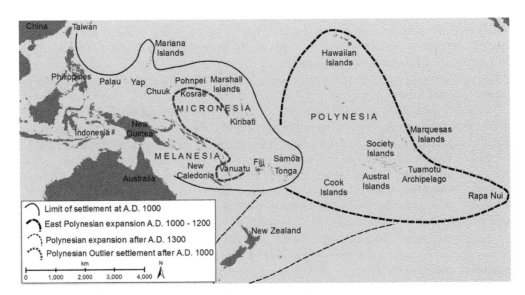

Figure 12.1 Map of the inhabited Pacific after A.D. 1000, noting movements into East Polynesia and the Polynesian Outliers, as well as later movement into New Zealand at A.D. 1300.

climate conditions, and competition among dense populations within the limits of their islands. Each of these factors contributed to the outcomes of formalized cultural expressions throughout Pacific Oceania. Regardless of theoretical interpretations, the emergent patterns at A.D. 1000 are best understood through cross-regional examples accounting for the region-wide results which are furthermore essential toward discussing the varied economic, social, and political developments of the next several centuries.

Monuments and monumental traditions

References to "monumental architecture" in Pacific Oceania have not always involved elements of monumentality or of architecture in the strictest definitions. House structures traditionally have been made of wood and thatch, and the only surviving elements in archaeological contexts are the stonework ruins of foundation terraces or platforms, mounds, and fences or walls. In a few places, features were constructed of earthen mounded material, typically with adjacent ditches or depressions. The durable stone or earthen remnants can be impressive in their size and footprint across the landscape. Regardless of total volume of material, the constructions often entailed special efforts in design and arrangement of stones with particular characteristics of size, shape, texture, color, and inter-fitting of the individual pieces. In many cases, individual stones served specific cultural functions, frequently in upright position and epitomized in the use of statues.

Monuments may be understood as large-scale and long-lasting constructions intended to commemorate an event, person, or idea. Eventually, monuments are used or appropriated by whole communities, even if they had originated for a single person or for a small group. All monuments share an intention of enduring through the future, beyond the lifetimes of the people who made them, and accordingly they become "public property," at least in an intellectual sense, while still recognized as having been constructed or owned by individuals of the past. In theory, a monument of the distant past potentially can be claimed as part of the whole community's heritage, regardless of personal family lineage connection, and an extreme example might refer to a World Heritage Site.

Along with strictly defined "monuments," several other sites may be considered "monumental" in character, and indeed these sites have comprised the bulk of the evidence of formalization of expression in a purported A.D. 1000 Event. This looser category refers to sites that cover large areas of land and have endured as permanent parts of the landscape multi-generationally. Over time, sites or objects may be assigned monumental status or meaning in new contexts and frames of reference that did not exist initially when they were constructed.

Almost every island in Pacific Oceania bears at least one site that may be considered as a monument or as monumental, and often, several such sites are present in a single island. The most prominent examples of definite monuments include the stone city of Nan Madol in Pohnpei, pigeon-snaring mounds in Samoa and Tonga, and human-figure statues associated with religious precincts in East Polynesia. Other kinds of monuments refer to temples, large burial features, and other religiously charged sites. A broader "monumental" consideration may be applied to the unusually large examples of residential housing structures that clearly were meant to impress in the manner of monumental expression, as well as to the total combined footprints of large village complexes. Other potentially "monumental" sites include land-altering works such as formalized field systems and fish-trapping constructions.

Today, the ruins of stonework villages cover large areas of many islands, where they are regarded as reminders of the past. Entire village settlement systems are preserved in the footprints of former house foundations, pathways, and other constructions of land-consuming and long-lasting stonework. The archaeological ruins often are linked with oral histories of those specific villages. In many cases, the architectural designs and spatial relationships follow sets of rules of an island group's social structure, for instance, reflecting family lineages, status differential, men's versus women's activities, and other organizational units.

Similar to the land-altering effects of stonework village complexes, the habitat-transforming constructions of field systems and fish-trapping devices may be regarded as monumental. Most of the known instances in Pacific Oceania actually postdate A.D. 1400 and therefore cannot be considered as originating with the A.D. 1000 Event. Their details will be discussed in relation to issues of land-use expansion and intensification in Chapter 13, but importantly, they developed from traditions that were formalized about A.D. 1000 in terms of fixed territories linking people with defined units of land and sea. A few examples, such as in New Caledonia and possibly in Palau, demonstrate older instances of formalized field systems prior to A.D. 1000.

Indexing and profiling monumentality

As a subjective and qualitative characteristic, monumentality cannot always be measured in objective quantitative terms suitable for cross-comparison. Measurements of the total volume of moved material may offer one indication of how much labor was involved in a construction, but the attention to detail of design and positioning of individual pieces may be more meaningful for conveying the cultural impact of a construction. Moreover, the wood and thatch all have disappeared from the archaeological record, so those aspects of architectural design cannot be estimated except through educated guesswork. The use of raw material with desirable color or texture may be impressive in its own way, but its value is not directly comparable with other choices such as displaying one extraordinarily large boulder versus several small cobbles, cutting or dressing the edges of stones versus leaving them in their raw form, covering space with smooth-surfaced versus angular stones, or positioning individual stones with tighter versus looser degree of fitting.

Formulation of a measurable index of monumentality could appear at first to be a fool's errand, yet it may be attractive as a means toward discussing what makes any particular construction "monumental." A numerical index cannot realistically translate architectural expressions into numbers in a formula, like a scoring of a certain number of points for the use of special raw materials, another number of points for neatly right-angled corners, or other such calculations. At best, an attribute-based profile can help in identifying the specific elements that people used for expressions of monumentality in one context versus another, such as the kinds of elements used differentially in religious temples, burial features, residential complexes, or crop-growing field systems. In theory, the design choices could change through time or according to the local cultural traditions in one place versus another. Further complicating these matters, some characteristics depended primarily on the natural availability of raw materials, not necessarily reflecting the degree of monumental expression as a deliberate cultural action.

Calculation of artificially built volume can figure prominently in an estimate of the overall degree of monumentality, but the calculation is not as straightforward as it may seem, for at least three reasons.

- First, the surviving stone and earthen remnants represent only a portion of the total constructed volume, and the ratio of stonework to wood and thatch never can be known for sure. Even when making presumptions about one house structure per foundation element, the individual characteristics are unknown, and the types of implied structures would be quite different for residential sites versus religious compounds or field systems.
- Second, people often make use of the naturally contoured landscape, building over the tops of natural mounds or hills, so a minimal movement of raw material can create the illusion of an impressive volume of a construction.
- Third, techniques of moving stone and earth are not always easy to quantify, such as noting the positive and negative volumes involved in mound-and-ditch formations or in cut-and-fill terracing.

Even when making presumptions about how to calculate built volume as an approximate value, more or less reflecting the overall labor investment in a construction, important practical methodological issues need to be addressed. Perhaps most frustrating, the unit of analysis can be difficult to identify as a single architectural element, a feature incorporating multiple elements, or a site complex composed of multiple features (Figure 12.2). The issues of how to define a "site" here become crucial. A single stacked-rock mound may not convey much significance of monumentality, but a field of hundreds of mounds may be regarded as more impressive (Figure 12.3). If a collective set of features is to be considered, then more issues still need to be resolved about how to define the spatial limit of the site being analyzed, as well as about the potentially different ages of the component features. In any site complex, the contributing elements may have been built or rebuilt at different times and for unique reasons.

The choice of location for a monument can be more important than the actual technique of construction. A simple small mound or platform may embody profound meaning by virtue of occupying a hilltop in a highly visible position, a proximity to another preexisting monument, or religiously sacred place (Figure 12.4). The values about a location are not always known today in contexts far removed from the original site usage. In any case, these values are highly subjective and tend to be unique to each situation, and they cannot be reduced to a mathematical quantification.

Rather than propose a quantified index of monumentality, a qualitative attribute-based profile more effectively can capture a sense of the variable potential expressions of monumentality. In this approach, a profile consists of the range of attributes being evaluated, such as built volume, types of raw materials, degree of symmetry, and angle of fitting of materials. Each attribute is measured or evaluated in its own sense, and therefore the expressions in the graphic profile are not necessarily equal to one another numerically. The resulting comprehensive profile format allows each attribute to be viewed in its own terms.

An example from Samoa illustrates one possible way of composing a qualitative profile of monumentality (Figures 12.5 and 12.6). This example may be regarded as typical of many survey areas in the Pacific region, complete with the problems of how to identify comparable units of analysis. It refers to a set of stonework ruins all postdating A.D. 1000, within one portion of a larger surveyed area of Tutuila, including individual features of a star-shaped pigeon-snaring mound, segments of a stone-lined pathway, and several stone-filled house foundation terraces (Carson 2005). This particular portion of the survey area geologically consists of rough lava-flow rock, with little or no opportunity for subsurface deposits, such that the surface-visible features comprise the totality of the archaeological

260 *An A.D. 1000 Event? Formalization of cultural expressions*

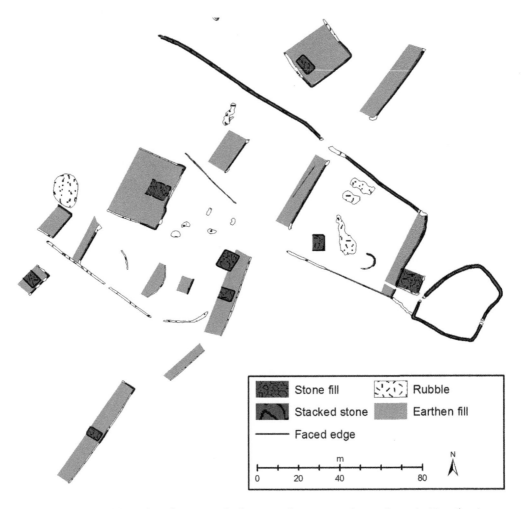

Figure 12.2 Variable scales of stonework elements, features, and complexes in Tutuila, American Samoa. Graphic is adapted from Carson (2005).

material all postdating A.D. 1000. All of the identifiable stonework constructions are composed of the immediately available raw materials of angular basalt rocks, manipulated into varied dry-stacked compositions.

In this one example from Tutuila in Samoa, the qualitative profiles reveal differential values for each stonework construction. The pigeon-snaring mound is the only feature that typically would be regarded as a monument, intended as an enduring physical marker of a special-use context in this location. This mound's distinguishing aspects of monumentality include the specialized shape with starlike arms in plan view, the height above adjacent terrain, and perhaps the total built volume. By comparison, the stone-lined pathway potentially could be regarded as conveying a monumental quality in its sheer volume, although its other aspects appear to involve minimal attention to quality of construction. The stone-filled house foundations include a few opportunities for individual expressions of architectural values that may suggest general labor input more than monumentality

An A.D. 1000 Event? Formalization of cultural expressions 261

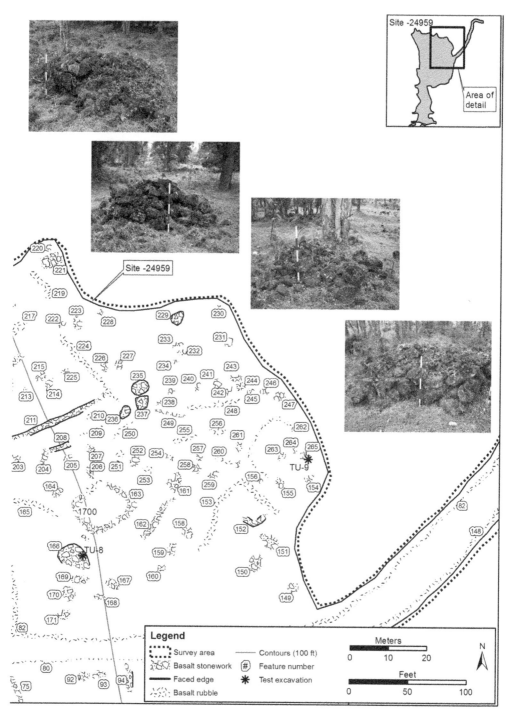

Figure 12.3 Stacked-stone mounds in Honokōhau, Hawai'i Island. Graphics are adapted from Carson (2006).

262 *An A.D. 1000 Event? Formalization of cultural expressions*

Figure 12.4 Stone-filled platform at the edge of Haleakalā Crater, Maui. Scale bar is in 20 cm increments.

specifically, for instance, with variable investment in the closeness of stone fitting, demarcation of numbers of internal activity areas, and incorporation of special-purpose stones such as an adze-grinding basin.

The foregoing attribute-based framework was intended to encourage new ways of thinking about architectural remnants and monuments, while acknowledging that the qualities often differ from one case to another in terms of cultural meaning, artistic expression, technical expertise, and monumentality. This approach could be applied in any survey area or time period, possibly with statistical analysis for identifying the key driving factors through principal components analysis (PCA). Nonetheless, a full cross-regional comparison study would be outside the scope of this book, and the current chapter concentrates instead on the characteristics of a postulated A.D. 1000 Event in the Pacific.

Issues of monumentality are relevant toward interpreting the structuring of village settlements, values of burial commemorations, creation of religious space, and investment in culturally significant landscapes. The A.D. 1000 Event involved more than monumentality, and more broadly it may be viewed as a formalization of cultural expression that often but not always was manifested in terms of monumentality. Overall, investments in stonework and other long-lasting constructions gained prominence after A.D. 1000, involving monumentality as one important aspect among this context.

Stonework villages

Extensive stonework villages comprise the majority of the detectable Pacific Oceanic archaeological record after A.D. 1000. Given the fact that the entire eastern portion of the Pacific was settled within this late time range, stonework features have constituted the

An A.D. 1000 Event? Formalization of cultural expressions 263

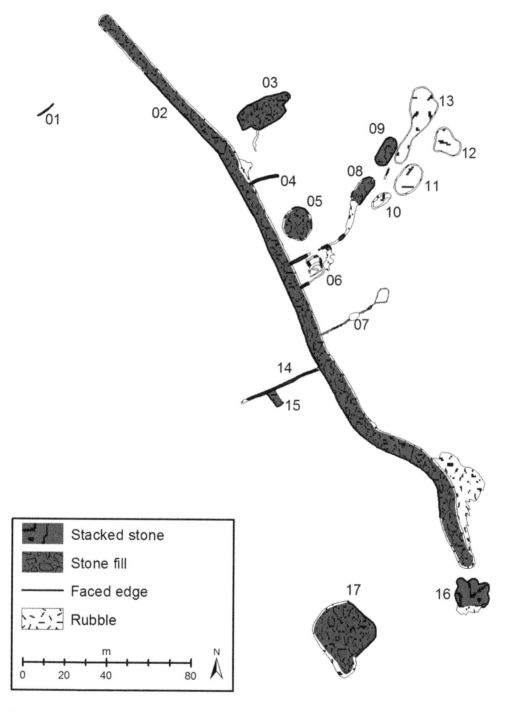

Figure 12.5 Portion of map of surface-visible stonework ruins in Tutuila, American Samoa. Graphic is adapted from Carson (2005).

264 *An A.D. 1000 Event? Formalization of cultural expressions*

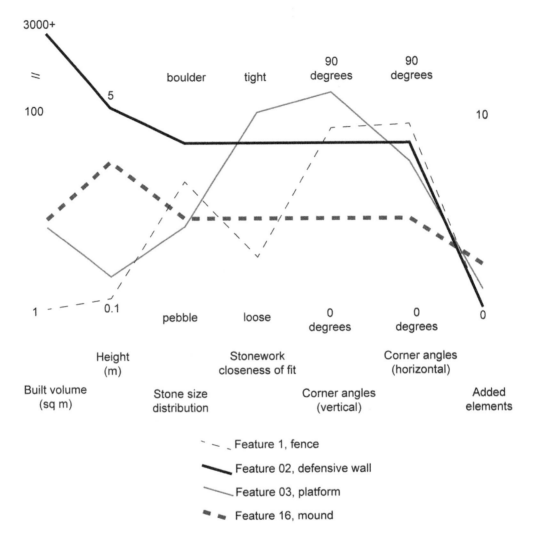

Figure 12.6 Monumentality profile, applied to surface-visible stonework ruins in Tutuila, American Samoa. The specific features are shown in Figure 12.5.

primary focus of archaeological attention in the Pacific as a whole. Furthermore, even in the older-settled islands of the western and central Pacific with subsurface layers of ancient housing features, the ground surfaces are covered with stonework remnants of the last few hundred years, thus constituting the most abundant and accessible archaeological materials throughout the region.

Dry masonry stacked-stone features and whole villages are known in every island group, not only as archaeological ruins but also as parts of historically and ethnographically documented traditions as late as the A.D. 1800s or even later in some cases. The later-aged archaeological remnants accordingly can be interpreted through the richness of ethnohistories and other traditions, yet caution is advised when using information from the last 200–300 years to interpret sites that belong to contexts of 500 years age or 1000 years age. Any abandoned archaeological site, by definition, has not sustained its original context into the present day.

Ethnohistorical and archaeological contexts certainly overlap in Pacific Oceania, yet they are by no means replicative of each other or interchangeable. As Rouse (1972) cautioned, archaeologists can examine only the durable material remnants of settlement patterns, whereas ethnographers study the living settlement systems in action. In an ideal case, if the ethnohistorical knowledge of a village or traditional settlement is documented in its material characteristics, then potentially those materials can be shown to have parallels in the archaeological record. This approach allowed Roger Green (1967, 1970) to assign ethnographically informed cultural functions to the material manifestations of settlement ruins in Samoa and elsewhere in Polynesia, specifically referring to men's and women's dwelling houses, cooking houses, religious shrines, and community activity areas. Those archaeological material correlates so far have been documented as early as A.D. 1000, thus suggesting that the ethnohistorical knowledge of Polynesian village systems may be extended in some ways into this age range.

In a global perspective, all settlement systems at a minimum include individual household features and community-serving features, with possibilities of fulfilling functions of dwelling, food preparation, religious ceremony, and whatever other activities are necessary for the group. With this general awareness, the basic functional components of a Polynesian settlement pattern may not appear to be so informative after all. More important are the specific material signatures that distinguish unique categories such as the kinds of tools and foods at a men's house versus a women's house, the layout of stones in the foundation of a household dwelling versus a community-serving venue, or the inclusion of task-specific features such as an adze-grinding basin or a cooking hearth denoting other functional categories.

In practical terms, stone-filled foundations at ground level are constructed as terraces or as platforms (Figure 12.7). Terraces are the most frequent occurrences, made with an elevated edge on the front or downslope side, a filled interior space, and another edge flush with the naturally sloped ground surface at the back or upslope side. Platforms are made with the same principles, but they are raised on all sides.

In a typical core-filled construction technique, the perimeter outlining stones of a terrace or platform are the most important structurally, as they surround the interior filled space. The perimeters tend to display the largest individual pieces, with attention paid to the strength of their setting or planting into the ground, closeness of inter-fitting of the stones, right-angled corners of the construction, and straight-sided exterior faces. The perimeter stones may be stacked in two or more courses in order to achieve the desired height of the foundation. With the perimeter set or framed in this manner, the interior space next is filled with rubble and sometimes with mixed earth and stone, and then finally the surface may be covered with paving stones. The surface paving typically shows a smooth quality, often comprised of many waterworn beach cobbles and pebbles known as 'ili'ili in Samoa and by other cognate terms elsewhere in Polynesia (Figure 12.8), but occasionally the paving stones are smooth-topped boulders.

Beyond the technological requirements of a terrace or platform as a structural foundation, plenty of options were available for artistic expression, displays of wealth, or other investment making a unique character in any stonework feature. Any such "extra" investment may be viewed as a sign of status or of the specialized cultural association of an individual feature. Footprint size and height may serve as initial proxies of labor input, but other aspects may be more telling of an individual character as expressed in the angle

266 *An A.D. 1000 Event? Formalization of cultural expressions*

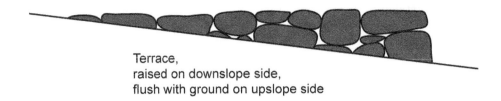

Terrace,
raised on downslope side,
flush with ground on upslope side

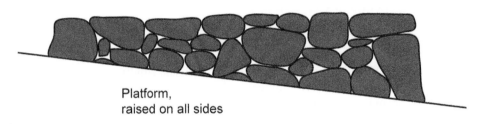

Platform,
raised on all sides

Figure 12.7 Schematic diagrams of terrace and platform constructions.

Figure 12.8 Pebble and shell floor paving in Mouly, Ouvéa in the Loyalty Islands of New Caledonia, 1999. Left: documenting time-limit collections of beach pebbles and shells. Right: pebble and shell paving at a cooking shed.

An A.D. 1000 Event? Formalization of cultural expressions

of fitting of stones, closeness to perfect right angles, and overall symmetry of design. The most visible perimeter stones and paving stones carry the greatest potential as expressive signals, for instance, when using stones of unusually large size, unique color, or smoothed faces.

House foundations potentially can accommodate divisions of internal space, such that they reflect more than just a direct outline of the house structure footprint. In many cases, the interior living space was paved with one type of stone or earthen fill, while the exterior front patio was paved with a different format of stonework. The interior floor often was intended to be covered by layers of comfortable woven mats, whereas the exterior floor was exposed to the elements and open for public viewing.

An example from the Marquesas Islands of East Polynesia illustrates the combined technical and artistic expressions embodied in stacked-stone terrace and platform foundations, locally known as *paepae*. In particular, the extensive stonework ruins of an abandoned village have been documented in the interior valley of Vaitahu in Tahuata (Figure 12.9), last used perhaps as recently as the A.D. 1800s but with archaeological deposits dating at least as early as the A.D. 1400s (Rolett 2010). Often, the floors of interior living areas consisted of earthen fill, occasionally with stone paving, and typically they were fronted by patio areas composed of massive stonework (Figure 12.10). The *paepae* displayed the usual construction technique of a strong and presentable outer frame around a loosely core-filled interior, wherein the perimeter front-facing stones and the top paving stones often were impressively large, about 1 m in length. Waterworn boulders were taken from the adjacent river drainage, and the individual pieces were positioned carefully with tight inter-fitting and flat surfaces facing outward. In the front edge of large paving boulders, often one flat-topped boulder showed adze-grinding slots and cuplike depressions (Figure 12.11). In some cases, certain of the front-facing perimeter boulders had been quarried from tuffaceous rock and transported to the site (Figure 12.12). The tuffaceous rock, known as

Figure 12.9 Vaitahu valley stonework ruins during 1997 survey in Tahuata, Marquesas Islands.

268 *An A.D. 1000 Event? Formalization of cultural expressions*

Figure 12.10 View of massive front patio stonework in Vaitahu valley of Tahuata, during 1997 documentation, Marquesas Islands.

keʻetu, occurs naturally in reddish or yellowish color, and its special cultural significance implies higher social status or religious contexts in Polynesia. The tuffaceous material can be gouged and chiseled with evenly cut or dressed edges and faces.

The dozens of *paepae* in Vaitahu together acted as an ensemble of the contributing features of a village complex, but the precise functional associations are not immediately obvious as dwelling houses, cooking areas, community assembly areas, or religious ceremonial venues. The construction and design principles are the same for each foundation feature, such that their functional categories do not have uniquely distinguishing material correlates (Rolett 2010). The specific cultural functions can be ascertained only through additional information, such as according to expectations of the amount of sq m of surface needed for a sleeping house versus a community-serving area. Contextual information may be more revealing, based on observations of associated artifacts and midden, indicators of extra labor investment, and position of a feature within the layout of the village.

An A.D. *1000 Event? Formalization of cultural expressions* 269

Figure 12.11 Grinding basins in patio stonework in Vaitahu valley of Tahuata, during 1997 documentation, Marquesas Islands.

Figure 12.12 Tuffaceous stone *keʻetu* incorporated into front-facing stonework in Vaitahu valley of Tahuata, during 1997 documentation, Marquesas Islands. This particular stone was carved with a *tiki* image.

Some of the most definitive studies of Polynesian settlement patterns have been reported in Samoa, where the post–A.D. 1000 record is abundantly accessible in surface-visible stonework ruins of numerous villages. Overall impressions and familiarity with Samoan settlement ruins figured prominently in Roger Green's (1967, 1970) depictions of the basic functional components of Polynesian settlement structure. Very importantly, ethnohistorical traditions are well remembered about Samoan villages, including stories attached with place-names and histories of family lineages. Archaeological maps of villages indicate the dwelling houses, cooking houses, community-serving ovens, pathways, group assembly areas, religious shrines, and ceremonial activity features. Detailed examples have been recorded throughout the Samoan islands, and some of the most extensive documentation has been at Mount Olo in 'Upolu (Holmer 1980; Jennings et al. 1982), Faleniu and Tafuna in Tutuila (Carson 2005), Alega in Tutuila (Clark 1993), Saua in Ta'u (Bayman and Calugay 2014; Hunt and Kirch 1987, 1988), and the Salua area of Manono (Sand et al. 2018). As a recent development, remote-sensing technology has revealed stonework ruins beneath the forest cover, and accurate maps have been possible through light detection and ranging (LiDAR) surveys in parts of the Samoan landscape (Jackmond et al. 2018).

Settlement patterns have been documented in countless field surveys of surface-visible stonework ruins all across Polynesia, and ideally they can serve as substantive baselines for further studies of how people had organized their cultural landscapes, how they interacted with each other and their environments, and how these systems may have changed through time. As just one example, observations in the southern Cook Islands have enabled a detailed view of an apparently typical Polynesian settlement pattern, but Richard Walter (1996) cautioned about needing more information before being able to address other research questions, especially concerning historical process. In this case, Walter (1996) recognized that the spatial patterns as evident in the surface-visible stonework ruins were not necessarily suitable for addressing chronological issues, yet they remained greatly informative about the later periods.

Without a means of assigning specific ages to each identified feature or component of an overall settlement pattern, the individual occurrences would need to be regarded as referring to a generic all-encompassing period such as the post–A.D. 1000 landscape. This level of temporal resolution may be acceptable for certain research questions about cultural use of space during broad time intervals. Finer resolution would be necessary for addressing questions about how the inhabited landscape evolved, how people adapted to changing circumstances, and how the settlement structure in one time period may have affected later developments.

While ground-level housing foundations flourished in Polynesia, parallel developments of stonework complexes emerged in western Micronesia with the continuation of post-raised housing. The heights of the elevated house floors generally were lower than 1 m, accessible by a step-cut coconut log ladder or other means. As seen even today in Palau, Yap, and Chuuk, the house posts were braced in position with stones, and those stones were incorporated within larger forms of terraces or platforms (Figures 12.13 and 12.14). Additional stonework features included pathways, boundary fences or walls, and other constructions (Figure 12.15). Deceased individuals were buried at houses, either beneath the stone-filled features or within specifically designated stacked-stone mounds just outside the house footprints.

Detailed archaeological maps have been prepared for many of the stonework villages of western Micronesia. In fact, nearly all archaeological work in these islands has entailed surface recording, with limited test pits and trenches primarily for augmenting knowledge

Figure 12.13 Example of traditional *bai* in Babeldaob, Palau.

Figure 12.14 Detail of stone-filled platform beneath *bai* in Babeldaob, Palau.

272 *An A.D. 1000 Event? Formalization of cultural expressions*

Figure 12.15 Detail of stonework pathway in Babeldaob, Palau.

about the surface-visible ruins. Several area-specific surveys have been reported in islands such as in Ulithi (Craib et al. 1980) and Yap (Cordy 1986), but the most thorough survey coverage has probably been in Palau, with numerous government-sponsored updates of Osborne's (1966) classic compilation. Ethnohistorical traditions refer to different villages and their dwelling houses, men's club houses, women's menstrual houses, group assembly areas, and other components of how each village had operated. Most villages include prominent features such as burial mounds or stone monoliths that served as elements of ritual attraction or commemorative reminders. Additionally, stone money discs or *rai* were displayed as signs of wealth and status in Yap. The discs were quarried from limestone sources in Palau and transported overseas back to Yap (Figure 12.16).

In places where survey coverage can account for large contiguous areas, village layouts can reflect the social or political order of a group. Often, one house is larger than others or situated in a prominent location, thus identifiable as the house of a leader or of a community assembly area. In the North Province of New Caledonia, for example, circular hut foundations are clustered around a pathway (Sand 2002), and often, one slightly larger foundation is positioned at the end of the pathway with a large stone or set of stones at the location of its entrance. The size differential of hut foundations can be miniscule, or in some cases the only distinction may be in the positioning of one hut foundation compared to the others (Figure 12.17), for instance, as illustrated in the post–A.D. 1000 village ruins in the areas of Vavouto and Pouémbout (Carson 2003).

The post–A.D. 1000 record in the Mariana Islands has revealed abundant and widespread ruins of pillar-raised houses locally known as *latte* (Carson 2012), which are among the more extreme examples of size differential in housing features. In every village cluster,

Figure 12.16 Photographs of pathway lined with *rai* discs on display in Yap. Photographs are from the Japanese collections, approximately 1925–1935, curated at the Micronesian Area Research Center, University of Guam.

274 *An A.D. 1000 Event? Formalization of cultural expressions*

at least one *latte* very obviously was constructed much larger than its counterparts. *Latte* were constructed from stone pillars called *haligi*, each topped by a capital stone called a *tasa*, arranged in parallel paired rows, originally supporting wood and thatch superstructures (Figure 12.18). The largest *latte* ever standing was the House of Taga in Tinian (Figure 12.19), more than 3 m in height and occupying the center of the village at the most protected natural canoe-landing area of the island (Figure 12.20). Only one other example would have been larger, but its stone elements were not yet removed from the limestone quarry at As Nieves in Rota before this project was abandoned for unknown reasons (Figure 12.21). While some of the larger *latte* in each village may have served as meeting halls, others, such as the House of Taga, were designed to impress the public.

Individual designs of *latte* may have expressed a household's identity and personality in a variety of ways, not necessarily constrained to notions of status or hierarchy conveyed

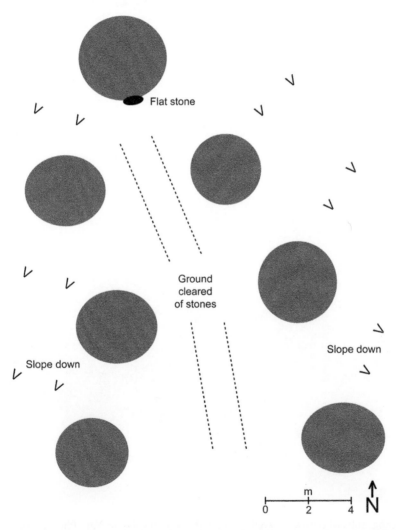

Figure 12.17 Arrangements of circular hut foundations in Vavouto and Pouémbout, northern province of New Caledonia. Graphic is based on documentation by Carson (2003).

An A.D. 1000 Event? Formalization of cultural expressions 275

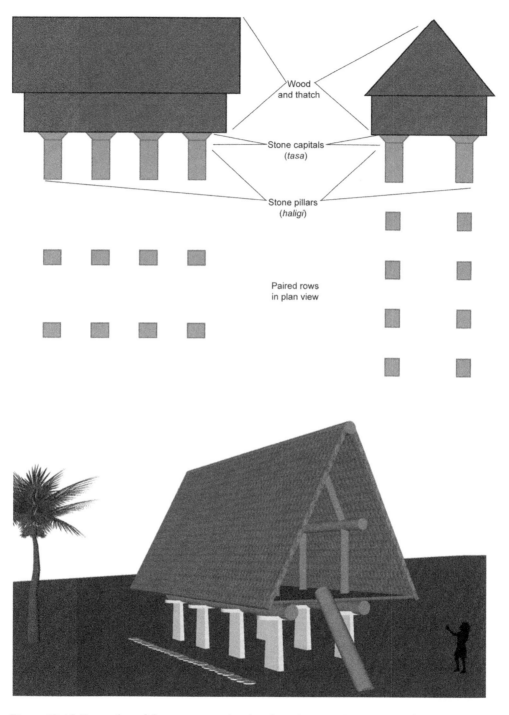

Figure 12.18 Examples of *latte* construction in plan view, section view, and reconstruction model.

276 *An* A.D. *1000 Event? Formalization of cultural expressions*

Figure 12.19 *Latte* of House of Taga in Tinian in 2013.

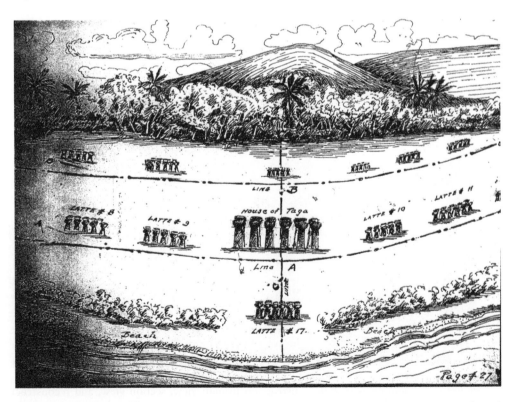

Figure 12.20 Setting of the House of Taga in Tinian. Illustration was by Hans Hornbostel (1925).

An A.D. 1000 Event? Formalization of cultural expressions 277

Figure 12.21 Latte quarry at As Nieves in Rota.

in overall size of the structures. The architectural designs varied somewhat according to the availability of raw materials, such that unique textures, colors, shaping, and size were possible when working with quarried blocks of limestone, cut and dressed tuffaceous rock, or natural unworked volcanic rock cobbles and boulders (Figure 12.22). The associated activity space of each *latte* could be organized in variable ways with simple cleared terrain, arrangements of stone pavings or borders, and grinding mortars (Figure 12.23). Additional information about the cultural use of space in and around each *latte* can be seen in the spatial distributions and relative concentrations of artifacts, food middens, and burial features.

While all *latte* functioned in a technological sense as elevating supports for ancient houses (Laguana et al. 2012; Thompson 1940), each case may have been recognized specifically as a dwelling house, high-status residence, meeting hall, or other possible association (Hornbostel 1925; Spoehr 1957). The specific functional categories may be inferred at least partially according to the position of each *latte* within a settlement cluster, as well as according to the characteristics of size and design, but more detailed information may be obtained from the inventories of function-specific artifacts and compositions of food middens at each *latte*. In theory, material signatures of higher density of pottery or luxury types of food remains may be expected at the larger *latte* as signs of prestige, or task-specific indicators such as tool-making debris versus cooking refuse may be associated with different *latte*. Presumed indicators of higher or lower status so far have not

278 *An A.D. 1000 Event? Formalization of cultural expressions*

Figure 12.22 Range of material types of *latte* in the Mariana Islands. Those in Guam, Rota, and Tinian were made of quarried limestone. Those in Pagan were made of beach cobbles (Apansamne'na) or of carved tuffaceous stone (Apansantatte). All scale bars are in 20 cm increments.

been demonstrated to correspond with overall size of *latte* (Craib 1986; Graves 1986), so the many design factors other than size will need to be considered in future research. When examining two adjacent *latte* at Ritidian in Guam, Bayman et al. (2012a, 2012b) documented strongly contrasting compositions of artifacts and midden, suggestive of a division of labor tasks between the two areas, even though the two *latte* structures were virtually identical in their stone constructions.

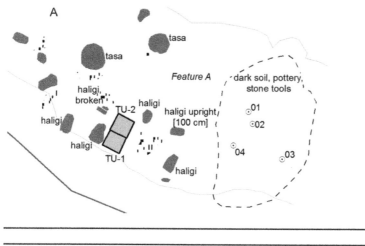
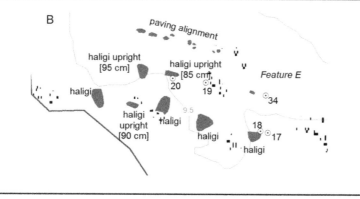
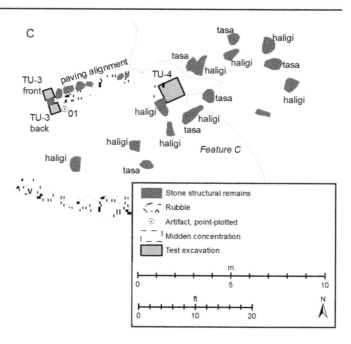

Figure 12.23 Different element configurations of *latte* sets with cleared areas, pavings, borders, grinding mortars, midden areas, and burial pits. All examples (A, B, and C) are from Ritidian, Guam.

280 *An A.D. 1000 Event? Formalization of cultural expressions*

The tradition of *latte* emerged about A.D. 1000 throughout the Mariana Islands as part of a larger pattern of formalization of culture expression consistent with the region-wide A.D. 1000 Event. Previously, house posts had been made of cut tree trunks or thick branches, such that the stone versions of house posts as *latte* represented an investment in permanence of place of the household and its associated lineage. Further stressing permanence of place, a tradition of burial at the house began with the construction of *latte* villages. At the same time, grinding mortars called *lusong* were made in stone, likely replacing older traditions of wooden pounding boards. The *lusong* could be made in semi-portable small boulders positioned at *latte* (Figure 12.24), or they could be made in immovable bedrock formations or outcrops in locations suitable for cave rituals or other special-use contexts (Figure 12.25). Meanwhile, pottery made of coarse paste and temper inclusions was produced in great quantity, yet at overall low quality as compared to earlier periods, with thick walls and even thicker rims of large, incurved bowls, showing either no decoration at all or else coarsely combed exteriors (Figure 12.26).

The preference for stone instead of wood signified the long-lasting intention of each *latte*, especially when considering how quickly the wood and thatch degrade in the humid

Broken *lusong*, showing section view, Unai Bapot, Saipan

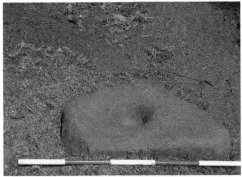

Typical *lusong*, Apansantatte, Pagan

Unusually small stone but with large *lusong* depression, Apansantatte, Pagan

Large basin-like *lusong*, Apansantatte, Pagan

Figure 12.24 Examples of semiportable household-related *lusong* grinding basins in the Mariana Islands. All scale bars are in 20 cm increments.

Setting of immovable *lusong*, central Pagan

Detail of immovable *lusong*, central Pagan

Immovable *lusong* outside "Upper Cave" at Ritidian, Guam

Immovable *lusong* outside small cave near boundary of Ritidian and Urunao, Guam

Figure 12.25 Examples of immovable permanent bedrock *lusong* grinding mortars in the Mariana Islands. All scale bars are in 20 cm increments.

tropical climate of the Marianas. Perhaps more importantly, recurrent typhoons may be expected to destroy the superstructures, while the stone elements persisted in their intended locations and with their associated burial features. The stone elements of each *latte* could be sustained multi-generationally in their designated places, despite repeated rebuilding of the wood and thatch components.

The realistic structural stability of *latte* is curious, and probably the sets of pillars and capitals could not stay upright unless they were bearing the weight of a wooden superstructure. The design could be a stone version of older wooden post structures with rat guards or structural support discs that are known ethnohistorically in parts of Island Southeast Asia, Taiwan, and Okinawa (Figure 12.27). Other potential purposes of the design of a pillar with capital could be for resisting typhoons and earthquakes, wherein the capitals could absorb vibrations without toppling. In some but not all instances, stability was achieved through slight sockets carved into the bases of the *tasa* capitals that rested over their associated *haligi* pillars (Figure 12.28). Other stabilizing options were possible through the use of bracing stones, as well as through slight notch shaping in the bases of the *haligi* set into the ground (Figure 12.29).

282 *An A.D. 1000 Event? Formalization of cultural expressions*

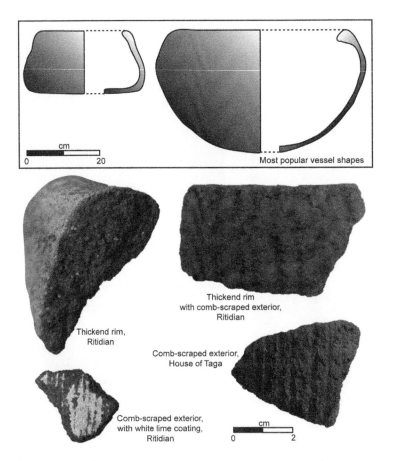

Figure 12.26 Examples of pottery from the *latte* period, A.D. 1000–1700 in the Mariana Islands.

Figure 12.27 Rat guards on a reconstruction of a traditional Austronesian house in Taiwan. Display is at the Formosan Aboriginal Cultural Village in Nantou, Taiwan.

An A.D. 1000 Event? Formalization of cultural expressions 283

Figure 12.28 Example of notch at the base of *haligi* pillar, with surrounding bracing stones in a *latte* set at Ritidian, Guam.

Composed of support pillars topped by capitals, all made of stone, *latte* of the Mariana Islands are unique in the Pacific and indeed in the world. Elsewhere as noted, wooden pillars and discs were used as rat guards, but nowhere else outside the Marianas was this design made of stone elements. In this context, the design of *latte* in stone must have developed locally within the Mariana Islands, or else it would have existed in at least one other location. This specific design in stone evidently never spread from anywhere else into the Marianas, nor did it spread from the Marianas to any other area.

In a few rare cases in Pacific Oceania, stone pillars were used as house supports yet without the topping capital stones seen in *latte* of the Marianas, and these rarities can be appreciated as anomalies in their cultural areas. One such rare example is the set of tall stone pillars at Badrulchau in Babeldaob of Palau (Figure 12.30), mentioned in local traditions as having been transported from the bottom of the ocean by gods, then used as the supporting pillars of a large meeting hall. Another curious example is the set of prismatic basalt columns known as Fale o le Fe'e (literally "house of the octopus," although Fe'e in this case may refer to a personal name or a title of a person) in 'Upolu of Samoa (Figure 12.31), remembered in Samoan ethnohistorical traditions as the house of a possibly high-ranked person or chief named Fe'e who had sailed to Samoa "from the west" (Freeman 1944).

Stonework features characterized the Pacific Oceanic landscape cross-regionally beginning at A.D. 1000, although each island group developed its own unique expressions.

284 *An A.D. 1000 Event? Formalization of cultural expressions*

Figure 12.29 Example of slight socket in *tasa* capital to fit over *haligi* pillar in a *latte* set at Ritidian, Guam. Scale bar is in 20 cm increments.

The cross-cultural consistencies involved an investment in permanence of place as well as new opportunities for monumental creations in the landscape. Monumental constructions at ceremonial sites tended to be unique in each cultural area. Other localized traditions included the *latte* of the Mariana Islands, extensive stone-paved villages of Palau and Yap, circular hut foundations in New Caledonia, and ground-level housing foundations in Polynesia, among others.

Everlasting burials

Among the potential ways of signifying a permanence of place, nothing can equal the construction of a burial feature, especially when a person is buried at a house site. The place of burial becomes a permanent part of the landscape, persistently reminding future generations of an inalienable connection between this particular place and a specific person or family lineage. Later generations of individuals may be buried at or around the site, adding to the permanence of place and implying a cross-generational heritage.

An A.D. 1000 Event? Formalization of cultural expressions 285

Figure 12.30 Badrulchau in Babeldaob, Palau.

Burial sites older than A.D. 1000 have been rare in the archaeological record of Pacific Oceania. The few known burial sites prior to A.D. 1000 have been found in special-use designated areas separate from their contemporary residential habitation sites, either in caves or in open-area cemeteries. Evidently, the region-wide house burial tradition gained popularity only later with the emergence of structured stonework villages about A.D. 1000. This correspondence is seen in all island groups, but it has been demonstrated most clearly in the Mariana Islands and in Palau with well preserved habitation layers long prior to A.D. 1000 yet not demonstrating abundant village systems with numerous at-house or near-house burials until after A.D. 1000. Regarding the older Austronesian or Malayo-Polynesian ancestral burial traditions of people who moved from Island Southeast Asia into Remote Oceania prior to 1000 B.C., no house burial features have been found at all in Island Southeast Asia until after 500 B.C. and later contexts. In other words, burial at the house has not been documented as part of the most ancient Malayo-Polynesian traditions prior to 1000 B.C., but rather the practice gained popularity in Island Southeast Asia about 500 B.C. and then independently in Pacific Oceania about A.D. 1000.

The house burial tradition may be contrasted against the instances of burials in caves. Cave burial certainly preceded the emergence of house burial, and then it continued to be practiced for some individuals after A.D. 1000. In these later cases, cave burial may have been reserved for people who did not yet complete rites of passage or initiation into a specifically recognized house lineage. Accordingly, many, but certainly not all, burials at caves include the remains of children. Anyone living an unusual lifestyle, like a shaman

286 *An A.D. 1000 Event? Formalization of cultural expressions*

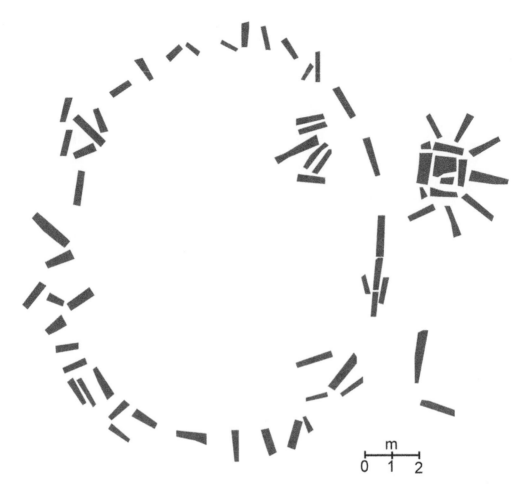

Figure 12.31 Map of Fale o le Fe'e in 'Upolu, Samoa. Graphic is based on documentation by J. Derek Freeman (1944).

or priest, could be buried in a cave associated with ritual contexts outside the realm of ordinary residential life. At least in some island societies, such as in the Hawaiian Islands, the most potent chiefs would need to be buried in secure places where the power in their bones would not pose a threat to the living.

Often, house burials were included in designated parts of the house floor or in marked features such as mounds at the front side of a housing complex. The intention was to be in a known spot, often visible to the public. Some higher-ranked individuals were buried not at the front of their dwelling house but rather at the front of a larger housing complex or at the edge of the entire village settlement, so that the permanent link between person and land was extended over a much larger area.

Religious complexes and components

As part of the A.D. 1000 Event of formalizing cultural expressions into the permanent landscape, locations of religious activities became more visible with the preponderance of stonework features and monuments. Ritual and ceremony often were incorporated into daily life at households, family compounds, and other sites that left no tangible archaeological trace except perhaps for small dedicated shrines or individual offerings. A quite different form of religious site was intended for the assembly of groups coming from multiple households and necessitating a larger space to accommodate more numerous participants. Often, the site was situated in a publicly accessible and culturally significant place, with capacity for the intended participants. Priests or other religious specialists may have performed the ceremonies or certain parts of the ceremonies.

As portrayed here, religious complexes after A.D. 1000 were made in the context of the rising popularity of stonework constructions used for making designated areas of dwelling houses, workshops, ritual space, and other functional categories. Religious and ceremonial sites surely existed prior to A.D. 1000, but the later structures were incorporated into the emergent social emphasis on stonework and permanence of place. Most instructively in Polynesia, the essential "building blocks" of community settlement organization must have existed already by A.D. 1000 in order to account for their widespread distribution into East Polynesia (Green 1986), and one such "building block" entailed a generalized category of ceremonial structure, possibly with variants of household-level, community-serving, and specialized-purpose venues.

The archaeological signatures of religious features or complexes superficially appear very similar to other stonework foundations and structural ruins. They tend to be designed with greater investment in appearance and durability of construction, similar to the expectations of a high-status residential construction. For instance, religious sites often include fully upraised platforms with tightly inter-fitted boulders, rather than low terraces with loosely stacked-stone retaining facing. Contextual findings of special-use foods and community-serving ovens do not necessarily equate with religious functions, but rather they could reflect group assemblies at feasting events, social or political meetings, or displays of wealth.

Whether at the household level or at the community-serving level, religious beliefs can be used toward justifying why the world exists in the way it does, including a group's social and political organization. The regular rituals at a household, family compound, cultivation field, or other daily activity venue may be regarded as necessary acts that continually reassure the beneficial operation of the world in terms of productive crop growth, safe and bountiful fishing trips, births of healthy children, and other desirable outcomes directly affecting individual people or families. Meanwhile, the ceremonies at community-serving religious sites are designed as affirmation of the social order, protection of a population, and productivity at an interfamily scale or even at a multigroup level. The community-serving contexts potentially can be commandeered by individuals seeking to justify their authority of rulership, while the household-serving venues typically would not affect the larger social groups.

Consistently through time, caves were used as specialized places, closely linked with religious ceremonies, rites of passage, mortuary rituals, and other events separated from the realm of ordinary daily life. After A.D. 1000, however, other opportunities outside caves became more frequently and conveniently available for religious and ritual events. The formalized village structures, including internal ordering of households, provided for permanently designated shrines and burial features used multi-generationally within the scope of regular residential life. At a larger scale, the structured villages and landscapes provided for uniquely identifiable community-serving religious sites or precincts. These possibilities always had existed, but they became formalized with stonework elements of monumental quality after A.D. 1000.

A family or household shrine may occur in varied manifestations, perhaps informal and not necessarily with its own stonework platform or distinguished material signature. The defining characteristic relates to the context within daily routines of a household or residential group, wherein a ritual locality may be situated within a specific part of a house or within the larger residential layout. Based on ethnographic knowledge and archaeological examples in the Marquesas Islands, Ottino (1990) portrayed Polynesian house layouts as involving public space at the exterior, transitioning into sacred space at the interior. Those farthest interior and private spaces were associated most strongly with religious contexts. A parallel situation may be proposed in the Mariana Islands, where the least publicly seen interiors of houses were reserved for keeping family heirlooms, including ancestral skulls among other religiously charged objects (Farrer and Sellmann 2014).

The religious components within households and residential complexes are not always identifiable in their archaeological material remains, and moreover, they can occur at different scales depending on what level of the society is being serviced as an individual household, set of households, or other organization. Most obvious are the occurrences of single upright stones or of small platforms that were too small to have been used as foundations for dwelling houses, workshops, or other activity spaces. Similarly, house burials can be integrated into the regular activities of households. All of these possible religious components, however, could operate at the scale of a single household, community, or other group.

A classic example of religious feature is the *fale aitu* (literally "god house" in Samoan, with direct cognates in other Polynesian languages) in most Polynesian settlement sites. A god house may be described as a place where religious idols and other objects are stored. Those objects are essential for their roles in religious ceremonies, but their storage within the house is equally important for preserving their potency (often understood as *mana*) and maintaining their efficacy separate from daily life contexts. The sacred storage may be understood in reference to notions of *tapu*, often involving the "binding" or "wrapping" of an object (or sometimes of a person) figuratively or literally, thereby preventing the sacred entity from touching the ordinary world. Only under certain circumstances can the *tapu* be removed or lifted, usually only for a limited duration.

A god house could be built within a family compound, or it could be constructed as part of a larger community-serving area. The specialized house typically stands atop a formally designed stonework platform, sometimes with an additional durable marker such as a stone upright or a statue. Roger Green (1970) noted that a god house most often functioned at a community-serving level, yet the scale of community organization could vary.

Areas for group assembly are not exclusively religious in function, but rather they can involve council meetings, feasting events, and other contexts. A distinction may be drawn between West and East Polynesian societies, wherein a more formalized religious context developed in East Polynesia. In West Polynesian areas such as in Samoa and Tonga, a group assembly area is traditionally known as a *malae*, referring to an open space with no permanent structural indicators, other than perhaps a god house at the periphery of a large cleared space. Alternatively, in West Polynesia, a single large meeting hall may be constructed, often without walls and instead open at its sides. In East Polynesian areas, the cognate term *marae* refers to a definitely religious complex made for accommodating participants from a whole village or sometimes from a set of villages, formalized in large stonework features.

In terms of the stonework structural remains, religious sites such as *marae* can resemble other kinds of community assembly areas. In both West and East Polynesia, council meetings occur at large group-accommodating houses or other designated areas. The same is true for all island groups, where meeting halls are made as larger versions of regular houses, usually with open perimeters lacking full walls. Additionally, areas for dance and music performance can entail very similar group-serving attributes and investments in permanence of place, yet they do not necessarily involve religious beliefs or activities. For these reasons, Rolett (2010) referred to stonework ruins in the Marquesas Islands as reflecting "blurred boundaries" between religious and residential contexts, wherein the technical forms of individual terrace or platform foundations could have supported ordinary dwelling houses (*paepae*), dance platforms (*tohua*), or religious temples (*meae*, cognate of *marae*).

Most frequently in East Polynesia, the religious associations of *marae* are known from ethnohistoric traditions, in many cases identifying the specific religious group or cult, deity, place-name history, and other attributes of a site. Jennifer Kahn (2010) illustrated one such example for sets of *marae* belonging to the 'Oro Cult in Mo'orea, an island near Tahiti. The associated stonework ruins, however, did not always display obvious signs of religious function, as they did not consistently exhibit the same traits of their overall size, attention to construction, or incorporation of ritual objects. In this case, the ethnographic documentation allowed confident interpretation, as well as an opportunity to explore more about the material correlates of the known cultural behaviors and contexts.

In terms of linking to the proposed A.D. 1000 Event, today's known *marae* of East Polynesia must be acknowledged as mostly postdating A.D. 1400, and very little actually is known about the older ceremonial structures. For instance, all of those ethnographically attested *marae* of the Oro Cult in Mo'orea entirely postdated A.D. 1400, and the cultural layers mostly postdated A.D. 1600 (Kahn 2010), thereby suggesting that the traditional knowledge of older religious sites may have been forgotten or overwritten. In a large-scale regional review, most of the recorded *marae* in Tahiti and the Society Islands were constructed after A.D. 1400, with only a faint record of the pre–A.D. 1400 structures (Martinsson-Wallin et al. 2013). Surveys of *marae* in the Society Islands and of their counterpart *moai* in Rapa Nui (Easter Island) have revealed different categories of construction techniques and architectural designs, expressed both geographically and chronologically (Martinsson-Wallin 1994; Wallin 1993), thereby indicating a long-term and region-wide shared tradition with a range of variation around the central theme.

A further research program will need to contend with issues of extending the interpretive framework of *marae* into older site contexts. The older ceremonial structures or antecedents of today's known *marae* have become overprinted by the post–A.D. 1400 record. Nonetheless, a shared ancestral tradition must have existed prior to the geographic distribution of *marae* all across East Polynesia, at least by A.D. 1400 if not from the beginning of East Polynesian settlement at A.D. 1000. Most tellingly, some of the buried cultural layers at religious sites in Rapa Nui (Easter Island) have yielded radiocarbon dates confirmed at A.D. 1000–1200 (Martinsson-Wallin and Crockford 2001), equal with the most secure dating of initial human settlement in this notably isolated island at the far eastern margin of Polynesia (Mulrooney 2013).

In the absence of ethnographic knowledge about a site, a potential religious association may be inferred from contextual clues. These clues may involve the placement within a site complex or an investment in construction technique, but most convincing are the admittedly rare occurrences of artifacts specially designated for religious performance. Perishable items of wood and thatch, plants, and trees may have served as the most visible symbols of a religious context during the lifetime of a *marae* or other ceremonial site, but they have not survived in most archaeological contexts today. Banyan trees are associated with spiritual places in most parts of Pacific Oceania, and their descendants tend to survive at the same sites yet not consistently.

Among the clearest examples of religious artifacts are stone uprights and stone statues typically defining *marae* in East Polynesia (Figure 12.32). The stone uprights are imbued with spiritual power, sometimes perceived as representing ancestors or spirits, and similar traditions may be reflected in the use of statues. Certain uprights are known by personal names, and they can play roles in ceremonies. For instance, at Koutu Ariki Taputapuatea in the Cook Islands (see Figure 12.32), a prospective chief must prove that he or she stands taller than the upright stone, possibly using ceremonial feathered head dressing to achieve the necessary height.

Statues of human figures are well known in East Polynesia as *tiki*, often made in wood but occasionally in stone. Sometimes only the head is represented, perhaps linked with traditions of curating or consulting with ancestral skulls. At one apparent religious site in Tahuata of the Marquesas Islands, a collection of four carved stone *tiki* heads served as the final indisputable evidence of a religious association (Figure 12.33). Each carved life-size head displayed its own unique personal characteristics (Rolett 2010).

The most extreme expressions of the *tiki* tradition are seen in the *moai* giant statues of Rapa Nui (Figure 12.34). A staggering amount of labor was dedicated to each statue weighing multiple tons, for its quarrying and transportation into its designated site (Hunt and Lipo 2011). Given the large-scale investments in the numerous *moai* of Rapa Nui, they must have been regarded as essential for life in this remote setting with overall marginal habitat for crop growth. As seen generally of *tiki*, the *moai* of Rapa Nui were fashioned with their individual personalities or characteristics. Furthermore, the statues can be appreciated as prominent features within their larger site settings, accentuating the monumental qualities of the associated sites.

A few categories of religious features serve only some members of a society who are engaged in particularly specialized or dangerous activities, such as when undertaking extended voyages at sea for fishing expeditions, overseas trade, or other purposes. Given the inherent dangers and unpredictability of open-ocean fishing and of long-distance seafaring, several ritual aspects may be expected for ensuring safe journeys and productive results, performed before, during, and after the events at sea. In the Hawaiian Islands, before and after fishing trips, prayers and offerings traditionally were made at a "fishing shrine" known as a *koʻa* (also the word for "coral"), typically constructed as a small stone-filled platform with small pieces of coral incorporated into the interior fill material. Sometimes pieces of coral were used as dedicatory offerings. One such small platform shrine (Figure 12.35) was documented at Kiʻilae Village on the leeward (west) rocky coast of Hawaiʻi Island (Carson et al. 2004), and nearby, a carved stone "fish god" idol (Figure 12.36) was identified through local oral traditions (Carson 2007). Another relevant example was documented in the Vavouto area of New Caledonia (Carson 2003), where local fishers reported a tradition of scraping on two small stones prior to venturing out to sea, specifically referring to stones with artificial grooves found in the intertidal zone of a post–A.D. 1000 village settlement (Figure 12.37). These stones at Vavouto may have served a different purpose in the more distant past, yet the attested role in fishing ritual during the last few generations can be appreciated as reflecting similar traditions of deeper antiquity.

Another case of a restricted group monument is the category of a pigeon-snaring mound (Figure 12.38), known in Samoa (Herdrich 1991; Herdrich and Clark 1993) and in Tonga

Figure 12.32 Examples of *marae* with an upright slab, at Koutu Ariki Taputapuatea, Cook Islands. Images provided by Dr. Hiro Kurashina.

Figure 12.33 Four *tiki* heads, carved in stone in real-life size with personal attributes, discovered during 1997 in Vaitahu valley of Tahuata, Marquesas Islands. These *tiki* are now in a curation display at the Tahuata Museum.

(Burley 1996). These mounds were not necessarily religious in context, but they involved ritualized actions and created monumental impositions in the landscape. According to the few available radiocarbon dates and total absence of pottery, these mounds are regarded as belonging to post–A.D. 1000 contexts (Carson 2014). Several tons of stacked stones and earthen material were arranged in mounds 1.5 m or taller, star-shaped in plan view and hence sometimes called "star mounds." The armlike extensions of the star shapes served as the supports for the participants to hide behind hunting blinds while waiting for the best moment to trap a pigeon in a net. These events were regarded as ritualized sports (rather than as subsistence activities) reserved for chiefs or people with leisure time who could devote the hours needed for the pigeon-snaring activities and associated rituals. The associated rituals and ceremonies are quite varied in the different surviving oral traditions. In some cases, they are viewed as mirroring a man's sexual prowess, his ability to act as a community leader, or simply his skill in the sport of pigeon-snaring.

Perhaps the most richly documented example of a fused religious and political statement in a stonework monument of Pacific Oceania has been preserved in the site of Nan Madol in Pohnpei of eastern Micronesia (Figure 12.39). Associated with the Saudeleur ruling class, the "stone city" was constructed of dozens of artificially mounded and modified

An A.D. *1000 Event? Formalization of cultural expressions* 293

Figure 12.34 Moai at Ahu Tongariki, Rapa Nui, in 1984. Image was provided by Dr. Hiro Kurashina.

islets, with canal-like shallow-water passageways between them. Each islet was modified by platforms, enclosures, and other constructions. According to the Pohnpeian traditions, a ritual performance at Nan Madol periodically renewed the authority and legitimacy of the Saudeleur rulers. Specifically, the ritual involved the sacrificial killing of a turtle, feeding its stomach to an eel that lived in the water beneath the islet of Idehd, and distributing the remaining turtle meat among the high-ranking chiefs and priests. The oral traditions about Nan Madol were recorded in the most detail by Luelen Bernart (1977), with annotations by Fischer et al. (1977) and extra notes by Bernart's grandson Masao Hadley (1981). These and other traditions were incorporated into a larger study of Pohnpeian history by David Hanlon (1988). In particular, Hanlon (1988: 14–15) regarded the turtle and eel ceremony at Idehd as symbolically reaffirming the ability of the Saudeleur rulership to underwrite the survival of the Pohnpeian people.

Due to the overwhelming size and complexity of Nan Madol, archaeological documentation for the most part has entailed technical mapping, with limited test excavations (Figure 12.40). Although not intended as an archaeological study per se, Paul Hambruch's (1911) historical documentary map has been useful for recording the traditional names of each islet that furthermore can be linked with oral traditions. Several detailed archaeological mapping projects have been undertaken (e.g., Athens 1980; Ayres 1983; McCoy et al. 2015). Additionally, an airborne remote-sensing survey has revealed an extensive surrounding landscape of cultivation features that likely supported the complex at Nan Madol (Comer et al. 2019).

294 *An A.D. 1000 Event? Formalization of cultural expressions*

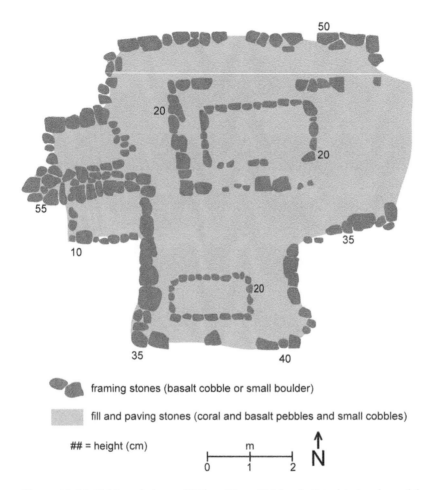

Figure 12.35 Fishing shrine at Kiʻilae, Hawaiʻi Island. Graphic is adapted from Carson et al. (2004).

The most informative excavation at Nan Madol was in 1984 but published decades later (Athens 2007), at the key ritual performance area in the islet of Idehd, showing that the stonework construction began around A.D. 1200 and subsequently underwent a change in cultural context after another few centuries. The findings were interpreted as reflecting the operation of the Saudeleur religious-political context primarily during the A.D. 1200s through 1400s (Athens 2007). More recent research has confirmed the same sequence at Nan Madol, by direct dating of coral used in the stonework construction (McCoy et al. 2016). In prior decades, however, other research had been conducted under the auspices of the Smithsonian Institution in 1963 by Saul Reisenberg, Clifford Evans, and Betty Meggers, documented only in an unpublished typescript letter (Reisenberg et al. 1963) and a copied set of photographic prints donated to the Micronesian Area Research Center, University of Guam.

Following the established monumental traditions and formalization of cultural expressions after the A.D. 1000 Event, monuments became entrained into overt materialization

An A.D. 1000 Event? Formalization of cultural expressions 295

Figure 12.36 Stone object of a fish god idol at Ki'ilae, Hawai'i Island.

of power after A.D. 1400. These later contexts involved issues of economic and social stress linked with political ambitions, as will be discussed in Chapter 13. Sites throughout the region and especially in the Hawaiian Islands offer spectacular examples of events overlapping with written histories of later periods and offering vivid details of how chiefs gained power. These later developments could not have occurred without the preexisting conditions following the A.D. 1000 Event as presented here.

Linking lands and lineages

Starting at A.D. 1000, formalized village construction, house burial, and monument building all shared a theme of fixing these actions into a landscape, directly linking specific

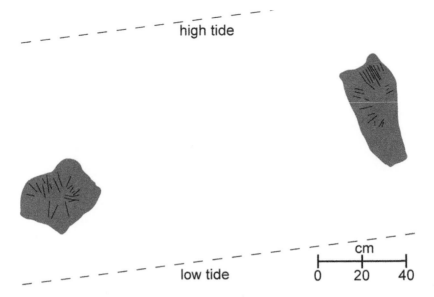

Figure 12.37 Stones associated with fishing lore at Vavouto, New Caledonia. Graphic is based on documentation by Carson (2003).

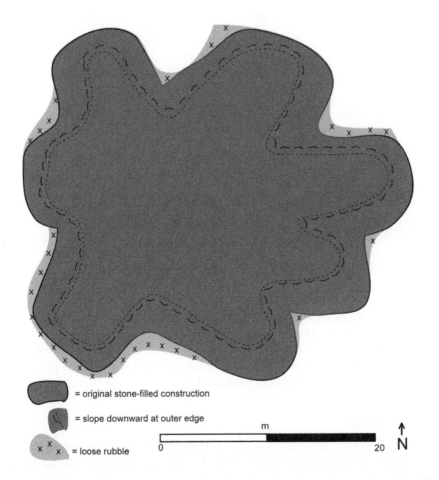

Figure 12.38 Pigeon-snaring mound in Tutuila, American Samoa. Graphic is based on documented by Carson (2005).

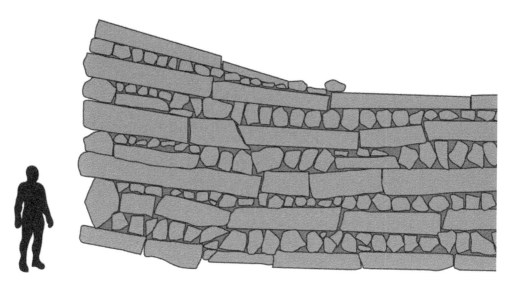

Figure 12.39 Portion of the stone city of Nan Madol in Pohnpei.

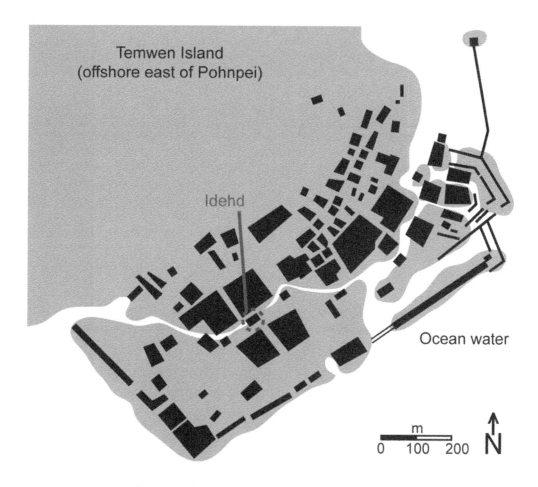

Figure 12.40 Map of stonework ruins of Nan Madol.

groups of people with defined areas of land and sea. Thereafter, successive generations of people were connected with their territories. Although the territories may not have been subject to ownership in a strict sense, they clearly were associated with identifiable groups of people who could claim rights of access and responsibilities of caretaking.

With the A.D. 1000 Event, communities became more tightly associated with specific lands, thus implying a need for people at this time to control access to the inherently limited resources of islands. By extension, the absence of such a material signature prior to A.D. 1000 indicates that people previously lived with acceptable social and economic buffers, for instance, with access to enough resource zones to overcome periodic stress. Only after A.D. 1000 did Pacific Oceanic societies approach the limits of population growth understood as involving social relations as well as the practical use of land and resources. Prior to this time, people periodically expanded into new portions of a growing sea of islands that eventually became fully inhabited.

The linking of lands and lineages is most clear in the Hawaiian Islands, where the ancestral Polynesian word of *kaainga for "family" was transformed to mean the "land" as 'aina in Hawaiian. Everywhere else in Polynesia, the word *fenua* refers to an inhabited landscape in a general sense, linked to an older Oceanic word of *vanua* traceable at least as old as the Lapita expansion at 1100–800 B.C. This anomalous development in the Hawaiian Islands most likely strengthened after A.D. 1400 in the context of competitive chiefdoms controlling land and resources (that will be discussed in Chapter 13), but it implies a longer trend that eventually reached a critical point by A.D. 1400.

Given this portrayal of linking land and lineages, other hypothetical notions about kinship, extended family structure, and "house societies" may be applied, although they are extraneous to the actual archaeological evidence. Among the more popular explanatory schemes, Claude Lévi-Strauss (1982, 1987) proposed that certain social groups lived according to lineage descent, wherein each lineage belonged to a "house" such as the House of Windsor, blending both cognatic kinship and social class ranking. In theory, ethnographic and other information of a "house society" (or *société à maison* in the original French) could help toward studies of the social functioning and relationships of people who lived in the formally structured and territorial village complexes after A.D. 1000 in Pacific Oceania, applying knowledge from the present backward into the past. On the other hand, a chronological view is necessary in order to understand how the formalized village complexes developed to support those kinds of societies, in this case stressing that people cross-regionally approached a critical threshold in their ability to manage community structuring about A.D. 1000.

The notion of a "house society" does not necessarily equate with a physical building or with an archaeological set of house foundations, although naturally, the members of the society in question must have lived in houses and therefore maintained households. The word "house" is perhaps unfortunate, as in this case, it refers to a social concept of a kind of lineage (such as the House of Windsor, as noted) and not to a material house construction. In practice, a lineage could accommodate both blood relatives and extended kinship relations, encompassing all of the people sharing in a "house society," regardless of where they built their individual houses. The same people could maintain their households with varying forms and scales of social units, wherein only one of those social structures involved the "house society" concept.

Especially after A.D. 1000 in the Pacific Islands, the linking of lands and lineages became increasingly evident in the archaeological record, here described as part of an A.D. 1000 Event. The reasons for this linkage, however, can be interpreted in various ways. In one view, the linkage fits with expectations of how a "house society" functions in a synchronic sense, irrespective of how this functioning may have developed in the first place. By default, these studies rely on ethnographic knowledge applied to sets of archaeological ruins as a way to validate that the essence of a "house society" persisted through a length of time. For instance, in this view, Jennfier Kahn (2014) argued that surface-accessible stonework ruins in Hawai'i reflected a *longue durée* of "house societies." In another view, the linkage between lands and lineages became visible archaeologically as part of the A.D. 1000 Event, resulting from the incentives for people to claim territories and resources becoming increasingly urgent with escalating population density in inherently limited island environments. These two perspectives do not contradict one another, but rather they approach the archaeological record from different directions.

When looking at the patterns of archaeological ruins over a land area today, those patterns may be interpreted as reflecting the operation of a "house society," but they equally could reflect the workings of a matrilineal clan or other kinship structure, differential social status, or separation of economic tasks. Often, these hypothetical models have been suggested by ethnographic knowledge and written histories of the last few centuries. All of those proposals are useful for applying independent theoretical notions to the real-life sets of archaeological data, but these kinds of studies tend to be inconclusive due to the limits of the physical evidence that do not directly reveal social behaviors. At best, the archaeological patterns can be evaluated as fitting or not fitting an expected model of a "house society" or other notion of how social groups behave, while the reasons are unknown for the existence of the social lineage, matrilineal clan, or other contextual scheme.

As outlined here, the linkage between lands and lineages can be situated in a chronological context, with attention to the records of how people related with their landscapes through a sequence of different time periods. The records of habitation and land-use patterns became most abundant and widespread after A.D. 1000, but they differed from older patterns, overall becoming more fixed and formalized after A.D. 1000. In this view, the outcome of an A.D. 1000 Event followed some centuries of population growth, concurrent with increasing reliance on land-based foods and resources, variable degrees of localized independence of communities, and strengthening of area-specific cultural traditions and languages in each island group.

Climate stability and instability

The proposed A.D. 1000 Event coincided with the beginning of a sustained and reliable period in world climate known as the Little Climatic Optimum (LCO) or the Medieval Warm Period (MWP), which was generally warmer and wetter than usual at a global scale (Lamb 1965, 1982). The overall favorable conditions of the LCO may not have contributed to the origins of monumental traditions and cultural formalization, but, more realistically, they provided the long-term stability and reliability to sustain these habituated customs for a few hundred years. With the predictable climate and weather patterns over an extended time period, behaviors of cultural formalization and monumentality could persist and become strong traditions enduring across generations. If the climate conditions instead had been more wide-ranging in patterns of variability and unpredictability, then the cultural behaviors emerging at A.D. 1000 might not have perpetuated in their overall unified outcomes as had happened.

If the LCO is viewed as a supporting context for maximizing cultural formalization, then the limits of a society's capacity may have been threatened by the disappearance of those supporting conditions a few centuries later. Beginning about A.D. 1300, world climate transitioned into the unstable conditions and cooler temperatures of the Little Ice Age (LIA). Along with overall cooler temperatures at a global scale, climatic instability entailed repeated incidence of storminess as well as droughts, both occurring unpredictably against the usual annual weather patterns (Grove 1988). By the time when this shift into LIA conditions had occurred, many of the Pacific Island populations were approaching a maximum growth capacity that could not be sustained for very long without the enabling climate reliability of prior centuries (Nunn 2000). In these cases, as will be discussed in Chapter 13, the unpredictability and punctuated extremes of storminess and drought posed the greatest threat to island societies after the LCO to LIA transition.

The LCO may not have been favorable for everyone in Pacific Oceania. According to some estimates, globally warmer temperatures of the LCO were sufficient to have caused sea level to rise, for instance, with 1 degree C of warmer temperature equating to 1 m of higher sea level (Nunn 1999). In this scenario, the LCO may have brought adverse effects of massive coastal erosion as well as a salinized water table in the atolls and other small low-elevation islands of Micronesia and Polynesia. These effects would have decreased the ability of each island to sustain populations, such that some people may have migrated into other islands with higher land masses, while only smaller numbers of people could continue to live in the low-lying islands affected by sea-level rise.

References

Athens, J. Stephen, 1980. *Archaeological Investigations at Nan Madol: Maps and Surface Artifacts*. Pacific Studies Institute, Mangilao, Guam.
Athens, J. Stephen, 2007. The rise of the Saudeleur: Dating the Nan Madol chiefdom, Pohnpei. In *Vastly Ingenious: The Archaeology of Pacific Material Culture in Honour of Janet M. Davidson*, edited by Atholl Anderson, Kaye Green, and Foss Leach, pp. 192–208. Otago University Press, Dunedin.
Ayres, William S., 1983. Archaeology at Nan Madol, Ponape. *Bulletin of the Indo-Pacific Prehistory Association* 4: 135–142.
Bayman, James M., and Cyril G. Calugay, 2014. *Archaeological Overview and Assessment of the National Park in American Samoa*. Western Regional Office, U.S. National Park Service, Honolulu.
Bayman, James M., Hiro Kurashina, Mike T. Carson, John A. Peterson, David J. Doig, and Jane Drengson, 2012a. Latte household economic organization at Ritidian, Guam National Wildlife Refuge, Mariana Islands. *Micronesica* 42: 258–273.
Bayman, James M., Hiro Kurashina, Mike T. Carson, John A. Peterson, David J. Doig, and Jane Drengson, 2012b. Household economy and gendered labor in the 17th Century A.D. on Guam. *Journal of Field Archaeology* 37: 259–269.
Bernart, Luelen, 1977. *The Book of Luelen*. Translated and edited by John Fischer, Saul Riesenberg, and Marjorie Whiting. Pacific History Series 8. University of Hawai'i Press, Honolulu.
Burley, David V., 1996. Sport, status, and field monuments in the Polynesian chiefdom of Tonga: The pigeon snaring mounds of northern Ha'apai. *Journal of Field Archaeology* 23: 421–435.
Carson, Mike T., 2003. *Phase Two Archaeological Study, Koniambo Project, Regions of Voh, Koné, and Pouémbout, Northern Province, New Caledonia*. Report prepared for Projet Koniambo. International Archaeological Research Institute, Inc., Honolulu.
Carson, Mike T., 2005. *Archaeological Data Recovery for the American Samoa Power Authority Sewer Collection System in Tualauta County, Tutuila Island, American Samoa*. Report prepared for American Samoa Power Authority. International Archaeological Research Institute, Inc., Honolulu.

Carson, Mike T., 2006. *Archaeological Inventory Survey in a Portion of Upland Honokōhau, North Kona District, Hawai'i Island*. Report prepared for Lanihau Partners, LLC. International Archaeological Research Institute, Inc., Honolulu.

Carson, Mike T., 2007. *Archaeological Surface Survey in a Portion of Ki'ilae Village, Pu'uhonua o Hōnaunau National Historical Park, South Kona District, Island of Hawai'i*. Report prepared for U.S. National Park Service. International Archaeological Research Institute, Inc., Honolulu.

Carson, Mike T., 2012. An overview of latte period archaeology. *Micronesica* 42: 1–79.

Carson, Mike T., 2014. De-coding the archaeological landscape of Samoa: Austronesian origins and Polynesian culture. *Journal of Austronesian Studies* 5: 1–41.

Carson, Mike T., 2016. *Archaeological Landscape Evolution: The Mariana Islands in the Asia-Pacific Region*. Springer International, Cham, Switzerland.

Carson, Mike T., Timothy Rieth, and William Burdick, 2004. *An Intensive Surface Survey of a Portion of Ki'ilae Village, Pu'uhonua o Hōnaunau National Historical Park, South Kona District, Island of Hawai'i*. Report prepared for U.S. National Park Service. International Archaeological Research Institute, Inc., Honolulu.

Clark, Jeffrey T., 1993. Prehistory of Alega, Tutuila Island, American Samoa: A small residential and basalt-industrial valley. *New Zealand Journal of Archaeology* 15: 67–86.

Comer, Douglas C., Jake A. Comer, Ioana A. Dumitru, William S. Ayres, Maureece J. Levin, Katherine A. Seikel, Devin A. White, and Michael H. Harrowers, 2019. Airborne LiDAR reveals a vast archaeological landscape at the Nan Madol World Heritage Site. *Remote Sensing 2019*: 2152. https://doi.org/10.3390/rs11182152

Cordy, Ross, 1986. *Archaeological Settlement Patterns Studies on Yap*. Micronesian Archaeological Survey Report 16. Historic Preservation Office, Commonwealth of the Northern Mariana Islands, Saipan.

Craib, John L., 1986. *Casas de los Antiguos: Social Differentiation in Protohistoric Chamorro Society, Mariana Islands*. Ph.D. dissertation. University of Sydney, Sydney.

Craib, John L., Josede Figirliyong, and Samuel T. Price, 1980. *Archaeological Survey of Ulithi Atoll, Western Caroline Islands*. Pacific Studies Institutre, Mangilao, Guam.

Farrer, D. S., and James D. Sellmann, 2014. Chants of re-enchantment: Chamorro spiritual resistance to colonial dominion. *Social Analysis* 58: 127–148.

Fischer, John L., Saul H. Riesenberg, and Marjorie G. Whiting, 1977. *Annotations to the Book of Luelen*. Pacific History Series 9. The Australian National University Press, Canberra.

Freeman, J. Derek, 1944. O Fale o le Fe'e. *Journal of the Polynesian Society* 53: 121–144.

Graves, Michael W., 1986. Organization and differentiation within late prehistoric ranked social units, Mariana Islands, western Pacific. *Journal of Field Archaeology* 13: 139–154.

Green, Roger C., 1967. Settlement patterns: Four case studies from Polynesia. In *Archaeology at the Eleventh Pacific Science Congress*, edited by Wilhelm G. Solheim, II, pp. 101–132. Asian and Pacific Archaeology Series 1. Social Science Research Institute, University of Hawai'i, Honolulu.

Green, Roger C., 1970. Settlement pattern archaeology in Polynesia. In *Studies in Oceanic Culture History*, edited by Roger C. Green and Marion Kelly, Volume 1, pp. 13–32. Pacific Anthropological Records Number 11. Department of Anthropology, Bishop Museum, Honolulu.

Green, Roger C., 1986. Some basic components of the Ancestral Polynesian settlement system: Building blocks for more complex Polynesian societies. In *Island Societies: Archaeological Approaches to Evolution and Transformation*, edited by Patrick V. Kirch, pp. 50–54. New Directions in Archaeology. Cambridge University Press, Cambridge.

Grove, Jean M., 1988. *The Little Ice Age*. Methuen, London.

Hadley, Masao, 1981. *A History of Nan Madol*. Translated and edited by Paul M. Ehrlich. Unpublished manuscript on file, Micronesian Area Research Center, University of Guam, Mangilao.

Hambruch, Paul, 1911. Die ruinen von Ponape. *Korrespondenzblatt fur Anthropologie, Ethnologie und Urgeschichte* 42: 128–131. (in German).

Hanlon, David L., 1988. *Upon a Stone Altar: A History of the Island of Pohnpei to 1890*. University of Hawai'i Press, Honolulu.

Herdrich, David J., 1991. Towards an understanding of Samoan star mounds. *Journal of the Polynesian Society 100*: 381–435.

Herdrich, David J., and Jeffrey T. Clark, 1993. Samoan tia 'ave and social structure: Methodological and theoretical considerations. In *The Evolution and Organisation of Prehistoric Society in Polynesia*, edited by Michael W. Graves and Roger C. Green, pp. 52–63. Monograph Number 19. New Zealand Archaeological Association, Auckland.

Holmer, Richard N., 1980. Mt. Olo settlement pattern interpretation. In *Archaeological Excavations in Western Samoa*, edited by Jesse D. Jennings and Richard N. Holmer, pp. 93–103. Pacific Anthropological Records 32. Department of Anthropology, Bernice Pauhi Bishop Museum, Honolulu.

Hornbostel, Hans, 1925. *Unpublished Field Notes, 1921–1924*. Record on file, Bernice Pauahi Bishop Museum, Honolulu.

Hunt, Terry L., and Patrick V. Kirch, 1987. *An Archaeological Reconnaissance of the Manu'a Islands, American Samoa*. Report on file at American Samoa Historic Preservation Office, Pago Pago.

Hunt, Terry L., and Patrick V. Kirch, 1988. An archaeological survey of the Manu'a Islands, American Samoa. *Journal of the Polynesian Society 97*: 153–183.

Hunt, Terry L., and Carl Lipo, 2011. *The Statues That Walked: Unraveling the Mystery of Easter Island*. Free Press, New York.

Jackmond, Gregory, Dionne Fonotī, and Matiu Matāvai Tautunu, 2018. Sāmoa's hidden past: LiDAR confirms inland settlement and suggests larger populations in pre-Contact Sāmoa. *Journal of the Polynesian Society 127*: 73–90.

Jennings, Jesse D., Richard N. Holmer, and Gregory Jackson, 1982. Samoan village patterns: Four examples. *Journal of the Polynesian Society 91*: 81–102.

Kahn, Jennifer G., 2010. A spatio-temporal analysis of 'Oro cult *marae* in the 'Opunohu Valley, Mo'orea, Society Islands. *Archaeology in Ocenia 45*: 103–110.

Kahn, Jennifer G., 2014. Household archaeology and "house societies" in the Hawaiian Archipelago. *Journal of Pacific Archaeology 5*: 18–29.

Laguana, Andrew, Hiro Kurashina, Mike T. Carson, John A. Peterson, James M. Bayman, Todd Ames, Rebecca A. Stephenson, John Aguon, and Harya Putra, 2012. Estorian i latte: A story of latte. *Micronesica 42*: 80–120.

Lamb, Hubert H., 1965. The early medieval warm epoch and its sequel. *Palaeogeography, Palaeoclimatology, Palaeoecology 1*: 13–37.

Lamb, Hubert H., 1982. *Climate, History and the Modern World*. Methuen, London.

Lévi-Strauss, Claude, 1982. *The Way of the Mask*. University of Washington Press, Seattle.

Lévi-Strauss, Claude, 1987. *Anthropology and Myth: Lectures 1951–1982*. Translated by Roy Willis. Basil Blackwell, Oxford.

Martinsson-Wallin, Helene, 1994. *Ahu, the Ceremonial Structures of Easter Island: Analyses of Variation and Interpretation of Meaning*. Aun 19. Societas Archaeologica Upsaliensis, Uppsala, Sweden.

Martinsson-Wallin, Helene, and Susan J. Crockford, 2001. Early settlement of Rapa Nui (Easter Island). *Asian Perspectives 40*: 244–278.

Martinsson-Wallin, Helene, Paul Wallin, Atholl Anderson, and Reidar Solsvik, 2013. Chrogeograohic variation in initial East Polynesian construction of monumental ceremonial sites. *Journal of Island and Coastal Archaeology 8*: 405–421.

McCoy, Mark D., Helen A. Alderson, Richard Hemi, Hai Cheng, and R. Lawrence Edwards, 2016. Earliest direct evidence of monument building at the archaeological site of Nan Madol (Pohnpei, Micronesia) identified using 230Th/U coral dating and geochemical sourcing of megalithic architectural stone. *Quaternary Research 86*: 295–303.

McCoy, Mark D., Helen A. Alderson, and Adam Thompson, 2015. A new archaeological field survey of the site of Nan Madol, Pohnpei. *Rapa Nui Journal 29*: 5–22.

Mulrooney, Mara A., 2013. An island-wide assessment of the chronology of settlement and land use on Rapa Nui (Easter Islands) based on radiocarbon data. *Journal of Archaeological Science 40*: 4377–4399.

Nunn, Patrick D., 1999. *Environmental Change in the Pacific Basin: Chronologies, Causes, Consequences*. Wiley-Blackwell, London.

Nunn, Patrick D., 2000. Environmental catastrophe in the Pacific Islands around A.D. 1300. *Geoarchaeology* 15: 715–740.

Osborne, Douglas, 1966. *The Archaeology of the Palau Islands: An Intensive Survey*. Bernice Pauahi Bishop Museum Bulletin 230. Bishop Museum Press, Honolulu.

Ottino, Pierre, 1990. L'habitat des anciens Marquisiens: Architecture des maisons, evolution et symbolism des forms. *Journal de le Société des Océanistes* 90: 3–15.

Reisenberg, Saul H., Clifford Evans, and Betty J. Meggers, 1963. *Preliminary Report of Anthropological Research Conducted on Ponape, Caroline Islands, from January 29 to March 8, 1963, Under Sponsorship of the Smithsonian Institution with Support from the National Science Foundation*. Unpublished document on file. Micronesian Area Research Center, University of Guam, Mangilao.

Rolett, Barry V., 2010. Marquesan monumental architecture: Blurred boundaries in the distinction between religious and residential sites. *Archaeology in Oceania* 45: 94–102.

Rouse, Irving, 1972. Settlement patterns in archaeology. In *Man, Settlement and Urbanism*, edited by Peter J. Ucko, Ruth Tringham, and G. W. Dimbleby, pp. 95–107. Duckworth, London.

Sand, Christophe, 2002. Creations and transformation of prehistoric landscapes in New Caledonia, the southernmost Melanesian Islands. In *Pacific Landscapes: Archaeological Approaches*, edited by Thegn N. Ladefoged and Michael W. Graves, pp. 11–34. Bearsville Press, Los Osos, CA.

Sand, Christophe, David Baret, Jacques Bolé, André-John Ouetcho, and Mohammed Sahib, 2018. Sāmoan settlement pattern and star mounds of Manono Island. *Journal of the Polynesian Society* 127: 91–109.

Spoehr, Alexander, 1957. *Marianas Prehistory: Archaeological Survey and Excavations on Saipan, Tinian and Rota*. Fieldiana: Anthropology, Volume 48. Chicago Natural History Museum, Chicago.

Thompson, Laura, 1940. The function of latte in the Marianas. *Journal of the Polynesian Society* 49: 447–465.

Wallin, Paul, 1993. *Ceremonial Stone Structures: The Archaeology and Ethnohistory of the Marae Complex in the Society Islands, French Polynesia*. Aun 18. Societas Archaeologica Upsaliensis, Uppsala, Sweden.

Walter, Richard, 1996. Settlement pattern archaeology in the southern Cook Islands: A review. *Journal of the Polynesian Society* 105: 63–99.

13 Expansion and intensification, A.D. 1000 through 1800

'A'ohe hana nui ke alu 'ia (Hawaiian proverb), translates into English as
"No task is too big when done together by all."

Cooperation is essential in any society, with an exaggerated role in islands where issues of population density and potential conflicts are magnified and closely tied with processes of expansion and intensification. Whether amicably or forcibly, teamwork can accomplish impressive tasks, as stressed in the quoted Hawaiian proverb and illustrated abundantly in the Hawaiian archaeological landscape's legacy of stonework monuments, walled fishponds, field systems, and other labor-intensive constructions. Similar examples are found throughout Pacific Oceania, most prominently at sites postdating A.D. 1000 after the region-wide formalization of cultural expressions as presented in Chapter 12. These sites embody the sentiment that "no task is too big when done together by all," but they raise questions about the nature of the cooperative acts as reflecting peaceful collaboration or imposed political authority.

While very much aware of the powers of cooperation and conflict, island societies after A.D. 1000 tested the limits of expanding into new lands and of intensifying their usage of those lands. After people inhabited the farthest margins of Pacific Oceania and found no further potential for occupying new territories, patterns of intensification emerged in each island group at varying degrees of consuming the land and resources, building intercommunity networks, and establishing means of economic, social, and political controls. Pathways to power proceeded in epic proportions, as seen in the ideologically charged political economies of the Hawaiian Kingdom, the erection of grand stone statues of Rapa Nui, and the expansive maritime networks of trade and tribute across the islands of Micronesia and elsewhere.

These later periods have produced extraordinary examples of how societies can develop high degrees of complexity and complication within a compressed time frame, with equally notable cross-regional variation in how those developments occurred. Every case is unique, and different overarching explanatory theories refer to social complexity, definitions of chiefdoms and states, and the functional relationships among economics, politics, and ideology. Additionally, issues of climate change, population density, and island carrying capacity need to be considered, while the general processes of expansion and intensification always can be applied but need logical interpretation.

The islands of East Polynesia provide especially informative records of how people engaged in processes of expansion and intensification within brief time intervals. East Polynesian settlement has been dated no earlier than A.D. 1000 in most islands and as late as A.D. 1300 in Aotearoa (New Zealand), yet dramatic political economies had been established during the centuries prior to the burst of European historical observations in the late 1700s. Even more of a chronological constraint can be noticed for these processes when realizing that the archaeological signatures of conflict, competition, and control of land and resources all began to emerge or amplify markedly about A.D. 1400–1600.

The rapid pace and sometimes radical displays of social and political complexity were predicated by the preexisting context of formalized cultural expression, traditions of monumentality, and fixing of lineages with defined units of land that had operated since A.D. 1000 (Chapter 12). With those formalities and constraints in place, island societies could manage impressive cooperative undertakings, yet the potential for conflict and competition always would persist. These traditions already had been established when island societies underwent continued processes of expansion and intensification, both in the long-inhabited islands of the west and central Pacific and in the newly settled island frontiers of East Polynesia.

Processes of expansion and intensification

Islands comprise ideal settings for studying the processes of expansion and intensification in settlement and land-use patterns. Most of the documented area-specific cultural chronologies involve a sequence of initial settlement in the maximally productive zones, followed by expansion into less preferable areas and then later processes of intensification within all inhabited zones (see Figure 3.1). In this familiar scheme, initial habitations targeted the most resource-rich habitats and places with the most reliable sources of fresh water, and then gradually people expanded into less desirable areas. When people reached the limits of expansion, then they may have intensified their use of the lands that they occupied. In this view, people could expand to the extent of a particular island's carrying capacity for whatever mode of subsistence economy was being practiced, and then only later did they invest in intensifying the land-use patterns within the constrained island spaces.

The general trend of incremental expansion followed by later intensification may be applied to individual islands, collective archipelagos, or even the Pacific region as a whole. In a long time scale, people gradually expanded to inhabit more and more of Pacific Oceania through time, with a final expansion into the last remaining inhabitable islands after A.D. 1000 (see Figure 12.1). Only in later periods did the archaeological record reveal instances of people intensifying their use of island ecosystems, after the options of expansion had met their end.

Issues of expansion and intensification are linked closely with modes of land use and with a given environment's carrying capacity. Horticultural and arboricultural farmers, as in most Pacific Oceanic societies, can harvest more food per unit of land than would be possible by hunter-gatherers who generally need to range over much larger areas. Extending this example, root-tuber crops potentially can provide even greater calorie yields per unit of land than is possible with tree crops, but the farmers would need to invest in constructing and then maintaining labor-intensive field systems for the maximum effects. Moreover, a reliance on too narrow of a range of crops would involve a risk of total failure, whereas mixed crops would allow options of overcoming periodic shortfalls in any single category.

The parameters of expansion and intensification after A.D. 1000 can be appreciated as significantly different from the situation of lower densities of populations living much earlier and with easier options of expansion. At the beginning of human settlements in Remote Oceania, as early as 1500 B.C. and continuing through at least 800 B.C., people lived in shoreline-oriented communities and relied heavily on a narrow range of near-shore resources. This lifestyle proved unsustainable with a changing coastal environment (Chapters 8 and 9), and people responded by expanding their land-use patterns into a broader and more generalized use of mixed coastal and land-based habitat zones that allowed reliable use of more options of available lands. Increasingly evident after 500 B.C., this early adaptational shift effectively broadened the cultural use of the landscape, thus implementing a form of expansion. A similar strategy would not be possible during later periods when people already lived in the available habitat niches and made use of diverse resource zones with little or no remaining option for expansion.

With each set of Pacific Oceanic population expansions by sea-crossing migrations, people targeted the most naturally productive resource zones of their newly settled islands but gradually expanded to inhabit more marginal zones. This pattern repeated itself with each of the major episodes of migratory expansions as outlined in prior chapters of this book. Following a final such episode beginning at A.D. 1000, no more options remained for geographic expansion, and instead people needed to intensify within their given land areas.

Intensification in the most general sense refers to the increase of productivity per unit of available resource. In terms of food productivity, intensification typically involves efforts to grow more edible crops per land area, often by high-density planting but also by other means of manipulating water and nutrients to maximize yields and to increase the frequency of harvesting. In terms of other labor, such as stone toolmaking, intensification could involve a greater output of the tools made by a single workshop per day, week, or year. Intensification of house construction could entail higher density of houses within a constrained land footprint. In other words, intensification includes subsistence food production as well as potentially everything else that contributes to an economic system.

Intensification may be enacted by devoting more labor to a task, but it often involves the adoption of different technology to make certain tasks more efficient. Simply by adding more people or extending the number of work hours devoted to a task, such as tending to a taro field, the output can be increased, but this strategy involves clear limits of the number of people available and the number of hours that realistically can be reserved just for the task when so many other tasks need attention. Other necessary daily labor in the islands could include childcare and education, house-building and maintenance, producing essential tools, fishing and shellfishing, and more. Practical limits are met in terms of the amount of land available for a taro farm or for any kind of garden or orchard, especially in islands where land is finite and only certain ecological zones are suitable for growing specific crops such as taro, yams, or others.

Increased work efficiency typically entails the use of specialized technology targeting a particular task or sometimes a set of tasks that otherwise would consume significant numbers of work hours. For instance, weighted digging sticks can loosen more soil per hour than simple tree branches, raw rocks, or bare hands. Slashing and burning in a plot of land can provide usable space for growing crops, as well as introduce essential nutrients for soil productivity. Construction of terraces and mounds can enable the control of water flow, retention of water and sediment, and overall balance of soil properties for optimal growth of diverse crops. A walled fishpond can provide reliable access to large numbers of fish without the time and labor of fishing expeditions. Each of these examples would require an up-front investment and repeated maintenance effort working toward a return on the investment in the form of increased total productivity.

When increasing the labor product output, people actually become busier overall. The face value of increased efficiency may appear to be to provide more leisure time, at least in principle, but in reality, people are expected to produce more with their luxurious efficiency. In a modern analogy, high-speed internet can transmit large amounts of data quickly and thereby enable more work to be accomplished within a shorter amount of time. The resulting efficiency allows people to share more information and process more data each day, and the level of expected daily output accordingly grows higher. In a sense, people have become busier than ever because they have intensified their labor output and therefore are expected to produce more work on a daily basis.

Especially regarding food productivity, many of the technological solutions for intensification involve an initial investment in a massive construction such as a field system or a fishpond, followed by continual devotion of labor for ongoing maintenance. In these cases, people devote more total labor than in the less intensive systems of managed forests and informal gardens. This kind of high-density use of the land occurs only when people are forced to use limited territory, within which they face constraints on the ability of their available land to produce food or other resources.

As outlined in Chapter 12, traditions of territory-based lineages were established throughout Pacific Oceania about A.D. 1000, so the parameters for intensifying land use within those territories already existed long prior to the most obvious material manifestations of high-density field systems after A.D. 1400. When originally formulated at A.D. 1000 or perhaps earlier, territories of land units were not necessarily used intensively, but rather they served to define boundaries of the social groups or lineages associated with those separate lands. In fact, many land-use systems were sustained with low-labor input modes of managed forests and informal household gardens, such as in most of Micronesia without any formalized agricultural fields at all. High-density land-use patterns mostly developed as characteristic of East Polynesian societies, with a few notable instances in the western and central Pacific.

Individual examples of formalized high-density field systems and fish-trapping constructions will be presented later in this chapter, but first these permanently fixed complexes need to be understood as different from the more flexible systems of managed forests and household gardens. In the later formalized developments, large portions of territories were transformed permanently into food-producing complexes, enduring in their chosen places by the creation of walls, berms, mounds, and other features. The quality of permanence differed from older patterns of managed ecosystems that could be restructured within the range of a given territory. The chosen footprint of such a construction would need to occupy a place where the territory's group as a whole approved or at least did not reject the permanent transformation, possibly suggesting a group-level benefit at whatever scale the group may be defined.

Major cooperative work projects have resulted in the many field systems and stonework monuments throughout Pacific Oceania, achieved primarily by adding as many people and work hours as possible to a singular event. Considerable knowledge and skill were necessary to design and plan the constructions of field systems as well as statues, religious temples, burial mounds, and other monumental output. The actual labor of carving and hauling large stones or of moving thousands of individual stones, however, required mass labor. These group-collective labor activities potentially can build a sense of community bonding and pride, but more importantly, the resulting structures endure in the landscape as permanent commemorations. People forever are reminded that "no task is too big when done together by all," but later generations may wonder about how the labor had been amassed and dedicated to the project.

When a monumental construction creates a benefit for the public, as in a field system or fishpond that theoretically can provide more food for everyone, then the mass labor is easy to comprehend as a worthwhile investment for everyone's advantage. On the other hand, many of these constructions were controlled by individual people or elite groups, or sometimes the increased food yields served for fulfilling obligations of tax or tribute. Certainly, the instances of chiefly royal residences and burial monuments can be understood as magnifying the elite status of particular people, although they may be justified as beneficial for the public according to religious and ideological beliefs.

The long-lasting qualities of monuments are linked with their ability to legitimize or propagandize a ruler's authority, enacted most effectively when these constructions are designed as large and imposing in their landscapes. DeMarrais et al. (1996) refer to this process as a "materialization of power," in essence fixing a leader's claims to power into a permanent monument as part of the landscape itself. As presented in Chapter 12, religious rites at the complex of Nan Madol in Pohnpei periodically renewed the authority of the Saudeleur ruling class. Likewise, ritual performance at Hawaiian *heiau* temples could be viewed as justification of a leader's claims to power, for instance, if an offering to Kū (god of war) was followed later by victory in battle or if an offering to Lono (god of fertility, agriculture, rain, and peace) was followed later by productive crop yields. The Hawaiian ritual performances, in any case, became commemorated in the long-lasting *heiau* monuments designed for the specific god being propitiated and, in a sense, fused with the identity of the responsible chief.

Expanding to the margins of Pacific Oceania

Before considering the processes of intensification, the run-up of expansion needs to be clarified in terms of the timing and scale of population movements. A major sea-crossing population expansion into East Polynesia began at A.D. 1000 and continued over the next few centuries (see Figure 12.1), followed by several smaller-scale expansions within individual archipelagos or across the ecological zones of specific islands. Each such instance of geographic expansion resembles a momentous event as a horizon of diagnostic artifacts appearing in new areas, although a closer look reveals an extended process over a period of time in each case.

East Polynesian expansion involved the longest-distance ocean-crossing migrations in the Pacific – impressive not only for the distance but also for the number of island groups all settled at approximately the same time. The timing now is accepted around A.D. 1000 for nearly all island groups and as late as A.D. 1300 for Aotearoa (New Zealand). The overall pattern demonstrates rapid long-distance dispersal of populations sharing a Polynesian ancestry moving into separate island groups and archipelagos in one of the world's clearest examples of a treelike phylogeny. Historical linguistics, biological genetics, and archaeological material assemblages all point clearly to a shared ancestral origin in West Polynesia, with branching subgroups in the subsequently settled areas of East Polynesia (Kirch and Green 2001).

The Polynesian expansion primarily involved settlement of East Polynesia, but it also entailed movements westward into the Polynesian Outliers, all following A.D. 1000 (Carson 2012a). The Polynesian Outliers refer to scattered locations in Micronesia and Melanesia where people today speak Polynesian languages and live in the remaining available unutilized or underutilized habitat zones that were not already occupied by the long-established Micronesian and Melanesian communities. Linguistically, these populations came from two major groupings within West Polynesia, including a northern and a southern grouping

Expansion and intensification, A.D. 1000 through 1800 309

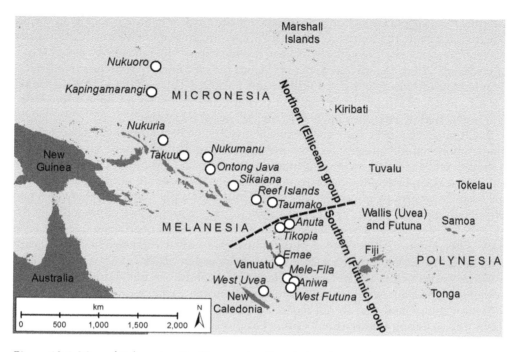

Figure 13.1 Map of Polynesian Outliers, noting linguistic subgroupings.

(Figure 13.1). The northern "Ellicean" group relates most closely to the speech communities in Tuvalu and Tokelau, whereas the southern "Futunic" group relates most closely to the speech communities in Futuna and Wallis. Where archaeological dating is available, the results are consistently after A.D. 1000 and thereby stress that the late Polynesian expansion involved simultaneous movements of several groups into different areas. The Micronesian and Melanesian language groupings must have been developed prior to this time and distinctly different from the Polynesian languages, or else the incoming Polynesian-speaking groups would not have been identifiable as the Polynesian Outliers.

The Polynesian expansion after A.D. 1000 most likely involved several groups sailing from various starting points in West Polynesia and migrating into equally diverse destinations all around the same time. Oral traditions in some of the Polynesian Outliers mention origins in different parts of West Polynesia, further corroborated by the linguistic differences between northern and southern Outlier groups (Carson 2012a). In East Polynesia, the language communities have retained mostly the linguistic features of West Polynesian origins, as well as some elements that characterized the northern Outliers, most likely reflecting some of the diversity of groups of people at the time of the expansion from West Polynesia around A.D. 1000. The known timing, essentially all at once after A.D. 1000, involved a newly emerged cultural context within West Polynesia, described as a dynamic and diverse setting of "polygenesis" (Burley 2013) and marked by the prominence of ground-level stonework housing and the disappearance of pottery-making traditions (Chapters 11 and 12).

The cross-regional radiocarbon dating evidence indicates a multidirectional population expansion from West Polynesia around A.D. 1000, and indeed the Outliers and East

Polynesian languages are closely related. Potentially, the linguistic similarities could be interpreted as supporting a hypothesis that some of the Outliers, specifically in the northern grouping, were the sources of the East Polynesian languages (Wilson 2021), yet neither the interpretation nor the hypothesis have found support in archaeology or in other lines of evidence. So far, the archaeological evidence indicates nearly simultaneous Polynesian population movements into the Outliers and into East Polynesia, and the chronological order cannot be distinguished except for perhaps slightly earlier movement into East Polynesia and slightly later movement into the Polynesian Outliers.

Rapid settlement over such a widespread seascape of East Polynesia has been regarded among humankind's greatest achievements, prompting questions of how it could have occurred. Of course, the remote-distance voyages were achievable and probably intentionally undertaken, or else the far margins of East Polynesia could not have been inhabited successfully by groups of people with sufficient biologically viable numbers, diversity of skills, and imported suites of plants and animals that endured multi-generationally. Moreover, Polynesians must have reached as far as the American continents in order to bring back sweet potato and perhaps a bottle gourd that now are verified at least as early as A.D. 1300 in the islands of East Polynesia (Ladefoged et al. 2003). In total, this body of evidence corroborates the notion of intentional exploratory and information-gathering voyaging against the wind from west to east, followed by later episodes of actual island settlement by groups who were prepared with advance knowledge of the sailing routes. Revival of seafaring traditions effectively has dispelled any lingering doubts of the ability of Pacific Oceanic navigators and sailors, for instance, as popularized by the Polynesian voyaging canoe Hōkūleʻa and others.

This portrayal of East Polynesian settlement has become well established (Kirch 2010a), yet it still occasionally needs to be defended against claims of sea-crossing migration from the Americas, as in Thor Heyerdahl's sensationally popular adventure of the Kon Tiki (Heyerdahl 1968). In 1947, Heyerdahl and his crew directed a raft with a sail, named the Kon Tiki, from South America to Rapa Nui (Easter Island). Part of the motivation was to consider if South America may have been the source of people who made the large *moai* statues in Rapa Nui. Today, the notion of a South American source has been discarded, and instead all evidence linguistically, biologically, and archaeologically points to an expansion from West to East Polynesia. Polynesians brought sweet potatoes back from South America, but Polynesian cultural origins definitely were from the west.

Although now broadly accepted as orthodox, dating of East Polynesian dispersal at A.D. 1000 previously had been regarded as a "short chronology" that overturned prior proposals of a "long chronology" (Spriggs and Anderson 1993). By using stricter protocols of interpreting the regional database of radiocarbon dates, the few older dates closer to A.D. 100 could be rejected, and instead the preponderance of evidence pointed to East Polynesian settlement after A.D. 1000. Increasingly popular since the 1990s, programs of "chronometric hygiene" brought attention to the need to clarify stratigraphic context, the nature of the material being dated, and the ability to refine a date range by multiple corroborating samples obtained from the same contexts and from clearly predating and postdating contexts. Today, these procedures constitute standard conventions of archaeological practice, and the results have substantiated the chronological sequence as presented in this book.

No systematic search yet has been attempted for finding the earliest settlement sites in most parts of East Polynesia, and in fact the record of oldest sites close to A.D. 1000 has been sparse. The situation has not changed at the time of the second edition of this book. The usual approach in field research involves a survey of surface-visible site ruins,

Expansion and intensification, A.D. 1000 through 1800

with little or no attention to the possibility of subsurface layers in contexts different from today's conditions of the physical landscape. Decades of field research have shown repeatedly that the surface-related materials date to the last time when people occupied an area, often with no underlying cultural deposits or else only scattered remnants of disturbed older materials in uncertain contexts.

Efforts of redating anomalous "old" site layers consistently have concluded that the previously dated materials had involved problems of inbuilt old age, unclear association with actual cultural events, or other issues. In one such redating exercise, apparent old dates of A.D. 1000 or even earlier were revealed as owing to natural ash falls from volcanic activity in leeward Hawai'i Island (Figure 13.2), while the verifiable hearth features and cultural deposits associated with the surface-visible stonework ruins dated primarily after A.D. 1400 (Carson 2012b). Using stricter protocols of the selection of short-lived wood taxa in the most secure contexts of convincingly cultural features, redating results repeatedly have pointed to much more recent ages, such as when redating individual pieces of bottle gourd in the leeward Hawai'i Island case.

With the frustrating paucity of site layers related to the oldest settlement periods, researchers have relied on paleoenvironmental proxies and on statistical modeling of island-wide or region-wide inventories of radiocarbon dates. This strategy has been developed most robustly in the Hawaiian Islands (Figure 13.3), where rat bones, avifaunal extinctions, and impacts on native vegetation in lake-bottom and swamp-bottom sediments, noncultural caves and sinkholes, and other non-site or off-site contexts dated as early as A.D. 1000 are compelling indictors of human presence (Athens et al. 2002). Additionally, the numerous radiocarbon dating results can be processed in terms of their collective statistical weight

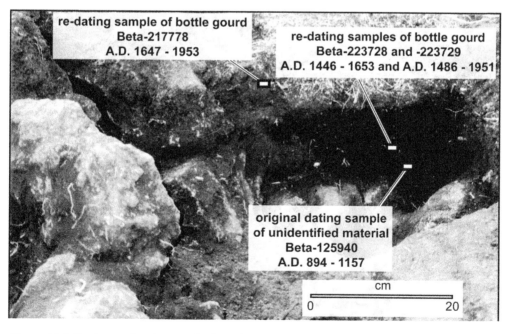

Figure 13.2 Dating and redating of a hearth feature at Puapua'a, Hawai'i Island. Graphic is based on documentation by Carson (2012b).

312 *Expansion and intensification, A.D. 1000 through 1800*

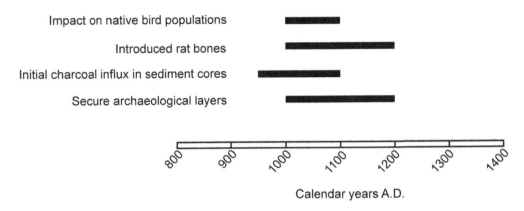

Figure 13.3 Proxies of earliest Hawaiian settlement dating. Graphic is based on information from Athens et al. (2002).

and probability to indicate a settlement date prior to A.D. 1000, 1200, or other arbitrary age (Figure 13.4) and then evaluated according to the most probable scenario (Dye 2015).

The contributions of paleoenvironmental and statistical proxies have been instructive, but this approach should be recognized as making the best of a poor situation. Certainly, direct information would be preferable from actual archaeological site layers dated to the earliest settlement contexts. In this regard, a paleo-terrain approach (Carson 2014), as presented in prior chapters, can be applied in East Polynesia when searching for the locations and depths of ancient coastal landform surfaces that most likely had been targeted during the initial settlement period of A.D. 1000–1400.

At least a few instances of earliest East Polynesian settlements have been verified, thus providing hard data about their original locations, depth, and settings in relation to the modern conditions. These archaeological deposits now are found buried usually 60 cm or deeper beneath more recent coastal sedimentary units, and they tend to be found 30 m or farther landward from today's shorelines. The habitation layers were emplaced over beach ridges, berms, and other formations that had stabilized after A.D. 100 yet had transformed somewhat by A.D. 1000. Some of the best documented examples have been at Hanamiai in the Marquesas Islands (Rolett 1998), Anakena in Rapa Nui (Hunt and Lipo 2006), Wainiha in Kaua'i (Carson 2004), Kualoa in O'ahu (Carson and Athens 2007), Kawela in Moloka'i (Weisler et al. in press), and Kawaihae in leeward Hawai'i Island (Carson 2012c). Other sites potentially could be added to this list, although the excavation records and occasional renewed excavation testing have not yet been able to confirm early dating associated with specific cultural layers, such as at Waimanalo in O'ahu (Tuggle and Spriggs 2000). Otherwise in the Hawaiian Islands, purported early site collections have been reexamined and redated, with results of considerably more recent age postdating A.D. 1400 or even 1600 (e.g., Kahn et al. 2014; Mulrooney et al. 2014). All of the confirmed early settlement examples, however, were discovered in subsurface layers unrelated to the surface findings, and future research may yet seek similar kinds of subsurface layers in order to overcome the scarce record of the earliest settlement period.

Among the few confirmed early Hawaiian coastal habitation sites (Figure 13.5), each instance has been documented in a subsurface layer directly applicable for understanding the ancient context and, furthermore, for seeking additional site layers of the same age.

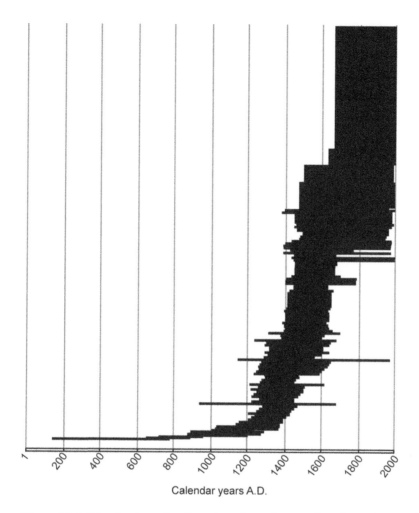

Figure 13.4 Distribution of radiocarbon dates from archaeological sites of Kaua'i, Hawaiian Islands. The weight of statistical probability increases steadily through time, notably after A.D. 1000–1200. Graphic is based on data from Carson (2005a, 2006a).

At Wainiha on the north shore of Kaua'i, people lived on an ancient beach surface that was about 30 m from the shoreline at A.D. 1040–1400, but today it has become buried 60–80 cm deep and stranded at more than 100 m from the modern shoreline (Figure 13.6). At Kualoa in O'ahu, another ancient beachfront habitation at A.D. 1040–1280 has become buried and stranded more than 500 m inland due to massive coastal enlargement (Figure 13.7). At Kawela in Moloka'i (see Figure 13.5), a present-day mounded surface contains internal layers that originally had formed over an ancient beach berm, including the deepest cultural layer as old as approximately A.D. 1100–1300 (Weisler et al. in press). At Kawaihae in leeward Hawai'i Island, people used two very narrow beach fringes along rocky coasts on opposite sides of a narrow inlet at approximately A.D. 1200–1400, but today this inlet has been infilled by more recent sediments along with a larger buildup of coastal sedimentary units (Figure 13.8).

314 *Expansion and intensification, A.D. 1000 through 1800*

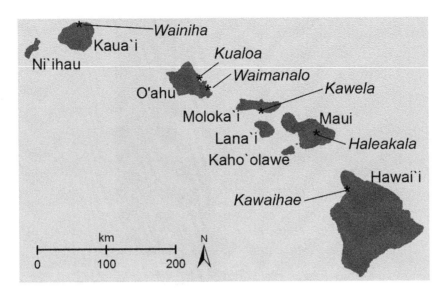

Figure 13.5 Locations of known early Hawaiian sites. Graphic is based on information from Carson (2004).

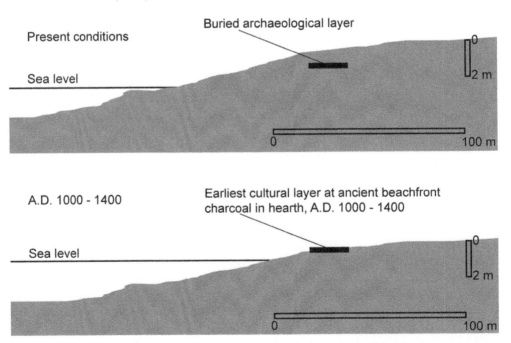

Figure 13.6 Wainiha Beach profile chronology. Graphic is based on information from Carson (2004).

Given that a time frame of A.D. 1000–1400 was not too radically different from today's conditions, the site layers of this period, in theory, should be detectable by observing present-day settings and accounting for the accumulation of sedimentary units. As noted, key information is already available about the positions and depths of buried layers that have become covered by more recent formations of accretional and expanded coastal

Expansion and intensification, A.D. 1000 through 1800 315

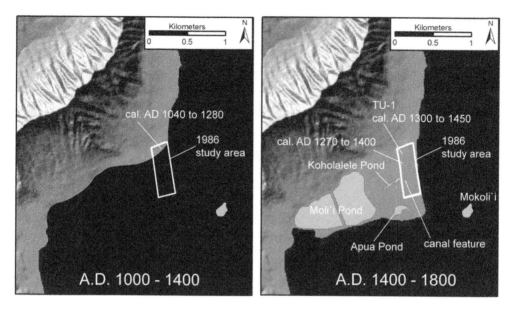

Figure 13.7 Kualoa plan map chronology. Graphic is adapted from Carson and Athens (2007).

plains within the last several centuries. Of additional concern, the time range of A.D. 1000–1300 may have brought a slightly higher sea level due to warmer global climate of the Little Climatic Optimum (LCO) that released more water from ice sheets melted into the world's oceans, thereby directly affecting the shapes of beaches during the earliest settlement in East Polynesia. Potentially, superficial indications of these older coastal sites may be identified as slightly mounded or ridged portions of the new land surfaces that have formed over ancient beach berms or ridges that once existed during the conditions of different sea level and coastal ecology prior to A.D. 1300.

These proposals of how to identify early settlement sites in East Polynesia may have been understood implicitly by many researchers, yet so far, no attempt has been made for a systematic search. Realistically, such a search today would need to contend with the fact that modern housing, roads, and other constructions already occupy the most likely areas of finding these oldest sites. Additionally, a large effort of labor and funding would need to be expended for digging through deep deposits in numerous locations, with no guarantee whatsoever of actually finding intact archaeological layers. Even with those practical constraints, new discoveries may be expected in the near future that will add to the information as presented here. At the time of preparing this book's second edition, however, no such new findings have been reported.

Generally in East Polynesia, the known site layers of A.D. 1000–1400 are restricted to a few localities in subsurface contexts of coastal zones, whereas abundant sites postdating A.D. 1400 are found throughout coastal and inland areas in association with surface-visible stonework ruins. The earlier sites therefore have been outnumbered and arguably underrepresented, while considerably more knowledge has been available about the later sites. The later-aged sites, especially after A.D. 1600, can be linked with vastly informative ethnohistorical knowledge and traditions, further corroborated by the profuse amounts of historical documentation as popularized with the voyages of Captain James Cook and others since the late 1700s. The older site contexts of A.D. 1000–1400 have been viewed as

316 *Expansion and intensification, A.D. 1000 through 1800*

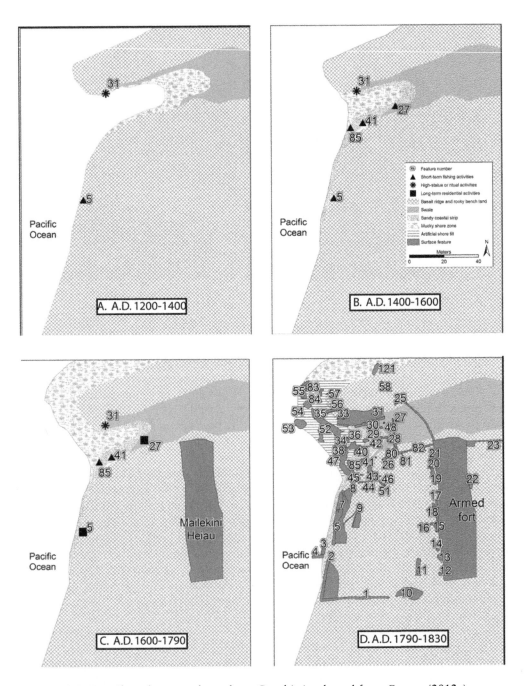

Figure 13.8 Kawaihae plan map chronology. Graphic is adapted from Carson (2012c).

"archaic," such that some of the forms and styles of fishing gear, food pounders, personal adornments, and other artifacts did not survive into the later ethnohistorical records.

The reality of sparse evidence of earliest East Polynesian settlement could be interpreted as starting around A.D. 1000 or perhaps most cautiously as starting at some point within the range of A.D. 1000 through 1400. An irresponsible view, however, would suggest that East Polynesian settlement occurred closer to A.D. 1400, and then the probability ranges of the radiocarbon dates of A.D. 1000–1400 could be pushed through statistical modeling to cluster closer to A.D. 1400. An equally irresponsible view would claim that East Polynesian settlement occurred prior to A.D. 1000 with little or no realistic opportunity to find the preserved evidence. Both of those proposals would misrepresent the factual evidence.

Given the paucity of the earliest dating results, anyone can cast doubt on radiocarbon dates prior to A.D. 1400 that appear to be "too old" or "anomalous," simply because they are few in number when compared with the corpus of later-dated site layers. Critics can point to the varieties of possible ways for a radiocarbon date to produce an older result, such as due to taxonomically unidentified charcoal of potentially old wood, unknown measurement of marine reservoir effect in marine shell samples, lack of corroborating dating samples, and other criteria. Importantly, these possibilities are rarely, if ever, proven, but rather they can be raised as cautions against accepting the older dating measurements. Similar argumentative devices tend to be forgotten in regards to dating results that appear to be "too young," and later-aged sites do not attract much scrutiny anyway.

Regardless of using terms like "chronometric hygiene," ultimately, all critical reviews of island-wide and region-wide radiocarbon dates do not actually prove or explain anything. Rather, they depend on the information already collected from prior excavations, and at best they illustrate overall trends and patterns with more clarity than might have been recognized previously. Indeed, most of the radiocarbon compilations so far have concluded that the first centuries of island settlement were poorly represented and thus vulnerable to misinterpretation. In one example, a compendium of radiocarbon dates from Kaua'i (Figure 13.9) showed scant evidence in the range of A.D. 1000 through 1400, as compared to overwhelmingly abundant dating results thereafter (Carson 2005a, 2006a). A similar scenario was noticed in Rapa Nui (Easter Island), confirming sparse cultural presence around A.D. 1000, followed by an extraordinary increase in site dating around A.D. 1400 (Mulrooney 2013).

While accepting a consensus of a "short chronology" in East Polynesia, issues of population growth and the later stages of neighbor-island and within-island movements must have occurred within time frames postdating settlement at A.D. 1000. In theory, the rates of population growth can be inferred by the numbers and sizes of habitation sites dating to specific time periods. Following the initial expansive movements of island settlement episodes, later descendant populations engaged in further expansive growth. As populations increased, some people needed to move into new locations of neighboring islands or different parts of the same islands, and eventually some groups moved to occupy even the most marginal ecological zones. No matter how reasonable these scenarios may be, they tend to lack tangible supporting data from the older ages that have been underrepresented, and instead they need to be inferred primarily from the later-aged sites postdating the presumed period of population growth and expansion.

Throughout East Polynesia, but especially evident in the Hawaiian Islands, island-wide chronologies show very few sites prior to A.D. 1400, compared to nearly all postdating this time, which perhaps suggests population growth needing yet closer scrutiny. This chronological pattern resulted in large part from an overrepresentation of later-dated

318 *Expansion and intensification, A.D. 1000 through 1800*

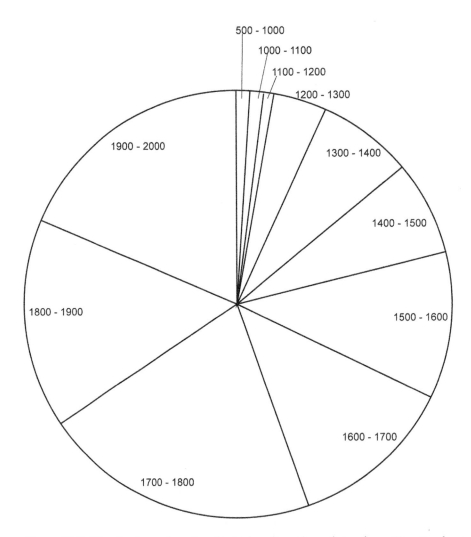

Figure 13.9 Distribution of archaeological radiocarbon dates from Kaua'i, shown as pie-slice percentage in 100-year increments. The overall probability becomes larger through time, with most probable habitation established by A.D. 1200–1300. Graphic is based on data from Carson (2005a).

sites that are conveniently surface-accessible today, although it does reflect at least some degree of a real population growth. In any case, the later sites consisted of larger-sized and longer-lasting stonework structures, and often, no older cultural layers are found beneath the surface-related materials. The older pre–A.D 1400 site layers have been found only rarely, but enough information is available to depict those site contexts in coastal zones slightly different from today's conditions.

Based on practicalities of resource zones, theoretically, the earliest settlements would have targeted wet windward areas, followed by later usage of dry leeward areas. So far, not enough information is available from earlier periods to confirm or deny these views, and at least a few contradicting examples are known. One such exception was documented at

Hanamiai in the Marquesas Islands (Rolett 1998), and another was reported at Kawaihae in Hawai'i Island (Carson 2012c). Both of these sites were situated in definite dry leeward locales but with access to localized freshwater sources sufficient for small groups. Also important for early settlement sites, leeward sides of islands were easier for canoe landings and launchings. Many islands do not even possess such strongly differentiated wet-versus-dry zonation, where instead the preferences of site settlement may have depended more on the availability of fresh water in accessible lenses and cave openings, the direction of prevailing winds for sailing, and the cultural perceptions of coastal ecological habitats.

Regarding the pace of expansion into marginal areas of an island, one instructive example comes from the archaeological sequence in alpine and subalpine zones of Haleakalā (Figure 13.10) atop Maui Island (Carson and Mintmier 2006a, 2006b). At a collection of sites at 2030 through 3030 m elevation above sea level (Figure 13.11), people could not have lived year-round in regular habitations, but rather they must have engaged in sets of short-term activities with imported supplies of food and fresh water. In the highest elevations of the alpine zone, crops cannot be grown, and no sources of fresh water are available. Nevertheless, as early as A.D. 1200–1400, people visited in this inhospitable setting repeatedly while camping at caves (Figure 13.12), hunting birds (Figure 13.13), obtaining high-quality basalt from a quarry source (Figure 13.14), following stone cairn-marked trails (Figure 13.15), and performing ritual ceremonies at stone-filled platforms along the rim of the volcanic crater (see Figure 12.4). After A.D. 1400, these and other activities intensified with more numerous sites in evidence, along with a large open-air (non-cave) campsite possibly servicing as a military outpost at a strategic island-crossing location (Figures 13.16 and 13.17).

The archaeological sequence at Haleakalā verifies that people were using marginal resource areas as early as A.D. 1200–1400, very shortly after the oldest proposed Hawaiian settlement dating about A.D. 1000. Later, people intensified their use of this marginal area, primarily after A.D. 1400, consistent with the archipelago-wide trends. Although regular habitation was not possible in the alpine zone, the intensified cultural use of such an inhospitable area may be viewed as part of a larger pattern of people using more marginal resource zones after A.D. 1400.

Among the last places ever inhabited in the Pacific, Aotearoa ("long white cloud"), also known as New Zealand, was settled by Polynesian groups about A.D. 1300 (Wilmshurst et al. 2008). For the first time, Polynesians settled into a temperate climate zone, with unique challenges of adapting to this environment (see Figure 2.10). This particular settlement expansion was enabled by importing sweet potatoes that could grow well in the cool temperatures that otherwise were unsuitable for the usual Polynesian tropical and subtropical crops. Certain varieties of taro and yams could be cultivated in the warmer parts of the North Island of Aotearoa, while the South Island proved to be too cold for those

Figure 13.10 View of Haleakalā crater, Maui.

320 *Expansion and intensification, A.D. 1000 through 1800*

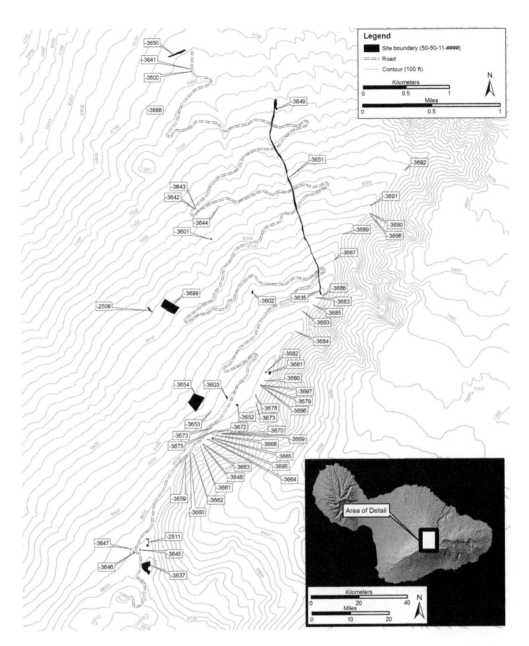

Figure 13.11 Map of site distribution at Haleakalā summit, Maui. Graphic is adapted from Carson and Mintmier (2006a).

crops other than the resilient sweet potato. At the same time, large flightless birds such as the *moa* (taxonomic order Dinornithiformes) provided ample protein and evidently were easy to hunt (Figure 13.18), as seen in the records of mass-killing sites and rapid depopulation (Anderson 1989).

Aotearoa presented marvels in its size, diversity, and range of resources and conditions not known anywhere else in Polynesia. These aspects of the environment may have

Expansion and intensification, A.D. 1000 through 1800 321

Figure 13.12 Example of a cave campsite at Haleakalā, Maui, during excavation. Scale bar is in 20 cm increments.

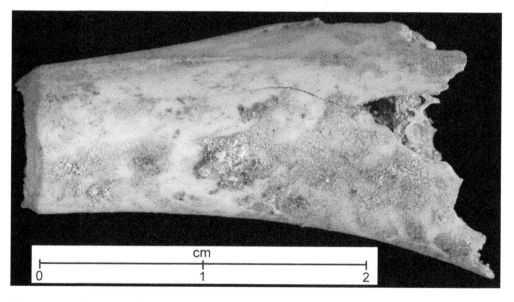

Figure 13.13 Example of bird bone with butchering or other artificial mark from Haleakalā, Maui.

Figure 13.14 Example of basalt flake chipping debris at Haleakalā, Maui. Scale bar is in 20 cm increments.

Figure 13.15 Stacked-stone cairns at Haleakalā, Maui. Scale bar is in 20 cm increments.

Expansion and intensification, A.D. 1000 through 1800   323

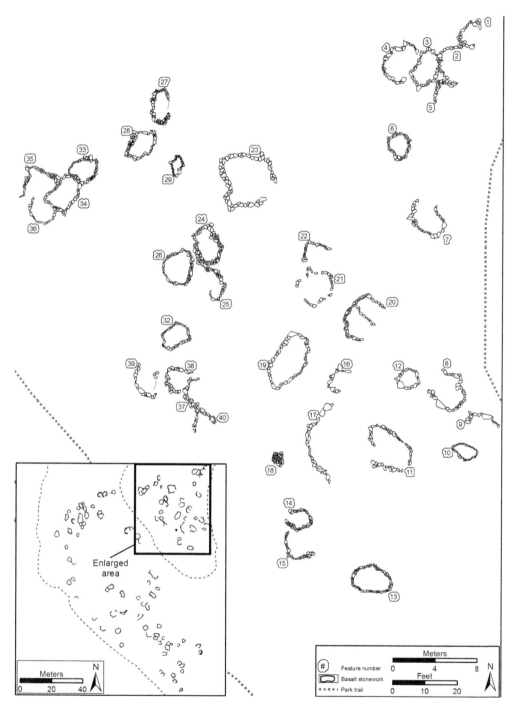

Figure 13.16 Map of stone-ringed campsite complex at Haleakalā, Maui. Graphic is adapted from Carson and Mintmier (2006a).

Figure 13.17 Example of stone-ringed campsite feature at Haleakalā, Maui, during excavation. Scale bar is in 20 cm increments.

been viewed more as attractive opportunities than as the daunting obstacles that may be implied when portraying Polynesian settlement here as overcoming the cool to cold conditions. Large river valleys offered reliable water supplies, and they supported an impressive biomass of plants and dozens of species of birds. Seashores were attractive for their abundance of shellfish, more birds, access to fishing zones, and hunting of seals and sea lions. Additionally, the coasts supported healthy populations of abalone (*Haliotis* spp.), useful for their meat and for their nacreous shells, either unknown or exceptionally rare in other islands of Remote Oceania. Precious greenstone (nephrite or "jade") could be found in certain parts of this ancient continental land mass of Gondwana origins.

The successful settlement of Aotearoa involved at least two major adaptations in Polynesian subsistence economy, with further effects in the local natural and cultural history.

- First was an adjustment to the local climate and seasonality, such as that seen in a reliance mostly on sweet potatoes for the bulk of carbohydrates and calories.
- Second was a shift to engage in more hunting and gathering than had occurred during the few immediately preceding centuries in other parts of Polynesia, most notably in this case while taking advantage of the numbers of large birds and sea mammals in Aotearoa (Smith 1985, 2004).

Expansion and intensification, A.D. 1000 through 1800 325

Figure 13.18 Silhouette model of large flightless *moa* bird of New Zealand, with hunter for relative scale.

Another unusual adaptation in Aotearoa entailed the development of communication networks over land, as compared to the usual reliance on coastal and sea-crossing routes throughout most of Polynesia and Pacific Oceania generally. Richard Walter (1988) outlined how the seasonal weather patterns and environmental conditions made canoe and sailing voyages less reliable, more risky, and sometimes impossible, while overland routes could be faster and more accommodating year-round, especially in the North Island. Overland communications networks very likely enhanced the ability to establish residential sites in far inland settings and to develop trading partnerships between groups living in different ecological zones. Additionally, overseas travels and contacts may have been less frequent than in other Polynesian islands, thus leading to stronger traditions of local intergroup relations rather than external sea-crossing networks.

The unique developments in Aotearoa influenced the land-use patterns and the process of converting the immense landforms into an inhabited landscape. Site locales prior to A.D. 1500 were more geographically widespread, especially in the colder areas of the South Island, during the time range when people were hunting appreciable numbers of the large flightless *moa* and other birds that became massively depopulated in later centuries.

During those later periods with less bird hunting opportunities, most but not all of the habitation sites were concentrated farther north in warmer places.

Another form of settlement expansion may be noted in the Mariana Islands after A.D. 1000. Although people had been living at sites in the larger southern-arc islands since at least 1500 B.C. and gradually spreading into more lands continually through time, a profound change occurred about A.D. 1000 with notably widespread expansion as attested in numerous *latte* village complexes (Carson 2012d). The material signature of the *latte* period entailed the creation of formalized villages and territories throughout the coastal and inland zones of all islands in the southern arc and for the first time in the northern arc of the Marianas. The northern-arc islands lack natural water sources, and they so far have yielded no evidence at all of any kind of human settlement prior to A.D. 1000. Limited camping and resource-gathering visits likely occurred on repeated occasions, but materially traceable settlement in the northern-arc islands apparently did not occur until after the initiation of the *latte* period. Chapter 12 offers more information about the *latte* sites of the Marianas.

Among the more spectacular expansions to the limits of the island world were the artificial constructions of islands or islets. In Pacific Oceania, these artificial constructions were typically in shallow water, close to the shorelines of natural islands. They consisted of soil and rubble, usually with deliberate plant growth for increased stability, and they often supported stonework house foundations or other structures (Nunn 2021: 294–295). Most notable was the canal-accessible complex of artificially raised features at Nan Madol in Pohnpei (see Figures 12.39 and 12.40), dated around A.D. 1200 (Athens 2007; McCoy et al. 2016). Several other examples have been at smaller scales of individual foundations for houses or clusters, and they often have been undated by archaeological layers while known through ethnohistories in parts of Micronesia, Melanesia, and Polynesia (Bryant-Tokalau 2011). The contexts appear to postdate about A.D. 1000, and many cases could be much later.

The artificial islands reflect a context of people exploring the extremes of inhabiting Pacific Oceania, possibly prompted by stress due to changing climate, sea level, or population density. Some sites, such as at Nan Madol in Pohnpei, were associated with religious beliefs and political groups, likely connected with the ability to predict high versus low tidal access conditions. Other sites have been linked with ethnohistories of people preferring to live with the mosquito-free sea breeze or preferring to reserve the limited natural island terrain for agricultural fields without consuming this precious land for a house (Nunn 2021: 295).

Field systems

Intensive field systems most importantly increase the amount of food produced per unit of land area, and some strategies can enhance the ability to continue using a parcel of land continually with shortened or less frequent fallow periods. These kinds of systems were developed most spectacularly in the Hawaiian Islands and a number of places in Polynesia, each independently after A.D. 1400 (Kirch and Lepofsky 1993), as well as in New Caledonia primarily after A.D. 1000 (Sand 2002). Meanwhile, most island communities engaged in variable degrees of managed forests with mixed informal growing of tree and root-tuber crops. Often, families managed their gardens and orchards in various land parcels, in total creating extensively cultivated landscapes as seen in Samoa (Carson 2006b), but the spatially widespread usage of the land did not necessarily constitute an intensification of food production per unit of land area as seen in irrigated pond fields or high-density rain-fed mound complexes.

People potentially could grow varied crops in almost any setting with some degree of success, but the ability to create intensified field systems with optimal edible yields would require focusing on the particular crops most suitable for a given area's soil properties, temperature regime, rainfall pattern, and other conditions. Land management traditions, in theory, could account for large territories and whole ecosystems with several internally defined zones or subzones, but the level of intensity could vary considerably within each of the recognized zones or subzones. In some but not all cases, population growth eventually exceeded the ability of the land to provide enough food for the resident population, thereby forcing people to intensify their land-use practice if they did not have any remaining options of expanding into new lands. Evidently, this threshold was crossed only rarely in Pacific Oceania as a whole, yet the known examples have resulted in vastly impressive archaeological signatures. In a large-scale view, the cases of non-intensive production are just as revealing, if not more informative, than the instances of intensive field systems.

Managed forests, horticultural gardening, and other non-intensive land-use practices overall have characterized most food production throughout time and across Pacific Oceania. These operations occurred at a family level or community level not necessarily involving political control or organization of multiple participating groups. Each land parcel potentially can be related to the individual person, household, family lineage, or multifamily grouping responsible for its management. The managing units could be hierarchical or egalitarian, with variable possible configurations. In any case, the potential existed for someone to seize control of the lands or of the food being produced from those lands, although it may not have happened as an overt political maneuver.

An example in the Mariana Islands can illustrate spatially extensive but non-intensified land management. Communities since 1500 B.C. gradually had expanded to inhabit more total land (Figure 13.19), yet they consistently engaged in low-labor input strategies of forest management and informal gardens. Even after A.D. 1000, when populations had expanded to occupy all of the islands, the Marianas archaeological landscape consisted of formalized villages surrounded by lands lacking any intensive field systems yet traditionally used for orchards, family gardens, hunting of birds and bats, and other low-intensity and low-impact resource usage.

A similar example of traditional land-use pattern is seen in Samoa. The Samoan landscape consists of innumerable parcels of land, each belonging to a family collective lineage, often divided and subdivided in order to accommodate each participating household. Access to a land parcel, in theory, is regulated by a family leader or chief of a lineage group, and individual people often attend to orchards and gardens in numerous separate places. Stacked-stone boundary fences or walls demonstrate the extent of land divisions and subdivisions (Figure 13.20), where people can choose to grow taro, yams, breadfruit, bananas, and other crops as well as raise pigs or chickens. Despite the formally demarcated territorial boundaries, the food production within each land parcel is not necessarily intensified as would be seen, for example, in Hawai'i with irrigated pond fields or high-density mound complexes.

At the time of this book's second edition, survey maps of cultivation-related features and field boundaries have become more efficient throughout the Pacific and indeed throughout the world, due to the ability of remote-sensing technologies to gather high-resolution data through thick forest cover. Previously, traditional on-the-ground surveys have been possible in some but not all areas, and now the remote-sensing options have allowed more thorough

328 *Expansion and intensification, A.D. 1000 through 1800*

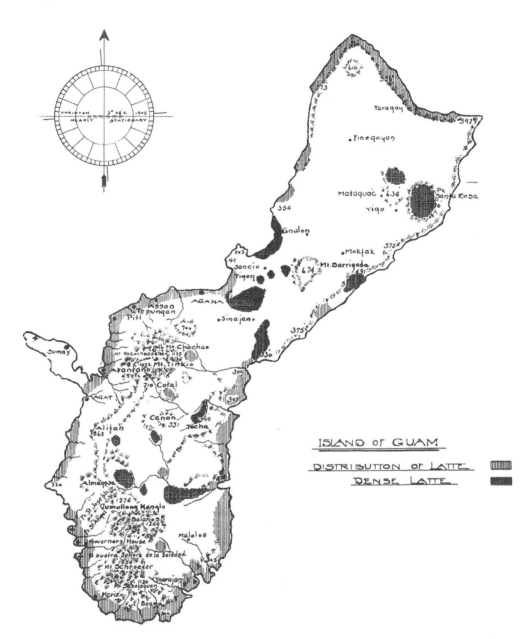

Figure 13.19 Guam island-wide settlement sites. Map is by Erik Reed (1955), modified from notes by Hans Hornbostel (1925), on file at the Micronesian Area Research Center, University of Guam.

coverage. In particular, surveys with airborne light detection and ranging (LiDAR) have revealed more examples of the cultivated landscapes in parts of Samoa (Jackmond et al. 2019) and of Pohnpei (Comer et al. 2019). In both the older and newer forms of surveys, ideally closer inspection and test excavations can obtain refined information about specific functions and associated time periods of the inferred cultivation activities.

Expansion and intensification, A.D. 1000 through 1800 329

Figure 13.20 Stacked-stone fence boundary in Tutuila, American Samoa. Scale bar is in 10 cm increments.

As in all parts of the world, Pacific Island farmers are intimately familiar with the optimal use of each of their ecological zones for growing different kinds of plants, even though they may not create formalized field systems with durable material structures such as irrigation channels, mounds, walls, and other constructions. People certainly are aware of their ecological zones, but these conditions do not always translate into strictly controlled or zonally defined field systems. Rather, some of the identifiable ecological zones may or may not be suitable for different kinds of intensification through the field systems that developed only in later periods and only in some island groups.

In Pacific Oceania, field systems often are categorized as wet versus dry adaptations. Wet and dry settings, by their nature, encourage differential strategies of land use, notably pronounced in high islands with rain shadows, but these conditions are not always so strongly influential in every case. Accordingly, the most substantial and formalized examples of wet versus dry field systems are found in the larger island masses with clear rainfall gradients, stream-cut valleys, and differential soil properties as in the Hawaiian Islands and in New Caledonia. The wet settings potentially can support intensive crop growth in pond fields serviced by irrigation channels, especially if streams or rivers are available as natural sources of flowing fresh water. The dry settings potentially can be transformed with high-density constructions of mounds and other features that retain and concentrate soil and nutrients for rain-fed crop growth.

In Southern Melanesia, wet and dry field systems developed in the ecologically diverse land mass of New Caledonia, primarily after A.D. 1000 in association with structured village territories (Sand 2002). As a broken piece of ancient Gondwana, New Caledonia's geology may be described as "continental," including rugged mountainous interior terrain with deep stream-cut valleys and enough tall mass to create a rain shadow effect of wet windward versus dry leeward sides of the island. In the wet zones and close to streams and rivers, irrigation systems feed high-intensity pond fields used primarily for growing taro but also for growing other crops in lesser amounts (Figure 13.21). In the dry zones of large, mostly plain-like landforms, people created elongate earthen mounds for growing yams made of piled earth 1–2 m in height and often more than 20 m in length, organized in high-density configurations (Figure 13.22). In the nearby coral formations of the Loyalty Islands, where cultivable lands were scarce and with very limited sedimentary units, the

330 *Expansion and intensification, A.D. 1000 through 1800*

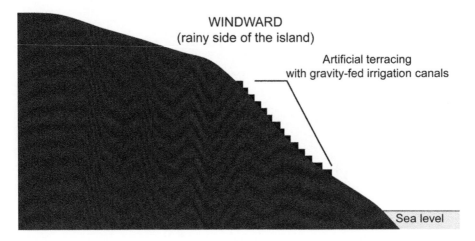

Figure 13.21 Schematic diagram of an irrigation field complex, New Caledonia.

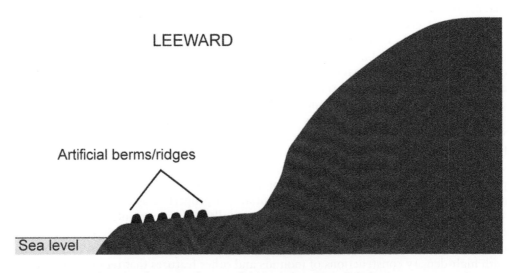

Figure 13.22 Schematic diagram of a yam field complex, New Caledonia.

yam-growing mounds traditionally have been much smaller piles about 15–30 cm in height and 80–120 cm in diameter (Figure 13.23), but they are maintained in extremely high density and with clearly marked property fencing (Figure 13.24). Some of these field systems may have started a few centuries prior to A.D. 1000, but their dominance of the landscape for the most part coincided with the establishment of formalized village structures and territories securely dated by radiocarbon and by associated pottery types after A.D. 1000.

Among the many irrigated pond field systems in the Hawaiian Islands, one case in particular has been well documented in the Halele'a District on the north shore of Kaua'i (Figure 13.25). The stream-cut valleys here are replete with irrigated terraces for growing taro, and they have been described as exemplary of the economic basis of complex

Figure 13.23 Yam field in Ouvéa, Loyalty Islands of New Caledonia.

Figure 13.24 Fencing border of yam field in Ouvéa, Loyalty Islands of New Caledonia.

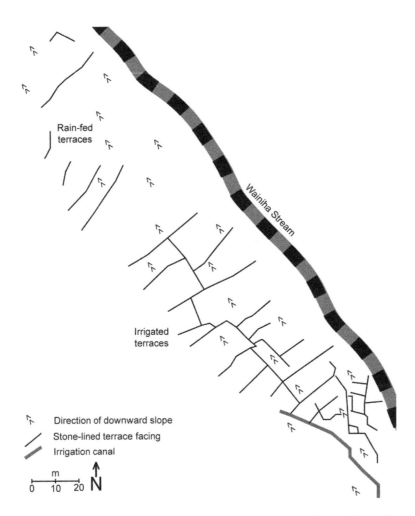

Figure 13.25 Map of agricultural sites in a portion of Wainiha Valley, Haleleʻa District of Kauaʻi, Hawaiian Islands. Graphic is adapted from Carson (2003).

chiefdoms (Earle 1978). The extensive transformation of the valley into a taro-producing landscape entirely postdated A.D. 1400 (Carson 2005b, 2006a). Beneath the constructions of taro fields, remnants of older cultural layers have revealed a qualitatively different and less intensive form of land use with scattered charcoal flecking, occasional hearth features, and little or no investment in long-lasting stonework architecture seen in the later periods (Carson 2003). The creation of larger-sized and longer-lasting stonework complexes throughout Haleleʻa postdated A.D. 1400 (Figure 13.26) and marked the beginning of a significantly different land-use pattern, population demography, and social context.

The archaeological sequence at Haleleʻa accords well with tales of the *Mū* people of this particular part of Kauaʻi but not known elsewhere in the Hawaiian Islands, which refer to "times when (or places where) bananas and other tree crops were more important in a local diet and landscape that otherwise came to be dominated by taro and other root crops" (Carson 2003: 100). The *Mū* or the *Mū ʻai maiʻa* ("banana-eating *Mū*") are remembered in local traditions as the older inhabitants prior to the more recent ethnohistoric contexts. Furthermore, Kauaʻi is known for its unique forms of stone food-pounder artifacts

Expansion and intensification, A.D. 1000 through 1800   333

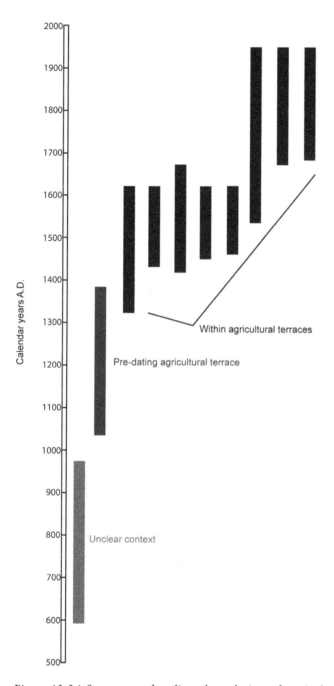

Figure 13.26 Summary of radiocarbon dating of agricultural sites in Halele'a District of Kaua'i, Hawaiian Islands. Graphic is based on data from Carson (2006a).

with "stirrup" shapes and other characteristics (McElroy 2004) not seen in other of the Hawaiian Islands and thus suggesting a different use than taro-pounding documented extensively in the Hawaiian record outside Kaua'i (Figure 13.27). Indeed, throughout the Hawaiian ancestral homeland region of Central East Polynesia, food pounders were (and still are) used for making breadfruit paste (Figure 13.28), and the paste known as *poi* traditionally has referred to breadfruit in all of these islands except in Hawai'i where it refers to taro paste today.

Concurrently with the irrigated pond field systems, Hawaiian dryland rain-fed complexes developed in high-density fields primarily after A.D. 1400. The classic example is seen in the Kona Field System of leeward Hawai'i Island (Figure 13.29), where the geologically young volcanic terrain lacks stream-cut valleys. The broad slopes of the Kona District are situated in a rain shadow zone, with very little rainfall annually at the coast, yet the rainfall gradient increases steadily in accordance with elevation and distance from the coast moving upland into rainier zones toward the mountainous island interior. Soil development overall is very weak, and thin and rocky silts are found in scattered pockets over rough volcanic bedrock. This landscape traditionally is regarded as consisting of four cultivation zones, wherein each zone is defined primarily by its elevation and rainfall as the essential determining factors for crop growth.

The four ecologically defined cultivation zones in the Kona District often are viewed as interrelated components of a traditional settlement system, wherein each zone, in theory, could contribute its own resources toward the larger community. The four zones have been described according to ethnohistorical information (Handy and Handy 1972; Kelly 1983; Major 2001: 25–28; Newman 1970), arranged from the coast to the upland interior.

- The *kula* zone nearest the coast was used mostly for growing sweet potatoes in lowland areas with less than 1000 mm mean annual rainfall.
- The *kalu'ulu* zone for the most part supported growth of breadfruit trees at elevations receiving between 1000 and 1400 mm mean annual rainfall.
- The *'apa'a* zone was suited for dryland (rain-fed) taro planted where mean annual rainfall ranged 1400 to 2000 mm.
- The *'auma'u* zone was known for cultivation of bananas and assorted useful trees in upland forests with mean annual rainfall in excess of 2000 mm.

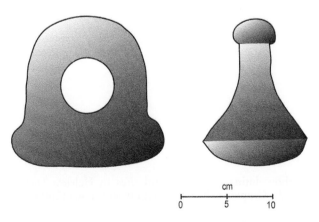

Figure 13.27 Varieties of food pounders in Kaua'i, Hawaiian Islands.

Figure 13.28 Pounding breadfruit paste in Tahuata, Marquesas Islands, 1997.

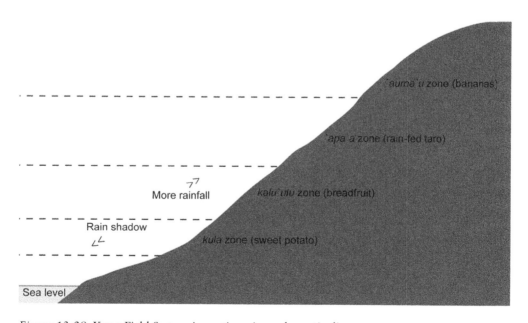

Figure 13.29 Kona Field System in section view schematic diagram.

336 *Expansion and intensification, A.D. 1000 through 1800*

Each of these ecological zones in the Kona District entails its own natural conditions and opportunities for intensification. The evidence of intensified dryland cultivation features has been documented most abundantly in the lower elevations nearest to the coast within the *kula* and *kaluʻulu* zones, where population densities were apparently the greatest according to the distributions of habitation site complexes. The dryland features consisted of stacked-stone mounds as naturally mulched planting areas, stone pilings as retaining faces along natural slope edges, small rings of stones piled around tree trunks, larger rings or enclosures of stacked stones that defined specific garden areas, and even larger stone-piled fences or walls that defined larger field plots (Figure 13.30).

Overall in the Kona District, both habitation sites and cultivation fields proliferated after A.D. 1400, where extremely sparse evidence so far can verify cultural use of this dry and rocky landscape prior to A.D. 1400. This timing coincided with the rise to power of land-controlling and conquest-driven chiefs, as attested in genealogical reckoning (Cordy 2000). In some views, the dryland zones became the most critical areas for chiefs to gain power over large collections of land and people, where these chiefs amassed expansive territories after A.D. 1400 and increasingly engaged in competitive warfare after 1600

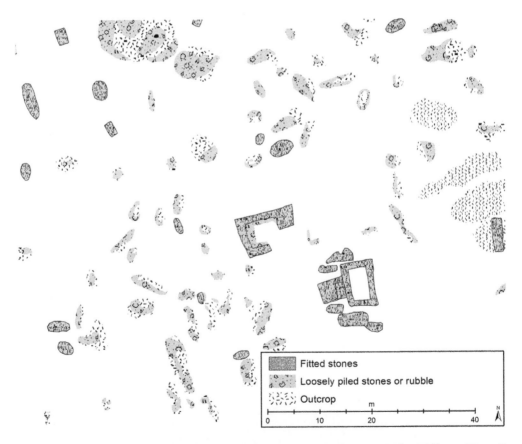

Figure 13.30 Portion of map of surface-visible stonework ruins at Kiʻilae Village, Hawaiʻi Island, incorporating dryland cultivation features among a habitation complex. Graphic is adapted from Carson et al. (2004).

(Cordy 2004). Traditionally, the Hawaiian chiefs originally from dryland areas were the most fiercely involved in seizing and "eating" the lands, whole districts, and even entire islands through warfare and compulsory tribute, epitomized in Kamehameha's interisland conquest during the late 1700s.

Animal foods

While crop production provided the most effective means of increasing annual yields of calories and nutrition, options were limited for intensifying animal food products. Pigs, dogs, and chickens were among the few domesticated animals in the Pacific that certainly contributed reliable amounts of protein yet could not compare with the potential of fish and shellfish resources. In theory, marked increase in animal bones could reflect intensification, but the situation is complicated by the fact that pigs in particular were regarded as luxury foods and signs of prestige in many island societies, quite different from practical dietary fulfillment. Meanwhile, depopulation of native birds and bats may be viewed as a result of intensified resource targeting, in many cases with an initial impact immediately at first human settlement but then followed by later periods of increasing effects.

Undoubtedly in island settings, fish and shellfish provide the most long-term reliability of animal food protein. Even through periods of coastal instability and transforming ecologies, fish and shellfish have contributed significantly in island diets. Technological developments of fishing gear, netting, and basket traps can act as forms of intensifying fishing, but artificial fish trap constructions constitute the most dramatic forms of intensification. Walled fishponds are known most clearly in Hawai'i and dated mostly after A.D. 1400 (Figure 13.31). Fish weirs are well known in Yap (Jeffery and Pitmag 2010), although not dated but associated with oral histories suggestive of the last few centuries (Figure 13.32).

Hawaiian fishponds almost all postdated A.D. 1400, with just a few possible radiocarbon dates extending as early as A.D. 1300 (Carson 2005c; Kikuchi 1976). The fishponds were made with stacked-stone walls enclosing shallow water along shorelines, with wooden gates that could be lifted to allow fish to enter during high tide and then lowered to trap the fish inside the pond during low tide. In some cases, watchtowers were constructed for the caretakers. One of the largest fishponds can be seen at 'Alekoko in Kaua'i (Figure 13.33). About 850 m long, it was attested by local traditions to be constructed by mythical small-statured *menehune* people and left unfinished at the end of their overnight labor (Wichman 1997: 27–32). According to a study of sediments at the bottom of the fishpond, an enclosed artificial pond environment began here about A.D. 1400 or perhaps a few decades earlier (Burney 2002).

Interaction and exchange networks

In addition to food production, trade and exchange networks can extend the reach of a group's economy, and these activities often follow the principles of expansion and intensification as seen in land-use patterns. Polished adzes, stone money discs, and other items can be traced to known geological formations and thus illustrate the geographic configuration of their mobilization during different time intervals. Depending on how much source-identifiable material is found within each time period, the results potentially can illustrate processes of expansion and intensification.

Volcanic islands of Polynesia naturally contain formations of basalt and volcanic glass that are ideal for toolmaking, as well as ideal for geochemical tracing of their origins.

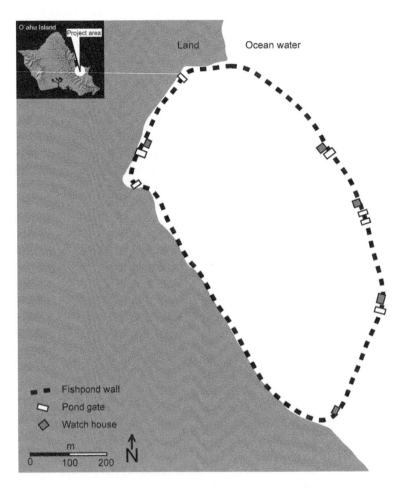

Figure 13.31 Map of Heʻeia Fishpond in Oʻahu, Hawaiian Islands.

X-ray fluorescence (XRF) analysis in particular has supported maps of the distributions of these artifacts that happen to constitute the major material categories in East Polynesia where pottery is famously absent. Certain geological sources were renowned for their quality, where large-scale quarries and workshops can be found, such as at Haleakalā in Maui (Mintmier et al. 2012), Mauna Kea in Hawaiʻi (Mills et al. 2008), Vitaria in Rurutu (Rolett et al. 2015), Tatagamatau in Samoa (Clark et al. 1997), and many others (Weisler 1997). In all of these instances, the long-distance transported adzes are found in contexts after A.D. 1000, and the evidence is most abundant after A.D. 1400.

Basalt adze quarries and workshops can be identified at varied scales from households to industrial complexes in terms of the acquisition of raw materials, initial tool shaping, polishing and sharpening, possible export, and ongoing maintenance. Some quarries contain a few cubic m of flaking debris and not much else. Others contain tons of flaking debris, spatially separated work stations, and outlying areas of supporting campsites and occasionally fortifications.

The larger industrial-scale complexes tend to be associated with the more fine-grained basalts that were traded over long distances. Serious investments in the quarrying activity,

Expansion and intensification, A.D. 1000 through 1800   339

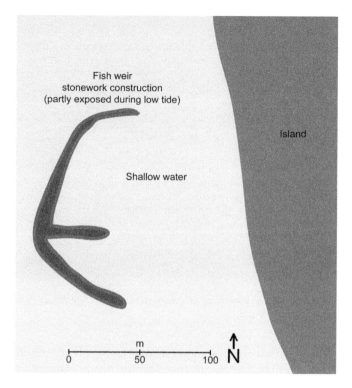

Figure 13.32 Example of fish weir in Yap.

Figure 13.33 View of 'Alekoko Fishpond in Kaua'i, Hawaiian Islands.

Figure 13.34 View of *foʻaga* adze-grinding basins near coast in Tutuila, American Samoa. Machete provides scale reference.

defense, and trading economy all imply that the raw material was worth all of this effort. Further indicative of an industrial complex, separate task-specific work stations could reflect overarching organization, for instance, as seen in the high-density clusters of adze-grinding basins in Samoa, removed from the actual quarries and instead carved into rocky seashore formations with access to saltwater as a grit and coolant (Figure 13.34).

A household scale of labor is most clear in the daily maintenance features of polishing and sharpening stones that occur frequently at residential complexes. For instance, in the Marquesas Islands, most house foundations display their own grinding basin where each family was responsible for its own adze maintenance work (see Figure 12.11). Occasionally, only one or two of the households in a village contained such daily maintenance features, along with copious flaking debris, for instance, as seen in some Samoan villages (Figure 13.35) and suggestive of community specialists.

Basalt adzes potentially can act as items of prestige (Figure 13.36), and they are easily portable in networks at all geographic scales within and between islands. The prestige factor is noticed especially in Polynesia, where the concept of *mana* typically refers to the potency of someone or something. The potency of an adze could apply to the raw material source, to the work of a master adze crafting specialist, and to the intended use in a specially recognized act such as the ceremonial first carving of a canoe. Further power or respect is acknowledged for objects that have traveled a long distance from a known high-quality source.

Beginning about A.D. 1400, basalt adze industries showed their most intensive production, as well as their most geographically extensive networks, linking numerous sites across Polynesia. This timing coincided with the region-wide evidence of people having expanded to live in the limits of their available environments and beginning to intensify their usage of those environments. In this context, overseas networks offered a means to extend island economies, meanwhile underwriting claims of status or strengthening social and political alliances.

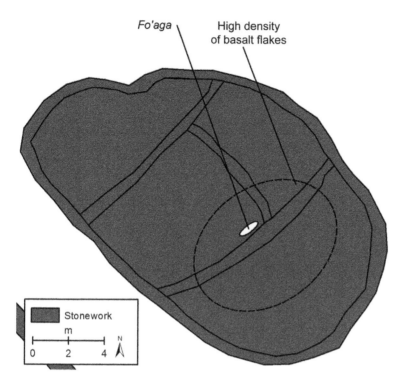

Figure 13.35 Map of house foundation with *fo'aga* adze-grinding basin and adze-working debris in Tutuila, American Samoa. Graphic is adapted from Carson (2005d).

Adzes and other commodities were not necessarily items of economic trade per se, but rather they were involved in broader contexts of interaction and exchange. Ethnographic and historical records frequently refer to gifts and presentations of woven mats, decorated bark cloth, food, and social performance. Additionally, among island societies with strong traditions of long-distance seafaring, opportunities were numerous for interisland networking and other encounters, including economic trade as just one of the activities.

Whether for trade or for other purposes, networks can increase the productivity and growth of societies with limited land, biomass, and other resources. Especially for people living in atolls and other small and vulnerable islands, overseas networks can provide critical supplements beyond the capacity of what their islands can offer. This potential follows the practical use of overseas contacts and alliances for securing relief from the effects of severe tropical storms, droughts, poor crop yields, warfare, and other catastrophic events.

Complex networking systems have operated in many parts of Pacific Oceania, best known historically in the islands of Micronesia. While documented in written and oral histories, these networks have shown only limited archaeological parallels due to the non-durable nature of many of the mobilized objects. Micronesia is famous for a formalized circulation of tribute known as *sawei* (Figure 13.37), wherein items of prestige were circulated from one community to another in a complicated interisland network (Descantes 2005; Descantes et al. 2002; Sudo 1996). So far in Micronesia, items of translocated pottery have been dated as early as A.D. 1400 (Descantes et al. 2004). Other specially prized objects of stone money discs or *rai* were quarried in Palau and transported to Yap

342 *Expansion and intensification, A.D. 1000 through 1800*

Figure 13.36 Collection of basalt adzes, presented by Barsinas family in Tahuata, Marquesas Islands, 1997, prior to entering into exhibit in the Tahuata Museum.

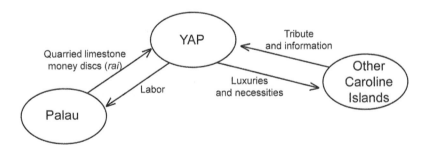

Figure 13.37 Generalized model of the *sawei* exchange network.

(Figure 13.38; see also Figure 12.16), and the known quarries have been associated with dates no earlier than A.D. 1400–1600 (Fitzpatrick 2002).

Micronesian contacts apparently extended into Melanesia as well. Examples are seen in shared oral traditions and localized creation of Micronesian styles of stonework features within Melanesia (Glenn Summerhayes, personal communication, 2022). Furthermore, a stone adze was found in Pohnpei of Micronesia that came from a geological source in Melanesia (Nagaoka and Sheppard 2023).

Expansion and intensification, A.D. *1000 through 1800* 343

Figure 13.38 Yap chief standing with *rai*. Image is from the Georg Fritz collection, approximately 1899–1911, curated at the Micronesian Area Research Center, University of Guam.

A similar context of overseas contacts may apply to the oral traditions of Tongan involvement in overseas raiding and trading adventures in neighboring islands of Fiji and Samoa, linked with genealogical reckoning about a Tongan maritime empire (Campbell 2001). Additionally, within the range of ethnohistorical traditions, people had constructed new hillforts and defensive walls in Fiji and in Samoa (Best 1993). Simultaneously, increased numbers of overseas-transported adzes have been documented coming from geological sources in Samoa.

Population growth and climate change

Population growth definitely affected the rate and magnitude of expansion and intensification, but these processes were influenced by the level of food production, furthermore linked with issues of climate stability and other factors. As mentioned in Chapter 12, a period of overall climate stability at A.D. 1000 through 1300 contributed to food productivity and population growth, by extension encouraging expansion of groups into increasingly larger territories. After this "time of plenty" of the LCO, a shift into climatic instability at A.D. 1300 through 1850 by comparison was a "time of less" of the Little Ice Age (LIA), bringing potential stress to the populations that had grown dependent on their extensively inhabited landscapes for food production (Nunn et al. 2007).

Although a globally defined shift in climate conditions occurred about A.D. 1300, the effects in cultural terms were not manifested in material archaeological records until somewhat later, after a few generations of people had been adjusting to the unpredictable and generally unfavorable conditions of the LIA. In archaeological records, Pacific Oceanic societies cross-regionally experienced substantial population growth and expansion after A.D. 1000, and then different groups engaged in variable forms of competition and potential intensification of economic production after A.D. 1400. In the absence of knowing about the global climate trends, the archaeological patterns after A.D. 1400 could be interpreted as the outcomes of population growth and increasing conflicts at the limits of island carrying capacity, but in reality, the role of an unstable climate cannot be ignored.

Making and remaking chiefdoms

As presented in Chapter 12, permanent territories developed in formalized structures throughout Pacific Oceania after A.D. 1000, and descendant populations expanded and eventually intensified to levels creating complex political systems. Processes of expansion and emergent intensification resulted in variable ways of managing population density and diversity with complex economics, social relations, politics, and ideological beliefs. In some islands, after A.D. 1400 and with increasing intensity after A.D. 1600, competition and conflict reached critical levels of warring chiefs who held extreme power by divine right, who "ate the land" in Hawai'i, and who claimed maritime empires from bases in Tonga. In other islands, leaders exercised less radical control but with just as much, if not more, legitimate authority.

Scholars have wrestled with notions of how to define, classify, or even quantify the categories of chiefdoms and other kinds of polities in Pacific Oceania, in particular addressing how the political systems could have developed so differently in at least two ways.

- First, some leaders were bestowed with ultimate power and authority, often justified through religious beliefs, while others lived with little or no differentiation from the group.
- Second, island societies exhibit great variation in the numbers of levels or layers in leadership hierarchy, from single leaders to potentially dozens of pyramid rank-ordered leaders.

The balance of power and the numbers of hierarchical levels can be viewed as proxies of the degree of complexity in a political system, such that the exact formulation in any particular case can be matched against definitions of chiefdoms, states, or other types of polities. The logical problem, of course, is that the proposed definitions ultimately are self-fulfilling, for instance, when a "state" is defined as having land ownership, religious legitimization of authority, and at least two levels of hierarchy. According to these or similar criteria, almost any society in the world can be equated with a state. For instance, Patrick Kirch (2010b) argued for the in situ development of a state polity in the Hawaiian Kingdom, although this particular expression of a state differed qualitatively in its functioning, degree of power, internal levels of hierarchy, and layers of complexity when compared to other polities known as states of the Roman Empire, Han Dynasty, and others.

Definitional maneuvering has produced scholarly claims of state-level society in the historically known Hawaiian Kingdom and in a proposed Tongan Maritime Empire, furthermore stressing how these developments occurred in primary and self-contained contexts without external influence. As noted, the criteria of being a state, kingdom, or empire in these cases are satisfied by virtue of starting with terminological definitions that already fit with the situations that are being examined. As outlined by Hommon (2013), Hawaiian leaders operated within impressively powerful and complex political and ideological systems that could be called "states." Conventionally, political systems in the Pacific are known as "chiefdoms" in most areas, as "big man" societies in New Guinea and some parts of Melanesia, and occasionally other terms of locally specific meaning. In any case, the words in themselves need to be regarded as terms of convenience for discussion, and the precise meaning always needs to be interpreted critically.

In a cross-regional view, different political systems developed across Pacific Oceania in large part depending on the intensity of land use that created demands on the limited island resources and on social relationships. Complexities existed previously, but they escalated after the establishment of conditions of formalized village layouts, permanence of house burial traditions, monumental expressions, and rights of land use within defined territories after A.D. 1000. In many places, the identifiable territories contained stonework ruins of villages adjacent to large expanses of managed forests and informal household gardens, implying that the members of each village shared access to the varied resource zones of their total territory, possibly with demarcated subunits or patchworks of smaller land holdings. In a few places, however, the territorial units contained multiple residential complexes, often with permanently marked croplands and field systems reflecting hierarchical divisions and subdivisions of food-producing lands.

The cases of the most concentrated political power, such as in Hawai'i, correspond with the most intensified land use, as seen in complex field systems, walled fishponds, and manifestations of power in large monuments. These instances of intensification postdated A.D. 1400 and emerged only after a period of expansion, all following from older traditions of group usage of formalized territories that operated at least since A.D. 1000. The period of A.D. 1000 through 1400 therefore may be viewed as crucial for population growth and expansion and resulted in no further opportunities of expansion by A.D. 1400, when instead people needed to intensify their land-use patterns in increasing density.

The extremities of social complexity and political power in Hawai'i emerged from an ancestral Polynesian system shared with communities elsewhere and traceable at least to A.D. 1000, with uniquely localized Hawaiian characteristics beginning about A.D. 1400. As mentioned in Chapter 12, Hawai'i is the only place in Polynesia where the word 'aina (cognate of Proto Polynesian *kaainga*) has been applied to the land itself, whereas elsewhere, the cognates of this word consistently mean "family." This shift in the cultural role of the land (and of the family) must have occurred locally within the Hawaiian Islands. Hawaiian land tenure, as known historically and reflected in the post–A.D. 1400 archaeological landscape, was focused on the land as the source of food and providing for the people as well as the source of a chief's power. Hawaiian chiefs (*ali'i*) could gain status as the "chiefs who eat the land" (*ali'i 'ai 'aina*) or who eat the whole district (*ali'i 'ai moku*). Each food-producing land unit was called an *ahupua'a*, literally "pig altar," where the people (*kama'aina* or "children of the land") were required to pay tribute in the form of food (especially pigs as the most prestigious item) for high-ranking chiefs. Hawaiian chiefs ruled in hierarchical ranks over individual *ahupua'a*, over collections of *ahupua'a* within districts (*moku*), and potentially over increasing scales of multiple *moku* or whole islands.

The strongest example of Hawaiian chiefly power refers to the historically known Hawaiian Kingdom of the Kamehameha Dynasty. During the late 1700s, Kamehameha's archipelago-wide conquest resulted in control of all of the Hawaiian Islands, redistribution of land among his allies and supporters, and imposition of political and ideological propaganda. Much of the dynasty's legacy today has been remembered through an effective strategy of materialization of power, which created large and long-lasting monuments tied with historical events and traditions, and furthermore imbued with propaganda justifying the authority of Kamehameha and of his supporters and descendants. His royal residence in Kawaihae (Figure 13.39) overprinted an older religious temple of Mailekini that was converted into an armed fort (Figure 13.40), and a new temple called Pu'ukoholā (Figure 13.41) was constructed specifically for the purpose of commemorating Kamehameha's power permanently in the landscape (Carson 2012c). Kamehameha was not present during the killing and sacrifice of his cousin and rival Keōua that served as the inaugural dedication of Pu'ukoholā, although the orthodox oral traditions delicately circumvent and reinvent these details, with implications that the temple was intended from the beginning as the site of sacrificial ceremony symbolizing Kamehameha's divine right to rule as paramount chief.

The renaming of Hawaiian places, along with reinvention of oral traditions about those places, greatly extended the effectiveness of Kamehameha's authority. Stonework

Figure 13.39 View of Kamehameha Dynasty royal residence at Kawaihae, Hawai'i Island.

Expansion and intensification, A.D. *1000 through 1800* 347

Figure 13.40 Mailekini Heiau at Kawaihae, Hawaiʻi Island. Puʻukoholā Heiau is in the background.

Figure 13.41 Puʻukoholā Heiau at Kawaihae, Hawaiʻi Island.

monuments created permanent markers in the landscape, while the place-name traditions brought those material entities into the immediate contexts of people's daily lives. The royal residence at Kawaihae today is remembered as Pelekane, the Hawaiian word for "British" in reference to the role of British representatives in supporting the Kamehameha Dynasty, while the original Hawaiian name has been lost. An older name may have been Kikiakoi or another similar word, mentioned unclearly in traditions associated with prior chiefs who had lived several generations before Kamehameha. Additionally, the Hawaiʻi Island localized dialect pronunciation of *honu* for "bay" replaced the usual Polynesian word of *hana* in most of the places where Kamehameha's allies were installed throughout the archipelago, hinting at the likelihood of a number of other reinvented place-names and traditions that are difficult to unravel from the surviving history as remembered by those in power. Critical counterpoint narratives persist as definite minority voices, for example, in Kauaʻi where the paramount chief Kaumualiʻi famously conceded to Kamehameha without a military confrontation, leading to different and often controversial interpretations of the "separate kingdom" of Kauaʻi.

Kamehameha's conquest followed after some prior generations of other interisland military campaigns, largely perpetrated by the chiefs of dry leeward districts seeking to control other lands. Genealogical reckonings of warring chiefs point to hostile actions in leeward lands since A.D. 1400–1600, consistent with the dating of complex dryland field systems (Cordy 2000). The same timing, however, refers to the construction of irrigation complexes found in wet windward areas, as well as walled fishponds found in all areas, thus suggesting that all communities were engaged in high-density intensification of land-use and food production after A.D. 1400 yet with differential emphasis on warfare as one possible means to control land, people, and resources. At the same time, increased activity is evidenced in marginal and inhospitable environments for access to specialized resources, such as for acquiring high-quality basalt material and birds in the alpine zone at the summit and crater of Haleakalā in Maui.

If widespread expansion and intense conflict can emerge within a few hundred years in the Hawaiian Islands, where apparently nobody had lived prior to A.D. 1000, then similar but less extreme situations very likely had developed in older contexts of longer-settled and much smaller islands in the western and central Pacific. Communities in the Mariana Islands since 1500 B.C. or in Tonga since 900 B.C. certainly faced the constraints of their small islands to support growing populations, where the total biomass and also the available water sources were far less than in the Hawaiian Islands. Unlike the case in Hawai'i, though, these groups demonstrated long-term sustainability through traditions of low-intensity managed forests, informal household gardens, and access to large nonresidential supplemental resource zones.

Flexibility and sustainability tend to be more prominent among groups in smaller islands and atolls that are the most vulnerable to major storms, famine, and other crisis events. In these settings, the political and social leadership may be flexible, involving a temporary shift into alternative structure and rules, such as for disallowing the use of certain areas or foods for an ordained length of time. These temporary shifts could occur when protecting an important food resource or ecological habitat during a time of threat or vulnerability, overall supporting long-term sustainability for people living in island environments (Cramb and Thompson 2022).

All Pacific Oceanic groups lived with degrees of social and political ranking, manifested in different ways and levels of intensity and closely linked with the processes of expansion and intensification. The long-term chronologies are not entirely clarified, but the most relevant material records became obvious after A.D. 1000 with larger and longer-lasting stonework features of formalized villages, recognized territories, and monumental expressions. The most elaborate and complex outcomes all postdated A.D. 1400 in contexts of intensified land use, necessarily postdating periods of expansion.

Warfare

Wars could occur at any time for a variety of reasons, but an increased incidence would suggest that people have extended to the limits of what their physical and social environments can support, and they thereby enter more frequently into competition and conflict. Fortified settlements, weapons, and other material indicators of warfare have been preserved in some but certainly not all Pacific Oceanic archaeological records, in some cases at least as early as A.D. 1000 but mostly postdating A.D. 1400. The timing corresponds with contexts of when populations had been expanding within formally defined territorial land units, with dwindling opportunity for migrating into other parts of an island, into neighboring islands, or into farther places overseas.

Warfare was not the only option for resolving conflicts, and indeed people could engage in ritualized confrontation, diplomatic discussion, or, in some cases, institutionalized mediation. In the Mariana Islands, an indigenous Chamorro conflict-resolving practice of *inafa'maolek* (literally meaning "to make good") was used to restore order to a broken social relation. In many island traditions, battles involved shows of force with very few or sometimes no physical casualty at all. Chiefs and other leaders could participate in competitive feasting and monument building, remembered in traditions across the Pacific, regardless of whether or not they occasionally waged wars.

Archaeological evidence of warfare for the most part has been implied through fortified sites and weapons. Beginning about A.D. 1400 and continuing in use through the 1700s, hilltop forts in Fiji and Samoa incorporated walls and ditches around house foundation features (Best 1993; Kumar et al. 2006), and at least one major basalt adze quarry was modified with defensive features at Tatagamatau in Tutuila of American Samoa. Additionally in Tutuila, a large stacked-rock wall was built more than 2 m high and extended more than 100 m in length, and it is remembered today as part of a battlefield associated with invading forces from Tonga (Carson 2005d). At the summit of Haleakalā in Maui, dozens of temporary shelters were constructed about A.D. 1400–1600 (Carson and Mintmier 2006a), and one of those shelters revealed an extremely rare cache of slingstones (Figures 13.42 and 13.43), possibly related to a military watch post, overland marching

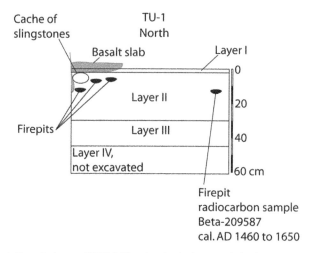

Figure 13.42 Excavation profile and dating of stone-ringed campsite feature at Haleakalā, Maui. Graphic is adapted from Carson and Mintmier (2006a).

350 *Expansion and intensification, A.D. 1000 through 1800*

Figure 13.43 Slingstone cache from excavation at stone-ringed campsite feature at Haleakalā, Maui.

campsite, or command of the nearby high-quality basalt quarry at this inhospitable high elevation more than 2.5 km above sea level (see Figures 13.16 and 13.17). In New Zealand, more than 5000 sites known as *pā* consist of arrangements of ditches and remnants of palisades in strategic positions of higher ground near villages (Figure 13.44) associated with traditions of refuge-seeking defense and occasionally with specific battles, generally postdating A.D. 1500 and clearly some generations after initial settlement of New Zealand about A.D. 1300 (Schmidt 1996). Similar hilltop retreats were mentioned by foreign visitors in the Marquesas Islands, although the physical archaeological traces have become ambiguous today (Rolett 1998; Suggs 1961).

The only sites possibly hinting at warfare substantially prior to A.D. 1400 are the large earthwork complexes in Palau (see Figure 11.5), dated generally in the range of 500 B.C. through A.D. 1000 (Liston 2009). These sites appear to have been used as regular habitations, with added defensive qualities by virtue of their positions on hilltops and the construction of surrounding ditches and probable palisades (Wickler 2002). Larger versions of the hilltop forts and retreats are described for much later contexts in Fiji, Samoa, and

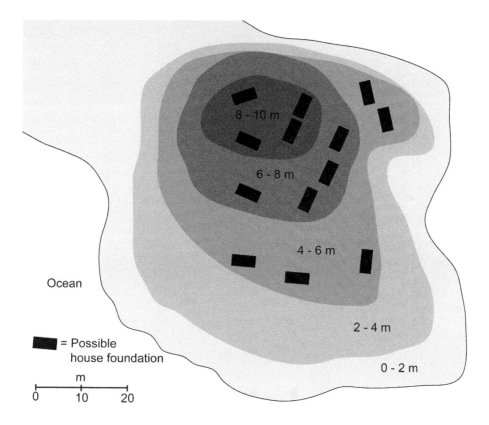

Figure 13.44 Approximation of *pā* at Dacre Point, New Zealand.

elsewhere. Regarding the Palauan earthwork sites, no definitive traditions exist about their past involvement in battles or warring activities. Excavations have recovered general habitation debris, and no other sites of this period have been discovered that would indicate residential habitation in other places outside the earthwork complexes. By default, these sites in Palau appear to be the residential habitations of their time period, including potential elements of defense.

While most refuge sites are in hilltop positions, many in Hawai'i were created inside lava tube caves. The entrances often were camouflaged by stacked rocks, and internal walls and barriers were constructed inside the lava tubes (Figure 13.45). Most of these refuge caves contain burned remnants of candlenut torches, dated as recently as the 1700s and occasionally as old as the 1400s (Kennedy and Brady 1997). At least one such refuge cave has been documented in Samoa at Seuao Cave, associated with oral histories of past warfare most likely around A.D. 1600 (Freeman 1943), and further corroborated by radiocarbon dating of the cave deposit (Golson 1969).

A unique "city of refuge" operated at Pu'u Honua o Hōnaunau in Hawai'i Island (Figure 13.46), which is attested in ethnohistories as functioning during the 1700s and probably earlier. Associations with chiefly lineages can suggest an age at least as early as A.D. 1600 and possibly as early as A.D. 1400 (Cordy 2000). According to the traditions, people could enter into a safe zone within the city boundary, where they potentially could

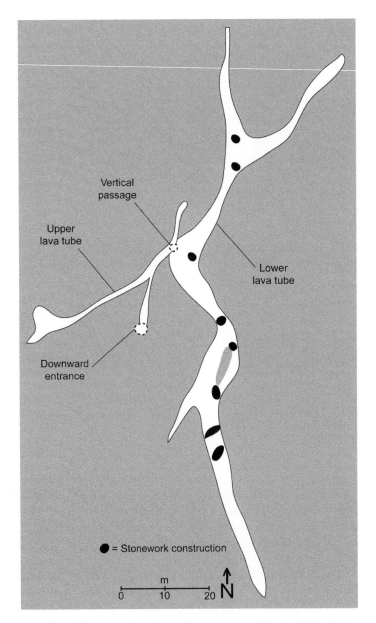

Figure 13.45 Map of a refuge cave site in Keauhou, Hawai'i Island.

undergo rites of purification (Stokes 1986a, 1986b). Archaeological layers and a series of superimposed stonework constructions reveal at least a few distinct periods of the site complex (Ladd 1969, 1987), and accordingly, the details of the refuge tradition may have transformed through time as warfare escalated. Of nine radiocarbon dates from the 'Āle'ale'a Temple Site within the *pu'uhonua* complex, eight results were modern, and the one pre-modern result was calibrated in a broad potential range of A.D. 1400–1950 (Ladd 1969).

Expansion and intensification, A.D. 1000 through 1800   353

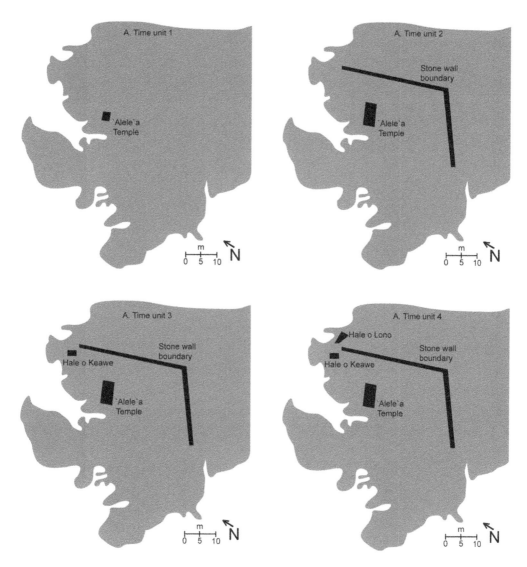

Figure 13.46 Map of Puʻuhonua o Hōnaunau, noting possible chronological sequence of construction episodes.

Weapons overall are scarce in Pacific Oceanic sites, and they could signify prestige more than warfare. Slingstones and carved bone spear tips are characteristic of post–A.D. 1000 contexts in the Mariana Islands (Figures 13.47 and 13.48), but they are absent or extremely rare everywhere else. The spear tips in particular were considered deadly for their magic and connection with the ancestors whose bones were used for making the objects. Other historically known weaponry in the Pacific included clubs with inset rows of shark teeth, but these items so far have not been identified in archaeological layers. Similarly, the most popular use of a carved wooden war club has been clear in historical periods, yet so far these objects have been invisible archaeologically, due to their perishable raw materials.

Figure 13.47 Slingstones of the Mariana Islands. Left: limestone. Right: volcanic stone. Both items are from Tumon, Guam.

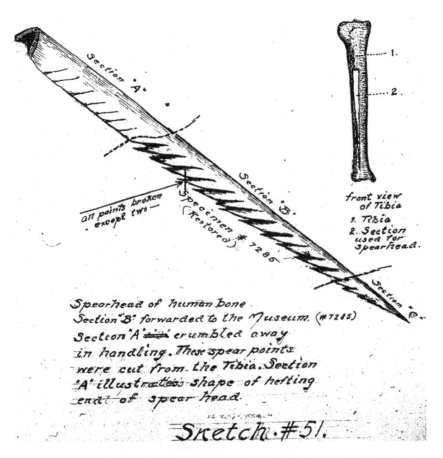

Figure 13.48 Diagram of carved bone spear tip from the Mariana Islands. Illustration was by Hans Hornbostel (1925).

Carved wooden clubs and staves signified rank and status, and they were used potentially but not necessarily in acts of violence. In any case, they have not survived in archaeological contexts. Historically, the dense wood of the ironwood tree (*Casuarina equisetifolia*) was the preferred material for war clubs. Throughout Polynesia, *toa* (or other cognate word for ironwood) literally means "hard" and was used as the term for a warrior. Ironwood was among the taxa imported by Polynesian settlers in all islands except notably in Hawai'i where the term *koa* instead refers to an entirely different genus and species (*Acacia koa*). Ironwood pollen first appeared in the Mariana Islands paleoenvironmental records at 1500 B.C. at the time of initial settlement (Athens and Ward 2006), thus indicating that people deliberately transported ironwood as part of the oldest cultural contexts in Pacific Oceania.

The sparse archaeological trace of warfare in part relates to the likelihood that many battles occurred at sea rather than on land. War canoes are well known historically, although no wreckage yet has been reported archaeologically. Naval battles may be represented in the collections of slingstones occasionally observed on the edges of coral reefs around the Mariana Islands, although the contexts so far have been unclear. Underwater surveys have been limited and mostly aimed at documenting debris from World War II and other historical contexts, so the possibility remains open for finding relics of older periods.

Inside and outside a globalized economy

Overseas contacts and trade formed critical parts of networking in Pacific Oceania, yet somehow these networks during later periods did not connect with neighboring areas such as in Island Southeast Asia. While iron tools, bronze ornaments, glass beads, and other valuables were well circulated in Southeast Asia long prior to A.D. 1000, none of these materials have been found in the islands of Micronesia, Melanesia, or Polynesia until much later contexts of European contacts. Instead, Pacific interisland networks operated independently of the developments in Southeast Asia, despite the likelihood that people were aware of activities in neighboring waters and islands.

While Pacific Oceania grew into an extensively inhabited sea of islands, some of the world's oldest globalized economies emerged just outside this region, specifically in Island Southeast Asia. Indian traders had established contacts as far as Bali in Indonesia by A.D. 100 (Ardika and Bellwood 1991), followed by greater numbers of trading outposts in several locales of Indonesia and the Philippines, linked with Indian, Southeast Asian, Chinese, and Islamic networks as mentioned in temple inscriptions, recordkeeping materials, and historical chronicles. Other networks had connected communities all around the edges of the South China Sea and involved partners in Taiwan, Mainland Southeast Asia, and Island Southeast Asia in continually greater intensity at least since 500 B.C. (Hung et al. 2013). In A.D. 1293, a Mongol fleet famously failed a naval invasion of Java in Indonesia (Hung et al. 2022), hinting at the importance of global shipping trade extending into Island Southeast Asia but not into Pacific Oceania. Dutch, Spanish, and other European powers increased their presence in Indonesia, the Philippines, and eventually in the Mariana Islands during the A.D. 1600s, again not venturing farther into the remote Pacific Islands until later and in a limited extent.

The independent regional networks very likely overlapped or were aware of one another peripherally, but the material records indicate no cross-movement of the known trade materials. Conceivably, the Southeast Asian and Pacific networks were incompatible in terms of their management structures as they involved foreign imperial capitalism in

Southeast Asia in contrast to formalized lineage-controlled and chief-controlled social exchange systems in Micronesia and elsewhere in the Pacific. Cross-regional contacts did exist in low frequency during much earlier periods prior to 500 B.C., as attested in the long-distance transfers of volcanic glass and certain styles of pottery decorations, but these low-frequency traces rapidly diminished. By the time of the major activity of globalized economy growing in Island Southeast Asia after A.D. 100, contacts reaching into Pacific Oceania seem to have been lost. Oral traditions do not refer to trade between Island Southeast Asia and anywhere in the Pacific.

After A.D. 1600, sea voyaging declined and contracted in East Polynesia, while it actually increased in frequency and network complexity farther west in the Pacific. According to European observations of the late 1700s, sea voyaging had been reduced primarily to short-distance travel in East Polynesia, while remote-distance travel persisted elsewhere, most notably in Micronesia. The shift to primarily short-distance sailing in East Polynesia can be traced back to A.D. 1450 (Rolett 2002), corresponding to the time when populations already had expanded to inhabit the extent of their available lands. The contraction of Polynesian voyaging occurred in a context of greater reliance on land-based food production, high density of villages and field systems, escalating intercommunity hostilities, and emergence of warring chiefs since A.D. 1400 and reaching critical levels by A.D. 1600. While some of those factors applied elsewhere in Pacific Oceania, the societies based in smaller islands such as in Micronesia relied heavily on the options of overseas contacts for a broad range of economic, social, and political considerations.

Given the key cultural role of interisland trade and exchange in Micronesia and many parts of Melanesia, the apparent separation from concurrent networks in Island Southeast Asia deserves more research. In one view, perhaps these groups did exchange with one another cross-regionally, but their interactions did not happen to involve the iron, bronze, glass, gold, jade, and other materials that circulated through Southeast Asia. In another view but not necessarily contradicting the first, perhaps the different exchange systems followed significantly different rules and standards that proved incompatible. Alternatively, the Pacific networks may have expanded and intensified to their functional limits, unable to accommodate the new links, materials, and contexts through Southeast Asia unless first undergoing a deep structural change. In any case, these issues at present are speculative and not yet connected to relevant evidence.

European powers at first regarded Pacific Oceania as marginal to their imperialistic developments of globalized economy and political ambitions. Long-established contacts and sea lanes in Island Southeast Asia offered access to vast supplies of prized spices and other commodities, and by comparison, the Pacific Islands were regarded as too small and too remotely situated to be brought into the shipping trade until considerably later. Foreign interests in the Pacific strengthened mostly in the late 1700s and even later in the 1800s, continuing today with the legacies of imperialism throughout the region. Traditional trade and exchange systems were affected profoundly by the new international market and foreign affairs, yet they have persisted in modified forms as integral parts of Pacific Oceanic societies.

References

Anderson, Atholl, 1989. *Prodigious Birds: Moas and Moa-hunting in Prehistoric New Zealand.* Cambridge University Press, Cambridge.

Ardika, I. Wayan, and Peter Bellwood, 1991. Sembiran: The beginning of Indian contact with Bali. *Antiquity* 65: 221–232.

Athens, J. Stephen, 2007. The rise of the Saudeleur: Dating the Nan Madol chiefdom, Pohnpei. In *Vastly Ingenious: The Archaeology of Pacific Material Culture in Honour of Janet M. Davidson*, edited by Atholl Anderson, Kaye Green, and Foss Leach, pp. 192–208. Otago University Press, Dunedin.

Athens, J. Stephen, H. David Tuggle, Jerome V. Ward, and David J. Welch, 2002. Avifaunal extinctions, vegetation change, and Polynesian impacts in prehistoric Hawai'i. *Archaeology in Oceania* 37: 57–78.

Athens, J. Stephen, and Jerome V. Ward, 2006. *Holocene Paleoenvironment of Saipan: Analysis of a Core from Lake Susupe*. Micronesian Archaeological Survey Report Number 35. Commonwealth of the Northern Mariana Islands Division of Historic Preservation, Saipan.

Best, Simon, 1993. At the halls of the mountain kings: Fijian and Samoan fortifications: Comparison and Analysis. *Journal of the Polynesian Society* 102: 385–447.

Bryant-Tokalau, Jenny, 2011. Artificial and recycled islands in the Pacific: Myths and mythologies of "plastic fantastic." *Journal of the Polynesian Society* 120: 71–86.

Burley, David V., 2013. Fijian polygenesis and the Melanesian/Polynesian divide. *Current Anthropology* 54: 436–462.

Burney, David A., 2002. Late Quaternary chronology and stratigraphy of twelve sites on Kaua'i. *Radiocarbon* 44: 13–44.

Campbell, Ian C., 2001. *Island Kingdom: Tonga Ancient and Modern*. Revised edition. Canterbury University Press, Christchurch.

Carson, Mike T., 2003. Integrating fragments of a settlement pattern and cultural sequence in Wainiha Valley, Kaua'i, Hawaiian Islands. *People and Culture in Oceania* 19: 83–105.

Carson, Mike T., 2004. Resolving the enigma of early coastal settlement in the Hawaiian Islands: The stratigraphic sequence of the Wainiha Beach Site in Kaua'i. *Geoarchaeology* 19: 99–118.

Carson, Mike T., 2005a. A radiocarbon dating synthesis for Kaua'i. In *Na Mea Kahiko o Kaua'i: Archaeological Studies in Kaua'i*, edited by Mike T. Carson and Michael W. Graves, pp. 11–32. Special Publication 2. Society for Hawaiian Archaeology, Honolulu.

Carson, Mike T., 2005b. Halele'a agricultural systems reconsidered. In *Na Mea Kahiko o Kaua'i: Archaeological Studies in Kaua'i*, edited by Mike T. Carson and Michael W. Graves, pp. 109–116. Special Publication 2. Society for Hawaiian Archaeology, Honolulu.

Carson, Mike T., 2005c. Alekoko Fishpond. In *Na Mea Kahiko o Kaua'i: Archaeological Studies in Kaua'i*, edited by Mike T. Carson and Michael W. Graves, pp. 66–71. Special Publication 2. Society for Hawaiian Archaeology, Honolulu.

Carson, Mike T., 2005d. *Archaeological Data Recovery for the American Samoa Power Authority Sewer Collection System in Tualauta County, Tutuila Island, American Samoa*. Report prepared for American Samoa Power Authority. International Archaeological Research Institute, Inc., Honolulu.

Carson, Mike T., 2006a. Chronology in Kaua'i: Colonisation, land use, demography. *Journal of the Polynesian Society* 115: 173–185.

Carson, Mike T., 2012a. Recent developments in prehistory: Perspectives on settlement chronology, inter-community relations, and identity formation. In *The Polynesian Outliers: State of the Art*, edited by Richard Feinberg and Richard Scaglion, pp. 27–48. Ethnology Monographs Number 21. University of Pittsburgh, Pittsburgh.

Carson, Mike T., 2012b. Re-examining anomalous early dates of settlement in leeward Hawai'i Island. *Radiocarbon* 54: 59–64.

Carson, Mike T., 2012c. Ethnohistoric and geoarchaeological landscape chronology at Kawaihae, leeward Hawai'i Island. *Geoarchaeology* 27: 385–409.

Carson, Mike T., 2012d. An overview of latte period archaeology. *Micronesica* 42: 1–79.

Carson, Mike T., 2014. Paleoterrain research: Finding the first settlement sites of Remote Oceania. *Geoarchaeology* 29: 268–275.

Carson, Mike T., and J. Stephen Athens, 2007. Integration of coastal geomorphology, mythology, and archaeological evidence at Kualoa Beach, windward O'ahu, Hawaiian Islands. *Journal of Island and Coastal Archaeology* 2: 24–43.

Carson, Mike T., and Melanie A. Mintmier, 2006a. *Archaeological Site Documentation in Front Country Areas in the Summit District of Haleakalā National Park, Maui Island, Hawai'i.* Report prepared for U.S. National Park Service. International Archaeological Research Institute, Inc., Honolulu.

Carson, Mike T., and Melanie A. Mintmier, 2006b. Radiocarbon chronology of prehistoric campsites in alpine and subalpine zones at Haleakalā, Maui Island, USA. *Radiocrbon* 48: 227–236.

Carson, Mike T., Timothy Rieth, and William Burdick, 2004. *An Intensive Surface Survey of a Portion of Ki'ilae Village, Pu'uhonua o Hōnaunau National Historical Park, South Kona District, Island of Hawai'i.* Report prepared for U.S. National Park Service. International Archaeological Research Institute, Inc., Honolulu.

Clark, Jeffrey T., Elizabeth Wright, and David J. Herdrich, 1997. Interactions within and beyond the Samoan Archipelago: Evidence from basaltic rock geochemistry. In *Prehistoric Long-Distance Interaction in Oceania: An Interdisciplinary Approach*, edited by Marshall I. Weisler, pp. 68–84. Monograph 21. New Zealand Archaeological Association, Auckland.

Comer, Douglas C., Jake A. Comer, Ioana A. Dumitru, William S. Ayres, Maureece J. Levin, Katherine A. Seikel, Devin A. White, and Michael H. Harrowers, 2019. Airborne LiDAR reveals a vast archaeological landscape at the Nan Madol World Heritage Site. *Remote Sensing 2019*: 2152. https://doi.org/10.3390/rs11182152

Cordy, Ross, 2000. *Exalted Sits the Chief: The Ancient History of Hawai'i.* Mutual Publishing, Honolulu.

Cordy, Ross, 2004. Considering archaeological indictors of the rise of appointed chiefs and the feudal land system in the Hawaiian Islands. *Hawaiian Archaeology* 9: 1–24.

Cramb, Justin, and Victor D. Thompson, 2022. Dynamic sustainability, resource management, and collective action on two atolls in the Remote Pacific. *Sustainability* 14: 5174. https://doi.org/10.3390/su14095174

DeMarrais, Elizabeth, Louis Jaime Castillo, and Timothy Earle, 1996. Ideology, materialization, and power strategies. *Current Anthropology* 37: 15–31.

Descantes, Christophe, 2005. *Integrating Archaeology and Ethnohistory: The Development of Exchange Between Yap and Ulithi, Western Caroline Islands.* British Archaeological Report International Series Number 1344. Archaeopress, Oxford.

Descantes, Christophe, Michiko Intoh, Hector Neff, and Michael D. Glascock, 2004. Chemical characterization of Yapese clays and ceramics by instrumental neutron activation analysis. *Journal of Radioanalytical and Nuclear Chemistry* 262: 83–91.

Descantes, Christophe, Hector Neff, and Michael D. Glascock, 2002. Yapese prestige goods: The INAA evidence for an Asian dragon jar. In *Geochemical Evidence for Long-Distance Exchange*, edited by Michael D. Glascock, pp. 230–256. Bergin and Garvey, Westport, CT.

Dye, Tom S., 2015. Dating human dispersal in Remote Oceania: A Bayesian view from Hawai'i. *World Archaeology* 47: 661–676.

Earle, Timothy K., 1978. *Economic and Social Organization of a Complex Chiefdom: The Halelea District, Kaua'i, Hawaii.* Anthropological Papers 63. Museum of Anthropology, University of Michigan, Ann Arbor.

Fitzpatrick, Scott M., 2002. A radiocarbon chronology of Yapese stone money quarries in Palau. *Micronesica* 34: 227–242.

Freeman, J. Derek, 1943. The Seuao Cave. *Journal of the Polynesian Society* 52: 101–109.

Golson, Jack, 1969. Preliminary research: Archaeology in Western Samoa, 1957. In *Archaeology in Western Samoa*, edited by Roger C. Green and Janet M. Davidson, Volume 1, pp. 67–76. Bulletin 6. Auckland Institute and Museum, Auckland.

Handy, E. S. Craighill, and Elizabeth Handy, 1972. *Native Planters in Old Hawai'i: Their Life, Lore, and Environment.* Bernice Pauahi Bishop Museum Bulletin 233. Bishop Museum Press, Honolulu.

Heyerdahl, Thor, 1968. *The Kon-Tiki Expedition.* Rand McNally, Chicago.

Hommon, Robet J., 2013. *The Ancient Hawaiian State: Origins of a Political Society.* Oxford University Press, Oxford.

Hornbostel, Hans, 1925. *Unpublished Field Notes, 1921–1924.* Record on file, Bernice Pauahi Bishop Museum, Honolulu.

Hung, Hsiao-chun, Kim Dung Nguyen, Peter Bellwood, Mike T. Carson, 2013. Coastal connectivity: Long-term trading networks across the South China Sea. *Journal of Island and Coastal Archaeology* 8: 384–404.

Hung, Hsiao-chun, Hartatik Tisna Arif Ma'rifat, and Truman Simanjuntak, 2022. The Mongol fleet on the way to Java: First archaeological remains from the Karimata Strait in Indonesia. *Archaeological Research in Asia* 29: 100327. https://doi.org/10.1016/j.ara.2021.100327

Hunt, Terry L., and Carl Lipo, 2006. Late colonization of Easter Island. *Science* 311: 1603–1606.

Jackmond, Gregory, Dionne Fonitī, and Matiu Matāvai Tautunu, 2019. Did Sāmoa have intensive agriculture in the past? New findings from LiDAR. *Journal of the Polynesian Society* 128: 225–243.

Jeffery, Bill, and William Pitmag, 2010. *The Aech of Yap: A Survey of Sites and Their Histories.* Yap State Historic Preservation Office, Yap.

Kahn, Jennifer G., Timothy M. Rieth, Patrick V. Kirch, J. Stephen Athens, and Gail Murakami, 2014. Re-dating of the Kuli'ou'ou Rockshelter, O'ahu, Hawai'i: Location of the first radiocarbon date from the Pacific Islands. *Journal of the Polynesian Society* 123: 67–90.

Kelly, Marion, 1983. *Nā Māla o Kona: Gardens of Kona: A History of Land Use in Kona, Hawai'i.* Department Report Series 82-2. Department of Anthropology, Bernice Pauahi Bishop Museum, Honolulu.

Kennedy, Joseph, and James E. Brady, 1997. Into the netherworld of island earth: A reevaluation of refuge caves in ancient Hawaiian society. *Geoarchaeology* 12: 641–655.

Kikuchi, William K., 1976. Prehistoric Hawaiian fishponds. *Science* 193: 295–299.

Kirch, Patrick V., 2010a. Peopling of the Pacific: A holistic anthropological perspective. *Annual Review of Anthropology* 39: 131–148.

Kirch, Patrick V., 2010b. *How Chiefs Became Kings: Divine Kingship and the Rise of Archaic States in Ancient Hawai'i.* University of California Press, Berkeley.

Kirch, Patrick V., and Roger C. Green, 2001. *Hawaiki: Ancestral Polynesia: An Essay in Historical Anthropology.* Cambridge University Press, Cambridge.

Kirch, Patrick V., and Dana Lepofsky, 1993. Polynesian irrigation: Archaeological and linguistic evidence for origins and development. *Asian Perspectives* 32: 183–204.

Kumar, Roselyn, Patrick D. Nunn, Julie S. Field, and Antoine de Biran, 2006. Human responses to climate change around AD 1300: A case study in the Sigatoka Valley, Viti Levu Island, Fiji. *Quaternary International* 151: 133–143.

Ladd, Edmund J., 1969. 'Alele'a Temple site salvage report. In *Archaeology on the Island of Hawai'i*, edited by Richard Pearson, pp. 95–130. Asian and Pacific Archaeology Series 3. Social Science Research Institute, University of Hawai'i, Honolulu.

Ladd, Edmund J., 1987. *Excavations at Site A-27: Archaeology at Pu'uhonua o Hōnaunau National Historical Park.* Publications in Anthropology 33. Western Archeological Conservation Center, National Park Service, U.S. Department of the Interior, Tucson.

Ladefoged, Thegn N., Michael W. Graves, and James H. Coil, 2003. The introduction of sweet potato in Polynesia: Early remains in Hawai'i. *Journal of the Polynesian Society* 114: 359–373.

Liston, Jolie, 2009. Cultural chronology of earthworks in Palau, western Micronesia. *Archaeology in Oceania* 44: 56–73.

Major, Maruice, 2001. An agricultural history of Kealakekua. In *Gardens of Lono: Archaeological Investigations at the Amy B. H. Greenwell Ethnobotanical Garden, Kealakekua, Hawai'i*, edited by Melinda S. Allen, pp. 23–46. Bishop Museum Press, Honolulu.

McCoy, Mark D., Helen A. Alderson, Richard Hemi, Hai Cheng, and R. Lawrence Edwards, 2016. Earliest direct evidence of monument building at the archaeological site of Nan Madol (Pohnpei,

Micronesia) identified using 230Th/U coral dating and geochemical sourcing of megalithic architectural stone. *Quaternary Research* 86: 295–303.

McElroy, Windy K., 2004. Poi pounders of Kauaʻi Island, Hawaiʻi: Variability through time and space. *Hawaiian Archaeology* 9: 25–49.

Mills, Peter R., Steven Lundblad, Jacob G. Smith, Patrick C. McCoy, and Sean P. Naleimaile, 2008. Science and sensitivity: A geochemical characterization of the Mauna Kea Adz Quarry Complex, Hawaiʻi Island, Hawaii. *American Antiquity* 73: 743–758.

Mintmier, Melanie A., Peter R. Mills, and Steven Lundblad, 2012. Energy-dispersive x-ray fluorescence analysis of Haleakalā basalt adze quarry, Maui, Hawaiʻi. *Journal of Archaeological Science* 39: 615–623.

Mulrooney, Mara A., 2013. An island-wide assessment of the chronology of settlement and land use on Rapa Nui (Easter Islands) based on radiocarbon data. *Journal of Archaeological Science* 40: 4377–4399.

Mulrooney, Mara A., Kelly S. Esh, Mark D. McCoy, Simon H. Bickler, and Yosihiko H. Sinoto, 2014. New dates from old samples: A revised radiocarbon chronology for the Waiʻahukini Rockshelter Site (H8), Kaʻu District, Hawaiʻi Island. *Hawaiian Archaeology Special Publication* 4: 17–26.

Nagaoka, Takuya, and Peter J. Sheppard, 2023. New data from an old discovery: Geological analysis of a stone adze found on Pohnpei, Micronesia. *Journal of Island and Coastal Archaeology* 18: 136–146.

Newman, T. Stell, 1970. *Hawaiian Fishing and Farming on the Island of Hawaiʻi in A.D. 1778.* Division of State Parks, Honolulu.

Nunn, Patrick D., 2021. *World sin Shadow: Submerged Lands in Science, Memory and Myth.* Bloomsbury, London.

Nunn, Patrick D., Rosalind L. Hunter-Anderson, Mike T. Carson, Frank Thomas, Sean Ulm, and Michael J. Rowland, 2007. Times of plenty, times of less: Last-millennium societal disruption in the Pacific Basin. *Human Ecology* 35: 385–401.

Reed, Erik K., 1955. *General Report on Archaeology and History of Guam.* Report prepared for Governor of Guam. U.S. National Park Service, Washington, DC.

Rolett, Barry V., 1998. *Hanamiai: Prehistoric Colonization and Cultural Change in the Marquesas Islands, French Polynesia.* Department of Anthropology and the Peabody Museum, Yale University, New Haven.

Rolett, Barry V., 2002. Voyaging and interaction in ancient East Polynesia. *Asian Perspectives* 41: 182–194.

Rolett, Barry V., Eric W. West, John M. Sinton, and Radu Iovita, 2015. Ancient East Polynesian voyaging spheres: New evidence from the Vitaria adze quarry (Rurutu, Austral Islands). *Journal of Archaeological Science* 53: 459–471.

Sand, Christophe, 2002. Creations and transformation of prehistoric landscapes in New Caledonia, the southernmost Melanesian Islands. In *Pacific Landscapes: Archaeological Approaches*, edited by Thegn N. Ladefoged and Michael W. Graves, pp. 11–34. Bearsville Press, Los Osos, CA.

Schmidt, Matthew, 1996. The commencement of *pā* construction in New Zealand prehistory. *Journal of the Polynesian Society* 105: 441–460.

Smith, Ian, 1985. *Sea Mammal Hunting and Prehistoric Subsistence in New Zealand.* Doctoral thesis. Department of Anthropology, University of Otago, Dunedin.

Smith, Ian, 2004. Nutritional perspectives on prehistoric marine fishing in New Zealand. *Newa Zeland Journal of Archaeology* 24: 5–31.

Spriggs, Matthew, and Atholl Anderson, 1993. Late colonization of East Polynesia. *Antiquity* 67: 200–217.

Stokes, John F. G., 1986a. Report 13. Archaeological features of the Puʻuhonua area. In *Natural and Cultural History of Hōnaunau, Konia, Hawaiʻi*, edited by E. H. Bryan, Jr. and Kenneth P. Emory, pp. 163–210. Departmental Report Series 86-2. Department of Anthropology, Bernice Pauahi Bishop Museum, Honolulu.

Stokes, John F. G., 1986b. Report 14. Features pertaining to early life in the Hōnaunau area. In *Natural and Cultural History of Hōnaunau, Konia, Hawai'i*, edited by E. H. Bryan, Jr. and Kenneth P. Emory, pp. 211–223. Departmental Report Series 86–2. Department of Anthropology, Bernice Pauahi Bishop Museum, Honolulu.

Sudo, Ken-ichi, 1996. Rank, hierarchy and routes of migration: Chieftainship in the Central Caroline Islands of Micronesia. In *Origins, Ancestry and Alliance: Explorations in Austronesian Ethnography*, edited by James J. Fox and Clifford Sather, pp. 57–72. Department of Anthropology, Research School of Pacific Studies, Australian National University, Canberra.

Suggs, Robert C., 1961. *Archaeology of Nukuhiva, Marquesas Islands, French Polynesia*. Anthropological Papers, Number 1. American Museum of Natural History, New York.

Tuggle, H. David, and Matthew Spriggs, 2000. The age of the Bellows Dune Site O18, O'ahu, Hawai'i, and the antiquity of Hawaiian colonization. *Asian Perspectives* 39: 165–188.

Walter, Richard, 1988. The development and use of communication networks in theprehistoric North Island of New Zealand. *Archaeology in Oceania* 23: 71–77.

Weisler, Marshall I. (editor), 1997. *Prehistoric Long-distance Interaction in Oceania: An Interdisciplinary Approach*. Monograph 21. New Zealand Archaeological Association, Auckland.

Weisler, Marshall I., Quan Hua, Sara L. Collins, Ashleigh J. Rogers, and Walter P. Mendes, in press. Dry, leeward regions support colonizing period sites: Stratigraphy, dating, and geomorphological of one of the earliest habitations in the Hawaiian Islands. *Journal of Island and Coastal Archaeology*. https://doi.org/10.1080/15564894.2023.2165200

Wichman, Frederick B., 1997. *More Kaua'i Tales*. Bamboo Ridge Press, Honolulu.

Wickler, Stephen K., 2002. Terraces and villages: Transformation of the cultural landscape in Palau. In *Pacific Landscapes: Archaeological Approaches*, edited by Thegn N. Ladefoged and Michael W. Graves, pp. 63–96. Bearsville Press, Los Osos, CA.

Wilmshurst, Janet M., Atholl J. Anderson, Thomas F. G. Higham, and Revor H. Worthy, 2008. Dating the late prehistoric dispersal of Polynesians to New Zealand using the commensal Pacific rat. *Proceedings of the National Academy of Sciences* 105: 7676–7680.

Wilson, William, 2021. East Polynesian subgrouping and homeland implications within the Northern Outlier-East Polynesian hypothesis. *Oceanic Linguistics* 60: 36–71.

14 Living with the past

Life, lore, and landscape in Pacific Oceania

A cherechar a lokelii (Palauan saying), translated into English as
"The distant eras will reveal."

Colloquial sayings such as "the past informs us about the future" have become cliché, yet they retain relevance today as expressed in this opening Palauan quote. Knowledge about the past can address current issues, and by extension, a person's actions today will create further effects. In this view, all of us are ancestors in training. Each generation is tasked with respecting the work and accomplishments of predecessors while fulfilling obligations for later descendants. These sentiments are familiar in Pacific Oceanic societies and potentially reflect worldwide human values of respect and responsibility.

The islands of Pacific Oceania offer exceptional potential for learning about the past in general and about human-environment relations in particular. These qualities ideally can satisfy the growing global concerns for all of us as human beings to learn about our place in the world and within the long-term evolution of natural and cultural history, so that we can be equipped to cope with problems of how to sustain healthy coexistence with our environments and with each other. Toward these goals, archaeology provides essential material records directly from the past, linked with other approaches such as ethnohistory, linguistics, genetics, and assorted paleoenvironmental studies for the most holistic view of how "the distant eras will reveal."

Potential values of the past can vary considerably, depending on views of long-term continuity versus transformation, as well as the given time depth, such as more than 3000 years in some islands versus less than 1000 years in many others. The scope of "distant eras" thus varies greatly from one viewpoint to another. In the older-settled western islands of the Pacific, archaeological records transcend a series of periods of changing climate, sea level, and other conditions along with observable change in pottery styles, housing forms, and other aspects of material culture. All of these variables found much less opportunity to exhibit chronological trends in the later-settled islands of East Polynesia, where instead the material records may be interpreted to support notions of overall steady cultural continuity and minimal influence of environmental change on societies. With awareness of these extreme examples as bookends around the range of variation between them, a cross-regional view most realistically discloses the relativity of time scales and the potential for multiple concurrent paces and magnitudes of change through time.

At any single point in time, people live in a world shaped by the inherited results of preceding natural and cultural history, and these factors continue to shape the future. The actions and contexts of any time period depend on what already had happened in the past. For instance, the first settlers in the remote Pacific Islands brought their experience of living in Island Southeast Asia with them to the Mariana Islands at 1500 B.C., resulting

DOI: 10.4324/9781003399025-14

in a targeting of specialized shoreline niches that were familiar to them, and later generations needed to adjust to the disappearance of precisely those earliest settled habitats after 1100 B.C. and eventually developed entirely different kinds of settlement systems in later centuries. The Marianas example provides one especially high-resolution illustration of how landscapes have evolved through complex natural-cultural histories over multiple time scales (Carson 2016), and the same approach has been applied at a region-wide scale in this book. The circumstances and consequences of the choices of first island settlers varied greatly across Pacific Oceania, such that the subsequent long-term records unfolded very differently in the Marianas after 1500 B.C., in Southern Melanesia and West Polynesia after 1100 B.C., in central and eastern Micronesia after A.D. 100, and in East Polynesia after A.D. 1000.

While most people can acknowledge that the past can be useful in the present and the future, the extent of usefulness may be questioned in practical terms. After all, past cultures and lifeways belong to the past because they have not survived through a changing world, so in fact they have lost some of their relevance in modern contexts. Nonetheless, the fundamental principles of cultural behaviors and the laws of natural and physical sciences have not changed, so indeed archaeology and other lines of evidence have much to offer, especially with access to long chronological sequences that otherwise are outside the view of modern life and beyond the reach of written histories.

People experience the past in a very real sense whenever stumbling across site ruins in a forest, viewing rock art in a cave, and remembering stories about how a place earned its name. In Palau, the stonework foundations of abandoned houses and pathways remind visitors about the traditional villages where their ancestors once lived as much as 1000 years ago, and even older ruins of earthwork complexes serve as reminders of an era of an additional 1000 years earlier. When people inhabited the stonework villages, they experienced the abandoned earthwork sites as tangible parts of their landscape and connections with the past, whereas today all of these remnants act as windows into different parts of a multicomponent past. In addition to the material site components, these places are known by traditional names, and stories about those place-names can reveal layered meanings beneath their apparent face values.

In order to build a factual understanding of the past, the preceding chapters have presented a chronological narrative of Pacific Oceania as a whole, drawing on diverse lines of evidence for a holistic view of a long-term evolving inhabited landscape in the broadest sense. The contexts of each time period thus can be appreciated in their own terms of how they came to exist. Moreover, the varied scales, paces, and magnitudes of change can be perceived in the full chronological scope of the combined chapters. This format allows clarity of chronological trends cross-regionally as a necessary baseline for addressing larger research issues such as regarding landscape heritage, the roles of concurrently changing elements of natural and cultural histories, and the interrelations of processes of transformation and continuity.

In addition to a summary discussion of the major themes of this book, the concluding chapter here considers the practicalities of bringing Pacific Oceanic archaeology into modern relevance for the public at large. If archaeologists want to contribute to the idealism of how "the distant eras will reveal," then they will need to enhance the values of their work and practical output as perceived by living communities, wherein archaeologists potentially can be recognized as contributing members and stakeholders. Some of the practical issues involve the roles of archaeologists in the operations of museums, collections management, and general sharing of information.

Overview of trends and patterns

Only with clarity of site dating and regional chronology can archaeologists decipher what happened in any particular island, archipelago, or cross-regionally during a measured time interval, through an extended period, or over long time scales of several centuries or millennia. These concerns are especially crucial for tracing the sea-crossing migrations of founding settlements, occurring at significantly different ages and with separate contexts, across the Asia-Pacific region. The differential time depths have created variable effects on population growth, the kinds of environmental challenges that people faced, and the ability of groups to interact cross-regionally while developing independent identities. With this awareness, no single island or island group alone can represent the totality of the regional archaeological record, but rather a cross-regional analysis is necessary for identifying overall trends and patterns, as well as for verifying what makes each case unique.

The Pacific-wide settlement chronology involved a series of long-distance migrations, followed by networks of cross-contacts and exchange. This book has depicted the regional settlement chronology as a set of incremental growths, including not only the settled islands but also the cultural knowledge of the associated inhabited seascape or sea of islands. The depiction of incremental growth can accommodate the movement of people to and from broad zones rather than pinpointed nodes, as well as the potential for subsequent interaction and cross-contacts throughout the inhabited zone spaces. Furthermore, the timing of each expansionary growth can be acknowledged as having occurred over a duration, measured within the limits of archaeologically detectable and datable materials.

Contrary to prior contentions about punctuated events of migrations or of a long pause or short pause between sea-crossing migration episodes, a large-scale view reveals a multistep movement of people into new parts of Pacific Oceania. Regarding the major population movements with obvious material archaeological signatures, these events occurred every few centuries. The only exception was for the final expansion into the margins of East Polynesia after A.D. 1000, with no further options for migrating into previously uninhabited islands thereafter, thus contributing to varied developments of stress and competition within fully inhabited and sometimes crowded islands. Now with a stronger region-wide settlement chronology, more research questions can be addressed that previously were ambiguous and debatable.

Islands, by their nature, offer convenient settings for detecting the material traces of first human settlement horizons, but the meaning of "first settlement" may be more complicated than it seems at face value. Dates of first settlement refer to the time when definite archaeological layers became prominent in an island or island group, always with an unknown possibility of eventually finding something slightly older. In recognition of these uncertainties, island settlement may be understood as a process involving at least three components of initial discovery, founding migration movement, and establishment of a population that is viable both biologically and culturally. A time lag may occur between the events of discovery and migration, allowing for sharing of information and practical preparations. Migration itself may have occurred in more than one episode, but the sets of episodes can become viewed as if they were singular in nature when they proceed in quick succession and without any diagnostically different material culture signatures between them. In any case, the establishment of a viable population is evident only after it already has happened, so that the archaeological records in many islands may be dated somewhat later than the actual occurrence of an initial foundational migration.

The exact motivations of the sea-crossing migrants are unknown today, and most likely they were variable. Possible scenarios may have involved overcrowding in homelands, allure of better opportunities overseas, escape from environmental catastrophe, refuge from warfare or persecution, or compulsion to start a new lineage. Realistically, the incentives may have differed for each person, and they certainly varied when considering the numbers of migrations involved in the entirety of a Pacific-wide settlement chronology. People with different motivations and backgrounds certainly could participate in the same voyage. In this view, any one-size-fits-all explanation cannot account for the diversity of instances of island settlement across the Pacific. Additionally, as expressed in this book, people may not have been seeking remote islands per se, but rather, scholars may need to rethink these ancient scenarios in terms of coastal habitats and other kinds of ecological settings that just so happen to exist in the remote islands of the Pacific.

By knowing more about the mechanics of how people migrated, each episode such as a remote island settlement can be placed in a larger context and potentially compared with other instances. In one such mechanical model, mentioned in Chapter 6, a migration in general terms is understood as a transformational process (Carson and Hung 2014), linking three variables:

- an inhabited home becomes viewed as a place that can be exited and potentially remembered as a homeland;
- a natural entity such as an ocean, river, or mountain ridge is converted conceptually from a barrier or resource zone into a potential conduit for a migration; and
- a faraway place is perceived as suitable for receiving migrants.

All three components need to be transformed conceptually from inert to active modes, but the activation may occur for different reasons and at separate times. Eventually, the three components are activated in unison, but the details are different in each case, as seen in the extended chronology of population movements across Pacific Oceania.

In a Pacific-wide view of settlement chronology, people expanded in incremental growth at several points in time, ranging from 1500 B.C. in the Mariana Islands through A.D. 1300 in New Zealand. The timing of each island settlement can be contextualized in reference to regional climate, sea level, and other environmental factors of the given time and place. Undoubtedly, the circumstances of first settlement in the Mariana Islands were very different from those of much later settlement in New Zealand. Between those extremes, several other situations can be portrayed about the kinds of environments that migrants encountered in separate islands at 1000 B.C., at A.D. 100, or at A.D. 1000. Depending on the time period involved and on the particular islands being incorporated into an inhabited seascape, people found different configurations of coastal habitats and resource zones. Likewise, they departed from homelands with specific kinds of social and environmental circumstances that directly influenced their actions in newly settled places.

The varied contexts of island settlements, in principle, could result in differential impacts on natural environments, divergent trends in population growth relative to island resources, and unique social-political systems. Cross-comparative studies have not yet accounted for all of the relevant variables from every island group, but the general processes of population expansion and land-use intensification can be outlined as a framework to identify consistencies and inconsistencies in the overall patterns and trends. A consistently low level of environmental impact has been identified in the oldest settlements in the Mariana Islands at 1500 B.C., as compared to vast extinctions of native birds and replacement of native forests in other parts of Remote Oceania with Lapita-associated settlements after 1100 B.C., followed by apparently even more drastic impacts in the later-settled islands of East Polynesia after A.D. 1000. Additionally, land-use patterns in many of the longer-settled islands of the Pacific were sustained with low-labor input strategies of managed forests and informal household gardens, as compared to the rapid development of high-density field systems in the later-settled islands such as Hawai'i which entirely postdated A.D. 1000. Moreover, social and political conflicts and complications developed at different paces and levels of intensity, and sometimes they were avoided.

Concurrent with the sequence of island settlement, several other chronological trends are evident, including both natural change in climate and sea level as well as cultural change in pottery forms and styles, housing formats, land-use patterns, and other factors. Without repeating the details as presented in the chapters of this book, the major points can be summarized here in 11 time periods.

1. Hunter-gatherers lived in broad ranges in the land masses of Sunda, Wallacea, and Sahul at least 50,000 years ago, when sea level was much lower during the Pleistocene with massive amounts of the world's ocean water trapped in ice sheets.
2. After 10,000 B.C., glacial melting elevated the global sea level and flooded coastal lowlands, effectively creating isolation of groups in separate land masses and islands across the region now known as Island Southeast Asia, Australia, and New Guinea. Localized distinctions in DNA lineages likely developed in the separate populations by 8000–6000 B.C.
3. People with pottery-making traditions, residential habitation formats, and mixed use of fishing, foraging, and farming moved to settle in Taiwan at least as early as 4000 B.C., where they met with established groups of hunter-gatherers whose ancestors effectively had been isolated there during the previous few thousands of years.
4. During and immediately after a sharp but short-lived dry climate episode about 2200 B.C., some members of the pottery-making groups in eastern Taiwan moved to settle in the northern Philippines. At that time, a mid-Holocene highstand in sea level was about 2 m higher than present, such that many coastal lowlands and river terraces of today's landscapes did not yet exist. The pottery-bearing sites of this period in eastern Taiwan and in the northern Philippines were situated on low hills overlooking watery zones, as well as occasionally in stilt-raised housing areas over watery or mucky wetland habitats. These population movements into the Philippines would have brought people from a generalized eastern Taiwan homeland source into contact with preexisting hunter-gatherer populations that already had developed localized distinctions in the Philippines and elsewhere in Island Southeast Asia, Australia, New Guinea, and Near Oceania at least since 8000–6000 B.C. This population movement, as well as other population movements over the next several centuries, involved elements of biological, linguistic, and cultural traits ultimately from a Taiwan homeland with counterpart elements of the communities that had developed with varying degrees of distinction from one another throughout Island Southeast Asia and Near Oceania.
5. By 1500 B.C., traditions of pottery-making, residential habitation structures, and mixed horticultural land-use patterns spread into more parts of Island Southeast Asia. Meanwhile, these traditions accompanied the first people who migrated into the Remote Oceanic world, specifically in the Mariana Islands. Initial Marianas settlement at 1500 B.C. targeted particular seashore niches and reflected aspects of older homeland lifestyles in Island Southeast Asia.

Living with the past 367

6 Over the next few centuries of human-caused impacts on island environments, the shoreline-oriented cultural traditions continued in the Marianas and extended with the Lapita-associated communities moving into Near and Remote Oceania. The anthropogenic impacts on native birds, other animals, and natural forest composition evidently were strongest in the Lapita-associated Remote Oceanic islands of Southern Melanesia and West Polynesia.

7 Following the beginning of sea-level drawdown after 1100 B.C., people needed to adjust their relationships with coastal environments, and eventually they abandoned their prior preference for certain narrowly defined nearshore habitat niches by 500 B.C. The shift by 500 B.C. involved a broadening of reliance on varied resource zones in both coastal and landward settings, coincident with a loss of finely decorated pottery styles.

8 By A.D. 100, communities in separate island groups began to develop locally distinctive material culture inventories enhanced by the growing dependence on land-based resources bringing people into closer relationships with definable territories. Meanwhile, sea level had lowered enough to make the many small islands of Central and Eastern Micronesia habitable for the first time, leading to further opportunities of localized cultural developments in separate island groups of a growing total inhabited seascape.

9 By A.D. 1000, the locally specific cultural developments across Pacific Oceania were distinguishable in their archaeological materials, when each island group expressed formalized village layouts, bounded territories, and monument-making traditions of a purported "A.D. 1000 Event." Stonework constructions, in particular, became most prominent by A.D. 1000. Another important material change was the decline and loss of pottery-making in Polynesia and in Eastern Micronesia. The timing after A.D. 1000 coincided with one more major population expansion, in this case bringing people into East Polynesia and into the Polynesian Outliers, followed by a final movement into New Zealand at the south margin of East Polynesia about A.D. 1300.

10 Within the context of the formalized cultural expressions after A.D. 1000, populations in each island group grew rapidly, partly encouraged by sustained conditions of warm, wet, and annually predictable climate through the next three centuries. Communities expanded to inhabit more and more territories, first making use of their most preferred habitats and ecological zones, eventually expanding into less preferable areas until no further options were available.

11 By A.D. 1400, people were expanding into the less preferable living areas in nearly all islands. Meanwhile, since about A.D. 1300, the stable and reliable climate had shifted into less favorable conditions of unpredictable storminess and periodic drought that no longer could support the rapid population growth and expansion of prior centuries. Island societies after A.D. 1400 followed rather diverse strategies for coping with these challenges, such as by intensifying their land-use strategies, investing in high-density use of land and resources, increasing overseas networking, and engaging in social and political competitions.

This chronological outline has remained intact from the first to second editions of this book, although it was designed deliberately with the capacity to be refined through continued investigations. The regional chronology should be viewed as a framework to pursue new questions and ideas. The currently proposed time periods each span some centuries, according to available radiocarbon dating associated with artifacts and other materials that are diagnostic of those periods. New excavations, and possibly new dating techniques, may yet clarify narrower periods or subperiods within the overall sequence. Additionally, research inevitably will identify more of the localized differences and cross-regional variation, potentially prompting rethinking of the overall patterns and trends.

This book advocates an approach of situating material evidence within a solid chronological sequence as the requisite starting point for building any kind of significant archaeological research program. While this mode of research is understood implicitly in most regions, it has been slow to develop in Pacific Oceania where, instead, most of the regional synthesis summaries of the last several decades have followed an area-by-area approach. By focusing on each area separately, some important aspects of the larger picture are missed in terms of cross-regional similarities and differences, and a cohesive sense of chronology is lost when treating each island group by itself. Furthermore, the area-by-area strategy creates an unfortunate effect of narrow views of each island or archipelago unrelated to larger research issues, and these narrow views effectively marginalize the region of nearly one-third of the world's surface known as Pacific Oceania as compared to the rest of the world.

Defendants of the area-by-area approach may caution that any large-scale view tends to miss some of the locally specific details, but these nuances always can be added to the larger framework. The research framework in this book has served an entirely different purpose than a literature review. An accurate starting framework does not need to be overly burdened with site-specific records, as it always can accommodate more information and increasing levels of refined data. The starting framework does, however, need to be based on a realistic comprehension of the cross-regional data, even if the synthesis summary format does not allow recapitulation of each detail already reported elsewhere. Toward this goal, the preceding chapters have provided real archaeological examples in sufficient detail to illustrate the points being made and to leverage the material findings into other research questions. Furthermore, the chronological approach has endured into this book's second edition without needing to be overturned in any way, and the newest discoveries have added extra clarity while reinforcing the overall chronological sequence of the region-wide incremental growth model.

Chronology has been overlooked in many Pacific Oceanic archaeological studies, as considerable effort instead has been devoted to the documentation of surface-accessible and ethnohistorically known sites. Indeed, many sites contain single undifferentiated layers of shallow time depth and limited duration of perhaps a few centuries or less, where notions of long-term chronological change are only minimally relevant. These sites tend to be identified through surface-visible ruins that relate strongly with ethnohistorical knowledge and traditions. The majority footprint coverage of terrain in Pacific Islands consists of inland zones that are the least likely to contain older settlement layers, and instead they most often have supported very little or no sedimentary deposits that overrepresent the preservation of later-aged materials. Stratified layers of older ages exist only in certain kinds of settings that are not always detectable on the surface, and they can be found just in a small percentage of the total land areas of islands as compared to the more extensive opportunities for finding later-aged surface-related sites in the vast majority of the existing landforms.

A default emphasis on surface-related sites has created an under-appreciation of chronological sequences, and moreover, it has encouraged a way of looking at the past as a single entity connected with ethnohistory. Many ethnographically and historically known traditions are traceable to material correlates in surface-visible sites and are arguably as old as the A.D. 1000 Event of formalized cultural expressions throughout Pacific Oceania. These studies are greatly valuable for their rich interdisciplinary information and immediate connections with important cultural traditions of modern relevance. Despite these advantages in contextualizing the past, the role of chronological change has been overlooked, leading to notions of a slow-moving or unchanging *longue durée* that can be accessed from the present reaching into the past.

A paleo-terrain approach allows past contexts to speak for themselves and in chronological order. This approach begins with reconstruction of ancient landforms and habitat zones of measured time intervals, hence the "paleo-terrain" name in recognition of the starting point of the research model (Carson 2014a). Within each time interval, archaeological records can reveal how cultural groups lived in the associated contexts as they changed through time. As many lines of evidence as possible are marshalled to build a comprehensive view of the natural and cultural setting of each time interval, furthermore situated in chronological order to reveal the overall landscape evolution in the most liberal sense of an integrated natural-cultural history.

People can experience or appreciate the past through the artifacts, sites, place-names and traditions, and other forms of evidence that are embedded or encoded in today's landscapes, not only in Pacific Oceania but also worldwide. The Pacific Islands happen to comprise ideal models for studying landscapes as social and ecological systems that operate everywhere in the world. As illustrated in this book, research can recapture the chronological sequence of how the many different island landscapes changed or evolved through time as a general framework for contextualizing diverse studies about the past. One such framework has been presented in these pages, primarily from the perspective of archaeology, as a way to substantiate a chronological sequence that can incorporate diverse information.

Long-term continuity and transformation

Archaeologists have portrayed the Pacific Oceanic past in at least two contradictory ways stemming from incompatible opinions about how the archaeological record refers to long-term continuity versus transformation. All archaeological records reveal at least some degree of chronological change, but archaeologists have disagreed about the role of such change as superficially absorbed into society, as causing deep restructuring of a society, or as some other degree between those opposite conditions.

- Advocates of long-term continuity or coherence may stress the role of deep social structure that is unlikely to change through time, as most vividly documented in societies of East Polynesia where archaeological sites are linked with ethnohistories, place-names and traditions, and language histories.
- Proponents of chronological transformation may point to the innumerable examples of changing natural environments and material culture inventories, as most abundantly demonstrated in the longer-settled islands of the western and central Pacific but also including smaller magnitudes of change in the later-settled islands of East Polynesia.

In the perspective of long-term continuity, the most visible instances of chronological change can be regarded as ultimately not affecting the deep structure of a society. As mentioned in Chapter 3, some aspects of society are slow-moving and change very little over long time scales, while other aspects can change more rapidly. In one view, popularized by Braudel (1949) following Simiand (1903), those slow-moving aspects are regarded as the *longue durée* that can define the essence of a society, while the fast-moving aspects are regarded as *histoire événementielle* that are merely superficial.

Archaeological records have shown indisputably that deep structural change has occurred at least a few times over the course of Pacific Oceanic culture history. Those occurrences cannot be classified as either the *longue durée* or *histoire événementielle*, and therefore they need to be interpreted through other viewpoints. Most importantly, they need to be recognized as real phenomena within the scope of archaeological study, and they do not need to be dismissed as inconsequential to social history or anthropology.

An extremist stance with the *longue durée* proposes that the unchanging aspects of culture should be studied as the essence of a human society, while other evidence of change is regarded as superficial and inconsequential to the long-enduring traditions that define a society. Certain aspects of culture have persisted through long periods, as exemplified in the tight coherence of Polynesian language, ethnographic traditions, and material culture found in the diverse and remotely separated islands all across Polynesia and traceable to a shared ancestry about A.D. 1000. Within the last 1000 years, however, at least some change has occurred in the coastal morphologies, slope erosion-deposition patterns, processes of expansion and eventual intensification of land-use practices, social and political structuring, and other variables in each island group, even within the closely related Polynesian societies, resulting in notably variable outcomes verifying that each society changed through time according to different circumstances. Furthermore, the ancestral traits of Polynesian society traced to A.D. 1000 evidently had developed after serious transformations in prior centuries with the decline and eventual total loss of pottery, change from stilt-raised to ground-level housing, popularization of large communal earth ovens and feasting events, formalization of village layouts and territorial land-use systems, and development of monument-making traditions. Looking deeper in time, the descendants of Lapita pottery-making groups in West Polynesia since 1100–800 B.C. had abandoned their shoreline-oriented settlements and their finely decorated pottery traditions, and instead by 500 B.C. the later generations had shifted to more broad-spectrum usage of coastal and inland resource zones, preference for general-utility pottery, and other developments that marked a deep restructuring of society. Additional examples of profound societal change are evident in all other island groups of the Pacific and manifest in different forms, as outlined in the preceding chapters.

Records of significant chronological change are undeniable, but a hard-line view of long-term continuity always can point to the fact of an unbroken human habitation in each island group as evidence of consistency from initial founding settlement through present-day traditions. Regardless of whatever change has occurred, the biological populations have persisted multi-generationally, and the modern descendants still sustain their own languages and cultural traditions today, traceable to ancient shared ancestry that unites all groups of Pacific Oceania at a deep level. On the other hand, chronological change must be acknowledged in the fact that all of the island groups have developed their own distinctive versions of their ancestral languages, cultural traditions, and material culture expressions. If no significant change had occurred through time, then the divergence and subgroupings of languages and cultures could not have developed.

This book has portrayed ongoing change in an integrated natural-cultural history, enacted in concurrent paces and scales of change in a multitude of factors. When these factors change at a slow rate or small magnitude, then they can be absorbed into the larger operating system. The instances of extreme degree of change, however, surpass a threshold of how the overall system operates, thereby triggering a deep structural change at a systemic level. Fundamental restructuring is more likely to occur when two or more factors are affecting one another, whether directly or indirectly.

At a Pacific-wide scale, at least three deep restructuring events have occurred.

1. First and most essentially, initial island settlement events brought people into contact with remote island environments that otherwise had been uninhabited, thus enabling several profound changes in the island ecologies and in the social groups who now inhabited those places. These processes recurred several times in very different contexts, beginning 1500 B.C. in the Mariana Islands and continuing as late as A.D. 1300 in New Zealand, with several other examples associated with major population movements at 1000 B.C., at A.D. 100, and at A.D. 1000 in different parts of Pacific Oceania.
2. A second deep restructuring episode began after 1100 B.C. with the combined effects of sea-level drawdown, changing coastal ecology, and the aftermath of initial targeting of narrowly defined shoreline-oriented habitats, resulting in substantially transformed natural landscapes, settlement and land-use patterns, and material signatures of pottery and other artifacts by 500 B.C. in all of the inhabited islands of Remote Oceania at that time.
3. The third deep restructuring episode was the purported A.D. 1000 Event of formalization of cultural expressions and stonework monuments throughout Pacific Oceania corresponding with the emergence of distinguishable localized differentiation of each island group.

These three major events have been substantiated with even more evidence in this book's second edition. Future research may yet clarify about other periods of change that have characterized Pacific Oceanic archaeological chronologies, with variable magnitudes of effects.

Future directions of enhancing archaeological values

When considering the future of Pacific Oceanic archaeology, many points follow worldwide trends and concerns, but the details, of course, are specific to the region. Issues of education, training, and heritage management are at the forefront of international agendas, and Pacific Oceania needs to be brought more prominently into these discussions rather than marginalized, as has been the case over the last several decades. The region's global relevance has increased only now with this book's second edition. The Pacific region happens to occupy a place of high visibility of the effects of changing climate and sea level, population densities, and sustainable development of economies that are reportedly urgent in the global arena, so more of the Pacific regional investigations, in theory, can make significant advancements in global research. Further regarding global research significance, islands have been promoted as ideal settings or models for studying general processes of ecological and social functioning and change, but archaeologists still need to improve on how realistically any island-specific research can represent larger issues.

Education and training are ongoing concerns, not only for students but also for the public overall. In many places, fears of site vandalism and looting dictate strict protection to the extent of disallowing the sharing of site documentation with the public. In these cases, more efforts in public education and outreach will be needed. Community-based groups have been encouraging, although they sometimes can struggle to sustain as essentially volunteer programs. Free online educational videos and other resources have been productive as well, although people always should be encouraged to exercise their critical thinking skills when evaluating the sources. Even if peer-reviewed scientific publications are regarded as inaccessible to the public, then people still should be able to access a peer-reviewed summary of the key points.

A large part of educations, training, and public engagement involves direct experience with archaeological sites. Practical opportunities are available year-round for community involvement in archaeological research, heritage resource management, government offices, museum operations, and programs of public access to archaeological sites and cultural landscapes. While these opportunities are available, many people face difficulty in justifying time away from their jobs, families, and other obligations without first having firm reassurance of a beneficial outcome of their investment.

Efforts of public engagement tend to be constrained by insufficient funding and by the same laws that originally were intended to protect archaeological sites and cultural heritage resources. Despite these difficulties, several examples illustrate positive outcomes due to the exceptional efforts and dedication of motivated individuals. The strongest programs are funded by governments, for instance, as in New Caledonia with its own Institute of Archaeology. Funding from the U.S. National Park Service has supported several exemplary programs in Micronesia, such as the ongoing database management and thorough surveys performed and updated annually in Palau integrating oral histories and archaeological evidence. Similarly, all of the technical staff in Historic Preservation Office of the Commonwealth of the Northern Mariana Islands are well experienced in archaeological fieldwork, documentation, and data management, resulting in professional treatment of sites and promotion of innovative research despite the rapid and large-scale impacts of military buildup and private land-development projects. In most other parts of Micronesia, the local Historic Preservation Offices have developed similar strategies, currently in different stages of implementation and leading the way for bringing Pacific Islander communities into leadership roles of archaeological work.

Among the more successful programs of community involvement, the Ritidian Site in Guam has accommodated diverse interests (Figure 14.1) not only of archaeologists but also of cultural practitioners, historians, traditional healers, biologists, and others (Carson 2014b). The diversity in this case has been enabled by the large-scale conservation of a cohesive ecosystem, managed by U.S. Fish and Wildlife Service as the Ritidian Unit of the Guam National Wildlife Refuge. Although a military live-fire training range will restrict or eliminate public access to the area, Ritidian currently serves as a refuge not only for wildlife but also for researchers and for the community at large (Figure 14.2). Similar public access programs have been proposed or initiated in other government-managed ecosystems throughout the Pacific, with variable degrees of success, as well as with variable degrees of competing interests for building military complexes, hotels and resorts, high-density housing, and other land-use transformations. In any case, these programs always need realistic financial commitments in order to sustain ongoing research and the engagement of the public. Importantly, the public in this sense includes the local community residents as well as visitors and any others interested to learn or participate.

Opportunities for education and training need to be extended not only to the public but also to archaeologists as members of the public, even if they may resist this idea. While many working professionals can recognize the benefits of updated skills and ability to use the latest scientific devices and methods, they still need to be open to the possibilities of

Figure 14.1 Traditional Chamorro blessing ceremony during excavation at Ritidian, Guam, led by Jeremy Cepeda (left) with cultural group I Fanalai'an, May 2016.

learning more about how to share their information and how to support new experiences for the public. Archaeologists are irresponsible when they hoard their findings, and they may be seen in the public eye as guilty of producing much of the same result as if they were site looters or robbers. Knowledge about a site or an artifact always can be beneficial, but archaeologists need to devote more effort into identifying the significance of the find and, furthermore, communicating it to others. Sharing of information needs to encompass more than filing a bland technical report in a government office or presenting for ten minutes at an academic conference without peer review. Formal publication, news media reports, public site visits, museum exhibits, and other options always exist for archaeologists to pursue.

The public interaction with archaeology by convention exists in venues of museum exhibits, news media reports, documentary summaries, and site visits. In the Pacific, archaeologists may not be involved in any of these venues, but often the results of their work are appropriated and reinterpreted by others. In this regard, archaeologists can recognize an obligation to make their work easy to comprehend and suitable for public reference, and some practitioners may invest in "executive summary" formats of their major findings, suitable for press release and other purposes of public outreach.

Archaeological material collections are of special concern to the interconnecting issues of scientific research, curation, museum studies, and public access. Of course, the vast bulk of material is not at all suitable for museum exhibition, for instance, including sediment

Figure 14.2 Community site visit at Ritidan, Guam, March 2016.

samples, shellfish fragments, and tiny broken pieces of plain earthenware pottery. Additionally, many facilities at museums, universities, and private contracting offices are now facing practical issues of how to manage the "legacy collections" of materials inherited from prior decades (Figure 14.3), often with dubious research value due to the survival of little or no information about provenience or context. In any case, the materials need to be stored and curated for long-term stability, not only in terms of their physical properties but also in terms of data management allowing access for research, museum display, and other purposes.

Archaeological material in itself is not inherently valuable, but rather it relates to potential research significance. In this regard, research significance needs to consist of more than just doing something new that has not been done before. In fact, many studies are "new" simply because nobody has bothered to perform such trivial work, ultimately reinforcing Ingold's (1994: xx) observation that "we know more and more about less and less." Significant contributions often involve thinking in new ways, applying different ideas or methodology for improved results, or simply working in a place where archaeological knowledge has been blank or minimal. Most importantly, though, researchers need to learn how to make their results accessible to others and relevant in a larger context. Accordingly, much of this book has concentrated on presenting a coherent chronological narrative, based on primary data, toward addressing general-global research themes.

Consistently in its first and second editions, this book has emphasized how to contextualize island-specific findings within a Pacific-wide view and with reference to larger

Figure 14.3 Example of "legacy collection" before and after updated curation treatment at the Micronesian Area Research Center, University of Guam.

research issues. Toward this goal, the preceding chapters have presented a chronological narrative accounting for the region-wide information in a complete sequence of time periods. Each chapter thus allows for cross-comparison of real material findings, and in unison, these chapters enable a full chronological view for addressing questions about change through time. This approach highlights the values of primary datasets that can be leveraged into new investigations and directions in future work. In this regard, the second edition's most important contribution has been to add the newest substantive evidence for the most updated and thorough basis of knowledge.

Beyond the significance of building archaeological knowledge for its own sake, the lessons from long-term chronologies cannot be stressed enough while today's international society is struggling to develop a deep structural change of lifestyle in order to overcome the effects of global climate change. A sustainable future depends on the ability to make the same kind of deep structural change that evidently occurred more than once in past societies of Pacific Oceania, when people faced threats of changing sea level and coastal ecology, as well as rising population density at the limits of what their island environments could support. As emphasized in this book, islands are ideal places to examine human-environment relations, and long-term archaeological records can reveal the strategies that have been successful or unsuccessful for overcoming different types of challenges. Once again, societies have developed a strong dependency on a certain way of life that can no longer be sustained, and a fundamental restructuring will be necessary. Modern dependencies on fossil fuels, high-density urbanism, and marginalization of farming will need to be revised severely and replaced by more sustainable lifeways.

Regarding the ability to contribute to global research issues, the islands of Pacific Oceania have been proposed as ideal models potentially representing the most essential aspects of nature and society within easily observable island environments. Scholars have worked through ways of thinking about islands as laboratories, as microcosms of the world, and as model systems. The persistent challenge, however, has been to develop a truly significant research topic and then to identify the particular island case study (or set of island case studies) serving most effectively as a model for addressing the specific question at hand. This strategy requires familiarity with the materials, chronology, and parameters of the region's archaeology as outlined in this book.

As shown in this book's first and second editions, any narrative synthesis eventually needs to be updated, as new research inevitably will reveal more information. In this sense, archaeological research constantly is refining what is known and therefore building more precise statements. While the second edition has incorporated new refinements and nuances, a few key issues still have not yet been addressed that had been mentioned in the first edition. For instance, some of the date ranges of island settlement or other key points have been expressed in vague terms due to incomplete or inconclusive information, such as the currently unknown date of first settlement in Yap being in need of clarification. Other future refinements may target the contexts of earliest settlement sites in the Hawaiian Islands, potential cross-contacts among communities in West Polynesia and East Polynesia, and the concurrent operations of trade networks in Island Southeast Asia and different parts of Pacific Oceania. Discussions about these topics so far have been imprecise and inconclusive, ripe for a cumulative refining approach.

A strategy of ongoing refinement must not be viewed as a free license for researchers to make erroneous conclusions. In a truly scientific paradigm, the same techniques and methodological procedures should produce the same outcome, or else something is wrong with the methodology. Whenever a prior conclusion is proven incorrect, then something must have been different about the methodology or about the datasets involved in supporting the new conclusion. For instance, methodologies of relying on surface-visible site ruins are flawed for the purpose of identifying long-term chronological sequences, and new investigations mostly within the last few decades have been providing more complete information and more robustly defendable conclusions about archaeological chronologies. These more complete chronological frameworks can support further research questions that previously were impossible or misdirected.

The preceding chapters have shown that Pacific Oceania bears much to offer in learning about several enduring themes in world archaeology. Significant information already is available, yet more research will continue to refine knowledge about human migrations, long-term processes of human-environment interactions, and the potential for integrating archaeology with other perspectives and lines of evidence. The opening paragraphs of this book mentioned that the Pacific Ocean covers nearly one-third of the world's total surface area, yet its thousands of islands are scarcely known to the other two-thirds of the world. The foregoing pages hopefully have rectified this imbalance and opened new possibilities, such that "the distant eras will reveal."

References

Braudel, Fernand, 1949. *La Méditerranée et la Monde Méditerranéan à l'Époche de Philippe II.* 3 volumes. Armand Collin, Paris.

Carson, Mike T., 2014a. Paleoterrain research: Finding the first settlement sites of Remote Oceania. *Geoarchaeology* 29: 268–275.

Carson, Mike T., 2014b. *First Settlement of Remote Oceania: Earliest Sites in the Mariana Islands.* Springer, New York.

Carson, Mike T., 2016. *Archaeological Landscape Evolution: The Mariana Islands in the Asia-Pacific Region.* Springer International Publishing, Cham, Switzerland.

Carson, Mike T., and Hsiao-chun Hung, 2014. Semiconductor theory in migration: Population receivers, homelands and gateways in Taiwan and Island Southeast Asia. *World Archaeology* 46: 502–515.

Ingold, Tim, 1994. Preface. In *Companion Encyclopaedia of Anthropology: Humanity, Culture and Social Life,* edited by Tim Ingold, pp. xiii–xxii. Routledge, London.

Simiand, François, 1903. Méthode historique et science social. *Revue de Synthèse Historique* 16: 113–137.

Index

Note: Page numbers in *italics* denote figures.

adze 6, 15, 37, 47, 53–54, 73, 75, 97, 101, 162, 170, 180, 237, 238, 262, 265, 267, 337, 338, 340–343, 349
Ancestral Polynesian Society (APS) 48, 250
Aotearoa *see* New Zealand
archaeological culture 57–62, 100, 203
atoll formation 28–29
atoll highway of Micronesia 230–242
Australao-Melanesian genetics lineages 41–43, 45–46, 70, 194–197
Australia 4, 5–7, 12, 16, 19, 30, 31, 36, 40–43, 67–70, 73–74
Austronesian genetics lineages 42–45, 194–197
Austronesian language 7–8, 38–41, 69–70, 92, 99, 124, 181, 192–194

Batungan Caves, Philippines 116, 180
Bikini Atoll 230, 232, *234*
biogeography 5–6, 25, 48
Bismarck Archipelago 20, 42, 74, 84–89, 124, 128, 133–136, 138, 181, 185, 188, 190–191, 193, 195–196, 199, 203, 212
Borneo 14, 75–77, 85, 92–97, 123–124, 203
bottleneck effect 7, 38, 130, 137, 159
Bukit Tengkorak, Indonesia 75, 97, 123–124,

Cagayan Valley, Philippines 37, 79, 85, 112–120, 180, 226
Callao Cave, Philippines 67, 69, 117
Central East Polynesian (CEP) languages 40
Challenger Deep 26
Chamorro 40, 149, 173, 181, 349
chiefdoms, making and remaking of 344–348
China 7, 35, 41, 46, 78, 84, 91–92, 97–100, 104, 141
climate and weather patterns 17, 34–36, 299
Cook Islands 270, 290–292
cultural chronologies 55–64, 305

DNA *see* genetics lineages
domesticated animals 6, 8, 62, 77–78, 90, 170, 197, 218, 223, 225–226, 337

Easter Island *see* Rapa Nui
East Timor 74, 78
ecological imperialism 10–11, 137, 185–186, 198
edge-ground stone tool 73–74
edge species 16

farming 70, 76, 78, 90, 92, 95, 97–99, 103, 106, 108, 120, 173, 223–226, 366, 375
field systems 326–337
Fiji 33, 43, 124, 185, 188, 190, 199, *201*, 203, 212–213, 246, 249, 343, 349–350
founder effect 7–8, 38
Fushan-associated sites, Taiwan 105–108, 110, 112, 117, 120

genetics lineages (DNA) 3, 41–46, 68, 70, 88–89, 181, 194–197, 366
Gondwana 30, *31*, 324, 329
Guam 17, 29, 44, 130, 149–156, 171, 173–174, 181, 204, 223, 236, 278, *328*, 372

Haleakalā, Maui 17, *262*, 319–324, *328*, 348–349
haligi pillars 274, 281, *283*, 284
Han Chinese 7
Hawaiian Islands 7, 14, 26–27, 33–34, 37–38, 40, 47, 55, 62, 286, 290, 295, 298, 304, 308, 311–314, 317, 319, 326, 329–330, 332–334, 337, 345–348
histoire événementielle 59–60, 227, 370
Hoa Binh Culture 63, 72–74
Holocene period 30–31, 35, 43, 63, 72–74, 76, 88, 210–211, 366
Homo erectus 5, 69
house burial 285–286, 288, 295, 345
House of Taga, Tinian 126, 151–152, 154, *157*, 170, 274, *276*
house societies 298–299
hunter-gatherer 12, 14, 18–19, 36–37, 41, 57, 63–64, 67–79, 84, 87–88, 97, 117–118, 249, 305, 366
Huxley's Line 7, *68*

Index

Ice Age *see* Pleistocene period
Ille Cave 77
incremental growth model 13, 85–86, 89, 91, 181, 368
Indonesia 5, 7, 37, 43, 68–69, 74, 76, 78, 85–86, 89, 120–125, 128, 135, 139, 163, 180–181, 190, 195, 203, 204, 226, 237, 255
Intertropical Convergence Zone (ITCZ) 35

Java 69, 76, 355

Kamehameha 337, 346–348
Karama Valley, Indonesia 85, 120–123, 226
Kauaʻi, Hawaii 28, 53, 312–313, 317, 330, 332–334, 337, 347
kava 245–246, 249
Kawaihae, Hawaii 55, 312–314, *316*, 319, 346–347
kelp highway 16
Kona Field System, Hawaii 334–336
Kon Tiki 310
Kuliʻouʻou, Hawaii 47

Lang Rongrien, Malay Peninsula 72
Lapita 10–11, 20, 45, 47–48, 59–61, 64, 75, 84–89, 120, 123–124, 128, 133–138, 170, 179, 181–182, 185–204, 210–213, 216–218, 226–227, 230, 235, 239–242, 298, 366–367, 370
Last Glacial Maximum (LGM) 7, 31–32
latte 126, 272, 274–284, 326
linguistic histories 38–41, 100, 210
Little Climatic Optimum (LCO) 35, 299–300, 315, 344
Little Ice Age (LIA) 35, 300, 344
longue durée 2, 59–60, 62, 210, 227, 299, 369–370
Loyalty Islands 266, 329, *331*
lusong 280–281
Lydekker's Line 7, *68*

Magellan, Ferdinand 2, 37, 40, 64
Malayo-Polynesian (MP) language 7, 41, 124, 173, 181–182, 192–193, 196–197, 203, 230
marae 2, 288–291
Mariana Islands 10–11, 13, 20, 33–35, 37, 40–42, 44–47, 53, 56, 62, 84, 86–87, 95, 110, 120, 123, 125–135, 138, 140–141, 149–182, 192, 196, 198, 202–204, 212–217, 225–226, 230, 233, 235, 238, 242, 256, 272, 274–285, 288, 326–327, 348–349, 353–355, 362, 365–366, 371–372
Marianas Trench 26
Marquesas Islands 40, 47, 247, 267–270, 288–290, 292, 312, 319, *335*, 340, *342*, 350
Marshall Islands 230, 232–233, 236
Mesolithic Age 63, 79, 84

Metal Age 57, 64, 78, 100, 115–116, 118, 121
microliths 74–75
millet 97–99, 101, 103, 106, 108, 120, 138, 225–226
moai 2, 289–290, 29*3*, 310
monsoon weather patterns 34–35, 153
monumental sites 2, 18, 20, 46, 53, 56–57, 64, 126, 247, 249, 255–262, 264, 284, 287, 290, 292, 294–295, 299, 304–305, 307–308, 345–349, 367, 370–371

Nagsabaran Site, Philippines *112*, 114–116, 118–120
Nan Madol, Pohnpei 2, 257, 292–294, 297, 308, 326
Near Oceania 5, 7, 10, 19–20, 36–37, 41, 43, 57, 63–64, 70, 75–78, 84–89, 128, 135–138, 181, 185–186, 191–199, 202–203, 213, 223, 226, 230, 366–367
Neolithic Age 56–58, 62–64, 70, 74–79, 84–88, 90, 95, 105, 178
network-breaking model 193
New Caledonia 5, 30, 33, 43, 47, 53, 59, 61, 185, *187*, 190, 199–200, 202, 212–214, 223, 225, 258, 272, 274, 284, 290, 296, 326, 329–330, 372
New Guinea 4–5, 14, 16, 19, 30–31, 36, 40–43, 45, 67, 69–70, 72, 74–78, 87–89, 124, 138, 185, *186*, 190, 192, 194, 196, 223, 345, 366
New Zealand (Aotearoa) 5, 10, 30, 34, 40, 45–46, 53, 62–63, 304, 308, 319, 324–325, 329, 350–351, 365, 371
Niah Caves 76–77, 92–93, 95–96
non-Austronesian (NAN) language 40–41

Oceanic (Oc) languages 42, 192–193, 232

Pacific Plate 26
Pagan, Mariana Islands 27, *278*
Palau 40, 42, 138–141, 173, 192, 203, 230, 235, 238–239, 250, 252–253, 258, 270–272, 283–285, 341, 350–351, 362–363, 372
Paleolithic Age 56–58, 62–64, 70–71, 73–74, 79, 84
pigeon-snaring mound *see* star mound
Pleistocene period (Ice Age) 30–31, 40, 43, 58, 63, 67–68, 72–73, 76, 366
polygenesis 246–247, 251, 309
Polynesian problem 45–46, 240
pottery trail 13, 19, 41, 70, 84–142, 181, 197
Proto Malayo-Polynesian (PMP) languages 40–41
Proto Nuclear Polynesian (PNP) languages 40
Proto Oceanic (POc) language 40, 192–194, 196, 203

Rapa Nui (Easter Island) 2, 40, 45, 63, 289–290, *293*, 304, 310, 312, 317
refuge cave 351–352
Remote Oceania 5, 7, 10–13, 15–16, 18–20, 35–37, 40–43, *57*, 62–64, 70, 75, 78–79, 84, 86–87, 89–92, 97, 124–125, 128, 136–137, 150, 160, 170, 177–179, 185–186, 191–193, 195–200, 202–203, 209–213, 223, 226, 230, 249, 285, 305, 324, 366–367, 371
rice 36–37, 76, 92–95, 97–99, 101, 103, 106, 108, 117, 120–121, 138, 173, 225–226
Ritidian, Guam 17, *30*, 129–130, *132–133*, 150–153, 155–156, *158–159*, 162–164, *167–169*, *171*, 173, 175–176, 204, 212, 223–224, 278–279, *283–284*, 372–374

Sahul 7, 31, 35–36, 40–41, 67–69, 72–73, 366
Sa Huynh-Kalanay 116, 118, 121–122
Saipan 128, *133–134*, 150–154, *156*, *160*, 171
Samoa 15, 43, 59–61, 84, 190, 199, 202, 204, 213, 221, 225, 247–248, *251*, 257, 259–260, 263–265, 270, 283, *286*, 288, 290, *296*, 326–329, 338, 340–341, 343, 349–351
sawei 15, 238, 341–342
sea level 3, 7, 9–13, 16, 18, 20, 25–26, 28–33, 43, 55, 67, 88, 101, 106, 108, 118, 120, 130, 134–135, 138, 140, 153–154, 173, 198–199, 204, 209–216, 218, 221, 223, 227, 230–232, 234–236, 240, 345, 300, 315, 319, 326, 350, 362, 365–367, 371, 375
Solomon Islands 43, 136, 185, 188–190, 199
star mound (pigeon-snaring mound) 257, 259–260, 290, 292, *296*
stemmed tool 75
Sunda 7, 31, 35–36, 40–41, 67–69, 72–73, 366

Tahiti 40, 53, 63, 255, 289
Taiwan 7, 14, 35, 40–42, 45, 63, 72, 78, 84, 87, 89, 91–92, 97–110, 112, 117–118, 120, 130, 141, 158–159, 163–166, 168–170, 180–181, 194–195, 197, 281–282, 355, 366
Teouma Site, Vanuatu 190–191, 197, 217–218, 223
Thailand 72
tiki 269, 290, *292*
Tinian 126–129, *133*, 151–152, 154, *157*, 171–172, 274, *276*, *278*
Tonga 14, 42–45, 59, 185, 190, 195–196, 199, 209, 212–213, 247, 257, 288, 290, 343–345, 348–349
triangulation approach 48
Tumon, Guam 236–238, *354*

Unai Bapot, Saipan 128, *133–134*, 150–151, 153–154, *156*, *160*, 170

Vanuatu 42–45, 185, 190–191, 195–197, 212–213, 217, 223, 249

Waimea Canyon, Kaua'i *28*
Wallacea 7, 31, 35–36, 40–41, 67, 68–69, 72–73, 366
Wallace Line 6–7, 10, *68*
warfare 46, 336–337, 341, 348–355, 365
Weber's Line 7, *68*
Word War II 46, 233, 355

Yap 15, 141, 203–204, 230, 232, 235, 238, 250, 270, 272–273, 284, 337, *339*, 341, 343, 376

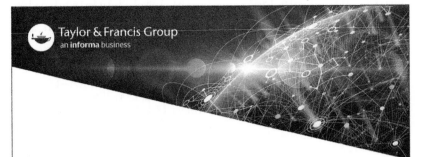